A Global Chronology of Conflict

A Global Chronology of Conflict

From the Ancient World to the Modern Middle East

VOLUME III: 1775–1860

Dr. Spencer C. Tucker
Editor

A B C CLIO

Santa Barbara, California
Denver, Colorado
Oxford, England

Library of Congress Cataloging-in-Publication Data

A global chronology of conflict : from the ancient world to the modern Middle East / Spencer C. Tucker, editor. — 1st ed.
      v. cm.
   Includes bibliographical references and index.
   Contents: v. 1. ca. 3000 BCE–1499 CE — v. 2. 1500–1774 — v. 3. 1775–1860 — v. 4. 1861–1918 — v. 5. 1919–1949 — v. 6. 1950–2008.
   ISBN 978-1-85109-667-1 (hc. : alk. paper) — ISBN 978-1-85109-672-5 (ebook) 1. Military history—Chronology 2. Chronology, Historical. I. Tucker, Spencer, 1937–
   D25.A2G57 2010
   355.002'02—dc22
                                 2009032434

ISBN 978-1-85109-667-1: hardcover
ISBN 978-1-85109-672-5: ebook

14 13 12 11 10   1 2 3 4 5

This book is also available on the World Wide Web as an eBook.
Visit www.abc-clio.com for details.

ABC-CLIO, LLC
130 Cremona Drive, P.O. Box 1911
Santa Barbara, California 93116-1911

This book is printed on acid-free paper ∞
Manufactured in the United States of America

Contents

List of Leaders

List of Weapons

List of Maps

A Note on the Text

Throughout the work the period introductory essays and chronology are supplemented with material intended to heighten the reader's awareness of important individuals and key technologies that have significant impact on the course of military history. This material is clearly identified within the main body of the work and can be found in a separate section at the end of each volume. For ease of use, entries are separated into Leaders and Weapons sections and are listed alphabetically within each category.

Volume III
1775–1860

February 1775

North America: American Revolutionary War (continued): Background (continued): The colonies on the brink of war. By the winter of 1774–1775 British North America has become a powder keg. Commander in North America Lieutenant General Thomas Gage reports to London that the situation is dangerous and that he lacks sufficient manpower to deal with events if fighting should break out. This does not deter King George III and his ministers. Convinced that the vast majority of the population is loyal to the Crown and that the agitation is the work of a small minority who will be easily rooted out and order restored, London takes a hard line. In February 1775 Parliament declares Massachusetts to be in rebellion.

Gage strongly disagrees with London's approach. In a report sent to the ministry but kept secret from Parliament, he estimates that if fighting begins, it will take a year or two and 20,000 men just to pacify New England. If these men cannot be supplied, Gage suggests a naval blockade and economic pressure as the best approach. London disagrees. The ministry holds that 10,000 troops, supported by Loyalists, will be sufficient.

See Leaders: Gage, Thomas

British Army lieutenant general Thomas Gage (1720–1787) was commander in chief of British forces in North America at the beginning of the American Revolutionary War and had a much more realistic appraisal of the situation in America than did British leaders in London. (Library of Congress)

April 19, 1775

North America: American Revolutionary War (continued): The clash at Lexington and Concord. Fighting begins in Massachusetts on April 19, 1775, when British commander in North America Lieutenant General Thomas Gage sends troops from Boston to destroy stores of arms that the radicals are stockpiling at Concord. Gage had successfully carried out similar operations in the past, but this time the militia are alerted. At Lexington, the British advance under Major John Pitcairn meets a hastily called-up militia company of 70 men under Captain John Parker. Someone opens fire ("the shot heard 'round the world"), and the British drive the militia from Lexington Common. The militia loses 8 dead and 10 wounded for only 1 British soldier wounded.

The British then continue their march to Concord and complete their mission. Their withdrawal to Boston becomes a nightmare, however. The local militia are now out in full force, and they snipe at the British from cover along the route. Gage sends out additional forces, but before the troops can reach safety in Boston, the operation has claimed 273 British casualties of some 1,800 engaged (73 killed, 174 wounded, and 26 missing). Ninety-five Americans are casualties (49 killed, 41 wounded, and 5 missing). Massachusetts militia forces then close around Boston. The American Revolutionary War, also known as the War for American Independence, has begun.

April 1775–March 1776

North America: American Revolutionary War (continued): Siege of Boston. The Massachusetts Provincial Congress calls up the colony's militia, supported by militia from Connecticut, Rhode Island, and New Hampshire, and some 15,000 militiamen begin the siege of Boston, held by British commander in North America Lieutenant General Thomas Gage with 3,500 men. Massachusetts major general Artemas Ward has initial command. Both sides seriously miscalculate the costs and possible duration of the war.

THE AMERICAN REVOLUTIONARY WAR, 1775–1783

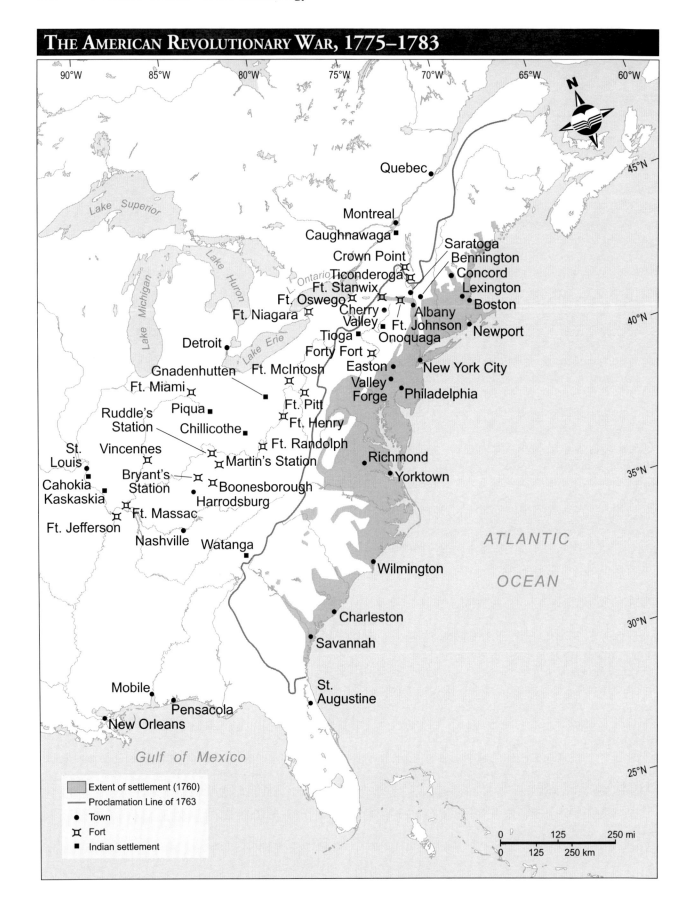

Quebec

Montreal

Caughnawaga

Crown Point

Saratoga
Bennington

Ticonderoga
Concord
Lexington
Ft. Stanwix
Ft. Oswego
Boston
Cherry
Valley
Albany
Ft. Niagara
Ft. Johnson
Newport
Detroit
Tioga
Onoquaga
Forty Fort
Gnadenhutten
Ft. McIntosh
Easton
New York City
Ft. Miami
Valley
Forge
Philadelphia
Piqua
Ft. Pitt
Ruddle's
Station
Chillicothe
Ft. Henry
St.
Vincennes
Ft. Randolph
Louis
Martin's Station
Richmond
Cahokia
Bryant's
Station
Boonesborough
Yorktown
Kaskaskia
Harrodsburg
Ft. Massac
Ft. Jefferson
Nashville
Watanga
Wilmington

Lake Superior
Lake Michigan
Lake Huron
L. Ontario
Lake Erie

Charleston

Savannah

Mobile
St.
Augustine
Pensacola
New Orleans

Gulf of Mexico

ATLANTIC

OCEAN

Extent of settlement (1760)
Proclamation Line of 1763
● Town
✸ Fort
■ Indian settlement

0   125   250 mi
0   125   250 km

May 10, 1775

North America: American Revolutionary War (continued). In a bold action, a small colonial force under colonels Ethan Allen and Benedict Arnold captures by surprise the poorly garrisoned British Fort Ticonderoga, on Lake Champlain. The Americans secure some 120 cannon and mortars and go on to take the British forts at Crown Point and St. Johns.

June 12, 1775

North America: American Revolutionary War (continued). In the first naval action of the war, Jeremiah O'Brien leads a party of lumbermen in capturing the British armed cutter *Margaretta.*

June 15, 1775

North America: American Revolutionary War (continued): Washington named to command the Continental Army. The rebellious colonies require some sort of regular military establishment, and on June 14, 1775, the Second Continental Congress, meeting in Philadelphia since May, authorizes the establishment of 10 rifle companies for the Continental Army (Army of the United Colonies). This is the first regiment and generally regarded as the beginning date for the U.S. Army. The next day, June 15, Congress appoints Virginian George Washington as general and commander in chief of the army. On July 2 Washington takes command at Cambridge, Massachusetts, just to the west of Boston.

June 17, 1775

North America: American Revolutionary War (continued): Battle of Bunker Hill. On June 15, 1775, the Massachusetts Committee of Safety resolves to move forces into Charlestown Peninsula, north of Boston. The area is dominated by Bunker Hill and the lower Breed's Hill in front of it. On June 16 the American militia occupies Bunker Hill, the highest ground and a favorable position as long as the adjacent land and narrow escape route can be held. They also occupy Breed's Hill, which is closer to Charlestown, lower, and more vulnerable to a flanking attack.

British forces in Boston had been reinforced in May with the arrival of 3,500 men under major generals John Burgoyne, Henry Clinton, and William Howe. They press British commander Lieutenant General Thomas Gage for offensive action, and on June 17 British troops under Major General William Howe cross over to Charlestown and mount a frontal

Lieutenant General Sir William Howe (1729–1814) commanded the British Army during 1775–1778 in the American Revolutionary War. He won several important battles but resigned his command in frustration over the lack of resources provided him. (Library of Congress)

assault on the colonial positions. Although the militias eventually break and run, this comes only after they have repulsed three British assaults and exacted a frightful toll on the British infantrymen.

The British lose almost half their strength. Of the 2,400 men engaged, 1,054 (including 92 officers) are casualties; 226 are dead. Probably some 1,500 Americans were engaged; of these, 140 are killed, 380 are wounded, and 39 are captured. In terms of percentage of casualties to force engaged, Bunker Hill is one of the most sanguinary battles of the entire century. The battle shakes Howe and may well have contributed to his failure as commander in chief to press home attacks.

See Leaders: Howe, Sir William

August–December 1775

North America: American Revolutionary War (continued). The Continental Congress decides to send expeditionary forces to Canada, hoping to secure its support against Britain and seal the back door to America. It sends two forces: one against Montreal (Montréal), the other against Quebec (Québec).

In the former, Major General Philip Schuyler departs Fort Ticonderoga with 1,000 men. Laying siege to St. Johns on the Richelieu River on September 6, he becomes ill and is replaced by Brigadier General Richard Montgomery. St. Johns surrenders on November 2, and Montgomery captures Montreal on November 13. British major general Sir Guy Carleton, governor-general of Canada, withdraws to Quebec.

Colonel Benedict Arnold meanwhile leads 1,050 men from Cambridge by sea to the Kennebec River on September 12 and then on a trek through the Maine wilderness toward Quebec. A letter from Arnold to Major General Schuyler falls into British hands, and Canada's governor, Major General Sir Guy Carleton, immediately bolsters the Quebec defenses.

Following considerable hardship, on November 9 Arnold finally reaches the St. Lawrence with only 600 of his force. A winter storm and a shortage of boats delay a crossing until November 13, allowing British reinforcements to arrive in the city. Governor-General Carleton now has some 1,200 men defending the city, but with his militia thought to be unreliable, he wisely refuses to engage the Americans outside the city. Montgomery arrives from Montreal on December 2 with 300 men and artillery and supplies captured from the British and assumes command.

See Leaders: Arnold, Benedict

December 9, 1775

North America: American Revolutionary War (continued): Battle of Great Bridge. Virginia governor John Murray, 4th Earl of Dunmore, withdraws from Williamsburg to Norfolk and leads British troops and Loyalists in attacking Patriot property. Murray also orders construction of a fort on the South Branch of the Elizabeth River across from Great Bridge, where Colonel William Woodford gathers some 850 Virginia and North Carolina militiamen.

Misinformed as to Patriot strength, Murray orders an attack across the river early on the morning of December 9, led by British captain Charles Fordyce with some 400 British and Loyalists with 2 cannon. They advance on what they believe to be an abandoned redoubt and close to about 50 yards when the concealed defenders suddenly rise and deliver a devastating volley. Fordyce is among the many attackers killed. The British and Loyalist force then withdraws, having suffered between 62 and 100 dead and wounded. Only 1 man is wounded on the Patriot side.

The Battle of Great Bridge ends royal authority in Virginia. Murray and some of his Loyalist followers seek refuge on a British warship off Norfolk.

December 13, 1775

North America: American Revolutionary War (continued). Congress authorizes construction of 13 frigates, the first purpose-built warships of the Continental Navy. Five are to be of 32 guns, 5 of 28, and 3 of 24 guns. Construction is parceled out for political reasons rather than the ability of a particular colony to construct them. Most of the frigates do not get to sea, and the brunt of the naval war is borne by privateers.

In addition to the Continental Navy, there is also a small naval force acquired by Continental Army commander General George Washington and the navies of the various colonies/states.

December 31, 1775

North America: American Revolutionary War (continued): American expedition against Quebec: Battle of Quebec. Lacking siege equipment and with all of Benedict Arnold's enlistments expiring at the end of the year and little hope of renewing them, Richard Montgomery and Arnold plan one desperate all-out attack. Waiting for a dark and stormy night, on December 31 they advance on Quebec (Québec) in a driving snowstorm.

The attack is a complete failure. Montgomery is killed, and Arnold is severely wounded in the leg. The British capture 426 Americans; another 50 are killed or wounded and not captured. British losses are 5 killed and 13 wounded. The remaining Americans are too few in number and in any case cannot sustain a siege in the Canadian winter, although they try to do so.

ca. 1775

West Africa: Benin. Successionist struggles that become civil war bring the decline of Benin.

1775–1776

Southeast Asia: Siam. Siamese king P'ya Taksin, having failed to take back Chiengmai from Burma (present-day Myanmar) in 1769, reconquers it in 1775, then defeats a Burmese invasion in 1776.

ca. 1775–1795

South Africa. The Boers easily defeat the Khoisa and San tribes, either killing or enslaving the natives.

February 17–April 8, 1776

North America: American Revolutionary War (continued): New Providence Island Campaign. In January 1776 the Naval Committee of the Continental Congress orders Continental Navy commander Commodore Esek Hopkins to sail his small squadron to Chesapeake Bay and end British/Loyalist operations under Virginia royalist governor John Murray, 4th Earl of Dunmore. Hopkins commands the flagship *Alfred* (24 guns), the *Columbus* (20 guns), the brigs *Andrew Doria* (14 guns) and *Cabot* (14 guns), the sloops *Providence* (12 guns) and *Hornet* (10 guns), and the schooners *Fly* (8 guns) and *Wasp* (8 guns). Hopkins departs Philadelphia on January 17, but ice in the Delaware River prevents him from reaching the Atlantic until February 17.

At sea, Hopkins takes advantage of discretion granted by his orders and sails not to the Chesapeake but to the Bahamas to carry out his own plan to raid New Providence Island. The squadron arrives off New Providence on March 3 minus two of the smallest ships, which collided and had to return home. A landing force goes ashore on March 3 and advances on Fort Nassau. It is taken the next day with 71 cannon, 15 bronze mortars, and 24 casks of powder (the slow approach enables the British to remove 150 casks of powder).

Over a two-week span the Americans load the captured stores into the impressed sloop *Endeavor.* Hopkins then orders the squadron to sail for Block Island Channel off Rhode Island. In Narragansett Bay the *Andrew Doria* and *Fly* capture the British armed schooner *Hawke* and the bomb brig *Bolton.* The *Hawke* is the first Royal Navy warship taken by the Continental Navy. On April 7 the squadron encounters the British frigate *Glasgow* (20 guns), but following a four-hour night engagement marked by poor American gunnery, the British ship escapes. Hopkins orders the squadron to sail for New London, Connecticut, where it arrives the next day.

February 27, 1776

North America: American Revolutionary War (continued): Battle of Moore's Creek Bridge. In response to Patriot agitation in North Carolina, some 700 Scots Highland immigrants and 800 Loyalist militia march toward the Atlantic coast in mid-February 1776 expecting to join British regulars. At Moore's Creek Bridge, about 20 miles north of Wilmington, some 1,000 Patriot militiamen and volunteers contest the Loyalist march.

At dawn on February 27, 1776, the Highland Scots under Lieutenant Colonel Donald McLeod and Captain John Campbell arrive at the bridge only to find the Patriots under colonels Alexander Lillington and Richard Caswell already there. The Loyalists rush the bridge but are cut down at close range. A Patriot counterattack forces the remaining Highlanders and Loyalists to flee.

The Loyalists sustain some 30 casualties, with both McLeod and Campbell among the dead. The Patriots suffer only 1 killed and 1 wounded. More than 850 Loyalists are captured over the next few days, including their commander, Brigadier General Donald MacDonald. This victory fans Patriot sentiment in the Carolinas.

March 17, 1776

North America: American Revolutionary War (continued): British evacuation of Boston. During the winter, Continental Army chief of artillery Major General Henry Knox brings down on sledges from Fort Ticonderoga 59 of the captured artillery pieces. In early March, Lieutenant General William Howe, now the British commander in North America, begins an evacuation to Halifax. Washington agrees not to harass the British with artillery fire, and Howe promises not to destroy the city. Howe completes the evacuation on March 17. The first stage of the war has ended in an American victory.

Washington immediately begins transferring resources south to New York City, which he believes will be the location of the next British move.

See Leaders: Knox, Henry

March 23, 1776

North America: American Revolutionary War (continued): Continental Congress authorizes privateering. During 1776–1783 the Continental Congress issues letters of marque for 1,697 privateers mounting 14,872 guns and manned by 58,400 crewmen. The state governments add many additional vessels. The United States sends to sea during the war at least

Continental Army major general Henry Knox (1750–1806) acquired his specialist knowledge largely from books. He ably commanded the artillery during the American Revolutionary War. Later he served as the new nation's first secretary of war. (National Archives)

2,000 privateers mounting some 18,000 guns and manned by 70,000 men.

The privateers carry the bulk of the naval war for the young republic. During the conflict, they capture some 3,087 British ships. A number of these are retaken, however, leaving 2,208 in American hands. The Americans also take 89 British privateers, of which 75 remain in American hands. (British privateers capture 1,135 American merchantmen, of which 27 are retaken or ransomed. The British also capture 216 privateers.) These figures compare with a total of 196 ships captured by the Continental Navy.

In addition to the important arms and stores captured, American privateers and Continental Navy ships may have taken prisoner as many as 16,000 British seamen, compared to 22,000 British soldiers taken by the Continental Army during the war.

April 7, 1776

Atlantic Ocean: American Revolutionary War (continued). Off the Virginia Capes, the Continental Navy brigantine *Lexington* (16 guns), commanded by Captain John Barry, captures the British sloop *Edward* (8 guns), tender to the frigate *Liverpool.* Each side has several men killed in the action. The *Edward* is the first Royal Navy vessel taken by a Continental Navy ship.

See Leaders: Barry, John

June 8, 1776

North America: Canada: American Revolutionary War (continued): Battle of Trois Rivières. Arnold retains a tenuous hold at Quebec (Québec) throughout the winter, but in May substantial British reinforcements arrive by sea via the St. Lawrence River under Major General John Burgoyne, and Arnold is forced to withdraw. Too late, the Americans reinforce their units in Canada with six regiments under Brigadier General John Sullivan. Smallpox ravages the American force.

On June 8, 1776, with 2,000 men Sullivan rashly attempts to attack the British at Trois Rivières, about halfway between Quebec and Montreal (Montréal). He is probably not aware of heavy odds against him. His force is soundly defeated by the professional British infantry.

The Americans suffer 25 dead, 140 wounded, and 236 captured. British losses are only 8 dead and 9 wounded. Caution on the part of British governor-general Sir Guy Carleton allows Sullivan's battered force to escape to Montreal. Sullivan hopes that he can hold Isle-aux-Noix, the last post in Canada, but this proves impossible. Desperately short of supplies of every kind and with much of his army sick and now opposed by 8,000 British regulars and Hessian mercenaries, Sullivan returns to Crown Point at the end of July with what little remains of his force.

The Canadian campaign is a complete failure. The mistake lies not in attempting it but in insufficiently supporting it. Had the campaign succeeded, it would have united Canada to the other British North American colonies and changed the course of the war.

Captain John Barry (1745–1803), considered the father of the U. S. Navy, was also the first Continental Navy officer to capture a British Navy ship during the American Revolutionary War. (National Archives)

June 28, 1776

North America: American Revolutionary War (continued): Battle of Sullivan's Island. In May 1776 five regiments from Cork, Ireland, arrive off Cape Fear to operate with Loyalists in North Carolina. This plan is dashed by the Battle of Moore's Creek Bridge, and the expeditionary force then joins some 2,000 troops from Boston under Major General Henry Clinton and a naval squadron under Commodore Sir Peter Parker. This latter force is scheduled to take part in Lieutenant General William Howe's attack on New York City, but with time available before that operation, Clinton and Parker decide to take the important port city of Charleston, South Carolina. The British depart Cape Fear on May 21 and arrive off Charleston on June 4.

Fort Sullivan, located on an island of the same name north of Charleston Harbor's mouth, has a garrison of 420 men. Colonel William Moultrie has command. Mounting 31 cannon, the fort guards the entrance to Charleston Harbor. The fort has 16-foot-thick dirt walls enclosed by palmetto logs, but only its southern and western faces are completed.

An immediate British attack might have been successful, but Parker delays to reconnoiter. Although most of the British ships cross the bar on June 7, the flagship *Bristol* (50 guns) has to be lightened by removing some of its guns and does not cross until June 10. By June 15 all British troops are ashore on Long Island, separated from Sullivan's Island only by a narrow channel. Clinton thinks that his men can wade across, but the channel turns out to be seven feet deep at low tide. Before Clinton can attempt a boat assault, the Americans fortify the opposite shore with field pieces and riflemen, preventing an assault there. Parker, though, is convinced that he can force the harbor with ships alone. Meanwhile, the Americans strengthen their defenses.

On June 27 the *Experiment* (50 guns) arrives. Lightened, it too gets across the bar and then takes on its guns again. On June 28 the British open fire on Fort Sullivan with eight warships mounting 260 guns and the bomb vessel *Thunderer.* The spongy ramparts absorb the cannonballs, and there is little damage. In the course of the bombardment, three British ships try to work around the end of the island in order to enfilade the fort but run aground. Although two are eventually refloated, the new 20-gun frigate *Actaeon* remains fast.

Fort Sullivan's gunners concentrate their return fire on the two largest British ships, the *Experiment* and *Bristol.* Finally at 9:00 p.m. Parker withdraws, having suffered 64 killed and 161 wounded (including Parker). The next morning its crew abandons and burns the *Actaeon.* American losses in the Battle of Sullivan's Island are only 17 dead and 20 wounded. British regular forces will not return to the southern colonies for another two and a half years.

July 3, 1776

North America: American Revolutionary War (continued): British expeditionary forces arrive by sea at New York. Reinforced with troops from Britain, not until June 1776 does Howe open the second phase of the war. He sets sail from Halifax with 32,000 ground troops in hundreds of transports convoyed by 10 ships of the line and 20 frigates, crewed by 10,000 seamen. It is the largest expeditionary force yet seen in British history. The advance elements arrive off New York on June 29, and on July 3 British troops begin coming ashore on Staten Island.

Continental Army commander General George Washington meanwhile has had ample time to prepare. His men erect earthworks and place artillery on Brooklyn Heights, in lower Manhattan, and on Governor's Island. Washington forms his 19,000 men in five divisions and positions three of them in New York City at the southern end of Manhattan Island, one at Fort Washington (Mount Washington, today Washington Heights) next to the Hudson River, and one on Long Island to protect Brooklyn Heights. Yet Washington has his men so far forward that they are in fact vulnerable to British flanking attack. Although Howe will mount such attacks, he will be too slow in pressing them home, allowing Washington to escape each time.

July 4, 1776
North America: American Revolutionary War (continued). Congress passes the Declaration of Independence from Great Britain.

August 27, 1776
North America: American Revolutionary War (continued): Battle of Long Island. Slow to move, British commander in North America Major General Sir William Howe does not land on Long Island until August 22. The American commander there, Major General Nathanael Greene, is ill, and Continental Army commander General George Washington appoints in his stead Major General Israel Putnam, who is largely unfamiliar with the defenses.

On the night of August 26, Howe with 20,000 men now feigns an attack on the American right, then turns the American left and the next day traps an American force on the Gowanus Road, forcing its surrender. Washington sends reinforcements, increasing his strength on Long Island to 9,500 men, and arrives to take personal command of the Brooklyn Heights line on Long Island.

Howe is slow to move, and Washington, realizing that the situation is lost, carries out a skillful evacuation on the night of August 29–30. In the Long Island

Campaign the Americans suffer 1,012 casualties, the British but 392.

September 6–7, 1776
North America: American Revolutionary War (continued): Attack by the submarine *Turtle.* Off New York City on the night of September 6–7, Sergeant Ezra Lee mans David Bushnell's submarine *Turtle,* attempting to sink Admiral Richard Howe's flagship *Eagle.* The attempt, the first modern instance of submarine warfare, miscarries.

See Weapons: *Turtle* Submarine

September 15–16, 1776
North America: American Revolutionary War (continued): Battles of Kip's Bay and Harlem Heights.

Model of American David Bushnell's submarine, the *Turtle,* used against the British in New York Harbor on the night of September 6–7, 1776, at the Science Museum, London. (The Art Archive/Science Museum London/Eileen Tweedy)

Following a council of war on September 11, 1776, Continental Army commander George Washington decides to remove his troops from lower Manhattan Island. The men begin moving north to Kings Bridge the next day. Washington transfers his headquarters to Harlem Heights.

Washington's decision to abandon lower Manhattan almost comes too late because on September 15, 4,000 British troops cross the East River from Long Island and land on Manhattan at Kip's Bay. The American withdrawal northward is not yet complete, and this threatens to cut off Major General Israel Putnam's division at the south end of the island in New York City from the remainder of the American army at Harlem Heights.

Despite Washington's personal intervention, the American brigade at Kip's Bay breaks and runs under a heavy but ineffectual British naval cannonade almost without firing a shot. Short of wagons, Putnam is forced to abandon a large number of his heavy guns and supplies in New York City as he rapidly marches the 12 miles north to rejoin the main army at Harlem.

September 16 finds the Americans in force at Harlem Heights. In the ensuing battle the British suffer as many as 70 dead and 200 wounded, while the Americans lose perhaps 30 killed and less than 100 wounded and missing. Although only a minor affair, the Battle of Harlem Heights helps restore Continental Army confidence. The battle is fought at close range, and the Americans do not quit the field until ordered to do so. Washington, however, withdraws again after the engagement.

October 11, 1776

North America: American Revolutionary War (continued): Battle of Valcour Island. Control of Lake Champlain is vital to the Americans for any future invasion of Canada and to the British for their plans to move south and isolate New England. Thus, following the American retreat from Canada the Continental Congress orders Major General Philip Schuyler to hold northern New York and authorizes the construction of galleys and gondolas on Lake Champlain and Lake George. Brigadier General Benedict Arnold has charge of the construction, with neighboring colonies supplying both materials and shipwrights.

The Battle of Valcour Island, October 11, 1776. This little-known but important naval engagement on Lake Champlain during the American Revolutionary War, while an American defeat, helped prevent a British invasion from Canada. (Naval Historical Society)

The British are also busy. Governor-general in Canada Major General Sir Guy Carleton is determined to control Lake Champlain as part of a British invasion of New York. The British have both larger vessels and more guns. What they do not have is time; winter will bring their operations to a halt. In early October, Carlton begins moving south with 13,500 men.

Engagements between the British and Americans begin at Valcour Island, about 50 miles north of Fort Ticonderoga, on October 11, 1776. Arnold's 800 men have 15 vessels: 2 schooners, 1 sloop, 4 galleys, and 8 gondolas. Their cannon have a combined throw weight of 703 pounds. Arnold positions his vessels in a crescent shape at the island so that the British will have difficulty bringing their superior firepower to bear and will have to tack into position to engage his anchored vessels.

The commander of the British squadron, Lieutenant Thomas Pringle, has more and larger vessels mounting heavier guns; his smaller vessels alone are nearly a match for those of the Americans. The British warships are served by trained Royal Navy crews and have a combined throw weight of 1,300 pounds, nearly double that of the Americans.

Battle is opened near noon on October 11, with Pringle's vessels pounding the Americans for six hours. The Americans lose 1 schooner and 1 gondola and have 3 others badly damaged. They have also used up most of their ammunition. Realizing that his small force will be destroyed if he remains in position, that night Arnold manages to slip his remaining 13 vessels through and past the British in an attempt to reach Fort Ticonderoga. But the wind shifts from the south, and the Americans have to resort to their

CANADA CAMPAIGN, 1775

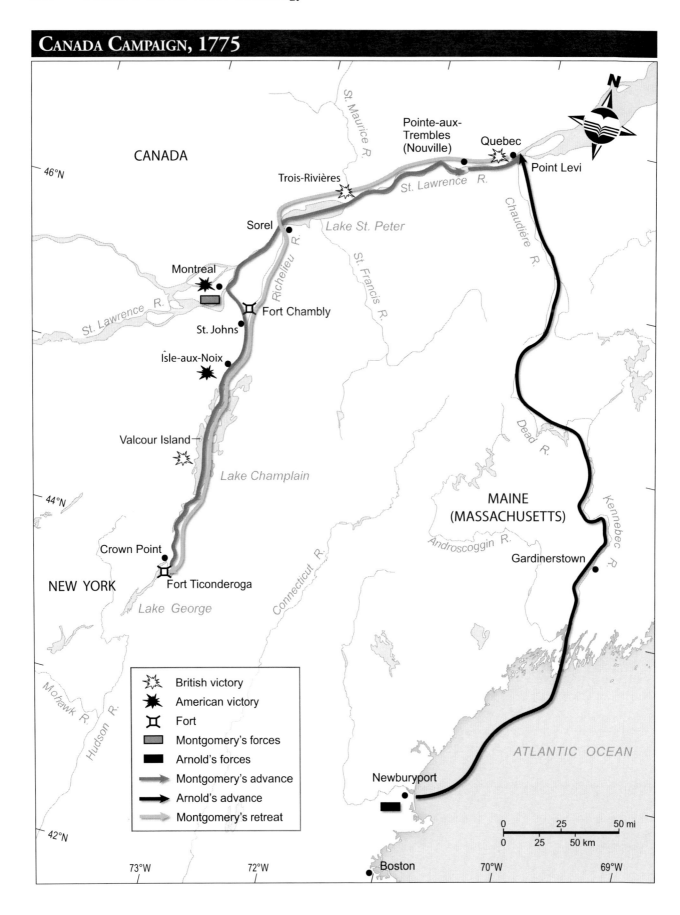

sweeps (oars). For a day the Americans keep ahead, but the British finally catch up, and a second engagement is fought on October 13 north of Crown Point. One American galley strikes to the British, and Arnold then beaches and sets afire another galley and 4 gondolas. Although most of their vessels have either been captured or sunk, the Americans lose only about 80 men. The others manage to reach Crown Point on foot, just ahead of pursuing Native Americans allied with the British.

Although both tactical defeats, the two small battles on Lake Champlain comprise a significant strategic American victory. Arnold has held up the British just long enough. Carleton now believes that it is too late in the year to begin a land campaign and withdraws, ending any possibility of a linkup in 1776 between his forces and those of Major General William Howe in New York. If the British had taken Ticonderoga and held it through the winter, their 1777 campaign would have been far easier and would have been more likely to succeed. Instead, the 1777 British thrust southward ends in American victory at Saratoga, the turning point of the war.

October 28, 1776

North America: American Revolutionary War (continued): Battle of White Plains. With British commander Lieutenant General William Howe carrying out another flanking attack at Trog's Neck, Continental Army commander General George Washington concludes that he cannot remain in Manhattan. He now withdraws north. Both armies head for White Plains. Washington, however, leaves Colonel Robert Magaw and some 2,000 men at Fort Washington in the hopes that this position, in combination with Major General Nathanael Greene's 3,500 men at Fort Lee across the Hudson River, might be able to block any British move up that river.

Washington and the rest of the army, some 14,000 men, arrive at White Plains on October 22. With a comparable force, Howe attacks the Continental defenses on October 28. Although the Continental Army fights well, the militia again breaks and runs, uncovering the American right flank and leaving Washington no option but to withdraw. Losses probably amount to several hundred killed and wounded on each side, although the British also take several hundred prisoners.

Major General Nathanael Greene (1742–1786) was arguably, next to George Washington, the greatest American military leader of the American Revolutionary War. His southern campaign of 1780–1783 was one of the most brilliant in U.S. military history. (National Archives)

Washington again withdraws north. Howe, reinforced to 20,000 men, does not pursue but instead turns west to Dobb's Ferry on the Hudson before moving south to envelop Magaw's force at Fort Washington. Washington leaves Major General Charles Lee and 6,000 men at Castle Hill to block the British from moving north and withdraws farther with the rest of his army, northwest to Peekskill. He crosses the Hudson to Haverstraw on November 10 and then marches south to Hackensack, New Jersey, several miles west of Fort Lee.

See Leaders: Greene, Nathanael

November 16, 1776

North America: American Revolutionary War (continued): British capture of Fort Washington on Manhattan Island. Continental Army commander General George Washington commits a major military error. Dividing his already inferior forces, he has left Colonel Robert Magaw and 2,000 men at Fort Washington on Manhattan on the east side of the Hudson where they might easily be cut off by the Royal Navy. Major General Nathanael Greene has overall command of Fort Lee and Fort Washington; believing that the garrison at Fort Washington can be easily evacuated if need be, he sends an additional regiment, bringing the garrison's strength to nearly 3,000 men.

On November 15 Howe sends 10,000 men against Fort Washington and demands its surrender. Magaw refuses, saying that the garrison will fight to the last man. Supported by fire from ships in the Hudson, Howe's forces storm Fort Washington on November 16. The British actually lose more killed and wounded in the fight: 59 Americans die and another 96 are wounded, while British losses are 78 killed and 374 wounded. But American losses in prisoners and supplies are staggering. The British capture 230 officers and 2,607 soldiers. They also secure 146 cannon, 2,800 muskets, 12,000 shot and shell, and 400,000 musket cartridges. It ranks with the surrender of Charleston as one of the two worst Patriot defeats of the entire war.

November 20, 1776

North America: American Revolutionary War (continued): British capture of Fort Lee, New Jersey. The fate that has befallen Fort Washington almost is repeated across the Hudson River at Fort Lee. That post is now useless, and its commander, Major General Nathanael Greene, has initiated the movement of its 3,000 men and considerable quantities of supplies and ammunition to the interior. In a bold flanking movement on the night of November 19–20, British major general Charles, Lord Cornwallis, leads some 4,000 troops across the Hudson at Closter, six miles above Fort Lee. Although Greene had posted patrols, the British exploit a gap in the American coverage. The attackers scale the Palisades on the New Jersey shore and then move south to get in behind Greene and pin him against the Hudson.

Warned by a farmer on the morning of November 20, Greene abandons Fort Lee, joining General

British general Charles Cornwallis served throughout the American Revolutionary War, most notably in the American South, in which theater he commanded all British forces during 1780–1781. Probably the best British field commander of the war, he was nonetheless forced to surrender at Yorktown in 1781. He went on to distinguish himself as governor-general of India. (National Archives)

George Washington at Hackensack that same day. Greene is forced to leave behind some 30 cannon, tents, and supplies. All of the garrison escapes except 8 men killed and 105 taken prisoner.

The New York campaign has been a disaster for the colonials. In all, the British have taken at Fort Washington, Fort Lee, and their dependencies 146 cannon, 12,000 shot and shell, 2,800 muskets, and 400,000 musket cartridges, not to mention tents and other equipment. More than 4,000 men have been lost.

See Leaders: Cornwallis, Charles

December 26, 1776

North America: American Revolutionary War (continued): Battle of Trenton. Continental Army commander George Washington leads what remains of his army southwest, across New Jersey, with British commander Lieutenant General William Howe's army in dilatory pursuit. On November 22 the Continentals arrive in Newark, and on December 2 they reach Trenton and the Delaware River. Major General Charles Lee now compounds Washington's problems. Disregarding orders, Lee is slow to cross the Hudson River and acts independently against British outposts in New Jersey. On December 9 Washington withdraws what remains of his army across the Delaware into Pennsylvania. On December 16 Lee is captured in Basking Ridge, New Jersey, by a British scouting force.

Both sides now go into winter quarters, with Howe setting up a string of outposts on the east side of the river at Trenton, Princeton, and other places. The most important of these is that at Trenton, held by Colonel Johann Rall's Hessian mercenaries. The war appears to be about over. Washington's position is critical. Smallpox is ravaging his force, and half of his 10,000 men are sick. To make matters worse, enlistments for most of his men will expire in a few days.

In these dire circumstances, Washington decides to risk everything with a surprise attack on Trenton. Logistical arrangements are critical. Success depends on getting the men across the icy Delaware at night in order to achieve surprise. Crossings by 5,500 men plus horses and artillery are to occur at three separate locations, with the forces then converging on Trenton. If circumstances favor, they can then advance on the British posts at Princeton and New Brunswick.

The attempt is planned for Christmas night, December 25. The crossing is to start at 5:00 p.m., with

Continental Army commander lieutenant general George Washington observing his troops crossing the Delaware River on Christmas night 1776. The men achieved surprise the next morning, defeating the Hessian garrison at Trenton and perhaps saving the revolution. (Library of Congress)

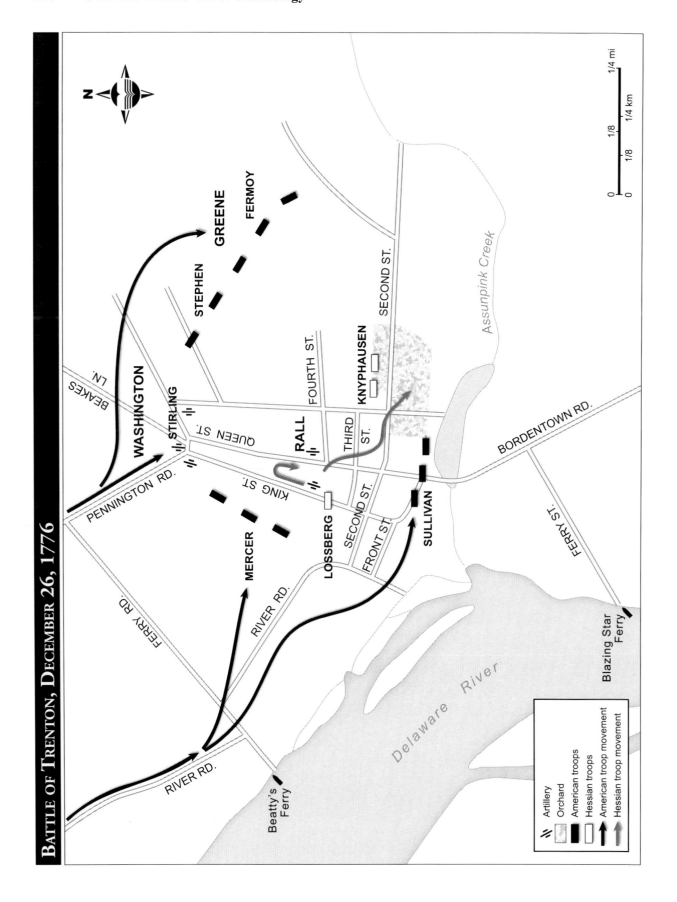

BATTLE OF TRENTON, DECEMBER 26, 1776

the attack at Trenton scheduled for 5:00 a.m. the next day. Weather conditions are terrible, and the troops are slow to reach their assembly areas. As a consequence, the men begin loading the boats an hour late. Shallow-draft wooden Durham boats, 40–60 feet long by 8 feet wide, transport the men across the river. Perfect craft for such an operation, they have a keel and a bow at each end. Four men, two to a side, use setting poles to push off the bottom and move the boats, which also have a mast and two sails. Horses and artillery go across in Delaware River ferries.

All does not go smoothly, however. A storm sweeps through, and of the three crossings only the major one at McKonkey's Ferry under Washington with 2,400 men occurs in time for the planned attack. That force is divided into two corps, under major generals John Sullivan and Nathanael Greene. Colonel Henry Knox commands 18 pieces of artillery. Conditions are horrible, with the men having to contend not only with the dark but also wind, rain, sleet, snow, and chunks of ice in the Delaware. The password for the operation, "Liberty or Death," reflects its desperate nature.

Washington planned for the crossing to be complete by midnight, but the last man is not across until after 3:00 a.m., and it is nearly 4:00 a.m. before the army is formed and begins to move. The men are poorly clad for such an operation, and some actually have no shoes, their feet wrapped in rags. After the army has formed, the men march the nine miles to Trenton.

Washington is determined that the attack will succeed. Informed in a message from Sullivan that the storm has wet the muskets, making them unfit for service, he replies, "Tell General Sullivan to use the bayonet. I am resolved to take Trenton." Washington's will keeps the men going. On nearing Trenton, Washington splits his force into two corps to follow two different roads for a converging attack on the British outpost.

The attack begins at 8:00 a.m., with the two columns opening fire within 8 minutes of one another. The battle lasts some 90 minutes. The Hessian garrison consists of 3 regiments, 50 Hessian Jägers, and 20 light dragoons, about 1,600 men in all, along with six 3-pounder guns.

The Continental Army soon drives the Hessians back. Artillery plays a major role, and here Washington enjoys a six to one advantage, with his guns deployed to fire down the streets of the town. The battle itself is a confused melee, with the men fighting singly or in small groups. Rall rallies his men with a bayonet charge down Queen Street, but the Hessians are cut down by individual Americans with muskets and rifles and by artillery fire.

In the battle the Hessians have 22 killed, 92 wounded (including Rall mortally), and 948 captured. The remaining Hessians would also have been taken had the other columns gotten into position in time. The Continentals also secure a considerable quantity of arms and booty. The Americans lose only 2 men (both frozen to death) and 5 wounded. With little food or rest for 36 hours, Washington's men need relief, and he is thus forced to suspend operations. On December 27 the Continental Army is back across the Delaware.

The Battle of Trenton changes the entire campaign. It helps end Continental fear of the Hessian troops and adds immensely to Washington's prestige, at such a low point a month before, establishing his reputation as a general and a leader of men. It also restores Patriot morale, which had been at its lowest point since the start of the war. Washington has snatched victory out of the jaws of death and fanned the dying embers of American independence into flame again.

1776

North America: American Revolutionary War (continued): French aid to the American revolutionaries. In 1776 King Louis XVI of France agrees to extend secret aid to the Americans. This is to weaken France's rival Britain but also to secure revenge for its humiliating defeat in the French and Indian War (1754–1763).

French playwright Pierre de Beaumarchais sets up in Spain a bogus trading firm known as Hortalez and Co. Ultimately Beaumarchais dispenses some 21 million livres in French government funds during 1776–1783. This includes more than 200 cannon, 20–30 mortars, 25,000 small arms, 100 tons of gunpowder, and clothing and tents sufficient for 25,000 men. Its importance cannot be overstated. One source estimates that in the pivotal Battles of Saratoga in 1777, nine-tenths of the arms used by the Americans are from France.

1776–1777

South America: Spanish-Portuguese War. Spanish troops capture Colona and other Portuguese territory in the Banda Oriental (present-day Uruguay and part of Brazil) and in southern Brazil. Ultimately the two nations agree that Spain will receive Colona and the Banda Oriental, with Portugal retaining the upper Uruguay River and Brazil.

January 3, 1777

North America: American Revolutionary War (continued): Battle of Princeton. Despite the victory at Trenton, Continental Army commander General George Washington struggles to hold the army together. Armed with a hasty congressional reenlistment bounty, Washington persuades 3,000 men to extend their term and recrosses the Delaware River on December 30. British commander Lieutenant General William Howe meanwhile gives Major General Charles, Lord Cornwallis, 8,000 men to crush the Americans.

Convinced that the Americans are about to mount another crossing, on January 2 Cornwallis stations three regiments totaling 1,300 men under Lieutenant Colonel Charles Mawhood to hold Princeton and about as many men at Maidenhead (now Lawrenceville) while he departs with the remaining 5,500 to seek out his adversary. Moving rapidly, that evening Cornwallis apparently traps Washington with about 5,200 men (including 3,600 unreliable militia) against the Delaware. Confident, Cornwallis disregards suggestions that he press forward and decides to rest his men and attack the next morning.

That night Washington leaves his campfires burning and slips around the British left flank, marching on Princeton. En route he encounters two of Mawhood's regiments moving to join Cornwallis and routs them. Washington's force suffers 35 casualties, and the British suffer 28 dead, 58 wounded, and 187 missing.

Before Cornwallis can arrive with his own troops, Washington moves on to the hilly terrain in the vicinity of Morristown, where the army goes into winter quarters. Howe recalls Cornwallis to New York, abandoning most of New Jersey.

In the span of only 10 days, Washington has restored confidence in the colonial cause. The small victories of Trenton and Princeton are rightly regarded as crucial battles, perhaps the most critical of the entire war. In place of despair, there is now confidence that the Americans can ultimately triumph. The victories also restore confidence within the army in Washington, so badly shaken by the New York debacle.

January 1777

North America: American Revolutionary War (continued): British plans of campaign for 1777. In London, Lord George Germain, secretary of state for the colonies and the man charged with actually running the war, approves two entirely different and even opposing plans for the 1777 campaign. In one, British commander in North America Lieutenant General William Howe will move against Philadelphia. Howe believes that this will force Continental Army commander George Washington to defend the capital and will give Howe the chance to destroy him.

In the second plan, Major General John Burgoyne will push south from Canada along the Lake Champlain corridor to Albany, New York, where he expects to meet part of Howe's army driving north from New York City up the Hudson. Burgoyne also plans a secondary campaign by Lieutenant Colonel Barry St. Leger (brevetted brigadier for this operation) in conjunction with Native American allies in the Mohawk Valley to force a dispersion of American resources.

Burgoyne hopes that by controlling the lakes and the Hudson he can isolate New England from the rest of the colonies, but his polycentric plan fails to take into account logistical considerations, problems of coordination and timing, and Howe's plan, which means that few of the latter's men will be available to move up the Hudson.

See Leaders: Burgoyne, John

April 26, 1777

North America: American Revolutionary War (continued): British raid on Danbury. In April 1777 British commander in North America Lieutenant General William Howe orders Major General William Tryon, royal governor of New York, to attack Danbury, Connecticut, and there destroy Continental Army military stores. Tryon commands about 2,000 men and several guns. Sailing from New York City, British ships enter the Saugatuck River; Tryon's men come ashore at Compo on April 25, 1777, and march to Weston.

On April 26 Tryon arrives in Danbury and destroys military stores there. Warned of the approach

British lieutenant general John Burgoyne. Arriving in Boston in 1775, he witnessed the Battle of Bunker Hill. In 1777 he led a disastrous invasion of New York from Canada that ended in the surrender of his army at Saratoga. (Library of Congress)

of militia forces, Tryon withdraws soon after midnight on April 27 but not before torching a number of Patriot residences and barns. Over the next two days Tryon experiences a near reprisal of the British withdrawal from Concord to Boston two years before; his men are severely harassed by local militia called out by Major General David Wooster along with some Continental Army troops. Brigadier General Benedict Arnold plays a leading role on the colonial side.

Timely British reinforcements rescue Tryon's force, but the British lose close to 200 men killed or wounded, including 10 officers. American losses are only about 20 killed and 40 wounded. Wooster is mortally wounded.

July 6, 1777
North America: American Revolutionary War (continued): British capture Fort Ticonderoga. Lieutenant General (brevetted this rank for the campaign)

John Burgoyne's army of some 7,200 regulars, along with some Loyalists and allied Native Americans, moves south from Canada and reaches Fort Ticonderoga on Lake Champlain on July 1. The next day Burgoyne begins positioning his artillery on high ground at Sugar Loaf (Mount Defiance). Well aware that cannon there could easily reduce the fortress, Major General Arthur St. Clair and his 2,500 poorly equipped troops abandon Ticonderoga on the night of July 5, crossing into Vermont on a bridge across Lake Champlain. St. Clair sends the sick and baggage via boat to Skenesboro (present-day Whitehall). The British occupy the fort on July 6, and Burgoyne immediately sends columns out after the Americans.

July 7, 1777
North America: American Revolutionary War (continued): Battle of Hubbardton. Continental Army major general Arthur St. Clair leaves a rear guard of some 1,200 men near the town of Hubbardton, Vermont, under Colonel Seth Warner. The pursuing British advance corps of 850 men under Brigadier General Simon Fraser attacks the Americans early on July 7. Despite being taken by surprise, the Americans repulse several vigorous British assaults until 150 Brunswick Grenadier reinforcements arrive and enter the fray. The Americans then give way.

The Americans lose 41 killed, 96 wounded, and 234 captured. British losses are 60 killed and 148 wounded. The stand at Hubbardton is nonetheless an important American tactical victory, as it purchases time for St. Clair's main body to reach safety. The British advance guard returns to Ticonderoga to rejoin the main British army.

July–August 1777
North America: American Revolutionary War (continued): Burgoyne's continued move south. The Americans under Major General Philip Schuyler practice a scorched-earth policy, destroying crops and stores that might be useful to the British and obstructing the roads. British lieutenant general John Burgoyne's advance, burdened by heavy baggage, slows, but despite the knowledge that Howe is not coming to meet him, he continues to push southward. Meanwhile, Schuyler receives reinforcements in the form of militia and Continental Army troops, including Colonel Daniel Morgan's rifle regiment, and capable subordinate commanders in major generals Benedict Arnold and Benjamin Lincoln.

August 6, 1777

North America: American Revolutionary War (continued): Battle of Oriskany. As part of the plan to disperse American forces in upper New York state, British brigadier general Barry St. Leger arrives at Oswego, New York, in late July with some 875 British, Hessian, and Loyalist forces and perhaps 1,000 allied Iroquois warriors under Joseph Brant. They advance to Fort Stanwix (present-day Rome, New York), held by some 750 Continentals and militiamen under Colonel Peter Gansevoort. When Gansevoort rejects a demand for surrender on August 3, St. Leger begins siege operations.

Brigadier General Nicholas Herkimer hurries to the relief of Fort Stanwix with some 800 militia. Some six miles from the fort, Herkimer is caught in a perfectly staged ambush by Brant and his Iroquois and the Loyalists. Herkimer's force sustains some 465 dead, wounded (he himself falls mortally wounded), and captured, while the Loyalists and Native Americans lose only 150. Most of Herkimer's force is able to withdraw. This Loyalist victory is offset by a concurrent sortie from Fort Stanwix that destroys St. Leger's camp.

August 16, 1777

North America: American Revolutionary War (continued): Battle of Bennington. With his force running short of supplies, British lieutenant general John Burgoyne sends out a foraging force of 700 Hessians under Colonel Friedrich Baum. Colonel John Stark, with 2,000 militiamen, cuts off and surrounds them at Bennington, Vermont. A Hessian relief force of 650 men under Lieutenant Colonel Heinrich von Breymann arrives later the same day; he too is met and defeated by Stark, aided by 400 Green Mountain Boys under Colonel Seth Warner. In all, the Hessians sustain 207 killed and 700 captured for American casualties of only 30 killed and 40 wounded. The Continentals also secure much-needed military supplies and weapons.

August 23, 1777

North America: American Revolutionary War (continued): Relief of Fort Stanwix. With a relief column of 1,000 men under Major General Benedict Arnold approaching, the allied Iroquois desert British commander Lieutenant Colonel Barry St. Leger, and he raises the siege of Fort Stanwix on August 23, 1777, abandoning stores and cannon in a precipitous withdrawal to Oswego.

September 11, 1777

North America: American Revolutionary War (continued): Battle of the Brandywine. On July 23, 1777, British commander Lieutenant General William Howe opens a new front when he sails from Sandy Hook, New Jersey, with 13,000 troops in some 260 ships. Washington is uncertain of the British destination, only clarified when the fleet sails into Chesapeake Bay. Washington now shifts the bulk of his forces south to meet Howe.

On August 25 British troops begin coming ashore at Head of Elk (Elkton), Maryland. Howe knows that Washington must fight to defend Philadelphia, the seat of Congress, and he anticipates destroying Washington's army in one large set-piece battle.

Washington takes up position north of Brandywine Creek and astride the road to Philadelphia to block Howe's access to the capital city. Washington has in place 16,000 men, but 3,000 of them are unreliable militia. Howe fixes Washington in place with a feint on the chief American position at Chadds Ford with 5,000 men under Lieutenant General Wilhelm von Knyphausen. Howe accompanies the main British body of 8,000 men, which swings wide around the American right and across an undefended ford to get in behind the defenders.

Again, though, Howe is slow to execute his attack, and in hard fighting Washington is able to parry the thrust and withdraw his army that night. American casualties are some 200 killed, 700–800 wounded, and almost 400 taken prisoner, as opposed to 99 killed, 488 wounded, and 6 missing for the British. American morale, however, remains high, although the British occupy Philadelphia on September 26.

September 19, 1777

North America: American Revolutionary War (continued): Battles of Saratoga: Battle of Freeman's Farm. British lieutenant general John Burgoyne's advance south, impeded at every turn by the Americans and slowed by his extensive baggage train and the need to construct dozens of bridges and causeways across swamps and creeks, slows to only a mile a day. On September 13–14, 1777, the British cross the Hudson River on a bridge of rafts. The troops at last reach Saratoga, New York, only a few miles from

John Trumbull's painting depicting the surrender of British lieutenant general John Burgoyne to Continental Army major general Horatio Gates at Saratoga on October 17, 1777. The American victory here marked a major turning point in the American Revolutionary War that led France to enter the war openly on the American side. (National Archives)

their goal of Albany, but there they find their way halted in a series of battles fought for control of the main Albany road. Collectively known as the Battles of Saratoga, these are the Battle of Freeman's Farm, or the First Battle of Saratoga (September 19), and the Battle of Bemis Heights, or the Second Battle of Saratoga (October 7).

Meanwhile, although Continental Army major general Philip Schuyler's scorched-earth strategy is a major factor in the ultimate American victory, dissatisfaction with his withdrawals leads Congress to replace him in command of the forces facing Burgoyne with Major General Horatio Gates.

The Battle of Freeman's Farm occurs on the afternoon of September 19. Some 6,000 American troops, their right flank anchored on the Hudson River, occupy a fortified position of redoubts and breastworks

on Bemis Heights south of a 15-acre clearing known as Freeman's Farm. Burgoyne opens the battle when he orders three of his regiments to attack across the clearing and dislodge the Americans from Bemis Heights. The British attack goes poorly. Brigadier General Daniel Morgan and Major General Benedict Arnold halt the advance, with Morgan's riflemen inflicting heavy casualties on the British, especially the officers. Fortunately for Burgoyne, Gates refuses to leave his entrenchments to support Arnold and Morgan, rejecting Arnold's request for reinforcements to mount a counterattack. Hessian forces turn the American right flank, and that night the British encamp in the field. However, they have failed to dislodge the Americans on Bemis Heights, the object of their attack. The British also sustain some 600 casualties to only 300 for the Americans.

SARATOGA CAMPAIGN, 1777

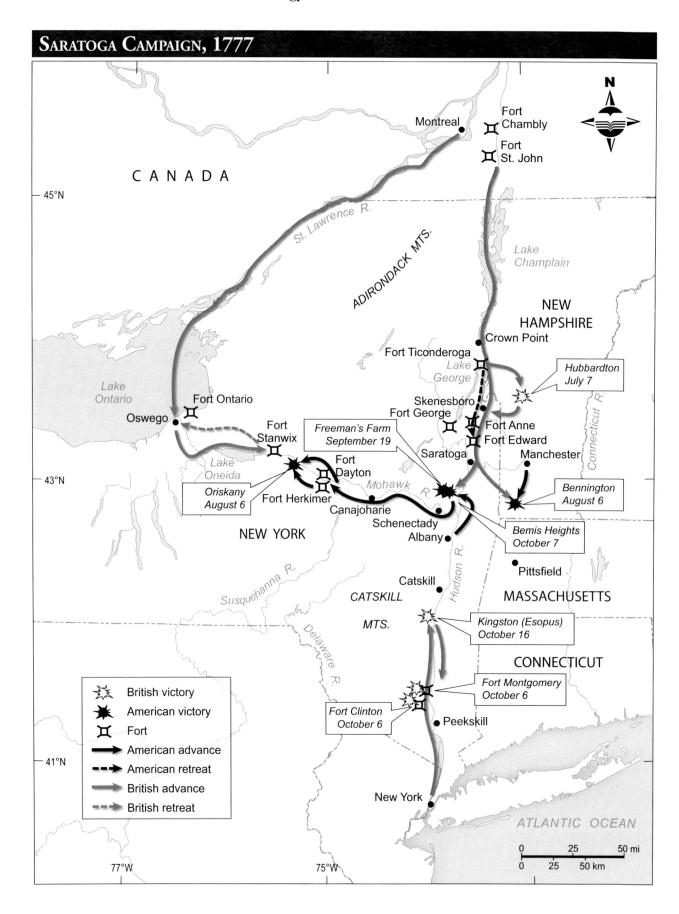

N

CANADA

45°N

St. Lawrence R.

Montreal

Fort Chambly

Fort St. John

Lake Champlain

ADIRONDACK MTS.

NEW HAMPSHIRE

Crown Point

Fort Ticonderoga

Lake George

Hubbardton July 7

Lake Ontario

Fort Ontario

Oswego

Skenesboro
Fort George

Fort Anne
Fort Edward

Connecticut R.

Fort Stanwix

Freeman's Farm September 19

Saratoga

Manchester

Bennington August 6

43°N

Lake Oneida

Fort Dayton

Oriskany August 6

Fort Herkimer

Canajoharie

Mohawk R.

Bemis Heights October 7

NEW YORK

Schenectady
Albany

Hudson R.

Pittsfield

Susquehanna R.

Catskill

CATSKILL

MTS.

MASSACHUSETTS

Kingston (Esopus) October 16

Delaware R.

CONNECTICUT

Fort Montgomery October 6

Fort Clinton October 6

Peekskill

41°N

✧ British victory

✴ American victory

Ⓧ Fort

→ American advance

⇢ American retreat

→ British advance

⇢ British retreat

New York

ATLANTIC OCEAN

0   25   50 mi
0   25   50 km

77°W   75°W

September 21, 1777

North America: American Revolutionary War (continued): Battle of Paoli. On September 21, 1777, Major General Charles Grey leads 5,000 British troops in a surprise attack on an American brigade of 1,500 men under Brigadier General Anthony Wayne camped at Paoli Tavern near present-day Malvern, Pennsylvania. The Americans claim that the British take no prisoners, and the engagement becomes known as the Paoli Massacre. The battle claims 53 Americans killed, 113 wounded, and 71 captured. British losses are only 4 killed and 5 wounded.

October 4, 1777

North America: American Revolutionary War (continued): Battle of Germantown. On the morning of October 4 Continental Army commander General George Washington, with 11,000 men, mounts a surprise attack on the main British army camp at Germantown, outside of Philadelphia. His plan of a night march and four converging columns proves too difficult for his men to execute, and the two columns of militia do not get into the battle at all. Blunders and poor discipline also contribute to the outcome.

British commander Lieutenant General William Howe rushes reinforcements from Philadelphia, and the American thrust is defeated. American losses are 152 killed, 521 wounded, and about 400 taken prisoner; the British lose 71 killed, 450 wounded, and 14 missing.

Both sides then go into winter quarters, the Americans at Valley Forge on the Schuylkill River some 25 miles from Philadelphia.

October 7, 1777

North America: American Revolutionary War (continued): Battles of Saratoga (continued): Battle of Bemis Heights. The Americans are reinforced, and by the time of the Battle of Bemis Heights (also known as the Second Battle of Saratoga), Continental Army major general Horatio Gates has some 11,500 men to only 6,617 for British lieutenant general John Burgoyne.

Meanwhile, Major General Sir Henry Clinton, commanding 7,000 men in New York City, answers Burgoyne's appeal for assistance by taking 4,000 men up the Hudson. On October 6 Clinton captures forts Clinton and Montgomery in the Highlands, but this British force returns to New York City after burning Esopus (Kingston), New York. Burgoyne will have

to fight on without the southern force on which he had counted.

At a council of war on October 5 Burgoyne's officers press him to retreat while there is still opportunity, but Burgoyne steadfastly refuses and orders a full-scale attack on October 7 in an attempt to turn the American flank. In the ensuing Battle of Bemis Heights, Gates commits Brigadier General Daniel Morgan's riflemen on the British right flank. Brigadier General Ebenezer Learned's brigade is in the center, and Brigadier General Enoch Poor's brigade is on the left. Gates's refusal to commit his entire force mitigates the British defeat, but Major General Benedict Arnold, who had quarreled with Gates and been removed from command, disregards orders and charges onto the field to lead a general American assault that captures two British redoubts. The Americans sustain only about 130 casualties to some 600 for the British.

On October 8 Burgoyne orders a general retreat, only to find that the Americans have blocked that possibility. Aware that Clinton will not be able to relieve him, on October 17 Burgoyne formally surrenders his army of 5,895 officers and men. Gates grants the British paroles on the condition that they not serve again in America. Congress, outraged at this agreement, shamefully repudiates the terms, leading to the imprisonment of the British troops.

In many ways, Saratoga is the turning point of the American Revolutionary War. Clinton now evacuates the Hudson Highlands as well as Ticonderoga and Crown Point. All the British have to show for a year's campaigning is the occupation of Philadelphia. The war now becomes a major issue in British politics.

More important, the Battles of Saratoga lead France to change its policy. News of the victory is a bombshell in France. Convinced that the Americans could win, France soon openly enters the war on the American side, and elements of France's army and navy will contribute substantially to the American victory.

October 22–November 20, 1777

North America: American Revolutionary War (continued): British forces clear the Delaware River. On September 26 British troops under Lieutenant General William Howe occupy Philadelphia. They will winter there and in the vicinity. The occupation of the American capital is a step devoid of military significance, however. To safeguard the passage of their supply ships to Philadelphia, British warships under Howe's brother, Rear Admiral Richard Howe, operate with land troops to clear the river of obstructions and forts. In hard-fought contests, the British force the evacuation of forts Mifflin and Mercer during October 22–November 20, 1777.

Winter of 1777–1778

North America: American Revolutionary War (continued): Winter encampment at Valley Forge. The American army passes a difficult winter at Valley Forge, near Philadelphia. At first the men are housed only in tents, and food is in short supply. As many as 2,500 Americans die, and many others desert.

This coincides with an unsuccessful effort (the Conway Cabal) within the army to replace General George Washington as commander in chief with Major General Horatio Gates. Washington appoints a new arrival from Europe, Frederick Wilhelm August Hendrik Ferdinand Steuben, a former staff officer in the Prussian Army who calls himself a baron, as the drillmaster (later inspector general) of the army. Steuben simplifies drill procedures and sets to work training the army, instilling new pride and discipline that will enable it to compete on an equal footing with the British Army.

February 8, 1778

North America: American Revolutionary War (continued): Franco-American alliance. France and the United States sign both a treaty of amity and concord and a formal alliance. The latter will take effect when war is declared between France and Great Britain (June 17, 1778).

April–May 1778

North Atlantic: Cruise of John Paul Jones. American captain John Paul Jones in the sloop *Ranger* (18 guns), the first ship to raise the Stars and Stripes flag (July 4, 1777), sails for France in November. In Quiberon Bay he receives the first official salute to the American flag in Europe, from French warships (February 14, 1778).

Jones then sails into the Irish Sea and brazenly attacks and captures the town of Whitehaven, England, holding it for several hours. It is the first foreign invasion of England since the Norman Conquest. Off

John Paul Jones (1747–1792) was the first great American naval hero. He achieved renown during the American Revolutionary War, especially for his victory while in command of the converted East Indiaman *Bonhomme Ricard* over the British frigate *Serapis* on September 23, 1779, one of the most celebrated single ship combats in history. (Library of Congress)

Carrickfergus on April 20, 1778, the *Ranger* engages and defeats the Royal Navy sloop *Drake* (14 guns), the first British warship taken during the war in home waters. Jones takes his prize to Brest, France, arriving there on May 8.

See Leaders: Jones, John Paul

June 17, 1778

North America: American Revolutionary War (continued). War begins between France and Great Britain, leading to the employment of major French naval and land units in America and significantly altering the course of the war.

June 28, 1778

North America: American Revolutionary War (continued): Battle of Monmouth. On June 18, 1778, new

British commander in North America Lieutenant General Henry Clinton evacuates Philadelphia and marches his troops to the coast to New Jersey in order that they be transported by ship to New York. Washington strikes camp at Valley Forge and pursues with 12,000 men, determined to attack a portion of the British force of 10,000 men en route.

On June 28 Washington sends a majority of his army under Major General Charles Lee against the British rear led by Major General Charles, Lord Cornwallis. Lee mishandles the attack so badly that there are suggestions that he had turned traitor while in British captivity. The battle ends with a furious Washington and the rest of the army blunting a British counterattack.

The Battle of Monmouth, which is fought in extreme heat, is the last major engagement in the north. American losses are less than half those of the British: 152 killed and 300 wounded versus British losses of 290 killed, 390 wounded, and 576 captured. Clinton returns to New York City, and Washington takes up station at White Plains. Lee is dismissed from the Continental Army.

July 3, 1778

North America: American Revolutionary War (continued): Battle of the Wyoming Valley. Colonel John Butler leads a force of some 800 Loyalists and allied Seneca warriors who attack and destroy a force of some 360 Patriot militiamen in the Wyoming Valley of Pennsylvania on July 3, 1778. More than half of the Patriot force are killed, including 30–40 who surrender and are tortured to death by the Native Americans after the battle. The attackers go on to terrorize and largely destroy settlements and crops in the valley.

July 27, 1778

Eastern Atlantic Ocean: Battle of Ushant. This first fleet action of the war between Britain and France occurs west of the French island of Ushant, in the Bay of Biscay in the Atlantic Ocean. French admiral Louis Guillouet, Comte D'Orvilliers, sails from Brest on July 8, 1778, with 32 warships, hoping to intercept two British convoys returning from the East Indies. On July 9 British admiral Augustus Viscount Keppel sorties with a similarly sized fleet of 30 ships of the line and 16 frigates from Portsmouth both to protect the convoys and to prevent a possible union between the French and a Spanish fleet preparing in Cádiz.

Keppel locates the French on July 23 some 100 miles off the French coast and due west of Ushant. Over the next four days the fleets maneuver for advantage. Battle is joined on July 27, with the two fleets on opposite tacks in line-ahead formation. As is their wont, the French fire into the rigging to incapacitate rather than destroy enemy ships. The British follow their usual procedure of firing into the hulls. The inconclusive battle lasts several hours.

That night the French, who have sustained more damage than the British, leave several small fast ships in place with lights on. The British plan to resume the fight the next day, only to discover in the morning that the French have sailed for home. Keppel is court-martialed but acquitted for his handling of the affair.

July–December 1778

North America: American Revolutionary War (continued): Patriot capture and loss of Vincennes. In a small operation of vast strategic importance, in mid-1778 George Rogers Clark convinces Virginia governor Patrick Henry to mount an expedition to secure British posts in the Old Northwest, including Detroit if possible. Commissioned a lieutenant colonel in the militia, Clark sets out with 175 men on his secret expedition. In July 1778 Clark surprises and captures both Vincennes (in Indiana) and Kaskaskia (in Illinois). He is successful in large part because the French-speaking inhabitants and Native Americans there refuse to support the British.

In December, however, Colonel Henry Hamilton, British commander at Detroit, recaptures Vincennes and rebuilds Fort Sackville there.

August 1778

North America: American Revolutionary War (continued): Newport Campaign. In Rhode Island, Continental Army major general John Sullivan tries to use the arrival off New England of French vice admiral Jean Baptiste Charles Henri Hector Theodat, Comte d'Estaing, and his squadron of 12 ships of the line carrying 4,000 ground troops to gain an advantage. Sullivan secures additional regulars from Continental Army commander General George Washington and calls out militia to eventually field 10,000 men. The plan calls for the Americans to cross to

Aquidneck Island (officially known as Rhode Island, but not to be confused with the state of Rhode Island) north of the city of Newport.

On August 9 the Americans cross to the island and move south on its east side. The French are to land on the west side and move with the Americans to attack the British garrison of some 3,000 men commanded by Major General Sir Robert Pigot at Newport. The plan goes awry.

Reinforced, British rear admiral Richard Howe sails north from New York with 13 ships to engage d'Estaing's 12. The Frenchman nevertheless has the advantage, as his ships are larger and have greater weight of broadside. D'Estaing sails out to engage the British, but a storm on August 11 damages both fleets. D'Estaing rejects appeals that he remain, even for a few days, and sails for Boston to refit. Sullivan might still have won a victory, but with d'Estaing's departure most of the American militiamen lose heart and also leave. Pigot then sorties from Newport to attack the Americans on August 28–29.

In what is known as the Battle of Newport, some 5,000 Americans hold off the 3,000 British troops. Sullivan withdraws his men from the island on the night of August 30. It is a wise decision, for the next day 4,000 British reinforcements arrive.

November 11, 1778

North America: American Revolutionary War (continued): Battle of Cherry Valley. Captain Walter Butler (son of Colonel John Butler, leader of the Wyoming Valley attack) leads some 400 Loyalists and 300 Seneca Indians in an attack on the fort and village of Cherry Valley, in eastern New York, on November 11, 1778. While the attackers are unable to take the fort, they do destroy the village. Forty-seven people are killed and scalped, including 32 women and children, in what the Patriots remember as the Cherry Valley Massacre.

November 13, 1778

Caribbean Basin: American Revolutionary War (continued). British forces under Vice Admiral Samuel Barrington capture St. Lucia in the West Indies.

December 29, 1778

North America: American Revolutionary War (continued): British capture of Savannah. On December 23, 1778, British forces land on Tybee Island, Geor-

gia, and on December 29 Lieutenant Colonel Archibald Campbell leads 3,500 men to defeat some 1,000 American Continentals and militiamen commanded by Continental Army major general Robert Howe and capture this important southern seaport. American losses total 83 men, with 450 captured; the British losses are 9 men killed and 4 wounded.

1778

Southeast Asia: Laos: Siamese invasion. Laos, divided into the two principalities of Luang Prabang and Vientiane, falls prey to intervention by Vietnam and Siam (present-day Thailand). In 1778 troops of Siamese king P'ya Taksin invade and conquer Vientiane, forcing it to acknowledge Siamese suzerainty.

1778–1779

Central Europe: War of the Bavarian Succession between Austria and Prussia. The death of Bavarian elector Maximilian Joseph in 1777 leads to a crisis. His ruling line is extinct, and Prussia and Austria support different candidates for the throne. Charles Theodore, the elector palatine, is the legal heir to the Bavarian lands. Habsburg emperor Joseph II persuades him to recognize certain Austrian claims to Lower Bavaria and the Upper Palatinate. As a consequence of the Treaty of Vienna of January 1778, Austrian troops occupy Lower Bavaria.

Charles Theodore is childless, though, and the heir presumptive is Charles Augustus Christian, duke of the palatinate of Zweibrücken (Deux-Ponts). King Frederick II of Prussia opens correspondence with him and, promising assistance, encourages him to dispute the Austrian claims. Frederick also incites the rulers of Saxony and Mecklenburg in the same fashion. When negotiations fail, Joseph II and Frederick II join their respective armies, already facing one another along the frontier between Bohemia and Silesia. Saxony joins Prussia.

This is a largely bloodless conflict, often called the Potato War for the soldiers' staple diet. Prussian troops invade Bohemia, but Frederick finds the Austrian positions too strong, and the war settles into a series of small skirmishes while both principal armies merely face one another. Correspondence between Empress Maria Theresa and Frederick, instigated by the former and assisted by Russian and French mediation, leads to the end of the conflict in the Treaty of Teschen of May 13, 1779.

1778–1779

West Africa: American Revolutionary War (continued). France reconquers from Britain the Senegal posts. The Treaty of Paris of 1783 ending the war divides the posts between France and Britain.

January–June 1779

North America: American Revolutionary War (continued): Fighting in the American South. In January, following the British capture of Savannah, British major general Augustine Prevost moves to Georgia from Florida with reinforcements. While British lieutenant colonel Archibald Campbell captures Augusta on January 29, Prevost attacks Port Royal Island (Beaufort). He is repulsed, however, by Patriot forces under Brigadier General William Moultrie.

At the same time, Patriot militia under Brigadier General Andrew Pickens defeat a Tory brigade at Kettle Creek on February 14, 1779. Patriot pursuit of the British, who had evacuated Augusta, is thwarted in the Battle of Briar Creek on March 3.

Major General Benjamin Lincoln arrives in South Carolina with Continental Army reinforcements and takes command of the Southern Department from Major General Robert Howe. Prevost tries and fails to take Charleston in May and returns to Savannah despite Lincoln's attack at Stono Ferry on June 20. Although there are regular forces there on both sides, in the South militia forces, both Patriot and Loyalist, play a much greater role than in the North.

February 25, 1779

North America: American Revolutionary War (continued): Patriot capture of Vincennes. Learning of the British recapture of Vincennes (in Indiana) and their rebuilding of Fort Sackville there in December 1778, Virginia Militia lieutenant colonel George Rogers Clark mounts a 180-mile winter march from Kaskaskia to retake the fort. Clark reaches Vincennes on February 23, 1779.

Clark warns the inhabitants of his approach and marches men back and forth with flags to create the impression of a far larger force. Following a brief fight, Hamilton surrenders on February 25. Although Clark is unable to take Detroit or completely halt Native American raids, his accomplishment helps secure for the United States the entire region from the Alleghenies to the Mississippi River, an area greater than that of the 13 original colonies.

May 13, 1779

Central Europe: War of the Bavarian Succession: Treaty of Teschen. Signed on May 13, 1779, in Teschen (present-day Cieszyn, Poland) between Austria and Prussia, the Treaty of Teschen abrogates the Treaty of Vienna of January 1778 between Emperor Joseph II and Charles Theodore, elector palatine, awarding Austria only the Innvertel district (territory between the Inn, Salzach, and the Danube) of Bavaria. Austria also agrees to the future union of Ansbach and Baireuth with the Prussian monarchy. Saxony secures some previously disputed rights and 9 million rix dollars. With the treaty, the electorships of Bavaria and the Palatinate are united.

The Treaty of Teschen is a diplomatic victory for Prussian king Frederick II and a setback for Joseph II, for had the Treaty of Vienna been allowed to stand it would have both strengthened Austria's western frontier strategically and enhanced his status among the German princes politically. It also frustrates his plan for ceding the Netherlands to the House of Wittelsbach in exchange for Bavaria five years later (1784).

June 4, 1779

Caribbean Basin: American Revolutionary War (continued). A French squadron carrying troops and commanded by Vice Admiral Jean Baptiste Charles Henri Hector Theodat, Comte d'Estaing, captures St. Vincent in the West Indies.

June 21, 1779–February 6, 1783

North America: American Revolutionary War (continued): Spanish declaration of war against Great Britain and Siege of Gibraltar. On June 21, 1779, Spain enters the war on the side of France, but it comes too late in the war to have much impact, and the decision is prompted primarily by a desire to recover Gibraltar from the British.

In one of the great feats of British arms, a defending force of 5,000 men (eventually 7,000), ably commanded by General George Augustus Eliott and supplied and supported by the British fleet, defends Gibraltar against an attacking force that grows by September 1782 to as many as 40,000 Spanish and French troops and 40 ships. The British employ hot shot to destroy 10 large French floating batteries. The 1,320-day siege claims 33 British troops lost to battle and 536 from illness. Spanish and French losses together total some 5,000 men.

July 4, 1779

Caribbean Basin: American Revolutionary War (continued): French capture of Grenada. French vice admiral Jean Baptiste Charles Henri Hector Theodat, Comte d'Estaing, reinforced from Brest to 25 ships of the line and several frigates, departs Port Royal and arrives off Grenada on July 2. French troops go ashore and capture the island, including a Royal Navy sloop and 30 merchantmen, by July 4.

July 6, 1779

Caribbean Basin: American Revolutionary War (continued): Battle of Grenada. On July 6, 1779, having learned that the French have taken Grenada, British vice admiral Sir John Byron, with 21 ships of the line and 1 frigate, escorts 28 transports to the island, arriving at dawn on July 6. Short of frigates and unaware of the true size of the French force, Byron details three ships of the line to guard the convoy and orders the remainder to attack d'Estaing's ships as they struggle out of Georgetown. To his dismay, Byron also finds himself engaging a superior force, and the three British leading ships of the line sustain heavy damage from French fire.

The cautious d'Estaing ends the battle in the afternoon, though, withdrawing to the south without having taken advantage of his superior numbers or attempted to take four English ships dismasted during the battle. The British lose 183 killed and 346 wounded; French losses are 190 killed and 759 wounded. Byron retires to St. Kitts to refit, returning to England in August. He is replaced as commander on the Leeward Islands Station by Admiral Sir George Brydges Rodney. The strategic advantage remains with the French until April 1782 and Rodney's victory in the Battle of the Saints.

July 16, 1779

North America: American Revolutionary War (continued): Battle of Stony Point. At the end of May, British troops had moved up the Hudson and on June 1 had captured Stony Point on the west side of the river and Verplanck's Point on the east side, both some 25 miles north of New York City. This allows them to close off King's Ferry, a narrow crossing point of the river.

On July 15, however, Brigadier General Anthony Wayne leads 1,350 men in a night attack against the 700-man British Stony Point garrison. The assault is carried out with unloaded muskets and bayonets,

Continental Army major general Anthony Wayne was one of the best tactical commanders of the American Revolutionary War. A thorough disciplinarian and meticulous planner, Wayne commanded the Legion of the United States and defeated a Native American force in the Battle of Fallen Timbers on August 20, 1794. Many regard Wayne as the father of the U.S. Army. (National Archives)

and the surprised British soon surrender. The Americans lose 15 killed and 80 wounded, but British losses are severe: 63 killed, more than 70 wounded, and 543 captured. Although Wayne is forced to abandon the post several days later, the attack secures much-needed arms, including 15 cannon, as well as supplies.

See Leaders: Wayne, Anthony

July 25–August 14, 1779

North America: American Revolutionary War (continued): Penobscot Expedition. In 1779 the British construct a fort on Bagaduce Peninsula, in the bay of the Penobscot River. Learning that 700 British regulars have arrived there on June 17 supported by 3 ships mounting 56 guns under Captain Henry Mowat, Massachusetts dispatches 18 warships and privateers mounting 108 guns under Captain Dudley Saltonstall and a land force of 900 men under Brigadier General Solomon Lovell. American operations proceed slowly, and the arrival of powerful British naval reinforcements brings ruin.

All the American ships are destroyed or captured. The survivors escape overland to return to Boston. Saltonstall is court-martialed and cashiered. The expedition failed from command problems, lack of planning and sufficient aggressiveness, and insufficient resources.

August 19, 1779
North America: American Revolutionary War (continued): Battle of Paulus Hook. Continental Army major Henry Lee leads an attack on a British outpost at Paulus Hook (present-day Jersey City), New Jersey. In a predawn assault on August 19, 1779, the Continentals storm and take the British works, killing 50 British troops and taking 158 prisoners at a cost of only 2 men killed and 3 wounded.

August–September 1779
North America: American Revolutionary War (continued): Expedition against the Indians. In order to end Loyalist and Native American depredations in western Pennsylvania and New York, Continental Army commander General George Washington authorizes a massive operation in the summer of 1779 commanded by Major General John Sullivan. The soldiers destroy some 40 Iroquois villages in central and western New York, including a large Cayuga settlement near present-day Ithaca, and burn thousands of bushels of grain. The expedition significantly reduces Loyalist and Native attacks in the region.

September 3–October 28, 1779
North America: American Revolutionary War (continued): American siege of Savannah. French vice admiral Jean Baptiste Charles Henri Hector Theodat, Comte d'Estaing, arrives from the West Indies off British-held Savannah, Georgia, with a fleet and 4,000 troops. Capturing several British ships, he disembarks his ground troops on September 12 and invests the city. The French are joined over the next week by Continental Army commander in the South Major General Benjamin Lincoln with more than 2,000 Continentals and militia.

British major general Augustine Prevost commands at Savannah with 3,500 men. The city's defenses are strong and can withstand a lengthy siege. Unwilling to wait too long lest his fleet encounter the hurricane season, d'Estaing insists on an assault. Alerted by a deserter as to the exact point of the attack (Spring Hill Redoubt), the British are waiting and hurl back the assault on October 9.

The allies lose 244 killed and 584 wounded, 20 percent of their total force and half of those actually in the fight. Among the mortally wounded is Brigadier General Polish Count Casimir Pulaski, known as the "Father of the American cavalry." British losses are 40 killed, 63 wounded, and 52 missing, which is certainly the most desperate battle since Bunker Hill and is well fought on both sides.

Refusing to remain longer, d'Estaing embarks his troops and sails away; Lincoln returns to Charleston.

September 23, 1779
North Sea: American Revolutionary War (continued): Battle between the *Bonhomme Richard* and the *Serapis*. In August 1779 Captain John Paul Jones departs France in the converted 40-gun East Indiaman *Bonhomme Richard* in concert with some French vessels. He circumnavigates the British Isles, taking 17 prizes.

On September 23 off Flamborough Head in the North Sea, off the east coast of England, Jones undertakes a desperate night engagement with the Royal Navy frigate *Serapis* (44 guns), commanded by Captain Richard Pearson. The two ships, lashed together, pound one another at point-blank range. With both ships on fire and the American ship sinking, Pearson calls upon Jones to surrender. Jones responds, "No, I'll sink, but I'll be damned if I will strike," later recalled as "I have not yet begun to fight." Within the hour, the *Serapis* strikes.

Of its crew of 284, the *Serapis* has 130 dead or wounded, while the *Bonhomme Richard* suffers 150 casualties out of 322. Jones moves his own crew to the *Serapis* and sails it to the Texel in the Netherlands.

September 1779
North America: American Revolutionary War (continued): Spanish operations on the lower Mississippi. Recognizing the threat posed to New Orleans by British posts on the Mississippi, Spanish governor of Louisiana Don Bernardo de Galvez and a small force

take Manchac (September 7), Baton Rouge (September 20), and Natchez (September 30).

December 26, 1779

North America: American Revolutionary War (continued): Opening of the British Charleston Campaign. As part of London's new strategy of concentrating on the American South, British commander in North America Lieutenant General Sir Henry Clinton leaves Lieutenant General Baron Wilhelm von Knyphausen in command in the North and sails with 8,500 men in 90 transports, convoyed by 5 ships of the line and 9 frigates. The ships assemble off Tybee Island, at the mouth of the Savannah River, and then sail for Charleston on February 10. The next day British troops come ashore on Johns Island, 30 miles south of Charleston.

See Leaders: Clinton, Sir Henry

1779–1781

South Africa: First Kaffir War. In 1778 white Boer settlers and black Bantu tribesmen, known as Kaffirs to the Boers, come into close contact. War begins in 1779 and lasts until 1781 but proves inconclusive.

1779–1782

South Asia: India: First Anglo-Maratha War. Raghunathrao has murdered his nephew and seized the throne as Peshwa of the Maratha Empire. He secures British support against a dozen Maratha chiefs, led by Nana Phadnis, who seek to replace him with Madhavrao, the posthumous legitimate heir to the throne. The Bombay government concludes a treaty with Raghunathrao that gives the British territorial concessions, but the Marathas subsequently repudiate. When the Maratha leaders grant the French a port on the western coast, this leads the Bombay government to send a force of 3,900 men (600 British troops) toward Pune. Raghunathrao joins them en route with several thousand more soldiers and artillery. The Maratha army is much larger, however, and has capable commanders in Tukojirao Holkar and Mahadji Shinde (Mahadji Sindia). Cut off from their supplies and harassed by Marathan cavalry at Talegaon near Pune, the British halt their advance and seek to withdraw at night, but the Marathas pursue and surround the British at the village of Wadgaon (now Vadgaon Maval), on January 12, 1779, forcing the Treaty of Wadagon on January 16 whereby the Bombay gov-

British lieutenant general Sir Henry Clinton (1730–1795) was commander in chief of British forces in the American colonies during 1778–1782. Clinton shifted the war to the American South. Although he forced the surrender of an entire American army at Charleston in 1780, Clinton was blamed for the capitulation of his own subordinate, Lieutenant General Charles Cornwallis, at Yorktown the following year. (Library of Congress)

ernment pledges to relinquish all territories acquired by it for the East India Company since 1773.

British reinforcements under Colonel William Goddard arrive too late to save the Bombay force, but Warren Hastings, British governor-general in Bengal, subsequently rejects the treaty on the grounds that the Bombay officials had no authority to sign it. He orders Goddard to restore British authority. Goddard's 6,000 men take Ahmedabad in February 1779 and Bassein in December 1780. Another Bengal force, led by Captain William Popham, captures Gwalior in August 1780, while yet another force under Major Jacob Camac harasses Mahadji Shinde and defeats him in a battle at Sipri in February 1781.

With the fighting inconclusive, Shinde proposes a new treaty with the British that will recognize the young Madhavrao as Peshwa and buy off Raghunathrao. The British agree, and the Treaty of Salbai is signed on May 17, 1782, guaranteeing peace for 20 years.

January 16–17, 1780
Eastern Atlantic Ocean: American Revolutionary War (continued): Battle of Cape St. Vincent. A British squadron of 18 ships of the line and 9 frigates under Admiral Sir George Rodney is escorting a large number of transports carrying reinforcements to Gibraltar, besieged by the Spanish since July 1779. On January 8 west of Cape Finisterre, the British spot a Spanish ship of the line and 6 frigates commanded by Commodore Don Juan di Yardi escorting 16 provision ships to Cádiz. Rodney orders a general chase, and his ships capture them all.

Resuming course for Gibraltar, on January 16 Rodney comes across a Spanish squadron of 9 ships of the line (2 others had separated from the squadron in a storm two days earlier) and 2 frigates under Admiral Don Juan de Lángara. Disregarding the Fighting Instructions, Rodney again orders a general chase.

The Battle of Cape St. Vincent, also known as the Moonlight Battle, begins at 4:00 p.m. and continues through increasingly stormy seas and darkness until almost 2:00 a.m. the next day. One Spanish ship of the line blows up with the loss of all hands. Four ships of the line and the 2 frigates escape, but the British capture 4 ships of the line. Continued storms the next day compel abandonment of two of them, retaken by their Spanish crews.

Rodney completes his resupply mission at Gibraltar before continuing on to the West Indies. Arriving at Saint Lucia on March 22, he assumes command of the station.

February–March 1780
North America: American Revolutionary War (continued): Mobile Campaign. Spanish governor of Louisiana Don Bernardo de Galvez lands a small force from New Orleans at Mobile (in present-day Alabama), the second-largest town in British West Florida, capturing it on March 14. A British relief force under Major General John Campbell returns to Pensacola.

February 11–May 12, 1780
North America: American Revolutionary War (continued): British siege of Charleston. With his troops from New York, British commander in North America Lieutenant General Sir Henry Clinton commands some 14,500 men before Charleston and enjoys significant naval support from the ships of the squadron under British commander in chief of the North American Station Vice Admiral Marriot Arbuthnot. Commander of Continental Army forces in the south Major General Benjamin Lincoln and the entire American army in the south take up position in Charleston. Lincoln, having agreed to an appeal from the city leaders, allows his forces to be bottled up in Charleston. But as soon as British shells began to fall on the city, the same leaders demand that he surrender.

Charleston capitulates on May 12, 1780. The British capture 5,466 officers and men (including 7 generals), 400 cannon, and half a dozen small warships in the biggest single defeat for American arms of the entire war and the greatest defeat for an American army before the fall of Bataan in the Philippines in 1942.

Believing that the campaign in the south is pretty much won and leaving behind his second-in-command Lieutenant General Charles, Lord Cornwallis, and 8,500 men to continue mopping up operations, Clinton returns with the remainder of the British troops to New York.

February 28, 1780
North America: American Revolutionary War (continued): League of Armed Neutrality. The British blockade of French and Spanish supply ships to America is dealt a serious setback when Czarina Catherine II announces that Russia will protect its trade against all belligerents. Denmark (July 9) and Sweden (August 1) join the so-called League of Armed Neutrality. Ultimately the Netherlands, Prussia, Portugal, Austria, and the Kingdom of the Two Sicilies all adhere to it.

May–August 1780
North America: American Revolutionary War (continued): British operations in South Carolina. Attempting to pacify the remainder of South Carolina, British lieutenant general Charles, Lord Cornwallis, conducts operations in the interior. British policies contribute to the horrific partisan warfare between Loyalists and Patriots in the south. Lieutenant Colonel Banastre Tarleton, commander of the British

Legion (known as the Green Dragoons for the color of their uniforms) is accused by the Patriots of killing those he captures. The phrase "Tarleton's quarter" is thus synonymous with no quarter.

In the one-sided British victory in the Battle of Waxhaws in South Carolina on May 29, 1780, the Patriots accuse Tarleton of perpetrating a massacre. His alleged actions help set the character of the southern fighting but work to Patriot advantage, alarming the inhabitants and driving the previously uncommitted into the Patriot camp. Lieutenant Colonel Francis Marion and brigadier generals Thomas Sumter and Andrew Pickens take the lead in the ensuing Patriot guerrilla warfare.

July 11, 1780
North America: American Revolutionary War (continued): French forces arrive at Newport, Rhode Island. French admiral Charles d'Arsac, Chevalier de Ternay, with 8 ships of the line and 2 frigates, escorts to North America 26 transports with 5,000 troops under commander of the King's Forces in America Lieutenant General Jean Baptiste Donatien de Vimeur, Comte de Rochambeau. The troops land at Newport, Rhode Island, on July 11, 1780. British ships, however, blockade the harbor, preventing Continental Army commander General George Washington from carrying out a Franco-American operation against New York City.

July 1780
South Asia: India: Second Anglo-Mysore War. Hyder Ali rules the vast southern India kingdom of Mysore, although he is not king. The British fail to honor their defensive alliance of 1769 with Mysore following the First Anglo-Mysore War; they do not come to Hyder Ali's aid when Mysore is attacked by Maratha in 1771. Furious, Hyder Ali commits himself to an alliance with France and seeking revenge against the British.

When France joins the United States in war against Britain early in 1778, the British resolve to drive the French out of India completely. The British capture Pondicherry and Mahé on the Malabar Coast in 1779. They then go on to annex certain lands belonging to a Hyder Ali dependent.

Hyder Ali then forges a joint front with Maratha and in July 1780, with 80,000 men and 100 guns, he attacks the Carnatic, threatening the entire British position in India. This begins the Second Anglo-Mysore War (1780–1784).

August 16, 1780
North America: American Revolutionary War (continued): Battle of Camden. Following Major General Benjamin Lincoln's capture at Charleston, South Carolina, Congress—without consulting Continental Army commander General George Washington—appoints Major General Horatio Gates to command what remains of the Southern Army. Gates joins Major General Johann de Kalb, sent south earlier, at Coxe's Mill, North Carolina, on July 25.

The army is in no condition for offensive operations, but instead of taking time to reorganize his forces and restore morale, Gates immediately sets out with only 4,000 men (about 2,000 regulars and a like number of militia) on a reckless 120-mile march to threaten the British post at Camden, South Carolina, held by Lieutenant Colonel Francis, Lord Rawdon, who calls on Cornwallis for assistance.

Cornwallis hurries up from Charleston and arrives at Camden on August 13. On the night of August 15 he marches from Camden with his 2,200 men, intending to attack Gates's camp. Instead Cornwallis encounters Gates's army marching southward.

In the ensuing Battle of Camden on August 16, the American militia run away. The regulars of the Delaware and Maryland line stand their ground and fight bravely under the able de Kalb, who dies from 11 wounds. Gates is routed.

The British suffer 68 men killed, 245 wounded, and 11 missing; American losses are on the order of 900 killed or wounded and 1,000 captured. The British also take 7 guns, many muskets, and all the American stores and baggage. Gates flees, riding 180 miles on a fast horse in only three days to avoid capture.

September 10, 1780
South Asia: India: Second Anglo-Mysore War (continued): Battle of Peranbakam. In July 1780 Hyder Ali attacks the Carnatic with 80,000 men and 100 guns; he is soon joined by French troops. The British government in Madras is slow to react to this dangerous threat. Not until late summer are troops previously dispatched to areas far from Madras hastily recalled to protect the city. Conjeeveram (present-day Kanchipuram), 40 miles south of Madras on the Arcot road, is the rendezvous point.

Among British forces ordered there is a detachment of 2,800 men under Colonel William Baillie. General Sir Hector Munro, overall commander of British forces and hero of the Battle of Buxar (1764), marches from Madras with some 5,600 men, reaching Conjeeveram on August 29.

Hyder Ali meanwhile sends his son Fateh Ali Tipu (Tipu Sultan, Tiger of Mysore) with 10,000 men and 18 guns to prevent the juncture of Baillie's force with that of Munro. Flooding of the Kortalaiyar River delays Baillie a week, and at Perambakkam, 14 miles from Conjeeveram, he is attacked by Tipu beginning on September 6. Munro, though aware of Baillie's situation, refuses to abandon Conjeeveram and the military stores gathered there. In fact, Munro also is anxious, for supplies promised by British ally Mohammed Ali, the nawab of Arcot, have not materialized.

Finally Munro dispatches a column of 1,000 men to assist Baillie. On September 10 Baillie's joint force is surrounded and totally destroyed in a fierce battle at Perambakkam, won by Hyder Ali's cavalry. The entire British force of some 3,800 men is either killed or captured. Baillie is among the prisoners. It is the most crushing blow the British have suffered in India. Munro abandons his guns and supplies and withdraws back into Madras, where Hyder Ali's army now moves.

September 23, 1780

North America: American Revolutionary War (continued): Treason of Benedict Arnold. Continental Army major general Benedict Arnold, commander of the strategic Hudson River fortress of West Point, having turned traitor, plans to surrender both the fortress and Continental Army commander George Washington (while at West Point on an inspection trip) to the British.

The plan is uncovered on September 23 when militiamen arrest intermediary British major John André with incriminating documents. Arnold escapes and enters British service as a brigadier general. André is hanged as a spy.

October 7, 1780

North America: American Revolutionary War (continued): Battle of Kings Mountain. This battle, which occurs some 30 miles west of Charlotte, North Carolina, is an all-American affair of Loyalist against Patriot. The Loyalists' commander, Major Patrick Ferguson, is the only British officer present. Militia colonels Isaac Shelby and William Campbell lead the Patriot side.

Ferguson takes a strong position at Kings Mountain, expecting reinforcements from the main army that never arrive. Instead, his force is surrounded and annihilated. Of Ferguson's 1,125 men, 1,105 are killed or captured. Ferguson is among the dead, having refused demands to surrender. Colonial losses are only 40 killed. This defeat temporarily halts efforts by British commander in the South Lieutenant General Charles, Lord Cornwallis, to secure North Carolina.

December 2, 1780

North America: American Revolutionary War (continued): Nathanael Greene takes command in the South. Following the debacle of the Battle of Camden, Congress decides to remove Major General Horatio Gates as commander in the South and this time allows Continental Army commander General George Washington to name his successor. On October 6, 1780, Washington selects Nathanael Greene, who had just taken command at West Point. Greene arrives at Charlotte, North Carolina, on December 2.

Greene finds that he has only 2,307 men, with 1,482 of these present for duty and only 800 equipped to fight. The army has provisions for only a few days, and even clothing is in short supply. His opponent, British lieutenant general Charles, Lord Cornwallis, commands some 3,224 well-trained veteran troops and thus outnumbers Greene in effective combat strength 4 to 1. There are also several thousand British and Loyalist troops in garrisons across South Carolina and Georgia.

Necessity forces Greene into a dramatic change of strategy. He divides his army. He will yield territory while he trains and rebuilds the army and awaits the right opportunity. He moves 1,100 men of his army to the Cheraw Hills near Cheraw, South Carolina, on the Pee Dee River. Greene also sends Continental Army brigadier general Daniel Morgan and 600 of his best troops some 140 miles to the west to take up position in western South Carolina between the Pacolet and Broad rivers. There Morgan is joined by 300 volunteers and up to 400 South Carolina and Georgia militiamen.

Morgan is thus in position to threaten British posts at both Ninety Six and Augusta, but Greene's decision is risky, for the two major units of his army are too far apart to be mutually supporting. Logistics plays a major role in the decision, for dividing the army makes it easier to feed and supply.

December 20, 1780

Northern Europe: Britain: American Revolutionary War (continued). As a consequence of clandestine Dutch trade with America, Britain declares war on the Netherlands.

December 30, 1780–May 26, 1781

North America: American Revolutionary War (continued): Operations in Virginia. On the orders of British commander in chief Lieutenant General Henry Clinton, British (formerly Continental Army) brigadier general Benedict Arnold and 1,600 men arrive in Hampton Roads with instructions to raid to the interior, rally Loyalist support, and cut supplies to Patriot forces to the south. Arnold burns Richmond on January 5 and then engages in inconclusive maneuvering with Continental Army forces commanded by Major General Frederick Wilhelm von Steuben.

In April, British major general William Phillips arrives at Williamsburg with 2,000 reinforcements and assumes command from Arnold. Following additional raids, Phillips and Arnold march to meet Lieutenant General Charles, Lord Cornwallis, moving up from North Carolina. Contracting typhoid fever, Phillips dies at Petersburg on May 13. Cornwallis arrives there on May 20 to take command of some 8,000 British troops in Virginia.

Both sides are reinforcing in Virginia. On April 29 Major General Marie-Joseph du Motier, Marquis de Lafayette, arrives in Richmond, sent by Continental Army commander General George Washington with reinforcements to take command in the state and attempt to bag Arnold. Lafayette has some 3,550 men, of whom 1,200 are veteran Continental troops. Washington later sends Brigadier General Anthony Wayne and 1,000 additional Continentals.

See Leaders: Lafayette, Marie-Joseph

1780

Caribbean Basin: American Revolutionary War (continued): Naval operations. In three indecisive engagements in April 1780, a British fleet under Admiral Sir George B. Rodney clashes with a French naval force of equal strength under Admiral Luc Ur-

Marie-Joseph du Motier, Marquis de Lafayette (1757–1834), was born into one of the greatest noble families of France. Seen here in a 1790 image, he volunteered to serve in America during the American Revolutionary War. A strong supporter of George Washington, he became a major general in the Continental Army and a highly effective field commander. Lafayette later played important roles in the French revolutions of 1789 and 1830. (Library of Congress)

bain de Bouexic, Comte de Guichen. A Spanish fleet reinforces Guichen, but disease and indecision prevent the allies from taking advantage of their numerical superiority.

In August, Guichen sails for France. Rodney then sails north to New York, preventing Continental Army commander General George Washington from realizing his plans for a joint French and American land and sea assault on the city. Rodney returns to the West Indies in December.

1780–1782

Southeast Asia: Siam. King P'ya Taksin of Siam (present-day Thailand) invades Vietnam in 1780. After going insane, he is overthrown and killed in

1782. His successor, General Chakri, becomes king as Rama I. He withdraws Siamese troops from Vietnam and establishes the modern city of Bangkok as his capital.

January 17, 1781

North America: American Revolutionary War (continued): Battle of the Cowpens. British commander in the South Lieutenant General Charles, Lord Cornwallis, having received 1,500 reinforcements under Major General Alexander Leslie, resumes offensive operations. In early January 1781 Cornwallis sends Lieutenant Colonel Banastre Tarleton and his crack British Legion, reinforced by infantry, to round up Continental Army forces in western South Carolina under Brigadier General Daniel Morgan. Once this has been accomplished, Cornwallis plans to move against the main American body under Major General Nathanael Greene.

Morgan takes up a defensive position at a place known as Cowpens, located near the North Carolina border and south of the Broad River. The Battle of Cowpens occurs on the morning of January 17, 1781. Counting militia, Morgan may have about 2,000 men; Tarleton has 1,100. Knowing of Tarleton's approach, Morgan selects a hill as the center of his position. His forces are in three lines: the riflemen in front, then the militia, and finally the Continental Line. His cavalry, under Lieutenant Colonel William Washington, is behind the hill.

An overly confident Tarleton fails to reconnoiter and immediately attacks. After firing, Morgan's first two lines withdraw on design. Tarleton, believing that victory is his, rushes forward to encounter the final American line, at which point the riflemen, militia, and cavalry come around both flanks and double envelop the British. In what is sometimes called the American Cannae, Tarleton loses 90 percent of his force.

Tarleton himself escapes along with some of his cavalry, but he leaves behind on the field 100 dead, 229 wounded, and 600 unwounded prisoners. Morgan's losses are only 12 killed and 60 wounded. Morgan also secures some 800 muskets, 2 cannon, 100 horses, and all the British supplies and ammunition. This brilliant victory completely transforms the situation in the South, which had seemed so close to disaster just weeks before. Patriot morale soars.

January 1781

North America: American Revolutionary War (continued): Spanish capture of Fort St. Joseph in Michigan. In late 1780 Spanish governor of Louisiana Don Bernardo de Galvez sends Captain Eugenio Pourré and a small force up the Mississippi River from St. Louis. In January 1781 Pourré's force of some 65 Spanish troops and 200 allied Native Americans capture British Fort St. Joseph on Lake Michigan. The Spanish then return to St. Louis.

January–February 1781

North America: American Revolutionary War (continued): Retreat to the Dan. Following the British disaster in the Battle of Cowpens, British commander in the South Lieutenant General Charles, Lord Cornwallis, pursues the American forces under Brigadier General Daniel Morgan, which are soon joined by those under Major General Nathanael Greene. In one of the most masterly withdrawals in American military history, Greene retreats north. Having arranged for the collection of all the watercraft on the unfordable Dan River, Greene barely escapes the fast-moving British forces into southern Virginia.

February 3, 1781

Caribbean Basin: American Revolutionary War (continued): British capture of St. Eustatius. Having returned to the West Indies from New York in December 1780, Admiral George B. Rodney moves against the island of St. Eustatius, or Statia, as it is then known. This small Dutch possession in the Caribbean, strategically located along shipping routes between Europe and the New World, is a prime trading location and is most active in the transshipment of military goods, especially gunpowder, to the Americans during the American Revolutionary War.

With the British declaration of war against the Dutch in December 1780, London orders Rodney to move against St. Eustatius and St. Martin. Rodney loses no time, moving three days after the orders arrive with 15 ships of the line and 3,000 ground troops under General John Vaughan to take the island. As Rodney hopes, Dutch authorities on the island are unaware of the recent declaration of war, and it is an easy matter for the British to take the island on February 3, 1781. They capture substantial military supplies, including illegal goods shipped by British merchants.

The British keep false colors flying on the island and within a short time capture additional ships that arrive there. In all, the British secure some 150 ships and also pursue and capture a Dutch convoy of 30 ships that had sailed for the Netherlands at the beginning of February. The captured goods are sold at auction, considerably below value. Goods reportedly worth some £3 million are shipped to England, although Hood will be tied up with legal procedures concerning them for years thereafter. Rodney also takes St. Martin and Saba, then returns to England, leaving Rear Admiral Samuel Hood in command. The French retake St. Eustatius in November 1781, and it is returned to the Dutch at the conclusion of the war.

See Leaders: Hood, Samuel

March 15, 1781

North America: American Revolutionary War (continued): Battle of Guilford Courthouse. Now reinforced, Continental Army commander in the South Major General Nathanael Greene takes the offensive and crosses the Dan River into North Carolina. The British commander in the South, Lieutenant General Charles, Lord Cornwallis, is also eager for a showdown.

The two opposing armies join battle at Guilford Courthouse on March 15, 1781, in one of the more important battles of the war. On paper, Greene has the superior force: 4,404 men, including 4,243 infantry and 161 cavalry, but only a third (1,490) are Continental troops, and only about 500 of them are trained veterans. The great majority of Greene's men are unreliable militia. Cornwallis has only 1,900 men, but they are regulars, and almost all are disciplined veterans, steady under fire.

Greene chooses the battlefield and arranges his men in three lines, similar to the system employed in the Battle of Cowpens. Although the battle is hard fought and the outcome in dispute for a time, Greene is unwilling to hazard his army and withdraws. The Americans sustain 264 casualties: 79 killed and 185 wounded, more than half of them militia. Another 160 Continentals are missing along with several hundred of the militia, most of the latter having deserted and returned home. British casualties are much higher: 93 killed and 439 wounded, a number mortally. This amounts to a quarter of the force engaged.

British admiral Sir Samuel Hood (1724–1816) fought in the War of the Austrian Succession, the Seven Years' War, the American Revolutionary War, and the French Revolution and Napoleonic Wars. (Library of Congress)

Two days after the battle, Cornwallis abandons the interior and marches to Wilmington, where he can be resupplied by the Royal Navy. At Wilmington he turns over management of the war in the South to Lieutenant Colonel Francis, Lord Rawdon, and marches north into Virginia with 1,500 men to join British troops there under Brigadier General Benedict Arnold.

Despite being a tactical defeat for Greene, the Battle of Guilford Courthouse changes the entire strategic situation in the South. With the exception of the British coastal enclave of Wilmington, Greene controls North Carolina and now prepares to move into South Carolina.

March 16, 1781

North America: American Revolutionary War (continued): First Battle of the Chesapeake. By early 1781 both the British and Americans have increasing numbers of land troops operating in eastern Virginia. On March 8, 1781, French commodore Charles René Sochet Destouches sails from Newport, Rhode Island, with 8 ships of the line and 3 frigates, carrying 1,120 ground troops and intending to land them in Virginia to operate with Continental Army forces under Major General Marie-Joseph du Motier, Marquis de Lafayette.

Learning that the French have sailed and correctly assuming their destination to be Chesapeake Bay, on March 9 British commander in chief of the North American Station Vice Admiral Marriot Arbuthnot sets out in pursuit with 8 ships of the line and 4 frigates. Because of recent coppering, the British ships are faster and reach the vicinity of the bay first.

In the First Battle of the Chesapeake (also known as the First Battle of the Capes), the fleets sight each other at about 6:00 a.m. on March 16, some 40 miles off Cape Henry. Complicated maneuvering follows; the British secure the weather gauge. The battle opens at around 2:00 p.m. Although the French are to leeward, this enables them to open their lower gun ports and employ the heaviest guns. As is their practice, the French fire high, disabling three of the British ships. Firing low, the British inflict more casualties.

Despite apparent success, Destouches breaks off the action after about an hour and stands out to sea. Arbuthnot chooses not to pursue. The British lose 30 killed and 73 wounded, the French 72 killed and 112 wounded. Strategically it is a British victory, for the French fail to capitalize on their success or land their troops. Destouches returns to Newport.

March 22, 1781

France: American Revolutionary War (continued): A powerful French fleet sails from Brest for the West Indies. On March 22, 1781, French admiral François Joseph Paul, Comte de Grasse, sails from Brest with 26 ships of the line, 14 frigates, and a number of troop transports. Off the Azores, Admiral Pierre André de Suffren separates with 5 ships to sail to the Cape of Good Hope while another ship of the line sails to North America.

De Grasse arrives off Martinique on April 28, and months of inconclusive operations follow involving the West Indian islands of both powers. De Grasse secures a slight advantage in the fighting over Royal Navy units under Rear Admiral Samuel Hood.

April 16, 1781

Eastern Atlantic Ocean: Cape Verde Islands: American Revolutionary War (continued): Battle of Porto Praya. Following the British declaration of war against the Netherlands, London decides to attempt the capture of the Cape of Good Hope, at the southern tip of Africa. A squadron of five small ships of the line and numerous smaller warships escorting a large number of transports duly sails from England under Commodore George Johnstone on March 13, 1781. Learning of the British plans, the French government sends Admiral Pierre André de Suffren and five ships of the line to reinforce the Cape of Good Hope. Suffren departs Brest on March 22 in company with French admiral François Joseph Paul, Comte de Grasse, and then separates to turn south. Although aware that the French are at sea, Johnstone anchors at Porto Praya in the Cape Verde Islands without preparations to repel an attack, which might be expected despite Portugal's neutrality.

Arriving at Porto Praya on the morning of April 16 to secure water, Suffren is surprised to find the English there but at once decides to attack. Although Suffren is poorly served by most of his captains, his attack damages Johnstone's squadron. Suffren then proceeds to the Cape of Good Hope; Johnstone calls off a pursuit. Suffren then lands the troops and fortifies the Cape of Good Hope against a British attack.

Johnstone arrives some time later and rejects any attempt to land. He sends three of his ships on to reinforce India and returns with the remainder to England.

See Leaders: Suffren Saint-Tropez, Pierre André de

April 25, 1781

North America: American Revolutionary War (continued): Battle of Hobkirk's Hill. In a daring move that risks being cut off from behind, Continental Army major general Nathanael Greene proceeds into South Carolina with his small force of about 1,200 Continentals, 250 militia, and fewer than 100

Pierre André de Suffren (1729–1788) was the greatest French admiral of the 18th century. He distinguished himself during the American Revolutionary War by winning a series of battles against the British off India during 1782–1783. (Library of Congress)

cavalry. Supported by guerrilla forces, he will try to clear the state of British outposts in the interior, especially Camden and Ninety Six.

In the days before the April 25, 1781, Battle of Hobkirk's Hill, Greene endeavors to surprise British commander in South Carolina Lieutenant Colonel Francis, Lord Rawdon, at Camden or lure him from the fortifications. However, Thomas Sumter, ordered by Greene to join with his militia, refuses. Rawdon meanwhile learns of Greene's advance and assembles 900 men to meet him, hoping to turn the tables and surprise Greene. The ensuing battle is basically a draw, although Greene leaves the battlefield to Rawdon.

Casualties are about even. The Americans lose 270: 19 killed, 115 wounded, and 136 missing. British casualties are 258: 38 killed and some 220 wounded or missing. Bitter as the pill of Rawdon's tactical victory might be, Greene's army is still in-

tact. It is this battle that prompts Greene to remark, "We fight, get beat, rise and fight again."

May 9, 1781

North America: American Revolutionary War (continued): Spanish capture of Pensacola, West Florida. Spanish governor of Louisiana Don Bernardo de Galvez, with his own naval squadron and supported by land troops from Havana and Mobile, on March 10, 1781, lays siege to Pensacola in West Florida. After a Spanish shell blows up the British magazine at Fort St. George there, Major General John Campbell surrenders the town and province on May 9.

May 22–June 18, 1781

North America: American Revolutionary War (continued): Siege of Ninety Six. Major General Nathanael Greene, Continental Army commander in the South, initiates operations against British outposts in interior South Carolina. In one month the Americans take four outposts and force the evacuation of two others. By May 24 Greene's men have taken 850 prisoners. Augusta surrenders on June 5, with the Patriot forces capturing its garrison of 350 provincials and Loyalist militiamen and 300 Creek Indians.

On May 22 meanwhile, Greene begins siege operations against Ninety Six, just west of the Saluda River, held by 350 provincial regulars and about 200 Loyalist militia. Greene is on the verge of success when he is forced to break off the siege by the approach of British lieutenant colonel Francis, Lord Rawdon, and a relief force of 2,000 men. With only 1,000 men, Greene makes one last effort to take the fort by assault on June 18 and then has no choice but to withdraw.

The first setback of the campaign, the siege of Ninety Six, lasts 28 days and costs the Americans 185 men killed or wounded. Despite Greene's failure to take the British fort, on July 3 Rawdon evacuates the garrison of Ninety Six to Charleston.

July 1, 1781

South Asia: India: Second Anglo-Mysore War (continued): Battle of Porto Novo. This battle is perhaps the most important for British rule in India. On July 1, 1781, at Porto Novo, south of Pondicherry, General Sir Eyre Coote and 8,000 British troops, sent by sea from Bengal, defeat Hyder Ali's army of 60,000 men, causing the latter to flee in disarray. The British suffer 400 casualties in the battle, while Hyder Ali sustains several thousand. This battle probably saves the Madras Presidency.

Porto Novo is followed by other British victories over Hyder Ali at Pollilur on August 17, 1781, and at Sholingarh in September. Fateh Ali Tipu (Tipu Sultan, Tiger of Mysore) seizes Chittur from the British in December.

July 6, 1781

North America: American Revolutionary War (continued): Operations in Virginia: Battle of Green Spring. Shortly after his arrival in late May 1781, in campaigning in eastern Virginia, British lieutenant general Charles, Lord Cornwallis, endeavors, without success, to bring Continental Army major general Marie-Joseph du Motier, Marquis de Lafayette, to battle and destroy him. With New York City now threatened by the combined American forces under General George Washington and French forces commanded by General Comte Jean Baptiste de Rochambeau, however, British commander in North America Lieutenant General Henry Clinton orders Cornwallis to send 3,000 of his men north.

Cornwallis sets out from Williamsburg on July 4 to embark the men from Portsmouth. Lafayette hopes to cut off the rear guard while the British are divided as they cross the James River. The British begin crossing at Jamestown Ford on July 5. On July 6 Lafayette detaches Brigadier General Anthony Wayne and 600 men (later increased to 900) to strike the British rear guard. Cornwallis, anticipating the American move, has sent across only his baggage and a minority of his men; he is lying in wait with the remainder. In the ensuing battle, Wayne is able to extricate his force in good order.

In the ambush, the Americans lose 145 killed, wounded, and missing and 2 guns; British losses are only 75 men. Nightfall probably saves Lafayette's nearby army from destruction. Cornwallis continues on to Yorktown.

August 4, 1781

North America: American Revolutionary War (continued): Cornwallis moves to Yorktown. Receiving new orders from British commander in North America Lieutenant General Henry Clinton that allow him to keep all his troops in Virginia, British lieutenant general Charles, Lord Cornwallis, retires with 7,000 men to the port of Yorktown, at the mouth of the York River on Chesapeake Bay, where he can be in communication by water with Clinton in New York. Continental Army commander in Virginia Major General Marie-Joseph du Motier, Marquis de Lafayette, with 4,500 men, keeps watch on the British from West Point on the York, informing Continental Army commander in chief General George Washington of developments.

August 5, 1781

North Sea: American Revolutionary War (continued): Battle of the Dogger Bank. British vice admiral Sir Hyde Parker, with 7 ships of the line and 12 frigates and smaller warships, is escorting a large British merchant convoy from the Baltic when it encounters Dutch admiral Johann A. Zoutman's squadron of 7 ships of the line, 10 frigates, and smaller warships convoying Dutch merchant ships to the Baltic. Parker orders his own convoy to make for England and changes direction to engage the Dutch.

The engagement of August 5, 1781, while inconclusive, is a strategic victory for the British, as their convoy makes port, and the Dutch convoy returns to the Texel. Casualties are 142 killed and 403 wounded for the Dutch and 104 killed and 339 wounded for the British. One badly damaged Dutch ship sinks the next day.

August 21, 1781

North America: American Revolutionary War (continued): Washington marches south, beginning the Yorktown Campaign. Continental Army commander General George Washington and Commander of the King's Forces in America Lieutenant General Jean Baptiste Donatien de Vimeur, Comte de Rochambeau, are in agreement that if the powerful French fleet in the West Indies under Admiral François Joseph, Comte de Grasse moves north, it could isolate British troop concentrations in New York or Virginia and enable the allied land forces to concentrate against one of them. Washington prefers a campaign against New York, but de Grasse sends word that he will sail north to Chesapeake Bay, bringing an additional 3,000 French land troops, and that he will be able to support allied land operations until mid-October. Rochambeau meanwhile moves his army south from Newport and places it under the American's command. Washington receives word of de

Grasse's plan shortly after the Continental Army commander in Virginia, Major General Marie-Joseph du Motier, Marquis de Lafayette, informs him that British lieutenant general Charles, Lord Cornwallis, has moved his army to Yorktown.

Washington at once recognizes that if de Grasse can control Chesapeake Bay, Cornwallis can be cut off and destroyed. Ordering Lafayette to try to contain Cornwallis's larger force and leaving Brigadier General William Heath and 2,000 men to watch Clinton and his 17,000 men in New York, on August 21 Washington sets the allied armies in motion in forced marches south toward Yorktown. De Grasse arrives off Yorktown on August 30 and sends ashore the ground troops under Major General Claude-Ann, Marquis de Saint-Simon. De Grasse then detaches transports and smaller ships to carry the allied armies down the bay from Head of Elk (Elkton), Baltimore, and Annapolis. The allied troops assemble at Williamsburg during September 14–26.

September 5–9, 1781

North America: American Revolutionary War (continued): Second Battle of the Chesapeake. French admiral François Joseph, Comte de Grasse, with a powerful fleet of 28 ships of the line, has been campaigning in the West Indies, where both France and Britain have deployed major fleet units in an effort to secure the lucrative sugar trade of the other. De Grasse, however, plans to bring his fleet north during hurricane season and will thus then be free to act to support Continental Army and French Army land operations in North America during that time. Washington hopes to retake New York, but de Grasse decides to sail instead to Chesapeake Bay. He departs the West Indies on August 13. Washington immediately sees the possibilities of bagging the sizable British force of Lieutenant General Charles, Lord Cornwallis, at the port of Yorktown on Chesapeake Bay.

On August 27, three days before the arrival of de Grasse, British rear admiral Samuel Hood with 14 ships of the line stands into Chesapeake Bay on his way north from the West Indies. With no sign of de Grasse, Hood sails to New York. There he joins Rear Admiral Thomas Graves with 5 ships of the line. Graves also has heard nothing of de Grasse but informs Hood that French admiral Jacques Comte de Barras, with 8 ships of the line and 18 transports, has sailed from Newport, Rhode Island, the day before.

Hood correctly assumes that Barras is headed south, probably for the Chesapeake.

On August 31 Graves puts to sea from New York to intercept Barras. The day before, de Grasse had arrived in the Chesapeake with 28 ships of the line, 4 frigates, and 3,000 land troops under Major General Claude-Ann, Marquis de Saint-Simon. Disembarking the troops, de Grasse orders the transports and boats up the bay to ferry Washington's forces south.

Graves, sailing faster than Barras, arrives in Chesapeake Bay first. On September 5 at the beginning of the Second Battle of the Chesapeake (also known as the Second Battle of the Capes), a French frigate signals the British approach. Instead of swooping down on the unprepared French ships, Graves, hampered by an inadequate signaling system and unwilling to risk a general action against a superior enemy (19 ships to 28), forms his ships into line ahead and waits for de Grasse to come out. Shorthanded with 90 of his officers and 1,500 sailors on ferrying duties up the bay but aware of his poor position, de Grasse immediately stands out with 24 ships of the line to meet the English. Hood and his officers have not had time to assimilate Graves's signals, and in any case Graves and Hood are rivals. Two signals—close action and line ahead at half a cable—are simultaneously flown. Thus, while the British van bears down on the French, the British center and rear follow the van instead of closing. Both vans became engaged at 3:45 p.m., but the rest of the two fleets remain out of action.

At 4:27 p.m. the British signal of line ahead is hauled down, yet it is not until 5:20 p.m. that Hood attempts to close with the French. But the French avoid close engagement. The battle ends at sunset. The British have sustained 336 casualties, the French 221. No ships are lost on either side.

On the morning of September 6 there is only a slight wind, and Graves chooses to effect repairs to his squadron's masts and rigging. On September 7 and 8 the French bear to windward and refuse to engage. Then Graves learns that Barras has slipped into the bay with his 8 ships of the line and transports with siege artillery and stores. This increase in French strength to 36 ships of the line leads Graves to hold a council of war with his captains and to the decision to return to New York to gather additional ships.

The Second Battle of the Chesapeake dooms the British forces at Yorktown. Thus, the tactically

SECOND BATTLE OF THE CHESAPEAKE, SEPTEMBER 5–9, 1781

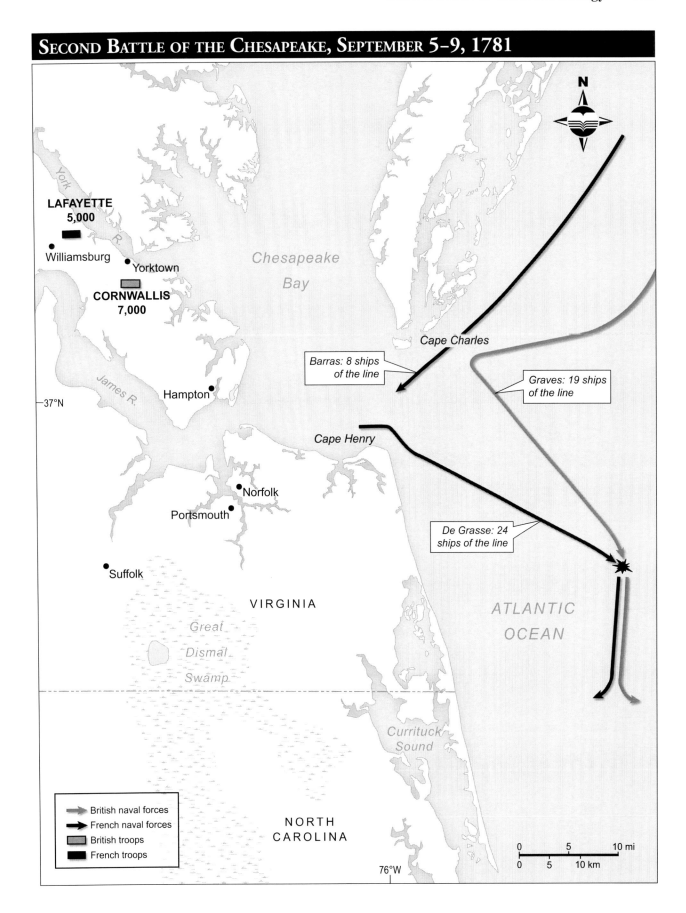

LAFAYETTE
5,000

Williamsburg

Yorktown

CORNWALLIS
7,000

York R.

Chesapeake
Bay

Cape Charles

Barras: 8 ships
of the line

Graves: 19 ships
of the line

James R.

Hampton

37°N

Cape Henry

De Grasse: 24
ships of the line

Norfolk

Portsmouth

Suffolk

VIRGINIA

ATLANTIC
OCEAN

Great
Dismal
Swamp

Currituck
Sound

British naval forces
French naval forces
British troops
French troops

NORTH
CAROLINA

76°W

0   5   10 mi
0   5   10 km

The Second Battle of the Chesapeake on September 5, 1781, between the British and French, while itself indecisive, had immense ramifications. It made possible the subsequent land victory by the Americans and French over the British in the Battle of Yorktown. (DeA Picture Library/Art Resource, NY)

inconclusive Second Battle of the Chesapeake ranks among the most important strategic victories in world history.

September 8, 1781
North America: American Revolutionary War (continued): Battle of Eutaw Springs. Although he has won no pitched battles during April–July 1781, Continental Army commander in the South Major General Nathanael Greene now controls the entire South Carolina interior. In July, dispirited and in poor health, Lieutenant Colonel Francis, Lord Rawdon, hands over command at Charleston to Lieutenant Colonel Alexander Stewart.

On August 22 Greene, with 2,000 men, begins a 70-mile march against Stewart at Eutaw Springs with a force of equal size. In the battle on the morn-

ing of September 8 Greene appears on the verge of a decisive victory, but when the hungry Americans overrun the British camp with its abundant food and stores, they stop to loot and gorge themselves. This enables Stewart to reestablish his line. With his own men utterly exhausted after four hours of battle and thoroughly disorganized, Greene withdraws.

Eutaw Springs is another draw, but Greene has come very close to a decisive victory. It is the hardest fought of all battles in the American South during the war. With 522 casualties, the Americans lost some 25 percent of their force: 139 killed, 375 wounded, and 8 missing. Stewart's losses are much heavier: more than 40 percent of his force. The British sustain 866 casualties: 85 killed, 351 wounded, and 430 missing, including prisoners. Indeed, Stewart is so weakened by the battle that he has no option but to withdraw to Monck's Corner, just north of Charleston. Eutaw Springs is the last major engagement of the war in the South.

September 28–October 19, 1781
North America: American Revolutionary War (continued): Siege of Yorktown. Marching from Williamsburg, Continental Army commander General George Washington's combined American and French army arrives at Yorktown on September 28. Washington has at his disposal in all some 9,000 American troops—3,000 of whom are militia, who play no role in the battle—and 7,500 French under Lieutenant General Jean Baptiste Donatien de Vimeur, Comte de Rochambeau. Washington also has both French field and siege artillery and the services of French military engineers, who now direct a siege of Yorktown with European-style zigzag trenches and parallels dug toward the British defenses.

On October 9 the Americans and French open a bombardment of the British lines. Two days later, on October 11, the allies begin construction of a second siege line, only 400 yards from the British line. On the night of October 14 the allies storm two key British redoubts, the French taking No. 9 and the Americans seizing No. 10, completing the second siege line and sealing the fate of the British. The allies are thus able to establish new firing positions that compromise the British defensive line.

On October 16 the allies repulse a desperate British counterattack. Too late, Cornwallis attempts to escape across the York River to Gloucester Point, which Washington has largely neglected. The plan is thwarted by a severe storm.

Now running low on food, on the morning of October 17 Cornwallis asks for terms, seeking parole for his men. Washington insists that the British surrender as prisoners of war, and Cornwallis agrees. On October 19 the formal surrender of 8,077 British—840 seamen, 80 camp followers, and 7,157 soldiers—occurs. During the siege the British lose 156 killed and 326 wounded; the allies suffer 75 killed and 199 wounded (two-thirds of them French).

Too late, on October 24 British commander in North America Lieutenant General Sir Henry Clinton arrives with a powerful fleet and 7,000 land troops. French admiral François Joseph, Comte de Grasse, has already departed with his fleet to return to the West Indies. The British had lost control of the American seaboard for one brief period, and as a result they lose the war.

The consequences of the British defeat at Yorktown are momentous. A terrific shock in Britain, it brings down the government of the hard-liner Lord North and ushers in a British policy of cutting its losses immediately, even to the point of granting concessions to America, including independence, in order to separate it from its French ally.

December 12, 1781
North Atlantic Ocean: American Revolutionary War (continued): Second Battle of Ushant. On December 10, 1781, French admiral Luc Urbain de Bouexic, Comte de Guichen, sails from Brest with 19 ships of the line escorting a large convoy with military and naval stores for the East and West Indies. The British, aware of the French preparations, send to sea 13 ships of the line and several frigates under Rear Admiral Richard Kempenfelt. The British intercept the French in the Bay of Biscay, about 150 miles southwest of Ushant, on December 12. Guichen errs in allowing his squadron to be leeward and ahead of the convoy, allowing the British to take 15 of the merchant ships before the French warships can intervene.

A severe storm several days later disperses the remainder, all of which return to Brest except for two ships of the line and five transports that make it to the West Indies.

1781 and 1784
East Asia: China. The Qing easily put down revolts against Manchu rule in Gansu (Kansu). These are part of a pattern of revolts during the period 1774–1797 signifying a gradual deterioration in Qing (Ch'ing) dynasty power.

1781–1782
North America: American Revolutionary War (continued): Final land operations. Following the allied victory at Yorktown in October 1781, Continental Army commander General George Washington marches back to New York, establishing his headquarters at Newburgh on the Hudson River. Commander of the King's Forces in America Lieutenant General Jean Baptiste Donatien de Vimeur, Comte de Rochambeau, winters with his army in Virginia

YORKTOWN CAMPAIGN, AUGUST–OCTOBER 1781

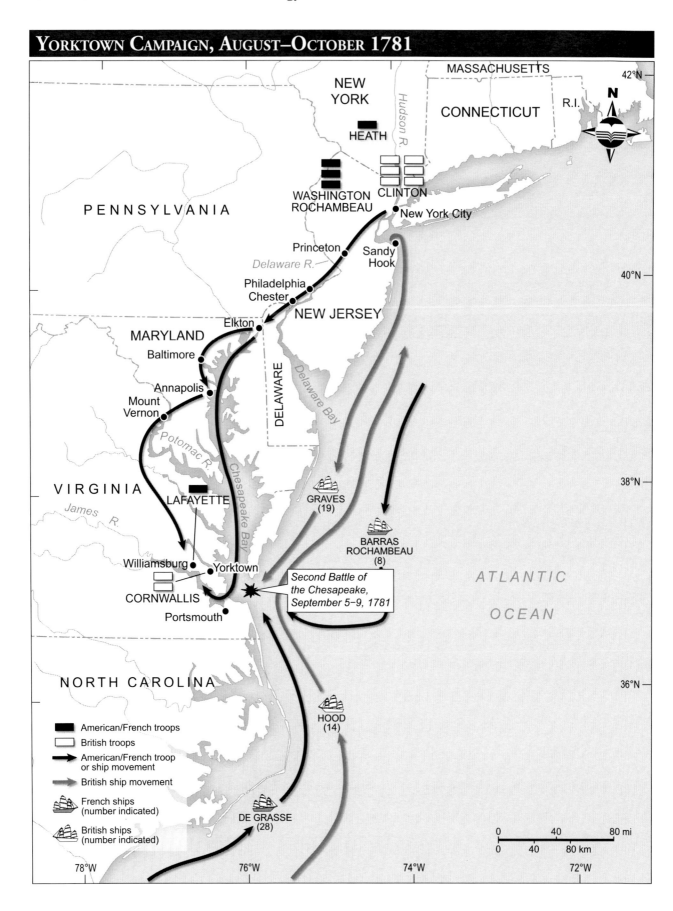

and then returns to Rhode Island in the autumn of 1782. His forces sail for France that December.

In the South, American commander Major General Nathanael Greene sends Brigadier General Anthony Wayne into Georgia, which he secures in a few minor engagements. Terrible partisan warfare, reprisals, and atrocities continue in that region between Loyalist and Patriot militiamen.

The British defeat at Yorktown helps bring down the British ministry of Lord North in March 1782, and peace negotiations open the next month. On May 6 Lieutenant General Sir Guy Carleton lands in New York, succeeding Lieutenant General Henry Clinton as British commander in chief in North America. Carleton concentrates all British troops at New York. The British have already evacuated Wilmington (January); they depart Savannah on July 11 and Charleston on December 14.

February 5, 1782

Mediterranean Sea: American Revolutionary War (continued): French and Spanish forces conquer Minorca. An allied force under General Duc Louis de Crillon lands on Minorca and during July–August 1781 conquers all the island except for Port Mahon. Besieged beginning on August 19, it finally surrenders on February 5, 1782.

February 18, 1782

South Asia: India: Second Anglo-Mysore War (continued): Battle of Annagudi. On February 18, 1782, Fateh Ali Tipu (Tipu Sultan, Tiger of Mysore) defeats a British East India Company force of some 1,800 men and 10 guns under Colonel Braithwaite at Annagudi, near Tanjore. Tipu takes the entire force as prisoners and seizes the guns.

April 12, 1782

Caribbean Basin: American Revolutionary War (continued): Battle of the Saints. The Battle of the Saints (also known as the Battle of the Saintes) takes its name from the Îles des Saintes, a small archipelago between Dominica and Guadeloupe in the West Indies. The battle is fought between a French fleet commanded by Admiral François Joseph Paul, Comte de Grasse, and a British fleet under Admiral Sir George Brydges Rodney. The Caribbean sugar islands are vital to both sides for revenue from their sugar production. Indeed, the presence of substantial French and British naval forces in the West Indies show how much more important they are than North America in naval considerations.

On April 8, 1782, de Grasse sails from Martinique with 35 ships of the line, 6 frigates, and 150 unarmed ships for an invasion of Jamaica. Rear Admiral Sir Samuel Hood, Rodney's second-in-command, immediately departs St. Lucia with 36 ships of the line and accompanying frigates. On the morning of April 9 the British catch up with the French off Dominica. De Grasse orders his 2 50-gun ships to escort the convoy to safety at Guadeloupe, trusting that the superior sailing qualities of his ships will enable them to escape and rejoin his convoy.

French admiral François Joseph Paul, Comte de Grasse, surrenders his sword to British admiral Sir George Brydges Rodney following the former's defeat and capture in the Battle of the Saints in the West Indies on April 12, 1782. (Library of Congress)

BATTLE OF THE SAINTES, APRIL 12, 1782

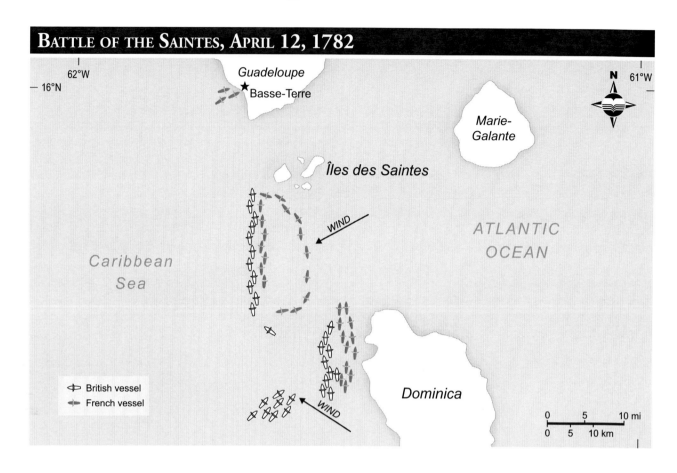

An indecisive engagement ensues when Hood's van of 8 ships separates from the rest of the fleet, whereupon de Grasse orders 15 French ships under the Marquis de Vaudreuil to attack. The French withdraw, however, when the remainder of the British ships close. One French ship is forced into Guadeloupe for repairs. Although some of his own ships are badly cut up, none of Rodney's ships has to depart.

After making repairs that night, Rodney continues the pursuit. It appears that de Grasse will escape, but on September 11 two French ships separate from the rest and drop behind. With Rodney closing and hoping to cut off the two ships, de Grasse drops back to protect them. That night one of the two French ships, the *Zélé,* accidently rams the French flagship the *Ville de Paris* (110 guns), said to be the finest ship then afloat. The *Zélé* loses its foremast and bowsprit, and de Grasse orders the frigate *Astrée* to take it in tow and head for Guadeloupe.

The British pursuers have been carrying a press of sail and, at dawn on September 12 Rodney can see

both French ships making for Guadeloupe and the main body of the French fleet beyond. The two fleets are now between Dominica and the Saints. Rodney has 36 ships of the line to only 30 for de Grasse.

The battle opens with the two fleets in parallel lines exchanging broadsides. When the wind suddenly shifts, however, the French formation begins to break apart, and the ships bunch up. Here superior British seamanship comes to play, as Rodney quickly orders his flagship, the *Formidable,* through a gap in the French line. Five other British ships promptly follow, raking the French ships on either side. The *Duke* also pierces the French line in another place, as does the *Formidable,* followed by other ships. The French formation is thus shattered, cut into three separate divisions. In the melee that follows, the British inflict serious damage to a number of French ships.

When the wind picks up again, de Grasse attempts to escape to westward; the British pursue. Three crippled French ships are quickly taken, and late that afternoon the British capture two additional French warships, including the *Ville de Paris* with de Grasse himself aboard. It is the first time that a French commander in chief has been captured at sea. At 6:45 p.m. Rodney signals an end to the pursuit, and the remainder of the French fleet, now under de Vaudreuil, manages to escape to Cap François.

Hood is appalled and criticizes Rodney for his failure to continue the chase that night and finish off the French in the morning. Hood claims that had he been in command, 20 ships would have been captured rather than 5. Rodney acknowledges that he has been cautious, but many of his ships have been badly cut up aloft and are short of ammunition.

Following the battle, survivors on the captured French 74-gun *César* break into the spirit stores, and someone upsets a candle. The ship catches fire and explodes, killing 400 Frenchmen and 60 members of the British prize crew. Total French casualties in the battle are more than 3,000; the British lose 243 dead and another 816 wounded.

The British spend the next four days repairing damage. On April 17 Hood captures four additional French ships: the two 64-gun ships badly damaged in the April 9 engagement, a frigate (32 guns), and a sloop (18 guns).

The important British victory of the Saints, the last major naval battle in the Caribbean of the war, comes too late to affect the outcome. It is sufficient, however, for the British to retain all their West Indian islands in the resulting Treaty of Paris and to place Hood and Rodney in the ranks of British naval heroes.

August 19, 1782

North America: American Revolutionary War (continued): Battle of Blue Licks. A force of some 50 British rangers under Captain William Caldwell and 300 allied Indians under Alexander McKee and Simon Girty raids across the Ohio River into Kentucky. Their goal is the destruction of the settlement at Bryan's Station. Warned of their approach, on August 15 the settlers repulse the attack. The raiders then lay siege to Bryan's Station but withdraw on August 17 on the approach of a large Patriot militia force under Colonel John Todd and lieutenant colonels Stephen Trigg and Daniel Boone. Todd orders a pursuit.

On August 19 at Lower Blue Licks on the Licking River near present-day Mount Olivet, Kentucky, Todd calls a war council. Boone warns that they are walking into an ambush, but his sound counsel is ignored.

In this last major battle of the war, 72 of the 182 Kentuckians are killed, including Todd and Trigg, and 11 men are captured. The allied British and Indians lose only 11 men killed. Boone distinguishes himself in the battle, which also claims his son.

September 3, 1782

South Asia: India: Second Anglo-Mysore War (continued): Battle of Trincomalee. Commodore Pierre André Suffren de Saint-Tropez arrives in the Bay of Bengal with a French squadron of 14 ships and fights four inconclusive battles with a British squadron of 12 ships of the line under Vice Admiral Sir Edward Hughes: Sadras (February 17, 1782), Provedien (April 12), Negapatam (July 6), and Trincomalee (September 3). All are hard-fought but indecisive engagements—in part owing to the ineffectiveness of Suffren's subordinates—with no ship losses on either side.

The last battle, Trincomalee, is a French strategic victory, however, for the brilliant Suffren drives off the British and lands French troops, who take Trincomalee. Suffren then retains a shaky control of the Indian Ocean until the conclusion of peace.

November 1782

North America: American Revolutionary War (continued): Patriot militia raid against the Shawnees. In November 1782 in retaliation for the August British raid into Kentucky, militia brigadier general George Rogers Clark launches a strike of more than 1,000 men into the Ohio Country. In the last major offensive of the war, they destroy five Shawnee villages on the Great Miami River. There are no battles, however, for the Native Americans refuse to stand and fight, instead withdrawing to their villages on the Mad River.

December 2, 1782

South Asia: India: Second Anglo-Mysore War (continued). Hyder Ali dies and is succeeded by his son, Sultan Fateh Ali Tipu (Tipu Sultan, Tiger of Mysore).

Spring of 1783

South Asia: India: Second Anglo-Mysore War (continued). French commodore Pierre André Suffren de Saint-Tropez proceeds to Mauritus and returns to India with French troops under Marquis Charles de Bussy, landing them at Cuddalore.

September 3, 1783

Western Europe: American Revolutionary War (continued): Treaty of Paris. Signed in Paris on September 3, 1783, and formally ratified by the Congress of the Confederation on January 14, 1784, the Treaty of Paris definitively ends the American Revolutionary War. The treaty recognizes the full independence of the United States. Eager to woo the United States away from France, the British agree to the American demand for land beyond the original 13 colonies, extending to the Mississippi River. The treaty also grants the Americans full rights to the Newfoundland fisheries and recognizes the binding nature of lawfully contracted debts, which are to be paid by both sides. The Americans also agree that Congress will recommend restoration of lands confiscated during the war from Loyalists, but this provision is never implemented.

Both Great Britain and the United States are to enjoy free navigation on the Mississippi River. Treaty differences over the northeastern and northwestern boundaries of the United States lead to subsequent trouble with Britain, just as southern boundary disputes create problems with Spain.

1783

Eastern Europe: Russia. Russia annexes the Crimea. British and Austrian leaders prevail on the Porte not to go to war with Russia.

March 11, 1784

South Asia: India: Second Anglo-Mysore War (continued): Treaty of Mangalore. Both sides are now tired of the war, and Sultan Fateh Ali Tipu (Tipu Sultan, Tiger of Mysore) is willing to conclude peace because the end of France's war with Britain means the withdrawal of French aid. The Treaty of Mangalore restores the status quo ante bellum, and both sides agree to return all prisoners taken. The treaty is the last occasion when an Indian state dictates terms to the British. The British in India now work hard to reverse the treaty.

1784–1785

Southeast Asia: Burma. Burmese forces invade and conquer Arakan.

January 19, 1785

Southeast Asia: Vietnam: Tay Son Rebellion and civil war (continued): Battle of Rach Gam-Xoai Mut. In 1784, the last Nguyen prince, Nguyen Anh, having been defeated in the south several times by the Tay Son, calls in the Siamese. In 1784 they send into the western Mekong Delta an army of between 20,000 and 50,000 men, along with 300 ships. The Siamese invaders treat the Vietnamese badly, leading many Vietnamese to support the Tay Son.

In January 1785, Tay Son leader Nguyen Hue lures the Siamese into an ambush on the Mekong River in the Rach Gam Xoai Mut area of present-day Tien Giang Province. Nguyen Hue positions infantry and artillery along a five-mile stretch of the river between the Gam and Xoai Mut arroyos, which run at right angles to and north of the Mekong River. He also positions troops on islands in the river and places his ships in the two arroyos behind islands on the other side of the main river channel and at My Tho.

On January 18 Nguyen Hue sends some ships west to provoke the Siamese. Feigning flight, on January 19 they lead the Siamese toward My Tho. Nguyen Hue then springs his trap, sending his ships out of the two arroyos and cutting off the Siamese from advance or retreat. At the same time his land artillery opens fire on the Siamese ships.

According to Vietnamese sources, all 300 Siamese junks are destroyed, and only 2–3,000 Siamese escape, fleeing westward across Cambodia to Siam by land. Vietnamese regard this battle as one of the most important in their history because it halts Siamese expansion into southern Vietnam. It also greatly benefits Nguyen Hue, now regarded as a Vietnamese national hero.

1785

Central Europe: Transylvania. A revolt occurs by Romanian peasants, who massacre many Magyar nobles. The revolt is crushed with great severity.

1785–1786

North Africa: Egypt. A revolt in Egypt is put down by Ottoman forces sent overland and by the Mediterranean.

1785–1792

Southeast Asia: Burma: Renewed war between Burma (present-day Myanmar) and Siam (present-day Thailand). A Burmese invasion of Siam during 1785–1786 meets with little success, although following protracted fighting the Burmese do annex the border areas of Tavoy and Tenasserim.

August 1786–February 1787

North America: United States: Shays' Rebellion. Poor economic conditions lead to a rebellion by debt-ridden former Continental Army soldiers who have not received promised pay and are in danger of losing their property. Daniel Shays of Massachusetts, a former Continental Army captain, is the reluctant leader. The rebellion begins on August 29, 1786. In January 1787 the rebels, afraid that they will be indicted for treason by the Massachusetts Supreme Court at Springfield, try to prevent its sitting and to secure arms from the arsenal there.

On January 26 some 1,200 state militia disperse the rebels there after one volley, killing 4 and wounding 20. Another militia force of 4,400 men under Major General Benjamin Lincoln pursues the rebels, defeating them on February 4, 1787, and ending the revolt. Massachusetts acts with moderation; 14 leaders, sentenced to death, are ultimately pardoned or given light prison terms.

1786

North Africa: Egypt. A revolt in Egypt against Turkish rule is suppressed by the Ottoman Army.

1786–1787

East Asia: China: Taiwan (Formosa). A revolt against Manchu rule in Taiwan is put down by the Chinese. It is, however, one of a series of revolts during the period 1774–1797 that signify a gradual deterioration in Qing (Ch'ing) dynasty power.

1787

West Africa: Sierra Leone. Britain secures Sierra Leone.

1787

Eastern Europe: Russo-Turkish War: Background. Czarina Catherine II of Russia, anxious to secure further territory at the expense of the Ottoman Empire, initiates the Russo-Turkish War of 1787–1792, the second war of her reign against the Ottoman Empire, which was urging the Crimean Tatars to rise against Russia. In a secret treaty, Austria agrees to join Russia. War is actually declared in 1788.

June–July 1788

Eastern Europe: Russo-Turkish War (continued): Battles of the Liman. A series of naval actions occur along the coast of what is now Ukraine as warships of both navies support their forces ashore in the struggle for control of Ochakov. Actions take place on June 17, 18, 28, and 29 and July 9, 1788. On July 14, another engagement also occurs some 100 miles to the south.

Prince Grigori Potemkin has overall command of the Russian Navy, but on June 6 American John Paul Jones, now a rear admiral in the Russian Navy, takes command of some 14 Russian sailing ships, the largest mounting 48 guns. Rear Admiral Prince Charles of Nassau-Siegen commands the Russian gunboat flotilla.

At the end of May a large number of Turkish ships (their types and numbers are in dispute, but there may have been as many as 80) arrive at the Liman (a series of lagoons at the mouth of the Danube River). Kapudan Pasha Hassan el Ghazi has command of the Turkish ships.

A minor action occurs on June 17, and on June 18 there is a larger clash in which the Turks lose several ships. Another clash occurs on June 28, in which the Turks lose 2 capital ships, and on June 29, in which they suffer the loss of 8 of their largest ships along with 7 smaller ones.

On July 9 the Russian Army begins the assault of Ochakov at the entrance to the estuary of the Dnieper River, and the Russian flotilla attacks the Turkish warships there, capturing two Turkish gunboats and a galley and burning many others. On July 14 the Turks engage the Russian Sevastopol fleet in the Battle of Fidonisi to the south.

The decisive factor in these Russian naval victories is apparently the use of explosive shell. It is the first time it has been tried at sea to such an extent. Englishman Samuel Bentham equipped the small Russian gunboats with one gun each to fire explosive and incendiary shell.

1788

Eastern Europe: Russo-Turkish War (continued): General land operations of 1788. In the Crimean theater of war, Russian general Aleksandr Suvorov turns back the Turks at Kinburn, rebuffing their effort to recover the Crimea. In Moldavia the Russians are also successful, capturing the Turkish-held cities of Chocim and Jassy. Following a six-month-long siege, on December 6 Russian forces led by Prince Grigori Potemkin and Suvorov take Ochakov at the entrance to the estuary of the Dnieper River, held by Ottoman forces under Hasan Pasha. Potemkin apparently orders the massacre of all inhabitants of the captured cities.

The Turks enjoy success only in Serbia and Transylvania, where they turn back the Austrians led by Emperor Joseph II.

July 17, 1788

Northern Europe: Russo-Swedish War: Battle of Hogland. In June 1788 Swedish king Gustavus III begins the Russo-Swedish War (1788–1790) with an invasion of Russian Finland. This is for domestic political reasons in order to rally the opposition to the Crown but also to offset a possible military move by either Russia or Prussia against Sweden and with the hope of securing territory lost to Russia in the Great Northern War. Gustavus plans a multipronged advance on St. Petersburg by land and sea.

On July 17 off Hogland Island in the Gulf of Finland, a Swedish fleet of 20 ships of the line mounting some 1,180 guns and under the overall command of Vice Admiral Gustav Wachtmeister meets a Russian fleet of 17 ships of the line with 1,220 guns under the command of Admiral Samuel Greig. The Russians capture the Swedish flagship, the *Prins Gustaf,* while the Swedes capture the Russian *Vladislav.* Both are 70-gun ships.

The Russians suffer some 1,806 casualties, the Swedes 1,151. The Battle of Hogland is indecisive, but the Russians effect sufficient damage to thwart the Swedish landing.

Despite Gustavus's hopes, the war proves deeply unpopular in Sweden and also in Finland, where it has not been sanctioned by the Assembly. News of the failure at Hogland triggers a revolt among some of the Finnish arm officers, known as the League of Anjala.

September 1788–July 1789

Northern Europe: Theater War. The Theater War (known in Norway as the Lingonberry War) occurs between Denmark-Norway and Sweden. Because of obligations under its treaty of 1773 with Russia, on September 24, 1788, Denmark enters the war against Sweden. A Norwegian army briefly invades Sweden, the attack being directed toward Bohuslän. The Norwegians meet little resistance before being stopped at Gothenburg. Winter weather, lack of food supplies, and disease force the Norwegians to withdraw in mid-November.

British, Dutch, and Prussian pressure ultimately leads Denmark to conclude peace on July 9, 1789. Denmark-Norway declares itself neutral in the Swedish-Russian War, bringing the Theater War to an end.

January 25–30, 1789

Southeast Asia: Vietnam: Tay Son Rebellion and civil war (continued): Battle of Ngoc Hoi-Dong Da. In late 1788 King Le Chieu Thong, who has fled from Hanoi to far northern Vietnam, calls on Qing assistance in recovering his throne against the Tay Son Rebellion, led by Nguyen Hue. Qing Viceroy Sun Shiyi (Sun Shi-yi) in Canton supports military intervention, believing that it will be an easy matter to establish a protectorate over an area weakened by a long civil war. Emperor Qianlong agrees but in public pronouncements claims that he is intervening simply to restore the Le dynasty to power.

In November 1788 Sun Shiyi, assisted by General Xu Shiheng, leads an expeditionary force of up to 200,000 men in an invasion of northern Vietnam. There is little Vietnamese opposition. Tay Son forces withdraw, and on December 17 the Qing enter Hanoi. The establishment of an extensive logistical base indicates that the Qing intend to remain in Vietnam. Sun Shiyi plans to renew the offensive against the Tay Son southward after the lunar new year celebrations. Because of the scant Vietnamese resistance, the Qing commanders believe that it will be an easy matter to bring all Vietnam under their control.

Events worked to undermine the Qing, however. Their treatment of Vietnam as captured territory, their subordination of King Le Chieu Thong, and a series of typhoons and disastrous harvests all lead northerners to believe that the king has lost the so-called Mandate of Heaven.

Nguyen Hue lays careful preparations for offensive operations. Taking the name of Quang Trung, he proclaims himself king, abolishing the Le dynasty. Appealing to Vietnamese nationalism, he assembles an army of some 100,000 men, supported by several hundred elephants, while at the same time throwing the Chinese off by calling for peace talks.

Following a month of preparations, on January 25 Quang Trung begins what is sometimes referred to as the First Tet Offensive (Tet, the Vietnamese new year, based on the Chinese lunar new year). Expecting to soon resume the offensive themselves, the Qing are caught off guard with their forces in offensive rather than defensive positions. Quang Trung forces the Qing to disperse their superior resources by sending his men against them in five separate columns. His intelligence is excellent, his men are well trained and highly motivated, and he launches attacks generally at night, catching the Qing off guard. On January 30 following five days of battle, the Tay Son enter the capital. The Qing forces flee north, with thousands drowning when a pontoon bridge collapses under their weight as they try to cross the Red River. The offensive covers some 54 miles and takes six forts, a rate of more than 10 miles and a fort a day. Vietnamese know this series of victories as the Victory of Ngoc Hoi-Dong Da, the Emperor Quang Trung's Victory over the Manchu, or the Victory of Spring 1789. It is still celebrated as the greatest military achievement in modern Vietnamese history

Quang Trung now consolidates his control over Vietnam, restores peaceful ceremonial relations with China (allowing the Qing also to declare victory in this war), and introduces extensive reforms. Unfortunately, he dies of illness in the spring of 1792. He is succeeded by his 10-year-old son, who is overthrown in 1802 by forces led by the last surviving Nguyen prince in southern Vietnam, Nguyen Anh, who takes the imperial name of Gia Long.

January 1789–December 1790
Western Europe: Austrian Netherlands: Brabant Revolt. This popular uprising against Habsburg rule comes in reaction to centralizing policies instituted by Vienna that infringe on civil rights. Two factions appear: the Statists, who oppose the reforms, and the Vonckists, who initially support the reforms but then join the opposition because of the way in which the reforms are implemented.

The revolt begins in Brabant, which in January 1789 declares that it no longer recognizes the authority of Vienna. The leader of the Statists, Hendrik Van der Noot, raises a small army in the Dutch Republic and invades Brabant. He defeats Austrian forces in the Battle of Turnhout on October 27. He then goes on to capture Ghent on November 13 and Brussels several days later. Remaining Austrian forces withdraw to Luxembourg and Antwerp.

Van der Noot now declares Brabant independent. All other provinces of the Austrian Netherlands (Belgium) except for Luxembourg follow Brabant's lead,

and on January 11, 1790, they establish a confederation known as the United States of Belgium. Recognizing that the new state will require allies if it is to survive, Van der Noot seeks an arrangement with the Dutch Republic but with little success. Also, the two factions of Statists and Vonckists soon fall into conflict that borders on civil war.

Meanwhile, Joseph II dies (February 20, 1790) and is succeeded as Holy Roman emperor by his brother Leopold II, who moves decisively to restore Austrian rule. Austrian troops retake Namur on October 24, and by December they have secured the entire Austrian Netherlands. The former constitution and privileges are restored, however.

May–June 1789
Western Europe: France: French Revolution. The great French Revolution of 1789 results from many factors but chiefly from the economic crisis caused by the heavy debt incurred through France's costly participation in the American Revolutionary War along with bad weather and poor harvests. France is by far the wealthiest nation in Europe, but the government is chronically poor as a consequence of its inability to tax the nobles and the church, which together control about half the land of France. With the government bankrupt, however, the Crown has no choice but to tax the privileged classes.

Their resistance forces the calling of the historic parliament of France, the States General, that last met in 1615 and that the nobles expect to control. There are three estates: church, nobility, and everyone else. Voting in the States General had traditionally been by order, not by head. But the Third Estate, with 90 percent of the population, receives the concession of having twice the number of delegates ("doubling the Third"), although voting is to be by order. The victory of the nobles in forcing the calling of the States General encourages the Third Estate. The patricians may have begun the revolution, but the plebeians finish it. Actually, it is the leaders of the middle class rather than the bulk of the population, the peasants, who dominate the French Revolution.

The States General meets at Versailles beginning on May 5, 1789. Imbued with the ideals of the Enlightenment and the example of the American Revolution, the delegates of the Third Estate insist on vote by head rather than order. Both the king and the other two orders resist this, however. When the

Set off by fears of a royalist coup by French king Louis XVI, Parisians took to the streets on July 13, 1789. The next day, they stormed the Bastille. (Library of Congress)

members of the Third Estate find themselves locked out of their meeting hall on June 20, they repair to a nearby tennis pavilion and declare themselves the true representatives of France. They vow to carry on until they draft a constitution for France. The Tennis Court Oath is one of the memorable events of the French Revolution.

On June 23 King Louis XVI addresses the deputies. While he expresses support for a number of reforms to include equality of taxation, freedom of press, individual liberties, and regular meetings of the States General, he sides with the nobility in insisting on vote by order, not by head. This is the high point of the so-called Aristocratic Reaction. The king has sided with the nobility despite the fact that it had fought him tooth and nail. Louis XVI's alliance with the nobility will prove fatal for them both.

The Third Estate stands firm, however, rejecting the vote by order. Some of the more liberal nobles now come over to it, which thanks to the doubling of the Third gives it a majority of the delegates. On June 27 Louis XVI reluctantly gives in and orders the other two estates to join the Third Estate in what is now the National Assembly.

July 14, 1789
Western Europe: France: French Revolution (continued): Storming of the Bastille. The traditional date for the beginning of the French Revolution, this event is the response to local conditions and the result of fear and anxiety.

A shortage of bread, brought on by a poor grain harvest, brings rioting in Paris. There are relatively few police in the city, and they are not armed. When

Louis XVI orders troops there and to Versailles, anxiety runs high among the citizenry. On July 12 news is received in Paris that King Louis XVI has dismissed his chief minister, Jacques Necker. This brings violence. The people now believe that the court intends to crush the revolution. Demands that the people be armed to be able to defend themselves bring rioting.

On July 14 after earlier seizing a large number of muskets but no powder from the Invalides (military hospital), the mob moves to the Bastille, which contains a sizable quantity of powder. The Bastille is a large medieval fortress with 80-foot-high walls that looms over the working-class district of St. Antoine. A large crowd of anxious neighborhood residents has already gathered at the Bastille, fearful that the cannon of the fortress might be used against the crowded neighborhood that had grown up around it. They demand that the Bastille's governor, the Marquis de Launay, surrender the powder. When he refuses, fighting breaks out. The besiegers have the worst of it, with some 80 dead, but they bring up some cannon. De Launay decides to surrender on the promise of safe conduct for him and his men. The French Guards, who had done most of the fighting, try to bring the prisoners along to safety at the Hotel de Ville, but de Launay, his 3 officers, and 3 of his men are killed. De Launay's head is cut off and subsequently paraded around Paris. Over the next few days the Bastille is demolished, stone by stone.

The assault on the Bastille is mistakenly interpreted at Versailles as a popular reaction against despotism and injustice and a show of solidarity of Paris with the Third Estate at Versailles, a myth so telling that July 14 later becomes the French national holiday. Louis XVI now gives way entirely. He recalls the incompetent Necker and withdraws troops he had ordered to Paris and Versailles. Another consequence of the fall of the Bastille is the organization of the Commune of Paris, the first autonomous government for the city. Yet another discovery is that mobs may be manipulated to achieve political ends.

The deputies at Versailles now write a constitution for France. The French Revolution, however, moves from moderate to radical. The leaders of the revolution justifiably distrust King Louis XVI, and the Constitution of 1791 gives the Crown little power and no effective check on the legislature. At the same time, revolutionary changes, although long overdue, heighten turmoil. The Civil Constitution of the Clergy of July 1790 that subordinates the church to the government and provides for election of clergy is strongly opposed by the king and more than anything else fuels counterrevolutionary forces. At the same time, there is opposition from the lower classes to the division of the populace into active and passive citizens, with the distinction based on wealth and passive citizens unable to vote. Government attempts to solve the financial crisis prove unsuccessful. Bonds known as assignats, secured by the 1790 confiscation of land belonging to the church, evolve into paper currency, but the government resorts to the printing press. With the assignats acting as a barometer of the revolution and their value exceeding that of the confiscated properties, France is swept by massive hyperinflation, leading to unrest and rioting. In these circumstances, a first wave of conservative emigrants (the Ultras), drawn largely from the nobility, departs France (the Joyous Emigration). They expect to soon return.

August 24, 1789
Northern Europe: Russo-Swedish War (continued): First Battle of Svensksund. At sea, the evenly matched Russian and Swedish battle fleets meet in inconclusive artillery duels in the Baltic in the battles of Hogland on July 17, 1788, and Öland a week later, on July 25. In early August the Russians take 1 Swedish ship of the line off Sveaborg and burn it. Then on August 24 a Russian fleet of 107 ships under mercenary admirals Prince Karl of Nassau-Siegen and Giulio Litta decisively defeat the Swedish coastal galley flotilla of 44 ships under fleet admiral Carl August Ehrensvärd in the First Battle of Svensksund (known to the Russians as the First Battle of Rochensalm) in the Gulf of Finland.

1789
Eastern Europe: Russo-Turkish War (continued): General land operations in 1789. In Moldavia the Ottomans are pressed by the Russians from the north and the Austrians from the west. Although the Russians are initially unsuccessful, a Russian army under General Aleksandr Suvorov defeats the Turks in the Battle of Focsani on August 1 and the Battle of Rimnik on September 22. Suvorov then advances to the Danube.

On the Serbian front meanwhile, Austrian forces under General Gideon E. von Laudon turn back an Ottoman invasion of Bosnia and go on to besiege and capture Belgrade.

1789

North America: Pacific coast dispute between Britain and Spain. When Spanish forces seize Nootka Island and some British ships in Nootka Sound (an inlet of the Pacific Ocean on the west coast of Vancouver Island, today part of the Canadian province of British Columbia), the two nations almost go to war. France refuses to support Spain, however, and the Spanish back down.

1789–1792

South Asia: India: Third Anglo-Mysore War. Sultan Fateh Ali Tipu (Tipu Sultan, Tiger of Mysore), ruler of Mysore in southern India and an ally of France, in 1789 invades Travancore, a British protectorate on the southwest coast of India, touching off the Third Anglo-Mysore War (1789–1792). France, embroiled in the revolution and thwarted by British command of the seas, is unable to provide as much assistance as Tipu expects. British governor-general Charles, Lord Cornwallis (from 1786), has carried out land reforms and greatly improved the British military and administration.

One notable military advance championed by Tipu is the use of mass attacks with rocket brigades in the army, especially in the Third Anglo-Mysore War and later in the Fourth Anglo-Mysore War. The effect of these weapons on the British impressed William Congreve, who then experimented with war rockets of his own design. They are insufficient, however, to halt the disciplined British infantry and artillery.

See Weapons: Rocket

Cornwallis invades Mysore, takes Bangalore (March 7–21, 1792), drives Tipu into Seringapatam, and then lays siege to it and takes it during September 6–7, 1792. Tipu is forced to conclude peace.

Mysore loses perhaps half its territories to the profit of the Marathas, the Nizam of Hyderabad, and the Madras Presidency, all either allied with the British or under their control. The Mysore districts of Malabar, Salem, Bellary, and Anantapur are ceded to the Madras Presidency. The war paves the way for British dominance in southern India.

July 9, 1790

Northern Europe: Russo-Swedish War: Second Battle of Svensksund. On April 30, 1790, Sweden sends to sea its largest fleet ever: 25 ships of the line of 70 and 60 guns each, 15 frigates, and 16 other ships, all mounting a total of 2,240 guns and manned by about 18,000 men under the command of Duke Carl. The aim is to prevent the Russian fleets at Kronstadt and Reval from uniting.

The fleet arrives at Reval on May 13, but Carl rejects sound advice to attack immediately, and two Swedish ships are lost when the attack occurs the next day. Following an unsuccessful engagement with the Russians off Kronstadt, Gustavus and Carl order the High Seas Fleet to protect the flank of the galleys of the Inshore Fleet. The Russians unite their own fleets and blockade the Swedes in Vyborg Bay.

While breaking out of the bay on July 3, the Swedes lose 10 ships, but the galleys of the Inshore Fleet escape to Svensksund Fjord, where Gustavus, fearing the loss of Finland and in consequence his throne, orders the Inshore Fleet's reluctant commanders to fight. Because Finnish-born captain C. O. Cronstedt is the only one of his commanders who supports this decision, Gustavus places him in command.

In the Second Battle of Svensksund, the Swedish fleet numbers 275 ships mounting some 440 guns and 860 swivels and manned by 13,000–14,000 men. The Russian fleet numbers 274 ships and boats with at least 850 heavy guns and 19,000 men. Russian admiral Prince Karl of Nassau-Siegen is slow to follow up his earlier victory at Vyborg and delays the attack with his more powerful fleet until the July 9 anniversary of Catherine the Great's accession to the throne. That morning he confidently sends his fleet into the fjord in three columns, anticipating an easy victory.

In the close quarters of the fjord, however, some of the Russian ships collide, owing to their mixed sailing qualities. As they press their attack, the confusion intensifies. The Swedes then counterattack, and many Russian ships are caught in a Swedish cross fire.

At daybreak the following day the Swedes resume their advance, and the Russians flee in confusion. In this greatest victory in the history of the Swedish Navy, the Swedes lose 1 larger ship and 5 smaller ones along with 171 killed and 124 wounded. The Swedes sink or capture 53 Russian vessels of every description, including 5 frigates. Some 3,000 Russians are killed in the battle or are drowned, and another 6,000 are captured.

Svensksund is the last engagement of the Russo-Swedish War and a boost to Swedish morale. Moreover, this largest naval battle in Scandinavian history helps secure a favorable end to the war for Gustavus, as the Russians thereafter are content to concentrate their efforts against Turkey. The ensuing Treaty of Värälä (August 14, 1790) restores the status quo ante, leaving Finland and Karelia in Russian hands.

October 18–22, 1790

North America: United States: Military expedition into the Ohio Valley. Tensions increase between white settlers and Native Americans in the Old Northwest because of squatters settling on lands belonging to the Miami and Shawnee tribes. Encouraged by the British, the Native Americans insist that the whites fall back to the Ohio River. In 1789 Brigadier General Josiah Harmar, commander of the Army of the United States, directs the erection of Fort Washington (present-day Cincinnati, Ohio), and in June 1790 governor of the Northwest Territory Arthur St. Clair and Harmar decide on force to intimidate the Native Americans.

This first major military expedition for the small (1,200 men) standing Army of the United States ends in disaster. President George Washington authorizes the calling up of the Kentucky and Pennsylvania militias. Harmar invades Shawnee and Miami territory in October 1790, but of his force of 1,133 men only 320 are regulars. Harmar foolishly divides his force twice.

During October 18–22, 1790, in several clashes not far from present-day Fort Wayne, Indiana, Harmar's men attack Miami villages along the Maumee River and engage the Native Americans led by Little Turtle in what is known as Harmar's Defeat, the Battle of the Maumee, the Battle of Kekionga, and the Battle of the Miami Towns. The militias perform poorly, and Harmar is forced to withdraw, having suffered some 300 casualties.

In 1791 Harmar is court-martialed for negligence at his own request. Exonerated, he nonetheless retires the next year.

1790

Eastern Europe: Russo-Turkish War (continued): General land operations. Turkey and Austria conclude a truce in July 1790 that extends into Sep-

tember. Meanwhile, revolt in Greece forces the Ottomans to divert resources there, severely crippling operations elsewhere. In December, Russian forces under General Aleksandr Suvorov capture the Ottoman fortress of Ismail, at the mouth of the Danube.

August 4, 1791

Central Europe: Russo-Turkish War (continued): Treaty of Sistova. Austria, which joined the war in 1778, has enjoyed some success, taking Belgrade. Prussia is now threatening intervention, the Russian effort has weakened because of their concurrent war with Sweden, and revolt has broken out in the Austrian Netherlands. In these circumstances, Austria concludes peace with the Ottoman Empire in the Treaty of Sistova. Austria gives back Belgrade in return for a strip of northern Bosnia.

August 27, 1791

Central Europe: Wars of the French Revolution: Background: Declaration of Pillnitz. At a meeting at Pillnitz in Saxony, called primarily to deal with Poland, King Frederick William II of Prussia and Emperor Leopold II of Austria, goaded by the French émigrés who have taken refuge in their territories and seeking to strengthen the hand of French king Louis XVI, issue what becomes known as the Declaration of Pillnitz. Intended as an expression of monarchical solidarity and a warning to the revolutionaries in France, it calls on the European powers to intervene if King Louis XVI is threatened.

The declaration states that the two powers are prepared to go to war against France if all the other major European powers will also do so. Leopold chooses this wording because he knows that Prime Minister William Pitt of Great Britain is strongly opposed to intervention. The French revolutionary leaders, missing this subtlety, interpret it to mean that Austria and Prussia are about to declare war. This greatly strengthens the war party of so-called Brissotins (for their leader Jacques Pierre Brissot) in the government.

November 4, 1791

North America: United States: St. Clair's Defeat. Following the October 1790 defeat by Native Americans of an expedition under Brigadier General Josiah Harmar into the Ohio Valley, Northeast Territory governor Arthur St. Clair is invested with command of the army and mounts another expedition. St. Clair, who is sick much of the time, does little to prepare his force. In October 1791, commanding some 2,000 men including the entire regular army of 600 men, he departs Fort Washington (present-day Cincinnati, Ohio), planning to build a fort among Native American settlements on the Wabash River to counteract British influence there.

On November 4, 1791, St. Clair's force is surprised and routed by a tribal confederation led by Miami chief Little Turtle and Shawnee chief Blue Jacket. The Native Americans inflict some 800 casualties, including scores of women and children who had accompanied the men, for a reported Native American loss of only 21 killed and 40 wounded. Known as St. Clair's Defeat, the Columbia Massacre, and the Battle of the Wabash, it is the greatest defeat of the U.S. Army by Native Americans in history.

Following the debacle, St. Clair resigns from the army at the request of President George Washington. St. Clair is ultimately cleared by court-martial and continues to serve as governor of the Northwest Territory.

1791

North Africa: Algeria. Spain abandons Oran but retrains some coastal towns in Morocco and western Algeria, however, including Ceuta and Melilla.

January 9, 1792

Eastern Europe: Russo-Turkish War (continued): Treaty of Jassy. Worried about Prussian activity in Poland and with its ally Austria already having concluded peace, Russia agrees to peace with the Ottoman Empire, ending the Russo-Turkish War of 1787–1792. Under the terms of the Treaty of Jassy, Russia returns both Moldavia and Bessarabia but secures Ochakov and territory along the Dniester River.

April 20, 1792

Central Europe: Wars of the French Revolution (continued): War of the First Coalition. France declares war on Austria and Prussia, beginning the War of the First Coalition (1792–1797). There is really little external threat to France at the time despite the loud posturing of the émigrés, known as the Ultras. The French declaration of war is caused by many factors. The leaders of the revolution believe that they must export the revolution, for they will not be safe until there are neighboring similar regimes. They also see a foreign war as a means of uniting the French people, who are badly divided over the course of the revolution, behind the government. Personal ambition on the part of the leaders of the revolution also plays a role, and ironically King Louis XVI supports the war because he believes that it will go badly for France and strengthen his hand. Toward that end, the Crown shares the French military plans with the Austrians.

For French revolutionary leaders the timing seems propitious, as the Austrians and Prussians are preoccupied with the partition of Poland. Indeed, the French leaders keep their best troops in the east, more afraid of each other and Russia than revolutionary France. In a very real sense, the French Revolution is saved at the expense of Poland, which undergoes a second partition in 1793.

April 28–May, 1792

Western Europe: Belgium: Wars of the French Revolution (continued): War of the First Coalition (continued): French invasion of the Austrian Netherlands. The initial fighting occurs along the frontier between France and the Austrian Netherlands (present-day Belgium). The French plan of campaign calls for striking into the Austrian Netherlands before the Austrians can prepare; this is unrealistic, as the French Army is hardly ready for war.

Mobilization proceeds slowly, there is confusion at the top, and there are only 28,000 men ready when three columns of the French Army of the North invade on April 28, 1792. Even by August 1792 there are only 82,000 men under arms along the frontier instead of the 300,000 originally envisioned. Many of the officers have emigrated, and the army itself is poorly trained, the result of several years of unrest and indiscipline.

The initial fighting goes badly for France. Two columns of the Army of the North panic during their advance on Tournai, even without being in contact with the Austrians. General Comte Théobald Dillon, commanding one of the columns, is murdered by his own troops when he tries to stem the retreat to Lille. The Austrians easily defeat French troops in fighting around Lille and proceed to lay siege to that city. Some foreign regiments in the French Army defect to the Austrians, taking their weapons with them. French marshal Jean-Baptiste Donatien de Vimeur, Comte de Rochambeau (a hero of the American Revolutionary War), resigns as commander of the Army of the North. He is replaced by Marie-Joseph Lafayette (another hero of the American Revolutionary War), who had commanded the Army of the Center.

June 20, 1792

Western Europe: Belgium: Wars of the French Revolution (continued): War of the First Coalition (continued). A mob invades the Tuileries Palace in Paris, confronting and threatening King Louis XVI before withdrawing.

July 1792

Western Europe: Rhineland: Wars of the French Revolution (continued): War of the First Coalition (continued): Allied forces assemble in the Rhineland. With the French invasion of the Austrian Netherlands at an end by late June, coalition forces commanded by Karl Wilhelm, Duke of Brunswick, opposed to France assemble at Koblenz (Coblenz) in the Rhineland. The allied force numbers some 84,000 men: 42,000 Prussians, 29,000 Austrians, 5,000 Hessians, and 8,000 French émigrés.

July 25, 1792

Western Europe: Rhineland: Wars of the French Revolution (continued): War of the First Coalition (continued): Brunswick Manifesto. Issued by allied commander Karl Wilhelm, the Duke of Brunswick, the Brunswick Manifesto threatens France—soldier and civilian alike—with destruction should any harm come to King Louis XVI or if there is resistance to the allied invasion. Intended to intimidate the revolutionaries and protect the king, the manifesto has the opposite effect. Known in Paris on August 3, the manifesto helps trigger the storming of the Tuileries Palace a week later.

August 10, 1792

Western Europe: France: Wars of the French Revolution (continued): War of the First Coalition (continued): Insurrection in Paris. Radical leaders, taking advantage of the arrival of a large number of militant recruits for the army from the provinces (the Fédérés from Brest and Marseille, who bring with them a marching song that becomes known as "La Marseillaise"), instigate an insurrection in Paris. The crowd attacks the Tuileries Palace. The king's loyal Swiss Guards of some 950 men along with some supporters are carrying the day when King Louis XVI, who has sought refuge in the Legislative Assembly, orders the Swiss to lay down their arms, condemning

the vast majority of them to death at the hands of the angry mob.

The storming of Tuileries ushers in the radical period of the French Revolution (August 10, 1792–July 28, 1794). After the king seeks refugee in the Legislative Assembly, he is suspended from office and then is imprisoned on August 13. The commander of the Army of the North, Marie-Joseph Lafayette, enjoys wide support in Paris and considers a march on the capital. Such an enterprise would be risky, however, and in any case he feels too great a loyalty to France to attempt it. Now fearing arrest by the new radical government in Paris, Lafayette flees across the border and is taken prisoner by the Austrians on August 14. Foreign Minister Charles-François du Perier Dumouriez replaces him.

See Leaders: Dumouriez, Charles-François du Perier

Frenchman Charles-François du Perier Dumouriez (1739–1823) was both a general and diplomat. As foreign minister of France, he supported the annexation of the Austrian Netherlands. Taking command in the field, he defeated the Austrians in the Battle of Jemappes on November 6, 1792, but was in turn bested by them at Neerwinden on March 18, 1793. Unsuccessful in a plan to overthrow the French government, he defected to the Austrians. (Photos.com)

August 19, 1792

Western Europe: France: Wars of the French Revolution (continued): War of the First Coalition (continued): Allied troops invade France. Coalition forces under Karl Wilhelm, Duke of Brunswick, cross the French frontier. Taking the fortresses of Longwy (August 23, 1792) and Verdun (September 2), Brunswick's army then advances slowly through the Argonne Forest toward Paris. He is opposed by French general François C. Kellermann, who takes command of the Army of the Center only on September 2.

September 2–6, 1792

Western Europe: France: Wars of the French Revolution (continued): War of the First Coalition (continued): September Massacres. With rumors rampant of a planned royalist uprising and the approach of the allied army, fear grips Paris. The Commune of Paris organizes a massacre of those held in the prisons. The radical leaders time the event to coincide with secondary elections to the new National Convention, seeking (and succeeding) to intimidate the moderate voters of Paris and secure political control of the city.

During September 2–6 in drumhead trials, more than 1,000 people are butchered. The September Massacres lead to the institution of the Revolutionary Tribunal and the Reign of Terror.

September 20, 1792

Western Europe: France: Wars of the French Revolution (continued): War of the First Coalition (continued): Battle of Valmy. The allied army under Karl Wilhelm, Duke of Brunswick, is slowly moving on Paris. Having taken Longwy and Verdun, Brunswick's forces move into the thickly wooded Argonne, terrain that favors the defender. Torrential rains also play havoc with Brunswick's lines of communication, and dysentery claims many men.

The French government in Paris orders General Charles-François Dumouriez to move his Army of the North south to block Brunswick. On September 1 Dumouriez marches the majority of his troops from Sedan to take up position in the passes of the Argonne. Although Dumouriez's men fight well and purchase valuable time, Brunswick manages to secure a lightly defended pass at Croix-aux-Bois and turn the French position. Dumouriez withdraws to Sainte-Manehould and Valmy, where he will be in position to threaten Brunswick's flank. French Army of the Center commander General François C. Kellermann joins Brunswick at Valmy, south of the Bionne River, on September 19.

The two French generals had planned to withdraw farther west, but the arrival of Brunswick's army from the north cuts off that route. While Brunswick is now closer to Paris than are Dumouriez and Kellermann, the Prussian must end the French threat to his supply lines, and he has only about 30,000–34,000 men to accomplish this.

Kellermann commands the first French line of some 36,000 men, drawn up along a ridge just west of Valmy. His troops consist of an equal mix of trained prewar soldiers and untrained but enthusiastic volunteers. Dumouriez's exhausted force of 18,000 men forms a second line behind Kellermann and east of Valmy.

Early morning fog on September 20 soon dissipates, and once he has identified the French positions, Brunswick prepares to attack. He has 54 artillery pieces, while Kellermann has only 36. Brunswick is confident, for his troops are far better trained than his French opponents.

The Battle of Valmy on September 20 is more a cannonade than anything else. The battle opens that morning when King Frederick William II orders the Prussian guns to bombard the French positions prior to an infantry assault. The French artillery, well handled by cannoneers of the prerevolutionary army, replies. The distance of some 2,500 yards between the two sides and soft ground from recent heavy rains mean that the exchange does little damage to either side. Nonetheless, the Prussians had expected the green French troops to break and run at the first volley and are thus surprised when they do not.

The Prussian infantry then begins an advance. Perhaps Brunswick hoped that the French would bolt, but when they fail to do so he halts his troops after about 200 yards. One French battalion after another takes up the cry of "Vive la nation!" Brunswick orders a second advance at about 2:00 p.m., but his men reach no farther than about 650 yards from the French. Brunswick then orders a halt, followed by a retirement. At 4:00 p.m. Brunswick summons a council of war and announces to his subordinate commanders, "We do not fight here."

The victory of the French over the Prussians in the Battle of Valmy on September 20, 1792, ended any allied hopes of crushing the French Revolution that year and is heralded as the first victory by a patriotic or "national" army over a dynastic army. (The Art Archive/Musée du Château de Versailles/Dagli Orti)

Personnel losses in the battle are slight. The Prussians lose 164 men, the French about 300. Brunswick had never been enthusiastic about the offensive and had wanted only to secure positions east of the Argonne in preparation for a major campaign the next spring; it was King Frederick William II, who was with the army, who had insisted on the movement farther west. Brunswick now uses the rebuff at Valmy as an excuse to withdraw. Prussian forces linger in the area for 10 days, but on the night of September 30–October 1 they break camp, crossing the French border on October 23.

The Battle of Valmy saves the French Revolution, at least to the extent of ending any hopes by the allies of crushing it in 1792. It is also important as marking the end of the age of dynastic armies and the arrival of the new age of patriotic national armies. Poet Johann Wolfgang von Goethe, present that day, understood this. When some Prussian officers asked him what he thought of the battle, reportedly he replied, "From this place, and from this day forth, commences a new era in the world's history, and you can all say that you were present at its birth."

September 21, 1792
Western Europe: France: Wars of the French Revolution (continued): War of the First Coalition (continued). In Paris, the new National Convention meets for the first time and on its first day votes to abolish the monarchy. A day later it proclaims France a republic and decrees that all official rulings will not be dated from the year 1 of the French Republic.

September–November 1792
Western Europe: France: Wars of the French Revolution (continued): War of the First Coalition (continued): Other French military operations. In the southeast, French forces invade Piedmont, overrun Savoy, and, on September 29, conquer Nice. On November

BATTLE OF VALMY, SEPTEMBER 20, 1792

Legend:
- French Infantry
- Prussian infantry
- French cavalry
- Prussian cavalry
- Towns

0   1,000   2,000   3,000
Yards

N

Dommartin sous-Hans

Neuville-au-Pont

Maffrecourt

Bionne River

Hans

BEURNONVILLE

Braux-St.-Cohière

DUMOURIEZ

to St. Ménehould

Somme-Bionne

STENGEL

DUMOURIEZ

Valmy

KELLERMANN

L'Etang-le Roi

KELLERMANN

KELLERMANN

Mill

RESERVE

DEPREZ-CRASSIER

Dommartin-la-Planchette

Orbeval

Dampierre-sur-Auve

Argiers

BRUNSWICK

CLERFAYT

VALANCE & CHAZOT

Gizaucourt

Maupertius

KELLERMANNS POSITION September 19

BRUNSWICK

Auve River

Fevre River

La Capelle

Voilement

from Châlons

Felcourt

Moncel

27 the National Convention declares Savoy the 84th department of France. From Alsace, meanwhile, French general Adam Philippe Custine mounts an offensive into Germany, capturing Mainz on October 21 and reaching as far as Frankfurt. French general Charles-François Dumouriez returns to northeastern France with his Army of the North and begins an invasion of Flanders.

November 6, 1792
Western Europe: Belgium: Wars of the French Revolution (continued): War of the First Coalition (continued): Battle of Jemappes. French general Charles François Dumouriez's Army of the North numbering some 45,000 men and 100 guns, having returned to the northeast following the Battle of Valmy, forces the Austrians to raise their siege of Lille and with-

draw from France. Dumouriez follows and invades the Austrian Netherlands (Belgium). The Austrians, with only 13,000 men under Marshal Albert of Saxe-Teschen, retire before the French and take up a defensive positon at Jemappes near Mons.

The French charge the Austrian positions and take heavier losses than their opponents but drive them from the field. The Austrians lose 1,500 men and eight guns, the French 2,000 men. Their victory here opens the whole of Belgium to the French, who capture Brussels on November 14. Some French forces then push up the Scheldt River to besiege Antwerp, setting off alarm bells in Britain and causing the Dutch government, on November 29, to request assistance from Britain.

December 1792

Central Europe: Western Germany: Wars of the French Revolution (continued): War of the First Coalition (continued): Allied military successes. While the French are overrunning Belgium to the north, Karl Wilhelm, Duke of Brunswick, is successful against French forces under General Adam Philippe Custine in western Germany. He retakes Frankfurt on December 2 and drives Custine back to the Rhine. Custine then goes into winter quarters at Mainz.

1792–1800

West Africa: Senegal: Wars of the French Revolution (continued). France and Britain battle over the coastal settlements in Senegal in the African portion of the Wars of the French Revolution. France initially recovers some of the posts lost during the Seven Years' War but then loses some of them back to the English.

January 21, 1793

Western Europe: France: Wars of the French Revolution (continued): War of the First Coalition (continued): Execution of Louis XVI. Former King Louis XVI is tried by the assembly, found guilty of a variety of crimes including sharing French military plans with the Austrians, and, by an absolute majority of one vote, sentenced to death. He meets his death by guillotine in Paris bravely. The execution of Louis XVI shocks King George III of Britain, and the French ambassador is expelled.

January 23, 1793

Central Europe: Poland: Second Partition of Poland. Following the First Partition of Poland, the more progressive Polish nobles realize that they must try to reform the state if Poland is not to be completely absorbed by its powerful neighbors. In 1791 they push through a new constitution that makes the kingship hereditary and not elective, creates a diet of two chambers, and abolishes the *liberum veto* whereby any noble could veto a decision of the diet.

While Austria and Prussia accept this change in Poland the Russians refuse to acknowledge it, and in May 1792 they invade to restore the old constitution. The Prussians also invade, and the two powers then agree to a new partition of Poland on January 23, 1793.

Russia receives most of Lithuania and most of western Ukraine, including Podolia, with a total of 3 million people; Prussia secures Gdańsk (Danzig) and Thorn (present-day Toruń, Poland) as well as Great Poland, with a total of 1.1 million inhabitants. In addition, Russia forces Poland into a treaty of alliance in which Russia is to have free entrance for its troops and the right to control Poland's foreign relations.

February 1, 1793

Western Europe: France: Wars of the French Revolution (continued): War of the First Coalition (continued): France declares war on Britain. Already at war with Austria, Prussia, and Piedmont, the French Republic declares war on Britain.

February–June 1793

Western Europe: France: Wars of the French Revolution (continued): War of the First Coalition (continued): Course of the Revolution within France. On February 10 a Revolutionary Tribunal comes into being. Created to try those accused of antirevolutionary crimes, it subsequently becomes a tool for Maximilian Robespierre and the Committee of Public Safety to carry out the Reign of Terror. Jacques Danton, whose energetic leadership perhaps saves France from being overrun by its enemies and who is instrumental in the tribunal's creation, eventually becomes one of its most famous victims.

On March 11 counterrevolutionary armed revolts break out in the Vendée in western France, and on April 6 the Committee of Public Safety—eventually numbering 12 men—is created to provide temporary strong leadership to meet the foreign and domestic threats to the revolution. It quickly becomes the most important part of the government. Elected on July 27, 1793, Maximilian Robespierre becomes its dominant member and eventually uses it as his power base during the subsequent Reign of Terror.

In late April the so-called Federalist Revolt, opposing the ascendancy of radical Paris over the rest of the country, spreads to Marseille and in early June to the cities of Bordeaux and Caen. In Paris meanwhile, the revolution becomes more radical. The moderate revolutionary leaders, the so-called Brissotins or Girondins, are purged from the Convention by June 2. The radicals, known as the Mountain (Montagnards) for the high benches they occupy in the Convention and who are only a minority of the population and centered in Paris, rule France during June 2, 1793–July 27, 1794, and usher in the Reign of Terror.

March 7, 1793

Western Europe: France: Wars of the French Revolution (continued): War of the First Coalition (continued). France declares war on Spain.

March 18, 1793

Western Europe: Belgium: Wars of the French Revolution (continued): War of the First Coalition (continued): Battle of Neerwinden. The French government decrees the annexation of Belgium and orders commander of the Army of the North General Charles François Dumouriez to invade the Dutch Republic. Over the winter of 1792–1793, however, the allies have built up their strength, and they now take the offensive. An Austrian army commanded by Friedrich Josias, Count Saxe-Coburg-Saalfeld, invades Belgium bent on recovering it for Austria; Karl Wilhelm, Duke of Brunswick, at the head of 60,000 men attacks French forces under General Adam Philippe Custine at Koblenz (Coblenz).

On Saxe-Coburg-Saalfeld's invasion of Belgium, Dumouriez hastily returns from his campaign in the Dutch Republic and counterattacks. Battle is joined between 41,000 Frenchmen and 43,000 Austrians. The French have more infantry, the Austrians more cavalry. Coburg is advancing toward Brussels when he encounters advance elements of Dumouriez's force. He then withdraws a short distance and takes up defensive position near the village of Neerwinden. Dumouriez attacks, hoping to turn Saxe-

Coburg-Saalfeld's left flank, but the French are repulsed. Although the French troops are enthusiastic, the Austrians are better trained and, with numbers about equal, this is the difference. The French lose some 4,000 men to 3,000 for the Austrians.

Dumouriez conducts a skillful withdrawal, but the Austrians go on to recapture Brussels and recover the southern Austrian Netherlands.

April 5, 1793

Western Europe: Belgium: Wars of the French Revolution (continued): War of the First Coalition (continued): Defection of Dumouriez. Commander of the French Army of the North General Charles François Dumouriez is falsely accused of treason by the radical leaders in Paris. Well aware of how the Convention treats its unsuccessful generals, he arrests the commissioners sent to investigate his role in the French defeat at Neerwinden. He then tries to convince his troops to march on Paris and overthrow the revolutionary government. When this fails, he deserts to the Austrians along with some of his generals, including future king of France Louis Philippe.

April–July 1793

Western Europe: France: Wars of the French Revolution (continued): War of the First Coalition (continued): Allied invasion of northeastern France and French defeats. Following the defection of General Charles Dumouriez, General Picot Dampierre takes command of the demoralized French Army of the North, France's largest field army. He is killed in action on May 8, however, during the siege of Condé in northeastern France by an allied army under Karl Wilhelm, Duke of Brunswick.

General Adam Philippe Custine now assumes command of the Army of the North. A defeat of May 21–23 near Valenciennes, also besieged by the allies, results in Custine's execution by order of the Committee of Public Safety. It is an occupational hazard borne by all French generals of the period. The allies take Condé on July 10 and Valenciennes on July 29. The Army of the North, now commanded by General Jean Nicolas Houchard (who himself will be guillotined in November), withdraws to Arras.

August 23, 1793

Western Europe: France: Wars of the French Revolution (continued): War of the First Coalition (continued): Levée en Masse. France appears on the brink of defeat. The allies retake Mainz, the Vendée is in full revolt, both Lyon and Marseille rebel against the central government, and a British-Hanoverian army under Frederick Augustus, Duke of York, lays siege to Dunkerque (Dunkirk). On August 1, therefore, the Convention implements a scorched-earth policy in the Vendée; on August 23 it issues the decree of a Levée en Masse, or national conscription, making every able-bodied male of military age liable for army service. This produces more than 600,000 recruits who will be formed into 14 field armies.

Most of the soldiers, for all intents and purposes, learn on the job. Former French Army captain Lazare Carnot, the member of the Committee of Public Safety charged with the direction of military affairs, develops tactics to take advantage of their elan and numbers, which simply overwhelm the allies facing them.

See Leaders: Carnot, Lazare

August 25, 1793
Western Europe: France: Wars of the French Revolution (continued): War of the First Coalition (continued). Marseille is recovered by revolutionary forces just as it is about to be handed over by the royalists to the English.

August 27–December 19, 1793
Western Europe: France: Wars of the French Revolution (continued): War of the First Coalition (continued): Allied capture and subsequent French siege of Toulon. At the start of hostilities the French Navy was not in the best condition. Revolutionary activities over the previous three and a half years had all but wrecked both the army and navy. As with the army, on the outbreak of the revolution virtually all senior professional naval officers are nobles. Most of these either flee France or are purged. Merchant captains are pressed into service as substitutes, but much more than with the army, enthusiasm proves to be no substitute for the long years of training required to operate, let alone to fight, warships at sea. In 1792 the crews are mutinous and poorly trained. Naval yards and shore facilities, having been starved for resources, are in poor repair. While the French possess some 76 ships of the line at the start of hostilities, fewer than half of these can be manned and gotten to sea.

The Royal Navy can send to sea 125 ships of the line, although seamen are in short supply. Spain adds another 56 ships of the line, their crews indifferently trained. The Dutch add 49 ships of the line, but these are somewhat lighter than most ships of the line in other navies.

In 1793 Admiral Lord Richard Howe commands the British Atlantic Fleet, while Vice Admiral Lord Alexander Hood commands in the Mediterranean. In the summer of 1793 Hood has at his disposal 21 ships of the line, including the first rates (100-gun) *Victory* and *Britannia.* Opposing him at Toulon, French rear admiral Jean Honoré, Comte de Trogoff de Kerlessy, commands 58 warships, representing nearly half the strength of the French Navy. Seventeen of these are ships of the line ready for sea, including the giant 120-gun *Commerce de Marseille.* Trogoff has another 4 ships of the line refitting and 9 repairing.

See Weapons: *Victory,* HMS

In August 1793 Hood is able to take advantage of royalist reaction in southern France against the radicalism of Paris. In July, Toulon had overthrown its Jacobin government and declared for the monarchy. When Paris dispatches troops, Toulon's counterrevolutionary leaders invite in Hood. Accompanied by a Spanish squadron of 17 ships of the line under Admiral Don Juan de Langara, Hood arrives off Toulon. Many of the French crews are willing to fight, but a great many simply desert.

On August 27 Hood's ships sail into the port, and Spanish and other allied troops then go ashore. The British disarm the French ships and place 5,000 captured French seamen on board 4 disarmed and unserviceable 74-gun ships of the line to sail under passport to French Atlantic ports.

In September, French Republican forces arrive at Toulon and invest the port from the land. Little is accomplished until December, however, when young artillery captain Napoleon Bonaparte convinces his superiors to employ land artillery from high ground to force the British from the port. On December 17 French troops finally secure the heights, and on the night of December 18–19 the British and Spanish sail away, bringing off with them the allied land force and some French royalists.

British captain Sir Sidney Smith meanwhile volunteers to burn the dockyard and those French ships that cannot be gotten off. His improvised effort is only partially successful. Although his men are able to fire some smaller storehouses, the large magazine

Siege of Toulon, August–December 1793

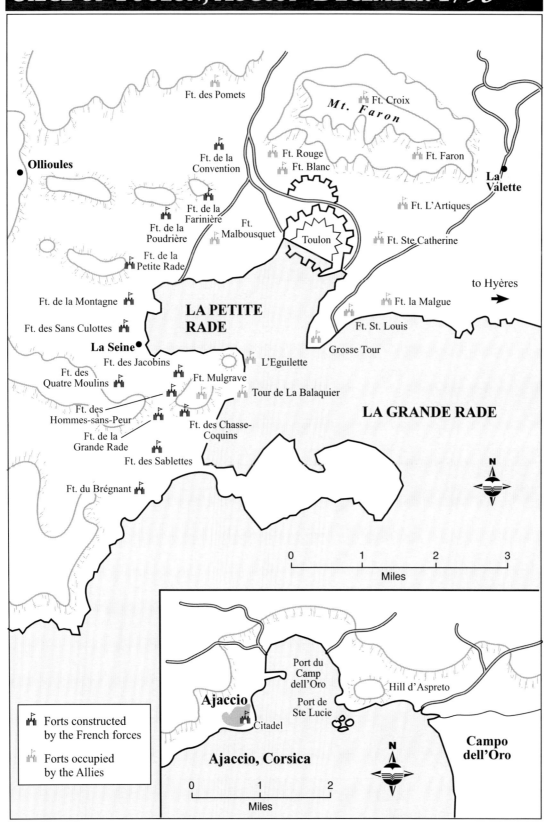

Ft. des Pomets

Mt. Faron

Ft. Croix

Ft. Rouge
Ft. Blanc
Ft. Faron

Ollioules

Ft. de la Convention

La Valette

Ft. L'Artiques

Ft. de la Farinière
Ft. Malbousquet

Ft. de la Poudrière

Toulon

Ft. Ste Catherine

Ft. de la Petite Rade

to Hyères

Ft. de la Montagne

Ft. la Malgue

Ft. des Sans Culottes

Ft. St. Louis

La Seine

LA PETITE RADE

Grosse Tour

Ft. des Jacobins

L'Eguilette

Ft. des Quatre Moulins

Ft. Mulgrave

Tour de La Balaquier

LA GRANDE RADE

Ft. des Hommes-sans-Peur

Ft. de la Grande Rade

Ft. des Chasse-Coquins

Ft. des Sablettes

Ft. du Brégnant

N

0   1   2   3
Miles

Port du Camp dell'Oro

Ajaccio

Hill d'Aspreto

Port de Ste Lucie

Citadel

Ajaccio, Corsica

Campo dell'Oro

N

0   1   2
Miles

Forts constructed by the French forces

Forts occupied by the Allies

escapes destruction. In all, 19 French ships (11 of them ships of the line), including those building, are destroyed; the Spanish take off 3 small French warships, and the British secure 15, including 3 ships of the line. Few of the captured ships prove to be of value. The *Commerce de Marseille,* which becomes the largest ship in the Royal Navy, is found too weak structurally for fleet service and is made into first a storeship and then a prison hulk.

The French recover largely intact at least 16 warships, including 13 ships of the line. These will later form the nucleus of the fleet for Bonaparte's expedition to Egypt. For the time being at least, however, the French have only their Atlantic fleet.

In addition to being a serious blow to the French Navy, the action at Toulon signals the beginning of the meteoric rise of young Bonaparte. It also marks the end of Spanish participation in the naval war on the British side.

> *See* Leaders: Hood, Alexander
> *See* Leaders: Bonaparte, Napoleon

September 5, 1793

Western Europe: France: Wars of the French Revolution (continued): War of the First Coalition (continued): Beginning of the Reign of Terror. News of the loss of Toulon, known in Paris on September 4, contributes to the decision of the Convention to adopt a resolution declaring "Let terror be the order of the day." Laws are passed allowing the arrest of large numbers of people, supposedly to protect the republic from its many enemies but also to maintain the radical minority in power. Among the most celebrated victims are Queen Marie Antoinette and the moderate revolutionaries, the Girondins.

Most of the victims of the Reign of Terror are in fact from the Third Estate. Between 35,000 and 40,000 people die in Paris and the provinces, with most executions taking place in the Vendée, in Lyon, and in other areas in open rebellion. This bloody period lasts from September 1793 through July 27, 1794. Not until its leader, Maximilian Robespierre, now seeking to install a so-called Republic of Virtue that will affect the daily lives of all Frenchmen, threatens the bulk of the deputies in the Convention do they finally rise up and overthrow him. The execution of Robespierre on July 28, 1794, ushers in the period in the revolution known as the Themidorean Reaction (1794–1795).

September 6–8, 1793

Western Europe: France: Wars of the French Revolution (continued): War of the First Coalition (continued): Battle of Hondschoote. In this battle, fought in far northeastern France just east of Dunkerque (Dunkirk) during September 6–8, 1793, 24,000 French troops under generals Jean Nicholas Houchard and Jean Baptiste Jourdan attack and defeat 16,000 well-disciplined British troops under Frederick Augustus, Duke of York. Sheer weight of French numbers carries the day. Each side suffers about 3,000 casualties.

Young French Army captain Napoleon Bonaparte directs artillery fire in retaking the Mediterranean port city of Toulon from Royalists and British and Spanish forces in December 1793. (Library of Congress)

September 13, 1793

Western Europe: France: Wars of the French Revolution (continued): War of the First Coalition (continued): Battle of Menin. French forces under General Jean Nicholas Houchard defeat Dutch forces under William V, Prince of Orange. Houchard fails to maneuver the Dutch forces out of the Austrian Netherlands (Belgium), however. He is arrested by the Convention and is tried and guillotined in November. General Jean Baptiste Jourdan takes his place.

October 15–16, 1793

Western Europe: France: Wars of the French Revolution (continued): War of the First Coalition (continued): Battle of Wattignies. In late September, Lazare Carnot, member of the Committee of Public Safety and for all intents and purposes minister of war, joins French general Jean Baptiste Jourdan in the field. Carnot orders Jourdan to relieve Maubeuge, then under siege by 30,000 Austrians under the command of Field Marshal Friedrich Josias, Count Saxe-Coburg-Saalfeld.

In the ensuing Battle of Wattignies, fought at present-day Wattignies-la-Victoire near Lille, the French attack on October 15 and are repulsed. The next day, however, the attack is renewed and results in victory, chiefly owing to the leadership of young General Florent Duquesnoy and superior French artillery of the Gribeauval system. This surprise victory forces Saxe-Coburg-Saalfeld to lift the siege of Maubeuge and withdraw to the east.

October–December 1793

Western Europe: France: Wars of the French Revolution (continued): War of the First Coalition (continued): Victories for French revolutionary forces. The revolt in the Vendée is largely quelled; Lyon is retaken by revolutionary forces on October 9, and Toulon is recovered on December 19.

On the Rhine, after being defeated by allied forces under Karl Wilhelm, Duke of Brunswick, at Kaiserslautern on November 28–30, a French army under General Louis Lazare Hoche turns the tables on Brunswick at Fröschwiller on December 22. Only four days later Hoche also defeats an Austrian army under General Dagobert Wurmser at Geisberg in Alsace. By year's end, the Prussians have been driven back across the Rhine, and the French have also retaken Mainz.

In northwestern Italy and along the frontier with Spain there is sporadic, indecisive fighting.

1793–1795

South Africa: Second Kaffir War. This second war between white Boer settlers and black Bantu tribesmen, known as Kaffirs by the Boers, proves as inconclusive as the first.

March 22, 1794

Caribbean Basin: Wars of the French Revolution (continued): War of the First Coalition (continued): British conquest of Martinique. At the end of January 1794 British vice admiral Sir John Jervis arrives at Barbados in the West Indies to take command there, accompanied by Lieutenant General Sir Charles Grey. On February 2 Jervis sails from Bridgetown with five ships of the line, a large number of frigates and smaller warships, and transports lifting about 6,100 men under Grey's command. On February 5

Portrait of Royal Navy admiral of the fleet John Jervis, Earl St. Vincent (1735–1823). Jervis won an overwhelming naval victory over the Spanish in the Battle of Cape St. Vincent, February 14, 1797. Later he was first lord of the Admiralty. (Photos.com)

the British arrive off Martinique, held by only some 600 French troops. The British come ashore in three separate places and, in several joint operations, take all of the island by March 22, 1794.

See Leaders: Jervis, John

March 27, 1794
North America: United States: Birth of the U.S. Navy. Following the twin pressures of merchant shipping losses to the North African (Barbary) states and being caught in the middle of the naval war between Britain and France, the U.S. Congress passes legislation for the construction of six frigates. The act is signed into law on March 27, 1794. The six ships are the *Constitution, United States, Constellation, Congress, President,* and *Chesapeake.* They enter service beginning in 1797. They fall under the control of the

secretary of war. Not until 1798 does a Department of the Navy come into being.

See Weapons: *Constitution,* USS

April 4, 1794
Central Europe: Poland: National uprising and Battle of Raclawice. Following the Second Partition of Poland in 1793, a popular uprising occurs in 1794, directed against both the Prussians and Russians. Tadeusz Kościuszko, a Pole who had played a major role in the American Revolutionary War, leads the revolt. On April 4, 1794, Kościuszko directs a force of some 2,400 troops and 2,000 poorly armed peasants with 11 guns in the defeat of a Russian force of 5,000 men and 30 guns under General Fiodor Denisov. The Russians sustain some 1,100 casualties, the Poles 500. This Polish success spurs uprisings elsewhere in

The U.S. Navy frigate *Constitution* shown saluting George Washington's birthday at Malta in 1837. The *Constitution,* easily the most famous ship of the U.S. Navy, remains in commission at Boston and is the world's oldest warship still afloat. (United States Navy)

Poland, and on April 17, after several days of fighting in what is known as the Warsaw (Warszawa) Insurrection, Poles drive the Russians from that city.

April 4–20, 1794

Caribbean Basin: Wars of the French Revolution (continued): War of the First Coalition (continued): British conquest of St. Luca and Guadeloupe. British vice admiral Sir John Jervis and Lieutenant General Sir Charles Grey leave a small squadron and garrison to hold Martinique and, on March 31, embark a force from Fort Royal to attack St. Lucia. Troops come ashore the next day, and on April 4 the French there surrender.

On April 5 most of the British troops return to Martinique; three days later Jervis sails from there against Guadeloupe. The British troops begin coming ashore at Guadeloupe on April 11. The British secure the surrender of the entire island on April 20.

The French are not prepared to accept the loss, and on June 4 a squadron of nine warships arrives off Cape François and begins landing troops. Most of the islanders rally to the French. Jervis and Grey return to the island on June 7 and effect a landing on June 19. Additional French reinforcements arrive and retake the entire island by December 10.

There is also inconclusive fighting involving the British, French, and Spanish on Santo Domingo, and both sides attack the other's merchant marine. The French suffer the heaviest losses.

May 11, 1794

Western Europe: France: Wars of the French Revolution (continued): War of the First Coalition (continued): Battle of Kortrijk. As part of a French offensive in Flanders, units of the French Army of the North commanded by General Charles Pichegru seize both Menin and Kortrijk. An allied army of Dutch and Austrian troops under Austrian field marshal Charles de Croix, Count von Clerfayt, forces the French from Kortrijk and establishes strong defensive positions there. The French counterattack, and although two French infantry attacks fail, a third succeeds, forcing back the Austrian left flank and threatening the entire line. At nightfall Clerfayt orders a withdrawal to Thielt. Each side loses some 700–800 men in the battle.

May 18, 1794

Western Europe: France: Wars of the French Revolution (continued): War of the First Coalition (continued): Battle of Tourcoing. In continued fighting near Tourcoing, a town just north of Lille in northeastern France, French general Charles Pichegru's Army of the North, temporarily commanded by General Joseph Souham, engages an allied force of Austrians, British, and Hanoverians under Austrian field marshal Friedrich Josias, Count of Saxe-Coburg-Saalfeld. Frederick Augustus, Duke of York, commands the British forces in the allied army.

In the battle the better-led 70,000 French troops outfight the 74,000 poorly managed allied troops, generating a French victory. The French suffer 3,000 casualties and lose 7 guns; the allies sustain 4,000 men killed or wounded and another 1,500 taken prisoner. They also lose 50 guns. Although hardly a decisive victory, the Battle of Tourcoing halts the allied advance from Flanders into northeastern France and causes the Austrians to go over on the defensive.

May 23, 1794

Western Europe: Belgium: Wars of the French Revolution (continued): War of the First Coalition (continued): Battle of Tournai. On May 22, 1794, French general Charles Pichegru's Army of the North attacks the fortress city of Tournai, in the western Austrian Netherlands (Belgium), with about 45,000 men. The French attack is blunted by some 50,000 Austrian forces under Austrian field marshal Friedrich Josias, Count of Saxe-Coburg-Saalfeld. The French sustain 6,000 casualties, the Austrians only 4,000. The battle proves to be only a temporary French setback. The French threat here forces the Austrians to pull forces from the southern sector of the allied front, helping to set up the decisive French victory at Fleurus in June.

June 1, 1794

Western Atlantic Ocean: Wars of the French Revolution (continued): War of the First Coalition (continued): Battle of the Glorious First of June. The French assemble some 170 merchant vessels loaded with purchased foodstuffs (mostly grain) in Chesapeake Bay in the United States. To ensure their safe arrival at Brest and perhaps the very survival of the French government, on December 25, 1793, French rear admiral Pierre Jean Van Stabel sails for the United States with 2 ships of the line and 2 frigates; he is expected to return with the merchantmen toward the end of May. Meanwhile, the French fleet rebuilding at Brest will put to sea and break the British blockade.

On May 16, 1794, the French fleet, with 22 ships of the line under Admiral Louis Villaret-Joyeuse, departs Brest; member of the Committee of Public Safety Jeanbon Saint-André sails with him. They hope to link up with the grain convoy some 500 miles west of Brest. Paris had given explicit instructions that the fleet's sole task is to protect the convoy, with Villaret-Joyeuse to avoid all action unless the convoy is positively in danger. The fleet must be preserved for a planned invasion of England.

The French fleet is anything but ready, as is obvious when the ships take to the sea. Captains lack experience handling ships in formation, maneuvers are indifferently executed, signaling is ineffective, and frigate commanders disobey instructions to chase isolated merchantmen on their own.

On the morning of May 28 the French sight British admiral Richard Lord Howe's fleet of 25 ships of the line in the distance. Villaret-Joyeuse seeks to withdraw, while Howe tries to force a battle. Howe manages to cut off the last ship in the French line, the 100-gun *Révolutionnaire*. It is badly damaged, but the French manage to tow it into Aix Roads. Two British ships are also forced to withdraw for repairs.

On May 29 the two fleets again came together, running parallel in the same direction. The engagement is destructive but inconclusive. The damaged British ships continue in service, however, while some French ships must depart for dockyard attention. French losses are made up the next day by the arrival of 4 additional ships of the line under Rear Admiral Joseph Maire Nielly. Villaret-Joyeuse now tries to draw Howe away to the northwest in the hope that Van Stabel will then be able to pass to the south with his convoy. On the afternoon of the May 31 both sides prepare for battle.

In the resulting engagement, known to the British as the Glorious First of June and to the French as La Bataille du 13 Prairial, the French have 26 ships of the line to the British 25. Howe wins a resounding victory by turning into the midst of the French line and piercing it in six separate places. In the resulting melee battle, some French ships are forced to fight both sides simultaneously, while others have nothing at which to shoot. Control is lost in the din and smoke of battle, and the contest becomes one of individual ship engagements.

Superior British leadership and gunnery win the day, while on many French ships enthusiasm gives way to panic. The French flagship *Montagne* is attacked by five and six British ships at a time, including Howe's flagship *Queen Charlotte*. The *Montagne*'s 129 guns enable it to survive despite more than 318 casualties. The battle ends in the afternoon, with Villaret-Joyeuse breaking off contact to return to Brest.

In all the British take six French ships. Another sinks as British ships approach it. The captured French ships have all sustained extensive damage, and two are judged not worthy of repair. Although the victory goes to Howe, Villaret-Joyeuse achieves his goal of drawing the Royal Navy away from the convoy.

The French Atlantic Fleet returns to Brest on June 11, but there is no sign of the grain ships. The fleet prepares to go to sea again, but Van Stabel is sighted the next day, and on June 13 the convoy arrives with 24 million pounds of flour. The French are lucky. Howe's vessels suffer such damage in the June 1 battle that he returns to Plymouth for repairs, but the remaining British squadron patrolling the coast is sufficient to deal with Van Stabel's warships; it is mere chance that the French convoy avoids detection.

June 26, 1794
Western Europe: Belgium: Wars of the French Revolution (continued): War of the First Coalition (continued): Battle of Fleurus. In early June, General Jean Baptiste Jourdan receives command of the Army of the Ardennes and four divisions of the Army of the North—about 80,000 men—later named the Army of the Sambre-Meuse. Assigned to take the city of Charleroi in the Austrian Netherlands (present-day Belgium), on June 12 his forces cross the Sambre River and invest the city. Austrian field marshal Friedrich Josias, Count of Saxe-Coburg-Saalfeld, having concentrated some 46,000 men north of Charleroi, on June 16 attacks the French lines around Charleroi, inflicting some 3,000 casualties and forcing Jourdan to withdraw back across the Sambre.

On June 18, however, Jourdan again crosses the Sambre and invests Charleroi, defended now by only about 2,800 men. The French bring up siege artillery this time, and the city surrenders on June 25. Jourdan then detaches some 2,000 men from his army to hold the city. Unaware that Charleroi has fallen, Saxe-Coburg-Saalfeld marches there with a considerable Austrian-Dutch army—as many as 103,000 men—to relieve the siege and destroy the French forces there.

Saxe-Coburg-Saalfeld organizes his force into five large columns with the intent of enveloping and destroying Jourdan's army.

On June 26 Saxe-Coburg-Saalfeld arrives around Charleroi. Jourdan decides to fight behind his entrenchments. The crew of a French reconnaissance balloon, *l'Entreprenant,* continuously informs Jourdan about Austrian movements.

The battle is actually a series of separate engagements, fought along a front of some 18 miles. On the right, French troops hold against at least three Austrian assaults. On the French left, Dutch troops under William V, Prince of Orange, achieve some success, pushing back their adversaries. In late afternoon, however, the French counterattack and drive back the Dutch. In the center, cavalry and horse artillery come to the assistance of hard-pressed French infantry, enabling them to hold the line.

Following some dozen hours of combat Saxe-Coburg-Saalfeld, now uncertain of the outcome, calls off the attacks, giving the French an unexpected victory. The French lose about 2,000 men, the Austrians about 2,200. After the battle, however, French cavalry take another 3,000 isolated Austrian infantry prisoner. Jourdan's army is too exhausted to pursue the Austrians, though.

Fleurus is a decisive French victory in that it deals a crushing blow to Austrian hopes of retaining the Austrian Netherlands. Following a pause to regroup, French forces advance rapidly through Belgium, taking Brussels on July 10 and Antwerp on July 27. By the end of the year, the French control the entire Austrian Netherlands.

The Battle of Fleurus also has important political repercussions in France. It ends the justification for the Reign of Terror (the military threat to France) and is a major impetus behind the overthrow of the radicals late the next month.

See Weapons: Air Gun

July 28, 1794

Western Europe: France: Wars of the French Revolution (continued): War of the First Coalition (continued): Overthrow of the Montagnards by the Convention. The end of the military threat and the desire of the leader of the radical Montagnards (Mountain) faction in the Convention Maximilian Robespierre to continue, and even expand, the Reign of Terror and his vague threats against the Convention

without naming names finally bring action against him. When he attempts a coup d'état, the forces of the Convention defeat him and his followers. Robespierre and other Mountain leaders are executed on July 28, 1794. This ushers in the period of the revolution known as the Thermidorian Reaction, named for the month of the new revolutionary calendar in which the new period begins. The instruments of the Reign of Terror are shut down, and the radical clubs are closed.

July–November 1794

North America: United States: Whiskey Rebellion. Opposition in western rural Pennsylvania to a whiskey excise tax (but also to taxes in general) becomes armed rebellion. On August 7, 1794, President George Washington declares the area in open rebellion. With the Legion of the United States occupied in Indian warfare to the west, Washington calls on the governors of Pennsylvania, New Jersey, Maryland, and Virginia to provide nearly 13,000 militiamen. This is the first test of the Militia Act of 1792 and presidential authority to call out militia to suppress insurrection.

Washington takes personal command of one column at Carlisle, Pennsylvania, and Virginia governor Henry "Light Horse Harry" Lee commands the other at Cumberland. The Whiskey Rebellion quickly collapses before this so-called Army of the Constitution. In the end a dozen individuals are brought to trial in Philadelphia and are later pardoned.

August 10, 1794

Southern Europe: Wars of the French Revolution (continued): War of the First Coalition (continued): British capture all Corsica. The British aid Corsican nationalist Pasquale Paoli, leading an uprising against the French. Vice Admiral Lord Alexander Hood sends 3 ships of the line and 2 frigates along with a number of transports lifting troops under Major General David Dundas. Hood lands the troops at Mortella Bay on February 8, 1794. Throughout the Corsican campaign the navy provides offshore gunfire support.

Mortella Tower is taken on February 18, and Bastia falls to the British on May 21 after a 37-day siege. British reinforcements arrive from Gibraltar, and Calvi is taken on August 10 following a 51-day siege.

August 20, 1794

North America: United States: Battle of Fallen Timbers. In the 1783 Treaty of Paris that ended the American Revolutionary War, the British government acknowledged U.S. claims west of the Appalachians. Incursions by American settlers into the Ohio Valley, however, led to serious problems because Native American leaders refused to acknowledge U.S. authority north of the Ohio. Encouraged by the British in their stance, leaders of the Miami and Shawnee tribes insisted that the Americans fall back to the Ohio River.

Following two disastrous forays into Native American territory, the first led by Brigadier General Joseph Harmar in 1790 and the second by governor of the Northwest Territory Major General Arthur St. Clair in 1791, in December 1792 Congress votes to establish a 5,000-man Legion of the United States, commanded by a major general and consisting of four sublegions of 1,250 men, each led by a brigadier general. President George Washington appoints retired general Anthony Wayne to command the legion.

Wayne establishes a training camp 25 miles from Pittsburgh at a site he names Legionville and there puts the men through rigorous training. In May 1793 he moves the legion to Cincinnati and then a few miles north to a new camp, Hobson's Choice. In early October Wayne moves north with 2,000 regulars to Fort Jefferson, the end of his defensive line. When Kentucky mounted militia arrive, Wayne moves a few miles farther north and sets up a new camp, naming it Fort Greeneville (now Greenville, Ohio) in honor of his Revolutionary War commander, Major General Nathanael Greene.

In December 1793 Wayne sends a detachment to the site of St. Clair's defeat on the Wabash. On Christmas Day 1793 the Americans reoccupy that battlefield and construct Fort Recovery on high ground overlooking the Wabash. Aided by friendly Native Americans, the soldiers recover most of St. Clair's cannon, which the Native Americans had buried nearby. These are incorporated into Fort Recovery, which is manned by an infantry company and a detachment of artillerists.

Wayne's campaign timetable is delayed because of unreliable civilian contractors, Native American attacks on his supply trains, the removal of some of his men elsewhere, and a cease-fire that leads him

In the Battle of Fallen Timbers on August 20, 1794, Major General Anthony Wayne's Legion of the United States ended Native American power in the eastern region of the Old Northwest and restored U.S. military prestige. (Library of Congress)

to believe that peace might be in the offing. But Miami chief Little Turtle, Shawnee chief Blue Jacket, and other Native American leaders reject peace negotiations, in part because of a speech by British governor-general in Canada Guy Carleton predicting war between Britain and the United States and pledging British support for the Indians. Indeed, in February 1794 Carleton orders construction of Fort Miami on the Maumee River to mount cannon larger than those that Wayne might be able to bring to bear, further delaying Wayne's advance.

On June 29, 1794, Little Turtle strikes first, at Fort Recovery, Wayne's staging point for the invasion. A

BATTLE OF FALLEN TIMBERS, AUGUST 20, 1794

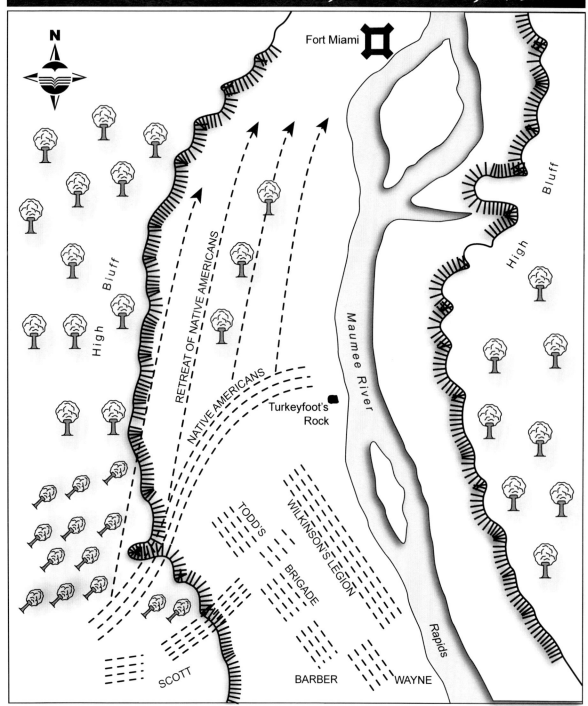

supply train had just arrived there and is bivouacked outside the walls when 2,000 warriors attack. Although a number of soldiers are killed, the Native Americans are beaten back with heavy casualties, and two days later they withdraw. Never again are they able to assemble that many warriors. The repulse here also prompts some of the smaller tribes to quit the Native American coalition and leads to the eclipse of Little Turtle, who is replaced as principal war leader by the less effective Blue Jacket.

Wayne now has 2,000 men. In mid-July some 1,600 Kentucky militia under Brigadier General Charles Scott arrive. Wayne can also count on 100 Indians, mostly Choctaws and Chickasaws from Tennessee. On July 28 Wayne departs Fort Greeneville for Fort Recovery. Washington warns that a third straight defeat "would be inexpressibly ruinous to the reputation of the government."

The Native Americans are concentrated at Miami Town, the objective of previous offensives, and the rapids of the Maumee River, around Fort Miami. A 100-mile-long road along the Maumee River Valley connects the two. Wayne intends to build a fortification at midpoint on the road, allowing him to strike in either direction and forcing the Native Americans to defend both possible objectives. By August 3 he has established this position, Fort Adams, and has also built a second fortified position, Fort Defiance, at the confluence of the Auglaize and Maumee rivers. Wayne then sends the chiefs a final peace offer. Little Turtle urges acceptance, pointing out the strength of Wayne's force and expressing doubts about British support. However, Blue Jacket and British agents want war, which a majority of the chiefs now approve.

Having learned of a Native American concentration near Fort Miami, Wayne decides to move there first. After a difficult crossing of the Maumee River, on August 15 Wayne's men are still 10 miles from the British fort. Sensing an impending fight, Wayne detaches unnecessary elements from his column to construct a possible fall-back position, Fort Deposit, manned by Captain Zebulon Pike and 200 men.

On August 20 Wayne again puts his column in motion, anticipating battle that day with either the Native Americans or the British. Indeed, more than 1,000 braves and some 60 Canadian militiamen are lying in wait in a position just south of present-day Toledo, Ohio, hoping to ambush Wayne's men from the natural defenses of what had been a forest before it was uprooted by a tornado and transformed into a chaos of twisted branches and broken tree trunks.

Blue Jacket had expected Wayne to arrive on August 19, not anticipating the day-long delay. In consequence of the impending battle, the Native Americans had begun a strict fast on August 18 and then continued it on August 19. When the Americans fail to arrive, many of the Native Americans, half-starved and exhausted, depart for Fort Miami.

Wayne marches his men so as to be ready to meet an attack from any quarter. His infantry are in two wings. Brigadier General James Wilkinson commands the right, and Colonel John Hamtramck commands the left. A mounted brigade of Kentuckians protects the left flank, while legion horsemen cover the right. Additional Kentucky horsemen guard the rear and serve as a reserve. Well to the front, Major William Price leads a battalion intended to trigger the Native American attack and allow Wayne time to deploy the main body.

When the Native Americans do open fire, Price's men fall back into Wilkinson's line. Wayne rallies his men and sends them to defeat the ambush with an infantry frontal attack driven home with the bayonet. At the same time, the horsemen close on the flanks. The Native Americans are completely routed and flee the battle toward Fort Miami. The killing continues to the very gates of the fort while the British look on. Wayne's losses in the battle are 33 men killed and 100 wounded (11 of them mortally), while Native American losses are in the hundreds.

Although Wayne disregards Fort Miami, he destroys Indian communities and British storehouses in its vicinity. The soldiers then march to Miami Town, occupy it without opposition on September 17, and raze it. They then build a fort on the site of Harmar's 1790 defeat, naming it Fort Wayne.

The Battle of Fallen Timbers breaks forever the power of the Native Americans in the eastern region of the Northwest Territory. It also does much to restore U.S. military prestige; Wayne is justifiably known as the father of the U.S. Army.

On August 3, 1795, chiefs representing 12 tribes sign the Treaty of Greeneville, Wayne having revealed to them that the British have now agreed to withdraw their forts and recognize the boundary set in the 1783 Treaty of Paris. The Treaty of Greeneville sets a definite boundary in the Northwest Territory, forcing the American Indians to give up once and for all most of the present state of Ohio and part of Indiana.

August 26–September 6, 1794

Central Europe: Poland: National uprising (continued): Siege of Warsaw. Following the Polish uprising and victory in the Battle of Raclawice, Prussian and Russian armies invade Poland. After a series of desperate smaller battles, the Prussians and Russians converge on Warsaw (Warszawa) and lay siege to the city. Prussian king Frederick William II commands in person 25,000 men and 179 guns, while Russian general Ivan Fersen commands 65,000 men and 74 guns. Another Russian army of 11,000 men controls the right bank of the Vistula (Wisła). During August 26–September 6, 1794, the Poles defend the city with 35,000 men and 200 guns, defeating two allied assaults and raising the siege.

August–December 1794

Western and Central Europe: Wars of the French Revolution (continued): War of the First Coalition (continued): French land victories against the allies. Crossing the Roer River, French general Jean Baptiste Jourdan clears the left bank of the Rhine of Prussian forces. General Jean Victor Moreau, having distinguished himself in the fighting in Belgium, takes command of the newly formed French Army of the Rhine and Moselle and lays siege to Mainz.

Meanwhile, another French army under General Charles Pichegru crosses the Meuse on October 18 and, after taking Nijmegen, drives the Austrians beyond the Rhine. Other French forces cross the Pyrenees into Spain and force the allies from Savoy.

October 10, 1794

Central Europe: Poland: National Uprising (continued): Battle of Maciejowice. On October 10, 1794, Polish general Tadeusz Kościuszko attempts, with 6,200 men, to prevent the union of two larger Russian armies: 12,000 men under Ivan Fersen and 12,500 men under General Aleksandr Suvorov. Kościuszko calls too late for support from Polish general Adam Poniński with 4,000 men, and the latter fails to arrive in time at Maciejowice, about 50 miles from Warsaw.

The Russians under Fersen attack the Poles and, after several assaults, defeat them. Kościuszko, seriously wounded, is taken prisoner. The Battle of Maciejowice is decisive; the Polish uprising now collapses.

November 19, 1794

North America: United States: Jay's Treaty. Following the British government Orders in Council of June 8 and November 8, 1793, the Royal Navy begins seizing American merchant ships trading with France and impressing American seamen. Many Americans favor honoring the treaty of alliance with France. With the United States and Britain teetering on the brink of war, President George Washington names Supreme Court chief justice John Jay as special envoy to Britain to negotiate outstanding differences between the two countries. These include the removal of forts in the Northwest, which had been stipulated in the Treaty of Paris of 1783 ending the American Revolutionary War but which the British have steadfastly refused to carry out pending payment of prewar debts owed to British citizens and compensation for the confiscation of Loyalist properties by state governments. The Washington administration also seeks to maintain trade with Britain, as import duties on British goods are the chief source of federal tariff revenue.

Under the terms of Jay's Treaty of November 19, 1794, the British agree to evacuate the northwestern forts by June 1, 1796. The treaty also opens the British East and West Indies to U.S. merchant trade under certain restrictions and refers to a joint commission the settlement of prerevolutionary debts, the Northwest boundary, and compensation for illegal maritime seizures by the Royal Navy. There is nothing in the treaty regarding the issue of impressment, the Native American question (British authorities have been encouraging creation of a Native American buffer state in the Northwest, and many Americans there believe that the British are behind Native American raids against their settlements), or compensation for the slaves removed from the American South by the English during the Revolutionary War.

There is considerable opposition to the treaty in the United States, especially in the South by Republicans but also among New England shipping interests. Nonetheless, the treaty is narrowly approved by the Senate on June 24, 1795.

January–March 1795

Western Europe: Wars of the French Revolution (continued): War of the First Coalition (continued): French invasion and conquest of the Netherlands. Instead of going into winter quarters after taking Nijmegen, French general Charles Pichegru prepares for a winter campaign, facilitated by one of the coldest winters on record and his ability to transit frozen rivers and lakes with his cavalry. On December 28, 1794, he crosses the Meuse on the ice and storms the island of Bommel. He then crosses the Waal River and takes Utrecht (January 19) and Amsterdam (January 20).

The campaign sees a unique event in military history: the capture of a fleet by horse cavalry. On the evening of January 23 French hussars arrived at Den Helder, the northernmost point of the North Holland Peninsula. There the Dutch fleet is frozen in the ice, and the French cavalrymen take its surrender. Pichegru's army then goes on to take all of the Dutch Republic, which now becomes the French satellite Batavian Republic.

March 14, 1795

Mediterranean Sea: Western Europe: Wars of the French Revolution (continued): War of the First Coalition (continued). On March 15, 1795, British admiral Lord William Hotham's Mediterranean Fleet of 14 ships of the line engages 13 French ships of the line and takes 2 of them.

April 5, 1795

Western Europe: Wars of the French Revolution (continued): War of the First Coalition (continued): Treaty of Basel. On April 5, 1795, Prussia and France conclude peace. The French agree to withdraw their forces from Prussian territory east of the Rhine, while Prussia agrees to French retention of the left bank until peace with the empire is concluded. In secret provisions, Prussia recognizes the definitive acquisition by France of territory on the west bank of the Rhine and in return will receive financial compensation from the secularization of church lands on the right bank belonging to the ecclesiastical princes.

May 16, 1795

Western Europe: Wars of the French Revolution (continued): War of the First Coalition (continued): Treaty of The Hague. The treaty ends the war between France and the Dutch Republic. The new Batavian Republic organized by France from the former Republic of the United Netherlands concludes a defensive alliance with France.

June 23, 1795

Atlantic Ocean: France: Wars of the French Revolution (continued): War of the First Coalition (continued): British and French naval engagement off Groix in the eastern Atlantic Ocean. A British naval squadron under Commodore Sir John Borlase Warren sails from Portsmouth with an expeditionary force for Quiberon Bay in western Brittany, France. Admiral Sir Alexander Arthur Hood, Lord Bridport, commanding the British Channel Fleet, parts company with the expeditionary force near Belle Isle on June 19.

Learning that the French are at sea, Bridport detaches 3 ships of the line to reinforce Warren and continues with his remaining 14 ships, maintaining position between Warren and the French. On June 22 Bridport sights the French 12 ships of the line under Admiral Louis Thomas Villaret de Joyeuse. In an engagement on June 23 Bridport captures 3 of the French ships. The British continue their mastery of the English Channel, and during the remainder of the year both sides engage in trying to destroy the waterborne commerce of the other.

June 27, 1795

Western Europe: France: Wars of the French Revolution (continued): War of the First Coalition (continued): British landing in Quiberon Bay. A British naval squadron under Commodore Sir John Borlase Warren arrives unmolested in Quiberon Bay in western Brittany, France. It consists of 3 ships of the line, 6 frigates, and many other smaller warships escorting 50 transports carrying a French émigré force of 2,500 men under Joseph, Comte de Puisaye, and Louis Charles, Comte d'Hervilly.

The expeditionary force goes ashore without incident on June 27, 1795. The British also put ashore a considerable quantity of arms hoping that the royalist sympathizers of the region (Chouans) will join the émigrés, and thousands do so. The émigré cause is badly hampered by divided command, however.

D'Hervilly leads a largely peasant force of 12,000 men to take Penthièvre, the only fortress on the Quiberon Peninsula, but he refuses to advance farther, allowing General Louis Lazare Hoche and his 13,000-man republican Army of the West to seal off the peninsula. Although émigré reinforcements are landed on July 15, Hoche retakes Penthièvre on the night of July 20–21, then attacks and routs the remaining émigré forces.

British frigates, delayed by bad weather, manage to rescue only 2,000 of the force that ultimately totals 17,000. Hoche also captures arms sufficient for 40,000 men. Despite pledges of mercy, the republicans execute some 700 of the émigrés. The abortive Quiberon expedition, which is mounted too late, puts finis to prospects of other such émigré operations.

July 22, 1795

Western Europe: Wars of the French Revolution (continued): War of the First Coalition (continued): Treaty of Basel. Spain concludes peace with the French Republic. Under the terms of the Treaty of Basel, Spain cedes to France Santo Domingo, the eastern portion of the island of Hispaniola.

August 22, 1795

Western Europe: France: Wars of the French Revolution (continued): War of the First Coalition (continued): Constitution of the Year III. This constitution, the third of the revolution, creates the Directory, so-named for five directors who are the executive. There is also a legislature of two chambers—the Council of Elders (Ancients) and the Council of Five Hundred—but the framers, fearful of their own position and lives, rig this so that two-thirds of the members of the new government have to be taken from the Convention.

September 1795

South Africa: British conquest of the Boer settlement in South Africa. There is little opposition from the Boers, who in any case oppose the French who have overrun their homeland (the Netherlands). During 1796 the British extend their control over the interior territories, including several that freed themselves from control of the Capetown Boers.

October 5, 1795

Western Europe: Wars of the French Revolution (continued): War of the First Coalition (continued): 13 Vendémiaire. Widespread opposition in France to the Two-Third's Decree and the new government of the Directory leads in Paris to an uprising of the sec-

tions. Forewarned, the government places General of Brigade Napoleon Bonaparte in charge of troops in the city.

Bonaparte employs artillery—his "whiff of grapeshot," as he puts it—to crush the uprising of perhaps 30,000 people in Paris on 13 Vendémiaire (the date according to the revolutionary calendar). Perhaps 200 people are killed. The Directory is safe. Bonaparte is rewarded by promotion to general of division and receives command of the Army of Italy in March 1796.

October 7, 1795

Atlantic Ocean: Wars of the French Revolution (continued): War of the First Coalition (continued): Naval engagement between the French and English. The French have rebuilt their Mediterranean fleet at Toulon, now commanded by Admiral Pierre Martin. On October 7, 1795, 31 British merchant ships from the Levant and an escorting squadron of 3 ships of the line and 1 frigate fall in off Cape St. Vincent with a French squadron of 6 ships of the line and 3 frigates under Admiral Joseph de Richery that has escaped the British blockade of Toulon. The British convoy scatters while the squadron forms to do battle off Cape St. Vincent.

In the battle the French capture 1 British ship of the line, the French prize *Censeur* that had been jury-rigged and loses all three topmasts and is forced to strike. Two other British warships escape, but the French frigates capture 30 of the 31 merchant ships.

Another French squadron of one ship of the line, five frigates, and a smaller warship, all under Commodore Honoré Ganteaume, also escapes from Toulon at the end of September, owing to incompetence or poor management on the part of British admiral Lord William Hotham. The French squadron heads east, hoping to intercept the same British convoy, and regains Toulon with all but two of his ships in early February 1796. On November 1, 1795, Vice Admiral Sir Hyde Parker replaces the ineffective Hotham.

October 24, 1795

Central Europe: Poland: Third Partition of Poland. In this final partition, Poland disappears from the map. Russia receives what remains of Lithuania and the Ukraine with 1.2 million people, Prussia takes Mazovia with the city of Warsaw and 1 million people, and Austria takes the remainder of the Kraków (Cracow) region, with 1 million people. Courland, long under Polish suzerainty but under de facto control by Russia since 1737, is officially incorporated into Russia.

November 23, 1795
Southern Europe: Northern Italy: Wars of the French Revolution (continued): War of the First Coalition (continued): Battle of Loano. General Barthélemy Schérer, commander of the French Army of Italy, receives reinforcements that bring his strength up to some 25,000 men. He advances to the east into Liguria, which belongs to Genoa, along the Mediterranean coast. The opposing Austrian and Piedmontese forces on paper number some 43,000 men, but in actuality they are far smaller.

The principal battle occurs at Loano on November 23, part of a series of engagements during November 22–29. General André Masséna leads 13,000 French troops in an attack on the center of the Austrian defensive line. Allied losses in the battle total 5,500 casualties and four guns; French losses are 1,300 dead and wounded and 400 taken prisoner. This French victory consolidates their position in western Liguria and the Maritime Alps and throws Austrian and Piedmontese forces there on the defensive.

1795
Central Europe: Western Germany: Wars of the French Revolution (continued): War of the First Coalition (continued): French military operations along the Rhine. French general Jean Baptiste Jourdan's 100,000-man Army of the Sambre and Meuse operates west of Koblenz (Coblenz), opposing some 85,000 Austrians under Marshal Charles de Croix, Count von Clerfayt. French general Charles Pichegru's 90,000-man Army of the Rhine and Moselle operates to the south, in Alsace and the Palatinate, opposing another 85,000 allied troops under Marshal Dagobert Sigismund, Count Wurmser. After a prolonged siege, Luxembourg falls to the French on June 15, 1795. In early September, Jourdan invades Germany but is outmaneuvered by Clerfayt near Höchst in early October. Pichegru meanwhile loses Mannheim and all strategic advantage before concluding a general armistice on December 21.

The defeat of Jourdan's forces is undoubtedly the work of Pichegru. Although widely acknowledged as a hero of the Revolution, he betrays French military plans to the Austrians and is involved in a con-

spiracy seeking to secure the return of Count de Provence (Louis XVIII) as king of France, probably more from a desire for wealth and advancement than political conviction. Pichegru is widely suspected, and when he offers his resignation, much to his surprise the Directory quickly accepts it in 1796. Retiring in disgrace, he secures election to the Council of Five Hundred in May 1797 as a leader of the royalist faction.

1795–1796
Western Europe: Wars of the French Revolution (continued): War of the First Coalition (continued): French military operations in the Vendée. The Vendée, a hotbed of royalist and antirevolutionary sentiment in east-central France, again breaks into revolt. The British occupy the small Ile d'Yeu off the coast of Poitou, and in October 1795 they send warships under commodore Sir John Warren escorting transports lifting 4,000 British troops under Major General Doyle. The troops and supplies are landed on the Ile d'Yeu, but by the end of the year French troops crush the royalist uprising. The British then withdraw their men and stores. In the spring of 1796 French troops under General Louis Lazare Hoche savagely wipe out what remains of the uprising, although they cannot end unrest.

1795–1796
Southwest Asia: Persia: Persian conquest of Georgia. In 1795 Persian forces invade the Kingdom of Georgia, which had shaken off Persian rule following the death of Nadir Shah. The Persians defeat the Georgians and brutally maintain their control.

1795–1797
East Asia: China. Revolts against the Qing in Hunan and Guizhou are easily put down by the Qing. They are, however, part of a series of revolts during 1774–1797 that signify a gradual deterioration in Qing dynasty power.

1795–1798
Northern Europe: Ireland: Unrest and revolt against British rule. Continuing discontent in Ireland, fanned by United Irishmen leaders Wolf Tone and Napper Tandy, among others, brings revolt against British rule. Although the nationalists hope for French intervention, little aid materializes, and the uprising is suppressed with great brutality in the Battle of

Vinegar Hill (June 12, 1798) by British troops under General Gerard Lake.

February 15, 1796
South Asia: Ceylon: British conquest of Ceylon. As part of British East India Company operations against the Dutch in the East Indies, a British expeditionary force of three small warships escorting five Indiamen with troops arrives off Negombo near Colombo from the Cape of Good Hope. The British occupy the port, and the troops march on Colombo, which surrenders on February 15. The king of Kandy recognizes British sovereignty. (Two years later, in 1798, Ceylon, present-day Sri Lanka, becomes a Crown colony.) Also in February, another British squadron takes possession of Amboyna, in the Moluccas, and in March it secures the Banda Islands.

April 12, 1796
Southern Europe: Northern Italy: Wars of the French Revolution (continued): War of the First Coalition (continued): Battle of Montenotte. On March 27, 1796, Napoleon Bonaparte assumes command of the 45,000-man French Army of Italy, which is poorly equipped and badly provisioned. His troops occupy a line extending from Nice almost to Genoa. Opposing him are two allied armies: a Piedmontese force of 25,000 men under Baron Colli and an Austrian army of 35,000 men under General Jean Pierre Beaulieu. Bonaparte takes advantage of the fact that the allies, although more numerous, are both extended and separated, inviting a French attack.

For several weeks Bonaparte does nothing, but on April 6 he sends his cavalry and some of his infantry under General André Masséna toward Genoa, or so it appears. Beaulieu, as expected, dispatches men to Bochetta to counter this. Masséna then concentrates his forces at Savona on April 11 and, in a rapid night march, catches 4,500 Austrians still asleep at Montenotte on the morning of April 12. The resulting victory belongs to Masséna, for Bonaparte is five miles away, but Bonaparte gives his subordinate only a share of the credit.

April 14–15, 1796
Southern Europe: Northern Italy: Wars of the French Revolution (continued): War of the First Coalition (continued): Battle of Dego. Following the Battle of Montenotte, commander of the French Army of Italy Napoleon Bonaparte continues his drive north, widening the gap as he proceeds. He defeats the Piedmontese at Colli on April 13 and then pushes the Austrians from Dego on April 14. The Austrians counterattack and drive the French out. Bonaparte then rushes reserves forward and retakes the town. Austrian general Jean Pierre Beaulieu withdraws eastward toward Alessandria to regroup. With both allied armies withdrawing, Bonaparte decides to pursue the Piedmontese.

April 21, 1796
Southern Europe: Northern Italy: Wars of the French Revolution (continued): War of the First Coalition (continued): Battle of Mondovi. Pursuing Piedmontese forces under General Baron Colli, commander of the French Army of Italy General Napoleon Bonaparte pursues the Piedmontese. He defeats Colli at Ceva on April 18 and then, three days later, reunites all of his forces against Colli, now with 17,500 men, at Mondovi in Piedmont. Colli manages to hold off one French assault but then is driven out. Colli proceeds to Turin, where King Victor Amadeus of Piedmont-Sardinia concedes that further resistance is futile. He negotiates an armistice with the French on April 26 that effectively ends Piedmont's participation in the war. Bonaparte exacts a substantial indemnity in gold and silver specie and bouillon, promising the Piedmontese a speedy departure (hence less looting) in an immediate campaign against the Austrians.

April 23–May 8, 1796
Southern Europe: Northern Italy: Wars of the French Revolution (continued): War of the First Coalition (continued): French advance to and crossing of the Po River. Having concluded an armistice with Piedmont, commander of the French Army of Italy Napoleon Bonaparte shifts his forces to the northeast, advancing to the Po River against the Austrians. Austrian commander General Jean Pierre Beaulieu has his men spread out on the north bank of the river, covering all possible crossing points along a 60-mile front.

Bonaparte demonstrates on a wide front to confuse Beaulieu, then swiftly concentrates and crosses the Po in strength at Piacenza, threatening the Austrian flanks and Beaulieu's communications with Mantua. Beaulieu responds with a rapid withdrawal eastward, abandoning both Pavia and Milan.

May 10, 1796

Southern Europe: Northern Italy: Wars of the French Revolution (continued): War of the First Coalition (continued): Battle of Lodi. In pursuit of Austrian forces under General Jean Pierre Beaulieu, General Napoleon Bonaparte's French Army of Italy catches up with the rear guard under General Sebottendorf. The Austrians are defending a 200-yard-long bridge over the Adda River at Lodi. Bonaparte positions some 30 guns to fire on the Austrians at point-blank range, aiming and firing many himself, a corporal's job, for which his men thereafter call him the Little Corporal. A number of French officers lead charges, but General André Masséna leads the final effort that takes the bridge, although French cavalry that forded the river upstream and hit the Austrian flank just at that time may well have been the decisive factor.

The battle claims 350 French casualties for 153 Austrian dead and 1,700 captured, many of them wounded. Lodi is hardly important by itself, but it boosts Bonaparte's confidence and reputation. Recognizing the value of propaganda, he purchases two newspapers to trumpet his successes.

Bonaparte enters Milan in triumph on May 15. Austrian troops in the citadel there surrender on June 29. King Victor Amaedeus II now concludes a formal peace with France on May 21, surrendering Nice and Savoy to France outright and allowing France to garrison troops in Piedmont.

June–October 1796

Central Europe: Germany: Wars of the French Revolution (continued): War of the First Coalition (continued): Failed French Rhine Campaign. In 1796 French forces take the offensive. This is in part from revolutionary fervor and the belief that the French Republic will be safe only with the establishment of similar neighboring regimes but also because it is difficult for France to feed and maintain its own very large land force.

Lazare Carnot's plan of campaign calls for a pincer attack: the Army of the Sambre and Meuse is to advance and draw the Austrians north, while the southern Army of the Rhine and Moselle pushes into Bavaria. The two French armies are then to join for an advance on Vienna, with the Army of Italy coming up from the south. General Jean Baptiste Jourdan commands the Army of the Sambre and Meuse, and General Jean Victor Moreau commands the Army of

the Rhine and Moselle. Austrian field marshal Archduke Charles of Austria has charge of allied forces opposing the French. He has the advantage of complete freedom of action, while the two French armies are both poorly coordinated and subject to orders from Paris.

On June 10, 1796, Jourdan and 72,000 men of the Army of the Sambre and Meuse cross the Rhine at Düsseldorf. After reaching Wetzlar, his forces are repulsed by Charles on June 16; in accordance with plans, Jourdan withdraws back across the Rhine.

Moreau meanwhile begins his advance with the 78,000-man Army of the Rhine and Moselle. He crosses the Rhine at Strasbourg during June 23–27 and pushes the archduke's southern forces back to Neresheim, where the two sides fight an indecisive action during August 1–3.

August 3, 1796

Southern Europe: Northern Italy: Wars of the French Revolution (continued): War of the First Coalition (continued): Struggle for Mantua. Following the Battle of Lodi, General Napoleon Bonaparte's Army of Italy, reinforced by 10,000 men, moves east and takes Peschiera, Legnago, and Verona. Austrian commander General Jean Pierre Beaulieu withdraws into the Tirol (Tyrol), leaving some 14,000 men and 70 guns behind at Mantua, the strongest of the so-called Quadrilateral fortresses. For the next seven months Mantua is the centerpiece of the struggle between the French and Austrians for control of northern Italy. Bonaparte blockades Mantua in June and has it fully invested by July 15, but the way that the fortress is situated along the Mincio River makes a direct attack prohibitive. Bonaparte therefore decides to starve out the garrison. In the meantime his forces range over much of Italy, and his emissaries secure peace with the papacy and with Naples. The papacy cedes Bologna and Ferrara to France along with a sizable indemnity and important works of art; Naples makes a large financial contribution. All of this wins Bonaparte great credit with the Directory in Paris.

Marshal Count Dagobert von Wurmser meanwhile replaces Beaulieu as Austrian commander and is reinforced to some 55,000 men. In July 1796 he moves south to relieve the siege of Mantua but makes the fatal error of dividing his army. He moves down the eastern shore of Lake Garda through the Adige Valley with 35,000 men while General Peter

Quasdanovich and 20,000 men advance south down its western shore. Wurmser further divides his own forces, sending 5,000 to besiege Peschiera and 5,000 to approach Mantua by way of Verona.

Informed of Wurmser's movements, Bonaparte gambles. Trusting in the skill of his own subordinates and the ineptitude of his opponents, he recalls troops from the Adige and abandons the siege of Mantua to concentrate southwest of Lake Garda against Quasdanovich. This dangerous step makes it possible for the Mantua garrison to sortie against his rear.

August 3, 1796

Southern Europe: Italy: Wars of the French Revolution (continued): War of the First Coalition (continued): Battle of Lonato. General Napoleon Bonaparte concentrates his 47,000-man French Army of Italy against the 20,000 men of General Peter Quasdanovich, moving down the western shore of Lake Garda, leaving the second Austrian force under Marshal Count Dagobert von Wurmser free to join the Mantua garrison. Not only is Quasdanovich badly outnumbered, but he has split his force into three columns.

Cutting the Milan-Mantua Road on July 3, 1796, Quasdanovich swings to the southeast, expecting to reunite with Wurmser and crush the French in a double envelopment. Detaching one division under General Pierre François Charles Augereau to hold Wurmser, Bonaparte advances against Quasdanovich. On August 3, 1796, just north of the town of Losano, General André Masséna defeats Quasdanovich's main column and sends the other two reeling back north in confusion. This battle deprives Wurmser of 20,000 men and, by virtue of his own detachment of 10,000 men, allows Bonaparte to outnumber him 30,000 men to 24,000.

August 5, 1796

Southern Europe: Northern Italy: Wars of the French Revolution (continued): War of the First Coalition (continued): Battle of Castiglione. Following his victory at Lonato, commander of the French Army of Italy Napoleon Bonaparte concentrates 30,000 men against 24,000 Austrians under Field Marshal Count Dagobert von Wurmser, who is advancing southwest of Lake Garda. In the Battle of Castiglione on August 5, 1796, Bonaparte carries out some dangerous maneuvers. He orders both General Pierre François

Charles Augereau and General André Masséna to advance and then fall back. This French feigned retreat draws Wurmser forward. Not content merely to push forward, which could have given him victory, Wurmser attempts to turn the French flank, which spreads out his men and renders them vulnerable. Augereau and Masséna then turn about and mount a coordinated frontal attack, while the French cavalry hits the Austrian left (south) flank. Wurmser personally leads a series of effective cavalry charges to try to remove some of the pressure on his infantry but is probably saved by the arrival of the 5,000 men he had sent to besiege Peschiera. Wurmser then withdraws in good order up the Adige River.

The Austrians suffer some 3,000 casualties and lose 20 guns. The French sustain some 1,500 casualties. Bonaparte has won another victory, thanks in large part to his able subordinates. In both the Battle of Lonato and the Battle of Castiglione, Bonaparte had placed his own smaller army between two enemy forces, allowing him to concentrate first against one and then the other and defeat each in detail.

August 19, 1796

Southern Europe: Spain: Wars of the French Revolution (continued): War of the First Coalition (continued): Treaty of San Ildefonso. Spain joins France in the war against Britain. The combination of the Spanish fleet and the ships of the French Mediterranean Squadron forces the British to withdraw their naval forces in the Mediterranean, now under Admiral Sir John Jervis, to Gibraltar in December. From there they will operate against the Spanish Mediterranean coast.

August 24, 1796

Central Europe: Germany: Wars of the French Revolution (continued): War of the First Coalition (continued): Battle of Amberg. Austrian field marshal Archduke Charles of Austria, reinforced, leaves 30,000 men under General Maximilian Count Baillet von Latour to oppose the French Army of the Rhine and Moselle under French general Jean Victor and marches rapidly north with 27,000 men to oppose the French Army of the Sambre and Meuse under Jean Baptiste Jourdan. At Amberg on August 24 Charles finds Jourdan with 34,000 men pressing 19,000 Austrian forces under General Alexander H. Wartensleben. Charles strikes the right flank of Jourdan's army while Wartensleben attacks the French from the front. The outnumbered French are decisively defeated, suffering some 2,000 casualties to only 500 for the Austrians. Jourdan then retires. Learning that on the same day, August 24, Moreau has defeated Latour at Friedberg, Jourdan regroups his army near Würzburg, while Charles pursues.

September 3, 1796
Central Europe: Germany: Wars of the French Revolution (continued): War of the First Coalition (continued): Battle of Würzburg. Austrian field marshal Archduke Charles of Austria, with 44,000 men, marches against the French Army of the Meuse and Sambre under Jean Baptiste Jourdan with only 30,000 men. Charles carries out a double envelopment of the French, with the Austrian cavalry particularly distinguishing itself. Jourdan is able to disengage but at a cost of 3,000 casualties and seven guns. The Austrians lose 1,500 men.

Jourdan then withdraws on the Rhine, engaging in a series of running battles with the Austrians until Charles breaks off the pursuit and moves south to defend Bavaria. Commander of the southern Army of the Rhine and Moselle General Jean Victor Moreau, learning of Jourdan's defeat, hastily withdraws, safely crossing the Rhine on October 26.

September 5, 1796
Southern Europe: Northern Italy: Wars of the French Revolution (continued): War of the First Coalition (continued): French forces take Trent. Following his victory at Castiglione on August 5, commander of the French Army of Italy General Napoleon Bonaparte on August 24 restores the siege of Mantua, the Austrian garrison of which now numbers 17,000 men. The Directory, however, orders Bonaparte to march for southern Germany and join General Jean Victor Moreau for a drive on Vienna.

The Austrians are aware of the French plans, and Field Marshal Count Dagobert von Wurmser decides to surprise the French by an attempt to end the siege of Mantua. He will move east and then south via Vicenza, then turn southwest across the Adige to Mantua. If he is successful, he will have superior numbers with which to attack Bonaparte from the south.

Detaching 20,000 men under General Paul Davidovich to defend Trent and the approaches to the Tirol (Tyrol), on September 1, 1796, Wurmser moves south toward Bassano with another 20,000 men. He again makes the mistake of dividing this force into three columns some 15–20 miles apart.

Unaware of Wurmser's movements, Bonaparte drives on Trent, defeating Davidovich at Caliano on the upper Adige on September 2 and forcing him back through Trent on September 5. Only then does Bonaparte learn that he is not fighting Wurmser.

September 8, 1796
Southern Europe: Northern Italy: Wars of the French Revolution (continued): War of the First Coalition (continued): Battle of Bassano. Learning on his capture of Trent on September 5 that Austrian field marshal Count Dagobert von Wurmser is marching south with 20,000 men to raise the siege of Mantua, French Army of Italy commander General Napoleon Bonaparte orders first André Masséna and then Pierre François Charles Augereau in pursuit of the Austrians. Each commands more than 10,000 men, but they are separated by the Brenta River, which is not fordable.

On September 8 Masséna and Augereau catch half of Wurmser's army at the town of Bassano. Capturing the town bridge, they rout the Austrians under generals Sebottendorf and Quasdanovich. The Austrians suffer 3,000 casualties and lose 30 guns. French casualties number only about 400.

September 1796
Southern Europe: Northern Italy: Wars of the French Revolution (continued): War of the First Coalition (continued): Struggle for Mantua. Following the Battle of Bassano, without orders Austrian general Quasdanovich withdraws north with 3,000 men. Meanwhile, Field Marshal Count Dagobert von Wurmser withdraws to Vicenza. Joined by forces from Bassano under General Sabottendorf, Wurmser surprises General Napoleon Bonaparte, commander of the French Army of Italy, by continuing south. Wurmser is confident that he can still take Mantua.

On September 12 Wurmser succeeds in entering the fortress with 10,000 men, bringing the garrison's total strength to 25,000 men (20,000 effectives). The next day he seeks to expand the Mantuan perimeter, attacking French forces under General Jean Joseph François Léonard de Sahuguet d'Amarzit and driving them north. Then on September 14 Wurmser smashes a French corps under General André

Masséna advancing on Mantua from the east. On September 15 Wurmser sorties again; this time, however, Bonaparte has united his forces. He drives Wurmser back into Mantua, where he remains bottled up until forced to surrender in February 1797.

November 12, 1796

Southern Europe: Northern Italy: Wars of the French Revolution (continued): War of the First Coalition (continued): Battle of Caldiero. With Field Marshal Count Dagobert von Wurmser and 25,000 men besieged at Mantua, Vienna appoints Baron Jozsef Alvinczy von Bøtberek to command Austrian forces in Italy. As with his predecessors, he will have more men than Bonaparte—some 50,000 Austrians to only 30,000 Frenchmen—but he will demonstrate the same fatal propensity of dividing his forces. Bonaparte, however, has his own forces badly divided, violating what later became an ironclad rule of having forces march dispersed but within mutually supporting distance. It will take his men a week to concentrate. Thus, if Alvinczy had not divided his forces, he might have been able to smash Napoleon in detail. Instead Alvinczy moves in October from Trieste on Vicenza with only 30,000 men, having detached General Paul Davidovich south from the Tirol (Tyrol) with another 18,000 men. Alvinczy expects to join forces with Davidovich at Verona and drive on Mantua together.

Bonaparte is determined to prevent a juncture of the Austrian forces. Counting on General Charles Henry Vaubois, with 10,500 men, to delay Davidovich, Bonaparte moves with most of his remaining forces against Alvinczy, who accommodates him by further dividing his resources. On November 12 Bonaparte with some 14,000 men attacks Alvinczy's advance guard at Caldiero, hoping to surprise it. Alvinczy rapidly brings forward 18,000 men, giving him a numerical advantage. Also, the attacks by Napoleon's two divisions under General Pierre François Charles Augereau and General André Masséna are not coordinated. At dusk Napoleon withdraws to Verona, having sustained 2,000 casualties. Alvinczy, however, fails to exploit the situation. Had he had his entire 30,000 men with him he might well have destroyed Bonaparte. Even so, Alvinczy fails to take advantage of the favorable situation that presents itself over the next few days to finish off his opponent.

November 15–17, 1796

Southern Europe: Northern Italy: Wars of the French Revolution (continued): War of the First Coalition (continued): Battle of Arcole. Commander of the French Army of Italy General Napoleon Bonaparte conceives a bold plan. Leaving only 2,600 men to hold Verona while making it appear that his entire army is there, he plans to moves south of the Adige to Ronco, cross the Alpone, and attempt to get in behind Baron Jozsef Alvinczy von Bøtberek's 30,000-man Austrian army and sever its lines of communication. Bonaparte now has some 19,000 men. Alvinczy considers the swamp ground north to the Adige in the Ronco-Arcole area impassable for a major attack force.

Battle is joined at Arcole (Arcola) on November 15 as the French repeatedly attempt to storm a bridge over the Alpone. Although Bonaparte leads a charge with French flag in hand, attempts to get over the causeway are unsuccessful. On the third day, however, the French finally succeed. General Pierre François Charles Augereau crosses on a trestle bridge that the French construct just below the village.

As General André Masséna attacks on the main bridge, Bonaparte orders a feint on the Austrian rear with several buglers blowing. Believing they are encircled, the Austrians break. The French suffer 4,600 casualties; Austrian losses are 6,000. Bonaparte then drives both Austrian forces back north.

December 1796

Northern Europe: Ireland: Wars of the French Revolution (continued): War between France and Britain (continued): Attempted French invasion of Ireland. In 1796 Irish nationalist leader Wolfe Tone convinces the French government to send an expeditionary force to Ireland, expecting that the Irish will rise up and support it. The French fleet prepares at Brest. Admiral Louis Thomas Villaret-Joyeuse is replaced as its commander by Admiral Justin Bonaventure, Comte de Morard de Galles, because Villaret-Joyeuse protests that the fleet, as it is then manned, is in no condition to encounter winter storms.

The fleet of 43 ships, including 17 ships of the line and 14 frigates and lifting some 15,000 French troops under General Louis Lazare Hoche, sails on December 16 for Ireland. On leaving Camaret Roads, 1 ship of the line runs aground and is lost with all but 60 of its 1,400 men.

At sea the French split into squadrons to avoid detection by the British, but in increasingly bad weather, only a small portion of the fleet under Admiral François Joseph Bouvet de Précourt manages to reach Ireland and the rendevous point of Bantry Bay on December 21. None of the Frenchmen go ashore, however; the continued bad weather induces Bouvet to order a return to France on December 30. In the undertaking five of the French ships are lost at sea, and the British capture six others.

January 14–15, 1797
Southern Europe: Northern Italy: Wars of the French Revolution (continued): War of the First Coalition (continued): Battle of Rivoli. In January 1797 forces of the French Army of Italy, commanded by General Napoleon Bonaparte, are besieging Mantua. While General Philibert Sérurier and 8,500 men maintain the siege, other French forces are situated to the north and east of the city to intercept any Austrian attempt to raise the siege. Bonaparte positions General Barthelemi-Catherine Joubert to the north with 10,000 men, General André Masséna at Verona with 10,000 men, and General Pierre François Charles Augereau at Adige with another 10,000 men. Another 4,000 French troops are scattered in garrisons at Brescia, Peschiera, and other locations at the south end of Lake Garda. The major French forces are thus spread as much as 70 miles apart.

Bonaparte is at Bologna with General Jean Lannes and 3,000 troops when he learns on January 10 that Austrian general Count József Alvinci von Borberek

French general Napoleon Bonaparte during his victory over the Austrians in the Battle of Rivoli in northern Italy during the War of the First Coalition, January 14–15, 1797. (Chaiba Media)

BATTLE OF RIVOLI, JANUARY 14–15, 1797

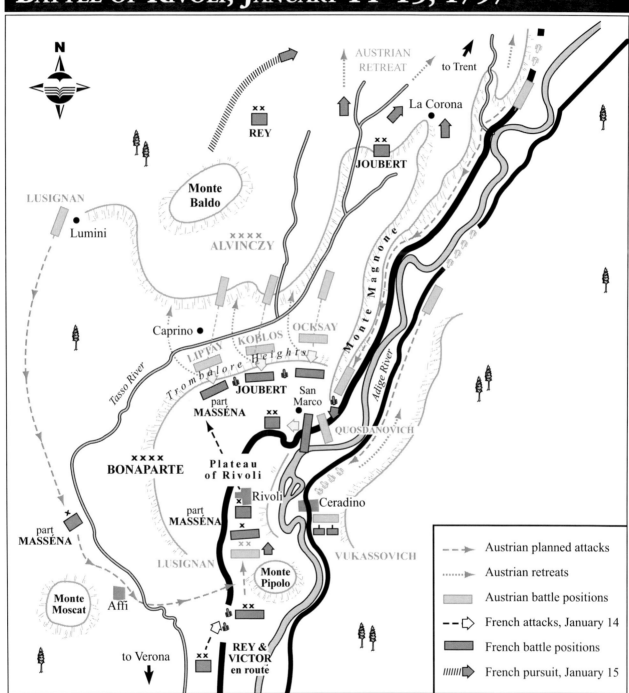

N

AUSTRIAN
RETREAT

to Trent

La Corona

XX
REY

XX
JOUBERT

LUSIGNAN

Monte
Baldo

Lumini

XXXX
ALVINCZY

Caprino

OCKSAY

KOBLOS

LIPPAY

Trombalore   Heights

Monte Magnone

Adige River

Tasso River

JOUBERT

part
MASSÉNA

San
Marco

XX

QUOSDANOVICH

XXXX
BONAPARTE

Plateau
of Rivoli

Rivoli

x

Ceradino

part
MASSÉNA

x

part
MASSÉNA

xx

LUSIGNAN

VUKASSOVICH

Monte
Moscat

Affi

Monte
Pipolo

to Verona

XX

REY &
VICTOR
en route

– – ▶	Austrian planned attacks
·······▶	Austrian retreats
▭	Austrian battle positions
– –▷	French attacks, January 14
▬	French battle positions
⦀▶	French pursuit, January 15

is on the move with a sizable force. The next day Bonaparte is at Roverbella, where he is informed of skirmishing between Austrian and French forces in the area between Legnago and Badia. Believing incorrectly that this is Alvinci advancing from Trieste, on January 12 Bonaparte orders both Masséna and Augereau to shift to meet an attack from the east. He also orders the garrisons at the south end of Lake Garda to join them.

Bonaparte learns of his mistake the next day, January 13, when Joubert reports that Alvinci is instead pushing south from the Tirol (Tyrol) with substantial forces and has forced him to withdraw southward to the vicinity of Rivoli. Bonaparte immediately orders Masséna and Augereau to make haste to Rivoli, where he also moves, joining Joubert there at 2:00 a.m. on January 14.

Bonaparte orders Joubert to position his troops on the Trombalora Heights, just north of Rivoli. The French are in position by dawn and are ready to meet the Austrians. Bonaparte hopes to be able to hold off Alvinci until the arrival of reinforcements. He is aided in this by Alvinci's tendency to carefully position all his forces prior to any attack. While the Austrian general has a total force of some 42,000 men, he arrives at Rivoli with only 12,000, having sent the remainder to circle around the French position and take it from the rear.

Bonaparte does not wait for his reinforcements or for the Austrians to concentrate. At dawn on January 14 he attacks the three Austrian divisions to his front, driving gaps between them. The battle is going badly for the French, with the Austrians having forced an opening in their lines, when at about 10:00 a.m. Masséna arrives with some 6,000 troops and takes up position on the French right. Supported by French cavalry, these troops attack and break through into the Austrian rear. Meanwhile, Alvinci's detachments sent to surround the French are also defeated, whereupon the Austrians withdraw northward. General Joachim Murat and 600 cavalry cross Lake Garda in gunboats and press the fleeing Austrians into the next day, adding substantially to the French prisoner count.

In the battle the Austrians suffer some 14,000 casualties, the French only 5,000. The Battle of Rivoli is the last and most important battle of Napoleon Bonaparte's Italian campaign and a significant step forward in his career.

Following the Battle of Rivoli, Vienna replaces Alvinczy with the Archduke Charles, younger brother of Emperor Francis II. Charles is the top Austrian field commander and is the same age (27) as Bonaparte. Charles is promised 90,000 men, evidence that the Austrians recognize that Italy is now the decisive theater of war and that Bonaparte must be defeated there.

February 2, 1797
Southern Europe: Northern Italy: Wars of the French Revolution (continued): War of the First Coalition (continued): Surrender of Mantua. While commander of the French Army of Italy General Napoleon Bonaparte is victorious at Rivoli, the other 15,000 Austrian troops under General Bejalich move in two columns toward Verona and Mantua. General Provera, with 9,000 men, reaches the outskirts of Mantua on January 16. He makes a determined effort to reach the fortress but is met and surrounded by the corps of General Pierre François Charles Augereau and is forced to surrender. Austrian field marshal Count Dagobert von Wurmser attempts a simultaneous sortie, but he is defeated and driven back into the fortress by General Jean Sérurier's besieging forces.

On February 2, 1797, having held out for six months, Wurmser surrenders Mantua. The Austrian garrison has been reduced from 25,000 to only 16,000 men through malnutrition and disease. The siege also claims 6,000 civilian dead.

February 14, 1797
Eastern Atlantic Ocean: Wars of the French Revolution (continued): War of the First Coalition (continued): Battle of Cape St. Vincent. In early 1797 the French and Spanish plan to combine naval assets for an invasion of Britain. In December, English admiral Sir John Jervis collects the Mediterranean Fleet at Gibraltar and concentrates its activities off the Atlantic coasts of Spain and Portugal. Meanwhile, the French gather their own ships at Brest.

On February 1, 1797, Spanish teniente general (admiral) José de Córdoba y Ramos departs Cartagena in the Mediterranean in command of 27 ships of the line, 12 frigates, a brigantine, and some smaller craft. He sails west, past Gibraltar and into the Atlantic. Córdoba plans to put in at Cádiz and take on supplies, then sail for Brest to rendezvous with the French and Dutch fleets for the invasion of England.

Defeat of the Spanish fleet at Cape St. Vincent by the British off the coast of Spain, February 14, 1797.
(Library of Congress)

Jervis, with 15 ships of the line, 5 frigates, a brig, and a cutter, has been cruising off Portugal to prevent such a concentration. Had not an easterly gale driven the Spanish ships well to the west, Córdoba would have gained Cádiz, and Jervis would have been forced to resort to a blockade.

Informed of the presence of the Spanish ships by his scouting forces, Jervis sails south and comes on the Spanish off Cape St. Vincent early in the morning on February 14. The Spanish ships are moving in two divisions, of 18 and 9 ships. Jervis forms his own ships from two columns into a single line formation in order to drive them between the two Spanish divisions. The Spanish crews are not well trained, and Córdoba knows that he cannot hope to unite the two parts of his fleet. Instead he brings his own more westerly division onto a northerly heading with the intent of escaping astern of the British. Jervis responds by ordering his ships to tack in succession, reverse course, and engage the Spanish rear.

In an hour of fighting, only a small number of the ships are engaged, and it looks as if Córdoba might be able to bring most of his ships astern of the British and escape. Jervis then orders his famous signal Number 41: "The ships to take suitable station for their mutual support and to engage the enemy as arriving up with them in succession." This signal abandons the traditional line of battle formation that is designed to take advantage of the broadsides firepower of ships of the line. Under it, the capital ships of the fleet would sail in line-ahead formation and blast away at close range with their broadside guns against the opposite in the enemy line. Jervis's signal frees each ship to act on its own to form a new line of battle as quickly as possible.

Already, Captain Horatio Nelson in the ship of the line *Captain,* the third ship from the end of the British line, has anticipated Jervis's command. Participating in his first fleet engagement, Nelson may or may not have seen the signal, but he has already acted and, in the process, turns the tide of battle. Breaking from the line of battle, he stands on the opposite tack into the path of the advancing Spanish line. Captain Cuthbert Collingwood in the *Excellent,* the last English ship in line, follows his friend Nelson's ship.

Almost at once the *Captain* of 74 guns falls in with the 130-gun four-decker *Santísima Trinidad,* the largest warship in the world and mounting nearly twice the firepower of Nelson's own vessel. Three other Spanish warships also join in: two of 112 guns

BATTLE OF CAPE ST. VINCENT, FEBRUARY 14, 1797

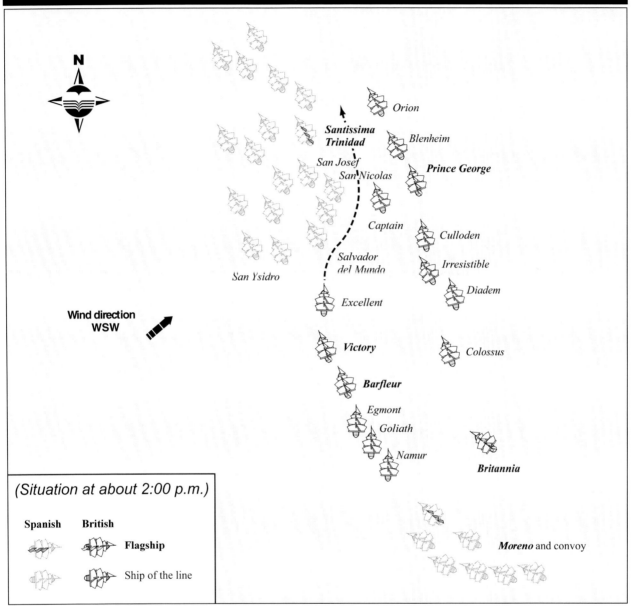

N

Orion

Santissima Trinidad

Blenheim

San Josef

San Nicolas

Prince George

Captain

Culloden

Salvador del Mundo

Irresistible

San Ysidro

Diadem

Wind direction WSW

Excellent

Victory

Colossus

Barfleur

Egmont

Goliath

Namur

Britannia

(Situation at about 2:00 p.m.)

Spanish	British	
		Flagship
		Ship of the line

Moreno and convoy

and one of 80. Soon Nelson's ship is a near wreck. But his action forces the Spanish ships to alter course, and this allows the remainder of Jervis's ships to close and join the fight.

In the ensuing melee battle, the British take four Spanish ships, two of which fall to Nelson. The 80-gun *San Nicolás* and 112-gun *San Josef* collide, and Nelson orders his ship to ram the *San Nicolás*. The three ships are soon locked together by spars and rigging. Nelson then leads with drawn sword a party of marines and sailors armed with pistols, pikes, and cutlasses to board the *San Nicolás*. Taking it, he then crosses from it to the *San Josef*. This exploit, unique in the history of the Royal Navy, becomes celebrated in the fleet as "Nelson's patent bridge for boarding first rates."

Vice-admiral Horatio Nelson, 1st Viscount Nelson. The best known figure in British naval history, Nelson won great victories in the Battles of the Nile (1798), Copenhagen (1801), and Trafalgar (1805), thereby confirming British naval supremacy. (Engraving by T. W. Harland after Lemuel Abbot from *History of Europe from the Commencement of the French Revolution to the Restoration of the Bourbons in MDCCCXV* by Archibald Alison. Edinburgh & London: William Blackwood, 1860, vol. 6.)

Although the remaining Spanish ships escape to Cádiz the next day, the Battle of Cape St. Vincent ends the possible allied invasion threat to Britain. It raises morale in Britain and convinces many that their nation can indeed triumph, even against great odds. The battle depresses the Spanish, making it less likely that they will be willing to take on the Royal Navy again. It also clearly demonstrates the superiority of the melee battle over the line of battle, at least for a more aggressive force with superior seamanship. Finally, the Battle of Cape St. Vincent marks the rise of Horatio Nelson.

See Leaders: Nelson, Horatio

March 10, 1797

Central Europe: Austria: Wars of the French Revolution (continued): War of the First Coalition (continued): French invasion of Austria from Italy. On taking command, new Austrian field commander Archduke Charles discovers that the reinforcements from Austria and Germany have not arrived and that, far from having the 90,000 men promised, he has at his immediate disposal only some 24,000 men (only 14,000 of them regulars) in the Tirol (Tyrol) and 27,000 more under his own immediate command along the Tagliamento River. General Napoleon Bonaparte, commander of the French Army of Italy, has been reinforced from France and commands some 53,000 men.

Not wishing to give Charles time to reorganize, Bonaparte orders an advance into Austrian territory. He seeks to place his own army between the two enemy forces in order to prevent their concentration and to allow him to destroy each in detail.

Leaving General Barthélemy Catherine Joubert with 12,000 men to operate against the Tirol, on March 10 Bonaparte advances against Charles on the Tagliamento. Defeated there, Charles retires behind the Isonzo but then has to fall back again to prevent encirclement. Bonaparte then crosses the Julian and Carnic Alps, moving toward Vienna. Bonaparte's army covers 400 miles in only 30 days, his forces uniting at Klagenfurt in Carinthia. Charles, with only 10,000 men, attempts to stop the French there, but he is again defeated.

On April 6 Bonaparte reaches Leoben, only 95 miles from Vienna. Joubert has also been successful in the Tirol and is on his way to meet Bonaparte at Vienna. On April 7, recognizing the hopelessness of his situation, Charles requests an armistice, which is granted and leads to the Preliminary Peace of Leoben. Although formal peace is not concluded until October, the war is for all intents and purposes over. War with Britain continues.

April 16–August 1797

Northern Europe: Britain: Wars of the French Revolution (continued): War of the First Coalition (continued): Mutinies in the Royal Navy. Beginning at Spithead on April 16 and spreading to the Nore on May 12 and to other ports, sailors in the Royal Navy react against the appalling conditions, miserable pay, and ferocious discipline in the fleet. The mutineers do, however, promise to return to duty should the French fleet put to sea. Although the mutinies are suppressed—the ringleaders are executed, and other men are flogged or transported to Australia—they focus attention on the terrible conditions in the fleet, and improvements follow.

April 18, 1797

Southern Europe: Northern Italy: Wars of the French Revolution (continued): War of the First Coalition (continued): Preliminary Peace of Leoben. With Venetia in open rebellion against the French and the Tirol (Tyrol) a threat, the French commander in Italy, General Napoleon Bonaparte, finds himself in danger of being cut off and opens negotiations with the Austrians, leading to the Preliminary Peace of Leoben. Austria cedes the Austrian Netherlands (Belgium) to France as well as the territory beyond the Oglio River, receiving in compensation Venetian territory between the Oglio, the Po, and the Adriatic; Venetian Dalmatia and Istria; and the fortresses of Mantua, Peschiera, and Palma Nova. Austria recognizes the Cisalpine Republic, established under French control in northern Italy.

Bonaparte's military success in the Italian Campaign of 1796–1797 is attributed to many factors: careful preparation and detailed planning; dogged aggressiveness; skill in motivating his men; exceptional subordinate commanders; the ineptitude of his opponents, steeped in 18th-century warfare; and finally the high motivation and excellent morale of his men, which the Austrian soldiers lack.

April 1797

Central Europe: Germany: Wars of the French Revolution (continued): War of the First Coalition (continued): Renewed French offensive across the Rhine. New French commander of the Army of the Meuse and Sambre General Louis Lazare Hoche moves his army along the Rhine to assist General Jean Victor Moreau in crossing the river at Kehl. General Maximilian Count Baillet von Latour commands Austrian forces opposing Moreau, while his subordinate, General Baron Werneck, defends the lower Rhine. Crossing the Rhine, Hoche attacks and defeats Werneck, first near Neuwied and again in the Battle of the Lahn on April 18. Moreau crosses the Rhine two days later, and the French force back the Austrians to Rastatt.

May 1797

Southern Europe: Northern Italy: Wars of the French Revolution (continued): War of the First Coalition (continued): France declares war on Venice. Using the pretext of an uprising in Verona, French troops invade and occupy Venetian territory, including the Ionian Islands. Abolishing the oligarchy, the French establish a popularly elected government.

July 9, 1797

Southern Europe: Northern Italy: Wars of the French Revolution (continued): War of the First Coalition (continued): Proclamation of the Cisalpine and Ligurian Republics. Established in accordance with the Preliminary Peace of Leoben, the Cisalpine Republic consists of Milan, Modena, Ferrara, Bologna, and Romagna. The Ligurian Republic is merely the former Republic of Genoa. Both republics are firmly under French control.

September 4, 1797

Western Europe: France: Wars of the French Revolution (continued): War of the First Coalition (continued): Coup of 18 Fructidor. Following the spring elections in France, a royalist conspiracy develops that is led by former general Charles Pichegru, presiding officer of the Council of 500, and one of the five directors, secret royalist François-Marie Barthélemy. Three of the other five directors are opposed, with the fifth, Lazare Carnot, attempting to heal the breach. When he fails, the three appeal to commander of the French Army of Italy Napoleon Bonaparte. A royalist victory would undo his conquests, so he sends his trusted subordinate General Pierre François Charles Augereau to Paris.

Appointed to command the National Guard, Augereau sets up a camp of 30,000 men on the outskirts of Paris. On September 4, 1797 (18 Fructidor by the revolutionary calendar), the three directors preempt the royalist plotters. Augereau's men invade the Tuileries Palace and seize control of the government. The elections of some 200 councilors are then annulled, and more than 50 individuals, including directors Barthélemy and Carnot, are deported.

The Coup of 18 Fructidor is a decisive event in the history of the French Revolution and Europe. Although the royalist threat is ended and the republic is preserved, the constitution has been violated, and the first free elections in the history of the French

Republic have been quashed. More than ever, the republicans are now dependent on the army.

October 11, 1797

North Sea: Wars of the French Revolution (continued): War of the First Coalition (continued): Battle of Camperdown. In 1795 after the French force the Dutch into an alliance, British vice admiral Adam Duncan instigates a blockade of Dutch warships in the Texel. In early October 1797, however, Duncan sails with the majority of his fleet to Great Yarmouth for repairs and provisions, leaving only a small squadron under Captain Sir Henry Trollope to continue the blockade.

Dutch admiral Jan Willem de Winter is ordered to engage the British blockaders. With the Dutch ships having been at anchor for two years, their seamen have little experience. Trollope informs Duncan of Dutch preparations, and Duncan immediately orders his ships to return to the Texel, joining Trollope on October 11, 1797, just as the Dutch fleet appears. The British have 16 ships of the line. De Winter, realizing that his 15 smaller ships of the line are outgunned and that their crews lack experience, plans to engage Duncan in the shallows along the coast near the Texel, hoping to cause the British ships to run aground. Duncan anticipates this and orders an immediate attack.

The two fleets come together some 9 miles northwest of the village of Kamperduin (Camperdown) on the Dutch coast. The British advance in two groups of 8 ships, each at right angles to the Dutch fleet in line of battle. Duncan orders his ships to break the Dutch line and engage them to leeward, placing his own ships between the Dutch fleet and the coast.

Fighting continues for several hours. Throughout, the British have the advantage not only in heavier ships and larger guns but also in training and gunnery drill. Nonetheless, the Dutch concentrate their fire on the hulls of the British ships, causing extensive damage and many casualties. By the end of the engagement, several of Duncan's ships are severely damaged, and on average his ships sustain 10 percent casualties. The British lose no ships, however, while capturing 11 Dutch ships—7 ships of the line (including the flagship *Vrijheid* of 74 guns with half its crew killed), 2 fourth rates, and 2 frigates—although the prizes have suffered so much damage as to be unusable. De Winter is among those taken prisoner. Dutch naval power never recovers from this blow.

October 17, 1797

Central Europe: Austria: Wars of the French Revolution (continued): War of the First Coalition (continued): Treaty of Campo Formio. On his own authority, commander of the French Army of Italy General Napoleon Bonaparte dictates peace with Austria. Austria cedes the Austrian Netherlands (Belgium) to France. Austria receives the territory of Venetia as far as the Adige, including the city of Venice along with Istria and Dalmatia (Austria assumes control on January 18, 1798). France retains the Ionian Islands. Austria recognizes the French puppet Italian state of the Cisalpine Republic (Milan, Modena, Ferrara, Bologna, and Romagna) and indemnifies the Duke of Modena with the Breisgau. A congress is to be convened at Rastaat to discuss peace with the empire; however, meeting from December 1797 to April 1799, it fails to reach agreement.

In secret provisions, Austria promises to cede to France the left bank of the Rhine from Basel to Andernach, including Mainz; princes who lose territory are to be compensated with German territory on the right bank of the Rhine. France agrees to use its influence to secure from Bavaria for Austria the city of Salzburg and some additional territory between Salzburg, the Tirol (Tyrol), and the Inn and Salza rivers. Both parties agree that Prussia is not to receive any compensation for lands it has lost on the left bank of the Rhine. The treaty in effect ends the War of the First Coalition, although France remains at war with Britain.

Was Campo Formio a major blunder for France? Some historians, including Napoleon biographer George Lefebvre, believe that it was, for the terms make an irreconcilable enemy of Austria, determined to strike France at every possible opportunity, setting the stage for the Napoleonic Wars to follow. Napoleon's subsequent defeats of and treaties with Austria only compound this problem.

In December, Bonaparte returns to Paris, a national hero in France and *stupor mundi* (wonder of the world) elsewhere. In only one year he has defeated five armies, each larger than his own, and taken 160,000 prisoners. He has also sent millions of francs in precious metals and artworks to Paris.

1797

Caribbean Basin: Hispaniola: Haiti: Toussaint Louverture takes power. There has been war and internal strife in the French colony of Haiti since 1791. The British occupy Haiti during 1793–1797. The war in Europe prevents the French Directory from dispatching a military force to Hispaniola. In 1797 François-Dominique Toussaint Louverture, a black of great military ability, combines lightning-quick strikes by his small number of men and adroit diplomacy to lead the blacks to victory over the whites and free coloreds. Louverture announces an end to slavery and establishes himself as dictator.

January 1798

Western Europe: France: Wars of the French Revolution (continued): War between France and Britain (continued): French preparations to invade Britain. In January 1798 General Napoleon Bonaparte assumes command of the French Army of England, intended to invade the British Isles. It is doubtful whether Bonaparte believes that such an enterprise is possible; he reports to the Directory that the forces assigned are totally inadequate. He also proposes several alternative plans, including the possibility of seizing Egypt in order to be in position for an overland attack on British India.

February 1798

Southern Europe: Italy: French forces occupy Rome. French forces strike south against Rome, taking Pope Pius VI captive and proclaiming a Roman Republic.

April 12, 1798

Western Europe: France: Wars of the French Revolution (continued): War between France and Britain (continued): Establishment of the Army of Egypt. The Directory appoints General Napoleon Bonaparte to command the French Army of Egypt. Bonaparte had actively advanced an invasion of Egypt, which had for several generations attracted French strategists. If the French were to control Egypt, they could threaten the British in Egypt with a land invasion. The venture also appeals to Bonaparte's romantic nature as an admirer of Alexander the Great. Bonaparte actively seeks the command, which he receives on April 12, 1798. On their part, members of the Directory are anxious to have their overly popular general out of France.

Bonaparte repairs to Toulon to oversee preparations, although the French continue their assembly of troops at Dunkerque (Dunkirk) in an effort to prevent the British from shifting naval assets to the Mediterranean.

April 1798

Western Europe: Switzerland. French forces occupy Switzerland. France annexes Geneva and proclaims the remainder the Helvetic Republic.

May 19, 1798

Western Europe: France: Wars of the French Revolution (continued): War between France and Britain (continued): French expedition sails for Egypt. General Napoleon Bonaparte departs Toulon on May 19, 1798, with 34,000 troops (for the most part veterans of his Army of Italy) and some 1,000 civilians, including a corps of 187 scientists (who will ultimately unlock the secrets of ancient Egyptian civilization), all lifted in 400 transports and escorted by 13 ships of the line and many other smaller warships. The expeditionary force proceeds first to Malta. Catching the island inhabitants by surprise, Bonaparte secures Malta (it is defended by only 300 Knights Hospitallers) in a day's token fighting on June 12. He incorporates some 6 million francs in treasure and sails for Egypt again on June 19.

Once again, Bonaparte's luck holds. Learning of the French plans and lacking a squadron in the Mediterranean, in April 1798 Lord St. Vincent dispatches a squadron of 14 ships of the line to the Mediterranean under Rear Admiral Horatio Nelson to locate and destroy the French armada. Without scouting vessels, Nelson narrowly misses his quarry on two occasions. On the foggy night of June 22–23, the British, moving at twice the speed of the French, pass their quarry only a few miles distant. Guessing that the French objective is Alexandria, Nelson arrives there on June 29. Finding no trace of the French, he departs that same morning. That evening an advance French frigate anchors at Alexandria, followed by the entire French fleet on July 1.

June 12, 1798

Northern Europe: Ireland: Battle of Vinegar Hill. In April 1798 unrest in Ireland becomes open rebellion when an armed mob storms Enniscorthy, County Wexford. General Gerard Lake assumes command of some 20,000 British troops in Ireland. He issues a proclamation demanding the surrender of all arms held by civilians in Ulster and unleashes a reign of terror known to the local population as the Dragooning of Ulster. Lake's troops surround the chief rebel force at Vinegar Hill, near Enniscorthy, and force their surrender following a brief struggle.

July 19, 1798

North Africa: Egypt: Wars of the French Revolution (continued): War between France and Britain (continued): French conquest of Egypt and Battle of the Pyramids. Learning that the British have recently been at Alexandria and fearing their imminent return, French general Napoleon Bonaparte immediately sends his troops ashore beginning on July 1. They quickly capture Alexandria, then endure a week's hellish march with little water to the Nile. On July 13 the French defeat a force of 4,000 Mamluk cavalry and 10,000 infantry. A week later on July 21, south of Cairo and near the great pyramid of Khufu (Cheops), the French engage a force of up to 40,000 Egyptian Mamluk cavalry and infantry commanded by Murad Bey.

Bonaparte forms his army into five hollow squares, and these hold against repeated Mamluk cavalry attacks. Bonaparte triumphs, and upwards of 7,000–8,000 Egyptians die; only 300 Frenchmen are killed. The Mamluks generally fight to the death. In his victory report to Paris, Bonaparte styles the engagement the Battle of the Pyramids (although they were not in sight). It is also known as the First Battle of Aboukir. The French take Cairo the next day.

July 1798–September 1800

Caribbean Basin: Quasi-War. The undeclared war between France and the United States grows out of deteriorating relations prompted by French seizures of American merchant ships trading with Britain, with which France is at war. July 7, 1798, may be taken as the starting date for the so-called Quasi-War. On that date, Congress rescinds the U.S. treaties with France. In additional legislation, Congress votes funds to purchase and convert merchant ships into warships, authorizes U.S. warships to attack and capture armed French ships, suspends trade with France, creates a separate Department of the Navy, grants letters of marque for privateers, and appropriates funds to complete construction of three frigates authorized

in 1794. Additional warships are built through private subscription.

The fighting, which begins in the summer of 1798, is entirely at sea and occurs with French warships and privateers off the American coast and in the Caribbean. There are 10 significant naval engagements and numerous encounters between privateers. The most important action is the capture of the French frigate *L'Insurgente* (40 guns) by the U.S. frigate *Constellation* (36 guns) on February 9, 1799. By early 1799 French ships are driven from the American coast and are largely eliminated from the Caribbean.

The French fear driving the United States into active collaboration with Britain, and new French leader Napoleon Bonaparte agrees to negotiations that begin in March 1800. These result in the Convention of Mortefontaine (or Convention of 1800) of September 30, 1800, ending hostilities.

August 1, 1798

North Africa: Egypt: Wars of the French Revolution (continued): War between France and Britain (continued): Battle of the Nile. After weeks of searching, on August 1, 1798, Rear Admiral Horatio Nelson and his squadron locate the French fleet riding at anchor in Abu Qir (Aboukir) Bay, a few miles east of Alexandria. Nelson has 13 ships of the line of 74 guns each, 1 ship of 50 guns, and a sloop.

French vice admiral François Brueys d'Aigalliers commands the French fleet of 13 ships of the line: 1 of 120 guns, 3 of 80 guns each, and 9 of 74 guns. Brueys also has 4 frigates of 36–40 guns each, 2 brigs, 3 bomb vessels, and several gunboats. Although the two sides are equal in number of ships of the line, many of the French vessels are thus larger than those of the English. The French, however, have been decimated by disease, and they are short of water and supplies. Some of the French ships are also weakly armed, and thus the French battle line is considerably less formidable than it appears.

The French are also unprepared for battle. Brueys, who flies his flag in the 120-gun *Orient,* believes that his position is secure. His ships of the line are anchored in a single line, protected by shoals, gunboats, and shore batteries, but part of his crews are ashore. He also has not ordered cables strung between the ships to prevent penetration by opposing ships, nor

BATTLE OF THE NILE, AUGUST 1, 1798

Fate of the French fleet
10 ships of the line captured;
1 burned; 2 escaped
1 frigate sunk; 1 burned;
2 escaped

Total French losses
11 ships of the line, 2 frigates
1,700 killed
1,500 wounded (1,000 of these captured)
2,500 taken prisoner

Total British losses
0 vessels
218 killed
678 wounded

do the French ships have springs attached to their anchor cables to prevent an opposing vessel from engaging them stern to stern. Also, the nearest French land batteries are three miles distant and thus quite unable to provide additional firepower to the fleet.

Nelson, who had written to his wife before the battle that "Glory is my object, and that alone," on seeing the French ships orders hoisted the general signal "Prepare for Battle." As the British ships close on the French, over dinner Nelson announces to his officers, "Before this time tomorrow, I shall have gained a Peerage or Westminster Abbey."

Nelson has foreseen the situation and has already explained to his captains what he expects; no new orders are therefore needed. His captains know him well, and all work well together (a "Band of Brothers," Nelson will call it). The attack occurs that same afternoon. The Battle of the Nile, also known as the Battle of Abu Qir Bay or the Battle of Aboukir Bay, is a disaster for the French.

Rear Admiral Horatio Nelson's decisive British victory over the French in the Battle of the Nile on August 1, 1798, cut off Napoleon Bonaparte's army in Egypt and firmly established Royal Navy dominance in the Mediterranean. (Engraving by J. Le Petit after J. Arnold from *The Life and Services of Horatio, Viscount Nelson . . . from his Lordship's Manuscripts by James Stanier Clarke and John McArthur*. London: Fisher, Son & Co., 1840.)

The French ships have been anchored so as to allow them sufficient room to swing with the current. Noting that if there is room for a French ship to swing then there is sufficient space for a British ship to maneuver and guessing that the French ships are unprepared to fight on their port sides, Nelson sends his leading ships in from that direction. The risk to the British side is revealed when the first British ship, the *Culloden,* promptly grounds. Nonetheless, three of Nelson's ships, led by the *Goliath,* manage to get in between the French battle line and the shore, where they anchor.

Nelson, in the *Vanguard,* takes the remainder of his ships down the outside of the French line. Brueys's ships can now be brought under attack from two sides. Such fighting is difficult in the best of circumstances, but it is made more so for the French because their ships are shorthanded. Systematically moving down the line, the British double up on one French ship after another.

The battle continues well into the night. The *Orient,* which was being painted when the British arrived, catches fire. The flames finally reach its magazine, whereupon the ship is destroyed in a great explosion that rocks the coast for miles. Brueys is among the dead. The flagship takes down with it most of Bonaparte's treasury, some £600,000 in gold and diamonds alone. By dawn only two French ships of the line remain; the rest have been burned, sunk, or captured. One of those that did get away carries Admiral Pierre Charles Villeneuve, Nelson's opponent at the later Battle of Trafalgar; the other takes Admiral Denis Decrès, subsequently Napoléon's minister of marine.

Bonaparte's army is now cut off in Egypt, in effect the prisoner of his conquest. The British victory in the Battle of the Nile also leads to the formation of a new coalition against France that added Russia, Austria, the Italian states, and Turkey.

August–October 1798
Northern Europe: Ireland: Wars of the French Revolution (continued): War between France and Britain (continued): French expeditionary forces land in Ireland. Disaffection in Ireland, nurtured by the French, leads the Directory to send an expeditionary force there. The French plan two independent expeditions, sailing simultaneously from Brest and Rochefort. The force from Brest is delayed, but on August 6, 1798, French commodore Daniel Savary sails from Rochefort with four ships transporting 1,150 French troops under General Jean Humbert. Savary anchors off Kilcummin Head, Ireland, at the mouth of Killala Bay, on August 22, and promptly disembarks his troops. He returns to France on September 9.

Although Savary enjoys some success, the French troops do not receive the anticipated Irish support and, after marching halfway across Ireland, are forced to surrender at Ballinamuck on September 8.

The second French expeditionary force is a more ambitious undertaking; it involves some 4,000 French troops under the command of general Jean Hardy. Commodore Louis Baptiste François Bompard commands the 10 ships (1 ship of the line and 9 frigates) transporting the ground force. The expedition sails from Brest on the night of September 16 hoping to avoid detection, but it is spotted the next day and shadowed by British ships. Efforts to deceive the pursuers fail, and the British anticipate a landing in Ireland. Commodore Sir John Warren is dispatched with his squadron to intercept, having 3 ships of the line and 5 smaller warships, all equal to or superior to the French.

Following an interval of bad weather, the British catch up with the French ships off the Irish coast on October 11. In the ensuing engagement the British capture four of the French ships, and in encounters during October 13–16 the British take three others in spirited engagements. Only three of Bompart's ships return to France, and no French troops from this second expedition are landed in Ireland.

August–December 1798
North Africa: Egypt: Wars of the French Revolution (continued): War between France and Britain (continued): Turkish preparations to invade Egypt. With French forces now cut off in Egypt thanks to the Battle of the Nile, the Ottomans assemble forces to defeat them there. One army, under Achmed Pasha, assembles in Syria, while another assembles on the island of Rhodes to be escorted to Egypt by a British naval squadron.

November–December 1798
Southern Europe: Italy: Wars of the French Revolution (continued): War of the Second Coalition: Preliminary operations in Italy. At the beginning of the War of the Second Coalition (1798–1800), French troops under General Barthélemy Catherine Joubert overrun Piedmont in November and early December, forcing King Charles Emmanuel IV to flee to Sardinia. Concurrently, a Neapolitan army under Austrian general Karl Mack von Leiberich marches into the Roman Republic and captures Rome on November 29, only to be driven out on December 15 by French forces under General Jean Etienne Championnet.

December 24, 1798
Eastern Europe: Wars of the French Revolution (continued): War of the Second Coalition (continued). The formation of an alliance between Britain and Russia is primarily the result of efforts by Czar Paul I, elected by the Knights of Malta as their grand master. This alliance leads to the formation of the Second Coalition against France that comes to include not only Britain and Russia but also Austria, Portugal, Naples, the Vatican, and the Ottoman Empire, the latter three states already at war against France.

The allied plan calls for a three-pronged assault on France. An Anglo-Russian army under the Duke of York is to drive the French from the Netherlands, an Austrian army under Archduke Charles is to force the French from Germany and Switzerland, and Austro-Russian forces under Russian general Aleksandr Suvorov are to expel the French from Italy. Not counting the unreliable Neapolitan forces, the allies outnumber the French some 300,000 to 200,000. Despite this disadvantage, French minister of war Lazare Carnot orders the French to advance.

1798
South Asia: Persia. Incited by the British, Persian Shah Fath Ali invades Afghanistan, beginning a series of wars that weaken both states.

January 23, 1799

Southern Europe: Italy: Wars of the French Revolution (continued): War of the Second Coalition (continued): French proclamation of the Parthenopean Republic. French forces under General Jean Etienne Championnet go on the offensive, and Neapolitan troops under Austrian general Karl Mack von Leiberich mutiny, forcing Mack to flee for his life. The French go on to take the island of Capua as well as the city of Naples. King Ferdinand IV flees to Sicily, and the French establish at Naples on January 23 the Parthenopean Republic, a satellite state of France.

February 10, 1799

Southwest Asia: Syria: Wars of the French Revolution (continued): War between France and Britain (continued): French invasion of Syria from Egypt. At the head of some 13,000 men in the Army of Egypt and with 52 guns, General Napoleon Bonaparte invades Syria. At first successful, he captures Jaffa on March 3. He discovers that many of the 2,000–2,500 Turks taken prisoner had been released on parole earlier. With such a small force of his own, he cannot spare troops to guard the prisoners, let alone escort them back to Egypt. In effect it comes to a choice of either continuing the invasion or calling it off. Bonaparte decides to continue the invasion and have the prisoners shot, a decision made easier by the fact that the Turks have killed French prisoners after torturing them. This decision provides considerable grist for the British propaganda mill, but in fairness to Bonaparte he is merely adopting the morality of his enemy.

March 25, 1799

Central Europe: Germany: Wars of the French Revolution (continued): War of the Second Coalition (continued): Battle of Stockach. In March 1799 General Jean Baptiste Jourdan, commanding the 47,000-man Army of Mayence on the upper Rhine, crosses the river at Kehl and begins operations against Archduke Charles's army of some 80,000 Austrians. Rebuffed at Ostrach on March 21, Jourdan nonetheless plans a bold strike against Charles. Charles is leading about half of the army forward in a reconnaissance in force when Jourdan surprises him at Stockach on March 25.

The initial French attack enjoys some success, but Charles manages to hold and purchase time for the remainder of his army to arrive. Now with a numerical superiority of some 46,000 men to only 38,000 for Jourdan, Charles drives into the center of the loosely organized French line, forcing a French retirement that night. Although Charles has sustained some 6,000 casualties (as opposed to only 3,600 for Jourdan), the French are forced to withdraw to the Rhine.

Jourdan resigns his command and is replaced by General André Masséna. The Army of the Middle Rhine is merged with Masséna's force. The Battle of Stockach brings to a close major military action in Germany for the remainder of the year.

See Leaders: Charles, Archduke of Austria

March–April 1799

Western Europe: Switzerland: Wars of the French Revolution (continued): War of the Second Coalition (continued): French offensive in Switzerland. As a part of general French offensive operations in the spring of 1799, General André Masséna advances from central Switzerland with an army of about 30,000 men in order to cover the right flank of Jean Baptiste Jourdan's army. Surprising the Austrians, Masséna crosses the upper Rhine and captures most of a 7,000-man Austrian force in the vicinity of Chur, in the Grisons. An Austrian garrison at Feldkirch, on Masséna's left flank, repulses French efforts to take that town on March 7 and 23. Masséna then halts operations. Awaiting the progress of Jourdan's army, Masséna sends General Claude Lecourbe and 10,000 men into the Tirol (Tyrol). Another small force from the French Army of Italy joins it, and together they wreak considerable havoc in the western Tirol area.

In April, defeats of French armies in Germany and Italy expose Masséna's northern and southern flanks, and the force in the Tirol is driven back to the upper Rhine.

March–May 1799

South Asia: India: Fourth Anglo-Mysore War. Fearful of a possible advance by the French Army of Egypt under General Napoleon Bonaparte against India, British prime minister William Pitt (the Younger) calls on Richard Wellesley, Lord Mornington, British governor-general in India, to end any vestiges of French influence on the subcontinent. The British send two armies, one from Madras and the other from Bombay, into the French-allied state of Mysore ruled by Sultan Fateh Ali Tipu (Tipu Sultan, Tiger of

Mysore), initiating the Forth Anglo-Mysore War. Indian states allied to the British provide assistance.

The British defeat Tipu at Sedaseer on March 5, 1799, and at Malvelly on March 27. Tipu then withdraws to his capital of Seringapatam, which is besieged by British forces under General George Harris. Counting allied troops the British have some 50,000 men, while Tipu has only 30,000. The result is the same as the first siege (in the Third Anglo-Mysore War): the city taken by storm. Tipu dies on May 4 bravely fighting to defend the city, which falls to the British the same day. Richard Wellesley's younger brother, Colonel Arthur Wellesley (the future Duke of Wellington), distinguishes himself in the campaign and is appointed governor of Seringapatam.

March 17–May 20, 1799
Southwest Asia: Syria: Wars of the French Revolution (continued): War of the Second Coalition (continued): French siege of Acre. French general Napoleon Bonaparte lays siege to the ancient fortress city of Acre, on the eastern Mediterranean coast. Acre is well constructed with massive stone walls and is defended by 250 cannon. Unfortunately for Bonaparte, he sends his siege guns by sea, and they are intercepted by British warships under Commodore Sir William Sidney Smith and then brought into Acre and turned against the French. Bonaparte's light field guns are unable to inflict material damage, and his only recourse is costly infantry assaults.

With the failure of these, his army short of ammunition, men falling prey to the plague, and reports of a large Turkish force massing against him, Bonaparte breaks off the siege and quits Acre on March 20, leaving behind the worst-off plague victims. Of the original 13,000-man force, 2,500 are dead (half from disease); another 2,500 are sick or wounded, and half of these will not reach Egypt.

April 5, 1799
Southern Europe: Italy: Wars of the French Revolution (continued): War of the Second Coalition (continued): Battle of Magnano. In northern Italy, French general Barthélemy Louis Joseph Scherer takes the offensive with 41,000 troops against 46,000 Austrians under General Paul Kray, hoping to defeat them before the arrival of Austrian reinforcements and Russian troops under Aleksandr Suvorov. Following a series of ineffective maneuvers, the two armies join battle at Magnano on April 5, 1799.

Scherer's initial attack is checked by Kray, who then sends his reserves in a flank attack on the French right. Scherer is forced into a disorderly retreat. The French lose 3,500 killed or wounded and 4,500 men captured, along with many guns and supplies. Austrian casualties are 4,000 men, with another 2,000 taken prisoner. General Jean Victor Moreau succeeds Scherer.

April 27, 1799
Southern Europe: Italy: Wars of the French Revolution (continued): War of the Second Coalition (continued): Battle of Cassano. Shortly after the Battle of Magnano, Russian general Aleksandr Suvorov arrives and assumes command of the allied forces in northern Italy. Advancing south with 90,000 men, he forces back French general Jean Victor Moreau.

Detaching Kray and 20,000 men to besiege Mantua and Peschiera, Suvorov (with 65,000 men) encounters Moreau, who has no more than 30,000 men, at Cassano, between Bescia and Milan. In the ensuing battle, Suvorov is victorious. Moreau loses 2,000 dead and 3,000 taken prisoner but is able to withdraw the remainder, thanks to effective French artillery fire, toward Milan.

Suvorov enters Milan on April 29, bringing an end to the French-sponsored Cisalpine Republic. On May 27 he occupies Turin and blockades what is left of Moreau's army at Genoa. Following differences with the Austrians, however, Suvorov gives up his pursuit of the French and scatters his men to lay siege to the remaining French garrisons.

May 1799
Eastern Mediterranean Sea: Wars of the French Revolution (continued): War of the Second Coalition (continued). A Russian-Ottoman fleet operating in the eastern Mediterranean takes the Ionian Islands from France. The Russians occupy the islands until 1807.

June 4–6, 1799
Western Europe: Switzerland: Wars of the French Revolution (continued): War of the Second Coalition (continued): First Battle of Zürich. In May, General André Masséna takes over command of General Jean Baptiste Jourdan's defeated army in addition to his own. With this new force, the Army of the Danube, Masséna is responsible for the defense of both Switzerland and the Rhine south of Mainz. Masséna

slowly withdraws his army of 45,000 men back on Zürich, followed by some 55,000 Austrians under Archduke Charles and General Friedrich von Hotze.

In the First Battle of Zürich (June 4–6), Masséna repulses an Austrian attack on his entrenchments. Superior Austrian numbers and the questionable loyalty of the Swiss, however, lead him to withdraw farther west on June 7. Switzerland is generally calm during the next several months, as Archduke Charles does not feel that he has sufficient numerical advantage to press the issue.

June 17–18, 1799

Southern Europe: Italy: Wars of the French Revolution (continued): War of the Second Coalition (continued): Battle of the Trebbia. French general Etienne Jacques Joseph Alexandre MacDonald hurries up from southern Italy with 33,000 men, and in mid-June 1799 Russian general Aleksandr Suvorov finds his force of 40,000 men caught between two French armies.

In the hard-fought Battle of the Trebbia on June 17–18, 1799, Suvorov defeats MacDonald. The French suffer about 11,500 killed, wounded, and taken prisoner; the Russians lose 5,500. MacDonald then manages to link up with General Jean Victor Moreau at Genoa but loses another 5,000 men while doing so.

In the interim, King Ferdinand IV returns to Naples and suppresses the Parthenopean Republic with savage reprisals, while the French-established Roman Republic suffers the same fate. Suvorov now drives the French Army of Italy back to the Riviera, causing the Directory in Paris to replace Moreau with General Barthélemy Catherine Joubert on August 5.

July 25, 1799

North Africa: Egypt: Wars of the French Revolution (continued): War between France and Britain (continued): Second Battle of Aboukir. French general Napoleon Bonaparte and his expeditionary force return from Syria to Egypt in early June. An Ottoman force of 20,000 men under Mustafa Pasha, supported by the Royal Navy, lands on July 10, takes the fortress of Abu Qir (Aboukir) at the end of a narrow peninsula, and digs in to fight a defensive battle. The Ottomans are supported by 30 guns and gunboats on both sides of the peninsula. Bonaparte has only 7,700 men and 17 guns.

Bonaparte nonetheless attacks, and he is victorious. Generals Jean Lannes and Joachim Murat particularly distinguish themselves. Fort Abu Qir surrenders on August 2. The Ottomans lose 2,000 killed in the fighting and 11,000 drowned; 5,000 others become prisoners of war, while 2,000 are missing and unaccounted for. French losses are only 900. British commodore William Sidney Smith negotiates withdrawal of the prisoners, including Mustafa Pasha.

August 14, 1799

Western Europe: Switzerland: Wars of the French Revolution (continued): War of the Second Coalition (continued): Second Battle of Zürich. In August 1799 commander of the French Army of the Danube General André Masséna resumes the offensive. Defeating Austrian commander Archduke Charles's left wing in the rugged territory of the upper Rhine and Rhone river valleys, Masséna advances on Zürich but is repulsed there in the Second Battle of Zürich on August 14. Two days later he blunts an Austrian attack on his left flank at Dottingen.

August 15, 1799

Southern Europe: Italy: Wars of the French Revolution (continued): War of the Second Coalition (continued): Battle of Novi. Advancing from Genoa with his 35,000-man French Army of Italy, General Barthélemy Catherine Joubert attacks 50,000 Russian and Austrian forces under Russian general Aleksandr Suvorov at Novi. The French are decisively defeated, suffering 11,000 casualties; Joubert is among the dead. Suvorov, who loses 9,000 men, promptly pursues the French, forcing them back across the Apennines.

Suvorov halts the pursuit, however, upon learning that the 30,000-man French Army of the Alps commanded by General Jean Etienne Championnet has entered Italy via Mt. Cenis Pass. Suvorov moves north to engage Championnet. Before Suvorov can accomplish this, though, he receives orders from Moscow to join his 20,000-man army with that of Russian general Alexander Korsakov, who has taken the place of Austrian commander Archduke Charles in Switzerland.

New allied plans call for Charles to march north through Germany, joining his army to British and Russian forces under the Duke of York in helping to drive the French from the Netherlands. The combined Russian armies of Suvorov and Korsakov will then drive French forces under General André Masséna from Switzerland. Suvorov leaves allied operations in Italy to Austrian marshal Michael Melas and 60,000 men.

August 24, 1799

North Africa: Egypt: Wars of the French Revolution (continued): War between France and Britain (continued): Napoleon Bonaparte sails from Egypt to return to France. During negotiations with French commander of the Army of Egypt General Napoleon Bonaparte regarding return of Turkish prisoners from the Battle of Aboukir (Abu Qir), British commodore William Sidney Smith provides Bonaparte with copies of the London *Times* to show him that thanks to allied forces of the Second Coalition, the French are doing poorly militarily in Italy, Switzerland, and the Netherlands. Without having received orders to do so, Bonaparte decides to abandon his command in Egypt. On August 24, 1799, he sails with his key aides for France aboard two French frigates. Bonaparte's luck holds, and after a stop at Corsica he lands in France at Fréjus on October 9.

Capable general Jean Baptiste Kléber assumes command in Egypt. The survivors of the Army of Egypt are not repatriated until after the conclusion of the Treaty of Amiens in March 1802.

September 16, 1799

Western Europe: Netherlands: Wars of the French Revolution (continued): War of the Second Coalition (continued): First Battle of Bergen. In August 1799 a British army of 27,000 men under the Duke of York lands in Holland, south of the Texel. On August 30 the Dutch fleet in the Texel surrenders to a British squadron without a fight. Reinforced by two Russian divisions, the Duke of York then takes the offensive against the French in the Netherlands.

In the First Battle of Bergen, French general Guillaume Marie Anne Brune, at the head of 22,000 French and Bavarian troops, meets the advancing British-Russian force of 35,000 men. The allies fail to coordinate their actions, and Brune halts their advance, inflicting some 4,000 casualties and sustaining 3,000 of his own.

September 25–26, 1799

Western Europe: Switzerland: Wars of the French Revolution (continued): War of the Second Coalition (continued): Third Battle of Zürich. In August the

allies develop new plans to attack France from the east. Archduke Charles of Austria will march north through Germany to assist British and Russian forces under the Duke of York in driving the French from the Netherlands. Two Russian armies, one of 27,000 men under General Alexander Korsakov and another of 21,000 men under Aleksandr Suvorov, sent north from Italy, will then take the place of Charles.

Korsakov's men begin arriving at Austrian headquarters at Kloten on August 12, and on August 28 Charles marches north with 30,000 men, leaving behind 16,000 Austrian troops under General Friedrich von Hotze. Seeing an opportunity to attack before the allies can concentrate against him, French general André Masséna advances with his 76,000-man Army of the Danube against the remaining allied forces in Switzerland. Sending General Claude Lecourbe with 12,000 men to hold the St. Gotthard Pass and block Suvorov, Masséna moves against Korsakov at Zürich.

Detaching some 10,000 men in each of two secondary thrusts to fix the Austrians in place, on September 25, 1799, Masséna and the remainder of his army attack Korsakov near Zürich. In this Third Battle of Zürich (sometimes called the Second Battle of Zürich, which ignores the fight near there in August) during September 25–26, the French are victorious.

In danger of being cut off, Korsakov withdraws his forces in some disorder toward the upper Rhine beginning on the morning of September 26. The Russians sustain some 8,000 casualties in the battle itself and another 3,800 in the ensuing retreat. They also lose 100 guns. The French suffer only 4,000 casualties. Masséna's victory helps save the French Republic and briefly reinvigorates the Directory, which nonetheless falls prey to a coup d'état the next month.

Suvorov meanwhile fights his way through the St. Gotthard at considerable cost and arrives at Zürich too late. He then manages to extricate his army, with considerable hardship, across the Alps to Ilanz on the upper Rhine. There he learns that Russian czar Paul I has removed him from command. Meanwhile, Masséna takes Constance.

October 2, 1799

Western Europe: Netherlands: Wars of the French Revolution (continued): War of the Second Coalition (continued): Second Battle of Bergen. The Duke of

York renews the offensive with his British-Russian army against French forces at Bergen under French general Guillaume Marie Anne Brune. Each side suffers about 2,000 casualties, but this time the allies are successful, and York pushes south.

October 6, 1799
Western Europe: Netherlands: Wars of the French Revolution (continued): War of the Second Coalition (continued): Battle of Castricum. In fighting along the North Sea coast at Castricum, allied forces under the Duke of York again engage French forces under General Guillaume Marie Anne Brune. Again, coordination between the British and Russian forces is poor, and the allies are defeated, losing some 3,500 men to only 2,500 for the French. Realizing that he lacks the strength to drive the French from the Netherlands and having accomplished his goal of surrender of the Dutch fleet, York withdraws north.

October 18, 1799
Western Europe: Netherlands: Wars of the French Revolution (continued): War of the Second Coalition (continued): Convention of Alkmaar. Under the terms of this agreement with the French, the British return some 8,000 French and Dutch prisoners held in England in exchange for their unhindered evacuation from the Netherlands. However, the British retain the ships of the Dutch Navy taken earlier.

October 22, 1799
Eastern Europe: Russia: Wars of the French Revolution (continued): War of the Second Coalition (continued): Russia leaves the war. Disgusted with the failure of the allies, especially the Austrians, to take advantage of favorable circumstances and crush the French, Czar Paul I withdraws Russia from the war.

November 4, 1799
Southern Europe: Italy: Wars of the French Revolution (continued): War of the Second Coalition (continued): Battle of Genoa. Austrian field marshal Michael Melas, commanding about 60,000 men, defeats General Jean Etienne Championnet and the French Army of the Alps (with about 30,000 men) at Genoa, driving the French back across the Alps.

November 9, 1799
Western Europe: France: Wars of the French Revolution (continued): War of the Second Coalition

(continued): Coup d'état of 18 Brumaire. General Napoleon Bonaparte returns from Egypt on October 9. Trumpeting his victory over the Ottomans in the Battle of Aboukir (Abu Qir), he is greeted as a conquering hero in one French city after another. Arriving in Paris on October 15, he sizes up the political situation and allies himself with directors Emmanuel Siéyès and Roger Ducos. With the assistance of Napoleon's brother Lucien, president of the Council of 500, the plotters overthrow the government and seize power. Not only is this a coup d'état, but it is Bonaparte's personal coup over the other plotters, for the new constitutional arrangement, known as the Consulate, sees Bonaparte effectively controlling the state as first consul for a term of 10 years. Ducos and Siéyès refuse subordinate roles and are bought off, replaced by Jean-Jacques-Régis de Cambacérès and Charles-François Lebrun as second and third consuls, respectively.

December 24, 1799
Western Europe: France: Wars of the French Revolution (continued): War of the Second Coalition (continued): Constitution of the Year VIII. The Constitution of the Year VIII is overwhelmingly approved by popular vote (supposedly more than 3 million votes to 1,567). Although maintaining a republican facade, it is in fact a vehicle for the dictatorship of one man, Napoleon Bonaparte. There is a window dressing of representative institutions, although they have little power. Bonaparte introduces a more efficient tax collection system and a new administrative system consisting of prefectures and subprefectures.

1799
Central Europe: Independence of Montenegro. Following an alliance between King Peter I of Montenegro and Russia, Ottoman sultan Selim III recognizes without qualification the independence of Montenegro.

1799–1802
South Asia: India: Rise of Maharaja Ranjit Singh. During three years of warfare from 1799 to 1802, young (b. 1780) Ranjit Singh unites the Sikhs and establishes control over the Punjab. He assumes the title of Maharaja in April 1801.

The Napoleonic Age

Overview of 1800–1850

This period sees the peak effectiveness of a number of weapons, including the smoothbore musket and bayonet. It also sees lighter smoothbore field artillery. By midcentury there are extensive experiments in new weaponry, from rifling and breech-loading in both small arms and artillery to revolutionary new projectiles such as the minié ball for small arms, and extensive use of improved-fused explosive shells for artillery. The period also produces important developments in transportation that will dramatically impact civilian society but also war on land and sea with the application of the steam engine. At the end of the period, governments are experimenting with iron ships for commercial and military use.

In tactics, by the early 19th century ground commanders have learned how to achieve maximum effectiveness from combinations of infantry, field artillery, and cavalry. At the same time the Industrial Revolution, generally accepted to have begun in Britain in the 1760s and then spreading to France and the rest of Europe, makes possible the deployment of the mass citizen armies that typify the era. Better roads and maps help bring campaigns of rapid movement.

Two men take maximum advantage of these developments and dominate warfare in the early 19th century: Frenchman Napoleon Bonaparte on land and Englishman Horatio Nelson at sea.

Land Warfare

Weapons. This period is marked not only by the improvement of existing systems but also by the development of new weapons systems. This is largely due to the application of science and technology but also to improved manufacturing techniques and better machine tools.

In small arms there are major changes, especially with the development of the percussion cap that employed fulminates of mercury as a primer and was patented by Alexander Forsyth in 1807. The percussion cap dramatically decreased the number of misfires with the old flintlock system of ignition and thus substantially increased firepower. Forsyth's invention also made possible a new weapon for close combat, the revolving chamber pistol or revolver.

> *See* Weapons: Percussion Cap
> *See* Weapons: Revolver

Particularly important was the marriage of the percussion system of ignition, rifling, and the minié expanding lead bullet in 1849. This resulted in vastly increased firepower and long-range accuracy that gave great advantage to the defense, a situation not well understood by the generals of the time, much to the misfortune of their men.

> *See* Weapons: Minié Ball

Major changes occur in artillery. The development of the shell gun by French general Henri Paixhans is especially important. Experiments also go forward in breech loading and in new casting techniques. Beginning in the 1820s, serious efforts are made to apply rifling to cannon. Among prominent ordnance designers in this period are Paixhans in France; Charles Lancaster, William G. A. Strong, T. A. Blakely, Joseph Whitman, and William George Armstrong in Britain; Martin von Wahrendorff in Sweden; Giovanni Cavalli in Italy; and John A. Dahlgren, Robert P. Parrott, and Thomas J. Rodman in the United States.

See Weapons: Parrott Gun
See Weapons: Dahlgren Gun

Another important development occurs in ammunition with the increased use of spherical case or shrapnel, credited to British lieutenant Henry Shrapnel of the Royal Artillery in 1784. Employed against infantry formations, it consisted of a fused hollow carcass packed with an explosive charge and small balls, with a fuse timed to explode when the shell was in the air to inflict casualties on troops in the open.

See Weapons: Shrapnel

One weapon, the war rocket, made a short reappearance. The modern war rocket, designed by the Englishman Sir William Congreve, revived a weapons system that had been employed in China in medieval times and more recently in fighting in India. Rockets saw use in the Wars of the French Revolution, the Napoleonic Wars, and the War of 1812 and for several decades thereafter. Rockets appeared in a variety of sizes, but their inaccuracy and maximum range of about 1,500 yards limited their employment. For area fire, though, particu-

An 11-inch Dahlgren gun on a pivot mount aboard the U.S. Navy sidewheel gunboat *Miami*. (Naval Historical Center)

larly if the intention was to burn out a city (as in the case of the British attack on Copenhagen in 1807), they proved quite useful.

Tactics. Large field armies engaging in set-piece battles were the rule. At the opening of the period, opposing forces employed linear formations in the field, and sieges were conducted according to precise rules that included the digging of parallels. Infantry, still armed primarily with the smoothbore flintlock musket and bayonet, dominated on the battlefield. Rifles were employed but, because of the far greater time required for reloading, were employed only in small numbers by specialized troops for long-range sniping fire. Cavalrymen were armed primarily with the saber, although some carried the short-barreled musket or carbine and others the lance.

Napoleon Bonaparte, who dominated this era, was, perhaps surprisingly, not a tactical innovator. His strength was in effectively applying lessons developed by others. His success lay in his strategic vision; careful preparation, including the study of maps and logistics; and attention to details, training, discipline, and the morale of his men and the effective use of available weapons. Usually outnumbered by the combined strength of multiple opponents, Napoleon sought to make the most of rapidity of movement, concentration, surprise, and deception. In these, he was blessed with having a number of able subordinates, many of them sergeants under the Old Regime who had been promoted during the Wars of the French Revolution on the basis of proven ability.

Napoleon's campaigns were based on rapid movement and effective maneuver to catch his opponent by surprise in adverse circumstances, achieve rapid concentration of his own forces, and destroy his enemy in detail. He pursued the strategy of the central position, placing his own main army between enemy forces to prevent their concentration against him. Destruction of the main enemy field army to decide a campaign or even a war in one stroke was usually his chief goal.

In battle, Napoleon had no tactical preferences aside from massing his artillery to provide maximum support for the infantry and create a breach in the enemy line. He often launched the main attack on the enemy center with the aim of breaking through and then swinging to one flank or the other, in conjunction with a secondary flanking attack. Cavalry was usually positioned on the flanks of his army but was also set against key points in an enemy line as part of the effort to break through.

Infantry. The Wars of the French Revolution had seen developments of highly effective flexible tactics, with many skirmishers employed to tie down enemy forces until massed assault formations could be brought forward against the enemy line. Both the French and British developed highly flexible light infantrymen capable of operating under less direct supervision by officers and marked by high esprit de corps. Pride in the regiment, revolutionary idealism, and nationalism became prime motivators. Napoleon was one of the first and most effective promoters of nationalism, but one of the consequences of this was its spread throughout Europe. Rational in his approach, with a passion for organization and proper administration, his consolidation of the patchwork of many small German and Italian states made him the stepfather of present-day Germany and Italy.

The French infantry attack in column, developed by Lazare Carnot early in the Wars of the French Revolution and perfected by Napoleon, was in fact a flexible formation (*ordre mixte*) that allowed a combination of infantry tactics. In the brief period of peace preceding the 1805 land campaign, the French Army developed a seamless blend of infantry tactics. Battalion columns normally deployed in ranks no more than nine men deep. They employed a combination of line for firepower, column for maneuver and shock, square to repel cavalry, and skirmisher screens to deplete the enemy force before the main battle was joined. The column could operate efficiently in difficult terrain, and it could easily change from marching column to attack column or rapidly form two- or three-rank firing lines or squares. The tactical superiority of the veteran French infantry dominated France's continental opponents.

The peak of Napoleonic efficiency came in 1805; by Napoleon's own admission, the men of that year were the best he ever led. Only later in his wars, with the substantial decline in the quality of his infantry, did Napoleon resort to employing his battalions as mere battering rams.

The British developed the most effective answer to the French infantry column formation. Sir Arthur Wellesley, the Duke of Wellington, was a master of defensive-offensive warfare. He employed the tactic of keeping his troops on the reverse slope of a hill, both to protect them from enemy fire and to conceal his troop dispositions and strength from enemy observation. The highly effective and well-disciplined British light infantry relied on massive aimed musket fire delivered on command that could be devastating to an attacking force.

The British placed a premium on accurate aimed fire and employed larger numbers of riflemen, who fired subcaliber bullets under rapid fire or full-sized bullets for individual aimed fire. Such well-trained infantrymen were capable of operating in close order or as individuals. The British represented the infantrymen of the future. The British retained a two-deep line in order to provide maximum firepower, however. Because the British were relatively weak in cavalry, Wellington also relied on natural obstacles and accurate infantry fire to destroy French cavalry formations.

Cavalry. Cavalry remained the principle shock arm in this period. Cavalrymen were armed primarily with the saber and lance. Cavalry were divided between heavy and light, with the former being sometimes partially armored and riding larger horses, while the latter were unarmored and rode smaller mounts. Heavy cavalry were employed primarily for shock action, while light cavalry could be used both to harass and to shock.

French cavalry was, generally speaking, the finest of any European army at the beginning of this period. This changed with the huge wastage of Napoleon's wars—especially the campaign in Russia in 1812, which saw the loss of tens of thousands of trained mounts—coupled with improvements in opponents' cavalry. This was particularly evident in the War of German Liberation of 1813 and in the campaigns of 1814 and 1815. Napoleon made excellent use of his cavalry at its peak, though, to break an enemy defensive formation, to exploit a battlefield victory with minimal losses to his own side, and for reconnaissance and screening.

The French light cavalry were known as *chasseurs à cheval,* dragoons, and hussars. The heavy cavalry was known as the *cuirassiers* and *carbiniers à cheval.* Army headquarters controlled the cavalry reserve of 20,000 men in 1805 to as many as 60,000 men in 1812. Napoleon's cavalry was commanded by the highly effective Marshal Joachim Murat.

Napoleon also established an elite formation, the Imperial Guard. Held in reserve, the Guard was his trump card to be inserted at the most critical point in the battle. It consisted of the Old Guard (proven veterans of three or more campaigns), the Middle Guard (the same requirements), and the Young Guard (after 1809, also veterans but younger tall, promising soldiers). More than a body guard for the emperor, the Guard was in effect an army in miniature, containing its own formations of infantry, cavalry, artillery, engineers, etc. The infantry (known as the *grognards,* or grumblers) stood as an intimidating formation behind the lines, often in full-dress uniform, and never failed the emperor in battle, until Waterloo. The Guard grew in size from some 8,000 men in 1805 to 80,000 in 1812. Although the Guard was headed by a marshal, in battle Napoleon commanded it himself.

Artillery. French artillery was, at the beginning of the period, superior to that of its opponents. Napoleon was a trained artillery officer. His tactic was to mass his guns, forming them into the *grand batterie* at a critical spot and using it to blast large holes in an enemy battle line prior to an infantry assault. Napoleon inherited the excellent artillery system developed by the preeminent French artillerist Jean Baptiste Vaquette de Gribeauval. The guns were of standardized caliber 4-, 6-, 8-, and 12-pounder guns and 6-inch howitzers. Gribeauval had slightly shortened and reduced the weight of the guns. Improved manufacturing techniques allowed the production of shot of greater sphericity, and this permitted a reduction in windage and the amount of powder charge required. Rapidity of fire and precision in the charge was ensured by the use of cartridges: cylinders, usually of flannel, containing the gunpowder charge.

Napoleon reduced the weight of the guns by further shortening the barrel and by employing a chamber at the bottom of the bore and smaller powder charges. This so-called System of the Year IX (1803) proved a failure, lacking both range and striking power. As a stopgap, the French employed a number of excellent 6-pounder Austrian and Prussian guns, secured by capture.

Horse artillery, with the artillerymen either riding on limbers or on horseback, proved highly effective. The lighter horse artillery guns (4- to 8-pounders) were highly mobile, quickly unlimbered, and effective in harassing an advancing or retreating enemy formation.

The British also improved their artillery during the period. Their standard field gun was the 9-pounder. They lightened it and made it more maneuverable by replacing its double trail carriage with a single trail. This single modification made the British 9-pounder field piece as maneuverable as the French 4- and 6-pounder guns. Unlike the French, the British did not mass their guns but used them for infantry support along the entire line.

Organization of the Napoleonic Grande Armée

Napoleon's major tactical innovations were to make the corps, rather than the division, the army's standard unit and to devise a new marching formation for it. In 1700 the basic military organization was the brigade; by 1760 it had become the division. By 1800 it was the corps. This came about because of the tremendous expansion in the size of field armies, which often approached 200,000 men.

The Napoleonic corps numbered some 20,000–30,000 men, was commanded by a lieutenant general or a marshal, and was an entirely self-contained battle unit. The corps was comprised of two or more divisions of 8,000–12,000 men each, a brigade of light cavalry numbering 2,000–3,000 men, and six to eight companies of artillery as well as engineers and medical and headquarters personnel.

Each corps had between 48 and 64 artillery pieces. Army headquarters (i.e., Napoleon) thus controlled 150 or more guns in the field. Contrary to myth, Napoleon, a trained artillerist, did not substantially increase the number of artillery pieces serving his infantry. They remained on average about 3 guns per 1,000 infantry, the same ratio as that maintained by the other major powers.

On the march, armies were organized in three or four corps about 20 miles from each other, that is, one or at most two days apart. This allowed for maximum foraging, helping to offset the large supply trains required and improving speed; it also allowed rapid concentration of force and movement in any direction.

Contrary to popular myth, until after the Russian disaster of 1812 Napoleon's army was essentially a regular force of professional soldiers—enlisted men as well as officers—rather than draftees. Although all French males were required to register for the draft at age 18 and were subject to being called up between ages 20 and 25, between 1800 and 1810 the average number raised in this fashion was only 73,000 annually. This changed with the defeat in Russia, and during the period 1812–1815 Napoleon called up 1.5 million men. The draft total was kept down in France in part because even in the early period, foreigners constituted a large percentage of the army. Thus, even the Grande Armée of 1805 was about a quarter foreigners, while of the 600,000 men whom Napoleon led into Russia in 1812 only a third were Frenchmen.

Officers were often from the lower classes, and more often than not, advancement was on the basis of demonstrated merit, the military counterpart of Napoleon's "careers open to talent" approach of utilizing men of ability, regardless of past affiliation, as long as they would be loyal to him. This gave Napoleon a tremendous advantage over his opponents, as did the fact that most of his army consisted of volunteers who followed him enthusiastically.

The Allied Armies

The armies of Napoleon's opponents had in common an aristocratic officer corps. The two exceptions were the specialist branches of artillery and engineers, where nonnobles were able to secure commissions. Many senior commanders were elderly, in their seventies or even eighties. Russia had a large number of foreigners in senior officer positions. While it would be wrong to say that all the senior commanders of this period were incapable, they were mostly comfortable with 18th-century warfare and generally opposed change.

Britain still retained the purchase system whereby nobles and commoners alike bought commissions. Nonetheless, aristocrats dominated the higher positions in both the army and navy. Parliament and government ministries, however, investigated cases of demonstrated incompetence, and the threat of this led a number of inefficient or elderly officers to retire. After Prussia's humiliating defeat at the hands of Napoleon, in 1807 the Prussian officer corps was opened to commoners, but aristocrats continued to dominate the senior positions into the Hitler era. Capable commoners nevertheless soon worked their way into staff positions and were thus able to improve the performance of some of the more senior aristocratic commanders.

The British retained their system of regiments and independent brigades and did not adopt the division until 1807. The British Army was essentially a volunteer force and, for its day, perhaps the world's best trained and most disciplined. The accuracy and volume of British infantry musket fire was perhaps Europe's best, enhanced by their use of a two-rank line. In the Peninsular War, Wellington made effective use of larger numbers of skirmishers to deal with the French *tirailleurs.*

Weapons were similar to those of the French and of like characteristics. The Austrian, Prussian, and Russian muskets were of .74 caliber, while the British Brown Bess was of .75 caliber. These were slightly larger than the comparable, excellent French .69-caliber Charleville. Allied and French artillery were also comparable except that the allied guns tended to be somewhat heavier and thus less maneuverable.

All governments worked to increase the size of their armies to match that of the French, and in this they were largely successful. Only the British Army remained small, a consequence of the vast manpower needs of the Royal Navy. The army was expanded to 200,000 men in 1812, but only 50,000 of these were committed to the fight on the continent in part because of the concurrent War of 1812 with the United States. None of the powers opposing France resorted to its system of conscription, though, as the monarchs considered it too democratic and even dangerous. Russia continued to rely on an annual levy of serfs, however, and both Austria and Prussia briefly adopted a *Landwehr* (national guard) system late in the Napoleonic Wars. All countries resorted to hiring foreigners to fill the ranks, mainly from the German states, the British having the smallest number.

The European armies, especially those defeated by the French, sought to copy the French organizational structure, including the corps system. The Austrian corps was generally smaller than that of the French, though, because they lacked a divisional structure, having only brigades of infantry and cavalry directly under corps command. The largest British formation was the division of 4,000–7,000 men with the notable exception of the Battle of Waterloo, when the Duke of Wellington temporarily organized two corps. The Austrians came up with one significant improvement over the French system: taking the 6-pounder guns from battalion control and placing them with the 12- and 18-pounders in corps reserve. As a consequence, the Austrians were able, in certain engagements, to concentrate more artillery than Napoleon, leading the emperor to copy the Austrians and increase the number of guns under direct independent command.

The Rise of Military Professionalism

The half century from 1800 to 1850 was also marked by the rise of military professionalism. France led, with the establishment in 1794 of the École Polytechnique (Polytechnical School) for the training of military and civil engineers and the military academy at St. Cyr in 1808. The British established the Royal Military College at Sandhurst in 1802, the same year the U.S. Military Academy at West Point was founded. The U.S. Naval Academy at Annapolis, Maryland, came into being in 1845. In Prussia, humiliated by Napoleon in 1806–1807, Count Gerhard von Scharnhorst established a school system to retrain the Prussian military; at the top was the Kriegsakademie, established in Berlin in 1810. This marked the first true approach to a modern professional school system for the military. Scharnhorst also created the first truly modern general staff.

The period was also marked by a proliferation of compendiums of military knowledge and manuals that covered every aspect of drill and warfare. Napoleon's mastery of the art of war also inspired a search for principles of warfare that might explain his success. Swiss Antoine Henri de Jomini, who had served for a time in the French Army and was later a general in the Russian Army, devoted himself to studying and analyzing Napoleon's operations. His seminal work was *Précis de l'Art de la Guerre: Des Principales Combinaisons de la Stratégie, de la Grande Tactique et de la Politique Militaire,* published in 1838 and translated into English as *Summary of the Art of War.*

    See Leaders: Jomini, Antoine Henri

    The work of the director of the Kriegsakademie in Prussia, Carl von Clausewitz, was published posthumously in 1831. He had written a number of studies of military campaigns, but *Von Krieg* (*On War*), a series of military maxims on war, might be the most important work on war ever written.

    See Leaders: Clausewitz, Carl Philipp Gottfried von

    In the United States, Dennis Hart Mahan, professor of military and civil engineering at West Point, initiated the American study of military theory. Mahan graduated from West Point and then went on to study military engineering in France before returning to his alma mater to teach. Because there was no textbook available in English, Mahan produced his own. Published in 1847, it was titled *An Elementary Treatise on Advance Guard, Out-Post, and Detachment Service of Troops;* the cadets called it simply *Out-Post.* Mahan's basic assumption was that war was a science and could be learned. An officer could become a professional only by acquiring a broad historical knowledge of war. Mahan stressed Napoleonic principles, especially one great battle deciding a war. Virtually all major American Civil War generals except Robert E. Lee studied in Mahan's classroom.

    See Leaders: Mahan, Dennis Hart

Naval Warfare

The British dominated the seas throughout this period. British naval mastery, confirmed by the Battle of Trafalgar in 1805, was unchallenged until the rise of German naval power in the 1890s. At sea as well as on land there was a trend away from the old formalist tactics, spelled out in the Fighting Instructions, in favor of the melee school, which allowed innovation and adaptation according to circumstances. This transition was furthered by commanders of great ability and proven professionalism, the most notable being British vice admiral Horatio Nelson. Nelson's tactics, combined with an innovative signal system capable of conveying as many as 30,000 words, developed by Royal Navy captain (later rear admiral) Sir Home Riggs Popham in the first decade of the 19th century, saw sailing ship warfare at its peak of perfection.

    The Royal Navy was by far the world's best led and best trained. Most of its crews were pressed; discipline was often ferocious and conditions aboard ship appalling, but long service at sea, including maintaining the blockade of continental Europe in all weather, translated into efficiency of operation.

Antoine Henri Jomini (1779–1869) was a Swiss citizen who became a general in the French and Russian armies. An unabashed admirer of French Emperor Napoleon I, Jomini achieved renown as a writer on military affairs who sought to identify principles of war. (Sloane, William M. *The Life of Napoleon Bonaparte,* 1896)

British naval gunnery was clearly superior to that of most of the world's navies, and the fact that the British crews could fire at double the rate of the Spanish and French counterparts in the Battle of Trafalgar was no small factor in its outcome and in many other engagements as well.

Changes in Naval Technology. Sir Robert Seppings, surveyor of the Royal Navy during 1813–1832, carried out a revolution in ship construction. Thanks to Seppings, Britain took the lead in structural design and held it until late in the 19th century. Seppings's system of diagonal framing in ship construction substituted a stronger triangulated plan for the old rectangular one. He also increased the use of knee pieces and employed iron straps. In exterior design Seppings developed stronger round bows and circular sterns, which were important given the new Nelsonian tactic of breaking an enemy line that exposed these relatively weak parts of a ship to fire more so than had the old tactic of broadside-to-broadside fire in the line of battle. Seppings's reforms produced ships that were a quarter larger and far stronger than their predecessors. The changes made possible construction of the 90-gun two-deck steam battleships of the 1850s.

Steam Warships. Even as it was reaching the peak of its development, the dominance of the wooden sailing ship was coming to an end. The introduction of steam engines revolutionized not only the construction of ships but also the entire practice of naval warfare. Steam engines freed warships from the whims of the wind and allowed a captain to take his vessel where he pleased. This was immensely important on inland waterways.

Prussian General Carl Philipp Gottfried von Clausewitz (1780–1831) was one of the most profoundly important military theorists of the modern age. As head of the Prussian Kriegsakademie, he constructed an analysis of war (published posthumously as *Von Krieg* (*On War*) that sought to understand the elemental forces shaping armed conflict. (Library of Congress)

Although primitive steam engines were known to the ancients, the modern steam engine evolved from the late 17th century to the second half of the 18th century, when it was largely perfected in 1764 by James Watt, an instrument maker at the University of Glasgow. Watt patented his steam engine in 1769.

Steamboats began appearing late in the 18th century, but American Robert Fulton's *Clermont* (1807), which plied the Hudson River in New York state, was the first commercially successful steamboat.

See Weapons: Steam Warship

Navies were slow to embrace the change. The British, with the world's largest sailing navy, opposed anything that would render it obsolete. As the lords of the Admiralty put it in 1828, "Their Lordships find it their bounden duty to discourage to the best of their ability the employment of steam vessels, as they consider the introduction of steam is calculated to strike a fatal blow at the naval supremacy of the empire" (R. Ernest Dupuy and Trevor N. Dupuy, *The Harper Encyclopedia of Military History,* 4th ed. [New York: HarperCollins,

1993], 812). Resistance to change prevailed in all navies, though. U.S. secretary of the navy James K. Paulding (1838–1841) said that he would "never consent to let our old ships perish, and transform our navy into a fleet of sea monsters" (Charles O. Paullin, *Paullin's History of Naval Administration, 1775–1911* [Annapolis, MD: U.S. Naval Institute, 1968], 179). The British, with by far the world's largest wooden sailing ship fleet, had to be forced into the technological changes of steam and ironclad, but once they entered the race, they led it.

The first steam warship was Fulton's floating battery, the *Demologos* (*Fulton I*), launched in October 1814 and commissioned in June 1815. The *Demologos* was a catamaran, with its paddle wheel protected by thick twin hulls.

See Weapons: *Demologos*, USS

Most early steam warships (known as paddlers) had their paddles to each side of the hull. This was both inefficient and vulnerable to enemy fire. Side wheels were also an inefficient means of propulsion, and their drag inhibited the ship's speed when under sail. The paddle wheels were also large and vulnerable to enemy fire, and they took up much room on the side of the vessel. This prevented standard broadside batteries, forcing location of the guns on the upper deck. Accommodating the engines, boilers, fuel, and boiler water also meant reductions in other areas, including the number of crewmen and thus men available to work guns. As a consequence, most early side-wheelers carried a few powerful guns on pivot mounts at bow and stern that were capable of much longer-range fire than the old broadside battery guns. Paddler fighting ships had only a brief period of service, and none fought in major battles.

With the advent of the screw steamer, paddlers became obsolete, although later types carried a heavy armament and had about the same capabilities as screw vessels. The chief accomplishment of the paddlers was to demonstrate conclusively the value of steam warships.

The solution to the inefficient side-wheel method of propulsion was the screw propeller. It is jointly credited to English innovator Francis Pettit Smith and Swedish engineer John Ericsson, both then working in London. It was brought into practical service in the late 1830s. The early screw propellers were quite large and created considerable drag when not in use (some could be retracted) but they were entirely underwater and thus far more efficient as well as more impervious to enemy fire. Ericsson later came to the United States, where he designed the machinery for the sloop *Princeton,* the world's first steam-driven screw warship. The ship incorporated such novel ideas as placement of engines below the waterline to shield them from enemy gunfire.

See Weapons: *Princeton,* USS

Doubts over which was the superior form of propulsion—the screw or the paddle wheel—were resolved by the Royal Navy in 1845. In a series of trials, the screw sloop *Rattler* proved faster than its rival, the paddle sloop *Alecto.* Proponents of the paddle wheel claimed that it had superior towing capabilities, but this too was disproved in a tug-of-war between the two ships on April 30, 1845, which the *Rattler* won.

All early steamers were hybrids incorporating both steam power and sail, a practice that continued until the end of the 19th century. This was due to the inefficiency of the early steam engines and the amount of coal that had to be carried. The engines frequently broke down, the ships were slow, and their high rate of fuel consumption reduced cruising range.

Steam warships conclusively demonstrated their great utility in the Mexican-American War (1846–1848) and the Crimean War (1853–1856). In 1856, summing up the lessons of the Crimean War, French minister of marine Vice Admiral Baron François Hamelin, who had commanded the French fleet in the Black Sea in 1854, opined, "Any ship that is not provided with a steam engine cannot be considered a warship" (quoted in Jack Sweetman, ed., *The Great Admirals: Command at Sea, 1587–1945* [Annapolis, MD: Naval Institute Press, 1997], 244).

Naval Ordnance. One trend in this period was a shift from many smaller guns to fewer guns of larger size. Others were the increasing use of shells at sea and the introduction of the shell gun. Wooden ships could absorb a tremendous amount of punishment from solid shot, the main effect of which was to produce splinters that caused human casualties. Hull hits, if they penetrated, produced a round hole that could be easily patched by a ship's carpenter, who had plugs available just for that purpose. Explosive shell, if it lodged in the hull of an enemy ship and exploded, might actually produce a large enough irregular hole to sink that ship.

Early shell was dangerous to friend as well as foe, however, and a premature discharge could wreak havoc in the close confines of a ship. Crews were reluctant to employ shell, and some captains thought that their use was a violation of the norms of naval warfare. In the early 1820s, though, French colonel Henri Paixhans began a series of ordnance experiments projecting shell at low velocity. Paixhans wanted to do away with solid shot altogether in favor of exploding shell fired in a flat trajectory from a few large-caliber guns. He argued for uniformity in caliber of guns; he wanted to replace the mixed armament then in place with 36-pounders of different weights for the various decks. All would fire charged shell. Tests in 1823 and 1824 proved conclusive. Armed with a few such guns, a frigate might actually sink a ship of the line.

That the French took the lead in developing a new system should not be surprising. They had less to lose than the British in adopting an entirely new naval ordnance system and could make up for having fewer ships with superior ordnance. The same applied to the introduction of the ironclad warship.

See Weapons: Explosive Shell and the Shell Gun

By 1850, ships mounted fewer and heavier guns. The standard broadside gun-deck armament in the British and American navies was the 32-pounder, while ships of the line carried 42-pounders as their lower-deck armaments. These might be coupled with a few large (8- or 10-inch) shell guns on pivot mounts fore and aft. Experiments went forward, with even heavier wrought-iron guns firing 12-inch shell.

Chronology (continued)

November 9, 1799
Western Europe: France: Wars of the French Revolution (continued): War of the Second Coalition (continued): Coup d'état of 18 Brumaire. Returning to France from Egypt, French general Napoleon Bonaparte arrives in Paris on October 15. There he allies himself with directors Emmanuel Siéyès and Roger Ducos, and with the assistance of Lucien Bonaparte, president of the Council of 500, the plotters overthrow the government and seize power.

Not only is this a coup d'état against the regime, but it is Bonaparte's personal coup over the other plotters, for the new constitutional arrangement, known as the Consulate, has Bonaparte effectively controlling the state as first consul for a term of 10 years.

For the next 15 years Bonaparte rules France, first as consul and then as emperor. November 1799 may thus be taken as the dividing point between the Wars of the French Revolution and the Napoleonic Wars.

January 1, 1800
Western Europe: Napoleonic Wars: War of the Second Coalition (continued): General military strategies for the spring of 1800. Britain and France remain at war on the seas. On land, the Austrians plan an offensive in Italy, where Field Marshal Baron Michael Melas with 100,000 men is to drive a French army of only 40,000 men under General André Masséna from the Riviera region of northwestern Italy. In Germany, General Paul Kray von Krajowa and 120,000 Austrian troops are to hold against any offensive by French general Jean Victor Moreau, who commands an army of equal size along the upper Rhine. Meanwhile, in the spring of 1800 Napoleon Bonaparte plans the second Italian campaign against Austria, the only continental power of weight holding out against France.

See Leaders: Moreau, Jean Victor Marie

French general Jean Victor Moreau (1763–1813) won a brilliant victory over the Austrians in the Battle of Hohenlinden on December 3, 1800. A jealous Napoleon Bonaparte later forced him into exile. (Chaiba Media)

January 28, 1800

North Africa: Egypt: Napoleonic Wars (continued): War of the Second Coalition (continued): Convention of El Arish. Following long negotiations, commander of the French Army of Egypt General Jean Baptiste Kléber, having concluded that the struggle in Egypt is irretrievably lost, arranges with the Turks, with the full concurrence of British commodore Sir William Sidney Smith (but without his signature), the Convention of El Arish. It provides for the evacuation of the French from positions in Egypt and withdrawal of all their forces to Alexandria, where they will be allowed free passage to France in ships provided by the Porte. The French are to be allowed to retain their arms, baggage, and equipment, with no restrictions on the men again fighting in any part of the world. The British government, however, instructs Vice Admiral George Keith Elphinstone,

Viscount Keith, commanding in the Mediterranean, that he is to permit no terms that do not end with the French laying down their arms and becoming prisoners of war.

March 8, 1800

Western Europe: France: Napoleonic Wars (continued): War of the Second Coalition (continued). French first consul Napoleon Bonaparte prepares to invade Italy from across the Alps, emulating Hannibal. Bonaparte hopes to catch the Austrians by surprise. Putting out the story (not true) that the constitution prohibits the first consul from going to war, he plans to cross the Alps and arrive in Italy at the rear of the Austrian army. Joining his 60,000-man Army of the Reserve at Dijon in early March, Bonaparte prepares it with special clothing and equipment.

March 20, 1800

North Africa: Egypt: Napoleonic Wars (continued): War of the Second Coalition (continued): Battle of Heliopolis. When Vice Admiral Lord Keith refuses to ratify the terms of the Convention of El Arish, commander of the French Army of Egypt general Jean Baptiste Kléber attacks a British-supported Turkish force at Heliopolis. Although he has no more than 10,000 men against a reported 60,000 Turks, Kléber defeats the Turks on March 20, 1800, then retakes Cairo, which had revolted against French rule.

April 6–20, 1800

Southern Europe: Italy: Napoleonic Wars (continued): War of the Second Coalition (continued): Austrian victories. French forces in northwestern Italy under General André Masséna are dispersed. Masséna has 27,000 men against Austrian field marshal Michael Melas with 51,000 men. Masséna personally commands 10,000 men besieged at Genoa by Austrian general Karl Ott with 21,000 men. Meanwhile, Melas and his remaining 30,000 men drive against French general Louis Gabriel Suchet and the rest of Masséna's 17,000 French troops beyond Nice in the Var Valley.

See Leaders: Masséna, André

May 15–30, 1800

Southern Europe: Italy: Napoleonic Wars (continued): War of the Second Coalition (continued): Bonaparte moves into Italy via the Alps. In mid-May

ITALY, 1800

Border of the Kingdom
of Italy, 1805

French territory

Controlled by France

Other territory

HELVETIAN
REPUBLIC
1798–1803

Geneva

TYROL
to Italy, 1810

AUSTRIA

Trent

46°N

VENETIA

Milan

Castlefranco

Trieste

PIEDMONT

CISALPINE
REPUBLIC

Venice

ISTRIA

Turin

Marengo

Mantua

FRANCE

Novi

PARMA

Bologna

Zara

44°N

Genoa

DALMATIA

OTTOMAN
EMPIRE

LIGURIAN
REPUBLIC
1797–1805

Lucca

Florence

Nice   Monaco

Pisa

Anacona

PAPAL
STATES

ETRURIA
1801–1808

Adriatic
Sea

Piombino

Elba

CORSICA
to France,
1768

Orbetello

ROMAN
REPUBLIC
1798–1799

ABRUZZI

42°N

Ajaccio

Rome

Pontecorvo

Gaëta

Benevento

Bari

Capua

PARTHENOPEAN
REPUBLIC
1798–1799

Naples

Brindisi

Salerno

Tyrrhenian
Sea

KINGDOM
OF
SARDINIA

40°N

Ionian
Sea

Cagliari

0   100 mi

0   100 km

Mediterranean   Sea

38°N

Trapani

Palermo

Messina

Reggio

Bizerta

KINGDOM
OF SICILY

Catania

Bône

Syracuse

Tunis

Pantelleria
(Sicily)

ALGERIA

MALTA
to France,
1798–1800

36°N   8°E   10°E   12°E   14°E   16°E   18°E

1800, Napoleon Bonaparte begins crossing the Alps with his Army of Reserve into Italy. By May 30 his army is on the Lombard Plain.

May–June 1800

Central Europe: Germany: Napoleonic Wars (continued): War of the Second Coalition (continued): French military operations against the Austrians in Germany. With his 120,000-man French Army of the Rhine, General Jean Victor Moreau makes steady progress, forcing Austrian general Paul Kray von Krajowa back into Bavaria. Moreau wins victories at Stockach on May 3, Möskirch on May 5, Ulm on May 16, and Hochstadt on June 19. Kray retires behind the Inn River, and Moreau advances on Munich.

June 2, 1800

Southern Europe: Italy: Napoleonic Wars (continued): War of the Second Coalition (continued): Bonaparte captures Milan. Moving quickly, French first consul Napoleon Bonaparte and his Army of Reserve capture the city of Milan. Restoring the Cisalpine Republic, Bonaparte moves on Lodi to prevent the Italians from reaching Mantua.

June 4, 1800

Southern Europe: Italy: Napoleonic Wars (continued): War of the Second Coalition (continued): Masséna surrenders Genoa. His army starving and having held out as long as he can, French general André Masséna takes advantage of favorable terms to quit the city under arms and on June 4, 1800, surrenders Genoa. Only 6,500 of his 10,000-man force survive. Austrian field marshal Michael Melas grants the terms so that he can garrison Genoa and concentrate on defeating the remaining French forces in Italy.

June 9, 1800

Southern Europe: Italy: Napoleonic Wars (continued): War of the Second Coalition (continued): Battle of Montebello. At Montebello in Lombardy, French general Jean Lannes, commanding a corps of 8,000 men, unexpectedly runs into Austrian general Karl Ott's army of 18,000 men moving north from Genoa. Joined by General Claude Victor's corps of 6,000 men, Lannes defeats Ott and drives him toward Alessandria.

See Leaders: Lannes, Jean

Jean Lannes (1769–1809) was one of the most capable of Emperor Napoleon's I marshals. Known as "the bravest of the brave," Lannes commanded a corps in the campaigns of 1805–1807 and captured Saragossa in Spain in 1809. He was mortally wounded later that same year during fighting against Austria. (Drawing by Jean Baptiste Guerin from *Life of Napoleon Bonaparte by William M. Sloane.* New York: Century Co., 1906, vol. 3.)

June 13, 1800

Western Europe: France. American Robert Fulton, employed by the French Directory, successfully tests his submarine, the *Nautilus,* in the Seine River at Paris.

> *See* Weapons: *Nautilus,* French Revolution Submarine

June 14, 1800

Southern Europe: Italy: Napoleonic Wars (continued): War of the Second Coalition (continued): Battle of Marengo. French first consul Napoleon Bonaparte hopes to catch Austrian forces under Field Marshal Michael Melas between his own army and that of General André Masséna, but although Masséna tries,

Engraving from May 1801 depicting the *Nautilus*, Robert Fulton's submarine built for the French government. (Photos.com)

he is unable to deliver his half-starved men. Undeterred, Bonaparte moves against Melas alone, with only 28,000 men, seeking a quick, decisive victory that will cement his political control of France. Melas meanwhile leaves 10,000 men in garrison at Genoa and concentrates 34,000 men at Alessandria, about halfway between Genoa and Milan.

Thinking that Melas is at Turin and not expecting the Austrians to stand and fight, Bonaparte separates his forces, sending two detachments totaling about 12,000 men to prevent the Austrians from escaping to Genoa (where they might be supplied by the British fleet) or to the Quadrilateral fortresses. He thus stumbles into Melas's numerically superior force at Alessandria. Bonaparte is heavily outnumbered, and his own army is widely dispersed.

At dawn on June 14 Melas and 34,000 Austrians fall on Bonaparte with only 15,000 men. Bonaparte is slow to realize the threat, but at about 10:00 a.m. he sends urgent appeals for his detached units to return. By 5:00 p.m. the Austrians have driven Bonaparte back some five miles, to the village of San Giuliano. The 71-year-old Melas, having sustained a minor wound early and believing that the battle won, retires to Alessandria and turns over command to his chief of staff General Anton Zach. The Austrians are strung out in pursuit formation.

At this point, French general Louis Charles Antoine Desaix arrives on the field with his corps and reportedly announces, "The battle is lost, but there is time to win another." When the French reorganize, Bonaparte orders an attack, and the French drive into the middle of the overconfident and disorganized Austrians. The Austrian front ranks fall back on the packed ranks to the rear, panicking the latter and turning the victory into a rout.

French casualties in the battle are 1,100 killed (including Desaix, who saved the day for Bonaparte), 3,600 wounded, and 900 captured. Austrian losses are 1,000 killed, 5,500 wounded, and 3,000 captured.

Convinced that his troops are too disorganized to continue the fight, Melas asks for an armistice, which Bonaparte grants on June 15. Bonaparte orders General Guillaume Marie Anne Brune to advance on Mantua and prevent the Austrians from seeking refuge there. On June 18 Bonaparte turns over the army to Masséna and returns to Paris. The fighting in Italy is over.

July 15–November 15, 1800

Central Europe: Germany: Napoleonic Wars (continued): War of the Second Coalition (continued). Following the French capture of Munich in July, French general Jean Victor Moreau and Austrian general

Paul Kray von Krajowa conclude an armistice. The Austrians rebuild their forces and, encouraged by a British subsidy, refuse to treat with Napoleon.

September 5, 1800

Mediterranean Sea: Malta: Napoleonic Wars (continued): War of the Second Coalition (continued): Malta taken by the British. An insurrection breaks out in Malta against the French led by General Claude Henri Belgrand de Vaubois. British rear admiral Horatio Nelson dispatches ships and men to assist the Maltese. Besieged at Valetta, the French are starved into surrender on September 5, 1800.

September 30, 1800

Western Europe: France: Quasi-War between France and the United States (continued): Convention of Mortefontaine. Worried that the United States might ally with Britain against France, French first consul Napoleon Bonaparte agrees to bring the Quasi-

War to a close. The resulting Treaty of Mortefontaine (also called the Convention of 1800) of September 30, 1800, ends hostilities between the two nations, restores normal diplomatic and commercial relations, and defers discussion of the alliance between the two states and American claims for the seizure of more than 830 ships. After congressional approval of the treaty, the two nations formally agree in 1801 that the alliance will be abrogated and that the United States will assume claims against France of up to $20 million.

December 3, 1800

Central Europe: Germany: Bavaria: Napoleonic Wars (continued): War of the Second Coalition (continued): Battle of Hohenlinden. At the beginning of December 1800, French general Jean Victor Moreau's Army of the Rhine of some 50,000 men is moving west in Bavaria, dispersed over a 30-mile front, when it encounters Archduke John's army of 64,000 men.

In a brilliant victory at Hohenlinden in Bavaria on December 3, 1800, French general Jean Victor Moreau defeated a numerically superior Austrian army commanded by Archduke John. (Historical Picture Archive/Corbis)

Moreau had assumed that he held the initiative and is therefore surprised when he comes under attack. John's chief of staff, Colonel Franz Weyrother, had convinced the archduke to go on the offensive.

Overwhelming Austrian numbers force French general Michel Ney and his 10,000 men into a fighting withdrawal from Ampfling on December 1. The Battle of Ampfling, however, costs the Austrians 3,070 casualties (1,077 prisoners) to only 1,707 (697 prisoners) for the French. These figures should have given John pause.

Believing that the French are in full retreat, Archduke John orders his forces, which are advancing west on parallel axes, to continue their movement toward München (Munich) and concentrate near Hohenlinden. John expects that if Moreau gives battle, the decisive encounter will occur the next day, near Haag, about eight miles east of Hohenlinden. Austrian patrols, however, discover that the French have

departed as the archduke pushes his principal column of some 22,000 men under Johann Kollowrat down the only hard-surface road, which runs through the Forest of Hohenlinden.

Weyrother, for his part, sends three smaller columns on parallel marches. One is just to the north under Maximilien Baillet with 11,000 men, another proceeds farther north just south of the Isen River (near present-day Erding, northeast of Munich) under Michael Kienmayer with 16,000 men, and the third column is to the south under Johann Riesch with 13,300 men. Moreau has 32,000 men in his main body, with two divisions to the south: one of 10,000 men under General Antoine Decaen and another of 8,400 under General Charles Richepence.

The Battle of Hohenlinden opens at about 7:00 a.m. on December 3 when Kollowrat's main body with the archduke and his staff comes under fire from French troops concealed in the forest on either side

BATTLE OF HOHENLINDEN, DECEMBER 3, 1800

Michel Ney (1769–1815), known as "the Bravest of the Brave," was one of Napoleon's most capable marshals. He displayed great courage, especially during the retreat from Moscow. His decision to rally to Napoleon in 1815, however, cost him his life. (Engraving by Gaildrau and Leguay, 19th c. The David Markham Collection.)

of the road. Moreau is able to concentrate the bulk of his forces against the Austrians, while John is unable to bring his own together in timely fashion. The Austrians nevertheless push forward. Ney and the forces of General Emmanuel de Grouchy to his right deserve great credit for the success of their two outnumbered divisions in repelling the main Austrian attack.

On the night of December 2 Moreau, aware of the broad outline of the Austrian plan, had ordered both Richepance and Decaen to flank the Austrian left with 18,000 men. Their attack late in the morning of December 3 now catches the Austrians by surprise and causes them to hesitate. Moreau, judging that the sudden collapse of Austrian momentum is the result of the flanking attack, now orders Grouchy and the rest of his forces to shift to the offensive. Under attack from the flank and the front, the more numerous Austrians withdraw in disorder. The limited road net and topography have both worked against an Austrian concentration of force.

The Austrians sustain some 13,500 casualties (1,750 taken prisoner) and lose 26 guns. The French probably lose 3,000 men and 1 gun. It is the greatest casualty ratio of any major battle of the Napoleonic Wars.

Moreau now moves southeast on Vienna. Another French force under General James Macdonald advances from Switzerland on the Tirol (Tyrol), while General Guillaume Marie Anne Brune moves up from Italy with a third army. Faced with these circumstances, on December 25 Austria sues for peace, in effect ending the War of the Second Coalition.

See Leaders: Ney, Michel

January 1, 1801
Northern Europe: United Kingdom. The Act of the Parliament of Great Britain and the Act of the Parliament of Ireland merge the Kingdom of Ireland with the Kingdom of Great Britain (itself a merger of the Kingdom of England and the Kingdom of Scotland) to create the United Kingdom of Great Britain and Ireland.

February 9, 1801
Central Europe: Napoleonic Wars (continued): War of the Second Coalition (continued): Treaty of Lunéville. This treaty between France and Austria reconfirms the provisions of the earlier treaties of Leoben and Campo Formio in 1797 and also practically dissolves the Holy Roman Empire. Austria cedes the left bank of the Rhine to France, the boundary being the middle of the river. The princes who lose lands in this are to be compensated elsewhere in Germany. Austria agrees to recognize the Batavian, Helvetian, Cisalpine, and Ligurian republics. Spain loses Parma and also cedes Louisiana to France, which then sells this vast territory to the United States in 1803.

February 1801

Northern Europe: Napoleonic Wars (continued): War of the Second Coalition (continued): Neutral League. In February 1801, following the Treaty of Lunéville (February 9) in which Austria is forced to sue for peace, Russia, Denmark, and Sweden (joined by Prussia in March) form the League of Armed Neutrality to protect their shipping against Britain. The British see this as a threat and decide on a show of force in the Baltic and, if necessary, a preemptive strike to break up the league.

March 2, 1801

North Africa: Egypt: Napoleonic Wars (continued): War of the Second Coalition (continued): Amphibious landing at Aboukir. A British fleet of 7 ships of the line and 12 smaller warships under Admiral Lord George Keith, lifting a British army of 16,150 men commanded by Lieutenant General Sir Ralph Abercromby, arrives in Aboukir Bay, Egypt, on March 2, 1801. That afternoon the troops begin going ashore. A total of 7,000 men, including a detachment of 1,000 seamen, defeat some 2,500 French troops under General Louis Friand. By the end of March 9, all the troops are ashore.

March 18, 1801

Northern Europe: Napoleonic Wars (continued): War of the Second Coalition (continued): Treaty of Florence. This treaty between France and the Kingdom of Naples gives the Neapolitan possession in central Italy and the island of Elba to France. Naples also agrees to the stationing of French troops in a number of Italian towns and to close its harbors to British and Turkish shipping.

March 21, 1801

North Africa: Egypt: Napoleonic Wars (continued): War of the Second Coalition (continued): Battle of Alexandria. Some 16,000 British troops, having landed at Aboukir, begin their advance on Alexandria on March 12. French forces, now numbering about 7,000 men, attack the British at Mandora on March 13 but are defeated, suffering about 750 killed or wounded. On March 18 Aboukir castle surrenders, and a Turkish squadron arrives. That same evening, French reinforcements under General Jacques Abdallah Menou arrive at Alexandria from Cairo, bringing the size of the French force opposing the British to about 14,000 men.

On March 21 the French launch a predawn attack at Alexandria. In the ensuing battle the French are defeated, sustaining some 1,500–3,000 casualties. British losses are 1,468. British commander Lieutenant General Sir Ralph Abercromby is mortally wounded by a musket ball to the thigh.

March–September 1801

North Africa: Egypt: Napoleonic Wars (continued): War of the Second Coalition (continued): British conquest of Egypt. Following their victory over the French in the Battle of Alexandria, the British proceed to conquer the rest of Egypt as units of the British and Turkish navies operate in conjunction with the army. General Jean Baptiste Kléber, commander of the French Army of Egypt, is stabbed to death by a Syrian student in Cairo on June 14 and is succeeded by General Jacques Abdallah Menou. The British take Cairo on June 27.

Although London has now decided to permit implementation of the Convention of El Arish, signed by Kléber 19 months earlier, Menou opposes this as shameless. Not until after additional bloodshed and the surrender of Alexandria on September 2 following a siege does Menou agree to the same terms. The French survivors are repatriated in cartels sent from France. In all, of Napoleon Bonaparte's original 34,000-man Army of Egypt and 16,000 French Navy sailors and marines abandoned in Egypt, few more than 25,000 return to France, and 5,000 of these are invalids. Egypt is now restored to Ottoman control.

One of the by-products of the Egyptian venture is, however, the discovery of a stone relief at Rosetta (Rashid), at the mouth of the Nile. French scientists accompany the relief, known as the Rosetta Stone, to Britain. The Rosetta Stone, which has resided in the British Museum since 1802, is written in three scripts, including ancient Greek and Egyptian hieroglyphs, and enables the deciphering of the latter and the unlocking of the secrets of ancient Egyptian civilization.

April 2, 1801

Northern Europe: Napoleonic Wars (continued): War of the Second Coalition (continued): Denmark: Battle of Copenhagen. Trade with the Baltic has long been important to Britain. This trade includes grain imports, but the Royal Navy also relies on the Baltic for timber and naval supplies, especially flax, which

BATTLE OF COPENHAGEN, APRIL 2, 1801

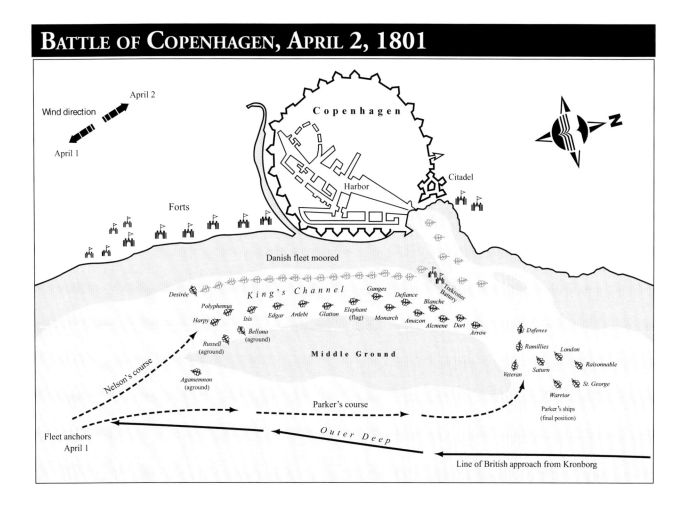

is used in the production of both sails and rope. Thus, in 1800 when Czar Paul of Russia abandons the war against France and moves to create a pro-French Armed Neutrality of the North, the British are alarmed. London regards the matter as sufficiently important to warrant military action.

The immediate problem arises with Denmark and its claimed right to convoy its merchant shipping through the British blockade without being subject to search. On July 25, 1800, a small British squadron brings a Danish convoy into port to search it for contraband. Pressured by the presence of a British squadron off Copenhagen, the Danes agree to allow their convoys to be searched. Although both the British and Danish governments declare themselves satisfied, the event pushes Denmark closer to Russia.

In December 1800, having learned of the British seizure of Malta to which Czar Paul had pretensions, Russia embargoes all British ships and signs a naval convention with Sweden in which the two powers re-

vive the Armed Neutrality of 1780 that would have allowed noncontraband goods, including timber and flax, to pass to France. In February 1801 after French first consul Napoleon Bonaparte has forced Austria to sue for peace in the Treaty of Lunéville, Russia expands the Armed Neutrality to include Prussia and Denmark, whereupon the British government decides on a show of force and, if necessary, a preemptive strike to break up the league.

Admiral Sir Hyde Parker receives command of the Baltic expedition. Vice Admiral Horatio Nelson, recently returned from the Mediterranean, is second-in-command. In March, Denmark embargoes British shipping, and its forces occupy both Hamburg and Lübeck. The only question now for the British is whether to descend on Denmark or to move up the Baltic against the source of the problem and attack the Russian fleet at Reval (Tallinn) while the remainder of Russian ships are icebound at Kronstadt. This would be the boldest, most certain course, but the cautious Parker rejects it in favor of a descent on Denmark.

Parker sails from Yarmouth on March 12 with 53 ships—20 of them ships of the line—and nearly two regiments of ground troops. The British have sent a diplomatic mission ahead, so the Danes have some idea of British intentions and time to prepare. Even on his arrival, Parker delays for a week, giving the Danes additional time.

Nelson asks to lead an assault on Copenhagen. On April 1 Parker agrees, giving him 30 ships including 10 smaller ships of the line, a 54- and a 50-gun ship, and 7 bomb vessels. Parker remains well offshore with 8 ships of the line, including the 98-gun ships *London* and *St. George.*

At dawn on April 2, taking advantage of a favorable southerly wind, Nelson's ships weigh anchor to attack. Noting that the Danish line is strongest in the north, close to a large land battery, Nelson decides on an attack from the south. It begins at 9:30 a.m. Danish commodore Johan Fischer commands 18 warships, armed hulks, and floating batteries that are moored north and south, paralleling the shore over about a mile and a half, all supported by several shore batteries.

From the start, things go badly for the British. Lacking adequate charts or pilots, 1 ship of the line grounds before the action begins. Two others ground on the other side of the channel at extreme range. The other 9 capital ships then close to relatively long range of about a cable length (240 yards) and engage the Danish ships and shore batteries. (Subsequently, the British learn that they might have improved their gunnery effectiveness by bringing their ships in much closer and even doubled the Danish ships, as at the Nile.)

Clearly Nelson has underestimated the Danish defenses, which are fought with great gallantry and effectiveness. The result is a long, slow slugfest, but following three hours of combat that includes even Nelson's frigates, superior British gunnery begins to tell. Parker, about four miles away with his larger ships of the line and very slow to close, now signals a recall to all ships.

Nelson ignores the order. Had it been carried out, it would probably have turned victory into disaster, for the only way for Nelson's ships to withdraw was up the channel and across the undefeated northern Danish defenses (indeed, two British ships of the line ground there after the cease-fire). An angry Nelson reportedly turns to his flag captain and remarks, "You know, Foley, I have only one eye, and I have a right to be blind sometimes." Placing the telescope to that blind eye, he remarks, "I really do not see the signal." Nelson's captains copy their commander and also refuse to disengage.

By 1:30 p.m., although several British ships are flying distress signals, Nelson has disabled a dozen Danish ships, including Fischer's flagship, and overwhelmed the southern shore defenses of Copenhagen. Nelson is thus in position to bring up his bomb vessels to shell the city. The Danes agree to a cease-fire an hour later.

Human casualties in the battle are heavy and approximately equal; of Nelson's battles only Trafalgar is fought at greater human cost. Copenhagen is also Nelson's most difficult battle, that in which he comes closest to defeat, but it stands as one of the three most remarkable of his victories at sea, along with the Nile and Trafalgar.

Nelson negotiates directly with Danish crown prince Frederick. On April 9, faced with a British threat to bombard Copenhagen, the Danes agree to a truce of 14 weeks. Denmark agrees to take no action under the Treaty of Armed Neutrality and also grants the British the right to secure water, food, and supplies from shore. (Nelson had demanded a truce of 16 weeks, sufficient time for the British fleet to deal with the Russians.)

The Battle of Copenhagen was unnecessary. Nelson understood from the start that Russia was the real enemy. He had wanted to descend on the Russians at Tallinn, leaving only a squadron to keep the Danes in check. Had this course of action been followed, the British would have discovered that Czar Paul had been assassinated on March 24 and that his successor, Alexander I, had changed policies. Indeed, news of this event, received at Copenhagen by the Danes in the course of the negotiations, enables them to conclude an agreement more satisfactory to their position. The Armed Neutrality now breaks up, and by June 1801 British trade in the Baltic is again moving without threat of hindrance.

May 14, 1801

North Africa: Tripoli: Tripolitan-American War. The Tripolitan-American War (1801–1805) occurs between Tripoli (present-day Libya) and the United

States and is known in the United States as the Tripolitan War or the Barbary Wars. U.S. independence in 1783 removes the protection of the British Royal Navy for American seaborne trade, which now comes under assault in the Mediterranean from the corsairs of the Barbary states of Tripoli, Tunis, Algiers, and Morocco. U.S. ships are seized, and American seamen are held for ransom. The U.S. government resorts to paying tribute, believing that this is cheaper than building and maintaining a navy. Treaties also establish consulates in Tangier, Algiers, Tunis, and Tripoli.

The United States fails to meet the promised payments, though, and in October 1800 bashaw of Tripoli Yusuf Karamanli demands a new treaty and an increase in the payment. When this is not forthcoming, on May 14, 1801, he orders the U.S. consulate flagpole chopped down, beginning hostilities with the United States. Unaware of this event but nonetheless anticipating hostilities, in June 1801 U.S. president Thomas Jefferson sends Commodore Richard Dale and a squadron of four warships to the Mediterranean. Over the next two years the United States makes only halfhearted efforts to bring the war to a conclusion.

Dale arrives in the Mediterranean in July to find war under way. Beginning offensive operations, he lacks the requisite force and orders an end to the conflict. Dale returns to the United States in his flagship in March 1802, leaving three warships on station.

Meanwhile, in February 1802 Congress authorizes force against Tripoli. That May, a second squadron of six ships under Commodore Richard V. Morris arrives off Gibraltar, giving the United States nine ships in the Mediterranean. Morocco also declares war on the United States but takes no hostile action. Morris restores peace with Morocco in August, but he spends most of his time at Gibraltar, 1,000 miles from Tripoli, which he is supposedly blockading. Morris also negotiates with Tunis, which is threatening war. Not until May 27, 1803, does Morris lead a poorly conceived attack against Tripoli, after which he concludes that a blockade of that place is unfeasible. Morris is called home that summer for his lack of accomplishment.

July 6 and 13, 1801

Western Mediterranean Sea: Napoleonic Wars (continued): War of the Second Coalition (continued): Battles of Algeciras. In mid-June 1801 French rear admiral Charles Alexandre Durand, Comte de Linois, sails from Toulon with three ships of the line and a frigate for Cádiz, where he is to join up with six French ships of the line, newly acquired from Spain, and six Spanish ships of the line under Vice Admiral Don Juan J. De Moreno. Learning of the presence of a British squadron of six ships of the line under Rear Admiral Sir James Saumarez, Linois puts into Algeciras. On July 6 Saumarez locates the French and attacks the French ships in the harbor, but one of his ships, the *Hannibal* of 74 guns, grounds and is captured.

Saumarez is successful a week later, on July 13, when he again attacks Algeciras, this time with five ships of the line and three smaller ships against the Spanish and French force of nine ships of the line and four smaller warships. One Spanish ship, the *Real Carlos* of 112 guns, catches fire and blows up. It sets fire to the other Spanish ship of like size, the *San Hermenegildo,* which also blows up. Only 300 of their combined crews of 1,700 men survive. One other ship is captured. The rest escape to Cádiz. The English have only one ship of the line badly damaged.

July 15, 1801

Western Europe: France: Concordat between France and the Catholic Church. Upon coming to power in France, First Consul Napoleon Bonaparte seeks to secure an understanding with the papacy in order to end the major breach caused by the Civil Constitution of the Clergy, the primary fuel for counterrevolutionary activity in France. Discussions proceed between representatives of Bonaparte and Pope Pius VII. Agreement is reached on July 15, 1801, following Bonaparte's victory over Austria and the conclusion of the Treaty of Lunéville and the Treaty of Florence. The pope is confirmed in possession of the Papal States, without Ferrara, Bologna, and the Romagna. The agreement also defines the status of the Roman Catholic Church in France. It recognizes the Roman Catholic faith as the religion of the "great majority" of the French people but not as the established religion of the state, thus retaining freedom of worship for Protestants and Jews. Bonaparte secures the right to nominate bishops, but they are to be confirmed by the pope. The government also undertakes to pay the salaries of the clergy, who now take an oath of allegiance to the state. The Church recognizes the confiscation of its property in 1790. The Concordat remains in effect until 1905 and does much to bridge the religious divide in France and bring to an end most of the counterrevolutionary agitation.

January 20, 1802

Caribbean Basin: Hispaniola: Haiti: French effort to reconquer Haiti. In 1797 François-Dominique Toussaint Louverture, a black of great military ability, leads the blacks of Haiti to victory, abolishes slavery, and establishes himself as dictator. He then expels the French. The French Directory considers a military expedition to take back Haiti but is stymied by the ongoing war with Britain. With the conclusion of the preliminary Peace of Amiens, however, First Consul Napoleon Bonaparte reactivates the project and appoints his brother-in-law, General Charles Victor Emmanuel Leclerc, to command the 25,000-man expedition.

The first troops come ashore on January 20, 1802, and the French soon control most of the south and the coastal towns. On May 7 Toussaint Louverture capitulates on the pledge of continued freedom for blacks. Three weeks later, Leclerc orders him seized. Accused of plotting an uprising, Toussaint and his family are sent to France, where Toussaint is confined and repeatedly interrogated. He dies of pneumonia in April 1803.

March 27, 1802

Western Europe: France: Napoleonic Wars (continued): War of the Second Coalition (continued): Treaty of Amiens. After the withdrawal of William Pitt (the Younger) from the cabinet, the British government reaches agreement with France. The Treaty of Amiens of March 27, 1802, ends hostilities between France and Britain and brings to a close the War of the Second Coalition. Britain returns to France and its allies all territories it has taken except for Trindad, ceded by Spain, and Ceylon (present-day Sri Lanka), which is ceded by the Batavian Republic (the Netherlands). France recognizes the Republic of the Seven Ionian Islands, and Malta is to be restored to the Order of the Knights of Malta. At the same time, peace is restored between France and the Ottoman Empire.

June–November 1802

Caribbean Basin: Haiti: French effort to reconquer Haiti (continued): Deterioration in the French military situation. In June 1802 French first consul Napoleon Bonaparte instructs his commander in Haiti, General Charles Victor Emmanuel Leclerc, to restore the former colonial system and slavery, violating a pledge made by Leclerc to black Haitian leader François-Dominique Toussaint Louverture. Blacks under Jean Jacques Desalines then resume fighting. By August, resistance to the French has sharply increased; by late October the French control only the larger cities. Leclerc dies of yellow fever in early November, one of many Frenchmen felled by the disease.

August 2, 1802

Western Europe: France. Napoleon Bonaparte is named consul for life with the right to name his successor.

October 1802

South Asia: India: Maratha Civil War. Baji Rao II, hereditary peshwa of the Maratha Confederacy, is defeated and overthrown by his nominal subordinate, Yaswant Rao Holkar of Indore, in the Battle of Poona on October 25, 1802. Holkar rejects a British demand that their ally, Baji Rao, be restored to the throne.

1802–1803

South Asia: Ceylon: British operations against Kandy. Although the British conquered coastal areas of Ceylon (present-day Sri Lanka) from the Dutch in 1796, they do not control the interior of the country. In 1802 they mount an expedition there against Kandy (Maha Nuvara). The British take the city but are driven out the next year.

1802–1812

Southeast Asia: Cambodia: Joint Siamese-Vietnamese protectorate over Cambodia. During much of the first half of the 19th century, Siam and Vietnam vie over who will control Cambodia. Cambodian king Ang Chan tries to play one power against the other and ends up paying tribute to each.

March 1803–1805

South Asia: India: Second Anglo-Maratha War. Angered by Yaswant Rao Holkar of Indore's refusal to return the throne of the Maratha Confederacy to their ally, the incompetent Baji Rao II, the British East India Company concludes in December the Treaty of

Bassein with Baji Rao. He agrees to cede territory to the British in return for military assistance in recovering his throne.

The treaty angers a number of the peshwa's powerful subordinate rulers, who repudiate it, beginning the Second Anglo-Maratha War (1803–1805). The British commander in chief in India, Lieutenant General Lord Gerard Lake, and Major General Sir Arthur Wellesley (younger brother of British governor-general in India Marquis Richard Wellesley and later the Duke of Wellington) carry out successful offensives in Hindustan and the Deccan, respectively.

Peace is concluded in 1805 under the terms of which the British acquire Orissa and portions of western Gujarat and Bundelkhand from the Maratha Confederacy, which then receives a free hand in much of central India. The rulers of Sindh ally with the British and retain control over much of Rajasthan.

March 20, 1803
South Asia: India: Second Anglo-Maratha War (continued): Deccan Campaign: Capture of Poona. Major General Sir Arthur Wellesley leads some 9,000 British East India Company regulars and 5,000 native troops into the Deccan, capturing the capital of Poona on March 20, 1803, and restoring Peshwa Baji Rao II. When the Sindh army refuses to withdraw, Wellesley proceeds deeper into Maratha territory.

April 1803
Caribbean Basin: Hispaniola: Haiti: French effort to reconquer Haiti (continued). The arrival of reinforcements gives the French their best chance of military success, but the next month the war between Britain and France is renewed. The French forces are now largely cut off and suffer increasingly from a lack of supplies and disease. Most French troops surrender to the British in November 1803, although some hold out on the Spanish side of the island of Hispaniola (Santo Domingo) until 1809.

May 2, 1803
North America: United States: Louisiana Purchase. With the failure of Napoleon Bonaparte's project to reconquer Haiti and revive the French empire in the Western Hemisphere, President Thomas Jefferson arranges to purchase the Louisiana Territory from France. The treaty is signed on May 2, 1803, but antedated to April 30. The purchase price is 60 million

francs (approximately $15 million), and the 828,000 square miles of territory doubles the territorial size of the United States.

May 16, 1803
Western Europe: Napoleonic Wars (continued): War resumes between France and Britain. Dissension increases when Napoleon Bonaparte is unwilling to make concessions, leading to war between France and Britain during 1803–1805. The Treaty of Amiens, which was disadvantageous to Britain, might not have lasted in any case, but Bonaparte gives it no chance, annexing Piedmont, Elba, and part of Switzerland to France and failing to implement his promise in the Treaty of Amiens to negotiate a trade agreement with Britain. Bonaparte also alarms the British by sending troops to Haiti.

Britain, on its part, refuses to evacuate Malta, which it was supposed to have accomplished under the terms of the Treaty of Amiens. In April 1803 the British withdraw their ambassador from Paris and resume the war at sea, without benefit of a formal declaration of war. Fighting formally resumes with a British declaration of war on May 16, 1803. French troops occupy King George III's possession of Hanover, which they ravage. Bonaparte also gathers several thousand vessels of all types along the coast and creates a large camp at Boulogne for the 200,000-man Army of England (the future Grande Armée) and a supposed invasion. That, however, depends on at least brief French control of the English Channel.

September 4, 1803
South Asia: India: Second Anglo-Maratha War (continued): Hindustan Campaign: Capture of Aligarh. Simultaneous with Major General Sir Arthur Wellesley's campaign against Maratha in the Deccan, the British make their major effort in Hindustan under commander in chief in India Lieutenant General Lord Gerald Lake. His so-called Grand Army numbers some 10,500 men, most of them native troops of the British East India Company. As with Wellesley, Lake is heavily outnumbered. The Maratha army opposing him contains perhaps 43,000 men with 464 guns. It is commanded by French adventurer Pierre Cuillier Perron. Other Frenchmen serve under him, and the army has undergone some European-style training.

Despite this, Lake captures the walled city of Aligarh on September 4. Maratha casualties are unknown, but the British side suffers 260 killed or wounded.

September 12, 1803

North Africa: Tripolitan-American War (continued). U.S. Navy commodore Edward Preble arrives at Gibraltar on September 12, 1803, and for the first time in the war the Americans carry out effective offensive action against Tripoli. Not only does he blockade Tripoli, but Preble also demonstrates before Tangier, forcing Morocco to maintain the peace. At the same time, American warships endeavor to hunt down the Tripolitan corsairs.

September 16, 1803

South Asia: India: Second Anglo-Maratha War (continued): Battle of Delhi. Following the capture of Aligarh in Hindustan on September 4, British commander in chief in India Lieutenant General Lord Gerald Lake sets his Grand Army in motion toward Delhi. En route, French adventurer Pierre Cuillier Perron, commander of the Maratha army, and a number of his subordinates desert and ride into the British lines to surrender. Louis Bourquien takes over as the senior foreign officer in the Maratha army.

Battle is joined between the two sides before Delhi on September 16. Lake is again victorious. Maratha casualties are again heavy but unknown, although the British capture 63 guns and considerable baggage. Lake occupies the city of Delhi and then pushes on after the retreating Marathas, toward Agra.

September 23, 1803

South Asia: India: Second Anglo-Maratha War (continued): Deccan Campaign (continued): Battle of Assaye. Pushing deeper into Maratha territory, British and native forces under Major General Sir Arthur Wellesley capture Ahmadnagar on August 11. Wellesley then proceeds to the junction of the Jua and Kelna rivers, where he discovers the combined armies of Sindh and the raja of Berar. Wellesley faces heavy odds. His enemies have some 20,000 infantry, 30,000 cavalry, and 100 guns. He has only 4,500 infantry and 2,000 cavalry, supported by 20 guns. The remainder of his force is beyond supporting range.

In the Battle of Assaye, which takes place near Jafrabad on September 23, 1803, Wellesley's men

discover an unprotected ford over the Kelna River. They cross the river and then attack the Sindhian army, which turns its flank to meet them. Although Wellesley's troops are greatly outnumbered, their superior discipline tells, and they break the Sindhian line. The Maratha cavalry then strike the British force from both flanks. Wellesley's cavalry engage and defeat the Maratha cavalry, however, and the Sindh army panics and flees.

The Sindh army has suffered 1,200 dead, 4,800 wounded, and 98 guns lost. Wellesley's losses are also heavy: some 428 killed and 1,156 wounded.

October 31, 1803

North Africa: Tripolitan-American War (continued): Loss of the *Philadelphia*. Captain William Bainbridge, commander of the frigate *Philadelphia*, which while rated a 38 guns actually mounts 44 guns and is the second most powerful warship in U.S. commodore Edward Preble's Mediterranean squadron, chases after a Tripolitan ship close to shore, grounding the frigate on an uncharted reef. Following unsuccessful efforts to free his ship and an engagement with Tripolitan gunboats that emerge from the harbor, Bainbridge surrenders, having taken only ineffective actions to scuttle the ship. The Tripolitans take the American crew prisoner, refloat the ship, and tow it into Tripoli Harbor, where they begin repairs with the intention of adding it to their navy.

November 1, 1803

South Asia: India: Second Anglo-Maratha War (continued): Hindustan Campaign (continued): Battle of Laswari. Following his victory in the Battle of Delhi in September, British commander in chief in India Lieutenant General Lord Gerald Lake moves south with his Grand Army of some 10,000 men to capture Agra. In the Battle of Laswari, the two sides are close in numbers. Lake commands something less than 10,000 men, while the Sindh army consists of 9,000 veteran infantry and 5,000 cavalry.

The Marathas form a defensive line behind cannon chained together. Lake attacks with his cavalry, which penetrates the line, but the Maratha infantry fight well until the arrival in time of Lake's own infantry, who carry the day. British losses in the battle are 834 killed or wounded. Maratha losses are unknown but are presumed to have been on the order of 7,000 men. The British also capture 72 guns and a large number of stores. Sindh sues for peace on December 20, 1803.

November 28, 1803
South Asia: India: Second Anglo-Maratha War (continued): Deccan Campaign (continued): Battle of Argaon. The concluding battle of the Deccan Campaign occurs at Argaon (Adgaon), a village some 32 miles north of Akola near Akot, on November 28, 1803. The Sindh army makes a final stand here. The outcome of the battle is in jeopardy when three of British major general Sir Arthur Wellesley's battalions break, but Wellesley rallies them, and the British and their native allies win the battle.

The Maratha suffer the loss of all their guns and baggage. Maratha casualties are unknown, but the British side suffers 346 killed or wounded. This British victory concludes the Deccan Campaign and establishes Wellesley's military reputation.

January 1, 1804
Caribbean Basin: Haiti: Independence of Haiti proclaimed. Black leader Jean Jacques Dessalines, leader of the latter stage of the resistance to the French, becomes governor-general-for-life of Haiti. On September 22, 1804, he proclaims himself emperor and crowns himself Jacques I on October 6. A former slave himself, he endeavors to keep the sugar plantations in production without slavery. He also orders the massacre of all remaining whites. He is in turn assassinated on October 17, 1806.

January 1804
Southwest Asia: Russo-Persian War: Russian invasion of Persia. In 1800 Russia annexes Georgia. The Persians then provide aid to those resisting the Russians, who in turn decide to punish the Persians. In January 1804 Russian forces under General Paul Tsitsianov (Sisianoff) invade Persia and storm the citadel of Ganjeh, beginning the Russo-Persian War (1804–1813). Tsitsianov renames Elizavetpol and joins it to Georgia. He then advances on Yerevan (Erivan).

February 16, 1804
North Africa: Tripolitan-American War (continued): Destruction of the *Philadelphia.* Concerned that the captured American frigate *Philadelphia,* once repaired, will shift the naval balance of power in favor of Tripoli, U.S. Mediterranean Squadron commander Commodore Edward Preble authorizes a daring at-

Stephen Decatur Jr. (1779–1820) was the youngest person to achieve the rank of captain in the history of the U.S. Navy. He became a national hero in the Tripolitan-American War and went on to distinguish himself in the War of 1812. (Library of Congress)

tempt to destroy the ship, now riding at anchor under the protection of shore batteries in Tripoli Harbor. Lieutenant Stephen Decatur leads the successful effort with 83 volunteers on the evening of February 16, 1804, in the *Intrepid* (formerly the Tripolitan *Mastico*), firing the frigate without the loss of a single man. Decatur is later advanced to captain for the deed, becoming (at age 25) the youngest captain in the history of the U.S. Navy.

See Leaders: Decatur, Stephen, Jr.

March 4–5, 1804
Australasia: Australia: Irish Convict Rebellion. The British government establishes New South Wales in 1788 as a penal colony ruled by a military governor. Many of the convicts sent to Australia are Irish political prisoners, deported after the Irish Rebellion of

1798. On March 4 some 400 convicts rise up in what becomes known as the Irish Convict Rebellion (or the Castle Hill Rising).

The rebels seize the New South Wales convict station at Parramatta, about 10 miles from Castle Hill. The next day, 57 members of the New South Wales Corps and a few local settlers attempt to negotiate with the convicts; when this fails, they open fire. The convicts suffer 15 dead and many wounded. The rebel leader, Philip Cunningham, is captured that same day and immediately hanged. Eight other convicts are later tried and hanged, and others are flogged.

March 21, 1804

Western Europe: France: Conspiracy against Bonaparte and murder of the Duc d'Enghien. In February 1804 Napoleon's minister of police Joseph Fouché uncovers a plot led by former French general Charles Pichegru and Georges Caudoual to assassinate First Consul Napoleon Bonaparte and replace him with a "prince of the blood." In a major mistake, Bonaparte orders the arrest in Baden of the Duc d'Enghien, the presumed but unnamed Bourbon prince to be placed on the throne after the assassination of Napoleon. French troops invade that independent state, arrest the entirely innocent d'Enghien, and transport him to France. There, without benefit of normal legal process, he is tried by a military tribunal and shot at Vincennes early on March 21. The deed arouses a wave of horror and anger at Bonaparte throughout Europe. Bonaparte meanwhile uses the plot on his life to move against all opposition, presumed or real. General Jean Victor Moreau, whom Bonaparte sees as a rival, flees to America.

April 1804

South Asia: India: Second Anglo-Maratha War (continued): British declaration of war against Indore. With Yaswant Rao Holkar, ruler of Indore in the Maratha Confederacy, intriguing against the British and encouraging Sindh and Bhonsle to rise up against their British overlords, governor-general in India Marquis Richard C. Wellesley makes preparations and then declares war on Indore in April 1804.

June 1804

Southwest Asia: Russo-Persian War (continued): Battle of Echmiadzin. Following the Russian invasion and capture of Ganjeh, Persian ruler Fath Ali Shah orders the governor of Azerbaijan, his 15-year-old son and heir apparent Prince Abbas Mirza, to assemble an army and defeat the Russians. The result is a three-day battle near Echmiadzin, the capital of Armenia. The able Abbas Mirza with 20,000 men forces the Russian army of 5,000 men led by General Paul Tsitsianov (Sisianoff) to withdraw. The Persian army then disbands for the winter.

August 24–30, 1804

South Asia: India: Second Anglo-Maratha War (continued): Monson's retreat. With Britain at war with Indore, British commander in chief in India Lieutenant General Lord Gerald Lake commences military operations, but after several months of skirmishes and demonstrating contempt for his enemy and not much military sense, in June Lake suspends military operations. Believing that he has Yaswant Rao Holkar, ruler of Indore, contained and that the Maratha army is disintegrating, Lake withdraws the main body of his army to cantonments in Agra and Kanpur, leaving Lieutenant Colonel William Monson and a mixed force of about 10,000 men to guard the passes of Bundi and Lakheri south of Tonk Rampura in order to hold Holkar's forces in Malwa. Encouraged by local support and perhaps lured forward by Holkar, in June Monson decides to advance to Khatowli on the other side of the Mokundra Pass, some 30 miles south of Kotah.

Holkar attacks Monson there in early July and forces him to retire, then strikes him in full force at the swollen Banas River beginning on August 24. Forced to abandon his baggage, his wounded, and later all of his guns and equipment, Monson carries out a fighting retreat all the way to Agra, which he reaches on August 30.

Following this withdrawal of some 250 miles during almost two months, only a few hundred men remain of Monson's original force of more than 10,000 (not counting reinforcements). This allows Holkar to advance to and threaten Delhi in September.

August 1804

North Africa: Tripolitan-American War (continued): Preble's operations against Tripoli. After quieting a restive Tunis, which was also threatening war with the United States, in May 1804 commander of the U.S. squadron in the Mediterranean Commodore Edward Preble secures the loan of two bomb ketches and six gunboats from Naples. Following the failure of negotiations with Tripoli, the aggressive Preble attacks Tripoli proper on August 3, 7, and 28, shelling the city's defenses and engaging some of its gunboats. The Americans capture three Tripolitan gunboats while losing one of their own to the explosion of its magazine. Preble returns home in September, succeeded by Captain Samuel Barron.

October 1, 1804
South Asia: India: Second Anglo-Maratha War (continued): Lake's relief of Delhi. Yaswant Rao Holkar, ruler of Indore, advances with his troops on Delhi. British commander in chief in India Lieutenant General Lord Gerald Lake orders his forces to leave their summer monsoon cantonments and march to Delhi, relieving it on October 1.

October 2, 1804
Western Europe: Napoleonic Wars (continued): War between France and Britain (continued). British Royal Navy captain Sidney Smith leads a raid with fire and explosion ships against the mouth of the Rhine, destroying a number of ships in the putative invasion fleet anchored there. Elsewhere, British naval units keep the French from concentrating their fleet for any cross-Channel attempt.

November 17, 1804
South Asia: India: Second Anglo-Maratha War (continued): Battle of Farrukhabad. Following his relief of Delhi, British commander in chief in India General Lord Gerard Lake pursues the Maratha cavalry with his own horsemen during a 17-day period, covering 350 miles and defeating the Maratha army under Yaswant Rao Holkar, ruler of Indore, at both Deeg on November 13 (where the British capture 84 guns) and Farrukhabad on November 17. Holkar flees into the Punjab.

December 2, 1804
Western Europe: France: Bonaparte crowned emperor. Napoleon Bonaparte summons Pope Pius VII to France for the coronation ceremony but, in a fitting gesture, takes the crown from the pope and crowns himself, as Emperor Napoleon I. The Crown is to be hereditary in the male line, with Napoleon having the right to adopt the children of his brothers. In default of this, the Crown will pass to his brothers. Napoleon's elevation is confirmed by a supposed popular vote of more than 3.5 million to 2,569. Despite trappings of representative institutions, Napoleon in effect restores a royal absolutist state in France but one of greatly increased administrative efficiency.

1804–1810
West Africa: Fulani War. The Fulani War of 1804–1810, which occurs in the area of present-day Nigeria and Cameroon, is also known as the Fulani Jihad or Jihad of Usman dan Fodio. The war results from the proclamation of a jihad (holy war) by Islamic reformer Usman dan Fodio. Expelled from Gobir by his former student Yunfa, Usman assembles a Fulani army that also includes many Hausa people to wage war against Gobir and the other Hausa kingdoms of the north under the promise of a renewal of Islam.

Initially the Hausa kingdoms enjoy military success, including victory in the Battle of Tsuntua in December 1804 in which Usman loses more than 2,000 men. In 1805, however, taking advantage of popular discontent caused by famine and heavy taxation, Usman's forces seize Kebbi and Gwandu. Then in 1808 the jihadists capture Gobir's capital of Alkalawa and kill Yunfa.

As a consequence of his military victories, Usman forms the Fulani Empire. His success inspires other would-be West African jihadists.

1804–1813
Central Europe: Balkans: Serbian insurrection. Serbian nationalists led by George Petrovich, known as Kara George, rebel against the Ottoman Turks, force the Turks from Belgrade, and proclaim the independence of Serbia in December 1806. Unfortunately for the Serbs, their independent state comes crashing down following a pact between the Russian and Ottoman governments in 1812. Ottoman armies then reoccupy Serbia, and Kara George and his followers take to the mountains.

January 1805
Western Europe: Napoleonic Wars (continued): War between France and Britain (continued): Spain joins the war on the side of France. Under the terms of the alliance, Spain agrees to provide no fewer than 25 ships of the line and 11 frigates by mid-March. The French and Spanish hope to concentrate their naval resources for a brief mastery of the English Channel and an invasion of England. Spain has 62 ships

of the line at the ports of Coruna, Ferrol, Cádiz, and Cartagena. A similar number of British ships of the line blockade the Spanish, with instructions that if the blockaded ships break free and avoid destruction, the blockaders are to fall back on the English Channel and add their resources to those of Admiral William Cornwallis and the Channel Fleet.

January–April 1805
South Asia: India: Second Anglo-Maratha War (continued): Siege of Bhurtpore. Following his victory over the Maratha army of Yaswant Rao Holkar, ruler of Indore, in the Battle of Farrukhabad on November 17, British general Lord Gerard Lake advances to the city of Bhurtpore, which he invests on January 1. Lake mounts four unsuccessful assaults on the city, all commanded by Lieutenant Colonel William Monson and all defeated. Lake lifts the siege in April. The attempts to take Bhurtpore cost the British 103 officers and 3,100 men.

March–July 1805
Eastern Atlantic Ocean: Napoleonic Wars (continued): War between France and Britain (continued): Background to the Battle of Trafalgar. French emperor Napoleon I plans to secure mastery of the English Channel long enough to transfer his 200,000-man Army of England. In the spring of 1805 Napoleon, who does not understand naval warfare, orders a deception that he hopes will cause the British to leave the Channel unprotected. He orders Admiral Pierre Charles Villeneuve's fleet at Toulon and Spanish naval units under Admiral Federico Carlos de Gravina to sail to the West Indies, drawing the Mediterranean fleet under Vice Admiral Lord Horatio Nelson after them. At the same time, Admiral Honoré Ganteaume and his 21 ships of the line are to break out from Brest and release Spanish ships at El Ferrol in northwestern Spain. The French fleets are to unite at Martinique under the command of Ganteaume, elude their British pursuers, and make for the Channel. Napoleon assumes that he will thus have available 60–70 ships of the line and at least a dozen frigates for the brief period of naval mastery sufficient for a host of small vessels to ferry his army to England.

On March 30 Villeneuve indeed escapes Toulon, sails west, and links up with de Gravina at Cádiz. Their combined 20 ships of the line, 8 frigates, and some smaller warships reach the West Indies in mid-May. Nelson meanwhile disregards his orders to fall back on the Channel Fleet; he pursues Villeneuve with his 10 ships of the line, believing that if necessary he can withdraw ahead of the French. Napoleon's orders are for Villeneuve to wait at Martinique no longer than 35 days. If Ganteaume cannot break free of Brest, Villeneuve is to proceed to El Ferrol, then on to Brest to release Spanish and French ships for the invasion attempt.

Following some inconclusive maneuvering that fails to lose Nelson, on June 8 Villeneuve departs Martinique for Europe. Nelson follows and makes a speedy return to Gibraltar, arriving there on July 20.

March–July 1805
North Africa: Tripolitan-American War (continued): Eaton's expedition against Derna and the end of the war. Former U.S. consul to Tunis William Eaton comes up with a plan to replace the bashaw of Tripoli, Yusuf Karamanli, with his brother Hamet, rightful heir to the throne. Eaton, with two midshipmen and seven marines, locates Hamet in Egyptian exile and signs a convention with him in February 1805.

On March 6 Eaton departs Alexandria with a small expeditionary force of 10 Americans, 300 Arab horsemen, 70 Christian mercenaries, and 1,000 camels. Advancing 500 miles across the Libyan desert, Eaton assaults Derna on April 27, supported by naval gunfire from three American brigs offshore under Captain Isaac Hull. Hamet and Eaton then take control of the town, and marine captain Presley O'Bannon raises the American flag, the first time the banner has flown over a captured foreign city. Yusuf's forces fail in attempts to retake the city on May 8 and June 10.

Command of the U.S. squadron has meanwhile again changed hands. In May, Commodore Samuel Barron falls ill and turns over command to Captain John Rodgers. On June 3 Bashaw Yusuf bows to pressure and agrees to peace. He accepts a $60,000 ransom for the release of the 300-plus American prisoners he holds from the frigate *Philadelphia* but renounces future tribute from the United States. The United States buys off Hamet Karamanli with a small annual tribute, but the two brothers reach accommodation, and Hamet becomes governor of Derna.

On August 1 Rogers, sailing to Tunis in the frigate *Constitution,* forces its ruler to conclude peace as well. Only Algiers of the Barbary states now still receives U.S. tribute. The Tripolitan War claims only 30 U.S. dead (including 13 killed in the ketch *Intrepid,* which Commodore Edward Preble hoped to explode under the fort in Tripoli Harbor but which blew up prematurely). The war creates a strong esprit de corps in the young U.S. Navy and helps to train its officers and men for a far more difficult test in 1812.

April 1805

Northern Europe: Napoleonic Wars (continued): Formation of the Third Coalition against France. In April 1805 Britain, already at war against France, enters into formal alliance with Russia against France. Austria and Sweden join in the next several months. The allied war plan calls for the Habsburg archduke Charles, their best commander, to advance with 90,000 men against French marshal André Masséna's 50,000-man Army of Italy and then drive against the main French concentration of the Grande Armée.

July 22, 1805

Eastern Atlantic Ocean: War of the Third Coalition: Background to the Battle of Trafalgar (continued): Battle of Cape Finisterre (Calder's Action). At the beginning of the War of the Third Coalition (1805–1807), on June 8 the combined French and Spanish fleet sails from Martinique to return to Europe and the port of Ferrol, Spain. British vice admiral Horatio Nelson pursues with his Mediterranean Fleet of 10 ships of the line, narrowly missing his opponent and arriving at Gibraltar on July 20. Nelson, however, had sent a fast brig to Britain with the news that Admiral Pierre Charles Villeneuve and his French and Spanish ships of the line are heading east. On July 9, therefore, the Admiralty orders a squadron of the Channel Fleet under Vice Admiral Robert Calder to patrol off Cape Finisterre, on the northwestern Spanish coast.

On July 22, 1805, Villeneuve arrives in the Bay of Biscay with 20 ships of the line, 6 frigates, and 2 smaller warships, only to discover Calder's 15 ships of the line and 2 frigates. Although visibility is poor, Calder attacks. The Spanish ships bear the brunt of the onslaught, with the English dismasting 2 ships and taking them as prizes along with 1,200 prisoners. Five other Spanish ships, including a frigate, are so badly damaged that they have to enter dry dock for repairs. Three British ships lose masts. The allies suffer 476 killed or wounded in the two prizes and 171 in the other ships. British personnel losses are only 198.

The following day the two fleets are still in visual contact, but Calder, conscious of the proximity of additional Spanish ships in Ferrol, decides not to renew the battle. The French and Spanish ships sail to Vigo and into Ferrol. On August 13 Villeneuve departs from Ferrol but not for the Channel. Taking advantage of a loophole in his orders, he proceeds south to Cádiz, abandoning any attempt to force the Channel and leading Napoleon to abandon any hopes of an invasion of England.

Although Calder has triumphed with an inferior force and won a major strategic victory, it is not the total tactical triumph that the British people expect, and there is an outcry in the press. Calder demands and gets a court-martial; to his surprise, he is reprimanded for not having renewed the action. He is never again employed at sea.

August 25, 1805

Western Europe: France: Napoleonic Wars (continued): War of the Third Coalition (continued): Napoleon invades Germany. In his earlier campaigns of 1796 and 1800, French emperor Napoleon I planned to make the main French military effort on the Danube but was sidetracked by operations in Italy. After learning the broad outline of his enemies' new plans, Napoleon abandons the effort (pretended or real) to invade England (although throwing off his enemies by making a great show of preoccupation with this and with winning control of the English Channel) and invades Germany instead. Marshal Guillaume Marie Anne Brune remains at Boulogne with 30,000 men to continue the charade and protect against any British invasion, while Marshal André Masséna and 50,000 men hold in Italy, and General Laurent Gouvion Saint-Cyr marches to Naples with 20,000 more.

On August 24–25 Napoleon orders the Army of England, now renamed the Grande Armée, to strike east. His intention is to surprise the Austrians with his 200,000-man army and defeat them—and the Russians if they arrive soon enough—before they have a chance to organize effectively against him.

October 20, 1805

Central Europe: Germany: Baden-Württemberg: Napoleonic Wars (continued): War of the Third Coalition (continued): Austrian capitulation at Ulm. On September 13, 1805, General Karl Mack von Leiberich invades Bavaria with an army of 70,000 men. The Bavarian army moves north to await the arrival of allied French forces. On September 26 meanwhile, unknown to Mack, Napoleon's Grande Armée of some 200,000 men crosses the Rhine River. Mack's army is located between Munich and Ulm, in present-day Baden-Württemberg on the Danube River. Mack has serious command problems, created by the presence of Archduke Ferdinand, who is there because the Russians insist that their aristocratic commanders deal with an equal. The nearest Austrian force to Mack is a 25,000-man army under Archduke John at Innsbruck, in the Tirol (Tyrol). The Russians are sending 95,000 men to assist the Austrians, and the advance force of 35,000 men under Field Marshal Mikhail Kutuzov is to link up with Mack at Ulm by October 20. The Austrians, however, underestimate by several weeks the time that it will take the Russians to arrive and overestimate by a similar amount the marching time of the Grande Armée.

On October 6 French forces reach the Danube. Over the next week most of the army crosses the river. Napoleon is still unaware of Mack's precise location. Mack meanwhile wants to cut through the French rear and join the Russians at Regensburg. Had this occurred, the Austrians would have caught the French artillery and ammunition trains and army treasury virtually unprotected with important consequences for the campaign, but Archduke Ferdinand refuses to authorize the move. In the middle of the night of October 12–13 Napoleon finally realizes his mistake (although he blames others for it) and orders the army back across the Danube to concentrate around Mack at Ulm.

On October 14 Archduke Ferdinand flees Ulm with 6,000 troops. Napoleon dispatches Marshal Joachim Murat and the cavalry after them, and half of the Austrians are cut down. Others from Mack's forces south of the Danube flee for Austria or the Tirol, leaving Mack with only 27,000 men.

By October 15 Napoleon has surrounded Mack's army at Ulm and the next day opens a bombardment. Mack refuses to treat with the French, but his generals overrule him and open negotiations. Mack surrenders his entire 27,000-man army and 65 guns on October 20. Mack is subsequently court-martialed and sentenced to 20 years in prison. He is pardoned by the emperor, but his military career is nonetheless ended.

See Leaders: Murat, Joachim

October 21, 1805

Eastern Atlantic Ocean: Napoleonic Wars (continued): War of the Third Coalition (continued): Battle of Trafalgar. In late August French admiral Pierre Charles Villeneuve arrives at Cádiz, where he is reinforced with additional Spanish ships. The British soon have this combined naval force under blockade. On learning the news, British prime minister William Pitt insists that Vice Admiral Horatio Nelson, then in England, take over command from Vice Admiral Lord Cuthbert Collingwood of the British ships opposing the French-Spanish fleet.

Arriving on station, Nelson rejects the previous, more cautious close blockade in favor of a loose arrangement that keeps his fleet out of sight of Cádiz. He uses a line of frigates to signal to the main body of the fleet over the horizon some 50 miles out. Nelson hopes that this tactic will entice the French and Spanish out of port. A loose blockade such as this is risky, however, because his enemies might get away. Nelson, however, prefers it to no action at all.

Nelson has no way of getting the French and Spanish to oblige him, but Napoleon arranges that. In mid-September Napoleon orders the combined fleet to the Mediterranean to support French operations in southern Italy, a recipe for disaster.

Villeneuve is well aware that his ships are not ready to do battle. Many of the Spanish crews are untrained, a large number of his own men are sick, and he cannot be certain of the strength of the British force lurking offshore. His Spanish colleagues urge him not to sail because of approaching bad weather. On the plus side, the wind is to the south, and Villeneuve is aware that Nelson has recently detached some of his ships to escort a convoy through the Straits. Nelson also commits the serious error of allowing Vice Admiral Robert Calder to sail home in

British admiral Horatio Nelson's overwhelming triumph over the combined Franco-Spanish fleet in the Battle of Trafalgar on October 21, 1805, firmly established Britain's domination at sea, not to be challenged until the end of the 19th century. (Sloane, William M., *The Life of Napoleon Bonaparte,* New York: Century Co., 1909)

a ship of the line, rather than a smaller warship, to a board of inquiry regarding the Cape Finisterre action. Yet in the final analysis, Villeneuve risks everything because he is stung by Napoleon's charges of cowardice, by the news from Madrid that Vice Admiral François Étienne Rosily-Mesros has been to Cádiz to succeed him, and by reports that he is to be ordered back to Paris to explain his conduct.

On October 19 the French and Spanish ships begin exiting Cádiz; in all 33 allied ships of the line (18 French and 15 Spanish) straggle out over that day and the next. Lookout frigates soon inform Nelson off Cape Spartel, who calls his captains to a council of war and explains his daring plan. Outnumbered by his opponents, who also boast the two largest ships, Nelson intends to split off the French and Spanish center and rear from the van by attacking in two or three columns so as to cut off some 20 or so ships in the van from the remainder. With the French and Spanish ships running before the wind, the others would find it difficult to tack back and rejoin the action. By the time they could come up, Nelson hopes

to have the battle decided. This bold plan promises either great success or disaster.

When Nelson's ships appear and approach the Franco-Spanish fleet, Villeneuve realizes the size of his opponent's force and orders the combined fleet to turn back toward Cádiz, a decision that astonishes his flag captain. The five-mile-long irregular allied line becomes even more ragged; in places ships of the line bunch up and even come abreast. Nelson's 27 ships, formed in two divisions, do not hesitate and instead drive directly into the center of the opposing line, cutting it in two.

The British have only 2,148 guns to 2,568 for the allies. The French and Spanish also have some 30,000 men as opposed to slightly more than 17,000 for the British. But Nelson's ships are far superior in terms of gunnery and seamanship. These factors and superior leadership more than compensate for any deficiencies in numbers.

In the resulting five-hour Battle of Trafalgar on October 21, 1805, the British take 19 allied ships. Another, the *Achille,* blows up. No English ship is

BATTLE OF TRAFALGAR, OCTOBER 21, 1805

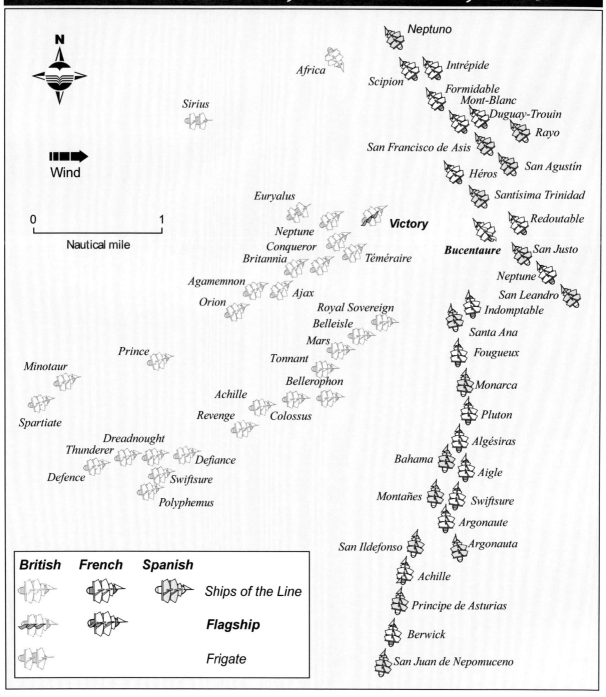

N

Wind

0   1
Nautical mile

Africa
Sirius

Neptuno
Intrépide
Scipion
Formidable
Mont-Blanc
Duguay-Trouin
Rayo
San Francisco de Asis
San Agustín
Héros
Santísima Trinidad
Euryalus
Redoutable
Neptune
Victory
Conqueror
Britannia
Téméraire
Bucentaure
San Justo
Neptune
San Leandro
Agamemnon
Ajax
Indomptable
Orion
Royal Sovereign
Santa Ana
Belleisle
Fougueux
Mars
Prince
Monarca
Minotaur
Tonnant
Pluton
Bellerophon
Algésiras
Achille
Bahama
Spartiate
Revenge
Colossus
Aigle
Dreadnought
Montañes
Swiftsure
Thunderer
Defiance
Argonaute
Defence
Swiftsure
Argonauta
San Ildefonso
Polyphemus
Achille
Principe de Asturias
Berwick
San Juan de Nepomuceno

British   **French**   **Spanish**

Ships of the Line

Flagship

Frigate

lost, but human casualties are heavy, and Nelson is one of them. His flag in the *Victory* was easily visible to ships in the van of the combined fleet, and the British flagship became a principal target for Spanish-French gun crews and sharpshooters. Pacing the deck in full uniform, Nelson fell early in the battle, mortally wounded by a sharpshooter in the *Rédoutable*. Carried below, he learned of the great victory before he died.

The British seamen do not have long to mourn their beloved leader or to savor their victory. A great storm blows in, and despite valiant efforts, most of the prizes are lost in the fierce tempest that lashes victor and vanquished alike. Crewmen who had just fought each other now fight just as desperately together to save their ships and themselves. Only four of the prizes are saved, a cruel disappointment to seamen who had hoped to profit from hard-earned prize money.

Not a single British ship is lost in the storm, but of the original 19 prizes, excluding 4 taken to Gibraltar, Collingwood orders 4 scuttled, including the giant Spanish ship of the line *Santísima Trinidad;* 2 other ships escape to Cádiz. The remainder either sink in the storm or are dashed on the rocks, with heavy personnel losses. Although 13 ships of the combined fleet make it back to Cádiz, 3 soon break up on the rocks. As a consequence of the Battle of Trafalgar, the Royal Navy has thus reduced its opponents by 23 capital ships.

Napoleon absurdly dismisses the Battle of Trafalgar in one sentence: "Some ships have been lost in a gale following an unwisely undertaken engagement." In truth, the Battle of Trafalgar shatters the French Navy and firmly establishes Britain as mistress of the seas, not to be seriously challenged until the end of the 19th century. The battle also marks the completion of the trend from the formalist school of fleet tactics to the melee school.

Trafalgar is quite possibly the most important naval victory in British history, and it raises Nelson as the greatest of Britain's military heroes. More immediately, it confines Napoleon to the land. To get at the British thereafter, Napoleon resorts to a war against their trade from the land side by denying British goods entry into all parts of Europe. This leads directly to the Continental System, which alienates many Europeans, and to the overextension of French military commitments.

October 30–31, 1805

Southern Europe: Italy: Napoleonic Wars (continued): War of the Third Coalition (continued): Battle of Caldiero. Following the Battle of Ulm, Napoleon sends several corps south to delay the Austrians in crossing the Alps from Italy while he drives east with the Grande Armée. On October 30, 1805, Marshal André Masséna with 37,000 men attacks an Austrian army of 50,000 men under Archduke Charles at and around the village of Caldiero, east of Verona. Masséna's men capture the heights nearby, but the village holds out. That night, however, Charles decamps, covered by a corps of 5,000 men under General Johann Frimont. In the Battle of Caldiero the Austrians suffer some 5,500 casualties, the French perhaps 5,000.

October–December 1805

South Asia: India: Second Anglo-Maratha War (continued): Pursuit of Holkar and end of the war. The failure to defeat Yaswant Rao Holkar, ruler of Indore, leads to the recall of British governor-general Marquis Richard C. Wellesley and his replacement by General Sir Charles Cornwallis, who also becomes commander in chief in India, replacing General Lord Gerard Lake. Cornwallis dies in October, however, and Lake replaces him in turn and begins a final campaign against Holkar, pursuing him into the Punjab. Unable to cause a general Maratha rising against the British, Holkar cannot continue the war.

Holkar surrenders at Amritsar in December 1805 and the next month signs a relatively favorable treaty with the British. The British acquire Orissa and portions of western Gujarat and Bundelkhand from the Maratha Confederacy, which then receives a free hand in much of central India. The rulers of Sindh ally with the British and retain control over much of Rajasthan.

November 4, 1805

Eastern Atlantic Ocean: Napoleonic Wars (continued): War of the Third Coalition (continued): Battle of Cape Finisterre. In a brief action on November 4, 1805, British captain Sir Richard Strachan with four ships of the line and four frigates encounters

French rear admiral Pierre Étienne René Dumanoir le Pelley's four ships of the line that have survived the Battle of Trafalgar. Dumanoir is about to escape when the two leading British frigates, in advance of the rest of the squadron, are able to overtake his rearmost ship and bring it under fire, forcing Dumanoir to form a line of battle. Ignoring custom, the British frigates join in, opposing ships of the line. All four French ships of the line are taken.

November 12, 1805
Central Europe: Austria: Napoleonic Wars (continued): War of the Third Coalition (continued): French capture of Vienna. Following his victory at Ulm, French emperor Napoleon I detaches some of his force to harry the Austrians moving north from Italy and others to protect his lines of communication to France, then drives east with the bulk of his Grande Armée. Marshal Mikhail Kutuzov reaches the Inn River with his 38,000 Russians (the advance element of 90,000 troops) but, following news of Napoleon's advance, burns the bridges over the Inn and withdraws east. Napoleon orders his cavalry under Marshal Joachim Murat to pursue. Crossing into Austrian territory, the French press forward, encountering growing numbers of Russians.

The Russians engage the French in effective delaying actions at both Dürnstein (November 11) and Hollabrunn (November 15–16). Murat and Marshal Jean Lannes nonetheless enter Vienna on November 12 (Holy Roman Emperor Francis II having declared it an open city), while Russian forces unite at Olmütz. Francis II supplies 15,000 Austrian troops, bringing allied strength up to 86,000 men. Twenty-eight-year-old Czar Alexander I arrives and takes personal command from Kutuzov. Following a brief stay in Vienna and leaving 20,000 men to garrison the city, Napoleon turns north. He now has 70,000 men under his direct command.

December 2, 1805
Central Europe: Moravia: War of the Third Coalition (continued): Battle of Austerlitz. The Austerlitz campaign opens with French emperor Napoleon I's move north into Moravia after his capture of Vienna. Minus those forces maintaining his lines of communication back to France and others garrisoning Vienna and preventing the movement of Austrian troops up

from Italy, Napoleon now has at his disposal some 70,000 men of the Grande Armée.

The allies have significantly more men. To the northwest, Austrian archduke Ferdinand commands 18,000 troops at Prague; to the northeast, Russian marshal Mikhail Kutuzov, with Czar Alexander I and Emperor Francis II in camp, has 90,000 Russians at Olmütz in Moravia. Another 80,000 Habsburg troops under archdukes Charles and John are to the south in Italy, trying to reach Austria. They are blocked from the Alpine passes by about 20,000 French troops under Marshal Michel Ney and General Auguste Marmont and harried by 35,000 other French troops under Marshal André Masséna as they attempt to move through Hungary.

As Napoleon moves toward the Russian frontier, he finds himself in the middle of more numerous enemy forces and must prevent them from concentrating against him. His supply lines lengthen, and his position becomes less satisfactory. With Napoleon now apparently vulnerable, on November 28, 1805, the Russian and Habsburg forces under Kutuzov at Olmütz move south to cut his communications with France.

Even though his forces are outnumbered, Napoleon is confident. He anticipated Kutuzov's move and now baits his opponents into battle by withdrawing from the seemingly advantageous high ground of the Pratzen Heights before them. Carefully concealing his own numbers, Napoleon extends his right flank to invite an allied attack there, confident that he can turn the tide of battle.

Supposedly impressed by the sight of his own troops marching in review, Czar Alexander I, who has taken personal command of the Russian forces, overrules the wise counsel of Kutuzov and orders the allied troops forward to attack the seemingly weak Napoleonic right wing and cut the French off from Vienna. Had the czar but waited, the allies might have obliged Napoleon to advance farther, dangerously extending his lines of communication and making him even more vulnerable to being cut off and annihilated, or to withdraw. Prussia might also have joined the allied coalition.

In the battle of December 2, 1805, the allies deploy some 86,000 men (71,000 Russians and 15,000 Austrians), the French 70,000. Because Austrian emperor Francis I (Holy Roman Emperor Francis II) is

French troops under Emperor Napoleon I defeat Russian and Austrian troops in the Battle of Austerlitz in Moravia on December 2, 1805. Because Russian emperor Alexander I and Austrian emperor Francis I were both present, it is sometimes called the Battle of the Three Emperors. (Library of Congress)

also present, it is sometimes known as the Battle of the Three Emperors, but more commonly, because it occurs west of the small village of Austerlitz in Moravia, the conflict is called the Battle of Austerlitz.

The battle opens at 7:00 a.m. when half of Alexander's troops move against the French right. The advance comes to a halt at the icy Goldbach, a stream between the two lines, due to the timely arrival of 6,000 French reinforcements from Vienna under Marshal Louis Nicolas Davout. By 9:00 a.m. a third of the allied force is engaged against the weak French right wing, with other forces moving laterally across the French front join them.

Napoleon now springs his trap on the allied right. Between 10:00 and 11:00 a.m. Marshal Nicolas Jean de Dieu Soult's corps retakes the high ground of the Pratzen Heights abandoned earlier, cutting off the

allied left. He then turns to the right to roll up the Russians attacking the French right, who have become mired in marshy ground. At the same time, on the French left Marshal Jean Lannes moves his corps east along the Olmütz highway while another French corps under Marshal Jean Baptiste Bernadotte drives into the gap created by Soult and pushes on directly for Austerlitz, cutting off the Russian left under Prince Pyotr I. Bragration, despite valiant resistance, is shattered.

Davout's forces also advance. By nightfall the allied army has completely broken up and ceased to exist as a fighting force, although many of the allied soldiers manage to escape the French trap. Napoleon's losses are some 2,000 killed and 7,000 wounded, while the Russians and Austrians lose 12,000 killed or wounded along with another 15,000

BATTLE OF AUSTERLITZ, DECEMBER 2, 1805

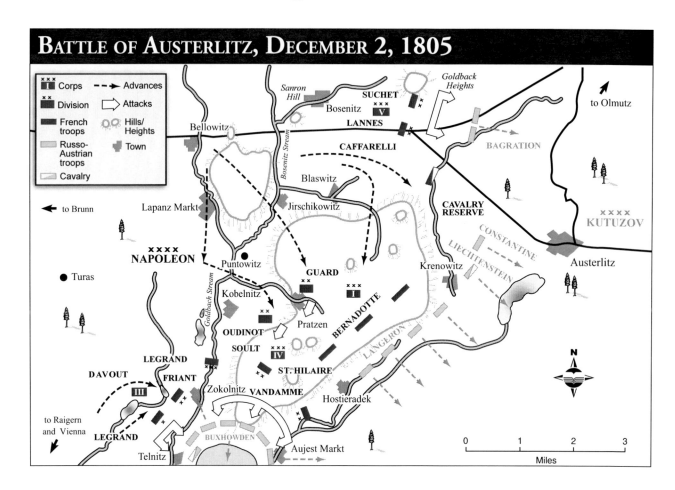

taken prisoner. Napoleon later causes the 180 allied guns taken that day to be melted down to form the Column of the Grande Armée that still stands in the Place Vendôme in Paris.

Alexander refuses to make peace and simply removes his forces back to Russia. British prime minister William Pitt remarks, on learning of the battle, "Roll up the map of Europe; it will not be needed these next ten years."

Nowhere is Napoleon's military genius better illustrated than in this battle. Unfortunately for France, Napoleon's skill in battle is not matched by his political and diplomatic sensibility. Foreign Minister Maurice de Talleyrand-Périgord urges Napoleon to conclude a generous peace with Austria in order to win its friendship. Talleyrand and others understand that if France is to have lasting peace, it must be content with hegemony over Europe rather than conquering all of it. Napoleon is not ill-served by his diplomats; he simply ignores their advice. His am-

bition drives all, and in the end the cost to France will be no territorial gains and hundreds of thousands of dead. In a sense, Austerlitz was too great a victory. The defeated had been humiliated, and Napoleon is now more convinced than ever that he cannot be beaten on the battlefield. His reach now begins to exceed his grasp.

See Leaders: Bernadotte, Jean Baptiste Jules
See Leaders: Kutuzov, Mikhail Illarionovich Golenischev

December 26, 1805

Central Europe: Austria: Napoleonic Wars (continued): War of the Third Coalition (continued): Treaty of Pressburg. On December 4, two days after the Battle of Austerlitz, Emperor Francis II agrees to unconditional surrender. The peace terms between France and Austria are signed at Pressburg (present-day Bratislava, Slovakia). France receives Piedmont, Parma, and Piacenza. The Kingdom of Italy receives

General Mikhail Kutuzov (1745–1813) was an able strategist who was greatly respected by his men. As commander of Russian forces during the French invasion of 1812, he practiced a scorched earth policy. Defeated in the great Battle of Borodino on September 7, 1812, his actions nonetheless helped bring the ultimate defeat of Napoleon. (George Dawe (1781–1929)/Hermitage, St. Petersburg, Russia)

all the territory that Austria had gained from the Treaty of Campo Formio as well as Venetian Istria and Dalmatia. Austria also agrees to recognize Napoleon as king of Italy.

France's ally Bavaria secures from Austria Vorarlberg, the territories of the Tirol (Tyrol), and the bishoprics of Brizen, Trent, Burgau, Eichstädt, Passau, and Lindau. Bavaria also gains the free city of Augsburg. Baden and Württemberg secure the remaining Austrian territory in western Germany. Austria receives in return Salzburg, Berchtesgaden, and the estates of the Teutonic Order, which are secularized.

The elector of Salzburg is compensated by receiving Würzburg. France now dominates western and southern Germany.

1805–1811

Southwest Asia: Russo-Persian War (continued). Despite their involvement in the war against Napoleon in Europe, Russian forces again invade Transcaucasia, again under General Paul Tsitsianov (Sisianoff). Once again, the Russians are inferior in numbers to the Persians. Sporadic warfare continues for the next half dozen years in Transcaucasia and along the coast of the Caspian Sea.

January 8, 1806

Southern Africa: Napoleonic Wars (continued): British capture of Cape Town. Following the allied defeat at Austerlitz, Britain strengthens its blockade of continental territory held by France and employs its seapower to assist its allies fighting on land. In the Peace of Amiens, Cape Town had been restored to the Dutch, now the Batavian Republic, under French control. The Cape Colony is governed by Lieutenant General Jan Willem Janssens, who is also commander of its small military force.

On January 6, 1806, a British squadron under Commodore Sir Home Riggs Popham lands two British infantry brigades north of Cape Town under the command of Lieutenant General Sir David Baird. They then begin marching on Cape Town. In the Battle of Blaauwberg (now Blouberg), Janssens with 2,049 men is defeated by Baird with 5,399. The Dutch sustain 353 casualties, the British 212. Surrender instruments for Cape Town and the Cape Peninsula are signed on January 10. Janssens, hoping for a French relief force, holds out until January 16.

Under the terms of capitulation, Janssens and Batavian officials and troops are returned to the Netherlands in March. The British remain in occupation until August 13, 1814, when the Netherlands cedes the colony to Britain.

February 6, 1806

Caribbean Basin: Napoleonic Wars (continued): Battle of Santo Domingo. On February 6, 1806, off Santo Domingo, British vice admiral Sir John Duckworth with seven ships of the line, two frigates, and two sloops defeats a French squadron under Vice Admiral Leissègues that had broken out of Brest the previous December and numbers five ships of the line (including the 130-gun *Impériel*), two frigates, and one corvette. Only the two frigates and the corvette escape. In March the British are also victorious over French naval units in the Indian Ocean.

July 2, 1806
South America: Argentina: Napoleonic Wars (continued): British capture of Buenos Aires. After landing troops who capture Cape Town in southern Africa, in April British commodore Sir Home Riggs Popham learns that the inhabitants of Buenos Aires and Montevideo are unhappy with Spanish rule. On his own initiative and without orders but after consulting with the shore commander Lieutenant General Sir David Baird, he sails from Cape Town for South America with two ships of the line and four other warships escorting five transports with a Highland regiment and some artillery under Brigadier General Sir William C. Beresford. At St. Helena, Popham secures some additional men, bringing the number of troops up to about 1,200 men.

The British expeditionary force arrives off Buenos Aires, and the troops, marines, and some seamen are sent ashore on June 25. Buenos Aires capitulates on July 2, and Popham sends home in the *Narcissus* more than $1 million in specie.

French colonel Jacques de Liniers (in Spanish service), however, puts together a force loyal to Spain, and on August 11–12 in bad weather when the British ships have to stand off the land, he leads an insurrection that retakes Buenos Aires. Having lost 48 killed, 107 wounded, and 10 missing, Beresford surrenders but secures most-favorable terms.

In October, Popham makes an attempt against Montevideo; he is forced to abandon it when his ships cannot close to sufficient range to engage the shore defenses. The British do take Maldonado (Uruguay) and the island of Gorrete. Learning what has occurred, the Admiralty recalls Popham to face a court-martial for leaving Cape Town without orders, but he is only reprimanded.

July 4, 1806
Southern Europe: Italy: Napoleonic Wars (continued): Battle of Maida. In July 1806 the British mount an amphibious attack in Calabria, Italy. On July 1 British ships commanded by Rear Admiral Sidney Smith put ashore in the gulf of St. Eufemia 4,800

troops under British major general Sir John Stuart. On July 4 near the village of St. Pietro di Maida a larger French force of about 6,200 men (128 cavalry) and four guns under Général de Division Jean Reynier attacks the British and is repulsed.

The British suffer 45 killed and 282 wounded. The French lose 500 killed, 1,100 wounded, and 400 taken prisoner. Stuart fails to follow up the victory, but the British force is not sufficiently strong to advance on Naples and is subsequently withdrawn to Sicily. The Battle of Maida removes the immediate threat of a French invasion of Sicily.

July 10, 1806
South Asia: India: Vellore Mutiny. The mutiny against the British of sepoys (native troops) at Vellore in the state of Tamil Nadu in southeastern India results from British changes in the dress code considered offensive for religious reasons. These changes prohibit Hindus from wearing religious marks on their foreheads and require Muslims to shave their beards and trim moustaches. The revolt on July 10, 1806, is one of the first uprisings against British rule in India, a forerunner of the great Sepoy revolt of 1857. The rebellious troops kill or wound 200 British soldiers at the Vallore Fort before the rebellious troops are suppressed by British reinforcements from nearby Arcot.

July 12, 1806
Central Europe: Germany: Napoleonic Wars (continued): Formation of the Confederation of the Rhine. In the spring of 1806 French emperor Napoleon I reorganizes the Germanies and on July 12 officially forms the Confederation of the Rhine, allied with France. All German princes join the confederation except for the rulers of Austria, Prussia, Brunswick, and Hesse.

August 6, 1806
Central Europe: Austria: End of the Holy Roman Empire. Recognizing the inevitable, Holy Roman Emperor Francis II, who has from 1804 already been calling himself Francis I, emperor of Austria, abdicates the Crown of the Holy Roman Empire, bringing it to an end.

September 1806
Europe: Napoleonic Wars (continued): Formation of the Fourth Coalition. Prussian king Frederick William III, who had held back joining Austria and Rus-

sia in 1805 when this might have spelled defeat for French emperor Napoleon I, is angered by the latter's reorganization of Germany and the French violation of the Prussian territory of Ansbach in 1805. In June 1806 Frederick William learns that Napoleon is considering taking Hanover from Prussia and returning it to Britain in order to secure peace. True, Napoleon would have compensated Prussia elsewhere, but the situation is so compromising to Frederick William's position that, joined by Saxony, he begins preparations for war against France. In this Fourth Coalition (1806–1807), Prussia therefore allies itself with Britain and Russia, which have remained at war with Napoleon. The coalition against France ultimately includes Prussia, Russia, Saxony, Sweden, and the United Kingdom.

The Prussian armed forces total about 150,000 men, with about 145,000 of these in the field army. To assist Prussia, Russia begins assembling two armies of 60,000 men each. Napoleon meanwhile has some 200,000 men in his Grande Armée, chiefly in southern Germany. Well aware of his adversary's scarcely concealed plans against him and unwilling to wait to be attacked on their terms, he rapidly and secretly masses forces in northeastern Bavaria for an invasion of Prussia.

October 8, 1806
Central Europe: Napoleonic Wars (continued): War of the Fourth Coalition: French emperor Napoleon I begins the campaign against Prussia. On October 6, Napoleon takes personal command of his forces concentrated around Bamberg. He has 180,000 French troops and can call on 100,000 from the allied German states. With Prussian forces already moving against him, on October 8 Napoleon begins his own movement north from Bavaria, proceeded by a cavalry screen and in three parallel columns on a front of about 30 miles at a rate of about 15 miles per day. This begins the War of the Fourth Coalition (1806–1807).

October 14, 1806
Central Europe: Germany: Thuringia: War of the Fourth Coalition (continued): Battles of Jena and Auerstadt. In late September 1806 the Prussian forces set out in the expectation of meeting the French in the Weimar-Jena-Erfurt region. Prussian king Frederick William III accompanies the army in the field,

but actual command is vested in 71-year-old Karl Wilhelm Ferdinand, Duke of Brunswick. Brunswick has three field armies: 75,000 men under himself, 38,000 under Friedrich Ludwig Prince von Hohenlohe, and 30,000 under General Ernst Rüchel. Coordination among the three armies is poor, with Brunswick and Hohenlohe hardly on speaking terms. Also, no decision is taken without the king and Brunswick spending long hours discussing it, a fact that is well known in the army and hardly inspires confidence in the leadership.

The Prussians advance west on two axes and, as in the 1805 Battle of Ulm, on October 14, 1806, the French come upon their adversary unawares. Prince Hohenlohe encounters French emperor Napoleon I at Jena, while 15 miles north at Auerstadt it is Brunswick and the king against able French marshal Louis-Nicolas Davout.

Learning of the French advance, Brunswick endeavors to shift his plan and move northeast to Auerstadt. Meanwhile, Hohenlohe is to protect the Prussian rear between Auerstadt and Jena. Napoleon, finally realizing that the Prussians are between Jena and Auerstadt, moves on the former, believing that the bulk of the Prussian army is there.

At 6:30 a.m. on October 14, Napoleon with 90,000 men (40,000 actually engaged) falls on Hohenlohe with 38,000 men at Jena (33,000 engaged). Hohenlohe calls on Rüchel with his 30,000 men to join him, but for some inexplicable reason Rüchel takes several hours and arrives only to have to fight a separate battle in which he tries to attack through the remnants of Hohenlohe's force. At Jena, Hohenlohe is easily defeated largely because he has camped on a plain without bothering to secure the surrounding high ground and faces superior French numbers. In the two battles at Jena, the French sustain some 5,000 casualties for 11,000 Prussians killed or wounded and 15,000 taken prisoner. The Prussians also lose 112 guns.

Although Napoleon will recall it differently, the major battle on October 14 takes place not under the emperor at Jena but rather at Auerstadt. Believing that he is confronting the entire Prussian army at Jena, Napoleon gives no attention to the (actually larger) part of the Prussian army under the Duke of Brunswick. But by striking early at Jena, Napoleon does prevent Hohenlohe from moving north against

NAPOLEON'S CAMPAIGN OF 1806

Neumünster

Rostock

Lübeck

Hamburg

Wittenburg

to Stettin
and River
Oder

Lüneburg

R. Elbe

Bremen

R. Weser

N

Oranienburg

Berlin

Potsdam

Hanover

Ziesar

to Frankfurt-
am-Oder

Magdeburg

R. Leine

Wittenberg

R. Elbe

Halberstadt

Dessau

R. Mulde

Torgau

Gottingen

Halle

Leipzig

Kassel

Merseburg

Freiburg

Mülhausen

Hassenhausen

Weissenfels

to Dresden

Auerstädt

Naumburg

Apolda

Dornburg

Zeitz

Eisenach

Erfurt

Weimar

Kappellendorf

Köstritz

Gorha

Umpferstadt

Jena

Gera

Blankenhain

Kahla

Reda

Rudolstadt

Neustadt

Weyda

Saalfeld

Mittel Pollnitz

Auma

Meiningen

Gräfenthal

Ebersdorf

Schleiz

Fulda

Lebenstein

Saalberg

Plauen

to Wesel and Coblenz

Hildburghausen

Hof

Frankfurt-am-Main

Neustadt

Coburg

Münchberg

Mainz

Kronach

Thüringer wald

R. Main

Schweinfurt

Bayreuth

Bamberg

R. Main

R. Rhine

Forcheim

Würzburg

to Ansbach

to Amberg

		✳ Site of engagement		
0	20		40	60
		Miles		

On October 14, 1806, French forces under Emperor Napoleon I and Marshal Louis Nicolas Davout defeat the Prussians in the battles of Jena and Auerstadt. This painting, *The Battle of Jena*, is by Horace Vernet from 1836. (The Gallery Collection/Corbis)

French forces under Davout, who with a single corps of 27,000 men engages and defeats Brunswick with 63,000 men.

The Battle of Auerstadt lasts six hours, and the cost is heavy for Davout, whose corps comes under heavy attack by the aggressive Prussian general Gebhard Blücher von Wahlstadt. The French hold, however, and Blücher withdraws. The Prussians then mount a four-division-strong frontal attack against only two French divisions, but the Duke of Brunswick is blinded and mortally wounded; the other Prussian generals are not privy to his battle plans, if he had any. The king also cannot make up his mind whether to command in person or appoint someone else, and in the end he does neither. As a result, sub-

stantial portions of the Prussian forces are not committed to battle, and although the Prussians almost turn the French left flank, their effort falls short.

At 1:00 p.m. after more than six hours of fighting, the Prussian troops break. Davout's infantry and cavalry pursue the fleeing Prussians for several hours before breaking off. In the wild retreat following the twin French victories, the two Prussian forces merge, heightening the confusion and sense of panic. Davout achieves a complete victory but at the cost of 8,000 French casualties. The Prussians lost 12,000 men killed or wounded as well as 115 guns, with a further 3,000 men taken prisoner. Napoleon at first disbelieves that Davout has defeated 64,000 men. "Your marshal . . . saw double today," he tells the messenger. This single day demoralizes the Prussian military, virtually ending resistance to the French.

See Leaders: Blücher, Gebhard Leberecht von
See Leaders: Davout, Louis Nicolas

October–November 1806

Central Europe: Napoleonic Wars (continued): War of the Fourth Coalition (continued): Following the twin defeats of Jena and Auerstadt, Prussia rapidly collapses militarily. Napoleon orders the Grande Armée forward. Marshal Joachim Murat takes Erfurt on October 15, Marshal Louis Nicolas Davout takes Berlin on October 24, and Murat bluffs Prince Hohenlohe into surrendering his larger force of nearly 10,000 men at Prenzlau on October 28. Most of the Prussian fortresses and their garrisons, including Magde-

Marshal Gerhard von Blücher came out of retirement twice to command Prussian forces in the campaigns of 1813–1815. He played a pivotal role in the Battle of Waterloo, June 18, 1815. (Unsigned print from *Life of Napoleon Bonaparte* by William M. Sloane. New York: Century Co., 1906, vol. 4.)

burg, fall quickly, with few shots fired. The last major Prussian force, under General Gebhard Leberecht von Blücher, surrenders at Ratekau, near Lübeck, on November 24. King Frederick William III flees to Königsberg (Kaliningrad) with his government.

November 6, 1806

Southwest Asia. The Ottoman Empire declares war on Russia, and Russian forces then invade Moldavia and Wallachia.

November 21, 1806

Central Europe: Napoleonic Wars (continued): War of the Fourth Coalition (continued): Berlin Decree. On November 21, 1806, Napoleon issues a decree from Berlin inaugurating what becomes known as the Continental System. It prohibits trade between the French Empire, including the German states, and Britain. In 1807 the system is extended to Russia, and the next year it is expanded to Portugal and Spain. Napoleon's intention is to deny Britain trade and force it into ruinous inflation. He also hopes that being deprived of British manufactured goods will stimulate continental, and especially French, industry.

November 30, 1806

Central Europe: Poland: Napoleonic Wars (continued): War of the Fourth Coalition (continued). At the end of November, French emperor Napoleon I with 80,000 French and allied Bavarian and Württemberger troops moves into Prussian Poland, up to the line of the Vistula (Wisła) River, and occupies Warsaw (Warszawa). Calling on the Polish people to rise up and ally themselves with France, he creates the Duchy of Warsaw. No doubt Napoleon intends (certainly most Poles believe this) to re-create the Kingdom of Poland, but the right moment for this never comes.

Meanwhile, Elector Frederick Augustus of Saxony abandons his ally Prussia, and on December 11 he allies himself with France. Napoleon rewards him with the title of king and shortly thereafter makes him ruler of the new Duchy of Warsaw.

December 1806

Central Europe: Poland: Napoleonic Wars (continued): War of the Fourth Coalition (continued): French and Russian forces begin to clash in Poland.

Frenchman Louis Nicolas Davout, Duke of Auerstadt and Prince of Eckmühl (1770–1823). One of Emperor Napoleon I's greatest generals, he was known as "the Iron Marshal." (Photos.com)

Russian marshal Count Alexander Kamenski commands some 100,000 men in Poland. Most are Russians, but there are also those members of the Prussian Army who have managed to escape Prussia. In heavy fighting at Pultusk on December 26, Marshal Jean Lannes's corps of 18,500 men gets the worst of it in an encounter with a Russian corps of 45,000 men under General Levin August Gottlieb Theophil, Count von Bennigsen.

On the same day, 15 miles away at Golymin, 18,000 Russians under Prince Golitsyn fight 31,000 French under Marshal Joachim Murat to a standstill. The weather is already very cold, and both sides now go into winter quarters. Meanwhile, Bennigsen replaces Kamenski as Russian commander.

1806–1807
West Africa: Gold Coast. The Ashanti conquer the Gold Coast.

1806–1812
Eastern Europe: Russo-Turkish War. Thanks to Napoleon's defeat of the Russians at Austerlitz and the

efforts of the French diplomat to the Sublime Porte, General Horace Sebastiani, the Ottomans end their alliance with Russia and Britain and in August 1806 depose the Russophile governors (*hospoidars*) of the Turkish vassal states of Moldavia and Wallachia. Simultaneously, the French occupy Dalmatia. Czar Alexander I of Russia responds by sending 40,000 Russian troops into Moldavia and Wallachia. The Ottomans then block access to the Straits to Russian ships and declare war on Russia. The war, largely a small-scale affair, plays out over the next six years.

January 1807
Northern Europe: Britain: Napoleonic Wars (continued): War of the Fourth Coalition (continued): Orders in Council. London responds to Napoleon's Berlin Decree with the Orders in Council of January 1807, which prohibit neutral ships from trading between French-controlled ports (i.e., the coasting trade) or those of its allies. Britain insists that neutral ships bound for a French or French-held port first discharge their cargoes in Britain before obtaining an export license.

January 1807
Central Europe: Poland: Napoleonic Wars (continued): War of the Fourth Coalition (continued). Russian general Levin August Gottlieb Theophil, Count von Bennigsen takes the offensive. This move catches French emperor Napoleon I by surprise. Not expecting any fighting until spring, Napoleon has his corps widely spread, with part of it two days' march from the main body. Cossacks have also captured French orders that give Bennigsen full knowledge of French plans and dispositions.

French forces under Marshal Jean Baptiste Jules Bernadotte and Michel Ney south of Königsberg (present-day Kaliningrad) fall back before the Russians. Napoleon orders a rapid concentration and pursuit, and Bennigsen withdraws.

February 3, 1807
South America: Uruguay: Napoleonic Wars (continued): War of the Fourth Coalition (continued): British capture of Montevideo. Rear Admiral Charles Stirling replaces Rear Admiral Sir Home Riggs Popham in command of British naval forces in the Río de la Plata, and Brigadier General Sir Samuel Auchmuty assumes command of ground forces from

Brigadier General T. J. Backhouse. The new British commanders decide to try to take Montevideo and, on January 16, land troops and about 800 seamen and Royal Marines about eight miles east of the city. Shelling commences and a breach in the defenses is made on February 2. The city is stormed and carried the next day. British casualties in the operation are 198 killed, 449 wounded, and 12 missing. The British maintain a force of some 10,000 men here until they proceed against Buenos Aires in late June.

February 8, 1807
Eastern Europe: East Prussia: Napoleonic Wars (continued): War of the Fourth Coalition (continued): Battle of Eylau. French emperor Napoleon I catches up with the Russians at Eylau-Preussisch (Bagrationowski), but only Marshal Louis Nicolas Davout is able to answer the emperor's orders to reinforce him. Bernadotte is two days' march away. Disdainful of the Russians, however, Napoleon attacks with only part of his force: 50,000 men and 200 guns. (Davout's 15,000 men do not arrive until the afternoon.) Russian general Levin August Gottlieb Theophil, Count von Bennigsen, commands 67,000 men and 460 guns, and he is reinforced during the battle to 75,000 men by the timely arrival of an 8,000-man Prussian corps under General C. Anton Wilhelm Lestocq.

The Russians are deployed on a long ridge east of Eylau. The battle opens with Russian artillery fire. Napoleon launches a premature pinning attack while Davout attacks the Russian flank piecemeal at 8:00 a.m. Fought beneath lowering clouds with occasional snow squalls, the battle sees one of the great cavalry charges in history when, close to defeat, Napoleon orders a desperate attack against the center of the Russian line by Marshal Joachim Murat's 5,000-man cavalry reserve and 1,600 Guard cavalry.

Napoleon is nearly captured in the desperate fighting, but Bennigsen remains unaware of how close he is to victory. Immediately upon Davout's arrival in the early afternoon, Napoleon orders him to attack and turn the Russian flank. Davout, ever dependable, seems to have accomplished this, threatening the destruction of the Russian army, when the arrival of Lestocq's Prussian corps restores the line and saves the day for the Russians. The battle ends in a draw at nightfall, although Bennigsen withdraws.

The cost is high for Napoleon. Two of his four corps are decimated. Napoleon admits to 7,600 casualties, but the true number is probably closer to 25,000. Russian casualties are even heavier. Napoleon encountered unprecedented opposition at Eylau, and he is fortunate that Bennigsen chose to retreat after the battle. Both armies now again retire to winter quarters, reinforcing and refitting.

February–March 1807
Southwest Asia: Napoleonic Wars (continued): War of the Fourth Coalition (continued): British Royal Navy effort against Constantinople. As early as November 1806, the British government, fearful that Turkish naval resources will be added to those of France, orders Mediterranean commander Vice Admiral Cuthbert Collingwood to detach a large squadron and send it to the Dardanelles, with Vice Admiral Sir John Duckworth in command. Collingwood does not receive the orders until mid-January 1807. His instructions to Duckworth are to proceed through the Dardanelles to Constantinople and there demand surrender of the Ottoman fleet, along with sufficient naval stores to maintain it. Should negotiations fail, Duckworth is to bombard Constantinople and capture or destroy the Turkish fleet.

Duckworth commands eight ships of the line, two frigates, and two bomb vessels. He weighs anchor on February 11, but one of his ships of the line catches fire and blows up. Duckworth also wastes valuable time, and his dilatory advance allows the Turks time to mobilize; his squadron passes through the Dardanelles only on February 17. Sultan Selim III rejects the British ultimatum, and in short order the Ottomans place some 1,000 guns along the shore at Constantinople and open fire on the British ships. Some of the Turkish guns are quite large, firing shot of up to 800 pounds.

Duckworth's ships sustain considerable damage in the exchange of fire, and two are lost. He withdraws on March 3, and his ships are further damaged in repassing the Dardanelles. A Russian squadron under Vice Admiral Dimitri Seniavin, which has far more success against the Turks in the eastern Mediterranean, then joins him. Duckworth rejects, however, the Russian's suggestion that they combine their squadrons and return to Constantinople while a second Russian squadron blockades Constantinople from the northern end of the Bosporus. The British expedition has been a total failure.

March 15–April 27, 1807
Eastern Europe: East Prussia: Napoleonic Wars (continued): War of the Fourth Coalition (continued): Siege of Gdańsk. The French capture the important Baltic port of Gdańsk (Danzig), beating back Russian and Prussian relief efforts.

March 21, 1807
North Africa: Egypt: Napoleonic Wars (continued): War of the Fourth Coalition (continued): British occupation of Alexandria. The British seek to support Vice Admiral Sir John Duckworth's squadron operating against Constantinople by opening another front against the Ottomans in Egypt, where Muhammad Ali has from 1805 established himself as ruler under Ottoman suzerainty. On March 3, 1807, the British send a naval squadron escorting 33 transports lifting 5,000 troops under Major General A. Mackenzie Fraser from Messina to Alexandria. The troops come ashore two weeks later. On March 20 the British secure Aboukir Castle, and on March 21 Alexandria surrenders.

Duckworth appears with part of his squadron on March 22, and Fraser decides to attack Rosetta. He is repulsed there on April 20 with 400 casualties. By September, the British position has deteriorated to the point that they conclude a convention allowing them to evacuate Egypt on September 14.

June 2 and 18, 1807
Eastern Europe: Russo-Turkish War (continued): Russian military successes against the Turks. Preoccupied with fighting Napoleon, Czar Alexander I of Russia is reluctant to commit major Russian resources to a war with the Ottoman Empire. Nonetheless, in the Battle of Obilesti on June 2, 1807, Mikhail Miloradovich and as few as 4,500 men turn back a large Ottoman offensive aimed at Bucharest. Two weeks later on June 18 at Arpachai in Armenia, Count Gudovich and 7,000 Russians defeat a Turkish army of 20,000 men.

June 14, 1807
Eastern Europe: East Prussia: Napoleonic Wars (continued): War of the Fourth Coalition (continued): Battle of Friedland. French emperor Napoleon I plans to take the offensive in the spring and destroy the Russian army under General Levin August Gottlieb Theophil, Count von Bennigsen. Raising conscription totals to 100,000 men—the highest level since 1799—and demanding additional manpower from his allies, Napoleon builds the Grande Armée to 200,000 men, supported by 100,000 in Germany and 300,000 in France. Bennigsen also has rebuilt his forces to 90,000 men under his command. On June 5, 1807, he moves against French troops under Marshal Michel Ney, a week before Napoleon's planned advance, in hopes of catching the French by surprise. Ney withdraws, and Napoleon advances with five corps, attacking Bennigsen and the Russians in strong defensive positions in the town of Heilsberg on the Alle (Lyna, Lava) River. Napoleon hopes to separate Bennigsen from Prussian corps commander General C. Anton Wilhelm Lestocq and cut him off from Königsberg (Kaliningrad).

On June 10 the French take Heilsberg and the Russian positions but at a cost of 8,000 casualties. Bennigsen withdraws toward Friedland the following day. Napoleon is convinced that he is making for Königsburg and moves in that direction, his forces spread out and paralleling the Alle River. Bennigsen, with his army reduced to 60,000 men because he detached 25,000 men to reinforce Lestocq at Königsberg, is moving on the other side of the Alle. Learning that a French unit, presumed to be a division, is widely separated from the rest of the army, on June 13 Bennigsen orders his army to cross the river. The unit turns out to be Marshal Jean Lannes's corps of 18,000 men on the right French flank. Lannes informs Napoleon that the Russians are crossing, and the emperor orders some forces to assist. Finally convinced early on June 14 that this is indeed the major element of the Russian army, Napoleon orders his entire army to mass at Friedland.

The Battle of Friedland of June 14, 1807, pits Napoleon with 80,000 men against Bennigsen with only 60,000. Lannes is forced back some three miles before Napoleon attacks with the entire army. Using his superior numbers, he crushes the Russians against the river, driving Bennigsen back into Friedland. There the Russian defense stiffens, but by 8:00 p.m. the French have driven the Russians across the river.

The battle is a decisive victory for Napoleon, made possible by Bennigsen's error in dividing his forces and occupying a position with his back to the

Alle. Russian casualties are some 30,000 men, half of them killed or drowned, and 80 guns lost. French losses are not inconsiderable, at 1,400 dead and 10,000 wounded. The next day Lestocq abandons Königsberg and attempts to join his forces to Bennigsen's remnants but is harried too much by Marshal Joachim Murat and the French cavalry. The campaign is in effect over. On June 19 Napoleon occupies Tilsit (Sovetsk). The Russians request a truce, which Napoleon grants.

June 22, 1807
Atlantic Ocean: *Chesapeake-Leopard* Affair. The U.S. frigate *Chesapeake,* bound for the Mediterranean under Commodore James Barron, is stopped on the afternoon of its sailing from Norfolk by the more powerful British fourth-rate *Leopard* by British captain Salusbury Humphreys, who has been ordered to search the ship for British deserters. When Barron refuses to allow this, Humphreys opens fire. Following several broadsides during which the unprepared Americans get off only one shot in return, Barron strikes. The British then muster the American crew and take off 4 men whom they claim are deserters. The badly damaged *Chesapeake* limps back to Norfolk with 3 dead and 18 wounded.

The *Chesapeake-Leopard* Affair brings an explosion of outrage in the United States. President Thomas Jefferson might easily have had a declaration of war, with much more public support and under better conditions than would be the case in 1812. However, he prefers economic pressure against Britain, which takes the form of an embargo. Barron meanwhile is court-martialed and suspended from the navy for five years.

July 1, 1807
Eastern Europe: Russo-Turkish War (continued): Battle of Lemnos. Aggressive Russian admiral Dmitry Senyavin leads a Russian squadron of 10 ships of the line and 2 frigates. He blockades the Dardanelles, takes Lemnos and Tenedos, and then destroys an Ottoman fleet off Lemnos.

July 5, 1807
South America: Argentina: Napoleonic Wars (continued): War of the Fourth Coalition (continued): British capture of Buenos Aires. Some 5,000 reinforcements are sent to British forces in the Río de la Plata with Lieutenant General John Whitelocke in command. On June 28 British troops are put ashore to take Buenos Aires. The British attack on July 5, but their warships are prevented by shoal waters from providing meaningful gunfire support. While the British take the city, it is a costly success that claims some 2,500 casualties. Confronted by Spanish troops, militia, and a popular uprising again led by French Colonel Jacques de Liniers (still in Spanish service), Whitelocke agrees the next day to terms whereby all prisoners held by the Spanish will be given up in return for which the British will cease all future attacks and evacuate the Río de la Plata within two months. In January 1808 Whitelocke is court-martialed, convicted, and cashiered.

July 7–9, 1807
Eastern Europe: East Prussia: Napoleonic Wars (continued): War of the Fourth Coalition (continued): Treaties of Tilsit. The Fourth Coalition effectively comes to an end with the Treaties of Tilsit between France on the one side and Russia and Prussia on the other. Napoleon meets with Czar Alexander I on a raft in the Niemen River, the boundary between Prussia and Russia.

In the treaty between France and Russia, the latter agrees to recognize the Grand Duchy of Warsaw, formed of territory taken from Prussia, under the king of Saxony. Gdańsk (Danzig) is restored as a free city. Russia receives part of East Prussia (Bialystock). Russia recognizes Napoleon's siblings as monarchs and also recognizes the Confederation of the Rhine. In addition, Russia accepts French mediation to end the war between it and the Ottoman Empire, while France accepts Russian mediation to end its war with Britain. In secret articles, Alexander agrees to an alliance with Napoleon against Britain should the British reject the proffered peace terms. The treaty thus costs Russia little.

Prussia suffers serious losses at Tilsit, however. It loses approximately half its territory (going from 89,120 square miles to 46,032). Prussia cedes to France all its territory east of the Rhine and west of the Elbe and yields to Saxony the circle of Cottbus, while the Grand Duchy of Warsaw receives all territory taken in the partitions of Poland since 1772. Prussia also gives up Gdańsk, to become a free city. Prussia recognizes Napoleon's siblings on their thrones and agrees to close its ports and lands to British goods until the conclusion of peace between

France and Britain. The Prussian Army is restricted to 42,000 men. Prussia further agrees to pay war indemnities, set in the subsequent Treaty of Königsberg (Kaliningrad) of July 12 at 120 million francs (in 1808 raised to 140 million). Until the indemnity is paid, Prussia must support a French occupation army of 150,000 men.

In many ways, Tilsit is the height of Napoleon's rule. He now is virtual ruler of all Western and Central Europe, and he commands an army of Frenchmen and allies that numbers 800,000 men, a size without parallel in European history. Only Britain opposes him, but Napoleon will now attempt the impossible and reach too far. In August, Napoleon establishes the Kingdom of Westphalia, with its capital at Kassel.

August 17, 1807

Northern Europe: Denmark: Napoleonic Wars (continued): British attack on Copenhagen. Following the Treaties of Tilsit, the British government, fearful that Denmark will add its fleet to that of France and Russia, decides to reprise its action of 1801 by striking first. Admiral James Gambier sails for Copenhagen in secrecy with a powerful fleet of 29 ships of the line and 53 frigates and smaller warships. Lieutenant General Lord Cathcart commands the land contingent of 29,000 men, lifted in 380 transports. Arriving off Vinga, Gambier detaches 4 ships of the line, 3 frigates, and 10 brigs into the Great Belt to ensure that no Danish reinforcements reach Copenhagen from the mainland, where most of their troops are stationed.

On August 3 the main British body anchors off Helsinger, where the transports join them. The Danish fleet numbers 20 ships of the line, 27 frigates, and 60 smaller ships. Three additional ships of the line are under construction and nearing completion. The British achieve such surprise that none of the Danish ships are ready for combat.

When the Danes refuse to negotiate, on August 15 Gambier moves the fleet off Skövshoved, four miles north of Copenhagen. The next day the British troops go ashore there and five miles to the north. Hostilities begin on August 17. There is a brief armistice during August 28–30, and then the fighting resumes.

On September 2 the British fleet begins a bombardment of Copenhagen. The British have learned from their experience against the Danes in 1801 and do not employ ships of the line in this. Rather, they use shore artillery and Congreve rockets. These latter prove highly effective in area fire, where accuracy is not required, and parts of Copenhagen are soon in flames.

On September 6 the Danes surrender, agreeing to hand over the entire fleet as well as all the cannon in the arsenal. Over the next six weeks the British remove the spoils of war and destroy what they do not take, including the three ships of the line and four other vessels on the stocks. Some other ships are also burned and sunk.

On October 21 the British sail off with their captures: 16 ships of the line, 20 frigates, and 43 other ships. The military booty that the British carried off in the transports is estimated at 3 million thalers. Severe storms on the return trip to Britain result in the loss of 25 ships, however. Only 4 ships of the line are eventually taken into the Royal Navy.

August 1807

Eastern Europe: Russo-Turkish War (continued): Armistice between Russia and the Ottoman Empire. Largely as a result of French meditation, agreed to in the Treaty of Tilsit, fighting between Russia and the Ottoman Empire is brought to a temporary halt. Russia agrees to remove its forces from Wallachia and Moldavia, and Ottoman forces retire to Adrianople. Desultory fighting resumes in 1809 and extends into 1812, however, with the Russians generally getting the best of it. The conflict is not resolved until the Treaty of Bucharest in May 1812.

September 5, 1807

Northern Europe: Denmark: Napoleonic Wars (continued). In early September the British also take the small Danish island of Heligoland (Helgoland) in the Heligoland Bight of the North Sea, important in the economic warfare that now dominates. The island remains in British hands until 1890.

November–December 1807

Southern Europe: Iberian Peninsula: Napoleonic Wars (continued): Background to the Peninsular War. Securing permission from the Spanish government, French emperor Napoleon I invades Portugal. His decision to intervene militarily in Iberia is probably the most disastrous of his career, for it results in a drain of 300,000 casualties in five years of fighting, "the Spanish ulcer" as he will call it. In November,

General Jean Andoche Junot sets out from Salamanca. Junot captures Lisbon on December 1, and Napoleon creates him a duke and appoints him governor of Portugal. These events lead to the Peninsular War (1808–1814).

December 17, 1807

Southern Europe: Italy: Napoleonic Wars (continued): Napoleon's Milan Decree. From Milan, Napoleon issues yet another decree tightening the Continental System, in effect closing the entire European continent to British goods. The decree also authorizes French warships and privateers to capture neutral ships sailing from any British port or from any country occupied by the British. Any ships submitting to search on the high seas by ships of the Royal Navy are to be considered lawful prizes if taken by the French. Efforts to close the entry of British goods into Europe, however, leads to his intervention in Portugal and Spain.

1807–1810

South America: Independence movements against Spain. Buoyed by the expulsion of British forces from Buenos Aires and a measure of autonomy during the Napoleonic Wars, portions of the Spanish Empire in South America rebel. Spanish troops put down the independence movements except in the Río de la Plata viceroyalty (Argentina), which becomes virtually independent of Spain in 1810.

February–December 1808

Northern Europe: Finland: Russian invasion of Finland. Following the Treaties of Tilsit, both Napoleon and Czar Alexander I call on Sweden to renounce its alliance with Britain. When the Swedish government refuses, in February 1808 Russian troops commanded by General Count Friedrich Wilhelm Buxhöwden invade Finland. The Swedes, unprepared for war with Russia, evacuate Finland in December, concluding the Treaty of Frederikshavn in September 1808. The Swedes cede to Russia both Finland and the Åland Islands.

March 1808

Southern Europe: Iberian Peninsula: Spain: Napoleonic Wars (continued): Peninsular War: French invasion of Spain. In March 1808 French emperor Napoleon I sends 100,000 French troops into Spain under Marshal Joachim Murat, designated lieutenant of the emperor in Spain and commander of the Army of Spain, on the pretext of guarding the coasts against the British. Spanish king Charles IV abdicates in favor of his son Ferdinand VII, but Napoleon calls both men to Bayonne in May and gets each of them to renounce the throne.

May 2, 1808

Southern Europe: Iberian Peninsula: Spain: Napoleonic Wars (continued): Peninsular War (continued): Dos de Mayo. An uprising against French rule occurs in Madrid on May 2, 1808. Known as Dos de Mayo (Second of May), the uprising is put down by the French with great savagery. Indeed, French emperor Napoleon I welcomes the insurrection as a means of securing Spanish submission to his authority. Napoleon now sends his elder brother Joseph, currently king of Naples, to Spain as king (from June 6, 1808), whereupon Murat takes Joseph's place at Naples. Meanwhile, a guerrilla war begins in Spain. (The word "guerrilla" in fact comes from the Spanish word *guerra* and is the diminutive, meaning "small war.") The British provide arms and assistance to the insurgents in both Spain and Portugal and then decide to send an expeditionary force to Portugal under Sir Arthur Wellesley.

June 15–August 17, 1808

Southern Europe: Iberian Peninsula: Spain: Napoleonic Wars (continued): Peninsular War (continued): First Siege of Saragossa. The French find themselves fighting a series of small uprisings throughout Spain, the most prominent being in Saragossa. The chief city of Aragon, Saragossa is about 200 miles northeast of Madrid on the Ebro River. In 1808 it has a population of about 60,000 people. General Don José Robolledo Palafox y Melzi has charge of the defense. He has only 300 royal dragoons, only a third of whom have horses. Palafox therefore recruits volunteers, calls up retired and half-pay officers, and organizes the city defenses to include establishment of a munitions factory. Although he has artillery, few of his men are trained in its use.

The first fighting for Saragossa occurs on June 8 at Tudela, where a French force of 5,000 infantry, 1,000 cavalry, and 2 artillery batteries sent to Saragossa under the command of General François Joseph Lefèbvre-Desnouettes clashes with some 6,000 Spanish levies and armed peasants who block their

The Defence of Saragossa by Scottish painter David Wilkie (1785–1841). The painting depicts Augustina Zaragoza, a heroine of the siege and lover of British poet Lord Byron who took the place of one of the members of a gun crew. (Photos.com)

way. The French soon scatter the defenders. A second and last effort to bar the French approach occurs shortly thereafter at Alagon, where Palafox leads in person 650 men and 4 guns against the French; he is wounded and his force defeated.

On June 15 Lefèbvre and his troops arrive at Saragossa and commence military operations against the city. Situated on a plain, Saragossa is protected by the Ebro to the north. Its buildings are sturdy and tightly packed, ideal for defensive purposes, and the city is surrounded by a 12-foot-high stone wall. Palafox now commands about 10,000 men.

Assuming that a determined attack will carry the city, Lefèbvre directs his artillery against the western walls while his infantry and some cavalry attack the southern Santa Engracia gate. Several French attacks encounter ferocious Spanish resistance, and the attackers sustain 700 casualties. Lefèbvre then decides

to await reinforcements. Learning that a force of 4,000 Spaniards is en route to the city, though, Lefèbvre feints an attack on Saragossa and slips away with most of his men, surprising and destroying the Spanish relief column.

On June 29 an additional French division with siege guns arrives at Saragossa under General Jean Antoine Verdier, who now assumes overall command of operations there. Verdier orders his men to drive the 300 Spanish defenders from Mount Torrero, a dominating hill south of the city, where the French then place their siege guns. From that position at midnight on June 30, 46 French guns open fire on Saragossa. Following a 12-hour bombardment, Verdier orders his infantry forward.

Desperate fighting ensues during which Augustina Zaragoza, a heroine of the siege, makes her appearance. Immortalized by British poet Lord Byron, who

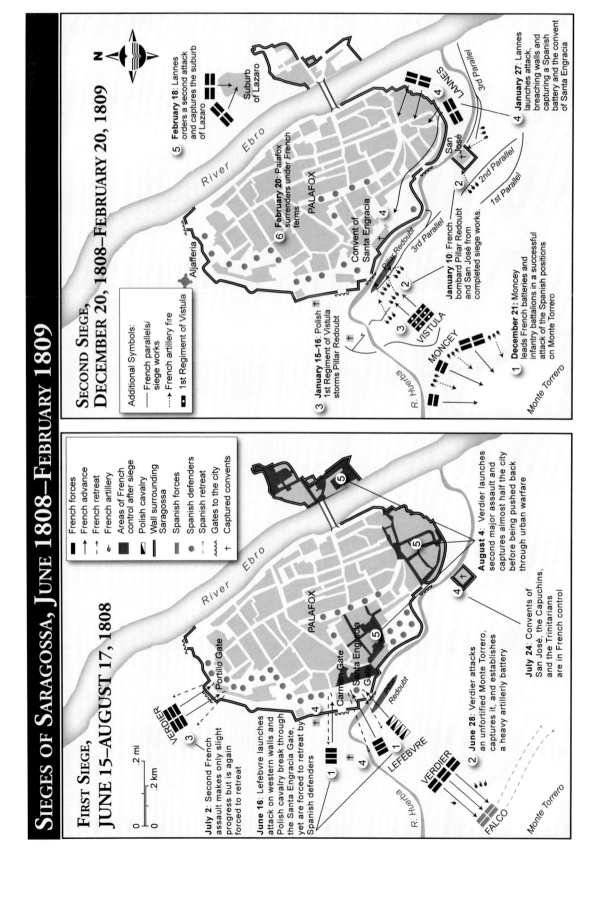

SIEGES OF SARAGOSSA, JUNE 1808–FEBRUARY 1809

SECOND SIEGE, DECEMBER 20, 1808–FEBRUARY 20, 1809

Additional Symbols:
— French parallels/siege works
→ French artillery fire
▪ 1st Regiment of Vistula

5 **February 18:** Lannes orders a second attack and captures the suburb of Lazaro

Suburb of Lazaro

LANNES

4 **January 27:** Lannes launches attack, breaching walls and capturing a Spanish battery and the convent of Santa Engracia

3rd Parallel

San José

2nd Parallel

1st Parallel

6 **February 20:** Palafox surrenders under French terms

PALAFOX

Convent of Santa Engracia

3rd Parallel

Pillar Redoubt

2 **January 10:** French bombard Pillar Redoubt and San José from completed siege works.

River Ebro

Aljafferia

3 **January 15–16:** Polish 1st Regiment of Vistula storms Pillar Redoubt

VISTULA

MONCEY

1 **December 21:** Moncey leads French batteries and infantry battalions in a successful attack of the Spanish positions on Monte Torrero

Monte Torrero

R. Huerba

FIRST SIEGE, JUNE 15–AUGUST 17, 1808

Legend:
■ French forces
↑ French advance
⇠ French retreat
⚑ French artillery
▬ Areas of French control after siege
▮ Polish cavalry
▌ Wall surrounding Saragossa
▨ Spanish forces
● Spanish defenders
↑ Spanish retreat
▬▬ Gates to the city
✝ Captured convents

River Ebro

Portillo Gate

PALAFOX

Carmen Gate

Santa Engracia Gate

Pillar Redoubt

VERDIER

3 **July 2:** Second French assault makes only slight progress but is again forced to retreat

June 16: Lefebvre launches attack on western walls and Polish cavalry break through the Santa Engracia Gate, yet are forced to retreat by Spanish defenders

LEFEBVRE

2 **June 28:** Verdier attacks an unfortified Monte Torrero, captures it, and establishes a heavy artillery battery

VERDIER

FALCO

Monte Torrero

R. Huerba

5 **August 4:** Verdier launches second major assault and captures almost half the city before being pushed back through urban warfare

July 24: Convents of San José, the Capuchins, and the Trinitarians are in French control

0   .2 mi
0   .2 km

N

was her lover, Zaragoza carries food to a gun crew and then takes the place of one of its members, reportedly firing the gun herself and shouting out that she will not leave the gun while she is still alive. A young boy seizes a banner from a wounded standard-bearer and waves it.

These actions rally the defenders, who are able to drive out those French troops who had penetrated the city. The attackers sustain 500 casualties.

Verdier now decides to conduct a conventional siege. With only 13,000 men, however, he is unable to seal off the city, and the defenders continue to receive both supplies and reinforcements. Gradually the French push their lines forward, though, and they continue their bombardment. On August 4 the French make another breach in the walls. That afternoon, 3,000 French troops attack, enter the city, and take about half of it. The fighting is desperate, with no quarter given by either side. Verdier demands that Palafox surrender, but the latter replies, "Guerra á chillo" ("War to the knife"), implying that he will fight to the last man. Desperate combat rages over the next days, with priests and monks fighting alongside the people.

On the morning of August 14 Verdier withdraws his troops from the part of the city that the French have captured, and on August 17 he breaks off the siege entirely. News of the major French defeat in the Battle of Bailén (Baylen) on July 19, his inability to seal off the city, and word that additional Spanish reinforcements are en route to Saragossa all cause Verdier to end the siege. Palafox finds himself the hero of Spain and Saragossa an example for the Spanish people.

July 19, 1808

Southern Europe: Iberian Peninsula: Spain: Napoleonic Wars (continued): Peninsular War (continued): Battle of Bailén. In May 1808 French general Pierre Dupont leads a French army corps south to occupy Cádiz, where Admiral François Rosilly's fleet lay at anchor. Dupont's corps numbers some 20,000 men, but most are inexperienced new recruits. The French advance to Córdoba, where they sack the city.

Upon learning of the approach of a much larger Spanish army under General Francisco Castaños, however, Dupont falls back on Andújar. Sick and

burdened with wagons of loot, he unwisely decides to halt and await aid from Madrid; unfortunately, his messengers are all intercepted and killed. A French division under General Dominique Vedel, dispatched by Dupont to clear the road to Madrid, becomes separated from the main body.

Spanish army forces come up, but unwilling to risk a frontal assault, Castaños divides his own larger force of 30,000 regulars and untrained levies in a risky maneuver. He sends forces under Generals Teodoro Reding and the Marqués de Coupigny in an attempt to surround the French. Dupont, left with 10,000 men, should have been able to break but, a halfhearted attempt in the Battle of Bailén (Baylen) on July 19 claims 2,000 French casualties, including himself wounded. With his men short of supplies and without water in sweltering heat, Dupont enters into talks with the Spanish.

Vedel now arrives, but it is too late. Castaños has placed sizable forces between the divided French, and it takes Vedel 12 hours to move 20 miles to Dupont's relief. In the talks Dupont agrees to surrender not only his own but Vedel's force. The 17,000 French troops are to be repatriated to France. In the actual fighting the French suffer some 3,000 casualties, the Spanish about 1,000.

The Spanish fail to honor the surrender terms. With the exception of Dupont and a few other officers, the men are transferred to the island of Cabrera, where most die of starvation. The surrender, the first of a French army under Napoleon, sends shock waves across Europe, invigorating opposition to French rule in other countries, especially Austria. It also is a tremendous boost to the continued Spanish resistance and to British hopes for it.

July 31, 1808

Southern Europe: Iberian Peninsula: Spain: Napoleonic Wars (continued): Peninsular War (continued): French evacuation of Madrid. Soon after the French defeat at Bailén, Marshal Bon-Adrien Jeannot de Moncey arrives in Madrid. His forces were supposed to seize Valencia, but he now reports that the opposing forces were too great. King Joseph panics. Although the French have 35,000 men in the capital and 20,000 along the route to Bayonne, Joseph decides to evacuate Madrid on July 31, withdrawing his forces above the Ebro River. French emperor Napoleon I in Paris is furious and now makes plans to go to Spain in person.

August 21, 1808
Southern Europe: Iberian Peninsula: Spain: Napoleonic Wars (continued): Peninsular War (continued): Battle of Vimeiro. On August 1 a British expeditionary force under Lieutenant General Sir Arthur Wellesley lands in Portugal north of Lisbon. French general Jean Andoche Junot marches up from Lisbon with 13,000 men and 24 guns to engage Wellesley's 17,000 men with 18 guns at Vimeiro. Devastating British musket fire against dense French attack formations decides the day in favor of the British. The French suffer some 2,000 casualties (450 killed) and 13 guns lost; British losses are only 720.

The road to Lisbon is now open, but the senior British commander, the elderly Lieutenant General Sir Harry Burrard (who arrived only the day before the battle), demurs. Despite Wellesley's pleas, the opportunity is allowed to pass.

See Leaders: Wellesley, Sir Arthur

August 30, 1808
Southern Europe: Iberian Peninsula: Spain: Napoleonic Wars (continued): Peninsular War (continued): Convention of Cintra. French governor in Portugal General Jean Andoche Junot now finds his position untenable due to British lieutenant general Sir Arthur Wellesley's victory at Vimeiro and a subsequent uprising in Lisbon against the French. Junot is in fact willing to offer complete capitulation, but elderly and inept commanders of the British expeditionary force in Portugal, lieutenant generals Hew Dalrymple and Harry Burrard, grant Junot far more generous terms than he had right to expect.

In the Convention of Cintra (Sintra) of August 30, 1808, the French army in Portugal is transported back to France by Royal Navy ships, complete with all of its weapons, equipment, and the loot acquired in Portugal. A tremendous storm of protest erupts in Britain over the terms of the convention, and after an official inquiry, both Dalrymple and Burrard are blamed. Wellesley, who had opposed the convention but was also recalled, is exonerated. Lieutenant General Sir John Moore takes command of British forces in Portugal.

British Army field marshal Sir Arthur Wellesley, Duke of Wellington, led British forces against the French and defeated Napoleon Bonaparte in the Battle of Waterloo in 1815. He subsequently commanded the army and was prime minister of Britain during 1828–1830. (Chaiba Media)

September 1808
Southern Europe: Iberian Peninsula: Spain: Napoleonic Wars (continued): Peninsular War (continued): British invasion of Spain. Following its victory in Portugal, the British expeditionary force is reinforced to 35,000 men. Lieutenant General Sir John Moore leaves 12,000 men in Portugal and invades Spain with the remainder to assist some 125,000 Spanish army and irregular forces.

French emperor Napoleon I in Paris sends reinforcements to Spain as he prepares to take command there himself.

September 27–October 14, 1808
Central Europe: Napoleonic Wars (continued): Congress of Erfurt. Napoleon seeks to prevent a restive Austria from again going to war against him by meeting with Russian czar Alexander I at Erfurt during September 27–October 14, 1808. Napoleon seeks a pledge that war between Austria and France will necessarily mean war between Austria and Russia. This undoubtedly would have prevented Austria from going to war, but after Alexander holds discussions with Napoleon by day he meets secretly with Napoleon's chief negotiator, Charles Maurice de Talleyrand-Périgord, Prince de Benevente. Talleyrand is secretly working against his master in the hopes that a balance of power might be restored in Europe and is able to persuade the czar against extending a guarantee to Napoleon. As such, Talleyrand is probably more responsible than any other individual for the war in 1809 between Austria and France. The Austrians, well aware of Napoleon's efforts and their failure, are much encouraged by the czar's stance.

December 4, 1808
Southern Europe: Iberian Peninsula: Spain: Napoleonic Wars (continued): Peninsular War (continued): French recapture Madrid. By the end of October 1808 French emperor Napoleon I has 300,000 French troops in Spain. He arrives at Vitoria on November 5, and on November 9 he advances south of the Ebro River with nearly 200,000 men, far outnumbering the forces opposing him. On November 30 he sends forward Polish lancers to defeat a force of 9,000 Spanish troops under General Benito San Juan that is blocking the road to Madrid.

On December 4 Napoleon enters Madrid and takes charge of the Spanish government, relegating King Joseph to the Pardo, a nearby hunting lodge. Napoleon abolishes monastic orders and the Inquisition, confiscates rebel property, and orders the sequestering of goods deemed necessary to France. After restoring Joseph to power, Napoleon suddenly departs Madrid on December 22 to deal with the English invasion in the north.

December 20, 1808–February 20, 1809
Southern Europe: Iberian Peninsula: Spain: Peninsular War (continued): Second Siege of Saragossa. After the First Siege of Saragossa, the capital city of Aragon, Spanish Army captain general Don José Ro-

bolledo Palafox y Melzi substantially improves the city's defenses, which are now manned by 34,000 regular Spanish troops and 10,000 levies. He also has 160 artillery pieces. French marshal Bon Adrien de Moncey leads the French attackers, reinforced by troops under Marshal Edouard Mortier. Moncey commands 38,000 infantry, 3,000 sappers and gunners, 3,500 cavalry, and 144 guns.

Again concentrating on Mount Torrero, the French capture it on December 20, driving its 6,000 defenders into the city and taking seven Spanish guns. Moncey calls on Palafox to surrender, but the latter replies, "Spanish blood covers us with honor and you with shame." French siege operations begin in earnest on December 23.

On January 2, 1809, General Jean Androche Junot arrives at Saragossa to replace Moncey and with orders to detach Mortier and 10,000 men to keep open the road to Madrid. Meanwhile, the French defeat a series of small Spanish sorties aimed at spiking the French guns, which now are concentrated against the southeastern walls of the city at close range. By January 26 the French have made several breaches in the walls, and the next day infantry assaults penetrate the Spanish defenses.

Learning that 20,000 Aragonese are marching to relieve Saragossa, French emperor Napoleon I, who is in Spain, sends reinforcements to the city and entrusts command of operations to Marshal Jean Lannes. He orders Mortier to move against the Spanish relief column, which the French surprise and scatter at Nuestra Señora de Magallón.

Inside Saragossa, bitter house-to-house fighting rages without letup for the next three weeks. With much of the city reduced to rubble and his main armaments factory destroyed by a mine, Palafox announces his readiness to surrender, which occurs on February 20, 1809.

Saragossa is by then largely a smoking ruin, with about a third of the city destroyed. Altogether the siege has claimed 54,000 Spanish lives, with only 8,000 of the Spanish garrison still alive. Some 10,000 French have died, 4,000 killed in action and 6,000 dead of disease.

Although the French have triumphed at Saragossa, the city's defenders again distinguished themselves. Saragossa's defiance becomes a symbol of resistance to French rule and a standard for other Spanish cities.

Napoleon is never able to solve the problem of Spanish nationalism. The so-called Spanish Ulcer continues to sap French manpower and encourage resistance elsewhere in Europe.

1808
Southeast Asia: Netherlands East Indies (Indonesia). The Dutch pacify Bantam, bringing all of western Java under their control.

1808–1809
Caribbean Basin: Hispaniola: Revolt in Santo Domingo. With British assistance, the colony of Santo Domingo, occupying the eastern half of the island of Hispaniola, revolts against the rule of the French-speaking blacks in Haiti to the west.

1808–1811
West Africa: Fulani attack on Bornu. Jihad (holy war) forces of Usman dan Fodio invade Kanem-Bornu and defeat its army in 1811. Mohammad al-Kamami then leads resistance forces that, by 1811, defeat and expel the Fulani.

January 14, 1809
South America: Guyane: Napoleonic Wars (continued): Capture of Cayenne. British and Portuguese seamen and marines take possession of Cayenne, capital of French Guiana (Guyane).

January 16, 1809
Southern Europe: Iberian Peninsula: Spain: Napoleonic Wars (continued): Peninsular War (continued): Battle of La Coruña. French emperor Napoleon I proceeds north from Madrid on December 22 to deal with the British invasion force from Portugal. British lieutenant general Sir John Moore commands some 23,000 men in Spain, hoping to assist the Spanish insurgents. With a 10-to-1 manpower advantage, Napoleon is anxious to seize the opportunity, but Moore realizes that he has blundered into the rear of an enormous French force and hurriedly withdraws north to La Coruña (Coruna), where his men might be lifted off by the Royal Navy. Napoleon moves toward Astorga with the Guard while ordering French forces already in the north into action. Marshal Nicholas Jean de Dieu Soult is to pursue Moore, while Marshal Michel Ney blocks the British escape route.

As Napoleon moves north, however, messages arrive from Paris that the Austrians are mobilizing. He

orders Soult to continue the pursuit, but Ney is unable to block the English retreat. Napoleon nevertheless departs Spain for Paris on January 16.

That same day Soult, with 24,200 men, engages Moore at La Coruña. The British repulse the French, but it comes at the cost of some 700–800 casualties including Moore, hit by a cannonball and mortally wounded. The attacking French, however, may have sustained 1,500 casualties. The next day, ships of the Royal Navy evacuate the expeditionary force.

February 24, 1809
Caribbean Basin: Napoleonic Wars (continued): British capture of Martinique. In late 1808, learning that Martinique is short of troops and provisions, the British prepare to invade this most important of the French West Indian possessions, then governed by French vice admiral Louis Thomas Villaret de Joyeuse. At the end of January 1809 a British expeditionary force of 44 ships, including 6 ships of the line, departs Barbados with 10,000 troops under Lieutenant General Sir George Beckwith. The troops begin going ashore on January 30, and land operations commence. On February 24 the British take Fort Desaix, and the entire island surrenders. Villaret de Joyeuse and some other French officers are court-martialed in Paris in December 1809 and dismissed. Britain controls Martinique until October 1814.

March 1, 1809
Central Europe: Prussia: Establishment of the Prussian General Staff. General Gerhard von Scharnhorst creates the first modern general staff system. As its first chief, Scharnhorst is the equivalent of a modern minister of defense.

> *See* Leaders: Scharnhorst, Gerhard Johann David

March 13, 1809
Northern Europe: Sweden: Coup d'état. Displeasure over the invasion and annexation of Finland by Russia leads to a coup d'état by the Swedish military against King Gustavus IV on March 13, 1809. Gustavus is forced to abdicate on March 29. His uncle becomes king as Charles XIII. By the Treaty of Fredriksham of September 17, 1809, Charles formally abandons much of Finland to Russia, and on January 6, 1810, Sweden signs the Treaty of Paris with France. Swe-

den regains Pomerania but at the cost of joining the Continental System against Britain.

March–May 1809

Southern Europe: Iberian Peninsula: Portugal: Napoleonic Wars (continued): Peninsular War (continued). Following the Battle of La Coruña, French forces under Marshal Nicholas Jean de Dieu Soult invade Portugal. The 12,000 troops the British left behind there during their invasion of Spain have been reinforced to 25,000 men. In addition, 16,000 Portuguese troops are available. On April 22 Lieutenant General Sir Arthur Wellesley, cleared of any charges of mishandling affairs in Portugal earlier, returns to command the allied forces there. Marching north, Wellesley surprises Soult at Porto (Oporto) on May 21, driving him from the city and forcing Soult to withdraw to Spain.

April 9, 1809

Central Europe: Napoleonic Wars (continued): War of the Fifth Coalition: Austrian forces invade Bavaria. The war in Spain leads Austria, already defeated three times by France, to go to war in April 1809 for a fourth time. The results of the Congress of Erfurt and the success of rebels in Spain encourage the Habsburg leadership in its mistaken belief that a widespread uprising will take place against the French in Germany. Archduke Charles, the leading Habsburg general, has built up the regular army to 300,000 men and the *Landwehr* to some 150,000. The troops are still poorly trained, and Charles opposes the war; however, the War Council prevails.

In March 1809 Charles calls for a German war of liberation. The response is disappointing. Prussia has still not recovered from its defeat in 1806–1807, and most of the major German princes have benefited handsomely from Napoleon's rearrangement of territory and have no wish to join a war against him. Only in the Tirol (Tyrol), where the peasants wish to return to Habsburg rule, is there an uprising in support of Austria.

On April 9, 1809, Charles nonetheless invades Bavaria, beginning the War of the Fifth Coalition. Britain continues at war with France, but Russia remains on the sidelines. Emperor Francis I decides to make the major effort in Germany. Archduke Charles moves against Regensburg with an army of 209,000 men.

April 15, 1809

South Asia: India: Treaty of Amritsar. Rising tensions between the British and Sikh Maharaja Ranjit Singh in the Punjab lead to the Treaty of Amritsar on April 15, 1809. The two sides agree that the Sutlej River will be the boundary between the Sikh territory and the lands seized by the British in the Second Anglo-Maratha War.

April 16, 1809

Southern Europe: Northern Italy: Napoleonic Wars (continued): War of the Fifth Coalition (continued): Battle of the Sacile. While the majority of Austrian forces are committed in Germany, Archduke John commands another army of some 72,000 men for operations in Italy. He detaches 10,000 to support rebels in the Tirol (Tyrol) and sends another 12,000 into Croatia. He then invades Italy across the Julian Alps from Bohemia with the remaining 50,000 men.

Prince Eugène de Beauharnais, French emperor Napoleon I's stepson, commands the French Army of Italy with 37,000 Italians and 15,000 French, but he too has detached formations. With only about 35,000 troops, Eugène attacks the Austrians at Sacile, east of the Tagliamento River, on April 16. The French sustain about 6,500 casualties and lose 15 guns. Austrian casualties are estimated at 4,000. For the first time since 1800, an Austrian army has defeated the French in the field. Eugène now withdraws his army behind the Piave River.

See Leaders: Beauharnais, Eugène de

April 17, 1809

Central Europe: Napoleonic Wars (continued): War of the Fifth Coalition (continued): Napoleon joins the army against Austria. French emperor Napoleon I, well aware of Austrian plans, in January 1809 had called up conscripts of the classes of 1809 and 1810, and at Donauwörth on April 17 he takes command of what he calls the Army of Germany. It numbers 200,000 men, including 50,000 German troops, but half of the French soldiers have never seen battle.

April 21–22, 1809

Central Europe: Napoleonic Wars (continued): War of the Fifth Coalition (continued): Battle of Eggmühl. French emperor Napoleon I meets the Austrian invasion with a superb improvised counteroffensive, crossing the Danube in order to strike the center of the extended Austrian army. On April 20 he wins a minor victory at Abensberg. Pushing forward, Napoleon splits the Austrian army in two the next day, pursuing what he believes to be the main Austrian force south toward Landshut, leaving both Marshal Louis Nicolas Davout and Marshal François Lefèbvre to deal with what Napoleon believes is the Austrian rear guard.

Davout actually confronts the main Austrian force under Archduke Charles near Eggmühl. Davout's repeated appeals finally bring Napoleon and French reinforcements to Eggmühl on April 22. Davout and Napoleon attack, and Charles orders a withdrawal across the Danube at Regensburg.

April 23, 1809
Central Europe: Napoleonic Wars (continued): War of the Fifth Coalition (continued): French capture of Regensburg. French emperor Napoleon I arrives at Regensburg on April 23. To cover his withdrawal, Charles leaves a strong force to defend the city. Rejecting a siege, Napoleon orders Marshal Jean Lannes to storm the walls. The first French attempt is thrown back, but the second succeeds. Napoleon, venturing too far forward in an effort to encourage his men, is slightly wounded when he is struck in the ankle by a spent musket ball, the second and last wound of his military career.

Most of Charles's army escapes. Gathering up the scattered Austrian units, Charles reaches the vicinity of Vienna with 100,000 men but on the north bank of the Danube, across the river from Napoleon.

April 1809–February 1810
Central Europe: Napoleonic Wars (continued): War of the Fifth Coalition (continued): Revolt in the Tirol. Peasants in the Tirol (Tyrol) region, wishing to return to Habsburg rule, rise up against Bavaria and receive some assistance from the Austrians. Following French emperor Napoleon I's victory over the Austrians, French troops under Prince Eugène de Beauharnais retake the region.

May 13, 1809
Central Europe: Napoleonic Wars (continued): War of the Fifth Coalition (continued): French capture of Vienna. Violating his usual rule, which is to pursue armies rather than to capture cities, Napoleon breaks off the pursuit of Archduke Charles to move on Vienna, hoping that this will cause the Austrians to sue for peace. Napoleon takes the city on May 13, but there are no Habsburg peace emissaries waiting to treat with him.

May 17, 1809
Southern Europe: Italy: Papal States formally annexed to France. Deteriorating relations between French emperor Napoleon I and Pope Pius VII, driven by Napoleon's high-handed measures in dealing with the Church in France and his seizure of some papal territories, lead to Pius's decision to remain outside the Continental System. On February 2, 1809, French troops occupy the city of Rome, and on May 17 Napoleon orders the Papal States incorporated with France. On June 10 Pius VII excommunicates Napoleon, and on July 6 the emperor orders Pius arrested. The pope is held first at Savona near Geneva and then, in 1812, at Fontainebleau, south of Paris.

May 21–22, 1809
Central Europe: Napoleonic Wars (continued): War of the Fifth Coalition (continued): Battle of Aspern-Essling. French emperor Napoleon I cannot locate the army of Austrian commander Archduke Charles. The permanent bridges across the Danube north of Vienna have been destroyed, and Napoleon looks for some way to cross the river, aware that he will face opposition in doing so. He settles on Lobau Island, five miles downstream from the city. Seizing it on May 18, his engineers begin building pontoon bridges to span the river at this point.

Unaware of just how close the main Austrian army is, Napoleon does not mass his forces on the island before crossing. This means that if either span goes down, he will not be able to reinforce the north bank. Napoleon has only 82,000 men. Charles has 100,000 men just north of Lobau Island and another 16,000 north of Vienna.

Napoleon is able to pass over the river only 66,000 men before the bridging breaks down under the force of the swollen waters and floating mines and other objects launched by the Austrians upriver. Unable to reinforce, Napoleon is defeated. Austrian casualties total 23,000; French losses are 25,000, including Marshal Jean Lannes, who is killed. This is Napoleon's first personal military defeat and is thus taken by Europe as a resounding event.

Karl Ludwig Johann Josef Lorenz, Archduke Charles of Austria and Duke of Teschen (1771–1847), was one of the most accomplished military leaders of his era. He reorganized and reformed the Austrian Army and, in the campaign of 1809, inflicted a serious defeat on French emperor Napoleon I in the Battle of Aspern-Essling on May 21–22 before losing to him at Wagram on July 5–6. (Imagno/Getty Images)

June 14, 1809

Central Europe: Napoleonic Wars (continued): War of the Fifth Coalition (continued): Battle of the Raab. Following his defeat in the Battle of Aspern-Essling, French emperor Napoleon I reorganizes and concentrates his manpower at Vienna.

Meanwhile in Italy, upon learning of Napoleon's early victories in Germany, Archduke John begins withdrawing his forces over the Alps to add them to those of the Archduke Palatine of Hungary and then march to join Archduke Charles at Vienna. Prince Eugène de Beauharnais, commander of the French Army of Italy, pursues the Austrian troops north, inflicting large losses on the Austrians as they cross the Piave and Tagliamento rivers. Eugène sends General Jacques Macdonald with 15,000 men in pursuit of

John into Hungary and moves with the remainder to join his stepfather Napoleon at Vienna on May 27.

Napoleon reinforces Eugène, giving him 45,000 men and assigning him the task of preventing Archduke John from joining his forces to those of Archduke Charles. John is moving north along the Raab River, which flows into the Danube 60 miles southeast of Vienna. John hopes to be reinforced by Hungarian troops, but few rally to him.

On June 14 Eugène catches up with John at Raab, forcing him to fight. Although his forces are inferior both in quality and number (35,000 Austrians to 45,000 French), John believes that he can win a defensive battle and prepares strong positions overlooking the river. French cavalry prove decisive in the battle, breaking the Austrian flank. John sends some of his men into the fortress at Raab and withdraws toward Bratislava with the remainder.

In the battle the Austrians lose some 6,500–7,000 men to only 3,000 for the French. Eugène surrounds the Raab fortress, which surrenders following an 11-day siege. While John is thus unable to join Charles for the decisive Battle of Wagram, Eugène is able to reinforce Napoleon there with about 30,000 men.

July 5–6, 1809

Central Europe: Napoleonic Wars (continued): War of the Fifth Coalition (continued): Battle of Wagram. French emperor Napoleon I now has built up his forces to some 198,000 men and 480 guns; Archduke Charles has 140,000 men and 450 guns. In contrast to his hasty improvised crossing in May, Napoleon makes meticulous preparations, including the erection of trestle bridges alongside a pontoon bridge across the Danube. With Prince Eugène de Beauharnais's forces now joined to his, Napoleon is determined to attack before Archduke John can arrive with 12,000 men to reinforce Charles. (Indeed, although John did arrived at Wagram, it is too late.)

Charles positions some 25,000 men along a fortified line between Aspern and Essling north of the Danube and Lobau Island. Charles expects a repeat of Napoleon's earlier effort at the same crossing point. Napoleon feints there, then surprises the Austrians by crossing farther downstream to outflank the defenders, who have the mission of delaying the French while Charles reorganizes and positions the bulk of his forces some six miles to the north at the Russbach River. Unfortunately for Charles, the 25,000 men in his delaying force are too many for an observation force and too few to halt the French. He would have been better served with fewer men, for they are quickly lost.

Napoleon crosses the Danube on the stormy night of July 4–5, 1809, ideal for a crossing by bridges. On the first day of fighting, July 5, Napoleon strikes the Austrian eastern (left) wing. The Austrians hold, and the day ends without a decision.

Knowing that Napoleon has the bulk of his forces on the Austrian left flank, Charles makes a bold attack against the western (left) flank of the French with forces under corps commander General Klaus von Klenau. The goal is to cut Napoleon off from his Danube bridgehead, destroy the bridges, and envelop the French. Although the Austrians are initially successful and Klenau seems to have clear access to the French rear, his indecision dooms the effort. Marshal André Masséna sweeps across the Austrian front with his corps and halts Klenau, who is also under flanking fire from French artillery on Lobau Island. Masséna then drives Klenau back, putting finis to Charles's plan.

Despite fierce resistance, the French attack on the Austrian left led by Marshal Louis Nicolas Davout makes steady progress. At the same time Napoleon masses artillery and troops under General Jacques Macdonald (created marshal for his role in the battle) for an attack on the Austrian center. The assault is preceded by the greatest concentration of artillery fire to that point in history, with the 112 guns that Napoleon has assembled there wreaking havoc on the Austrian line.

Napoleon then sends in Macdonald's infantry. Under the combined pressure of this center attack and Davout's flanking effort, the Austrians give way. The battle has been a near-run thing for Napoleon, and the Austrians withdraw in reasonably good order but are nonetheless decisively defeated.

With some 340,000 men engaged, Wagram is the largest of any Napoleonic battle to that point. Napoleon triumphs not by finesse but rather with bludgeoning tactics and artillery (his guns fire a record 71,000 rounds). In the sense of massive numbers of men and firepower, Wagram presages the later battles of the American Civil War and World War I. Napoleon may have won the battle, but the cost has been high, in part a reflection of the decline in the quality of his soldiers. In all, the French sustain 32,000 casualties and the Austrians 40,000, with the difference being primarily in prisoners taken by the French.

July 10, 1809

Central Europe: Napoleonic Wars (continued): War of the Fifth Coalition (continued): Armistice. With the Austrian defeat in the Battle of Wagram, Polish forces driving the Austrians from the Grand Duchy of Warsaw, the British of little assistance, and Russia remaining aloof, the Habsburg court has no choice but to request a halt in the fighting on July 10, 1809, pending a peace treaty.

July 13, 1809

West Africa: Senegal. British forces occupy the island of Gorée (now considered part of Dakar) in Senegal. The British remain in occupation of French posts in Senegal until January 1817.

July 27–28, 1809

Southern Europe: Iberian Peninsula: Portugal: Napoleonic Wars (continued): Peninsular War (continued): Battle of Talavera. In June 1809 Lieutenant General Sir Arthur Wellesley invades Spain and heads for Madrid. In July, King Joseph devises a plan that, had it been more forcefully executed, might have trapped and destroyed the British expeditionary force. Joseph calls for three corps of 60,000 men to move south from Salamanca and get in behind Wellesley while he marches out of Madrid with some 45,000 men to meet the British head-on. Unfortunately for the plan, the French troops from Salamanca are slow to arrive, so Joseph, Marshal Claude Victor, and the Madrid troops meet Wellesley alone.

In the Battle of Talavera, fought on July 27–28 some 70 miles southwest of Madrid, the two sides are thus almost evenly matched. Wellesley has some 20,600 British and nearly 35,000 Spanish troops under General Gregorio de la Cuesta, who proves to be almost as much a liability as an asset, and engages Joseph and Marshal Claude Victor with 46,000 French and allied troops. The battle is indecisive, with nearly equal casualties: 6,700 on the British side (5,300 of them British) and 7,270 on the French side. Warned of the approach of the Salamanca force under Marshal Nicolas Soult, Wellesley hastily retires, leaving some 1,500 British wounded with the Spanish, who then abandon them to the French.

Although the Spanish insurgents had promised food to the British if they invaded Spain, they renege, forcing Wellesley to withdraw all the way back to Portugal. The British in the peninsula never quite trust the Spanish again. Shortly thereafter Wellesley is ennobled as Viscount Wellington of Talavera.

July 28, 1809

Western Europe: Napoleonic Wars (continued): War of the Fifth Coalition (continued): British expeditionary force sails for the Netherlands. Believing that it must do something to support Austria and possibly divert French emperor Napoleon I from land operations there, the British mount a massive amphibious operation, known as the Walcheren Expedition, to seize the port of Antwerp. The British government pushes the plan, despite concerns raised by its military advisers. Even after news of Napoleon's victory over the Austrians at Wagram on July 5–6, the British government gives no thought to canceling the operation.

Rear Admiral Sir Richard John Strachan commands the largest task force in English history to that point. It numbers 245 warships, 37 of them ships of the line, escorting nearly 400 transports lifting nearly 40,000 troops (3,000 of them cavalry), along with 206 pieces of artillery. Lieutenant General John Pitt, Earl of Chatham and elder brother of the late William Pitt, has command of the land force. The British plan to attack up the West Scheldt estuary.

The first troops come ashore on July 19, but the expedition proves a dismal failure, repulsed not by significant battle but by heavy casualties from disease in the Scheldt islands. It also suffers from an appalling lack of army-navy cooperation. As a diversion for Austria, it was too little too late, and the British withdraw in December.

This operation, so costly in terms of men and money, does at least force the British to concentrate their efforts on land in the Iberian Peninsula. Here a combination of the Royal Navy and British merchant shipping proves invaluable in supplying troops under Sir Arthur Wellesley, Viscount Wellington.

September 17, 1809

Northern Europe: Sweden. Sweden, which has been forced to evacuate Finland, formally ends its war with Russia in the Treaty of Frederikshavn on September 17, 1809. It cedes to Russia both Finland and the Åland Islands.

October 14, 1809

Central Europe: Napoleonic Wars (continued): War of the Fifth Coalition (continued): Treaty of Schönbrunn. Following the Battle of Wagram, Austria is forced to come to terms with Napoleon. Much to its credit, the House of Habsburg has managed to survive a fourth defeat at the hands of the French without internal revolution. Nonetheless, the terms of the treaty, signed at the Schönbrunn Palace outside of Vienna, are severe. Austria is forced to cede Salzburg, Berchtesgaden, the Inviertel, and part of the Hausrückviertel to Bavaria. Napoleon's Grand Duchy of Warsaw receives western Galicia (which had been taken from Poland in the course of the partitions earlier). Russia gains Tarnopol in East Galicia.

In addition, Austria yields to France the territories of Dalmatia, Slovenia, and Croatia. Napoleon organizes the latter territories, along with the Ionian Islands, which had been taken earlier, into a new state known as the Illyrian Provinces. Marshal Auguste Marmont takes charge of the new state as the Duke of Ragusta. The French inroads in Poland and in the Balkans are especially alarming to Czar Alexander of Russia.

In all, Austria is forced to give up some 32,000 square miles of territory and 3.5 million people. Austria is also forced to break off all relations with Britain and join the Continental System. Austria must also pay an indemnity of 85 million francs and cut its armed forces to no more than 150,000 men. Although Austria has survived, it joins Prussia in being relegated to second-rate power status.

November 19, 1809

Southern Europe: Iberian Peninsula: Spain: Napoleonic Wars (continued): Peninsular War (continued): Battle of Ocaña. Taking command of Spanish insurgent forces from General Gregorio Garcia de la Cuesa, General Don Juan de Arizagua advances with 51,000 troops against 30,000 French troops under Marshal Nicolas Soult. At Ocaña near Madrid in their worst defeat in the Peninsular War, the Spanish are routed by the French cavalry. The Spanish suffer losses of 4,000 killed or wounded and 15,000 taken prisoner. French losses are only 1,700 killed or wounded.

November 23–December 17, 1809

Southern Europe: Napoleonic Wars (continued): Milan Decrees. To strengthen the Continental System, from Milan on November 23 and December 17, 1809, French emperor Napoleon I authorizes the seizure of ships that have called at British ports and the confiscation of cargoes not certified as originating outside of Britain or its colonies. London then warns that the Royal Navy will seize any ship that dares sail directly for a European port controlled by Napoleon. These policies directly affect the trade of all states and are a chief cause of war with the United States in 1812.

The Continental System not only does not work but is a major factor in Napoleon's defeat. It causes him to spread thin his limited resources and angers the peoples of Europe including the French middle class, who desire both trade with Britain and British goods. Also, exports to Britain are important to Russia, and a halt in this trade causes grumbling against Czar Alexander. Meanwhile, the British do everything they can to pry open the blockade. Corrupt French officials, including members of Napoleon's own family, violate the law and permit such trade, sometimes with Napoleon's approval.

To punish Russia for withdrawing from the Continental System, in 1812 Napoleon will embark on his most reckless enterprise, an invasion of that country.

November 1809

Central Europe: Southern Germanies: Napoleonic Wars (continued). The Tirolean peasants continue their resistance against both the Bavarians and the French. With forces numbering as many as 20,000 men, the Tiroleans had actually driven the Bavarians from the land in the spring of 1809. Habsburg emperor Francis I then promised never to surrender Tirol (Tyrol) again by treaty. In the Treaty of Schönbrunn, of course, the Tirol is once again ceded to Bavaria; the rebels, however, are promised amnesty. Tirolean leader Andreas Hofer, who styled himself "Commander of Tirol," soon renews the call for resistance.

1809

Eastern Europe: Russo-Turkish War (continued): Military operations. The Ottoman Empire and Britain conclude peace on January 5, 1809, and Britain withdraws from the war. Russian forces invade the Dobruja. Following the conclusion of the Treaties of Tilsit, Czar Alexander I of Russia is now able to concentrate more resources against the Turks. He

Russian general Prince Peter Bagration (1765–1812) fought in Poland and against the Turks, but he is best known for his actions in the Wars of the French Revolution and the Napoleonic Wars. He was mortally wounded in the Battle of Borodino on September 7, 1812. (George Dawe (1781–1929)/Hermitage, St. Petersburg, Russia)

increases the size of the southern forces to some 80,000 men. With Field Marshal Alexander Alexandrovich Prozorovsky doing little, in August 1809 Alexander replaces him with Prince Pyotr I. Bagration, who promptly crosses the Danube and overruns Dobruja. Bagration besieges Silistria but then, learning of the approach of a large Turkish army, decides to break off the siege and withdraw to Bessarabia.

See Leaders: Bagration, Peter Ivanovich

January 6, 1810

Western Europe: France: Treaty of Paris between Sweden and France. Sweden, which had joined the Third Coalition against France in 1805 only to see Swedish Pomerania occupied by French troops in 1807, agrees to join the Continental System and, in return, receives back sovereignty over Swedish Pomerania.

January 19, 1810

Central Europe: Napoleonic Wars (continued). Andreas Hofer, leader of Tirolean resistance to the Bavarian occupation, is captured; he is imprisoned at Mantua and executed in February 1810. Southern Tirol (Tyrol) is annexed to the Kingdom of Italy. Small particularist uprisings in several places in Germany are easily put down.

February 4, 1810

West Indies: Napoleonic Wars (continued). The British capture Guadeloupe, which they hold until 1816.

February 5, 1810–August 24, 1812

Southern Europe: Iberian Peninsula: Spain: Napoleonic Wars (continued): Peninsular War (continued): Siege of Cádiz. Following his victory in the November 1809 Battle of Ocaña, French marshal Nicolas Soult conquers all Andalusia except for Cádiz, site of the powerful Spanish naval base and the capital of the free Spanish government, which is defended by ships of the Royal Navy. On February 5, 1810, French forces commanded by Marshal Claude Victor begin a siege of Cádiz. British commander in Portugal Lieutenant General Sir Arthur Wellesley, Viscount Wellington, sends 8,000 British and Portuguese troop reinforcements. Also, in an operation extending into 1811, General Louis Gabriel Suchet establishes French control over all of Aragon and Valencia.

Spanish guerrillas continue operations in remote regions of Spain, attacking small French garrisons and supply columns where possible but posing no serious challenge to French rule. The French raise the siege of Cádiz on August 24, 1812, when, following their defeat the month before in the Battle of Salamanca, they fear that their forces there will be trapped.

April 1, 1810

Western Europe: France: Marriage of Napoleon and Marie Louise, Archduchess of Austria. The marriage of the 18-year-old Marie Louise, carried out by proxy on March 11, 1810, and formally celebrated in the Louvre in Paris on April 1, 1810, is arranged by Austrian foreign minister Klemens von Metternich with the support of Emperor Francis I as a means of cementing Austria to France while that nation rebuilds. Napoleon, who had earlier sought the hand of

Grand Duchess Anna, younger sister of Czar Alexander I of Russia, and been rebuffed by Alexander, wants the legitimacy of marriage into a prominent European ruling family. He also hopes to cement his position by fathering a legitimate heir. The revolutionary period has come full cycle, as Marie Louise is a niece of Marie Antoinette, who had been married to French king Louis XVI.

May 25, 1810

South America: Argentina: Independence of Argentina. Following confirmation that Emperor Napoleon I has overthrown Spanish king Ferdinand VII, the citizens of Buenos Aires create the First Government Junta (May Revolution), in effect making Argentina independent of Spain. Formal independence is declared on July 9, 1816.

May–September 1810

Eastern Europe: Russo-Turkish War (continued): Course of the fighting. Hostilities are renewed by two brothers, generals Sergei and Nikolay Kamensky, who defeat Ottoman reinforcements bound for Silistria and drive the Turks from Pazardzhik on May 22. With their situation now apparently hopeless, the Turkish garrison at Silistria surrenders on May 30. Russian efforts to take the two Turkish fortresses of Shumla and Rousse are both repelled, however, but with considerable loss of life.

The Russians finally take Rousse on September 9 after they surprise and destroy a large Turkish force at Batyn on August 26. Sergei Kamensky dies soon thereafter, and new Russian commander Marshal Mikhail Kutuzov evacuates Silistria and slowly moves northward.

On October 26, 1810, however, Nikolay Kamensky defeats a 40,000-man Turkish force under Osman Pasha at Vidin. The Russians suffer only some 1,500 casualties as compared to 10,000 for the Turks.

July 1, 1810

Western Europe: Netherlands: Abdication of King Louis of Holland. French emperor Napoleon I's younger brother Louis, refusing to obey orders to apply the Continental System completely to Holland because he believes that it will bring the economic ruin of his country, abdicates and flees. On July 9 Napoleon decrees the annexation of Holland to France. He also annexes part of the Kingdom of Westphalia, the northwest German coast including the Hanseatic cities, and the republic of Valais in Switzerland that controls the Simplon Pass into Italy. Napoleon hopes thereby to control the widespread smuggling that is occurring in violation of his new tariff laws. This means that France now embraces 130 departments and extends along the North Sea coast.

July 8, 1810
Indian Ocean: Napoleonic Wars (continued): War between France and Britain (continued). The British seize Réunion (then known as Bourbon), a French island in the Indian Ocean used as a base for commerce raiding.

July 10, 1810
Southern Europe: Iberian Peninsula: Portugal: Napoleonic Wars (continued): Peninsular War (continued): French invasion of Portugal. With French emperor Napoleon I's defeat of Austria in 1809, Britain is again largely fighting alone. Following his earlier withdrawal from Spain, Lieutenant General Sir Arthur Wellesley, Viscount Wellington, oversees construction of a powerful defensive system of mutually supporting fortresses to protect Lisbon. Known as the Lines of the Torres Vedras, the British defensive belt mounts some 600 guns and runs for about 30 miles from Torres Vedras on the coast north of Lisbon east to the beginning of the Tagus Estuary.

Napoleon believes that the key to stabilizing the situation in Spain is to drive the British from Portugal. Rather than campaign there himself, he gives Marshal André Masséna command of the 60,000-man Army of Portugal and orders him to clear the British from Iberia. As Masséna moves toward the Portuguese frontier, Wellington takes 32,000 men (18,000 British and 14,000 Portuguese) and moves to meet him.

On July 10 following a 24-day siege, Masséna captures Ciudad Rodrigo. Located in Salamanca Province, Spain, Ciudad Rodrigo occupies a key location on the road from Salamanca to Lisbon. Following his victory, Masséna invades Portugal on September 15. Wellington slowly withdraws before the advancing French.

August 23, 1810
Indian Ocean: Mauritius: Napoleonic Wars (continued): War between France and Britain (continued): Battle of Grand Port. Four British frigates engage three French frigates and two converted East Indiamen in a hard-fought naval battle. The British are commanded by Captain Samuel Pym, the French by Commodore Guy-Victor Duperré. In the only French naval victory over the British during the Napoleonic Wars, two of the British ships are destroyed by their crews to prevent their capture.

September 16, 1810
North America: Mexico: Revolt against Spanish rule. Led by Miguel Hidalgo y Costilla, a priest advocating social reform, this first real revolt in New Spain begins on September 16, 1810. It ultimately attracts some 80,000 peasants in southern Mexico who then march on and threaten Mexico City. The poorly armed and largely disorganized peasants are, however, turned back by the army under General Félix Calleja on November 6, 1810.

September 27, 1810
Southern Europe: Iberian Peninsula: Portugal: Napoleonic Wars (continued): Peninsular War (continued): Battle of Bussaco. In the course of his withdrawal into Portugal, British lieutenant general Sir Arthur Wellesley, Viscount Wellington, commanding 25,000 English and 25,000 men of the reconstituted Portuguese army, establishes a strong defensive position along the 10-mile-long ridge of Bussaco (Buçaco), near Luso, Portugal. Pursuing French marshal André Masséna, with 65,000 men, attacks Wellington there. Because the British commander has positioned his men on the reverse slope of the ridge, Masséna is uncertain as to the defenders' exact strength and dispositions, and the French direct-fire artillery is largely ineffective.

The French assaults are made by the corps of Marshal Michel Ney and General Jean Reynier. The French fail to dislodge the defenders and are driven off, with 4,500 killed or wounded. British and Portuguese losses are only about 1,250 men.

October 10, 1810
Southern Europe: Iberian Peninsula: Portugal: Napoleonic Wars (continued): Peninsular War (continued): Wellington occupies the Lines of the Torres Vedras. Wellington continues his withdrawal into Portugal, occupying the prepared Torres Vedras line before Lisbon on October 10. Testing the allied positions and finding them too strong to attack, Masséna stubbornly holds his position until, his army

starving, he is obliged to withdraw. Deprived of food and harried by British hit-and-run tactics, he loses an additional 25,000 men before withdrawing back into Spain early in 1811. All of Portuguese territory is now free of French control except Almeida, near the frontier.

October 27, 1810
North America: United States: Annexation of West Florida. The Louisiana Purchase treaty of 1803 makes no reference as to the status of the Spanish territories of East and West Florida, but U.S. president Thomas Jefferson holds that Louisiana includes that portion of Florida between the Mississippi River on the west and the Perdido River on the east. In 1810 American expansionists seize control of Baton Rouge and proclaim the independence of the Republic of West Florida (September 26). U.S. president James Madison responds with a proclamation of October 27, 1810, affirming Jefferson's position that the land between the Mississippi and Perdido belongs to the United States. He then sends in troops to hold it. On May 14, 1812, Congress passes legislation officially incorporating West Florida into the Mississippi Territory.

November 5, 1810
Northern Europe: Sweden. French marshal Jean Baptiste Bernadotte, Prince of Ponte Corvo, accepts the position of crown prince of Sweden, with the full support of French emperor Napoleon I. Adopted by King Charles XIII as Karl Johan (former French marshal Jean Baptiste Bernadotte), Bernadotte soon becomes the most powerful man in Sweden. He directs both Swedish military and political affairs but to the benefit of Sweden rather than France, as Napoleon had anticipated. Indeed, Bernadotte is the first of the Napoleonic inner circle to turn publically against the emperor. During the Russian campaign in 1812, if Sweden had joined against Russia and threatened St. Petersburg, the war might have turned out very differently. Napoleon claimed later that the Russian capital was at the mercy of "a small Swedish patrol." By 1812, however, Bernadotte had turned against his former master, whom he now referred to as "the monster."

December 3, 1810
Indian Ocean: Napoleonic Wars (continued): War between France and Britain (continued): British capture of Mauritius. The British land troops and on December 3, 1810, seize Mauritius, an island in the Indian Ocean used by the French for commerce raiding. Under the surrender terms, the French are allowed to retain their property, language, and legal system.

December 19, 1810–January 2, 1811
Southern Europe: Iberian Peninsula: Spain: Peninsular War (continued): Siege of Tortosa. French general Louis Suchet lays siege to the city of Tortosa, on the main highway connecting Catalonia with Valencia. It also contains the only bridge over the Ebro River still in Spanish hands. The walled city is defended by 7,000 Spanish troops under General Lilli. With the French artillery tearing out huge chunks of the city wall, Lilli surrenders unconditionally on January 2. The French take 4,000 prisoners. Another 3,000 Spanish troops are killed or desert. French casualties number only 400.

December 31, 1810
Eastern Europe: Russia: Czar Alexander I withdraws Russia from the Continental System. Russian leaders are increasingly unhappy with the French alliance. French emperor Napoleon I's ambiguous plans for Poland, his annexation of Oldenburg without consultation with Alexander and compensation (made all the worse by the fact that the duke's heir is married to Alexander's sister, whom the czar had refused to make available to marry Napoleon), and French troop movements in Europe all serve to alarm Alexander. In addition, there is considerable unrest among the Russian nobility over the forced participation in the Continental System, which cuts off the long-standing and important Russian trade with Britain. They also strongly oppose the Westernizing influences introduced by the French alliance. Alexander is well aware that his father, Paul I, had been assassinated in a noble conspiracy.

Napoleon meanwhile rejects the repeated suggestions of successive French ambassadors to Russia, Armand Augustin Louis de Caulaincourt and Jacques Lauriston, that the alliance can be preserved with a few French concessions. Caulaincourt strongly opposes war with Russia. In the case of Russia, Napoleon has appointed diplomats who will tell him the truth, but he repeatedly ignores their sage counsel.

An international collection of anti-Bonapartist émigrés meanwhile tells the czar that all Europe is looking to him for liberation from the Napoleonic yoke. On December 31, 1810, therefore, Alexander announces that Russia is leaving the Continental System, thus ending the alliance with France. Russian commercial relations with Britain quickly resume, and Napoleon resolves to crush the czar.

1810–1811

Southeast Asia: Netherlands East Indies (Indonesia): Napoleonic Wars (continued): British attack on the Dutch in Java. British governor-general in India Gilbert Elliot-Murray-Kynynmond, 1st Earl of Minto, mounts an expedition against the Dutch in Java. The British take Batavia in August 1811, and on September 17 the Dutch agree to the Capitulation of Semarang. They cede Java, Palembang, Timor, and Macassar to the British.

1810–1820

South Asia: India: Maharaja Ranjit Singh conquers all of the Punjab. Ranjit Singh defeats the Afghans and other Punjabi princes, taking control of the entire Punjab. With the help of French and Italian officers, he develops and trains the most powerful native military force in India, which he then uses to overrun Kashmir in 1819.

ca. 1810

East Africa: Battle of Shela. Probably in 1810, Lamu defeats the states of Mombasa and Pate in the Battle of Shela in East Africa (present-day Tanzania). This ends Pate's preeminence in the Lamu Islands and diminishes Mombasan influence along the coastal area. Indeed, the battle opens the way for the intrusion of Muscat into East African affairs when, after the battle, Muscat responds favorably to Lamu's appeals for a garrison from Muscat to assist it.

January 17, 1811

North America: Mexico: Revolt against Spanish rule (continued): Battle of the Bridge of Calderón. Near the city of Guadalajara at the Bridge of Calderón, on January 17 Spanish general Félix Calleja at the head of 6,000 troops routs the rebels under Father Miguel Hidalgo y Costilla. Hidalgo is taken prisoner and executed. The rebellion continues under his principal lieutenant José Maria Morelos y Pavón, also a priest. He wages a guerrilla war and, for a time, isolates Mexico City.

In 1813 Morelos calls a congress at Chilpancingo that declares Mexico independent and adopts a new constitution. His military fortunes continue to deteriorate, however, and royalist forces under General Augustin de Iturbide capture and execute Morelos in 1815.

March 1, 1811

North Africa: Egypt: Massacre of the Mamluks. To consolidate his authority, Egyptian ruler Muhammad Ali arranges by treachery the murder of most of the Mamluk chieftains and their men. He then makes peace with the Ottoman sultan, agreeing to recognize his suzerainty. At the same time, Muhammad Ali builds up a powerful military centered on Albanian mercenaries and a navy.

March 20, 1811

Western Europe: France: Birth of Napoleon's heir. On March 20, 1811, French empress Marie Louise gives birth to a son, Napoleon François Joseph Charles Bonaparte (1811–1832), known as the king of Rome and later the Duke of Reichstadt.

May 3–5, 1811

Southern Europe: Iberian Peninsula: Spain: Peninsular War (continued): Battle of Fuentes de Oñoro. In the spring of 1811 the French in Spain go on the offensive. While Marshal Nicolas Soult advances on Badajoz, which is besieged by the British under Major General William Beresford, Marshal André Masséna moves with his Army of Portugal to relieve Almeida, held by a French garrison of 1,300 men and besieged by a British-Portuguese army under Lieutenant General Sir Arthur Wellesley, Viscount Wellington.

Wellington prepares to meet the French relief force at the small village of Fuentes de Oñoro, Spain. He commands a combined British, Portuguese, and Spanish army of 34,000 infantry, 1,850 cavalry, and 48 guns. Masséna has 42,000 infantry, 4,500 cavalry, and 38 guns. The battle opens on May 3 with Masséna launching a frontal assault against British regiments in the village. After desperate fighting, the British retain possession. There is little fighting on May 4, but on May 5 Masséna launches an attack on Wellington's weakly held right flank near Pozo Bello. Wellington reinforces there and then carries out a fighting withdrawal.

The main French effort occurs against Fuentes de Oñoro, but in heavy fighting the British again hold. Short of ammunition, Masséna withdraws several days later. Allied losses in the battle are some 1,800, while the French lose perhaps 2,800.

Wellington is able to continue the siege of Almeida, but its 1,300-man French garrison manages to slip through the British lines at night. Only 360 of the French are captured. Napoleon now recalls Masséna to France and replaces him with Marshal Auguste Marmont.

May 5–July 1811

Southern Europe: Iberian Peninsula: Spain: Napoleonic Wars (continued): Peninsular War (continued): French capture of Tarragona. As part of the French pacification campaign, on May 5, 1811, French general Louis Suchet with some 17,000 men lays siege to the port city of Tarragona on the Mediterranean coast of Catalonia. Protected by formidable defenses, the city is held by 6,500 Spanish troops under General Juan Senen de Contreas and supported by an Anglo-Spanish naval squadron under Admiral Sir Edward Codrington. Additional allied troops arrive during the siege, bringing the defenders up to about 15,000 men.

Following a siege of nearly three months, Tarragona surrenders on July 28. Some 7,000 of its 15,000 defenders have been killed. The French lose 1,000 killed and another 3,000 wounded and sick. French emperor Napoleon I advances Suchet to marshal.

May 16, 1811

Southern Europe: Iberian Peninsula: Spain: Napoleonic Wars (continued): Peninsular War (continued): Battle of Albuera. Marshal Nicolas Soult, with a French army of 24,000 men and 40 guns advances on Badajoz, Spain, which is besieged by an allied force of 34,500 men under British major general (Portuguese field marshal) William Beresford and Spanish general Joaquin Blake. Beresford commands 9,900 British and 10,000 Portuguese; Blake has 14,600 Spanish.

The battle occurs about 12 miles south of Badajoz. Fighting is heavy. Spanish forces distinguish themselves, as do the Polish Lancers on the French side. The allies suffer 5,900 casualties, the French as many as 7,000. The battle is inconclusive but a strategic victory for the allies because Soult fails to break up Beresford's siege of Badajoz. The siege is abandoned, however, when Marshal Auguste Marmont joins his forces to those of Soult.

May 16, 1811

North America: United States: *President-Little Belt* Affair. On May 6 U.S. Navy captain John Rodgers is ordered to cruise in the frigate *President* to protect American merchant ships, which are being halted by British warships and suffering loss of crew members from impressments. On May 16 Rodgers gives chase to a ship that he thinks might be the British frigate *Guerrière,* which had impressed an American seaman earlier. That night he overhauls the ship in question off Cape Charles, and there is an exchange of fire. The ship, however, turns out to be the small British corvette *Little Belt* of only 20 guns. In the exchange, the British warship sustains 9 dead and 23 wounded.

The British are outraged, while the Americans consider it a measure of revenge for the *Chesapeake-Leopard* Affair of June 1807. A board of inquiry clears Rodgers of any misconduct.

June–November 1811

Eastern Europe: Russo-Turkish War (continued): Battle of Rousse. Ottoman general Ahmet Pasha leads a 60,000-man army against the Russians under Marshal Mikhail Kutuzov. Battle is joined near Rousse on June 22, 1811. Although Kutuzov turns back the Turks, he orders his army to cross the Danube to Bessarabia.

Several months later a Russian force returns and, on October 2, 1811, surprises Ahmet Pasha in a night attack, routing his army and inflicting more than 9,000 Ottoman casualties. Ahmet Pasha surrenders to Kutuzov on November 23.

July 5, 1811

South America: Venezuela declares independence: Beginning of Bolívar's campaigns. Under the leadership of Francisco Miranda, Venezuela declares its independence from Spain on July 5, 1811. Simón Bolívar takes command of Puerto Cabello but is defeated by Spanish forces under General Juan Domingo Monteverde, who then goes on to restore Spanish rule, capturing Miranda and forcing Bolívar into exile.

See Leaders: Bolívar, Simón

SOUTH AMERICA 1810–1914

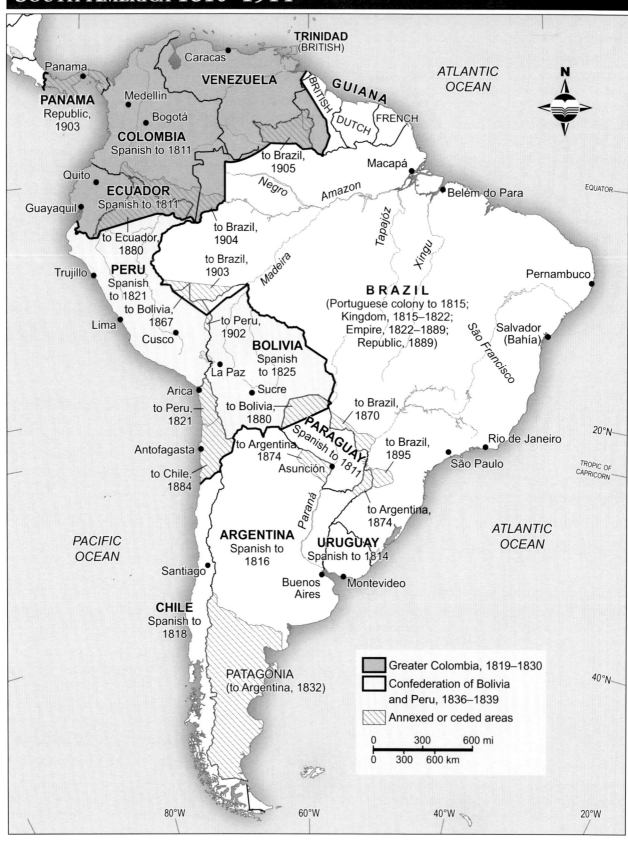

TRINIDAD
(BRITISH)

Caracas

VENEZUELA   GUIANA

Panama

PANAMA
Republic,
1903

Medellín

Bogotá

COLOMBIA
Spanish to 1811

BRITISH
DUTCH FRENCH

ATLANTIC
OCEAN

N

to Brazil,
1905

Macapá

Negro   Amazon   Belém do Para

EQUATOR

Quito

ECUADOR
Spanish to 1811

Guayaquil

to Ecuador,
1880

to Brazil,
1904

Tapajóz   Xingu

to Brazil,
1903

Trujillo   PERU
Spanish
to 1821
to Bolivia,
1867

Madeira

B R A Z I L
(Portuguese colony to 1815;
Kingdom, 1815–1822;
Empire, 1822–1889;
Republic, 1889)

Pernambuco

Lima   Cusco

to Peru,
1902

BOLIVIA
Spanish
to 1825

São Francisco   Salvador
(Bahía)

Arica
to Peru,
1821

La Paz   Sucre

to Bolivia,
1880

to Brazil,
1870

Antofagasta

to Argentina,
1874

PARAGUAY
Spanish to 1811

to Brazil,
1895

Rio de Janeiro

20°N

to Chile,
1884

Asunción

São Paulo

TROPIC OF
CAPRICORN

Paraná

to Argentina,
1874

ATLANTIC
OCEAN

PACIFIC
OCEAN

ARGENTINA
Spanish to
1816

URUGUAY
Spanish to 1814

Santiago

Buenos
Aires   Montevideo

CHILE
Spanish to
1818

PATAGONIA
(to Argentina, 1832)

40°N

Greater Colombia, 1819–1830

Confederation of Bolivia
and Peru, 1836–1839

Annexed or ceded areas

0   300   600 mi

0   300   600 km

80°W   60°W   40°W   20°W

South American revolutionary leader Simón Bolívar (1783–1830) was, more than any other individual, responsible for the liberation of Venezuela, Colombia, Ecuador, Peru, and Bolivia. (Library of Congress)

August 14, 1811

South America: Paraguay declares its independence. Following a popular uprising, this small subdivision of the Río de la Plata viceroyalty declares its independence both from Spain and the viceroyalty. Paraguay is soon ruled by a dictator, José Rodriguez de Francia.

1811

Eastern Europe: Russia: Napoleonic Wars (continued): French emperor Napoleon I prepares to invade Russia. All through 1811, Napoleon works to assemble a vast force of 611,000 men, 250,000 horses, and 2,000 guns in eastern Germany and Poland. It is the largest army under one command to that point in history. The first wave consists of 490,000 men, with 121,000 to follow. Additional forces, numbering more than 130,000 men, remain behind in the German territories.

The Grand Army of Russia is a European force, only about 200,000 of whom are from the France

of 1789 (that is, born citizens of France); another 100,000 come from the new departments of France such as the Netherlands, western Germany, and Italy. There are also 130,000 Germans from the Confederation of the Rhine, some 90,000 Poles and Lithuanians, 30,000 Austrians, 27,000 Italians and Illyrians, 20,000 Prussians, 9,000 Swiss, and 5,000 Neapolitans along with units from such nations as Spain and Portugal.

Napoleon's supply preparations are on a scale unprecedented in his previous campaigns, but they still fall far short. His army enters Russia with but three weeks of supplies available. He is counting on being able to live off the land and win one big battle in western Russia that will bring the czar to his senses and restore Russia to the fold. Napoleon does not anticipate a Russian army withdrawal deep into the vast stretches of Russia or Czar Alexander I embarking on a scorched-earth policy. Napoleon does not take into account the likely difficulties of securing adequate supplies for his men and fodder for the horses or problems of sickness, stragglers, and the indiscipline of the allied contingents. In the end it will be matters of supply rather than Russian winter weather and the Cossacks that destroy him.

November 7, 1811

North America: United States: Battle of Tippecanoe. Many Americans, especially in Kentucky and Ohio, believe that British agents are goading Native Americans to revolt. In fact, the settlers are doing it themselves; for the most part, the Indians are living up to their treaty obligations, while the settlers routinely violate them. Native Americans find redress impossible from settler juries. The Native Americans are also angry that between 1795 and 1809 William Henry Harrison, superintendent of the Northwest Indians and governor of the Indiana Territory, has secured the cession of some 48 million acres of land from them.

Two Shawnee brothers, Tecumseh and Tenskwatawa, lead the Indian opposition. They claim that the land is held in common and that no chief has the right to cede it. Tenskwatawa, a medicine man known as the Prophet, also calls on the Native Americans to reject the white man's ways. Tecumseh meanwhile travels widely to establish a confederation of all the tribes as the only way to resist further incursions. He has his work cut out for him. The Native Americans

U.S. and militia forces led by William Henry Harrison defeat warriors from Tecumseh's confederation led by Tenskwatawa in the Battle of Tippecanoe, November 7, 1811. The outcome drove many Native Americans of the Old Northwest to side with the British in the War of 1812. (Library of Congress)

have only 4,000 warriors in the territories between the Great Lakes, the Mississippi River, and the Ohio River, as opposed to some 100,000 white men of fighting age.

Tensions increase especially after September 1809 when Harrison is able to get a number of Potawatomi, Miami, and Delaware chiefs to cede a large amount of land to the United States. This action also fuels Tecumseh's efforts to build his confederation. In the summers of both 1810 and 1811 Tecumseh meets with Harrison at Vincennes, in Indian Territory, and warns him not to purchase additional land without general Native American approval. The 1811 meeting is particularly tense, as both sides arrive there with substantial forces. Tecumseh tells Harrison that his confederation merely emulates that of the United

States and that he is seeking to expand it by securing the support of Native Americans to the south.

Alarmed by Tecumseh's success and fearful of an expansion of the confederacy, Harrison decides in late September to take advantage of Tecumseh's absence to strike against the center of Indian resistance at Prophetstown. Harrison moves slowly north from Vincennes with a force of 970 men, including 350 soldiers of Colonel John Byrd's 4th Infantry Regiment, 484 Indiana militia, 123 Kentucky volunteers, and 13 guides. En route Harrison establishes a camp on high ground in a bend of the Wabash River (present-day Terre Haute, Indiana), completing this position, known as Fort Harrison, on October 27. He then moves to the mouth of the Vermillion River and erects a blockhouse. On November 6 he arrives in

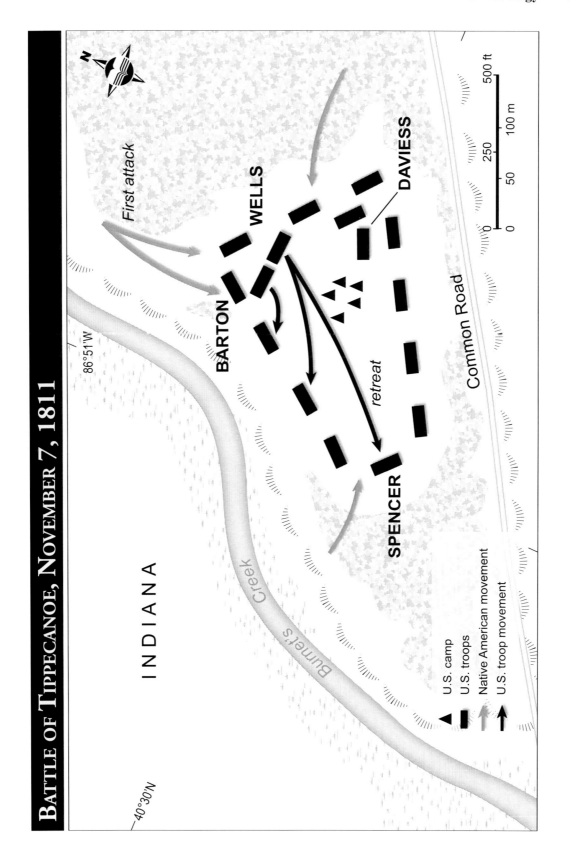

BATTLE OF TIPPECANOE, NOVEMBER 7, 1811

First attack

WELLS

BARTON

DAVIESS

retreat

SPENCER

Common Road

86°51'W

40°30'N

INDIANA

Burnet's Creek

U.S. camp
U.S. troops
Native American movement
U.S. troop movement

the vicinity of Prophetstown, which he is resolved to destroy.

That same day, Tenskwatawa sends emissaries to Harrison to inform him that he is prepared to meet the next day and discuss Harrison's demands. Against the advice of his commanders, Harrison decides to bivouac and meet the Prophet. The campsite is about two miles west of Prophetstown on a tree-covered knoll bordered by Burnet's Creek to the northwest and wet prairie to the southeast. Concerned about the possibility of a Native American attack, the men bed down for the night with their weapons loaded and bayonets fixed.

Harrison instructs that in case of attack, his men are to form a line of battle in front of their tents. He positions his mounted forces in the center of the camp as a mobile reserve. Although no breastworks are erected, Harrison does put out a guard force of 108 men.

That night at Prophetstown, egged on by two supposed British agents and informed that Harrison has no artillery but intends to attack the town, the Native Americans work themselves into a fury. At 4:00 a.m. on November 7, assured by the Prophet that the American gunpowder has already turned to sand and that the bullets will soon become soft mud, some 550 to 700 Chippewas, Hurons, Kickapoos, Ottawas, Mucos, Piankeshaws, Potawatamis, Shawnees, and Wyandots and possibly some Winnebagos surround Harrison's sleeping camp. An American sentinel manages to raise the alarm before he is shot dead.

As they struggle to form a line, many of Harrison's men are silhouetted before their campfires and become easy targets. The Native Americans employ the rare tactic, for them, of rushing forward in a group to fire and then withdrawing, while another group does the same. When it becomes light, however, Harrison sends out mounted troops against the Native American flanks and soon has the attackers in full retreat.

In the battle, the Americans suffer 62 killed and 126 wounded, a casualty rate of more than 20 percent. Native American casualties are about the same. On a report that Tecumseh is close by with a fresh force, Harrison orders his men to entrench, but a reconnaissance the next day reveals that the Native Americans have abandoned Prophetstown, however, and Harrison's men march in.

In Prophetstown, Harrison's men find new equipment provided by the British. After seizing food and other useful supplies, the men put the town to the torch. Harrison then withdraws the 150 miles to Vincennes. Tecumseh returns from his southern mission to find Prophetstown destroyed.

Harrison's victory over the Native Americans in the Battle of Tippecanoe, while it helps his presidential campaign in the election of 1840 ("Tippecanoe and Tyler Too"), has important negative short-term repercussions for the United States. It drives the Native Americans of the Old Northwest into an alliance with the British, who decide that they must now aid them. It also serves to convince the Americans on the frontier that they can never be safe as long as the British retain influence among the Native Americans, and this fuels demand for war with Britain. For these reasons, Tippecanoe is sometimes referred to as the first battle of the War of 1812.

December 25, 1811–January 8, 1812

Southern Europe: Iberian Peninsula: Spain: Napoleonic Wars (continued): Peninsular War (continued): French siege of Valencia. On December 25, 1811, French marshal Louis Suchet, with 33,000 men, lays siege to Valencia. Spanish general Joaquin Blake commands 20,000 defenders. The city surrenders on January 8, 1812. Suchet captures 16,000 Spanish troops (including Blake), 370 guns, and a considerable quantity of military equipment.

1811

Africa. Great Britain abolishes the slave trade. Similar action is subsequently taken by the Netherlands in 1814, France in 1815, and most other European nations thereafter.

1811–1818

Southwest Asia: War between Egypt and the Wahhabis. At the behest of the Ottoman sultan in Constantinople, Egyptian ruler Muhammad Ali invades Arabia. Having already occupied the Muslim holy places of Mecca, Medina, and Jidda, the Wahhabi religious sect is now threatening Syria, and the sultan calls on his powerful vassal Muhammad Ali, ruler of Egypt, to his aid. After seven years of war, some of it heavy, the Egyptians recover the holy places and also secure the eastern coast of the Red Sea.

January 8–19, 1812

Southern Europe: Iberian Peninsula: Spain: Napoleonic Wars (continued): Peninsular War (continued): Siege of Ciudad Rodrigo. Surprising the French, who had not expected him to stir before spring, British commander in Portugal Lieutenant General Arthur Wellesley, Viscount Wellington, invades Spain in early January. He begins the campaign by laying siege to Ciudad Rodrigo, which guards the route into northern Spain. The city is held by only 2,000 French troops under General Barré. The defenders have done little to improve Ciudad Rodrigo's defenses, apart from repairing breaches in the walls made during its capture. Following careful preparations, Wellington's troops storm and capture the city on the evening of January 19, 1812.

In the 12-day siege, the allies lose 195 dead, 916 wounded, and 10 missing; 2 major generals are mortally wounded. The French lose some 500 killed or wounded and 1,300 taken prisoner as well as a considerable number of guns. For his success, Wellington is elevated to Earl of Wellington.

March 17–April 6, 1812

Southern Europe: Iberian Peninsula: Spain: Napoleonic Wars (continued): Peninsular War (continued): British siege of Badajoz. Following his capture of Ciudad Rodrigo, British lieutenant general Arthur Wellesley, Earl of Wellington, moves his forces south to secure Badajoz on the Guadiana River, the southern gateway to Spain. By the end of March he has assembled on the frontier some 60,000 men and 58 siege guns.

The siege of Badajoz, the third of the war, begins on March 27. French general Armand Phillipon, commanding only 5,000 defenders, has worked hard to improve the city defenses.

Extensive allied shelling creates several gaps in the curtain wall, however, and with French troops under Marshal Nicholas Soult marching to the city's relief, Wellington orders an assault on the night of April 6, which succeeds following desperate fighting.

Some 4,800 British are killed or wounded against only 1,500 French. For more than a day after the French surrender, though, rampaging British troops subject the civilian population, Spanish and French alike, to savage reprisals.

April 25, 1812

Southeast Asia: Netherlands East Indies: British capture of Pelambang. Although the Netherlands East Indies (Indonesia) territory has been ceded by the Dutch to Britain in September 1811, the local sultan rejects the Capitulation of Semarang. A combined British land and naval force under Colonel Robert Gillespie then takes Pelambang on April 25, 1812.

May 28, 1812

Eastern Europe: Russo-Turkish War (continued): Treaty of Bucharest. This diplomatic agreement brings to an end the long, largely desultory war. Signed by Marshal Mikhail Kutuzov on May 28, the treaty cedes Bessarabia to Russia but provides for the retention of Moldavia and Wallachia by the Ottoman Empire.

June 18, 1812

North America: War of 1812: U.S. declaration of war and 1812 campaign plans. The War of 1812 (1812–1815) between the United States and Britain is a conflict that neither side sought or wanted. The conflict springs from Britain's long struggle against Napoleonic France, for in their effort to defeat Napoleon, British leaders push the Americans too far.

The chief causes of the war are maritime in nature. One is British impressment of American seamen. With conditions in the Royal Navy brutal and pay abysmal, many seamen desert when they have the opportunity, and a number of them find their way to American merchant ships and even U.S. warships. As a consequence, Royal Navy warships routinely stop U.S. merchant ships, supposedly to search for and take back these deserters but also to impress many native-born Americans.

Another cause of the war is the British Orders in Council that allow the Royal Navy to seize any ship sailing directly for a European port controlled by Napoleon. By 1812, the British have captured some 400 American ships and are playing havoc with the American export trade. Many Americans believe, rightly or wrongly, that national honor is at stake.

Other causes of the war are the American desire to conquer Canada and add it to the United States and the belief that British authorities are arming Native Americans against American settlers in the Old Northwest.

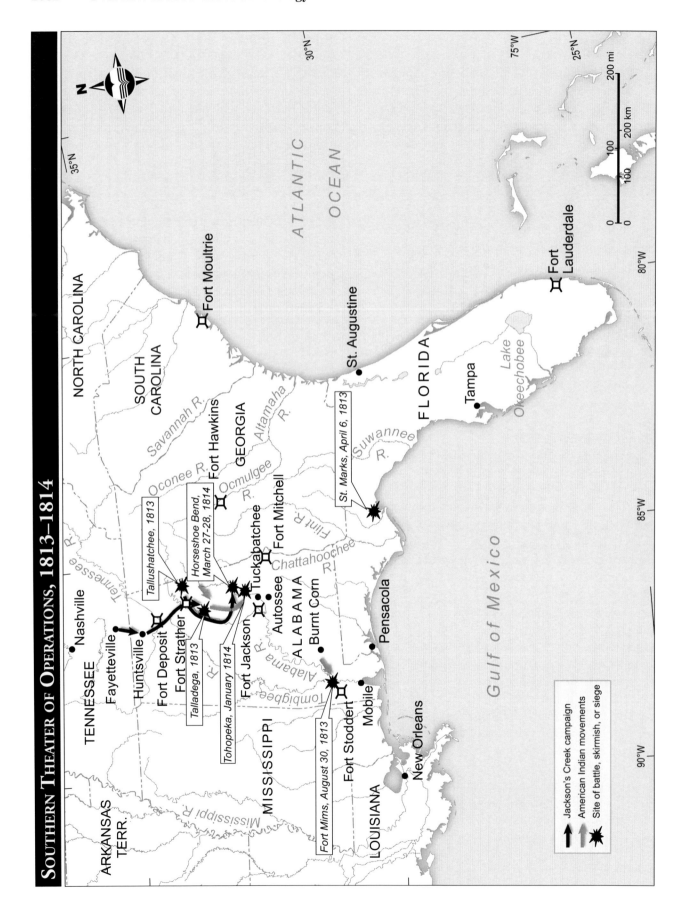

SOUTHERN THEATER OF OPERATIONS, 1813–1814

ARKANSAS TERR.

TENNESSEE

Nashville

Fayetteville

Huntsville

Fort Deposit

Fort Strather

Tallushatchee, 1813

Talladega, 1813

Tohopeka, January 1814

Fort Jackson

Horseshoe Bend, March 27–28, 1814

Tuckabatchee

Autossee

Fort Mims, August 30, 1813

Burnt Corn

ALABAMA

MISSISSIPPI

Fort Stoddert

Mobile

New Orleans

LOUISIANA

Fort Mitchell

GEORGIA

Fort Hawkins

NORTH CAROLINA

SOUTH CAROLINA

Fort Moultrie

St. Augustine

St. Marks, April 6, 1813

Pensacola

FLORIDA

Tampa

Lake Okeechobee

Fort Lauderdale

ATLANTIC OCEAN

Gulf of Mexico

Tennessee R.

Savannah R.

Oconee R.

Ocmulgee R.

Altamaha R.

Flint R.

Chattahoochee R.

Alabama R.

Tombigbee R.

Mississippi R.

Suwannee R.

35°N

30°N

25°N

90°W

85°W

80°W

75°W

N

200 mi

200 km

100

100

0

0

Jackson's Creek campaign

American Indian movements

Site of battle, skirmish, or siege

Finally, with U.S. economic measures taking a heavy toll in Britain, Foreign Secretary Lord Castlereagh announces suspension of the Orders in Council. Unaware of this, two days later on June 18, 1812, the U.S. Congress declares war. Ironically, this so-called War for Free Trade and Sailors' Rights is fought chiefly on land.

The American war hawks anticipate an easy victory. British North America numbers only about 300,000 people, while the United States has more than 8 million. The U.S. Navy is minuscule next to the Royal Navy, but the British are heavily committed against Napoleon, and it will be 1813 before major naval assets can be sent to North America. The U.S. regular army numbers about 7,000 officers and men, while British army strength in Canada is only about 5,000. Given British manpower commitments in Spain, there is little chance of reinforcement. The majority of the population in Upper Canada, moreover, is newly arrived Americans, expected to rally to any U.S. invasion.

In 1812 the British have no option but to remain on the defensive. The Americans plan to go on the offensive and conquer Canada. The U.S. strategic plan for 1812 calls for a three-pronged invasion. In the east, U.S. Army major general Henry Dearborn is to advance up the Lake Champlain route toward Montreal (Montréal). In the center, New York Militia major general Stephen Van Rensselaer is to attack along the Niagara River frontier, while in the west governor of Michigan Territory and U.S. Army brigadier general William Hull is to invade Upper Canada from Detroit. Unfortunately for the Americans, these attacks are not carried out simultaneously, and the British are able to defeat the offensive in detail.

There are three principal reasons for the American defeats on land in 1812. First, although the British regulars are few in number, they are well-trained professionals and have an able commander in Major General Sir Isaac Brock. Second, the Americans are poorly prepared for war. While enthusiastic, their army is both poorly trained and ineptly led. Third and by no means least, there is an alliance between many Native Americans with the British; Shawnee chief Tecumseh plays a key role.

June 24, 1812
Eastern Europe: Napoleonic Wars (continued): Napoleon's invasion of Russia. On June 24, 1812, French emperor Napoleon I sends the first wave of his army,

some 490,000 men, across the Niemen River into Russia. The invading French army group consists of three separate armies. Napoleon commands the northern wing of 250,000 men in East Prussia, his brother King Jérôme of Westphalia has command of the southern wing of 80,000 men at Warsaw, and his stepson Eugène de Beauharnais commands a center contingent, also of 80,000 men. The left flank is protected by French marshal Jacques Macdonald with 30,000 men and Prussian general Hans David Ludwig Count Yorck von Wartenburg with 20,000. Austrian field marshal Prince Charles Philip of Schwarzenberg and 30,000 men protect the right flank.

To oppose him, Czar Alexander has only about 450,000 men, but of this number only 130,000 are in position to contest the French advance. The Russian army facing Napoleon would have been even smaller were it not for the conclusion of an alliance with Sweden that allowed Alexander to remove 30,000 men from Finland and the end to the war with the Ottoman Empire, which permitted the withdrawal of 60,000 men from that front as well.

To oppose Napoleon, Russian czar Alexander I has only about 450,000 men, but of this number only 130,000 under Prince Mikhail Barclay de Tolly are in position against Napoleon. Opposite Jerome is Prince Pyotr Ivanovich Bagration with 48,000 men, while farther south and removed from the action are another 43,000 men under General A. P. Tormassov. Other Russian forces, totaling some 200,000 men, are forming to the east.

See Leaders: Barclay de Tolly, Mikhail Bogdanovich

June 26, 1812
Eastern Europe: Napoleonic Wars (continued): Napoleon's invasion of Russia (continued): French occupation of Vilna. Thus far unopposed by the Russians, Napoleon's troops occupy Vilna (Vilnius) on June 26. Napoleon tarries in Vilna for three weeks, turning it into a major base that could be supplied from Königsberg (Kaliningrad) and Gdańsk (Danzig) on the Baltic by way of the Niemen River. The Russian withdrawal is not by design; with so few troops available at this point, they have no choice.

July 12, 1812
North America: War of 1812 (continued). U.S. Army brigadier general and governor of the Michigan Territory William Hull leads 2,200 men across the Detroit

Russian marshal Prince Mikhail Barclay de Tolly (1761–1818) was a noted military reformer and general who distinguished himself in fighting against the Poles, Swedes, and Turks, as well as in the Napoleonic Wars. He later commanded the Russian Army. (Hulton Archive)

River in an invasion of Upper Canada. His forces soon occupy Sandwich. After the fall of Fort Mackinac and concerned about the large number of Native Americans aligned with the British, Hull withdraws to Detroit on August 8.

July 17, 1812
North America: War of 1812 (continued): British capture of Fort Mackinac. On July 17 British captain Charles Roberts leads a force of 600 (400 of them Indians) in an attack on U.S. Fort Mackinac on Michilimackinac Island, in the strait between Lake Huron and Lake Michigan. The Americans, commanded by Lieutenant Peter Hanks, do not know that the war has begun and are taken completely by surprise. All 61 surrender.

The capture of Fort Mackinac renders the American advance into Upper Canada under Brigadier General William Hull difficult, for control of the lake puts the British in position to cut him off. This initial

British success leads large numbers of Native Americans to join their side.

July 22, 1812
Southern Europe: Iberian Peninsula: Spain: Napoleonic Wars (continued): Peninsular War (continued): Battle of Salamanca. In June 1812 allied commander British lieutenant general Sir Arthur Wellesley, Earl of Wellington, advances into Castille intending to bring French forces there under French marshal Auguste Marmont into battle. On June 17 Wellington reaches the city of Salamanca. Both sides then maneuver for advantage. From mid-July, Marmont and 48,500 men outmarch and outmaneuver Wellington and his 50,000 troops.

Believing that he has no alternative but to withdraw, Wellington orders his baggage to the rear. Thinking that Wellington is in full retreat, Marmont orders a pursuit. Wellington, realizing that the French are overextended, seizes the opportunity. In the Battle of Salamanca, fought some five miles south of the city and also known as the Battle of the Arapiles, he turns and attacks the French advance units, driving them back into the main body. Marmont is wounded, and his army is driven from the field.

In what is Wellington's most brilliant victory to date, the French suffer 13,000 casualties, including 7,000 taken prisoner, and 20 guns captured; allied casualties are only about 4,800. This crushing French defeat opens the way for Wellington to take Madrid.

July 29, 1812
Eastern Europe: Napoleonic Wars (continued): Napoleon's invasion of Russia (continued): French capture of Vitebsk. French emperor Napoleon I lets Marshal Joachim Murat lead the way into Russia with his cavalry. With no sense of the limits of men and horses, Murat's pace condemns those following him to exhaustion. The price seems acceptable to Napoleon at the time if he can catch and destroy the Russians. Napoleon inserts his own army between the two Russian armies, hoping to destroy each in turn. He expects King Jérôme to prevent Russian forces to the south under Prince Pyotr Ivanovich Bagration from joining the army under Prince Mikhail Barclay de Tolly to the north but is unaware that Jérôme is chasing after Bagration, who has veered south. When Napoleon discovers this, he replaces Jérôme with Marshal Louis Nicolas Davout. An angry Jérôme deserts the army and returns to Westphalia. Amid

EUROPE IN 1810

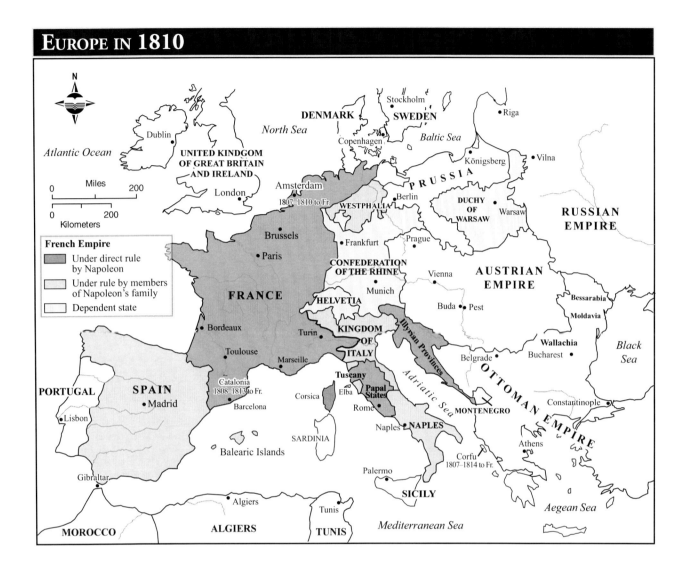

the confusion over the French change of command, Bagration escapes to the north to join Barclay near Smolensk.

Napoleon expects the Russians to fight for Vitebsk (present-day Belarus). They do not. Napoleon takes Vitebsk on July 29 but tarries there for two weeks, until August 12. He cannot help but notice that despite the fact that there had been very little fighting, the Grande Armée has already lost some 100,000 men through hunger, heat, disease, desertion, and straggling. Losses are particularly heavy among the army's cavalry and draft horses.

August 12, 1812
Southern Europe: Iberian Peninsula: Spain: Napoleonic Wars (continued): Peninsular War (continued): The Allies capture Madrid. Following his brilliant

victory at Salamanca, British lieutenant general Sir Arthur Wellesley, Earl of Wellington, advances on Madrid. With little means to defend the city, King Joseph flees to Ocaña, leaving behind 2,000 men in the Retiro arsenal and a large number of immovable sick. Wellington and his allied force enter the city on August 12, to general popular enthusiasm. Cut off from fresh water and with only limited food, the Retiro garrison surrenders on August 14. Wellington secures 180 guns and substantial quantities of military stores.

August 13, 1812
Southern Europe: Iberian Peninsula: Spain: Napoleonic Wars (continued): Peninsular War (continued): Allied French counteroffensive. Following his capture of Madrid, British lieutenant general Sir Arthur

Wellesley, Earl of Wellington, moves north in hopes of completely destroying the French Army of Portugal that he had shattered in the Battle of Salamanca. To Wellington's surprise, its new commander, French marshal Bertrand Clausel, has been actively reconstituting the army and resupplying it from the extensive depots at Burgos. On August 13, in fact, Clausel sets out on a counteroffensive with 25,000 men, relieving a number of French garrisons.

August 15, 1812

North America: War of 1812 (continued): British capture of Fort Dearborn. Brigadier General William Hull at Detroit orders Captain Nathan Heald, commander of Fort Dearborn (present-day Chicago, Illinois), to evacuate. On August 15, 1812, however, the evacuees are ambushed by some 500 Potawatomi Indians. Of the 148 soldiers, women, and children who evacuated the fort, 86 are slain in what becomes known as the Fort Dearborn Massacre. The Native Americans burn the fort the next day. Although this event brings more Native Americans to the British side, it shocks the American public and leads to calls for revenge.

August 16, 1812

North America: War of 1812 (continued): Surrender of Detroit. Afraid of being cut off, inept U.S. brigadier general William Hull withdraws to Detroit from Upper Canada. British commander of Upper Canada Major General Sir Isaac Brock arrives with a far smaller force of 730 British and Canadians and 600 Native Americans under Tecumseh. Brock parades his men to give the impression of greater numbers and calls on Hull to surrender, claiming that he will be unable to control the Native Americans if fighting begins. Knowing of earlier Indian massacres of Americans, the unnerved Hull surrenders on August 16, 1812. Brock then quickly marches back to meet the American threat on the Niagara front. Hull is subsequently court-martialed. Found guilty, he is sentenced to death; the punishment is remitted as a consequence of his Revolutionary War service.

August 17, 1812

Eastern Europe: Napoleonic Wars (continued): Napoleon's invasion of Russia (continued): French capture of Smolensk. At Smolensk on the Dnieper River, Russian forces under princes Mikhail Barclay de Tolly and Pyotr Ivanovich Bagration join and, for the first time since the invasion, stand and fight the French. On August 17 the French storm the fortified city and, at considerable cost, breach its high, thick walls. That night the Russians are able to withdraw in good order across the Dnieper, setting the city on fire on their departure. The Battle of Smolensk claims some 8,000–10,000 French casualties and 15,000 Russians.

It had been Napoleon's plan to spend the winter at Smolensk and organize his conquests, but the ease and speed of his advance leads him to decide to proceed to Moscow that autumn, convinced that taking the city will force Czar Alexander I to treat with him. Marshal Joachim Murat resumes the advance, again with a killing pace that has devastating effects on the rest of the army, which is trying to keep up. Morale among the troops is sharply declining, and discipline is collapsing.

August 19, 1812

Western Atlantic Ocean: War of 1812 (continued). The U.S. frigate *Constitution,* under the command of Captain Isaac Hull, captures the British frigate *Guerrière,* under the command of Captain James R. Dacres. The battle occurs about 400 miles southeast of Halifax. The British ship, a defenseless hulk after the battle, is torched and sinks the next day.

September 7, 1812

Eastern Europe: Napoleonic Wars (continued): Napoleon's invasion of Russia (continued): Battle of Borodino. French emperor Napoleon I's rapidly deteriorating Grande Armée advances on Moscow. Meanwhile, Prince Mikhail Barclay de Tolly's failure to halt Napoleon's advance leads Czar Alexander I to replace Tolly on August 20, 1812, with Field Marshal Mikhail Kutuzov. Alexander makes this appointment with the greatest reluctance, for the gulf between the two men is deep following the czar's decision over Kutuzov's objections that had brought Russian defeat in the Battle of Austerlitz in 1805, for which Kutuzov has borne the blame.

Kutuzov is now 67, bloated, and dissolute. He is also unflappable and cunning. Kutuzov had originally urged withdrawal and a scorched-earth policy to defeat the invaders. Now ordered to stand and fight, he plans a defensive battle behind well-fortified positions at Borodino, the last natural defense before Moscow. A defensive battle will play to the stolid nature of the Russian soldier.

The Battle of Borodino on September 7, 1812, gave Emperor Napoleon I and the French possession of Moscow but claimed as many as 76,000 lives and proved to be a hollow victory. (Library of Congress)

Kutuzov's lines are some four miles in length, and he deploys 640 guns. Napoleon has only 587 guns, but they are superior in quality to those of the Russians and are better handled. For the first time in his career, however, Napoleon, who relies primarily on mobility, will be forced to attack a well-entrenched enemy force. Because Napoleon has lost so many men on the march, the two armies are approximately equal in size: 130,000 in Napoleon's Grande Armée and about 120,000 on the Russian side.

French marshal Louis Nicolas Davout, impressed with the strength of the Russian position, urges Napoleon to turn it into an attack around the Russian southern flank. Napoleon, fearful that the Russians will simply slip away, rejects this sound advice in favor of a frontal assault to destroy the Russian Army. The emperor plans for massed French artillery fire to destroy the Russian redoubts, which will then be taken by infantry assault.

On September 6, with both armies in place, their commanders seek to inspire their troops. Napoleon

has just received a painting of his son, and he props it up on a chair for viewing by the men as they march by. Kutuzov rides among his men with an icon of the Holy Virgin of Smolensk.

At 6:00 a.m. on September 7 the French artillery opens up, beginning the battle. This fire fails to destroy either the Russian redoubts or their artillery. Successive French ground assaults against the Russian positions on high ground overlooking the battlefield gain ground only slowly and at heavy human cost in the face of determined Russian resistance and savage counterattacks. The attackers at last force the defenders from their redoubts in the late afternoon, only to see them re-forming to the rear.

It is one of Napoleon's principles to throw in his reserves at the decisive moment of battle. Marshals Joachim Murat and Michel Ney now urge him in person to do so, but here so far from home the emperor is reluctant to commit the Imperial Guard, the last unbloodied formation and his personal reserve. The battle thus ends without decisive tactical result. That

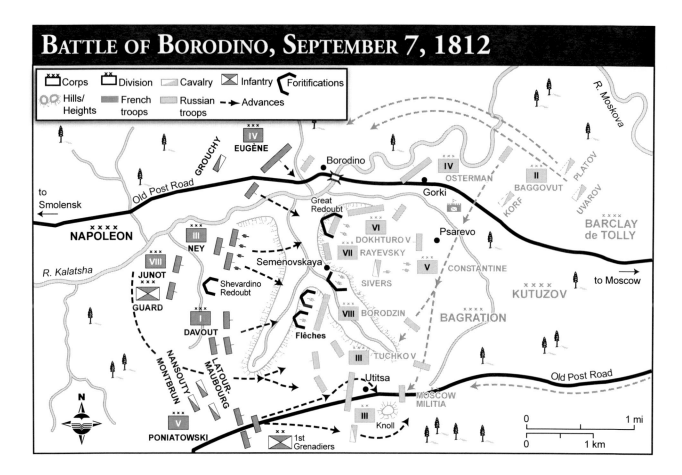

night both armies encamp on the battlefield, and the next day Kutuzov withdraws his army off toward Moscow, enabling Bonaparte to claim victory.

Borodino claims 28,000–31,000 casualties (including 47 generals) in the Grande Armée and upwards of 45,000 Russians. As usual Napoleon trumpets a great victory, minimizing his own losses while exaggerating those of the Russians. He and his men know better. The victory is a hollow one, for the Russian Army is still largely intact.

September 14, 1812
Eastern Europe: Napoleonic Wars (continued): Napoleon's invasion of Russia (continued): Napoleon enters Moscow. Russian marshal Mikhail Kutuzov now withdraws back into Moscow and then to the south followed by much of the city population, abandoning the ancient Russian capital to its fate. Napoleon enters Moscow on September 14 with 95,000 men. That night the city, largely of wood, is in flames. The conflagration is set by the Russians, who have also disabled much of the firefighting equipment. For the

next five days the French army is occupied fighting the flames; they succeed in saving the Kremlin.

Napoleon now waits for Czar Alexander I to come to terms. Kutuzov sends notes that make Napoleon believe that the Russians will treat with him, but Alexander delays. Fearful of the reaction of Europe should he withdraw without being able to claim victory, Napoleon rejects the advice of those who know the nature of Russian winter and delays the decision.

September 19–October 10, 1812
Southern Europe: Iberian Peninsula: Spain: Napoleonic Wars (continued): Peninsular War (continued): Allied siege of Burgos. British lieutenant general Sir Arthur Wellesley, Earl of Wellington, decides to take the major French supply depot of Burgos, investing it on September 19. General Jean Louis Dubreton and 2,000 men defend the fortress. The British try three mining attacks, but these cause little damage, and the allied assaults that follow all end in failure. With heavy rains and French reinforcements en

route, Wellington breaks off the siege. He is forced to leave behind many of his heavy guns. Debreton is relieved on October 22.

The French suffer 300 dead and a few seriously wounded in the siege, while British casualties are at least 2,100.

October 13, 1812
North America: War of 1812 (continued): Battle of Queenston Heights. After taking the surrender of Detroit, British commander of Upper Canada Major General Sir Isaac Brock rapidly marches back to the Niagara front to meet the American threat there. Brock arrives at Fort George on August 23, 1812, and prepares for an expected American attack. He has about 2,400 men but does not know where the Americans will strike. New York Militia major general Stephen Van Rensselaer commands a force of some 3,300 militia and 1,300 regulars.

On October 13 Van Rensselaer crosses the Niagara River. The Americans are poorly prepared, with only 13 bateaux to transport their army into Canada and with little ammunition and no entrenching tools. Van Rensselaer gets only about 1,350 of his force across the river to occupy Queenston Heights. Brock, Canada's first war hero, is killed in the ensuing fighting, but the Americans are crushed by superior British numbers, as the New York Militia refuses to cross the river into Canada. British losses are 20 killed and 85 wounded. The Americans suffer between 60 and 200 killed, more than 170 wounded, and 950 captured. Van Rensselaer resigns his commission. He is succeeded by the equally inept U.S. Army brigadier general Alexander Smyth, who makes an even more feeble attempt to cross the Niagara River on November 28, after which he is dropped from the army rolls.

October 18, 1812
Western Atlantic Ocean: War of 1812 (continued). The U.S. Navy sloop *Wasp* (commanded by Lieutenant Jacob Jones) defeats the British sloop *Frolic* (under Lieutenant Thomas Winyates). The American ship batters the British ship into a helpless wreck but is itself so damaged in the fight that it is unable to escape and is forced to strike to the Royal Navy ship of the line *Poitiers.*

October 19–24, 1812
Eastern Europe: Napoleonic Wars (continued): Napoleon's invasion of Russia (continued): The retreat

from Moscow and Battle of Maloyaroslavets. Finally, after five weeks of fruitless waiting in Moscow, on October 17 French emperor Napoleon I orders preparations for the withdrawal from Moscow. The next day Russian forces launch a strong attack against French forces under Marshal Joachim Murat across the Nara River. Surrounded, Murat is almost captured; however, he is able to cut his way out with most of his men and rejoin Napoleon at Moscow.

The retreat begins on October 19. The 100,000 French make use of every possible vehicle available and, had it been in normal weather conditions, might have been able to pull it off. Moving southwest from Moscow, for five days the French encounter little opposition. Then on October 24 at Maloyaroslavets the Russians appear in force behind the Luzha River.

The ensuing battle between 15,000 Russians (later reinforced to 25,000) under Marshal Mikhail Kutuzov and a French corps of some 20,000 men under Prince Eugène de Beauharnais is hard-fought. The town changes hands nearly a dozen times before the French secure it. In the battle the French sustain some 5,000 casualties, the Russians 6,000.

Napoleon now makes the fateful decision to turn back to the northwest and follow the same route by which he had advanced to Moscow. While more secure, this route has been stripped bare of resources by both the Russian and French armies in the earlier French advance east and thus is totally unable to sustain the army. With no forage available, the French army's logistical system collapses.

October 25, 1812
Eastern Atlantic Ocean: War of 1812 (continued). The U.S. Navy frigate *United States* (commanded by Captain Stephen Decatur) defeats Royal Navy frigate *Macedonian* (commanded by Captain John Carden). The engagement occurs near Madeira, but Decatur is able to bring his prize across the Atlantic and into port. The first British frigate taken by the Americans, the *Macedonian* is repaired and commissioned in the U.S. Navy.

October 25–November 13, 1812
Eastern Europe: Napoleonic Wars (continued): Napoleon's invasion of Russia (continued): The march to Smolensk. The Russians refuse to engage the French in pitched battle and instead attack isolated units. Cossack units harass the starving French whenever

possible. Winter sets in early and is unusually severe. The Russians are used to the conditions, but the French are utterly unprepared. Mud turns to snow and ice, and men and horses slip, starve, and freeze to death. Discipline collapses.

On November 13, 1812, some 50,000 Frenchmen, all that is left of the 100,000 who had departed Moscow, straggle into Smolensk. Perhaps only 30,000 men are capable of combat.

October 31, 1812

Southwest Asia: Russo-Persian War (continued): Battle of Aslanduz. On October 31, 1812, a Russian army under General Pyotr Kotlyarevsky surprises and defeats a far larger Persian army under Abbas Mirza on the Aras River at Aslanduz. This is the most important battle of the war. Shortly thereafter the Russians storm Lenkoran.

October 31–November 17, 1812

Southern Europe: Iberian Peninsula: Spain: Napoleonic Wars (continued): Peninsular War (continued): Allied retreat. French military commanders in Spain make major efforts and bring their strength to more than 110,000 men. Allied commander in Spain British lieutenant general Sir Arthur Wellesley, Earl of Wellington, has only 73,000 men and is soon forced into a withdrawal. The British abandon Madrid on October 31, destroying the Retiro and vast quantities of supplies and food. Wellington is forced into a precipitate retreat to Salamanca and then across the Huebra River on November 17, where the French abandon the pursuit. Wellington then goes into winter cantonments near Cuidad Rodrigo.

Wellington unfairly blames his subordinates and takes no responsibility himself. His army is now in a shambles, but he soon receives reinforcements from Britain, an enhanced subsidy, and appointment as general in chief of the Spanish Army and allied commander in the peninsula (a position thus far denied him by his stubborn and on occasion difficult Spanish allies). Wellington now assumes command of 160,000 Spanish troops. Reorganizing his resources, he is ready to resume offensive operations that spring.

November 15–18, 1812

Eastern Europe: Napoleonic Wars (continued): Napoleon's invasion of Russia (continued): Battle of Krasnoi. French emperor Napoleon I with about 16,000 men and 50 guns finds his way blocked at Krasnoi (Kransny) by as many as 35,000 Russians under General Mikhail Kutuzov. In a half dozen actions, collectively known as the Battle of Krasnoi, most of the French manage to cut their way through. Still, the Russians have taken 6,000 prisoners and a large number of guns.

Marshal Michel Ney, in command of the rear guard of perhaps 8,000 men, arrives in the afternoon of November 18 only to discover Napoleon gone and Russian general Mikhail Miloradovich at Krasnoi. Repulsed with heavy losses, Ney withdraws back toward Smolensk. The Russians do not pursue, and Ney then soon turns back toward the Dnieper and manages to get a number of his men across where the ice seems thick enough to permit a crossing that night near Syrokorenie. The ice gives way under the vehicles, however. Only 1,500 men manage to cross. The remainder and the vehicles remained behind. Ney's conduct in the retreat from Russia causes Napoleon to call him "the bravest of the brave."

November 19, 1812

North America: War of 1812 (continued): American advance on Montreal. The third prong of the American offensive into Canada in 1812 is also the largest. U.S. major general Henry Dearborn commands 5,000 men and, timing his own actions to coincide with those of Brigadier General Alexander Smyth on the Niagara front, moves down Lake Champlain from Plattsburgh to Rouses Point. On November 19, 1812, however, many American militiamen in the force insist on their constitutional right not to be forced to fight on foreign soil and refuse to cross into Canada.

November 20, 1812

North America: War of 1812 (continued): Battle of Lacolle Mills. On November 20, 1812, Major General Henry Dearborn and some 600 American militia attack the Canadian frontier Lacolle Mills blockhouse near Champlain, Ontario. It is defended by Lieutenant Colonel Charles-Michel d'Irumberry de Salaberry and some 520 British troops, Canadian militia, and Mohawk warriors. Although the Americans capture the blockhouse early on November 20, a second American militia force, unaware of what has transpired, attacks the first, and in the aftermath of American fighting American, Salaberry launches a counterattack that forces the Americans to withdraw to Champlain. The demoralized American militia refuse to renew the offensive, and on November 23 Dearborn returns his army to Plattsburgh.

November 26–29, 1812

Eastern Europe: Napoleonic Wars (continued): Napoleon's invasion of Russia (continued): Crossing of the Berezina River. At Orsha, French emperor Napoleon I orders the remnants of his army to take a more southerly approach to Vilna, even though this means that they will have to cross the Berezina River (near Borisov in present-day Belarus). This is because of the threat of a 30,000-man Russian army from the north commanded by General Ludwig Adolf Peter Wittgenstein. Marshal Mikhail Kutuzov meanwhile is two days' march to the southeast with 80,000 men; Admiral Pavel Chichagov, with 35,000 men, is to the west of the Berezina at Borisov. Napoleon then has only about 25,000 men, with as many or more stragglers, and perhaps only a dozen guns.

When Napoleon makes this decision the Berezina is frozen, but as the French approach the river, the Russian weather turns. An early thaw melts the ice and transforms the river into a formidable obstacle. At the Berezina, however, Napoleon is reinforced by troops under marshals Nicolas Oudinot and Claude Victor, bringing his effective strength to some 48,000 men. Russian forces still vastly outnumber his own, have far more artillery, and are better provisioned. Probably only Napoleon's presence saves the army, for the Russian commanders are wary of attacking him.

When the French arrive at the river, however, they discover that the bridge at Borisov has been destroyed. The more than 100-yard-wide river presents a formidable obstacle. Fortunately for Napoleon, military engineer commander General Jean Baptiste Eblé has managed to retain crucial forges and tools and needs only protection from Chichagov's troops on the west bank to bridge the river. Napoleon orders Oudinot to draw off Chichagov by making a move south against Tshetshakov. This works, while Eblé's engineers brave the frigid water to construct a bridge.

This accomplished, Napoleon's few cavalry quickly cross over, followed by infantry to hold the bridgehead. A second bridge is thrown across the river some hours later, and the few French guns remaining go across it to reinforce the bridgehead. Too late, Chichagov realizes that he has been duped and rushes north to attack the 11,000 French troops now holding the bridgehead.

By midday on November 27 the French rear guard east of the river is battling Wittgenstein's arriving army. Part of one of the two bridges collapses in late afternoon, but the French engineers manage to repair it by early evening. Davout and Prince Eugène de Beauharnais cross with their men, leaving only Victor's corps to hold off Wittgenstein's Russians on the east bank. Victor's men cross after midnight on November 28.

Wittgenstein now closes in, and by the morning of November 29 his artillery begins firing on the bridges. Eblé continues to hold so that as many French stragglers as possible can cross. By 9:00 a.m., however, he withdraws his last defenders and burns the bridges. A few hundred stragglers are caught on the bridges and die. Another 10,000 are left on the east bank to become victims of the Cossacks.

What remains of Napoleon's Grande Armée now pushes Chichagov aside and continues the retreat. The crossing of the Berezina claims some 15,000 French and 13,000 Russian casualties, not counting the stragglers caught on the east bank, but Napoleon has escaped with 100,000 men, half of them stragglers. The road to Vilna and safety is now open. Nonetheless, the word "Bérézinade" becomes a synonym for disaster.

December 5–19, 1812

Western Europe: France: Napoleonic Wars (continued): Napoleon's invasion of Russia (continued). At Smorgoniye on December 5, French emperor Napoleon I decides that he must return to Paris as quickly as possible, rally his resources, and also prevent a possible coup d'état. Indeed, ex-general Claude François de Malet had managed to convince part of the Paris garrison that Napoleon had died in Russia and for a few hours had managed to seize control of the Paris ministries. Traveling incognito by both sleigh and carriage, Napoleon arrives in Paris before dawn on December 19, having covered 1,300 miles in less than 15 days.

On December 8 meanwhile, elements of the Grande Armée reach Vilna, but there is no rest for the survivors. Not until they are across the Niemen River is there refuge at last. Gradually survivors trickle in, but of the force of some 460,000 men who entered Russia in June only as many as 100,000 return. A like number remain as prisoners in Russia, and the same number have perished in battle; the remainder are lost to disease, starvation, and the elements. On December 12 Marshal Alexandre Berthier informs Napoleon that of the 50,000-man Imperial Guard that had entered Russia, fewer than 500 survive.

Napoleon has been unable to conquer all Europe. It remains to be seen if all of Europe can conquer Napoleon.

December 29, 1812
South Atlantic Ocean: War of 1812 (continued). The U.S. frigate *Constitution* (commanded by Captain William Bainbridge) defeats the British frigate *Java* (commanded by Captain Henry Lambert) off Bahia, Brazil. Lambert is among the heavy British casualties, mortally wounded. Bainbridge burns the *Java,* a total wreck, on December 31.

December 30, 1812
Central Europe: Prussia: Napoleonic Wars (continued): Convention of Tauroggen. Prussian general Hans David Ludwig Count Yorck von Wartenburg, commander of the Prussian detachment in Napoleon's Grande Armée, on his own initiative and without the approval of King Frederick William III signs a truce with the Russian general Hans Karl von Diebitsch at Tauroggen (present-day Tauragè, Lithuania). Yorck agrees that his corps will await orders from the Prussian king and in any case will not fight against Russia for the next two months.

Yorck's act is a turning point in Prussian history. It makes the decision for the vacillating Frederick William and marks the beginning of the Prussian insurgency against Napoleon. This in turn leads directly to the so-called War of German Liberation.

1812
Southeast Asia: Cambodia: Civil war and Siamese intervention. Ang Snguon, brother of Cambodian ruler Ang Cha, revolts and calls in the Siamese to assist him in gaining the throne. Siamese ruler Rama II sends in troops, who quickly overrun Cambodia. Ang Cha then calls on Vietnam to assist him. Vietnamese emperor Gia Long sends in a Vietnamese army, which defeats the Siamese. Vietnam is then predominant in Cambodia.

1812–1813
North America: War of 1812 (continued): Naval Builders' War on the Great Lakes. Brigadier General William Hull's surrender at Detroit in August 1812 convinces Washington that command of the Great Lakes is essential. The British are determined to retain their naval superiority, though. The result is a so-called Naval Builders' War on Lakes Erie and Ontario during the winter of 1812–1813, with each side seeking to wrest control of the Great Lakes from the other.

January 22, 1813
North America: War of 1812 (continued): Battle of Frenchtown. In the western theater, the Americans are forced after the surrender of Detroit in August 1812 to fall back on the line of the Wabash and Maumee rivers. British forces, now commanded by Brigadier General Henry Proctor and assisted by Shawnee chief Tecumseh (commissioned a British brigadier general), hold the initiative. U.S. major general William Henry Harrison is ordered to retake Detroit, but he has few means with which to accomplish this.

While Harrison is trying to assemble adequate resources, Proctor takes a number of American outposts including Frenchtown on the River Raisin, held by Brigadier General James Winchester. American losses are heavy: 197 killed or wounded and another 737 taken prisoner. Native Americans in British service murder many of the American wounded.

The British also lay siege to Fort Meigs on the Maumee River (May 1–9) and attack Fort Stephenson on the Sandusky River (August 2). Neither effort is successful, however. Harrison meanwhile is unable to advance on Detroit until the Americans secure control of Lake Erie.

February 24, 1813
South Atlantic Ocean: War of 1812 (continued). The U.S. Navy sloop *Hornet* (commanded by Captain James Lawrence) engages the British Royal Navy sloop *Peacock* (commanded by Lieutenant William Peake) off the coast of Brazil. The *Peacock* is defeated and sinks following a lopsided 15-minute engagement.

March 3, 1813
Northern Europe: Sweden: Napoleonic Wars (continued). Crown Prince Karl Johan (former French

marshal Jean Baptiste Bernadotte) of Sweden concludes a treaty with the British government. In return for a substantial financial subsidy, Sweden remains among the allied powers opposing France.

March 16, 1813
Central Europe: Prussia: Napoleonic Wars (continued): War of German Liberation. Forced into double dealing by the large French troop presence on Prussian soil, Prussian king Frederick William III officially repudiates the Convention of Tauroggen, although it has already irretrievably compromised Prussian policy. After Russian troops cross the Oder River on February 28, he signs a treaty of alliance with Czar Alexander I. Russia pledges to continue the war against France until all of Prussia's former territory is restored.

On March 16, 1813, Prussia formally declares war on France. Frederick William issues a stirring declaration to "my people," and a wave of anti-French sentiment sweeps Germany, beginning the German War of Liberation.

The Prussian Army is vastly improved from that of 1806–1807. Since 1808, Prussian minister of war General Count Gerhard von Scharnhorst has carried out extensive reforms that include removal of inefficient officers; the opening of commissions to all, regardless of birth; an end to corporal punishment; the creation of a highly efficient general staff; national conscription and expansion of reserves; and the establishment of a militia (*Landwehr*).

March 1813
Central Europe: Napoleonic Wars (continued): War of German Liberation (continued): New coalition against France. Austrian field marshal Prince Charles Philip of Schwarzenberg has also defected from the Grande Armée with his corps and withdrawn into Bohemia. For the moment Austria remains neutral, waiting to see how the military balance shifts.

French emperor Napoleon I, who left impetuous Marshal Joachim Murat in charge of the army while he himself raced to Paris, now replaces Murat with the more steady Prince Eugène de Beauharnais. Napoleon also reinforces Eugène's troops to 68,000 men. Although many of his top commanders have lost faith in Napoleon, support for him remains strong in France. The country now faces a coalition

Austrian Karl Philip zu Schwarzenberg (1771–1820) commanded allied forces in Germany during the campaign of 1813 and won the decisive Battle of Leipzig over Emperor Napoleon I on October 16–19. (Engraving by Hassell and Rickards, 1814. The David Markham Collection.)

of powers against it consisting of Britain, Russia, Prussia, and Sweden, however.

See Leaders: Schwarzenberg, Karl Philip zu

April 27, 1813
North America: War of 1812 (continued): American offensive into Upper Canada: Attack on York. New U.S. secretary of war John Armstrong lays ambitious plans for a two-pronged invasion of Upper Canada. This commences with an amphibious operation on Lake Ontario headed by Commodore Isaac Chauncey and Major General Henry Dearborn. The original and sounder plan was to move against Kingston, but on the recommendation of Chauncey it is shifted to the presumed easier target of York (present-day Toronto), capital of Upper Canada. The Americans hope to seize or destroy shipping there, including several warships under construction, and wrest control of the lake from the British.

The American expedition sets out from Sackets Harbor on April 22. Chauncey commands 13 warships and a store ship, all manned by about 860 sailors and marines and carrying about 1,800 soldiers. The Americans arrive off York on April 27. To meet the attackers, British commander in Upper Canada Major General Sir Roger Hale Sheaffe has at York nearly 1,100 men, including more than 400 regulars, about 500 militia, nearly 100 dockyard workers and town volunteers, and 50 Ojibwa-Mississauga and Chippewa warriors.

Dearborn gives Brigadier General Zebulon M. Pike command of the landing force. York soon surrenders, and the Americans destroy one ship and capture another. More than 260 Americans are killed or injured, including Pike who is mortally wounded, when Sheaffe orders the powder magazine detonated. Against Dearborn's orders, the Americans loot some private homes, and the public buildings of York are burned. The British suffer 200 killed or wounded and another 340 taken prisoner. The raiders return to Sackets Harbor on May 8, having accomplished little beyond hardening Canadian resolve and resentment. The burning of York also gives the British the excuse to torch public buildings in Washington, D.C., during their raid of 1814.

May 2, 1813

Central Europe: Germany: Saxony: Napoleonic Wars (continued): War of German Liberation (continued): Battle of Lützen. French emperor Napoleon I has assembled a new army of 200,000 men that while for the most part enthusiastic (a characteristic not shared by its senior commanders) is almost totally untrained. Particularly grievous for the emperor is the loss in Russia of skilled junior officers and noncommissioned officers as well as trained horses. Equipment is also in short supply, including cannon and muskets. Many of the men do not receive muskets for the first time until they reach the German lands.

Meanwhile, the allies now have arrayed against Napoleon in the vicinity of the Elbe a force of some 100,000 well-trained veterans. On March 27 the Russians occupy Dresden.

Napoleon might have minimized his army's shortcomings by standing on the defensive behind the Rhine, but true to form he takes the offensive. On April 30, 1813, he reaches Naumberg in Saxony to take command of the new Grande Armée. Alto-

gether, he has some 300,000 men in Germany. Saxony is the natural meeting point for the allied and French armies, and all major battles of the campaign occur there.

Austrian foreign minister Klemens von Metternich rejects Napoleon's request that the Austrian army be placed at his disposal. Austria remains neutral for the time being, awaiting battlefield results. Thus on May 1, with about 120,000 men under his direct command, Napoleon orders his army across the Saale River toward Leipzig. The allies, as usual, are caught by surprise by the speed of his advance, but Napoleon is also unaware of their exact dispositions. Field Marshal Mikhail Kutuzov, who had been the allied supreme commander, died in April, and Czar Alexander has yet to name a successor. General Ludwig Adolf Peter Wittgenstein commands the allied force of some 110,000 troops opposing the French emperor.

At Lützen near Leipzig on May 2, Napoleon wins a hard-fought victory. On that day Wittgenstein and Prussian general Gebhard Leberecht von Blücher with 73,000 men surprise Napoleon, whose own army is widely separated and with only 45,000 men initially available. Napoleon is able to hold off the attackers until evening, when he has the numerical advantage (ultimately 110,000 men) and is able to defeat his enemy.

The fighting continues for several hours in the dark, but Napoleon lacks the cavalry to follow up the victory. Each side sustains about 20,000 casualties, but an exuberant Napoleon, who has hazarded his own person during the battle, is convinced that it is a turning point. "I am again the master of Europe," he proclaims.

May 20–21, 1813

Central Europe: Germany: Saxony: Napoleonic Wars (continued): War of German Liberation (continued): Battle of Bautzen. French emperor Napoleon I captures Dresden during May 7–8. With reinforcements from France, he now has 250,000 men. Napoleon detaches Marshal Michel Ney with four corps to march on Berlin and himself pursues the allied army with his main force. Learning that the allies are at the fortified town of Bautzen on the Spree River, Napoleon hurries there and orders Ney to redirect two of his corps south. In a fortuitous move, Ney misunderstands the orders and marches south with all four of his corps. By late on May 19 Napoleon has 115,000 men at Bautzen, while Ney has 85,000 more.

Russian general Ludwig Adolf Peter Wittgenstein commands 96,000 men in well-prepared defensive positions east of the Spree River. Napoleon's plan is to attack the Russians along the Spree front while Ney takes them from the rear. If the plan is properly executed, Napoleon should be able to destroy the entire allied army.

The battle opens at noon on May 20, 1813. Napoleon concentrates artillery against the center of the allied line and, throwing up bridges, sends men across the Spree under fire. By 6:00 p.m. the French have carried Bautzen and the first allied line. Both sides reorganize, with Ney approaching from the north.

Battle resumes the next day, May 21. By midafternoon Napoleon has pushed back Prussian general Gebhard Leberecht von Blücher's corps about one mile, but there the French attack stalls. Ney is slow to arrive and fails to cut the enemy line of retreat so that the Austrian and Prussian forces, far from being trapped, are able to stage a fighting withdrawal. A thunderstorm at 10:00 p.m. ends the battle, with Napoleon again lacking the cavalry to pursue. Each side has sustained about 20,000 casualties. Napoleon has two victories, but in each he has had to commit the Guard to achieve it.

May 22–June 2, 1813

Central Europe: Germany: Saxony: Napoleonic Wars (continued): War of German Liberation (continued): Increasing allied strength. Marshal Louis Nicolas Davout, whom French emperor Napoleon I should have had at Bautzen, takes Hamburg, securing the lower Elbe. Napoleon's problems are increasing, however. French cavalry is still unready; the Cossacks are raiding the French rear areas, disrupting and destroying supply trains; and there are a great many French sick and stragglers apart from the 40,000 men lost in the two French victories.

Allied strength is increasing. Swedish crown prince Karl Johan (former French marshal Jean Baptiste Bernadotte) is advancing into northern Germany with 120,000 men, prepared to enter the war on the allied side. The Austrians are mobilizing 240,000 men in northern Bohemia, close to Napoleon's line of communications. When on June 2 the allies ask for an armistice, therefore, Napoleon immediately agrees.

May 27, 1813

North America: War of 1812 (continued): Capture of Fort George. With Major General Henry Dearborn ill, command on the Lake Ontario front devolves upon U.S. Army colonel Winfield Scott. He teams with Commodore Oliver H. Perry, then operating on Lake Ontario, in an amphibious operation involving about 4,000 men against British Fort George, at the mouth of the Niagara River. Fort George is held by some 1,200 British troops and 500 militiamen, all under Brigadier General John Vincent.

The Americans attack the fort from the rear and take it, although most of the defenders are able to withdraw. The Americans lose 39 killed and 111 captured. British casualties are 52 killed, 44 wounded, and 262 captured.

This American success compels the British at Fort Erie, opposite Buffalo, to withdraw, thus freeing the American warships at the Black Rock navy yard.

May 28–29, 1813

North America: War of 1812 (continued): Battle of Sackets Harbor. Sackets Harbor, New York, becomes a major shipbuilding facility for Lake Ontario and the U.S. naval headquarters for the Great Lakes. There are some 5,200 troops stationed there and 3,000 men working at the shipyard. Sir George Prevost, governor-general of Canada, mounts an amphibious assault on the village while Commodore Isaac Chauncey, the American warships, and much of the garrison are at the western end of the lake operating against York and Fort George.

Prevost crosses the lake from Kingston with a land force of some 900 men under Colonel Edward Baynes in Commodore Sir James Yeo's squadron of 6 ships towing dozens of barges, bateaux, and smaller craft. On May 28, 1813, they intercept an American supply convoy bound for Sackets Harbor from Oswego. Twelve of the 19 supply boats and 70 men are captured, but the remaining 100 Americans make it overland to Sackets Harbor, raising the number of regulars there under Brigadier General Jacob J. Brown to 500 men. There are also some 600 militiamen.

Although the defenses are in poor condition, the Americans succeed in driving off the British. The defense is marred by mistaken orders to destroy naval storehouses and two warships, although one of the latter under construction is saved. American losses are 21 killed, 84 wounded, and 26 missing. British casualties are 48 killed, 195 wounded, and 16 missing; most of the wounded are taken prisoner.

May 1813–July 1814

South America: Venezuela: Bolívar's campaigns (continued): La Campaña Admirable. Securing a military command in New Grenada (now Colombia), Simón Bolívar leads an invasion of Spanish-controlled Venezuela in May 1813 and defeats the Spanish in six hard-fought battles, known as Campaña Admirable. The first is a victory over Spanish general Juan Domingo Monteverde in the Battle of Lastaguanes. Entering Mérida on May 23, Bolívar is proclaimed El Liberador. He then takes Caracas on August 6.

Civil war soon breaks out, however. Bolívar wins a series of battles over the royalists at Araure (December 5, 1813), La Victoria (February 1814), San Mateo (March 1814), and Carabobo (May 1814). He is then defeated by royalist general José Tomás Boves at La Puerta (July 1814), however, and forced to flee to New Grenada.

June 1, 1813

Western Atlantic Ocean: War of 1812 (continued). The British frigate *Shannon* (commanded by Captain Philip Broke) defeats the U.S. frigate *Chesapeake* (commanded by Captain James Lawrence). The British skein of single-ship-engagement losses is broken when the *Shannon,* with probably the best-trained gunnery ship in the Royal Navy, engages the *Chesapeake,* with a new and largely untrained crew. Lawrence foolishly accepts Broke's challenge and rejects maneuver in favor of a gunnery duel, only to be defeated in a sanguinary battle.

Although it lasts only 11 minutes, the battle claims 148 American and 83 British killed or wounded. Following its capture, the *Chesapeake* is repaired and taken into the Royal Navy. Whether or not he actually uttered them, the mortally wounded Lawrence's reported words—"Don't give up the ship!"—become a rallying cry for the U.S. Navy.

June 4–August 16, 1813

Central Europe: Germany: Saxony: Napoleonic Wars (continued): War of German Liberation (continued): Armistice of Poischwitz. On June 4, 1813, the allies and French emperor Napoleon I sign an armistice at Poischwitz to last until July 20. Both sides intend to use the time to rest and reinforce. The allies also hope to convince Austria to join the war on their side.

On June 14 Czar Alexander I of Russia, inspired by Austrian foreign minister Klemens von Metternich, proposes a peace conference at Prague. On June 24 Metternich concludes with Prussia and Russia the Treaty of Reichenbach. He promises to put four demands to Napoleon, and if he fails to meet these, Austria will enter the war.

On June 26 Metternich meets with Napoleon at Dresden. Napoleon rebuffs Metternich's demands, claiming that Austria will not dare to go to war against him and, if it does, will be beaten. Metternich reports later that he told Napoleon upon leaving that he was a lost man. That same evening, the Austrian decision to go to war is sealed by news of the British victory at Vitoria in Spain, marking the de facto end of French rule there and virtually ensuring a British invasion of southern France from Spain.

Despite the failure of the Napoleon-Metternich meeting, both sides agree to extend the armistice to August 16, and the peace talks open at Prague. While Napoleon sends Caulaincourt as his representative, he refuses any meaningful concessions. The allies demand that the Grand Duchy of Warsaw be ceded to Russia, that Austria receive back the Illyrian Provinces, that Prussia be restored to its 1805 territory, and that the Confederation of the Rhine be dissolved. With no agreement, both sides again resort to the court of war.

June 6, 1813

North America: War of 1812 (continued): Battle of Stoney Creek. Following the American capture of Fort George, a force of some 2,000 Americans under brigadier generals William H. Winder and John Chandler pursues the retreating British under Brigadier General John Vincent. In the predawn hours of June 6, 1813, Vincent turns on his pursuers at Stoney Creek (Stony Creek) some 10 miles from Hamilton and, with only 700 men, halts their advance. British losses in the battle are 22 dead and 134 wounded. The Americans suffer 55 dead and wounded and 113 captured. Chandler and Winder are among the prisoners. U.S. forces at Fort Erie withdraw on June 9, and the British reoccupy that post.

June 21, 1813

Southern Europe: Iberian Peninsula: Spain: Napoleonic Wars (continued): Peninsular War (continued):

Battle of Vitoria. In the spring of 1813, having re-organized his forces, allied commander in the Ibe-rian Peninsula Sir Arthur Wellesley, Earl of Welling-ton, takes the offensive. His Iberian forces total some 172,000 men against 200,000 French. In a series of maneuvers, the allies force the French back. On Na-poleon's orders, King Joseph again abandons Madrid on May 17 and withdraws north.

Napoleon orders Joseph to concentrate his forces at Valladolid to block an allied invasion of France from Spain. Joseph moves too slowly, however, and is outflanked at Valladolid and forced north of the Ebro River.

With some 60,000 men, Joseph establishes defen-sive positions south and west of Vitoria. Although outnumbered by Wellington's 80,000 men (50,000 British and 30,000 Portuguese troops), Joseph has more guns (150 to 90). Joseph and his chief of staff, Marshal Jean Baptiste Jourdan, compound their prob-lems by widely dispersing their defenders.

In the Battle of Vitoria on June 21, 1813, Welling-ton attacks simultaneously in four columns from the south and west, exploiting gaps in the allied line. The French fight hard, but the allies are completely victo-rious. Although casualties are relatively light for the number of men engaged—5,000 killed or wounded for the allies and 5,000 killed or wounded and 3,000 taken prisoner for the French—the battle is decisive, and the French precipitously retreat.

Joseph barely escapes and abandons 143 guns, baggage, a large treasury, vast amounts of stores, and even his crown. Fortunately for the French, the allies are not prepared for a rapid pursuit.

The Battle of Vitoria has far-reaching conse-quences. Not only does it mark the end of Napole-onic rule in Spain and enable Wellington to invade France, but it has a profound effect on the vacillat-ing Austrians and the war in Germany. Within a few weeks, Austria declares war on France.

July 14–August 10, 1813
Southern Europe: Iberian Peninsula: Spain: Napo-leonic Wars (continued): Peninsular War (contin-ued): Siege of San Sebastián. Following his victory in the Battle of Vitoria, allied commander in the Ibe-rian Peninsula Sir Arthur Wellesley, Earl of Welling-ton, decides to starve out Pamplona while concen-trating his efforts against the strategically important Basque city of San Sebastián, located on the French

border and the southern coast of the Bay of Biscay. Siege operations do not go well. A mining operation and assault on July 25 fails with the loss of 600 men in the attacking 5th Division. Wellington orders up more equipment and is preparing to intensify opera-tions when he learns that the French have launched a thrust toward Pamplona well ahead of when he thought possible. Wellington immediately suspends the siege, orders the heavy equipment withdrawn to ships offshore, and prepares to do battle with the French at Pamplona.

July 27, 1813
North America: War of 1812 (continued): Back-ground to the Creek War and Battle of Burnt Corn. Creek Native Americans in the area of present-day Alabama are restive in response to encroachments on their ancestral lands. In the autumn of 1811 Shawnee chief Tecumseh, whose mother is Creek, visits and speaks before the Creek Council in an effort to get the Creeks to join his proposed confederation.

Tecumseh's visit increases tensions between the Upper and Lower Creeks. A band of Upper Creeks (Koasatis) led by Little Warrior (Tuskeegee Tustun-nuggee) then travels north with Tecumseh on his re-turn home. They are soon under the influence of the spiritual teachings of Tecumseh's half brother Ten-skwatawa (the Shawnee Prophet), who preaches re-jection of white ways. On their return to Alabama, these Creeks spread this message.

In 1813, civil war breaks out when the Creek Coun-cil, dominated by Lower Creeks such as Big Warrior (Tustennuge Thlocco) and influenced by federal In-dian agent Benjamin Hawkins, orders the execution of six Upper Creeks (including Little Warrior), who have killed white settlers. In response, prowar Upper Creeks known as the Red Sticks (led by Menauway, Hopoie Tustanugga, Peter McQueen, and Hossa Ya-holo) lay siege to the council headquarters at Tuck-abatchee in June 1813, forcing Big Warrior and his followers to evacuate in July.

Meanwhile, some 200 Red Sticks led by Mc-Queen travel to Pensacola in an effort to secure am-munition from the Spanish authorities. Soldiers are then dispatched from Fort Mims on the east bank of the Alabama River, about 35 miles north of Mo-bile. They intercept and attack the Red Sticks at the village of Burnt Corn, about 80 miles north of Pen-sacola. The Red Sticks are scattered, but when the soldiers become preoccupied with looting the Red Stick packhorses, the Native Americans regroup and attack, forcing the troops to scatter.

Considering the attack at Burnt Corn a declaration of war by the American settlers, the Red Sticks, now led by William Weatherford (Red Eagle), mount an attack of their own on the source of the attack, Fort Mims.

July 28, 1813

Southern Europe: Iberian Peninsula: Spain: Napoleonic Wars (continued): Peninsular War (continued): First Battle of Sorauren. Following the French defeat in the Battle of Vitoria, Marshal Jean de Dieu Soult takes command of French forces that had fled Spain. He reorganizes the four separate armies that had fought at Vitoria into one Army of Spain. Although transport remains a problem and he is short of cavalry because of French emperor Napoleon I's exactions, Soult nonetheless disposes 73,000 infantry and 7,000 cavalry with 140 guns and 4,000 support troops. With his army operative by July 20, 1813— far faster than the allies thought possible—Soult returns to Spain. Allied commander in the Iberian Peninsula Lieutenant General Sir Arthur Wellesley, Earl of Wellington, quickly raises his siege of San Sebastián and marches to Pamplona to meet the French.

Soult proceeds south in three columns. Although the French initially enjoy local numerical superiority, the difficult terrain of the Pyrenees and tenacious allied resistance slow their advance and allow the allies time to bring up additional troops. Soult, moving with the main French column of about 30,000 men, heads toward Pamplona, where on the morning of July 27, 1813, he encounters some 17,000 British and Portuguese troops drawn up on a 1,000-foot-high ridge at the village of Sorauren, some eight miles northeast of Pamplona. Wellington rides along the ridge to great cheers from his men, which are audible to the French and apparently unnerve Soult, who postpones any attack that day. This allows allied reinforcements to come up, bringing Wellington's strength by the time of the battle the next day to about 24,000 men.

Soult seems to have lost his nerve, and he takes his time with his troop dispositions, not attacking until noon on July 28. The French have the difficult task of attaining the summit of the ridge, where Wellington has made his customary careful defensive dis-

positions. The fighting is intense, but the defenders hold. With the arrival of British reinforcements, Wellington mounts an assault on Soult's right flank, and the French commander soon orders a withdrawal.

The French sustain more than 3,000 casualties, while the British and Portuguese lose 2,650.

July 30, 1813

Southern Europe: Iberian Peninsula: Spain: Napoleonic Wars (continued): Peninsular War (continued): Second Battle of Sorauren. Two smaller battles occur on July 30 at Sorauren near Pamplona and at Lizaso, a bit farther to the northwest. With Allied strength steadily increasing, French marshal Jean de Dieu Soult abandons his effort to reach Pamplona and attempts to get his army between the main body of allied troops at Sorauren under Lieutenant General Sir Arthur Wellesley, Earl of Wellington, and San Sebastián to the north, allowing the French to relieve the latter. Both engagements are smaller than the First Battle of Sorauren.

In the Second Battle of Sorauren, Wellington holds off the French, who lose 3,000 men. In fighting at Lizaso where Soult commands in person, British lieutenant general Sir Rowland Hill is forced to withdraw at a cost of 1,000 casualties to 800 for the French. Soult is now in position to move to the north, but news of the rebuff at Sorauren causes him to reevaluate his situation. He decides to withdraw directly to France to prepare defenses against the anticipated allied invasion from the south.

August 12, 1813

Central Europe: Germany: Napoleonic Wars (continued): War of German Liberation (continued): Austria enters the war. On August 12, 1813, Austria declares war on France, with the Prussians resuming fighting the next day before expiration of the armistice. The allies put in the field four major armies totaling 515,000 men. This will soon grow to 600,000. French emperor Napoleon I's forces, in three major armies and scattered garrisons, total only 370,000 men. His main army never exceeds 250,000 and will steadily decrease in number as the fighting continues.

Napoleon's best course is to preserve his strength, concentrate his resources, and await an allied move; instead, he divides his resources with three armies operating independently. One of these, sent under Marshal Nicholas Oudinot against Berlin to destroy the Swedish army under Crown Prince Karl Johan (former French marshal Jean Baptiste Bernadotte), is beyond supporting distance. Giving command to Oudinot instead of the more reliable Marshal Louis Nicolas Davout proves a serious mistake and may have cost Napoleon the campaign.

Meanwhile, Napoleon and Marshal Michel Ney prepare to operate in Silesia against the Prussians under General Gebhard Leberecht von Blücher and in Bohemia against the Austrians under Field Marshal Prince Charles Philip of Schwarzenberg. Napoleon's generals are not optimistic about their chances.

The allies adopt the so-called Trachtenberg Plan, avoiding battle if Napoleon is present while at the same time isolating and destroying his subordinates. Eventually, their far superior numbers render this unnecessary.

August 14, 1813

English Channel: War of 1812 (continued). The Royal Navy brig *Pelican* (commanded by Commander John F. Maples) sinks the U.S. Navy brig *Argus* (commanded by Master Commandant William H. Allen). After delivering William H. Crawford, new U.S. minister to France, Allen had cruised in the English Channel and taken 19 prizes, the largest number for any American warship of the war. The *Argus* has just set alight its last prize on August 14, 1813, when the more powerful *Pelican* arrives. Following a 45-minute battle, Allen surrenders his badly battered ship.

August 23, 1813

Central Europe: Germany: Prussia: Napoleonic Wars (continued): War of German Liberation (continued): Battle of Grossbeeren. French marshal Nicholas Oudinot, dispatched by Emperor Napoleon I to take Berlin and defeat Prussian forces and the Swedish army under Crown Prince Karl Johan (former French marshal Jean Baptiste Bernadotte), is himself defeated south of Berlin, at Grossbeeren, by Prussian forces under Friedrich Wilhelm Baron von Bülow. The French suffer 3,000 dead and wounded, 1,500 captured, and 13 guns lost.

August 26, 1813

Central Europe: Germany: Saxony: Napoleonic Wars (continued): War of German Liberation (continued): Battle of Katzbach. Napoleon, having left a corps under Marshal Laurent Gouvion Saint-Cyr at Dres-

den, sets out after Prussian and Russian forces under General Gebhard Leberecht von Blücher on April 21, 1813. Blücher, in accordance with the Trachtenberg Plan, withdraws before him. Soon under attack by Austrian forces from Bohemia, however, Saint-Cyr calls for help, and Napoleon turns back with the Imperial Guard to assist. He turns command of the remaining forces over to Marshal Jacques Macdonald.

Napoleon having departed, Blücher turns and, on the Katzbach River near Liegnitz, Prussia, with 115,000 men engages and defeats Macdonald's 102,000-man Army of the Bober (River). The French sustain some 15,000 killed, wounded, and captured along with 100 guns lost. Prussian losses are only about 4,000 men.

August 26–27, 1813

Central Europe: Germany: Saxony: Napoleonic Wars (continued): War of German Liberation (continued): Battle of Dresden. Austrian forces under Field Marshal Prince Charles Philip of Schwarzenberg, accompanied by Austrian emperor Francis I and Prussian king Frederick William III and shortly joined by Russian czar Alexander I, attack a French corps under Marshal Laurent Gouvion Saint-Cyr holding Dresden. Saint-Cyr calls on French emperor Napoleon I for assistance. Napoleon breaks off his pursuit of Prussian general Gebhard Leberecht von Blücher and arrives unexpectedly at Dresden on August 26, breaking up the allied assault.

Both sides build up their resources. By August 27 the allies have 170,000 men and 400 guns, while Napoleon commands 120,000 men and 250 guns. Although outnumbered, Napoleon attacks both allied flanks and turns their left. Although failing to achieve the double envelopment that might have brought a strategic result, Napoleon wins a brilliant tactical victory. By the time Schwarzenberg breaks off the battle, it has claimed 38,000 allied casualties and 40 guns for French casualties of some 10,000. On the night of August 27–28 the allies withdraw. The Battle of Dresden is, however, Napoleon's last victory on German soil.

August 29–30, 1813

Central Europe: Bohemia: Napoleonic Wars (continued): War of German Liberation (continued): Battle of Kulm. Following the Battle of Dresden, Napoleon orders General Dominique Vandamme, south of the city, to cut off the Austrian route of retreat and destroy their supply trains. Vandamme encounters an Austrian corps under Alexander Ivanovich Ostermann-Tolstoy near the town of Kulm in northern Bohemia. Having superior numbers, Vandamme engages it.

On August 30, however, a Prussian corps under General Friedrich von Kleist arrives, withdrawing from Dresden. The French, now outnumbered 32,000 to 54,000, fight well but are defeated. The allies suffer 11,000 casualties, but half of the French force is either killed or captured. Vandamme is among those taken prisoner.

August 30, 1813
North America: War of 1812 (continued): Creek War (continued): Massacre of Fort Mims. U.S. Army Fort Mims is located on the east bank of the Alabama River, about 35 miles north of Mobile. In July 1813 soldiers had been sent from Mims to attack Red Stick Creeks who had gone to Pensacola to secure ammunition from the Spanish. The Red Sticks consider this a declaration of war and vow revenge against the source of the attack, Fort Mims.

Led by Peter McQueen and William Weatherford (Red Eagle), several thousand Red Stick warriors from a dozen Upper Creek towns attack there on August 30, 1813. There are some 550 people at Fort Mims, 175 of them militia and the remainder mixed-blood Creek families from the lower towns who have sought refuge there with the beginning of the fighting.

The Red Sticks lose 200 warriors killed in the attack, but the remainder capture the fort. The warriors then proceed to massacre as many as 500 of the men, women, and children in the fort.

August 31, 1813
Southern Europe: Iberian Peninsula: Spain: Napoleonic Wars (continued): Peninsular War (continued): British capture of San Sebastián. Following victories over French marshal Jean de Dieu Soult in the battles of Sorauren, allied commander in Iberia Lieutenant General Sir Arthur Wellesley, Earl of Wellington, resumes operations to capture the port city of San Sebastián on the Bay of Biscay. Although Wellington withdraws most of his troops and siege equipment to concentrate against the French thrust toward Pamplona, some British troops under Lieutenant General Sir Thomas Graham, Lord Lynedoch, continue the

siege. French commander at San Sebastián General de Brigade Louis Emanuel Rey is, for the most part, content to remain on the defensive (one French foray, however, costs the British 200 casualties and valuable equipment). Rey manages to bring in supplies and replacement manpower by boat while evacuating sick and wounded. The French are also able to repair damage caused by the earlier British mine.

By the time Wellington resumes siege operations in earnest on August 18, the city is defended by 3,000 French troops manning 60 pieces of artillery. British shelling recommences on August 26. One by one, the heavy British siege guns silence the French artillery, and the attackers open a 300-yard gap in the southeast wall. British and Portuguese troops storm the city on August 31. Fortunately for the English, a large French mine fails to explode. The French fight street by street and house by house. The British rampage through the city over a three-day period, burning almost all of it and destroying the port, despite the fact that the inhabitants were anti-French. Of the original city, only the street at the foot of the hill (now called 31st August Street) remains. Wellington refuses to intervene. The Spanish believed at the time, and still believe, that this was a deliberate act on the part of the British to ruin a leading Spanish port and rival to British commerce.

Rey, having retreated with 1,700 of his men to the citadel of La Mota, is bombarded there for days by 60 British guns. He finally agrees to surrender on September 8. The battle for San Sebastián claims 3,500 allied soldiers killed or wounded, 2,200 in the actual assault.

August 31, 1813
Southern Europe: Iberian Peninsula: Spain: Napoleonic Wars (continued): Peninsular War (continued): Battle of San Marcial. While allied forces are assaulting San Sebastián, serious fighting is also occurring to the east. French marshal Jean de Dieu Soult makes an attempt with nine divisions to relieve the San Sebastián garrison. Anticipating this, allied commander in Iberia Lieutenant General Sir Arthur Wellesley, Earl of Wellington, has substantially increased forces and defenses between the city and the Bidassoa River separating Spain and France.

On August 31, 1813, Soult's men ford the Bidassoa and establish a bridgehead. The French rank and file, clearly unenthusiastic, are soon locked in combat with the 16,000-man Spanish Army of Galicia commanded by Spanish general Manuel Freire. The Spanish give an excellent account of themselves, with most of the fighting occurring near San Marcial. A defeated and dispirited Soult withdraws back across the river.

At San Marcial the French lose 4,000 men; the allies lose 2,500, most of them Spaniards. This defeat and the concurrent loss of San Sebastián come as a great blow to Soult's men, who never regain their former zeal and skill.

September 4, 1813

Central Europe: Silesia: Napoleonic Wars (continued): War of German Liberation (continued). French emperor Napoleon I pursues Prussian forces under General Gebhard Leberecht von Blücher into Silesia in an effort to bring him to battle. The Prussian again swiftly withdraws and avoids combat.

September 5, 1813

Western Atlantic Ocean: War of 1812 (continued). Off the New England coast, the U.S. Navy sloop *Enterprise* (commanded by Lieutenant William Burrows) captures the Royal Navy sloop *Boxer* (commanded by Commander Samuel Blyth) after a 40-minute fight.

September 6, 1813

Central Europe: Brandenburg: Napoleonic Wars (continued): War of German Liberation (continued): Battle of Dennewitz. French emperor Napoleon I replaces Marshal Louis Oudinot with Marshal Michel Ney. Napoleon orders Ney to resume the offensive against the Swedes and Prussians. Ney engages the Swedes and Prussians under Swedish crown prince Karl Johan (former French marshal Jean Baptiste Bernadotte) and Prussian general Friedrich Wilhelm Baron von Bülow at Dennewitz in Brandenburg, some 70 miles north of Dresden. The allies are victorious, sustaining some 7,000 casualties to 10,000 for the French.

September 8, 1813

Central Europe: Bavaria: Napoleonic Wars (continued): War of German Liberation (continued): Treaty of Ried. Following the French defeat in the Battle of Dennewitz on September 6, Bavaria switches sides. In the Treaty of Ried in Bavaria of September 8 be-

tween Bavaria and Austria, King Maximilian I of Bavaria agrees to join the allies against Napoleon on the condition of a guarantee of his state's independence and territorial integrity. (By the first Treaty of Paris of June 3, 1814, however, he will cede the Tirol [Tyrol] to Austria in exchange for the former duchy of Würzburg.) On October 14 Bavaria formally declares war on France.

September 10, 1813

North America: War of 1812 (continued): Battle of Lake Erie. The battle for control of Lake Erie occurs on September 10, 1813. U.S. Navy master commandant Oliver H. Perry commands 450 men in nine warships of 54 guns with a broadside weight of 936 pounds. Perry flies his flag in the brig *Lawrence* (20 guns). His second-in-command, Lieutenant Jesse D. Elliott, commands the other American brig, the *Niagara* (20 guns). The other ships in Perry's squadron are the brig *Caledonia* (3 guns), the schooner *Somers* (2 guns), the sloop *Trippe* (1 gun), and four gunboats, the *Tigress, Porcupine, Scorpion,* and *Ariel* (each mounting 1 to 4 guns).

Royal Navy commander Robert H. Barclay commands 565 men in a squadron of 6 ships, armed with 64 guns and having a broadside weight of 496 pounds. Barclay flies his flag in the corvette *Detroit* (21 guns). The other ships in his squadron are the corvette *Queen Charlotte* (17 guns), the schooner *Lady Prevost* (13 guns), the brig *General Hunter* (10 guns), the sloop *Little Belt* (3 guns), and the schooner *Chippaway* (2 guns). At a disadvantage in the number of ships and their total throw weight of shot, Barclay also has in his squadron guns of many calibers and types that require different charges and shot.

On September 10, 1813, the two squadrons face off on roughly parallel axes. Barclay hopes to stand off at some distance and use his long guns to batter the American ships, which are armed principally with short-range carronades. Light winds initially work against the Americans, but Perry is able to take advantage of a shift to secure the weather gauge and close with his opponent. He orders the *Lawrence* to engage the *Detroit* and the *Niagara* to battle the *Queen Charlotte* while his smaller ships engage their British counterparts.

In the heavy fighting that follows, Elliott's *Niagara,* armed principally with carronades, fails to close. This allows the three largest British ships to

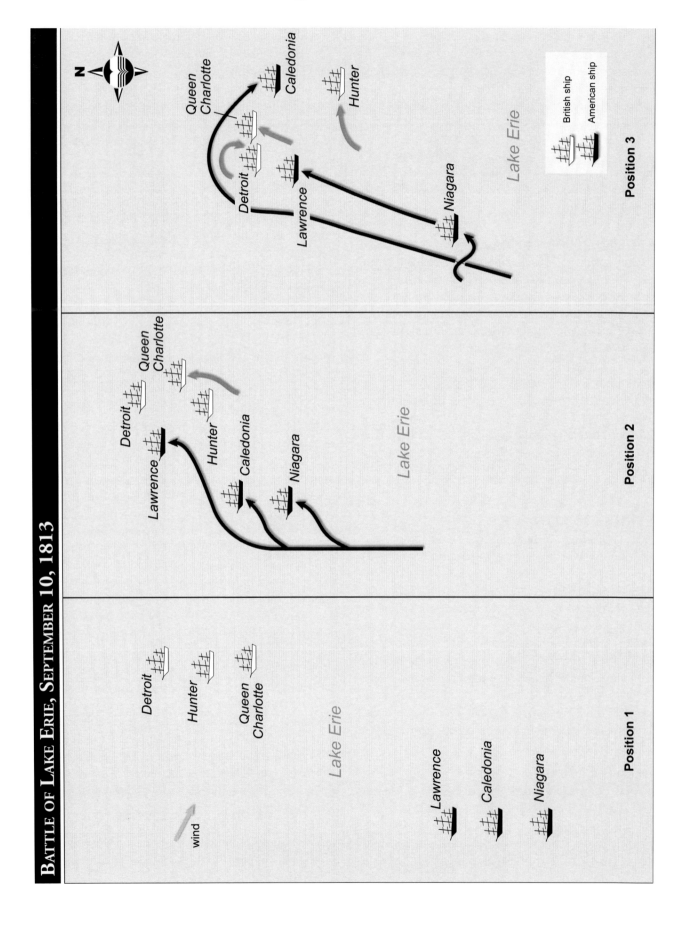

BATTLE OF LAKE ERIE, SEPTEMBER 10, 1813

Illustration depicting U.S. Navy Commodore Oliver Hazard Perry's decisive victory over a British squadron on Lake Erie, September 10, 1813. (Library of Congress)

concentrate on the *Lawrence,* which is badly damaged. Perry fails to signal Elliott to close, but he remains in his battle position behind the *Caledonia* rather than coming forward. After some two and a half hours of fighting with few men on the *Lawrence* still able to fight, Elliott brings the *Niagara* forward, and Perry transfers his flag to that brig. Sending Elliott in a boat to direct the trailing gunboats, Perry brings the undamaged *Niagara* into the fray.

Perry rallies his forces, and under a terrible pounding from the American broadsides, the British ships surrender one by one. The Americans lose 27 killed and 96 wounded, the majority of them on the *Lawrence,* which has taken terrible punishment. British losses are 41 killed and 94 wounded, with Barclay among the latter. Perry's battle report is laconic: "We have met the enemy and they are ours: Two Ships, two Brigs, one Schooner and one Sloop."

The Battle of Lake Erie marks a rare occasion in history when an entire British squadron has surren-

dered. Perry's ships are now able to transport U.S. ground forces across Lake Erie and keep them supplied, making possible the defeat of the British and their allied Indian forces. The Battle of Lake Erie also ignites a prolonged and bitter controversy between Elliott and Perry concerning their roles in the victory that divides much of the U.S. naval officer corps for years to come.

See Leaders: Perry, Oliver Hazard

September 29, 1813
North America: War of 1812 (continued): American recapture of Detroit. Informed of Commodore Oliver H. Perry's victory in the Battle of Lake Erie, U.S. major general William H. Harrison immediately sets his cavalry in motion around the lake toward Detroit. At the same time, Perry transports American infantry across Lake Erie to Amhertsburg. Assisted and supplied by Perry's ships, Harrison's ground forces converge on Detroit. British commander of Upper

Commander Oliver Hazard Perry (1785–1819) had charge of the U.S. Navy squadron on Lake Erie during the War of 1812. On September 10, 1813, he won the important Battle of Lake Erie over the British. (Navy Art Collection)

Canada, Brigadier General Henry A. Procter, over the protests of the Indian commander Brigadier General Tecumseh, withdraws his forces from Detroit and into Canada on September 18. On September 29 Harrison retakes Detroit.

October 5, 1813
North America: War of 1812 (continued): Battle of the Thames. U.S. Army major general William H. Harrison pursues British forces under Brigadier General Henry Procter into Canada. Harrison has a much larger force (4,500 men) than Procter (800 regulars and 1,000 Indians). Harrison catches up with the British and Indian force at Moravian Town, on the north bank of the Thames River. Harrison attacks, his infantry attacking straight ahead and his mounted Kentucky regiment sweeping in on the British right. Procter is defeated.

The British suffer 12 dead, 36 wounded, and 477 captured. The Indians stand firm until their leader, Tecumseh, is slain. They then flee, leaving behind 35 dead. American losses are light: only 15 killed and 30 wounded.

Tecumseh's death is a great blow, leading to major Native American desertions from the British side. The American frontier in the Northwest is now secure, with the British retaining only Fort Mackinac (kept by them until the end of the war).

October 7–9, 1813
Western Europe: France: Napoleonic Wars (continued): Peninsular War (continued): Allied troops invade France from Spain. Beginning on October 7, allied commander in Iberia Lieutenant General Sir Arthur Wellesley, Earl of Wellington, leads 24,000 allied troops from Spain across the Bidassoa River into southern France.

October 13, 1813
Southwest Asia: Russo-Persian War (continued): Treaty of Gulistan. The British offer to mediate between the Russians and the Persians, and on October 13, 1813, the war is brought to a close in the Treaty of Gulistan. Persia agrees to recognize Russian sovereignty over Georgia and surrenders to the Russians the Caspian districts of Daghestan, Baku, and Shirwan.

October 16–19, 1813
Central Europe: Saxony: Napoleonic Wars (continued): War of German Liberation (continued): Battle of Leipzig. The allies are now closing in on French emperor Napoleon I from north, east, and south. Napoleon is concerned that they might cut his communications west to France. Indeed, Cossack forces are already wreaking havoc on his supply lines.

On September 14 Napoleon orders a withdrawal behind the line of the Elbe River. Forced farther west, he leaves Marshal Laurent Gouvion Saint-Cyr to defend Dresden (surrendered on November 11). By mid-October Napoleon's main army is being driven toward Leipzig. Combat is joined there during October 16–19 in the Battle of Leipzig (also known as the Battle of the Nations). Numbers heavily influence the battle's outcome. Napoleon has 177,000 men in the area of Leipzig, while the allies have more than 254,000. Two days later, however, Napoleon has 195,000 men and 734 guns, and the allies

Emperor Francis I of Austria, King Frederick William III of Prussia, and Czar Alexander I of Russia after the Battle of Leipzig on October 16–19, 1813. Known as the Battle of the Nations, it was the largest engagement of the Napoleonic Wars and a major defeat for French emperor Napoleon I. (Archivo Iconografico, S.A./Corbis)

have 410,000 men and 1,335 guns. In terms of sheer numbers, the battle is probably the largest in history until the 20th century.

The Battle of Leipzig opens on October 16 when Napoleon attacks Austrian forces under Field Marshal Prince Charles Philip of Schwarzenberg south of Leipzig at Wachau. Although the French infantry are able to make advances, they are insufficiently supported by the few cavalry Napoleon can muster. That same day Prussian general Gebhard Leberecht von Blücher attacks French marshal Auguste Marmont at Möckern north of Leipzig. That evening, Marmont is forced to withdraw toward Leipzig.

On October 17 there is only light action. Napoleon makes a tentative attempt, without result, to negotiate. Both sides receive reinforcements. Napoleon gains 17,000 men under General Jean Louis Ebénézer Reynier, but the allies secure 70,000 men under Russian general Levin August, Count von Bennigsen, and 85,000 under Swedish crown prince Karl Johan (former French marshal Jean Baptiste Bernadotte).

Napoleon knows that he must withdraw to the west; he pulls his forces in tightly around Leipzig and secures his avenue of retreat west. The allies attack the French all along the line but the French

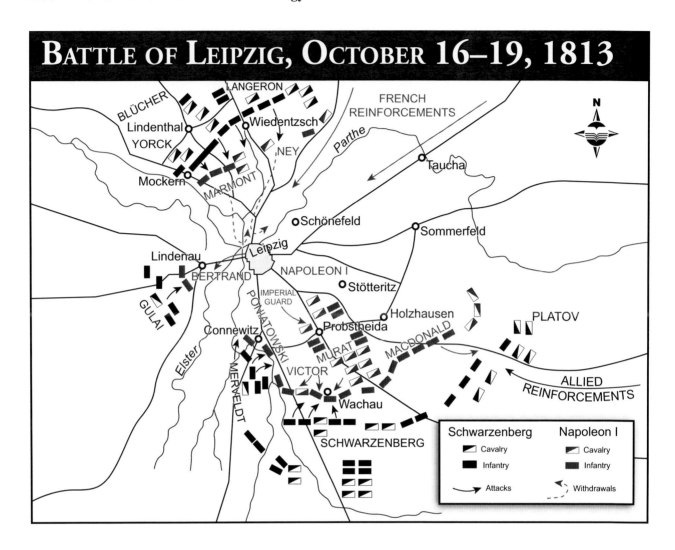

BATTLE OF LEIPZIG, OCTOBER 16–19, 1813

manage to hold despite the defection of the Saxons and some other German allies. That night, however, the French begin their withdrawal.

On October 19 the allies again attack and storm Leipzig. The French are withdrawing in good order over the Elster River bridge until a corporal prematurely blows the span, trapping on the Leipzig side the four corps of Marshal Jacques Macdonald, Marshal Józef Antoni Poniatowski (Prince Poniatowski), General Jacques Lauriston, and General Jean Louis Ebénézer Reynier. The French fight desperately but are driven into the river. Macdonald is able to swim to safety. Paoniatowski, wounded several times, tries to make it across on his horse but drowns. Lauriston and Reynier are taken prisoner.

In all, the French sustain 38,000 killed or wounded and another 30,000 taken prisoner. The French also lose 325 guns. The allies suffer about 54,000 casualties. As Napoleon makes for the Rhine, his German troops join the allies and throw off the rulers Napoleon had imposed. The liberation of Germany is now complete. The allies are now in position to invade France from the northeast as the Duke of Wellington and British forces invade southwestern France from Spain.

October 26, 1813

North America: War of 1812 (continued): Battle of the Chateauguay. In July 1813 the incompetent Major General Henry Dearborn is removed from command in the Northwest and is replaced by Major General James Wilkinson. At the same time, Major General Wade Hampton assumes command of forces on the southern shore of Lake Champlain. Secretary of War John Armstrong arrives at Sackets Harbor and, taking command in the field, develops a plan for a two-pronged U.S. assault on Montreal (Montréal). Wilkinson is to move from Sackets Harbor with 8,000 men and descend the St. Lawrence while Hampton marches north from Plattsburgh with 4,000 men. The two are to join for the assault on Montreal, held by 15,000 British troops. The plan is seriously marred, however, by the fact that the two generals hate one another.

Hampton enters Canada on September 19, but instead of moving north, he proceeds west to the Chateauguay River, where he awaits news of Wilkinson's progress. Ordered by Armstrong to move down the Chateauguay, by October 22 Hampton establishes a position about 15 miles from the river's mouth.

In the Battle of the Chateauguay on October 26, Hampton attacks a British force of 400 French Canadian militia and perhaps 170 Native Americans commanded by British lieutenant colonel Charles de Salaberry. Outnumbered some 8 to 1, Salaberry orders bugles blown and his men to cheer on the American left, tricking Hampton into believing that he is about to be enveloped. Hampton then calls off the attack. Ignoring Wilkinson's orders to continue the advance, Hampton withdraws back to Plattsburgh.

The British suffer only 22 casualties (2 killed). The Americans lose 85 (23 dead). Hampton resigns his commission in March 1814.

October 30–31, 1813
Central Europe: Hesse: Napoleonic Wars (continued): War of German Liberation (continued): Battle of Hanau. Believing that the French Grande Armée is effectively finished following the Battle of Leipzig, Bavarian general Prince Karl Philipp von Wrede moves to cut off the French withdrawal at the head of a Bavarian-Austrian army of 62,000 men. French emperor Napoleon I learns at Erfurt that Wrede is moving against him but does not expect the advance to be rapid. Wrede leaves Branau on October 15 and crosses the Danube four days later. On October 27 he sends 10,000 of his men toward Frankfurt and arrives at Hanau in Hesse on October 29.

With passage into the Main Valley now blocked, Napoleon appears to be trapped, for other allied armies are trailing him from the east. After some brilliant maneuvering, however, Napoleon defeats Wrede in two days of fighting during October 30–

31. The Bavarians suffer 6,000 killed or wounded and 4,000 taken prisoner. French losses are perhaps 5,000 men. The French reach Frankfurt on November 2, only 20 miles from their relatively safe rear base at Mainz. Most of the Grande Armée crosses the Rhine, although some men remain behind in garrisons and fortresses in Germany. Indeed, Marshal Louis Nicolas Davout holds Hamburg until after Napoleon's abdication in April 1814. Napoleon returns to Paris on November 9.

November 3, 1813
North America: War of 1812 (continued): Creek War (continued): Battle of Tallushatchee. News of the Red Stick massacre at Fort Mims on August 30, 1813, shocks Americans and heightens the urgency and intensity of the government response. Washington has already authorized the states of Georgia and Tennessee and the Mississippi Territory to call up militia in the belief that the Creeks have allied with the British in the War of 1812.

The white settlers can mobilize many more men than the estimated maximum 4,000 Red Stick warriors and have much better access to military supplies. In addition, the whites can rely on the assistance of allied Cherokees and Choctaws. The Americans plan a three-pronged invasion of Upper Creek Territory. Brigadier General John Floyd will move from Georgia with approximately 1,000 militiamen while Brigadier General Ferdinand L. Claiborne advances from Mississippi with a mixed force of 1,000 regulars and militiamen and 135 Choctaws. Finally, Tennessee Militia major general Andrew Jackson and Brigadier General John Coffee are to invade from Tennessee with 2,500 militiamen and some 600 allied Cherokees.

In late November, Floyd's Georgia militia destroy two Red Stick villages (Autosee and Tallassie), killing some 200 warriors. The militiamen then withdraw to the Chattahoochee River, where they construct Fort Mitchell. In December, Claiborne's Mississippians burn the Red Stick spiritual center of Ecunchate (near present-day Benton, Alabama) but withdraw after running short of supplies.

The Tennessee militiamen fight the major engagements of the war. Jackson proves an able military leader. After first drilling his men and stockpiling supplies, he advances into Alabama, establishing Fort Deposit on the Tennessee River and Fort Strother

Andrew Jackson (1767–1845) fought in the American Revolutionary War but gained renown in the Creek War and in the War of 1812, most notably for the Battle of New Orleans on January 8, 1815. Later he helped secure Florida from Spain. Jackson was president of the United States during 1829–1837. (Library of Congress)

on the Coosa River. On November 3, 1813, some 1,000 dragoons under Coffee surround and attack the Creek village of Tallushatchee (Tallassahatche, Talishatchee). They kill as many as 200 Red Stick warriors against their own losses of 5 killed and 41 wounded. Coffee then retires to Fort Strother.

See Leaders: Jackson, Andrew

November 8, 1813

Western Europe: France: Napoleonic Wars (continued): War of German Liberation (continued). On November 8, 1813, the allies, over British objections, offer French emperor Napoleon I generous peace terms. Austria and most of the German rulers, fearing the expansion of Russian influence into Central

Europe, would be content solely to have French rule ended in Germany and Italy. Czar Alexander I has already established control over Poland and is now championing the interests of Prussia, including the promise that it may have all Saxony. The czar also wants to place Swedish crown prince Karl Johan (former French marshal Jean Baptiste Bernadotte) on the French throne as his puppet in place of Napoleon. Other rulers would prefer that Napoleon retain the throne so that France would be a strong counterweight to Russia. Under the peace terms, France is to have its natural boundaries of the Rhine and the Alps.

Napoleon foolishly rejects the allied offer, claiming that it is a trick. On December 1, therefore, the allies resolve to continue the fight against Napoleon by an invasion of France.

November 9, 1813

North America: War of 1812 (continued): Creek War (continued): Battle of Talladega. Tennessee Militia major general Andrew Jackson receives an appeal for assistance from friendly Creeks at Talladega who are under siege by some 700 Red Stick warriors. On November 9, 1813, Jackson arrives at Talladega with 2,000 infantry and 800 dragoons. He drives the Red Sticks from the village. The Tennesseans kill some 300 Red Sticks while losing 15 killed and 85 wounded of their own. On November 18 Major General John Cocke's forces massacre some 60 Red Stick warriors who attempt to surrender at Hillaubee. Despite these successes, Jackson, short of supplies and forced to deal with a mutiny, withdraws to Fort Strother.

November 10, 1813

Western Europe: France: Napoleonic Wars (continued): Peninsular War (continued): Battle of the Nivelle. After crossing the Bidassoa River, allied commander in Iberia Lieutenant General Sir Arthur Wellesley, Earl of Wellington, leads his men north. By the beginning of November he has 82,000 men against only 62,000, many of them raw conscripts, for Marshal Jean de Dieu Soult, who can now only hope to delay the allied advance. Along the lower Nivelle River on November 10, 1813, Wellington orders a large-scale attack on Soult's positions.

The Battle of the Nivelle opens with an allied assault on Soult's two wings with 22,000 and 25,000 men, respectively, followed by a major assault by

33,000 men on the center of the French line. The demoralized French are driven back, losing 4,300 men for allied losses of only 3,400. Soult then begins a general withdrawal to the northeast.

November 11, 1813
North America: War of 1812 (continued): Battle of Crysler's Farm. Major General James Wilkinson and 8,000 men, the second prong of the American advance on Montreal (Montréal), set out from Sackets Harbor, New York, on October 17. On November 5 they begin the descent of the St. Lawrence River. The American flotilla halts at Crysler's Farm, Ontario, on the north bank of the river about 90 miles from Montreal. There Wilkinson orders Brigadier General John Parke Boyd and 2,000 men to attack a British force under Colonel Joseph W. Morrison moving against the American rear.

Although he commands only 800 men, Morrison routs the Americans in the November 11 Battle of Crysler's Farm, defeating their poorly executed piecemeal attack. The Americans lose 102 dead, 237 wounded, and 120 taken prisoner (106 of them wounded). British losses are only 31 dead, 148 wounded, and 13 missing.

Informed on November 12 that Major General Wade Hampton, who was to join him with 4,000 men, has broken off his advance on Montreal and is withdrawing to Plattsburgh, Wilkinson goes into winter quarters at French Mills on the Salmon River.

December 10–13, 1813
Western Europe: France: Napoleonic Wars (continued): Peninsular War (continued): Battle of the Nive River. When Spanish troops seek revenge for the atrocities and humiliations inflicted by the French over the past few years by attacking French civilians and destroying their property, allied commander Lieutenant General Sir Arthur Wellesley, Earl of Wellington, decides to leave most of them behind. Although this reduces his numerical advantage over the French, it also helps secure the tacit support of the population in southwestern France and prevents a nationalist uprising.

On December 9 Wellington begins a new campaign from St. Jean-de-Luz across the Nive River, aimed at Bayonne. He has 64,000 men; French marshal Jean de Dieu Soult has 63,000, but most of these men are untrained conscripts and reservists. Wellington divides his army into three columns crossing the Nive. Soult, however, is now operating on interior lines, and during the night of December 9–10 he secretly concentrates his forces.

The Battle of the Nive River opens at dawn on December 10. Although the French achieve tactical surprise and force the allies back, Soult lacks the resources to exploit the situation. The allies lose some 1,500 men before Soult calls off the attack. French losses are somewhat fewer. Other clashes occur over the course of the next two days, with the major fighting being the Battle of St. Pierre d'Irube on December 13.

On the night of December 12 a British pontoon bridge over the Nive washes away, isolating British lieutenant general Sir Rowland Hill's 14,000 men and 12 guns east of the river. Soult concentrates 40,000 men against Hill and attacks. Unfortunately for Soult, the terrain greatly favors the English and Portuguese defenders, and he is able to deploy only a part of his force at once. The French also mismanage the battle, and Hill is able to hold until the arrival of reinforcements under Wellington in midafternoon.

Soult then withdraws back on Bayonne, having lost as many as 2,400 men against British casualties of only 1,800. Deteriorating weather drives both sides into winter quarters.

December 18, 1813
North America: War of 1812 (continued): British capture of Fort Niagara. British brigadier general John Vincent sends a force to retake Fort George. New York militia Brigadier General John McClure evacuates the fort on December 10. But before withdrawing, McClure burns the village of Newark and part of Queenston.

On the night of December 18, British forces under Colonel John Murray carry out a surprise attack on Fort Niagara, taking that key American outpost. American casualties are 67 dead, 11 wounded, and 350 taken prisoner. The British also capture tons of stores, 27 cannon, and 3,000 stand of arms. The British occupy Fort Niagara for the remainder of the war.

December 21, 1813
Western Europe: France: Napoleonic Wars (continued): Campaign for France. Allied forces cross the Rhine River at both Mannheim and Koblenz (Coblenz).

December 29–30, 1813

North America: War of 1812 (continued): Burning of Buffalo. Following their capture of Fort Niagara, the British turn loose the Indians on the countryside; they ravage Lewistown and other places. Leading a column of 1,500 men, on December 29–30, 1813, British major general Gordon Drummond burns both Buffalo and Black Rock, destroying substantial supplies and shipping.

January 1, 1814

Western Europe: France: Napoleonic Wars (continued): Campaign for France (continued): Allied and French dispositions and strategic plans. French troops are fighting the allies in other countries besides France. Some 50,000 are in garrisons and fortresses in Germany, most of them under Marshal Louis Nicolas Davout at Hamburg. Another 100,000 men are in Spain, while Prince Eugène de Beauharnais has charge of 50,000 men in northern Italy. Of these forces, only a corps equivalent, to be commanded by Marshal Nicholas Oudinot, is withdrawn from Spain.

French emperor Napoleon I commands 118,000 men on French soil west of the Rhine. He is fighting on interior lines and seeks to get between the allied forces, attack them at their most vulnerable places, and destroy them piecemeal. The numbers are heavily against Napoleon, and his troops are largely untrained boys and National Guards. It is a risky strategy indeed, and it is to Napoleon's credit that he is able to accomplish so much with so relatively few resources.

The allies are moving in three main armies. Swedish crown prince Karl Johan (former French marshal Jean Baptiste Bernadotte) commands 100,000 men moving through the Low Countries. Prussian general Gebhard Leberecht von Blücher is advancing through the Moselle Valley with 110,000 men, and Field Marshal Prince Charles Philip of Schwarzenberg commands the largest force of 210,000 Austrian and Russian troops advancing through Switzerland and the Belfort Gap. The allied objective is the French capital of Paris.

January 22 and 24, 1814

North America: War of 1812 (continued): Creek War (continued): Battles of Emuckfaw and Enotachopco Creek. Following the Battle of Talladega, there is a lull in the fighting. As a consequence of desertions and the expiration of militia enlistments, by December 1813 Tennessee Militia commander Major General Andrew Jackson has little more than 100 men under arms. Reinforced by 900 inexperienced recruits, Jackson makes the risky decision of marching on the Creek village of Emuckfaw to support Georgia militia there.

Jackson departs Fort Strother on January 17, 1814, but is ambushed by Red Stick warriors about a dozen miles from Emuckfaw. The militiamen are able to drive off the Native Americans, but Brigadier General John Coffee, seriously wounded, is among the American casualties. Jackson has no choice but to return to Fort Strother.

On the way back, however, Jackson's force is again ambushed on January 24 while crossing Enotachopco Creek. He is prepared and attempts an envelopment, but the militia panic, and he is unable to carry it off. Nonetheless, Jackson returns to Fort Strother, where he remains until mid-March. In the two battles, Jackson loses 24 killed and 71 wounded. Red Stick losses are in excess of 50 killed.

January 29, 1814

North America: War of 1812 (continued): Creek War (continued): Battle of Calibee Creek. Georgia Militia brigadier general John Floyd departs Fort Mitchell with some 1,300 militia and 400 friendly Creek warriors, advancing toward the village of Tuckaubatchee. He expects to join Tennessee militia there under Major General Andrew Jackson. On January 29 Red Stick warriors attack Floyd's fortified camp on Calibee Creek. Although the militiamen drive off the attackers, Floyd withdraws back to Fort Mitchell, abandoning the line of fortified positions created in the course of the advance. Floyd's force suffers 17–22 dead and 132–147 wounded. Red Stick casualties are estimated at 37 dead. It is Georgia's last offensive operation of the Creek War.

January 29–February 1, 1814

Western Europe: France: Napoleonic Wars (continued): Campaign for France (continued): Early battles. On January 29, 1814, French emperor Napoleon I, with 30,000 men, surprises and defeats 59,000 Prussians under General Gebhard Leberecht von Blücher at Brienne. The Prussian is caught advancing on Paris with only part of his force. Blücher is able to reorganize, however, five miles to the east at La Rothière. Field Marshal Prince Charles Philip of Schwarzenberg reinforces him there to 110,000 men. Napoleon also reinforces to 40,000.

Napoleon attacks on February 1 but, surprised by Blücher's far greater strength, withdraws. Superior allied numbers now become significant. Blücher moves down the Marne Valley while Schwarzenberg advances down the Seine Valley. Both are headed to Paris.

February 10–14, 1814

Western Europe: France: Napoleonic Wars (continued): Campaign for France (continued): The Five Days. Prussian general Gebhard Leberecht von Blücher is advancing carelessly in the Marne Valley toward Paris when French emperor Napoleon I falls on him with only 31,000 men. In four successive battles—Champaubert (February 10), Montmirail (February 11), Château-Thierry (February 12), and Vauchamps (February 14)—Napoleon brilliantly maneuvers his small army to inflict four defeats on the Prussians, who lose about 9,000 men for only 2,000 French. Blücher now withdraws north of the Marne.

February 18, 1814

Western Europe: France: Napoleonic Wars (continued): Campaign for France (continued): Battle of Montereau. Having defeated the Prussians, French emperor Napoleon I turns his attention south to the Austrians and Russians. Leaving two corps on the Marne, each reduced to a division size of 6,000 men, Napoleon gathers 70,000 men and goes after the Austrians under Field Marshal Prince Charles Philip of Schwarzenberg. The Austrians are more concentrated than were the Prussians but are still somewhat vulnerable to being defeated in detail.

On February 17 Napoleon defeats one of Schwarzenberg's corps under Russian general Ludwig Adolf Peter Wittgenstein at Nangis. The next day Napoleon defeats the Prince of Württemberg at Montereau. Schwarzenberg, shaken, withdraws hurriedly some 40 miles to the south, having sustained losses of 6,000 men against only 2,500 French.

February 27, 1814

Western Europe: France: Napoleonic Wars (continued): Peninsular War (continued): Battle of Orthez.

Following the December Battle of the Nive River, bad weather forces both sides into winter quarters. Marshal Jean de Dieu Soult's troops winter at Bayonne, while Anglo-Portuguese forces under British lieutenant general Sir Arthur Wellesley, Earl of Wellington, winter along the Franco-Spanish border.

Hostilities resume in February 1814. Wellington has 70,000 men, Soult 60,000. Wellington advances around Bayonne, leaving 31,000 men to encircle the city with its 17,000-man French garrison while he drives Soult and the remainder of the French army to the north.

Wellington and Soult again clash at Orthez on February 27. Soult has 33,000 infantry, 3,000 cavalry, and 48 guns. Wellington has 40,000 infantry, 3,000 cavalry, and 54 guns. The battle opens in the morning with an allied attack. The battle is hard-fought. Initially the French have the upper hand, but the battle turns in the allied favor that afternoon. Soult executes a fighting withdrawal on Toulouse. The French suffer 4,000 casualties for only 2,200 for the allies. Wellington breaks off the pursuit, for the time being, to take Bordeaux.

February 27, 1814

Western Europe: France: Napoleonic Wars (continued): Campaign for France (continued): Battle of Bar-sur-Aube. Prussian general Gebhard Leberecht von Blücher regroups to the north and again drives on Paris. On February 27 he reaches La Forté, only 25 miles from the capital. Leaving Marshal Jacques Macdonald with 40,000 men to continue the pursuit of allied forces under Austrian field marshal Prince Charles Philip of Schwarzenberg, French emperor Napoleon I turns north with 30,000 men to deal with this new threat from Blücher. This decision proves unfortunate for the emperor, as Schwarzenberg turns back and defeats Macdonald on February 27, 1814, in the Battle of Bar-sur-Aube.

February 1814

Western Europe: France: Napoleonic Wars (continued): Campaign for France (continued): Allied offer of the frontiers of 1792. With their field armies once again defeated and in disarray, the allied leaders meet in the Congress of Châtillon (sur Seine) during February 5–March 19 and offer French emperor Napoleon I's representative, Armand Augustin Louis de Caulaincourt, the French frontiers of 1792 if the emperor will agree to peace. Buoyed by his recent military successes and against the advice of Caulaincourt, Napoleon refuses. This decision is perhaps the best example of his irresponsibility as a national leader.

March 7, 1814

Western Europe: France: Napoleonic Wars (continued): Campaign for France (continued): Battle of Craonne. French emperor Napoleon I moves rapidly north against a 30,000-man corps of Prussian general Gebhard Leberecht von Blücher's army on the Plateau of Craonne. Napoleon hopes to carry out a double envelopment, but the timing goes awry, and Marshal Michel Ney attacks before the French artillery is in position. Still, Blücher orders his troops to disengage and move toward Laon. Each side sustains about 5,000 casualties.

March 9, 1814

Western Europe: France: Napoleonic Wars (continued): Campaign for France (continued): Treaties of Chaumont. These treaties, arranged by British foreign secretary Robert Stewart, Viscount Castlereagh, finally forge the grand alliance that the British had so long sought. The four Great Powers (this descriptor now makes its way into diplomatic parlance) of Britain, Russia, Austria, and Prussia all pledge to continue the war until their policy objectives are achieved. These are identified as a confederated Germany, an enlarged and independent Holland, an independent Switzerland, a restored Spain ruled by a Bourbon king, and the restoration of the states of Italy.

Castlereagh promises the allied leaders that Britain will expend in prosecution of the war double the sum provided by any other power. The allies agree that the alliance will remain in effect for 20 years after the end of the fighting and that they will work together to prevent any disruption of the terms agreed to at a forthcoming general peace conference. Chaumont is, in effect, the cornerstone for the alliance system that will maintain the balance of power in Europe for decades thereafter.

March 9–10, 1814

Western Europe: France: Napoleonic Wars (continued): Campaign for France (continued): Battle of Laon. Prussian general Gebhard Leberecht von Blücher, having moved to Laon from Craonne, is

reinforced by troops from the army commanded by Swedish crown prince Karl Johan (former French marshal Jean Baptiste Bernadotte), bringing his strength up to some 85,000 men. Despite being outnumbered more than two to one, French emperor Napoleon I with 37,000 men attacks Blücher. The emperor is defeated, however. The allies lose about 3,000 men, the French perhaps 6,000.

French marshal Auguste Marmont, with 9,000 men, attempts to join Napoleon at Laon. Marmont gets only as far as the village of Athies before being driven off in a separate engagement. Napoleon orders Marmont to take up the defense of Paris and withdraws his own forces to Soissons.

March 12, 1814

Western Europe: France: Napoleonic Wars (continued): Peninsular War (continued). Anglo-Portuguese forces under British lieutenant general Sir Arthur Wellesley, Earl of Wellington, capture Bordeaux. This large city with historically strong commercial ties to Britain surrenders without a battle.

March 13, 1814

Western Europe: France: Napoleonic Wars (continued): Campaign for France (continued): Battle of Rheims. In a bold but dangerous move, French emperor Napoleon I marches 40 miles across the front of Prussian general Gebhard Leberecht von Blücher's army to defeat an isolated Russian corps at Rheims. Napoleon captures Rheims with the loss of only 700 men; the Russians suffer 6,000 casualties. With his confidence restored, Napoleon then moves rapidly south against Austrian field marshal Prince Charles Philip of Schwarzenberg, hoping to defeat the Austrians and Russians and force them back.

March 20–21, 1814

Western Europe: France: Napoleonic Wars (continued): Campaign for France (continued): Battle of Arcis-sur-Aube. French emperor Napoleon I moves south to Arcis-sur-Aube, reportedly held by a small allied force. Napoleon hopes to panic the allies and purchase additional time. Austrian field marshal Prince Charles Philip of Schwarzenberg, however, has concentrated his forces between Troyes and Acris for a major offensive.

Although the Battle of Arcis-sur-Aube opens on March 20 on near equal terms (20,000 French to 21,000 Allies), by the second day of the battle

Schwarzenberg's strength is up to 80,000 men, while Napoleon is able to increase his own numbers to only 28,000. Napoleon loses perhaps 3,000 men to 4,000 for the allies, but he is forced to withdraw eastward. More importantly, Schwarzenberg continues his westerly drive, as do the allies to the north under Prussian general Gebhard Leberecht von Blücher.

March 25, 1814
Western Europe: France: Napoleonic Wars (continued): Campaign for France (continued): Battle of La-Fère-Champenoise. French emperor Napoleon I develops a new plan. He will operate against the allied rear in hopes of cutting their supply lines and causing them to turn back from Paris. He therefore moves his own army and that of Marshal Jacques Macdonald to establish a line east of Vitry and orders marshals Auguste Marmont and Edouard Mortier to join him. This places them in the direct path of the vastly larger allied army under Austrian field marshal Prince Charles Philip of Schwarzenberg.

In the Battle of La Fère-Champenoise of March 25, Marmont and Mortier face odds of 5 to 1. They are driven back in the direction of Meaux and Paris. Two National Guard divisions are butchered in a rear-guard action, losing 4,500 of their 5,000 men. There is now no way that Napoleon can prevent the allies from attacking Paris, nor can he reach there before them, although he heads in that direction with what remains of his army via Bar-sur-Aube, Troyes, and Fontainebleau.

On March 28 Schwarzenberg unites his own army with that of Prussian general Gebhard Leberecht von Blücher at Meaux, near Paris; Napoleon is well off to the east. On March 29 Empress Marie Louise and Napoleon François-Joseph Charles, the King of Rome (Napoleon's son), leave the city and head south toward Orléans, followed the next day by Joseph Bonaparte and much of the government.

March 27, 1814
North America: War of 1812 (continued): Creek War (continued): Battle of Horseshoe Bend. In February, Tennessee Militia major general Andrew Jackson receives significant reinforcements in the form of Tennessee militia and some regular U.S. Army troops, allowing him to resume offensive operations against the Red Stick Creeks. He marches with 3,000 men to Horseshoe Bend of the Tallapoosa River, where

the Red Sticks have fortified a peninsula. Jackson defeats the Creeks in the Battle of Horseshoe Bend (Tohopeka) on March 27, 1814.

In the battle, an estimated 900 Red Stick warriors are killed, and 500 women and children are taken prisoner. Jackson loses 51 killed and 148 wounded. The American victory is decisive, for the Red Stick Creeks then enter into peace negotiations, culminating in the Treaty of Fort Jackson on August 9, 1814.

March 28, 1814
Eastern Pacific Ocean: Engagement between the British frigate *Phoebe* and sloop *Cherub* and the American frigate *Essex*. Following a highly successful 17-month Pacific cruise in which it took 16 British prizes, the *Essex* (commanded by Captain David Porter) falls in with the *Phoebe* (commanded by Captain James Hilyar) and *Cherub* (under Commander

U.S. Navy captain David Porter (1780–1843) enjoyed considerable success against the British while in command of the frigate *Essex* during the War of 1812 before being defeated and captured with his crew in a bloody, hard-fought engagement with the British warships *Phoebe* and *Cherub* near Valparaiso, Chile, on March 28, 1814. (Library of Congress)

Thomas T. Tucker) near Valparaiso, Chile. The *Essex* had lost its main topsail mast in heavy wind and is unable to close to use its short-range carronade armament. The British are thus able to stand off at long range and batter the American ship with their long guns. After a three-hour battle and heavy American casualties, the *Essex* surrenders. Of 255 men in the American frigate, 58 are killed and 66 are wounded in the battle, and 32 drown trying to make it to shore. The two British ships have in all only 5 killed and 10 wounded.

See Leaders: Porter, David

March 30, 1814

Western Europe: France: Napoleonic Wars (continued): Campaign for France (continued): Storming of Montmartre. French marshals Auguste Marmont and Edouard Mortier, with only about 22,000 men between them, contest the allied assault from the north on Paris with about 110,000 men. They are driven back to Montmartre, bringing allied artillery within range of the capital. French emperor Napoleon I, then with his army at Troyes, proceeds ahead with a small escort to Fontainebleau.

March 30, 1814

North America: War of 1812 (continued): Second Battle of Lacolle Mills. Following their naval victory on Lake Erie in September 1813, the Americans take the offensive. Major General James Wilkinson leads some 4,000 men from Plattsburgh and Sackets Harbor in a new invasion of Lower Canada on the Niagara front. Wilkinson vows to "return victorious, or not at all." On March 30, 1814, the Americans attack the small Canadian border fort of Lacolle Mills near Champlain, Upper Canada (Ontario). The blockhouse and a stone mill are held initially by only 80 men, although during the course of the day's fighting reinforcements arrive to bring the number up to 500.

The Americans subject the defenders to artillery fire, while the British employ Congreve Rockets and accurate rifle fire. With the arrival of the British reinforcements, the Americans withdraw back onto U.S. soil. The British suffer 59 casualties, the Americans 154. Wilkinson is relieved of command on April 12, and although acquitted in a court-martial, he is replaced by Major General Jacob Brown. Brown is ably assisted by newly promoted Brigadier Gen-

Lieutenant General Winfield Scott (1786–1866) was one of the greatest military commanders in U.S. history. He distinguished himself in the War of 1812 and led the campaign that captured Mexico City during the Mexican-American War. Commanding general of the army at the onset of the Civil War, he developed the broad outlines of the Anaconda Plan to defeat the Confederacy. (National Archives)

eral Winfield Scott and charged with U.S. operations along the Niagara frontier.

See Leaders: Scott, Winfield

March 31, 1814

Western Europe: France: Napoleonic Wars (continued): Campaign for France (continued): Allies enter Paris. Having put up a valiant fight for the capital and sustaining just 4,000 casualties for allied losses of 8,000, marshals Auguste Marmont and Edouard Mortier surrender Paris. French emperor Napoleon I is at Essones when he learns of events. He then returns to Fontainebleau, where on April 1 he has 36,000 troops.

April 6, 1814

Western Europe: France: Napoleonic Wars (continued): Campaign for France (continued): Napoleon's abdication. French emperor Napoleon I is at the chateau of Fontainebleau, just south of Paris. His army has now grown to some 60,000 men. Encouraged by the cheers of the troops and their calls for a march on Paris, Napoleon prepares such an operation. In Paris, however, Charles Maurice de Talleyrand-Périgord meets with allied leaders and then persuades the French Senate to depose Napoleon.

On April 4 Napoleon's marshals confront him and tell him that his cause is hopeless. Napoleon asserts, "The army will obey me!" Marshal Michel Ney replies, "The army will obey its chiefs." The other four marshals present side with Ney. Abandoned by his old comrades-in-arms, Napoleon reluctantly yields and that same day agrees to abdicate in favor of his three-year-old son Napoléon François Joseph Charles, the king of Rome. This is unacceptable to the allied leaders, however, and on April 11 Napoleon abdicates unconditionally.

Empress Marie Louise is at Blois awaiting Napoleon's orders to join him. No doubt she wants to do so, but he is waiting to see if she will come to him on her own now that he has been removed from power. On April 10 allied troops appear, and she and the king of Rome are delivered to her father, Austrian emperor Francis I. Napoleon never sees either of them again.

April 10, 1814

Western Europe: France: Napoleonic Wars (continued): Peninsular War (continued): Battle of Toulouse. British lieutenant general Sir Arthur Wellesley, Earl of Wellington, moves with some 50,000 Anglo-Portuguese forces against French marshal Jean de Dieu Soult with 35,000 troops, most of them raw recruits and National Guards. Soult receives some replenishment and reinforcements at Toulouse, a major army supply base.

On April 3 Wellington gets 19,000 men across the rain-swollen Garonne River below Toulouse by a pontoon bridge before the bridge is swept away. Fortunately for Wellington, Soult does not move against

the stranded allied divisions. Four days later, Wellington reestablishes communications with his forces on the left bank of the river.

On April 10 Wellington assaults the city with 49,000 men and 50 guns. Soult commands 42,000 men. As with Bordeaux, the city's inhabitants are Bourbon in sympathy and give the defending troops little assistance. Even so, in the assault Wellington loses 4,600 men, Soult only 3,200. On the night of April 11, however, Soult withdraws toward Carcassonne.

On April 12 word is received of Napoleon's abdication, and Soult and Wellington end hostilities. The Peninsular Campaign is over. Some commanders, however, remain unaware of what has transpired, and fighting continues at Bayonne.

April 11, 1814

Western Europe: France: Napoleonic Wars (continued): Campaign for France (continued): Treaty of Fontainebleau. Under the terms of the Treaty of Fontainebleau between Napoleon's representatives and those of the allied leaders, Napoleon is stripped of his powers as ruler of the French Empire, and the throne is denied to any of his relatives. He and Marie Louise are allowed to keep the courtesy titles of emperor and empress, however. Napoleon is granted full sovereignty of the island of Elba off the west coast of Italy. Marie Louise is to receive the duchies of Parma, Placentia, and Guastalla. Napoleon is to be furnished an annual subsidy of 2 million francs by the French government, and he is permitted to take 400 individuals with him into exile.

April 26, 1814

Western Europe: France: Napoleonic Wars (continued): Peninsular War (continued): French sortie at Bayonne. Unaware of what is transpiring elsewhere, the French commander at Bayonne, General Pierre Thouvenot, orders a sortie by his forces on April 14. It catches the besieging British forces by surprise, and the French take a number of prisoners, including British commander Lieutenant General Sir Rowland Hill, who is wounded. In all, the French inflict some 800 casualties and sustain an equal number themselves before they are driven back into the city by British reinforcements. Thouvenot refuses to surrender Bayonne until he receives a direct order from Marshal Jean de Dieu Soult on April 26.

April 29, 1814

Western Atlantic Ocean: War of 1812 (continued). The U.S. sloop *Peacock* of 18 guns (commanded by Master Commandant Lewis Warrington) defeats the Royal Navy brig *Epervier* of 18 guns (under Captain Richard H. Wales). This 45-minute battle off the coast of Florida is decided by superior American gunnery and ends with the surrender of the British ship. Warrington is able to bring his prize into Savannah.

May 30, 1814

Western Europe: France: Napoleonic Wars (continued): First Treaty of Paris. This treaty following the abdication of Napoleon and imposed by the allies on France is remarkably lenient. The allied leaders have claimed all along that Napoleon, not France, is the enemy, and the treaty is designed both to preserve a strong France and to get new Bourbon king Louis XVIII (r. 1814–1824) off to a good start. France is reduced to its frontiers of 1792, which include the addition of Avignon, Venaissin, parts of Savoy, and some border strongholds in the northeast, none of which had belonged to France in 1789. France agrees to recognize the independence of the Netherlands, the German and Italian states, and Switzerland. France also promises to abolish the slave trade. The allies eschew any indemnity.

Given the complexity of allocation of the newly reconquered territories, the allied leaders agree to a general peace conference to meet at Vienna. Britain announces that it will return the Netherlands Indies but retains Malta, Helgoland, Trindad, the Cape of Good Hope, and Ceylon (present-day Sri Lanka). Britain also secures a protectorate over the Ionian Islands (Treaty of November 1815). Britain agrees to return to France its overseas colonies except Tobago, St. Lucia, and Mauritius.

Of all former European colonial empires, the British is by far the largest and most dynamic. The British also maintain the world's largest navy.

June 28, 1814

English Channel: War of 1812 (continued). The U.S. Navy sloop *Wasp* of 18 guns (commanded by Master Commandant Johnston Blakeley) defeats the Royal Navy sloop *Reindeer* of 18 guns (under Commander William Manners). In this 17-minute battle of June

28, 1814, the *Reindeer* is virtually wrecked. Blakeley orders it burned.

July 2–3, 1814

North America: War of 1812 (continued): Upper Canada: U.S. invasion of Upper Canada and seizure of Fort Erie. New American commander on the Niagara front Major General Jacob Brown and his able assistant, Brigadier General Winfield Scott, weed out incompetent officers and reorganize and drill the American forces, which are also reequipped.

Secretary of War John Armstrong orders the major attack against Kingston, the main British base on Lake Ontario, with a diversionary strike on the Niagara front. Having failed to secure cooperation from Commodore Isaac Chauncey, who says that he cannot be ready with new ship construction before July, Brown decides to make the attack across the Niagara River his principal effort.

On July 2, 1814, Brown leads 3,500 men across the Niagara into Upper Canada (Ontario). Capable British commander in Upper Canada Lieutenant General Gordon Drummond has fewer than 4,000 men to garrison the border from Long Point on Lake Erie to York on Lake Ontario. On July 3 American brigades under Scott and Eleazar Wheelock Ripley capture Fort Erie.

July 5, 1814

North America: War of 1812 (continued): Upper Canada: Battle of Chippewa. Following the American capture of Fort Erie, on July 4 U.S. Army brigadier general Winfield Scott begins moving north along the Niagara River, easily driving back a British covering force under Lieutenant Colonel Thomas Pearson. Late that day, the Americans encounter British major general Phineas Riall's defensive line of about 1,500 men drawn up on the north bank on the Chippewa River, about 16 miles north of Fort Erie and near present-day Chippewa, Ontario. Scott then withdraws to Street's Creek.

Early on July 5 Riall, who is an aggressive commander, sends his 1,500 men across the Chippewa, routing an American militia brigade sent forward by U.S. commander Major General Jacob Brown under Brigadier General Peter B. Porter. The British then run into Scott's brigade, which Brown has hastily ordered up from Street's Creek. Riall believes that because of the brigade's gray uniforms, he is facing militia who will soon bolt and run. When the American line holds firm, Riall supposedly exclaims, "Those are regulars, by God!" (Scott is the source for the quote.)

Scott advances his two wings, forming a U-shape against the British advancing in line and catching them in a cross fire. After a hard-fought action lasting about a half hour, the British withdraw in good order. British losses are 148 dead, 350 wounded, and 46 captured. American losses are 61 dead and 255 wounded.

Chippewa is the only battle of the war where two regular army units of approximate size engage in close combat in extended order. It marks a turning point in the war for the U.S. Army, proving that U.S. regulars are a match for British regular troops.

July 22, 1814

North America: War of 1812 (continued): Treaty of Greenville. Reflecting the dramatic shift in the fighting, representatives of Native American tribes of the Old Northwest meet at Greenville, Ohio. They conclude with William Henry Harrison and Governor Lewis Cass the Treaty of Greenville on July 22, 1814. Under its terms, the Delawares, Miamis, Senecas, Shawnees, and Wyandots are forced to declare war on their former ally, Great Britain.

July 25, 1814

North America: War of 1812 (continued): Upper Canada: Battle of Lundy's Lane. Following Brigadier General Winfield Scott's victory in the Battle of Chippewa, American commander Major General Jacob Brown gets his men across the Chippewa River upstream, outflanking Riall's defenses and forcing him back to Fort George. Brown appeals to Commodore Isaac Chauncey, U.S. naval commander on Lake Ontario, to proceed with his squadron from Sackets Harbor at the east end of the lake and join him near Fort George on the west end for joint operations to conquer Upper Canada. Chauncey's refusal will force Brown to withdraw from Upper Canada. While Brown is unable to reinforce, the British rush reinforcements of their own to the Niagara front.

Brown now moves against Lundy's Lane, a village in present-day Niagara Falls, Canada. In the most bitterly contested land battle of the war, Brown, with 3,000 men and 9 guns, engages a British force of 4,000 men and 8 guns under Lieutenant General Sir Gordon Drummond and Major General Phineas Riall in a five-hour drawn battle. The Americans lose 171 killed, 572 wounded, and 110 captured or missing. British losses are 84 killed, 559 wounded, and 235 captured or missing. Brown, Scott, and Drummond are all among the wounded, while Riall is taken prisoner. The Americans then withdraw to Fort Erie.

July–August 1814

North America: War of 1812 (continued): British operations in Chesapeake Bay. The commander in chief of British naval forces in American waters, Vice Admiral Sir Alexander Cochrane, orders Rear Admiral Sir George Cockburn "to destroy and lay waste such towns and districts upon the coast as you may find assailable." In July and August 1814, therefore, Cockburn mounts a series of harassing operations in Chesapeake Bay. At the same time, London sends out a ground force of some 4,000 British regulars under Major General Robert Ross.

On August 15 Ross, Cochrane, and Cockburn meet aboard ship at the mouth of the Potomac River and devise a plan for a diversionary attack desired by London to take pressure off Canada. Their objective is the U.S. capital of Washington, D.C.

The British ships land Ross's troops at Benedict, Maryland, on August 19. The soldiers then begin their march against Washington, 40 miles distant. At the same time, smaller British warships move up the Patuxent River to destroy the small U.S. Chesapeake gunboat flotilla under U.S. commodore Joshua Barney that has sought refuge there.

On August 22 following a series of engagements with the British warships and with his gunboats in imminent danger of capture, Barney blows them up and withdraws overland with his men and some of his guns to take part in the defense of Washington.

August 9, 1814

North America: War of 1812 (continued): Creek War (continued): Treaty of Fort Jackson. Tennessee Militia major general Andrew Jackson is rewarded for his victory in the March 1814 Battle of Horseshoe Bend with a commission as a major general in the U.S. Army (May 22, 1814). He is also charged with negotiating peace terms with the Red Stick Creeks to end the war. In the Treaty of Fort Jackson of August 9, 1814, signed by only part of the Creeks, the Creeks lose some 20 million acres—approximately two-thirds of their land—in Alabama and Georgia. This cession removes a major obstacle to white migration in the Old Southwest.

August 24, 1814

North America: War of 1812 (continued): Battle of Bladensburg. British major general Robert Ross arrives at Marlborough, Maryland, on August 22. Brigadier General William Winder, commander of the Potomac Military District, issues a call for 75,000 militia to defend Washington, Baltimore, and Annapolis, all likely British targets. Barely 6,000 answer the appeal. Neither the incompetent Winder or Secretary of War John Armstrong makes any real effort to defend Washington.

The British are able to conceal their true objective until they march on Bladensburg, Maryland, on August 24. Winder takes position on the road near the town. There he is joined by Commodore Joshua Barney and his 400 flotillamen and 120 marines from the Washington Navy Yard, who bring with them five naval cannon.

The Battle of Bladensburg occurs that afternoon. Despite having the advantage of the defensive position, some 7,000 American defenders are routed by about 4,000 British troops. Most of the Americans flee, causing the battle to be known as the Bladensburg Races. Barney, his sailors, and the marines are the only ones to fight effectively. They delay the British advance for about half an hour. The Americans lose 26 killed and 54 wounded. British losses are 64 killed and 185 wounded. The way is now open to Washington.

August 24–25, 1814

North America: War of 1812 (continued): British occupation of Washington. Following their victory in the Battle of Bladensburg in Maryland, the British quickly move on Washington, D.C. In retaliation for the destruction of public buildings by the Americans in York (Toronto), the British torch the Capitol building and the White House. They also destroy other public buildings and a number of private homes. Secretary of the Navy William Jones orders the destruction of the Washington Navy Yard with its warships.

The British depart Washington on the night of August 25, marching to join their transports. Following the public outcry over the destruction of the nation's capital, James Monroe replaces John Armstrong as secretary of war.

August 31, 1814

North America: War of 1812 (continued): Lake Champlain Front: British invasion of New York. Substantial British reinforcements—veterans of the Peninsula Campaign in Europe—arrive in Canada in July, and Lieutenant General Sir George Prevost, governor-general of North America, leads 11,000 troops south in an invasion of upper New York state.

September 1, 1814

English Channel: War of 1812 (continued). The U.S. Navy sloop *Wasp* of 18 guns (commanded by Captain Johnston Blakely) defeats the Royal Navy 18-gun brig *Avon* (under Commander James Arbuthnot). Following an engagement of about 45 minutes, the *Avon* surrenders. Two other British warships then appear, forcing Blakely to relinquish his prize, but the badly damaged *Avon* sinks shortly thereafter. The *Wasp* disappears at sea the next month.

September 11, 1814

North America: War of 1812 (continued): Lake Champlain Front: Battle of Lake Champlain and Battle of Plattsburgh. Advancing south from Canada along the west side of Lake Champlain, the British 11,000-man land invasion force under Lieutenant General Sir George Prevost, governor-general of North America, is operating in conjunction with a naval force on Lake Champlain under Captain George Downie. Following some skirmishing along Beekmantown Road, the British reach Plattsburgh on September 6, 1814. Despite its importance, the town is defended by only a single brigade of U.S. regulars, under Brigadier General Alexander Macomb, along with about 800 New York and Vermont militia, a total of 3,000 men, at most.

Prevost is an inept commander. He fails to secure a ford across the Saranac River to his front and then, much to the consternation of his senior officers, suspends land operations pending the arrival of the supporting British naval squadron on Lake Champlain under Downie. Prevost is resolved to secure control of the lake before continuing his advance. Downie

Contemporary illustration depicting the fighting at Plattsburgh, New York, on September 11, 1814. U.S. Navy lieutenant Thomas Macdonough's victory in the Battle of Lake Champlain off Plattsburgh on that date led the British commander, Lieutenant General Sir George Prevost, to withdraw his land forces back to Canada. (Library of Congress)

had taken command of the squadron only on September 2, however; he is determined not to hazard it until his most powerful ship, the *Confiance,* is fully prepared and all of its guns mounted.

Prevost's land force thus remains inactive for nearly five days awaiting Downie's arrival, and Macomb uses this delay to strengthen his defensive position of three wooden forts and two blockhouses along the south bank of the Saranac River astride Lake Champlain. Although outnumbered 4 to 1, on the night of September 9 Macomb mounts a spoiling attack across the Saranac with 50 men against a British rocket battery. The raid is successful, and the American raiding force returns to its lines intact.

Prevost remains quiescent until the morning of September 11, when the British flotilla at last sails into Plattsburgh Bay. On Downie's arrival, Prevost orders two brigades to begin the land attack. As the British flotilla engages the U.S. Navy squadron on the lake, Major General Thomas Brisbane's brigade of 3,500 men attacks the American troops in front of Plattsburgh to fix the defenders in place. A second

British brigade of 3,500 men under Major General Frederick Robinson searches for a ford on the Saranac in an attempt to turn the American left. Prevost holds in reserve a third brigade under Major General Manly Powers, ready to exploit any opportunity.

Unfortunately for the British, Robinson is late in beginning his movement, and he loses additional time by marching down the wrong road. Brisbane also has difficulty in the face of determined American resistance. Just as the British troops are registering progress against the outnumbered Americans, however, at 10:30 a.m. they receive orders from Prevost to cease operations and withdraw immediately. Prevost takes this decision in consequence of what has occurred on the lake.

In the naval battle, Downie's squadron of 4 ships—the frigate *Confiance* (39 guns), brig *Linnet* (16 guns), sloop *Chubb* (11 guns), and sloop *Finch* (11 guns)—and 12 galleys mounting a total of 17 guns round Cumberland Head and stand in to engage the American flotilla. The defending American naval force consists of 4 ships (the frigate *Saratoga* [26

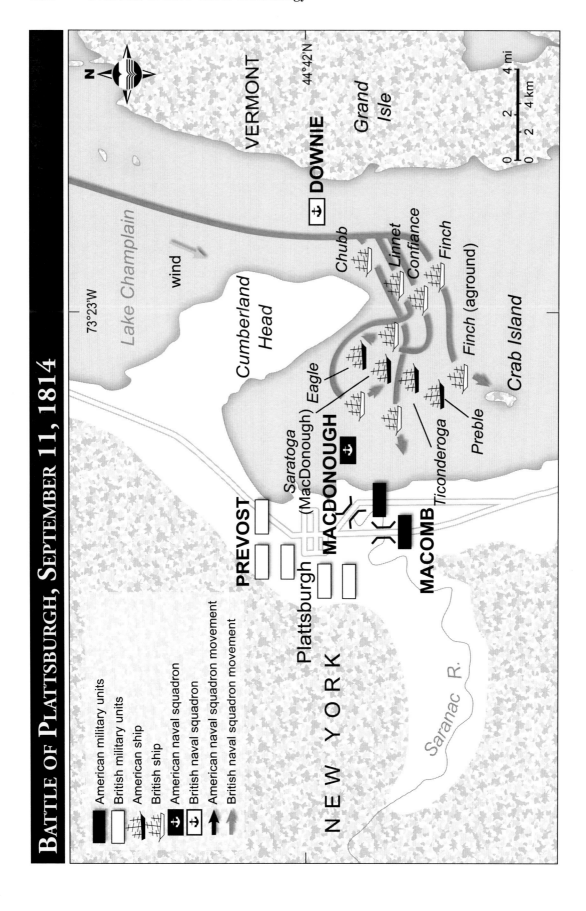

BATTLE OF PLATTSBURGH, SEPTEMBER 11, 1814

American military units
British military units
American ship
British ship
American naval squadron
British naval squadron
American naval squadron movement
British naval squadron movement

VERMONT

44°42'N

DOWNIE

Grand Isle

4 mi
4 km

73°23'W

Lake Champlain

wind

Chubb
Linnet
Confiance
Finch
Finch (aground)

Cumberland Head

Eagle

Crab Island

Saratoga (MacDonough)

MACDONOUGH

Ticonderoga

Preble

PREVOST

Plattsburgh

MACOMB

NEW YORK

Saranac R.

guns], brig *Eagle* [20], schooner *Ticonderoga* [17], and sloop *Preble* [7]) and 10 gunboats mounting a total of 16 guns. The two sides are evenly matched both in numbers of vessels and firepower.

Thomas Macdonough, however, has a significant advantage in that his ships are carefully positioned. In the week he had to prepare, he placed his ships in line, setting out anchors so that they might easily be swung in either direction to utilize their guns to maximum advantage. Because the American ships are anchored, their crews can concentrate all their energies on working the guns. The British crews, on the other hand, are forced to work both the sails and guns of their ships at the same time.

The naval battle lasts 2 hours and 20 minutes. The two largest ships, the American *Saratoga* and British *Confiance,* each inflict significant damage on the other. Downie is killed, and with heavy personnel losses, the *Confiance* strikes to the Americans. Three other British ships also surrender. Three British galleys are sunk, and the remainder pull off. With all of his own galleys in sinking shape, Macdonough is unable to pursue, however.

Macdonough has won a classic victory. American casualties are 47 dead and 58 wounded; British casualties total 57 dead and at least 100 wounded. The casualties in the fighting on land are also relatively insignificant—the British suffer perhaps 250 casualties, while American losses are only about 150—but the battle has immense consequences.

Deprived of his naval support and well aware of what had happened to a British invading army in this same region under Lieutenant General John Burgoyne during the American Revolutionary War in 1777, Prevost now orders a general withdrawal. Macomb's men are astonished. For his stand, Macomb receives a gold medal and promotion to major general. Prevost is recalled to England to face an official inquiry. Prevost's withdrawal ends all danger of a British invasion from Canada during the remainder of the war. News of the victory also influences the Ghent Peace Conference. Coupled with the American victories on the Niagara Front and at Baltimore, the Battle of Lake Champlain contributes greatly to the British decision to end the war status quo antebellum.

September 12–14, 1814

North America: War of 1812 (continued): British attack on Baltimore. Following their brief occupation of Washington, British troops under Major General Robert Ross withdraw to their ships and proceed to their next objective, the city of Baltimore, Maryland, long a major port and privateering base. Sailing from the Potomac on September 6, the British ships arrive at the mouth of the Patapsco River, about 16 miles from Baltimore. Ross's men go ashore at North Point on September 12. The British naval forces then move upriver to attack Fort McHenry. Unlike Washington, Baltimore is well defended by 13,000 regulars and militia and has an able commander in Maryland Militia major general Samuel Smith.

Some 3,200 well-entrenched militia under Brigadier General John Stricker engage the advancing British troops and fall back after having inflicted major casualties including Ross, who is mortally wounded. The British then halt on arrival at the well-defended heights, awaiting the outcome of the fleet's bombardment of Fort McHenry, which occurs on the night of September 13–14 and inspires eyewitness Francis Scott Key to write the verses of "The Star-Spangled Banner," which will become the national anthem.

With the failure of their naval bombardment, the British embark their troops. On October 14 the British expeditionary force departs Chesapeake Bay for Jamaica.

September 17, 1814

North America: War of 1812 (continued): Upper Canada: Battle of Fort Erie. Following the Battle of Lundy's Lane, U.S. forces in Upper Canada under Major General Jacob Brown withdraw back to Fort Erie on the Canadian side of the border. Beginning on August 2, some 3,500 British troops under Lieutenant General Sir Gordon Drummond besiege Fort Erie. Bringing up heavy siege guns, they subject the fort, held by about 2,000 Americans, to bombardment. The Americans repulse a British attack on August 15, inflicting heavy losses.

Then on September 17 Brigadier General Peter B. Porter leads a sortie by 1,600 of the defenders, attacking and destroying the British artillery positions. The Americans suffer 511 casualties during the sortie, the British 609. Drummond withdraws on September 21. The Americans hold Fort Erie until November 5, 1814, when they evacuate it and withdraw back across the Niagara River, bringing to an end major conflict on this front and closing out the American effort to seize Upper Canada.

September 1814–June 1815

Central Europe: Austria: Napoleonic Wars (continued): Congress of Vienna. In September 1814 representatives of virtually all European states—and those of a number that have passed out of existence—begin gathering at Vienna for one of the important diplomatic assemblies of modern times. Two emperors (Alexander I of Russia and Francis I of Austria) are present along with the kings of Prussia, Bavaria, Württemberg, and Denmark, but the real work of the congress is carried on by their first ministers, although Alexander retains full authority. The key players are Count Klemens von Metternich of Austria; Robert Stewart, Viscount Castlereagh, of Britain; King Frederick William III of Prussia and his chief minister Prince Karl August von Hardenburg; and Charles Maurice de Talleyrand-Périgord of France.

A serious split soon develops between Austria and Britain on the one side and Prussia and Russia on the other. Russia wants all Poland in a reconstituted Kingdom of Poland with Alexander as its ruler. Prussia, supported by Russia, seeks all Saxony. Austria and Britain fear the increase in Russian and Prussian influence. This controversy almost leads to war. Talleyrand moves into the breach, supporting Austria and Britain. Metternich then proposes a defensive alliance of Austria, Britain, and France, and this secret treaty is signed on January 3, 1815.

It is in these circumstances of discord that Napoleon decides to return to France from exile on Elba. The allies quickly compose their differences, however. On news of the secret treaty, Russia and Prussia back down. Prussia receives part of Saxony, and Russia most of Poland. This advances Russian influence 250 miles farther west.

In the Act of the Congress of Vienna of June 8, 1815, Austria receives Lombardy and Venetia, the Illyrian Provinces (former French kingdoms of Illyria and Dalmatia), and Salzburg and the Tirol (Tyrol), both from Bavaria. Austria, however, gives up its territory in the Netherlands.

Prussia gains about two-fifths of Saxony, Posen and Gdańsk (Danzig), Swedish Pomerania, and Rügen (for which Denmark gets Lauenburg). Prussia also receives territory in Westphalia as well Neuchâtel. In return, Prussia gives up Ansbach and Baireuth to Bavaria, East Friesland to Hanover, and part of its Polish territory before 1807 to Russia.

To offset any future French threat to the northeast, the Dutch Republic secures the former Austrian Netherlands (Belgium), the new enlarged state being known as the Kingdom of the Netherlands. Metternich hopes that this step will enhance the possibility of future cooperation between France and Austria. The new Kingdom of the Netherlands is, however, characterized by strong religious and linguistic difficulties.

One of the most difficult problems to resolve is the German states. Napoleon consolidated some 350 German states into a 10th that number (for good reason, Napoleon deserves to be considered the stepfather of present-day Germany). German nationalism, so evident in the German War of Liberation of 1813, is now deliberately set aside in favor of a loose-knit German Confederation of 39 states, including 5 free cities, with Austria as its president. The Act of Confederation is signed on September 8, 1815.

A new Polish state, known as Congress Poland, is created with much the same territory as Napoleon's former Grand Duchy of Warsaw with Czar Alexander as its king. He grants Poland a liberal constitution (which Russia does not have) with Polish as the official language and its own army. Kraków (Cracow) becomes a free state under the protection of Russia, Austria, and Prussia.

Sweden is confirmed in possession of Norway (acquired in the Treaty of Kiel of January 14, 1814), with Norway receiving a guarantee of its rights and a separate constitution. In the Act of Union of 1815, Norway is in fact confirmed as an independent kingdom, merely united with Sweden under the same ruler. Denmark is compensated by receiving Lauenburg.

Switzerland is reconstituted as an independent confederation of 22 cantons. Spain, Sardinia (which receives Genoa), Tuscany, and Modena, and the Papal States are all reconstituted. The duchies of Parma, Modena, Lucca, and Tuscany all are given to members of the Habsburg family. The Bourbons are not reestablished in the Kingdom of Naples until 1815 (then the Kingdom of the Two Sicilies), since its king, former Napoleonic marshal Joachim Murat, has deserted Napoleon. In Italy as in Germany, nationalism is deliberately stymied, with Habsburg predominance reestablished.

October 1–2, 1814

South America: Chile: Battle of Rancagua. In 1811 José Miguel Carrera leads Chilean nationalists in securing independence from Spain. After demonstrat-

EUROPE IN 1815

Boundary of the
German Confederation

```
0        250        500 mi
0    250    500 km
```

ing his incompetence, however, Carrera is replaced by Bernardo O'Higgins. On October 1 at Rancagua some 600 Chilean troops under O'Higgins turn back a Spanish expeditionary force of 1,200 men from Peru under Mariana Osorio. The next day the battle resumes, and this time Osorio is victorious. In large part, the Spanish triumph because Carrera refuses to lend his support to O'Higgins. Several days later, Osorio's troops enter Santiago and reestablish Spanish control of Chile.

November 9, 1814

North America: War of 1812 (continued): Jackson's seizure of Pensacola. In May 1814 Major General Andrew Jackson is named commander of Military District No. 7, which includes the area between Mobile, Alabama, and New Orleans, Louisiana, and U.S. forces in the southeast. Jackson prepares a campaign against Spanish Florida. Following a joint British-Indian attack on Fort Bowyer from Pensacola in East Florida, he disobeys President James Madison's instructions and seizes Pensacola on November 9, 1814. Jackson then withdraws to Mobile and from there proceeds to New Orleans, where he arrives on December 1.

November 1814–March 1816
South Asia: India: Gurkha War. Beginning November 14, 1814, the British East India Company sends Indian Army units into the Kingdom of Nepal to end Gurkha raids into northern India. The Gurkhas turn back the first British forays, but in 1815 British major general David Ochterlony achieves success. Taking one Gurkha fort after another, he penetrates the Kathmandu Valley and advances on Kathmandu itself. Ochterlony brings the war to a successful conclusion in the Treaty of Sugauli (Segowlee) of December 2, 1815.

Ratified on March 4, 1816, the treaty calls for Nepal to cede about one-third of its territory, including Sikkim, to British India. It also calls for the establishment of a British representative in Kathmandu (the first Westerner permitted to live there) and allows the British to recruit Gurkhas for military service, a practice that continues.

December 13, 1814
North America: War of 1812 (continued): New Orleans Campaign: Arrival of the British expeditionary force. Returning to New Orleans on December 1, U.S. Army major general Andrew Jackson is aware that the British are assembling an expeditionary force at Jamaica for a descent on the Gulf Coast, with the logical points of attack either Mobile or New Orleans. Jackson works to strengthen the New Orleans defenses and prepares works at Baton Rouge in case it should be necessary to fall back there.

On November 27, 1814, a large British task force of some 50 ships commanded by Vice Admiral Sir Alexander F. I. Cochrane sails from Jamaica with 7,500 seasoned veterans of the Peninsular War under the command of Major General Sir Edward Pakenham. The British objective is the rich port city of New Orleans. The British hope to secure control of the Mississippi River and its valley. The entire expeditionary force arrives in the Lake Borgne area, some 40 miles east of New Orleans, on December 13.

December 14, 1814
North America: War of 1812 (continued): New Orleans Campaign (continued): Battle of Lake Borgne.

The British plan to approach New Orleans not from the south but from the east through Bayou Bienvenue, which drains the area east of the city and reaches from Lake Borgne within 1 mile of the Mississippi. This route is far shallower than the British had believed, and it is 62 miles from Cat Island at the mouth of Lake Borgne to Bayou Bienvenue. Guarding this approach to New Orleans are five small American gunboats under Lieutenant Thomas ap Catesby Jones.

The British set out in 42 launches and other craft. British captain Nicholas Lockyer commands a force of more than 1,200 men, whereas Jones has only 183. Jones anchors his gunboats in the Malheureux Channel passage. The British attack on the morning of December 14 and take the American gunboats by boarding, one by one.

American casualties are 6 killed, 35 wounded, and 86 captured. The British report 17 men killed and 77 wounded. While a significant defeat for the U.S. side, the battle does delay the British arrival at New Orleans, giving Jackson more time to prepare the city's defenses.

December 24, 1814
Western Europe: Austrian Netherlands: War of 1812 (continued): Treaty of Ghent. Both sides in the peace talks at Ghent in the Austrian Netherlands (Belgium) initially take a firm stance. The United States demands an end to impressment and blockades and also demands resolution of other maritime matters. The British demand creation of a neutral Indian buffer state in the Old Northwest and territorial concessions in the northeastern United States to the benefit of Canada. Positions shift depending on the war news but, with both sides hurting financially, there is considerable pressure to reach a settlement.

Eventually the British accede to the U.S. position of status quo antebellum, the restoration of prewar borders. The Treaty of Ghent, signed on December 24, 1814, restores the prewar territorial situation. West Florida, taken by the United States from Spain during the war, remains in U.S. possession. There is no mention of an Indian state. The treaty provides for the release of all prisoners but says nothing about the maritime differences that were the chief causes of the war. It does provide for a commission to settle the matter of the disputed northeast border between the United States and Canada, and both sides agree to leave to future negotiation the matters of the military status of the Great Lakes and offshore fishing rights (the Rush-Bagot Agreement of April 28, 1817).

Fighting ceases immediately on news of the treaty, which is unanimously approved by the U.S. Senate on February 15, 1815. It is officially proclaimed by President James Madison on February 17.

1814

North America: War of 1812 (continued): The war at sea. In 1813 the British send significant naval reinforcements to America and soon close down most American ports and shipping. The blockade grows increasingly effective, and by 1814 the British are also carrying out major landings along the coast, resulting in considerable damage and property losses. Although the Americans win two key inland waters victories on lakes Champlain and Erie, they cannot in any way challenge British control of the oceans.

The U.S. Navy is, for all practical purposes, confined to port. Only occasionally does a warship escape the blockade, as with the *Constitution* near the end of the conflict. Thus, the situation at sea for the United States in 1813–1814 is much as it has been during the American Revolutionary War, with the British able to move land forces virtually at will.

The navy does achieve success on inland waters, however. In September 1813 the Americans win the Battle of Lake Erie, securing control of that important lake, and in September 1814 the navy is also victorious at Plattsburgh on Lake Champlain, turning back a powerful British land invasion from Canada. These two inland victories fortify the backdoor of the United States.

As during the American Revolutionary War, the Americans seek recourse in a *guerre de course,* largely conducted by privateers that prey on British shipping. Of 22 U.S. Navy ships, 18 are engaged in commerce warfare; they take 165 prizes. Of 526 registered privateers, only some 200 engage in extended operations on the high seas, but these take 1,344 prizes. This effort grows in intensity during the war, with 1,054 of the prizes taken in the last 18 months of the war, an average of 2 per day. British insurance rates soar. While the commerce raiding activities cannot win the war for the United States, they do provide a strong financial incentive for Britain to conclude peace.

January 8, 1815

North America: War of 1812 (continued): New Orleans Campaign (continued): Battle of New Orleans. Because of the shallowness of Lake Borgne, it takes British land commander Major General Sir Edward Pakenham more than a week to land all his troops below New Orleans. In a surprise move, though, Pakenham sends an advance force of 1,600 men under Major General John Keane down Bayou Bienvenue and Bayou Mazant to a point only 7 miles below the city, where there are no American defenses.

American commander Major General Andrew Jackson moves quickly, and with some 2,000 men supported by the schooner *Caroline* of 14 guns, on the night of December 23–24, 1814, he launches a raid on the British position. Rebuffed, Jackson withdraws to a point about 5 miles from the city. Taking advantage of a dry, shallow canal, Jackson sets up a line of breastworks. On January 1, 1815, an inconclusive artillery duel occurs between the two sides, with the Americans getting the better of it.

Pakenham now calls up reinforcements, who arrive on January 6. Unfortunately for the British, in that week's delay Jackson also receives reinforcement in the form of 2,000 Kentucky militiamen. Shortly before 7:00 a.m. on January 8, 1815, Pakenham launches a frontal assault on the American line with 5,300 men. Jackson has some 4,000 men across his front and 1,000 in reserve. The British troops prove easy targets for American artillery fire and steady rifle and musket fire delivered by a three-deep line of defending infantry. Pakenham rides forward to rally his men, and is shot and killed. The British then withdraw.

In a battle of only 75 minutes, the British sustain nearly 40 percent casualties: 291 dead, 1,262 wounded, and 484 taken prisoner. American losses are only 13 dead, 39 wounded, and 19 missing.

On January 18 the British withdraw to Lake Borgne, and on January 25 the men return to their ships and depart. The battle, although meaningless as far as the Treaty of Ghent is concerned, nonetheless proves a great boost for American nationalism and helps propel Jackson into the presidency.

January 15, 1815

Western Atlantic Ocean: War of 1812 (continued): Capture of USS *President.* While crossing the bar exiting New York Harbor for a planned Pacific cruise, the U.S. frigate *President* (under Captain Stephen Decatur) runs aground and is damaged. Although the frigate gets free, it is subsequently spotted by ships of the blockading Royal Navy *Majestic* squadron (commanded by Captain John Hayes) and, slowed by the damage, is chased down. In the course of a running fight, the *President* actually defeats the pursuing British frigate *Endymion* but is unable to outrun the four-ship squadron, and Decatur surrenders to avoid unnecessary bloodshed. Repaired, the *President* is taken into the Royal Navy.

February 20, 1815
Eastern Atlantic Ocean: War of 1812 (continued): Capture of HMS *Cyane*. Cruising off the Portuguese island of Madeira, U.S. frigate *Constitution* of 51 guns (commanded by Captain James Stewart) encounters the Royal Navy corvette *Cyane* of 34 guns (under Captain Gordon Thomas Falcon) and sloop *Levant* of 20 guns (under Captain George Douglas) and engages them both. Because the battle occurs after the end of the war, it never receives the notoriety of the war's other naval engagements.

March 1, 1815
Western Europe: France: Napoleonic Wars (continued): The Hundred Days: Napoleon returns to France from Elba. Taking advantage of allied divisions at the Congress of Vienna and dissatisfaction in France with the return of the Bourbons ("the illness and cure were in accord") and believing that he is justified by the failure of the French government to pay the annual subsidy promised to him under terms of the Treaty of Fontainebleau, Napoleon departs Elba with several hundred followers in his brig the *Inconstant* for France, landing again at Fréjus on March 1. This begins the period known as the Hundred Days (March 20–July 8, 1815).

March 3–June 30, 1815
North Africa: War between Algiers and the United States. During the War of 1812 between the United States and Britain, U.S. warships had been withdrawn from the Mediterranean. Encouraged by Britain, the dey of Algiers, Hadji Ali, breaks relations with the United States on the excuse that American naval stores sent as tribute are deficient. He expels U.S. consul Tobias Lear. The Algerines then seize a U.S. merchant brig and enslave its crew.

War with Britain precludes any action on the part of the United States against Algiers, and attempts to resolve the issue by negotiations through Spain fail. The conclusion of peace with Britain changes the situation dramatically, however. On March 3, 1815, Congress authorizes President James Madison to carry out operations against Algiers.

The administration sends two squadrons. The first, under Commodore William Bainbridge, the senior officer, assembles at Boston but is delayed. The second, under Commodore Stephen Decatur, departs New York. Decatur commands 11 ships, with his flag in the frigate *Guerriere* of 54 guns.

Arriving in the Mediterranean with 10 of his ships before Algiers is aware of the U.S. decision for war, Decatur captures two Algerine warships and then, on June 28, sails his squadron boldly into Algiers Harbor. There he dictates peace with the new dey, Omar Pasha. The treaty secures the cessation of all tribute and the release of American prisoners without ransom.

Decatur then sails to Tunis and Tripoli, securing similar guarantees as well as pledges of compensation for American merchant ships seized during the War of 1812. This closes the U.S. Barbary Wars. Bainbridge arrives with the second U.S. squadron after the conclusion of hostilities.

March 19, 1815
Southern Europe: Italy: Napoleonic Wars (continued): The Hundred Days (continued): Beginning of the Neapolitan War. Despite his earlier defection from Napoleon, king of Naples and former Napoleonic marshal Joachim Murat fears that the allies will not let him keep his throne (he had rendered little military assistance to them in 1814) and rallies to Napoleon. On March 19 Murat marches against the Austrians with his army (nominal strength of 100,000 men). Napoleon is furious, for this dashes any thin hopes he had that the allies would negotiate with him. He also knows that Murat's goal is to become ruler of all Italy.

Indeed, expecting a rush of volunteers to his cause, on March 30 at Reimini, Murat proclaims the independence of Italy. The response is disappointing, but Murat nonetheless outnumbers the Austrian forces two to one. The Neapolitan Army, however, is totally inept and absolutely unmotivated. Within short order, two Austrian armies under generals Adam Neipperg and Frederick Bianchi wipe out Murat's earlier gains and force him and his army to the southeast, into Ancona.

March 20, 1815

Western Europe: France: Napoleonic Wars (continued): The Hundred Days (continued): Napoleon returns to Paris. Napoleon makes his way north from the Mediterranean coast to Paris. Marshal Michel Ney, dispatched by King Louis XVIII to arrest Napoleon (he promises to bring Napoleon back in an iron cage), is unable to hold back his soldiers, who rally to their former commander. Ney also goes over to Napoleon. On March 19 King Louis XVIII flees to Ghent; the next evening Napoleon returns to the capital, beginning the period generally referred to as the Hundred Days.

There is no enthusiastic general welcome for Napoleon from among the French population, but he hopes to rekindle the revolutionary enthusiasm of the masses. To secure their assistance, he orders Benjamin Constant to prepare the Additional Act to the Constitution of the Empire. His survival will not rest on new constitutions, however, but on the battlefield. The leaders of Europe, still assembled in Vienna, resolve to crush him; on March 13, 1815, they declare Napoleon an outlaw. They act quickly to gather their armies while Napoleon puts together his own makeshift military force.

March 23, 1815

South Atlantic Ocean: War of 1812 (continued): Capture of HMS *Penguin*. The U.S. Navy sloop *Hornet* of 18 guns (commanded by Captain James Biddle) captures the Royal Navy brig-sloop *Penguin* of 18 guns (under Commander James Dickinson) off the Tristan da Cunha Islands. The war's last naval action, it occurs nearly three months after the official end of hostilities.

March–May 1815

Western Europe: Napoleonic Wars (continued): The Hundred Days (continued): Buildup of military forces. The governments of Austria, Britain, Prussia, and Russia each pledge to field a force of 180,000 men against France. Most other European powers join in, although not Sweden, which is then involved in the takeover of Norway. The initial forces

against Napoleon number 400,000 men. British field marshal Sir Arthur Wellesley, Earl of Wellington, receives command of the allied forces.

Napoleon meanwhile energetically prepares France for yet another war. He assembles an army of 300,000 regulars, but his field army, the Army of the North centered on Paris, numbers only 125,000 men. An additional 170,000 National Guardsmen are on interior duty. Other men undergo hasty military training. Many of his marshals either flee or refuse to rally to him, including the irreplaceable Alexandre Berthier. Napoleon makes some poor personnel choices, rejecting the services of Joachim Murat, who would have been useful to him, and making Marshal Louis Nicolas Davout, his best field commander, minister of war. Another capable field commander, Jean de Dieu Soult, is relegated to the position of chief of staff.

Facing formidable odds, Napoleon's only hope is to strike first and defeat the allies singly before they can concentrate against him. He plans to move first against the 110,000-man Anglo-Dutch force under Wellington at Brussels, then turn and deal with the 120,000 Prussians under Field Marshal Gebhard Leberecht von Blücher at Liège. Napoleon hopes that once he has bested these two, the allies will treat with him.

May 2–3, 1815

Southern Europe: Italy: Napoleonic Wars (continued): The Hundred Days (continued): Neapolitan War: Battle of Tolentino. By the end of April 1815, king of Naples Joachim Murat has lost all early gains of the Neapolitan War. Two Austrian armies in Italy under generals Adam Neipperg and Frederick Bianchi force Murat and the Neapolitan Army to withdraw from the north. With the Austrian armies temporarily separated by the Apennine Mountains, Murat hopes to defeat Bianchi to the west, then turn on Neipperg. Bianchi is aware of Murat's plan and seeks to avoid battle until Neipperg can come up, but Murat attacks.

The two armies do battle on May 2, 1815, at Tolentino in Macerata. Murat commands some 25,500 men and 58 guns; Bianchi has only 12,000 men and 28 guns but occupies strong defensive positions. The Neapolitans register modest gains in the first day of battle.

On May 3 things again are going well for the Neapolitans when Murat learns that Neipperg has defeated his blocking force in the Battle of Scapezzano and is closing on Tolentino. Murat also believes a false report that the Royal Navy has landed Sicilian forces in southern Italy, threatening his line of retreat. Murat therefore breaks off the battle and retreats south.

Austrian casualties at Tolentino are 100 killed and 700 wounded; Neapolitan losses are 1,120 killed, 600 wounded, and 2,400 taken prisoner. Murat returns to Naples, but the Austrians are approaching by land, and Queen Caroline Bonaparte has already surrendered Naples to the Royal Navy. Murat flees in disguise to France, where Napoleon refuses to see him. After some weeks Murat goes to Corsica, raises a small force, and returns to Naples, hoping that the people will rally to him. (In reality, he is probably seeking death.)

Defeated and captured by Bourbon troops at Pizzo in Calabria on October 7, Murat is tried by court-martial, convicted, and executed by a firing squad at Pizzo on October 13, 1815.

May 20, 1815
Southern Europe: Italy: Napoleonic Wars (continued): The Hundred Days (continued): Neapolitan War. The Treaty of Casalanza between Austria and Naples restores King Ferdinand IV to the throne.

June 15, 1815
Western Europe: France: Napoleonic Wars (continued): The Hundred Days (continued): Napoleon seizes Charleroi. On June 11 Napoleon leaves Paris with the Army of the North, moving before the allies imagine he is ready. He concentrates near Charleroi on June 14, hoping to strike and defeat the Anglo-Dutch forces and then deal with the Prussians. The next day Napoleon crosses the Sambre River, moving into Belgium at Charleroi with the aim of engaging British and Dutch forces under Field Marshal Sir Arthur Wellesley, Earl of Wellington.

Field Marshal Gebhard Leberecht von Blücher, commander of Prussian forces at Liège, acts promptly, moving his men from the northeast by that evening to near Sombreffe, 10 miles northeast of Charleroi. Wellington meanwhile moves more cautiously, concentrating his own forces some 15 miles to the west. The key point linking the two armies is the crossroads of Quatre Bras.

June 16, 1815
Western Europe: Belgium: Napoleonic Wars (continued): The Hundred Days (continued): Battles of Quatre Bras and Ligny. Napoleon sends Marshal Michel Ney along the road to Brussels with 40,000 men. Ney proceeds cautiously and, on the morning of June 16, is engaged with part of the Anglo-Dutch army under Field Marshal Sir Arthur Wellesley, Earl of Wellington, at Quatre Bras, 10 miles north of Charleroi. Meanwhile, with Prussian field marshal Gebhard Leberecht von Blücher having advanced too swiftly to Ligny 5 miles east of Quatre Bras with 85,000 men (had he waited a day, he could have had 35,000 more men on the field of battle), Napoleon moves his remaining 80,000 men to engage the Prussians there before they can join Wellington. At Ligny, battle is joined by noon on June 16.

Fortunately for Wellington, the Prince of Orange is near enough with 8,000 men and, with valiant actions, manages to hold Quatre Bras until Wellington can bring up reinforcements by early afternoon. By the end of the day Wellington has 36,000 men on the field. Ney, not aware of the size of the force confronting him, has moved too cautiously.

A British-Dutch counterattack that evening throws Ney back. Ney's confusing orders also result in the removal from the battle of an entire French reserve corps of 20,000 men under Marshal Jean Baptiste Drouet, Comte d'Erlon. It marches back and forth between the two French armies and aids neither. In the fighting at Quatre Bras, Ney loses perhaps 4,400 men, Wellington about 5,400.

At Ligny meanwhile, Napoleon defeats the Prussians, who then begin to withdraw with Blücher, who is injured. Had Drouet been able to assist, Napoleon might have destroyed the Prussians and then fallen on Wellington's flank and crushed him as well. As it is, the Prussians are able to withdraw to Wavre in good order, thanks in part to excellent work by Blücher's chief of staff, General August Neidhard von Gneisenau. The French have suffered 11,500 dead and wounded, the Prussians perhaps 14,000.

See Leaders: Gneisenau, August von

June 18, 1815
Western Europe: Belgium: Napoleonic Wars (continued): The Hundred Days (continued): Battle of Waterloo. It rains hard beginning on the evening of June 16 and all the next day. On the morning of June 17,

though, Napoleon makes what turns out to be a fatal error. He detaches Marshal Emmanuel de Grouchy and 33,000 men of the French right wing to pursue Gebhard Leberecht von Blücher and the Prussians. Napoleon and Grouchy mistakenly assume that the Prussians will withdraw back on their base of Namur.

Napoleon turns with the main body to assist Ney, planning to drive toward Brussels along the Charleroi road. Wellington meanwhile withdraws north and concentrates his men at the small village of Waterloo, north of Quatre Bras on the Charleroi-Brussels road. Wellington sends an appeal to Blücher, asking him to provide at least one corps. Blücher replies with a pledge to come to his assistance with two corps or more. Wellington will call this "the decision of the century."

Napoleon joins Ney at Quatre Bras and, on the afternoon of June 17, sets out after Wellington. Steady rain, quagmires of mud, and superbly executed hit-and-run tactics of British horse artillery under Lieutenant General Henry Paget, Lord Uxbridge, delay the French arrival at the village of Waterloo until midnight. Both sides are arrayed along ridge lines about a mile apart. Wellington plans to fight a defensive battle until Blücher and the Prussians can arrive.

The well-trained British Peninsular War veterans infuse the Anglo-Dutch army with confidence in Wellington's leadership. Wellington makes his dispositions carefully, confident in his veterans. Still, he is well aware that the key to an allied victory is whether the Prussians can arrive in time.

Napoleon is confident. Certain that the Prussians will not come to the aid of Wellington, Napoleon overrules his staff and does not recall Grouchy. This means that Napoleon has just 72,000 troops at Waterloo against 68,000 British and Dutch. Had he

In the Battle of Waterloo on June 18, 1815, British, Dutch, and Prussian troops under Field Marshal Sir Arthur Wellesley, Duke of Wellington, defeat French troops under Napoleon Bonaparte, bringing to a close his effort to return to power. *Napoleons Flucht in der Schlacht von Waterloo* by Rugendas. (Gianni Dagli Orti/Corbis)

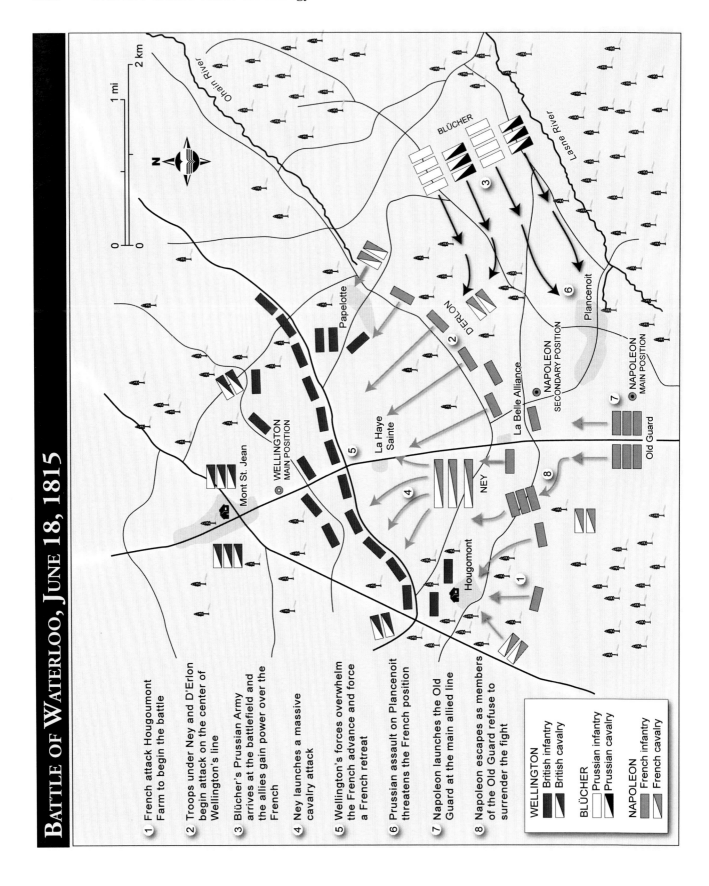

Battle of Waterloo, June 18, 1815

1. French attack Hougoumont Farm to begin the battle
2. Troops under Ney and D'Erlon begin attack on the center of Wellington's line
3. Blücher's Prussian Army arrives at the battlefield and the allies gain power over the French
4. Ney launches a massive cavalry attack
5. Wellington's forces overwhelm the French advance and force a French retreat
6. Prussian assault on Plancenoit threatens the French position
7. Napoleon launches the Old Guard at the main allied line
8. Napoleon escapes as members of the Old Guard refuse to surrender the fight

WELLINGTON
British infantry
British cavalry

BLÜCHER
Prussian infantry
Prussian cavalry

NAPOLEON
French infantry
French cavalry

recalled Grouchy, Napoleon would have had more than 100,000 men on the field of battle. If Blücher is able to join Wellington and Grouchy cannot join Napoleon, the allies will have an overwhelming advantage of nearly 140,000 men against only 72,000 for Napoleon.

The heavy rains have made the battlefield soggy. Napoleon had expected to open the battle at 6:00 a.m., but the pleas of his artillery commander who wants firmer ground for movement of the guns cause Napoleon to delay the attack. Battle is thus not joined until nearly noon, and it is after 1:00 p.m. when the grand battery of 80 French guns opens up. The first French infantry attacks do not occur until about 1:45. Had the ground been firmer, Napoleon might well have destroyed Wellington's forces and reached Brussels that evening.

The battlefield at Waterloo measures only about three square miles. Napoleon is certain that massed artillery fire followed by a frontal infantry assault will carry the day. Wellington, however, positions the bulk of his forces out of sight on the reverse slope of a ridge, protected from direct French artillery fire.

The French attack is launched against the center of the allied line. The English hollow squares withstand repeated French infantry assaults. In a battle within a battle, Napoleon's younger brother Jérôme disobeys orders only to occupy the approaches to the Château of Hougoumont, wasting an entire division in repeated unsuccessful charges against the building's thick walls. The French infantry and cavalry attacks are also not coordinated, and Ney, whose personal courage is unquestioned, leads his troops into battle piecemeal.

Despite savage fighting, British and Dutch forces manage to hold long enough to allow Blücher's Prussians to join them and save the day. Grouchy meanwhile fails to march to the sound of the guns and is held up by the Prussian rear guard at Wavre sufficiently long that he is unable to join the battle, less than 14 miles away. The retreat of the Imperial Guard—the first time this has occurred—signals the end of the battle. When word goes out that the Guard had retreated before massed British musket fire, in fact, there are cries of "*Sauve qui peut!*" (Every man for himself!), and the French retreat becomes a rout.

French casualties are 26,000 dead or wounded, with 9,000 more captured. The British-Dutch forces lose 15,000 men, and the Prussians lose some 7,000. Napoleon flees the field, his escape purchased with the lives of two regiments of his Old Guard. For Napoleon the loss at Waterloo is irreparable.

June 18, 1815

Western Europe: Belgium: Napoleonic Wars (continued): The Hundred Days (continued): Battle of Wavre. While the Battle of Waterloo is in progress to the west, Marshal Emmanuel de Grouchy has caught up with the rear guard of Field Marshal General Gebhard Leberecht von Blücher's Prussians marching to the aid of the Anglo-Dutch forces at Waterloo. Grouchy fights a rather dilatory action against the Prussians but then executes a skillful withdrawal south from Belgium, his force of 33,000 men largely intact.

June 22, 1815

Western Europe: France: Napoleonic Wars (continued): The Hundred Days (continued): Second abdication of Napoleon. Returning to Paris following his defeat in the Battle of Waterloo, Napoleon discovers that Joseph Fouché (his minister of police) has seized power, supported by the Chamber of Deputies. Crowds besiege the Tuileries Palace, however, urging Napoleon to fight on. He has the means to do so. Marshal Emmanuel de Grouchy's 33,000-man corps is largely intact, and Louis Nicolas Davout commands a force of some 120,000 men near Paris.

Even Napoleon now realizes, however, that he cannot win. Hoping to secure the throne for his family, he abdicates again on June 22, 1815, in favor of his son, Napoléon François Joseph Charles Bonaparte, king of Rome. Working through his brother Lucian Bonaparte, Napoleon tries to get the Senate to proclaim his son as Napoleon II, but several days later both the Senate and the Chamber of Deputies vote in favor of the return of King Louis XVIII. For most of the senators and deputies, it is an act of self-interest.

Making his way to the coast at Rochefort, on July 15 Napoleon surrenders to the British, who transport him into exile on the Island of St. Helena in the South Atlantic, 1,300 miles from the nearest land. There he lives out the remainder of his life, seeking to recast the historical record. He dies of stomach cancer on

May 5, 1821. In December 1840 during the reign of King Louis Philippe, Napoleon's remains are returned to France to be formally interred at Les Invalides in Paris.

September 26, 1815
Central Europe: Austria: Holy Alliance. At the insistence of Czar Alexander I of Russia, Austrian emperor Francis I and King Frederick William III of Prussia sign the Holy Alliance, a broad statement by which they agree to bind themselves and their states to act in accordance with Christian principles. It is ultimately signed by all European rulers save the king of England, the pope, and the Ottoman sultan.

November 20, 1815
Western Europe: France: Second Treaty of Paris. Napoleon's gambit of the Hundred Days proves costly to France, which is now treated more harshly than under the First Treaty of Paris. France is restricted to its borders of 1790. It also loses some of the key northeastern fortresses awarded to it earlier: Philippeville and Marienburg to the Netherlands and Saarlouis and Saarbrücken to Prussia. Landau becomes a fortress of the German Confederation. France is also obliged to give the Kingdom of Sardinia a part of Savoy that France had retained under the First Treaty of Paris.

The allies will now garrison 17 fortresses in the north and east of France for up to five years, at French expense. France is also saddled with an indemnity of 700 million francs for the expense of the war. In addition, all the art treasures taken back to France during the French Revolution and the Napoleonic Wars are to be returned to their country of origin.

November 20, 1815
Western Europe: France: Quadruple Alliance. Concurrent with the First Treaty of Paris, the major powers agree to the Quadruple Alliance, signed by the representatives of Britain, Austria, Prussia, and Russia. All four powers pledge to maintain for 20 years the arrangements they have made at Vienna and Paris. They also agree to meet periodically in order to discuss problems of common interest and to maintain the peace of Europe. Austrian foreign minister Klemens von Metternich sees this as a conservative arrangement that will maintain the status quo. The British government serves notice that it does not regard it as a license to meddle in the internal affairs of other states, however, and it will intervene only to maintain the territorial boundaries agreed to.

1815
South America: Venezuela: Bolívar's Campaigns (continued): Spain reestablishes control. In 1815 Simón Bolívar returns to Venezuela from New Grenada (Colombia) with a new army. Following some early successes, he is defeated by Spanish Royalist general Pablo Morillo at Santa Mara. With the defeat of Emperor Napoleon I in Europe, Spain is able to send substantial troop reinforcements to South America and crush the liberation movements there. Bolívar again flees, this time to Jamaica. He then mounts several unsuccessful raids against the Venezuelan coast.

1815–1817
Central Europe: Balkans. In 1815 a new uprising occurs in Serbia, led by Milosh Obrenovic. Followers of Obrenovic murder George Petrovich (Kara George), who had led a previous uprising against the Ottomans. This results in a bloody feud between adherents of the two families. The Turks take advantage of this to crush the revolt but recognize Obrenovic as hereditary prince of Serbia when he agrees to accept Serbian suzerainty.

1815–1818
South Asia: Ceylon. British forces, which have secured the coast earlier, now take control of the entire island of Ceylon (present-day Sri Lanka). They capture Kandy (Maha Nuvara) in 1815 and crush a Sinhalese revolt in 1818.

July 9, 1816
South America: Argentina. Argentina formally declares its independence from Spain.

July 27, 1816
North America: United States: Destruction of Negro Fort and beginning of the First Seminole War. In the early 18th century, a number of Creek Indians withdrew from the Creek Confederacy and settled in Spanish Florida. Known by the whites as Seminoles, they intermarried with runaway slaves and remnants of other Indian bands. During the War of 1812 the Seminoles sided with the British against the United States. They carried out cross-border raids from northern Florida, then still controlled by Spain, against settlements in southern Georgia. With Spain

powerless to prevent these outrages and seeing an opportunity to pressure Spain into ceding East Florida, the U.S. government decides on force.

Fighting begins in the spring of 1816 after U.S. Army brigadier general Edmund P. Gaines orders the construction of Fort Scott on the Flint River in southwestern Georgia. Gaines secures the cooperation of the navy for an operation up the Apalachicola River. U.S. Navy captain Daniel Patterson provides two gunboats and two schooners to operate against the so-called Negro Fort. This former British fort at Prospect Bluff on the Apalachicola, built during the War of 1812, was turned over by the British to their allies thereafter. Mounting 10 guns, it reportedly contains 700 kegs of gunpowder.

On July 27 the American gunboats reach the area of the fort and open fire. Their first heated shot strikes the fort's powder magazine, causing an enormous explosion and killing as many as 300 people in the fort. Troops and allied Native Americans then take the fort, seizing a reported 3,200 firearms. Although dates for the First Seminole War (1816–1818) vary, this event may be said to have begun it.

August 27, 1816
North Africa: Algiers: Allied naval bombardment. The Barbary states of North Africa take advantage of the Napoleonic Wars and distraction of the major naval powers to prey on their merchant shipping in the Mediterranean and eastern Atlantic. Algiers is the most active in this regard. Despite Commodore Stephen Decatur having dictated peace between the United States and Algiers, that North African state has been guilty of outrages against British merchant shipping. On July 28, 1816, a British squadron under Admiral Edward Pellow Lord Exmouth sails from Portsmouth to address the situation.

Arriving at Gibraltar, Exmouth encounters a Dutch squadron whose commander asks that his ships be included in the contemplated punitive action. Delayed by contrary winds, the combined fleet of 19 British warships (5 of them ships of the line) and 6 Dutch warships arrives off Algiers on August 27. Exmouth immediately demands the release of Christian slaves and peace with the Netherlands. When the dey of Algiers delays a response, Exmouth orders the fleet to stand in and commences an eight-hour bombardment of the port and its fortifications, firing more than 46,000 shot and shells. The Algerines reply with their shore batteries. This claims 141 killed and 742 wounded on the allied side, but much of the port and city are set ablaze.

The next morning, with the allies preparing to renew their attack, the dey agrees to all their terms. He frees 1,083 Christian slaves, promises to give up the slave trade, and restores peace with the Netherlands.

February 12, 1817
South America: Chile: San Martín's Campaigns: Battle of Chacabuco. Argentinean native José Francisco de San Martín, with more than two decades of military service as an officer in the Spanish Army, returns to Argentina after the Napoleonic Wars and joins Simón Bolívar in taking up the cause of Latin American independence. During 1814–1816 San Martín

Latin American liberator José Francisco de San Martín (1778–1850) led military forces against Spain that liberated Argentina, Chile, and Peru. (The Art Archive/ Museo Historico Nacional Buenos Aires/Gianni Dagli Orti)

recruits and trains the Army of the Andes at Mendoza. In January 1817 Martín leads his Argentian-Chilean force of 4,000 infantry and 600 cavalry with 22 guns to invade Chile from across the Andes, the first time that this has been attempted.

On February 12, 1817, San Martín encounters at Chacabuco, near Santiago, a Royalist force of 1,500 infantry and 7 guns under Spanish Brigadier General Rafael Maroto. San Martín immediately attacks, well aware that all Maroto has to do is to delay his advance, for Spanish Royalist reinforcements are en route.

General Bernardo O'Higgins, commanding the Chilean forces in San Martín's army, receives the assignment of holding Maroto in place while the other part of the army attempts to turn the defenders' flank. When the flanking attack is delayed, however, O'Higgins disobeys orders and attacks, breaking the defending line. San Martín now joins the flanking force, which completes the rout of Maroto. The Army of the Andes suffers 100 killed or wounded, while the Spanish force loses 500 killed or wounded, 600 taken prisoner, and all of its guns.

On February 15 San Martín occupies Santiago. Chile is now for all practical purposes independent, although that is not officially declared until February 12, 1818.

See Leaders: San Martín, José Francisco de

February 16–18, 1817

South America: Venezuela: Bolívar's Campaigns (continued): Battle of Barcelona. Simón Bolívar returns to Venezuela in December 1816, proclaimed as commander in chief of liberation forces of both Venezuela and New Grenada (Colombia). Haiti provides him troops on the promise that he will free the slaves. He then engages and defeats Spanish general Pablo Morillo in the Battle of Barcelona during February 16–18, 1817.

April 28, 1817

North America: United States: Rush-Bagot Agreement. In Washington, D.C., British minister to the United States Charles Bagot and Acting Secretary of State Richard Rush sign an agreement for disarmament on the Great Lakes. The United States and Britain agree to restrict their warships on inland waters to one each on lakes Champlain and Ontario and two warships each on the Upper Lakes, none of which may exceed 100 tons or armament of one 18-pounder gun. To allay British concerns that future adminis-

trations might not abide by the agreement, it is submitted to the U.S. Senate and there unanimously approved on April 16, 1818.

November 21, 1817

North America: United States: First Seminole War (continued): Battle of Fowltown. Seeking to avenge the destruction of Negro Fort, the Seminoles mount a series of raids in southern Georgia, leading to the deaths of some citizens there. U.S. Army brigadier general Edmund P. Gaines demands that Neamathla, chief of Fowltown, a Seminole village located just north of the Florida border, surrender those responsible. When Neamathla refuses, Gaines dispatches 250 soldiers from Fort Scott under the command of Major David Twiggs to arrest them.

The ensuing Battle of Fowltown is held by many to mark the beginning of the First Seminole War. A second conflict occurs at the village and nearby swamp on November 23, 1817. On January 4, 1818, the village is found deserted and destroyed.

1817–1818

South Asia: India: Third Anglo-Maratha (and Pindari) War. The war is caused by widespread raids against British territory by Pindaris (outlaws), many of whom are veterans of the earlier wars between the British and the Maratha Confederacy. Although they deny any responsibility, many of the Maratha princes secretly encourage the Pindari attacks on the British. Two major British armies totaling perhaps 20,000 men under British governor-general in India General Lord Francis Rawdon-Hastings, 1st Marquess of Hastings, and Sir Thomas Hyslop prepare to take the field against the Pindaris. It is a situation fraught with danger for the British, for the Maratha rulers control as many as 200,000 troops and 500 guns.

Indeed, major Maratha forces do go to war with the British, including Yaswant Rao Holkar of Indore, the Peshwa of Poona, and Bhonsle of Nagpur. The war is of short duration, however. On December 21, 1817, in the Battle of Mahidput, Hyslop and 5,500 men defeat Holkar with perhaps 35,000 men and 100 guns. Then, during January–June 1818, Rawdon-Hastings defeats the remaining Maratha opponents and the Pindaris. The Peshwa surrenders on June 2, 1818, in effect ending the war.

The Third Anglo-Maratha War sees the breakup of the Maratha Confederacy, and the British East India Company secures control of virtually all of India south of the Sutlej River. The Maratha kingdoms of

Indore, Gwalior, Nagpur, and Jhansi became princely states that accept British control.

March–May 1818
North America: United States: First Seminole War (continued): Jackson's invasion of Florida. In retaliation for the U.S. attacks on Fowltown, on November 30, 1817, Seminoles ambush a boatload of troops and their dependents on the Apalachicola River and kill 36 soldiers, 6 women, and 4 children. President James Monroe orders U.S. Army major general Andrew Jackson, commander of the Southern Division, to move into Florida and punish the Seminoles. Although there is no official authorization for Jackson to attack Spanish fortifications, he writes to Monroe in early January 1818 that he can occupy Florida within 60 days. Jackson chooses to interpret the lack of response from administration officials as an unofficial endorsement of his subsequent actions.

With 4,000 men, half of whom are allied Creeks, Jackson invades Florida in March. Arriving at the site of Negro Fort on March 15, Jackson orders it rebuilt as Fort Gadsden. He then moves overland to Fort St. Marks (San Marcos), where he demands and receives the surrender of the Spanish garrison on April 7. The Americans then attack and destroy a number of Seminole and fugitive slave settlements. Jackson takes Pensacola on May 24. With Spanish authority in Florida for all practical purposes at an end, Jackson installs a provisional U.S. government.

The Spanish are outraged at Jackson's actions; the British government is also upset, for Jackson has taken prisoner and executed two British subjects—former Royal Marine Robert Armbrister and Scots trader Alexander Arbuthnot—accused of providing arms to the Indians. Jackson departs Florida on May 30, bringing the First Seminole War to a close.

Despite official unease over Jackson's actions and calls for disciplinary action, no official steps are taken against him. Although the posts seized by Jackson in Florida are all returned to Spanish control, Secretary of State John Quincy Adams is able to use Jackson's actions as leverage to compel Spain to cede Florida to the United States (the Adams-Onís Treaty of February 22, 1819).

March 15, 1818
South America: Venezuela: Bolívar's Campaigns (continued): Battle of La Puerta. In the same location where he was defeated earlier, Simón Bolívar again is defeated at La Puerta on March 15, 1818, this time by Spanish troops under General Pablo Morillo. Bolívar now decides to concentrate on the liberation of New Grenada (Colombia), retaken by the Spanish.

March 16, 1818
South America: Chile: San Martín's Campaigns (continued): Battle of Cancha-Rayada. Spanish general Mariano Osorio moves south from Peru with 9,000 troops into Chile to engage José de San Martín's Army of the Andes of Chileans and Argentineans. In the Battle of Cancha-Rayada, fought near Linares, Chile, Osorio with 6,000 men surprises San Martín and defeats him. The Spanish lose 200 men killed or wounded, whereas the Army of the Andes suffers 120 killed and the loss of 22 guns.

April 5, 1818
South America: Chile: San Martín's Campaigns (continued): Battle of the Maipo. Following his defeat in the Battle of Cancha-Rayada, José de San Martín regroups his Army of the Andes. On April 5, 1818, he again engages Royalist forces under Spanish general Mariano Osorio, attacking them along the Maipo River. Turning the Spanish left, San Martín routs the Spanish force, which sustains casualties of 1,000 killed, 2,300 taken prisoner, and 12 guns taken. San Martín's army suffers only 100 killed or wounded. General Osorio gives up further campaigning in Chile and returns to Peru.

1818
West Africa: Macina jihad. A follower of Usman dan Fodio, Ahmadu ibn Hammadi at Macina preaches a jihad (holy war) and conquers the kingdoms of Segu, Djenné, and Timbuktu.

1818–1819
Southern Africa: Zulu-Ndwandwe War. In 1816 Shaku rises to prominence among the Zulus, then controlled by the Mtetwas. He becomes their chief in 1816. Shaku rebuilds the small Zulu army of only some 400 men. He retrains it and makes it into a formidable fighting force. Within a few years, Shaku has absorbed several neighboring clans and increased the size of the army to 2,000 warriors.

In 1818 Zwide of the Ndwandwe clan attacks the smaller Zulus. Shaku defeats him in the Battle of Gqokli Hill late that year. Regrouping, the next year Zwide again invades Zulu territory but, hampered by lack of supplies, tries to withdraw. In the course of a two-day battle, his army is destroyed by Shaku and the Zulus as it tries to get away. Zwide, however, escapes.

February 22, 1819

North America: United States: Adams-Onís Treaty. In this treaty, signed in Washington, D.C., on February 22, 1819, between Secretary of State John Quincy Adams and Spanish foreign minister Luis de Onís, Spain officially renounces all claims to West Florida and agrees to cede East Florida to the United States. In return the United States assumes all claims of its citizens against Spain, to the maximum amount of $5 million. The United States also renounces all claims to Texas.

The treaty also defines the disputed western boundary of the Louisiana Purchase territory as running from the mouth of the Sabine River on the Gulf of Mexico northwest along the Red and Arkansas rivers and then west along the 42nd parallel to the Pacific Ocean. In effect, Spain surrenders to the United States its claims to the Pacific Northwest.

August 7, 1819

South America: New Grenada: Bolívar's Campaigns (continued): Battle of Boyacá. Simón Bolívar develops a bold plan to induce the Spaniards to concentrate their forces in Venezuela. He will then march over the Andes, unite with guerrilla forces under General Francisco de Paula Santander, seize Bogotá, and force the Spaniards from New Granada (present-day Colombia). In June 1819 Bolívar leads 2,500 well-armed troops, including a number of Englishmen, across the Andes. Arriving in New Grenada, he unites with Santander, defeats the Spanish on July 1 in Tunja Province, and enters the town of Tunja on July 23.

On August 7 Bolívar, at the head of some 3,400 men, defeats Spanish colonel José María Barreiro with some 3,000 men in the Battle of Boyacá. In the ensuing rout, Bolívar's forces suffer 13 dead and 53 wounded, while Barreiro loses 100 killed, 150 wounded, and 1,600 taken prisoner in addition to much of his equipment. Barreiro is among those captured; he is later executed on the order of Santander.

Boyacá is the decisive battle in the liberation of South America from Spanish rule. On August 12 Bolívar makes a triumphal entry into Bogotá. All the provinces of New Granada now rise up against the Spaniards, who seek refuge in the fortified town of Mompox. Bolívar now establishes the Republic of Colombia, with himself as president.

1819

Central Asia: Afghanistan. Ranjit Singh, Sikh ruler of the Punjab, conquers the Afghan province of Kashmir.

1819

Southeast Asia: Burma. Following the Burmese conquest of Assam, Assamese rebels establish themselves in the British protectorate of Manipur. During 1820–1822, they raid into the territory occupied by Burma.

1819

Southeast Asia: Malay Peninsula: Founding of Singapore. Located on an island at the southern tip of the Malay Peninsula (Malaysia) at the mouth of the Singapore River, Singapore is a sparsely populated fishing village. Recognizing its potential, Sir Stamford Raffles, the British governor-general of Bencoolen (now Bengkulu) in Sumatra, founds a city there. Planned as a strategic trading post on the so-called spice route, Singapore grows by the 20th century into an important commercial center and the most powerful British base in Asia. This step angers the Dutch government, however.

1819–1828

Southern Africa: Creation of the Zulu Empire. Following his defeat of Zwide and the Ndwandwe clan, Shaku conquers other neighboring clans and steadily increases the size of his Zulu army to more than 30,000 men. The other clans are merely absorbed into the Zulu nation. Shaku is a cruel tyrant and increasingly given to irrational behavior.

On September 28, 1828, his half brothers Dingane and Mhlangana assassinate Shaku. The two soon disagree, however, and Mhlangana flees. Dingane becomes sole ruler.

January 1820

Southern Europe: Spain: Spanish Army revolt at Cádiz. King Ferdinand VII had been restored to power in 1814, promising to maintain the liberal Constitution of 1812. He refuses to keep his promise, however, and instead relies on force to stay in power and proceeds to persecute the liberals. Independence movements in Latin America deprive the Spanish Crown of valuable revenue, moreover, so Ferdinand resolves to reconquer them. Toward that end, he assembles army units at the port of Cádiz.

Disaffection among the army units leads to a revolt, led by Colonel Rafael del Riego y Núñez. The troops march on Madrid, where a revolt also breaks out. Taken prisoner, Ferdinand agrees to restore the Constitution of 1812.

February 3–4, 1820
South America: San Martín's Campaigns (continued): Cochrane captures Valdivia. José de San Martín wants to invade Peru, but to do this he must end Spanish control of the seas. The liberationist side therefore assembles a small naval squadron, including the Spanish frigate *Reyna Maria Isabel* of 40 guns that they capture and rename the *O'Higgins.* The squadron is commanded by a Chilean, Manuel Blanco Encalada, who had served as an officer in the Spanish Navy. In November 1818 the revolutionary navy receives a significant boost with the arrival of able Royal Navy officer Thomas Cochrane. Tried and convicted as a conspirator in the Great Stock Exchange Fraud of 1814 and forced to resign from Parliament and the Royal Navy, Cochrane accepts an offer to command San Martín's naval forces. Cochrane reorganizes the Chilean Navy and introduces British naval practices.

At the beginning of 1819 Vice Admiral Cochrane sails with his small squadron but is unsuccessful in his effort to draw the Spanish squadron at Callao and Valdivia into action. An effort to seize the Spanish fortress of Real Felipe at Callao fails, and Cochrane decides to attack Valdivia.

One of the most strongly fortified locations in South America, Valdivia is also a major Spanish base. On the night of February 3–4, 1820, Cochrane lands 350 men with the intention of capturing its seven Spanish forts, garrisoned by some 1,600 men and 118 guns. He quickly seizes two of the forts, and two others promptly surrender. The next morning the three remaining Spanish forts also surrender, followed by Valdivia shortly thereafter. (The Spanish troops sack the city before departing overland for Osorno.)

The Chilean side suffers 7 killed and 19 wounded; the Spanish lose 100 killed and 106 taken prisoner. The capture of Valdivia removes the last vestige of Spanish power in Chile and enables San Martín to proceed with his invasion of Peru.

See Leaders: Cochrane, Thomas

July 2, 1820
Southern Europe: Italy: Revolution in Naples. In May 1815 the Bourbon king Ferdinand I is restored to his throne in the Kingdom of Naples by force of Austrian arms. Despite promises of reform, he introduces a reactionary regime. On July 2, 1820, encouraged by news of the army revolt in Spain, General Guglielmo Pepe leads a revolt of troops in Naples against the government. On July 13 Ferdinand is forced to grant a liberal constitution similar to that introduced by the British in Sicily in 1812. Austrian chief minister Klemens von Metternich regards Italy as within the Austrian sphere of influence, however; he calls a meeting of representatives of the Great Powers at Troppau.

July 1820–1839
North Africa: Egypt: Egyptian conquest of the Sudan. In July 1820 Egyptian khedive Muhammad Ali Pasha sends forces under his son, Ibrahim Pasha, to conquer the Sudan. Capable Egyptian governor-general Ali Khurshid Agha (1826–1838) introduces reforms, and the Sudan prospers.

August 29, 1820
Southern Europe: Portugal: Porto Revolution. Influenced by the revolution in Spain in January 1820, revolutionaries in Porto (Oporto) overthrow the regency established by the British during the absence of King John VI, who is in Brazil. On July 4, 1821, John returns; he immediately agrees to the revolutionaries' demands that he become a constitutional monarch. The ensuing constitution of 1822 is the first in Portuguese history.

September 8, 1820
South America: Peru: San Martín's Campaigns (continued): Invasion of Peru. Escorted by the ships of Vice Admiral Thomas Cochrane's squadron, 16 transports carrying José San Martín's soldiers land at Pisco on September 8, 1820. Cochrane then sails to

Callao, Peru's most important port, where he block-ades the Spanish squadron.

November 5, 1820

South America: Peru: San Martín's Campaigns (con-tinued): Capture of the *Esmeralda*. After taking up position off the Peruvian port of Callao to blockade the Spanish squadron there, on November 5, 1820, Chilean Navy commander Vice Admiral Thomas Cochrane personally leads 250 men in small boats in a daring cutting-out operation against the ships of the Spanish squadron riding at anchor. The Span-ish ships are protected by chains and a great many shore batteries. The attackers succeed in cutting out the Spanish Navy frigate *Esmeralda* and take it out of the harbor as a prize. Cochrane is badly wounded, twice. He had intended to take other Spanish war-ships in the harbor as well, but this goes awry. The operation ranks as one of the most daring of its kind in naval history.

November 19, 1820

Central Europe: Silesia: Troppau Protocol. Austrian first minister Count Klemens von Metternich sum-mons representatives of the Great Powers to Trop-pau in Silesia. As Metternich sees it, the purpose of the conference during October–November is to se-cure support for military intervention to crush the revolution in Naples. The governments of Britain and France, unwilling to play Metternich's game, send only observers. Prussia, Russia, and Austria agree to the Troppau Protocol, a statement of collec-tive security against revolution. Issued on November 19, 1820, it asserts the right of the Great Powers to employ force if necessary to reverse revolutions in European states that pose a threat to the security of other states.

ca. 1820–1835

Southern Africa: The Mfecane. During this period there is a massive depopulation and forced migra-tion in Southern Africa and parts of Central and East Africa, with some estimates placing the number of deaths as high as 1–2 million people. Various rea-sons have been advanced for the Mfecane ("Crush-ing," also known by the Sotho name of *difaqane*), in-cluding the wars of Shaku and other Nguni conflicts that bring forced migrations of the Bantu peoples. This massive depopulation of native Africans gives the white (Boer) settlers an excuse for moving into lands that they regard as empty.

Today, historians question whether Zulu aggres-sion triggered the Mfecane. They cite archaeological evidence of both drought and environmental degra-dation that led to massive emigration. A more con-troversial, and largely unsupported, theory holds that the Mfecane was caused by illegal slave trading by white settlers.

February 1821

Central Europe: Insurrection in Wallachia and be-ginning of the Greek War of Independence. In Feb-ruary 1821 an insurrection in Wallachia (in present-day Romania) precipitates a revolt against Ottoman rule by the Greeks, leading to the Greek War of Inde-pendence (1821–1830). The Greek revolt is caused by many factors. Although Greece has been part of the Ottoman Empire since the mid-15th century, the Greeks have retained their national identity under loose Ottoman rule. The nationalism prompted by the French Revolution inspires the Greeks, but their ap-peal to the Congress of Vienna for self-determination is rejected by the Great Powers.

In 1814 therefore, Greeks in Odessa, Russia, founded the Hetairia Philike (Association of Friends) with the avowed aim of expelling the Turks from Eu-rope. The Greek nationalists receive aid from Greeks living abroad and from Russia. Czar Alexander I is keenly interested in an independent Greece under Russian protection as a means to secure access to the Mediterranean, and Russia has long used its claim to protect the right of Greek Orthodox Christians to in-tervene in the Ottoman Empire. Alexander Ypsilanti (Ypsilantis), a general officer in the Russian Army from a powerful Greek family in Moldavia, heads the movement. The Hetairia Philike hopes to estab-lish a Greek empire embracing other Ottoman terri-tories in Europe, including present-day Romania.

March 7, 1821

Southern Europe: Italy: Battle of Reiti. Acting under the authority of the Troppau Protocol of November 1820, Austrian troops march south to crush the rev-olution in Naples. Neapolitan forces under General Guglielmo Pepe move north to engage the Austri-ans. They are easily defeated in the Battle of Reiti in Latium, northeast of Rome, on March 7, 1821. The

Austrians then march to Naples and again restore the reactionary King Ferdinand I to the throne.

March–June 1821

Central Europe: Balkans: Moldavia: Greek War of Independence. Alexander Ypsilanti (Ypsilantis) leads an armed force from Ukraine into Moldavia. He then appeals for Russian assistance in a war to free Greece from Ottoman rule. Austrian first minister Klemens von Metternich is strongly opposed, however. The revolt, he says, should be allowed to "burn itself out beyond the pale of civilization." Czar Alexander is then under Metternich's influence, so the Russians disavow Ypsilanti.

Sultan Mahmoud II is therefore able to crush the uprising easily in June 1821. Yspilanti flees across the border into Austria, where he is arrested and imprisoned until 1827. Released at the insistence of Russian czar Nicolas I (r. 1825–1855), Ypsilanti retires to Vienna, where he dies in poverty in 1828.

April 8, 1821

Southern Europe: Italy: Battle of Novara. King Charles Emmanuel IV of Sardinia (Piedmont-Sardinia) abdicates on June 4, 1820. He is succeeded by his younger brother, Charles Felix. On March 10, 1821, revolutionaries seek to impose a constitution on the king, but a combined force of Royalists and Austrian Army troops defeat the revolutionaries in the Battle of Novara on April 8, 1821.

June 25, 1821

South America: Venezuela: Bolívar's Campaigns (continued): Battle of Carabobo. Following his triumph in achieving the independence of Colombia in 1819, Simón Bolívar and other leaders of the struggle for independence from Spain campaign against Royalist forces in Venezuela. After the expiration of an armistice (November 15, 1820–April 28, 1821), Bolívar leads 6,500 men (22,500 cavalry) against Spanish general Miguel de la Torre with 2,500 men in the valley of the Carabobo. Torre makes the mistake of dividing his force to meet a flanking attack, allowing Bolívar to defeat him in detail. The battle ends in a rout.

Bolívar suffers only 200 dead, while Torre has 1,900 dead and wounded. The remnants of Torre's force flee. With its defeat of the main Royalist force in Venezuela, the Battle of Carabobo is the deci-

sive engagement in the liberation of Venezuela from Spanish rule. Bolívar enters Caracas in triumph. Cartagena surrenders on October 1, 1821, following a 21-month-long siege.

July 9, 1821

South America: Peru: San Martín's Campaigns (continued): Capture of Lima. Liberationist forces under José de San Martín take Lima on July 9, 1821, and Callao on September 21.

September 28, 1821

North America: Mexico: Declaration of Mexican independence. In 1821 another rebellion occurs in Mexico. This time it is not a social upheaval but instead is sparked by news of the Spanish Army's revolt in Cádiz of January 1820. The revolt begins in February 1821.

The Plan of Iguala (also known as the Plan of the Three Guarantees) of February 24, 1821, worked out among the revolutionary leaders, calls for Mexican independence, full protection for Roman Catholicism, and equal rights for both creoles and peninsulares. The revolutionary slogan is "Religion, Independence, and Unity." The revolutionaries intend to maintain the old elites in power while creating an autonomous Mexican state with its own laws and institutions but within the Spanish monarchy. To accomplish this, the leaders seek the support of General Augustín de Iturbide, a Mexican-born Spaniard.

On September 21, 1821, Iturbide's troops occupy Mexico City. A Declaration of Independence is promulgated on September 28, 1821. When Ferdinand VII, the king of Spain, refuses to recognize Mexican independence, the Parliament proclaims Iturbide emperor of Mexico.

October 5, 1821

Southern Europe: Greece: Greek War of Independence (continued): Massacre of Tripolitsa. Inspired by Alexander Ypsilanti's rising against the Ottomans in Moldavia, Greeks in the Peloponnese Peninsula (southernmost Greece) rebel as well. The nationalists besiege the Ottoman garrison at Tripolitsa. Located in the middle of the Peloponnese, Tripolitsa is the largest city of southern Greece.

The attackers storm the city on October 5, and an orgy of violence ensues that results in the massacre over the next several days of some 10,000 Turks, including women and children. Many are tortured to death. Following savage Ottoman reprisals, all of Greece then rises up against their rule.

1821

Southeast Asia: Siam. The Siamese conquer the Malayasian Sultanate of Kedah. This action alarms the British and leads to a treaty between the two powers in January 1826. The Siamese agree not to expand further into Malaysia.

1821–1823

Southwest Asia: War between Persia and the Ottoman Empire. Although there are tensions between Persia and the Ottoman Empire because the latter has provided protection to rebellious tribesmen fleeing Persian Azerbaijan, Russia really instigates the war. Russia hopes to increase difficulties for the Ottoman Empire, which is then waging war with the Greeks, who are supported by Russia. The Russians induce Persian governor of Azerbaijan Abbas Mirza, son of Fath Ali Shah, to invade Ottoman territory. His troops occupy Kurdistan and the districts adjacent to Azerbaijan.

In retaliation, Ottoman forces under the pasha of Baghdad drive east into Persia. They are defeated and forced to withdraw back to Baghdad, which comes under a Persian siege for a time. In the Battle of Erzurum in 1821, Abbas Mirza and some 30,000 Persians triumph over an Ottoman force of more than 50,000 men. With a cholera epidemic hitting both sides, Persia and the Ottoman Empire agree to peace in the Treaty of Erzurum of July 28, 1823.

The treaty restores the status quo antebellum but also guarantees Persian access to the Muslim holy sites in Iraq and Arabia. The Ottomans also agree to work to halt Kurdish raids on Persian territory.

January 13, 1822

Southern Europe: Greece: Greek War of Independence (continued). Greek independence is proclaimed at Epidauros.

April–June 1822

Southern Europe: Greece: Greek War of Independence (continued): Occupation of Chios. The island of Chios (Scio) is located just off western Anatolia. In March 1822 several hundred armed Greeks from the nearby island of Samos land on Chios and attack the Turks living there. While a few Greek inhabitants join, most realize the precariousness of their position and refuse to participate.

A powerful Turkish naval squadron under Captain-Pasha Kara Ali soon arrives at Chios in response to these events. The Turks kill outright or starve to death some 42,000 Greeks. Another 50,000 are enslaved, and perhaps 23,000 are exiled. Fewer than 2,000 Greeks survive on the island. The event is later immortalized in a famous painting by French artist Eugène Delacroix.

The plight of the Greeks leads to a wave of sympathy for them in Europe. Known as Philhellenism, it is based in part on the democratic and artistic legacy of ancient Greece. Many Europeans, especially in Britain, France, and Germany, take up the Greek cause. The best known of them is the British poet George Gordon Byron, 6th Baron Byron, who dies of a fever there in 1824. Ultimately, the foreigners include capable British admiral Lord Thomas Cochrane, who commands the Greek Navy, and British general Sir George Church. The foreign officers, however, often find their efforts foiled by Greek infighting.

May 24, 1822

South America: Equador: Bolívar's Campaigns (continued): Battle of Pichincha. Patriot forces under Simón Bolívar move south to join with his lieutenant, General Antonio José de Sucre. Sucre is campaigning in Quito Province against Royalist forces led by Spanish governor-general Melchior Aymerich.

On May 24, 1822, the Battle of Pichincha, fought on the slopes of Pichincha next to the city of Quito, pits a Patriot army of 3,000 men under Sucre against a 1,900-man Royalist force under Aymerich. The battle ends in a Patriot victory. The Patriot side suffers 200 dead and 140 wounded, while the Royalists lose 400 dead, 190 wounded, and 1,260 captured along with 14 guns. The defeat of the Royalist forces brings the liberation of Quito the next day and secures the independence of the provinces belonging to the Real Audiencia de Quito, which then becomes the Republic of Ecuador.

June 18–19, 1822

Mediterranean Sea: Greek War of Independence (continued): Battle of Chios. On the night of June 18–19, 1822, Greek naval captain Constantine Kanaris sails into the middle of the Ottoman squadron off Chios (Scio) with two fire ships. He manages to blow up the Ottoman flagship with the loss of all aboard.

July 21, 1822
North America: Mexico: Proclamation of the First Mexican Empire. General Augustín de Iturbide accepts the throne as Augustín I, emperor of Mexico. The First Mexican Empire is short-lived, however, lasting only to March 19, 1823.

July 26–27, 1822
South America: Equador. The two great leaders of the liberation movement in South America, Simón Bolívar and José de San Martín, meet at Guayaquil and agree to join forces. There is disagreement over just what transpired at Guayaquil, but San Martín, from this point on, refrains from military revolutionary activities. Bolívar continues with the liberation of Peru.

July 1822
Southern Europe: Greece: Greek War of Independence (continued): Turkish invasion of Greece. Two Ottoman armies invade Greece, overrunning all Greece north of the Gulf of Corinth.

September 7, 1822
South America: Proclamation of the independence of Brazil. Growing tensions between Portugal and Brazil and also between Portuguese king John VI and his son Prince Regent Dom Pedro in Brazil lead to the proclamation of Brazilian independence on September 7, 1822. Dom Pedro is crowned Emperor Pedro I of Brazil on December 1.

October 20–December 14, 1822
Southern Europe: Italy: Congress of Verona. Representatives of the Quadruple Alliance meet at Verona, Italy, to discuss the situation in Spain. Although the British government opposes intervention, the other powers fear that the liberal contagion might spread. They authorize France to send troops and restore King Ferdinand VII to full authority.

October 25–December 31, 1822
Southern Europe: Greece: Greek War of Independence (continued): First Siege of Messolonghi. The Ottoman army under Omar Vrioni is halted before the strategically located Greek fort of Messolonghi

(Missolonghi). The Ottomans lay siege to the fort, which guards the entrance to the Gulf of Corinth, beginning on October 25, 1822. Both sides then reinforce.

A final Ottoman attack on January 6, 1823, is beaten back, and the Ottomans raise the siege and retire. A second siege of Messolonghi occurs during 1825–1826.

1822
East Africa: Muscat forces capture Pemba. Sayyid Said, ruler of Muscat, encouraged by his ally, the British, expands his influence in East Africa beginning with the capture of Pemba in 1822. Although he agrees (at British insistence) to halt the sale of African slaves to Christian countries, Muscati trade in slaves to Persian Gulf and Asian markets continues.

1822
Southeast Asia: Burma: Burmese invasion of Manipur and Cachar. Following raids by Assamese rebels from British-controlled Manipur, the Burmese invade both Manipur and Cachar. The British East India Company sends military aid, but the ensuing fighting is inconclusive.

1822
Caribbean Basin: Hispaniola. Under the leadership of Haitian president Jean Pierre Boyer, the Haitians drive the Spaniards out of Santo Domingo and reestablish their control of the entire island.

1822–1847
West Africa: Establishment of Liberia. Despite opposition from neighboring tribes, freed slaves from the United States establish the state of Liberia. The independence of the new state is formally declared on July 26, 1847.

March 19, 1823
North America: Mexico: Republican revolution. On March 19, 1823, Emperor Augustín I is forced from the throne. A federal republic is established on October 4, 1824.

April 17, 1823
Southern Europe: Spain: French military intervention in Spain. On April 17, 1823, French troops under the command of Louis, Duc d'Angoulême, cross the Bidassoa River into Spain. Moving through the

conservative countryside, the French are hailed as liberators by the peasants. The French take Madrid and drive south to Cádiz, where the rebel government has relocated. King Ferdinand VII moves with the French forces.

July 1, 1823
Central America: Formation of the United Provinces of Central America. Following its declaration of independence, Mexico comes to control most of Central America. With the republican revolution in March 1823, however, Mexican general Vicente Filosola calls a Central American assembly in Guatemala City. On July 1, 1823, it establishes the United Provinces of Central America, to include Costa Rica, Guatemala, El Salvador, Honduras, and Nicaragua.

July 4, 1823
Western Atlantic Ocean: Naval engagement between Brazil and Portugal. In March 1823 Englishman Thomas Cochrane, commanding the Chilean Navy, falls out with General José de San Martín and accepts command of the Brazilian Navy. With a small squadron of warships, both purchased and captured, Admiral Cochrane works wonders against the Portuguese Navy. He first blockades the port of Bahia, where Portuguese naval strength is concentrated.

On July 2 the Portuguese evacuate Bahia, departing in 60 transports with 17 escorting warships, far too powerful for Cochrane to attack with only 2 frigates. Cochrane pursues, however, and, by skillful seamanship in his flagship, the 50-gun frigate *Pedro I,* manages to cut out several of the transports and take several stragglers, which are sent on to El Salvador. Assuming that the Portuguese convoy is bound for Maranhão (São Luiz), Cochrane then races to that port ahead of the Portuguese and captures it.

As the Brazilian Army has occupied Bahia on July 4, there is no place for the Portuguese to go but on to Portugal. Some Brazilian warships harass the Portuguese ships as they cross the Atlantic. Cochrane is rewarded by being made governor of the province of Maranhão and created Marquess of Maranhão by Pedro I. Cochrane soon tires of the politics and revolutions, though, and returns to England.

July 24, 1823
South America: Venezuela: Bolívar's Campaigns (continued): Battle of Lake Maracaibo. The final battle in the struggle for Venezuelan independence is fought in Lake Maracaibo on July 24, 1823, between Patriot naval forces under Admiral José Prudencio Padilla and Royalist forces under Captain Ángel Laborde. It ends in a Patriot victory.

August 31, 1823
Southern Europe: Spain: Battle of the Trocadero. French forces advance on Cádiz and lay siege to rebel forces under Rafael del Riego y Núñez holding two fortresses. In the Battle of the Trocadero on August 31, 1823, the French defeat the rebels. King Ferdinand VII ignores French advice to institute a moderate constitutional regime, though, and proceeds to take harsh repressive measures against the liberals and other opponents of his regime. These continue until his death in 1833.

September 23, 1823
Southeast Asia: Burma: Beginning of the First Anglo-Burmese War. Burmese leaders are angered by British East India Company support for anti-Burmese rebels and take action. Fighting in the First Anglo-Burmese War (1823–1826) begins on September 23, 1823, when the Burmese attack the British on Shapura Island, close to Chittagong, killing or wounding six guards.

December 2, 1823
North America: United States: Proclamation of the Monroe Doctrine. President James Monroe, knowing that he has the full support of the British government and Royal Navy, issues the Monroe Doctrine during the course of his State of the Union address to Congress. Set against the background of the wars of independence in Latin America, Monroe states that the United States will not tolerate new European colonization, interference in the affairs of the newly independent nations of the Americas, or the transfer of existing colonies from one European nation to another. The United States plans to remain neutral in the wars between European powers and their colonies but expects the European powers not to intervene militarily in the Americas. If that were to occur, the United States would regard it as a hostile act. In effect, Monroe proclaims that the Western Hemisphere is closed to European intervention. British foreign secretary Sir George Canning, who would have preferred a joint British-U.S. declaration, none-

theless boasts that he has "called the New World into existence to redress the balance of the Old."

1823–1824

Southern Europe: Portugal: Civil war. King John VI's second son, Miguel, leads an unsuccessful effort to restore an absolutist monarchy.

January 1824

North Africa: Algiers: British naval expeditions against Algiers. The 1816 British bombardment of Algiers proves an insufficient (or forgotten) lesson, for Algiers continues to harass British and other European merchant shipping. London sends out two ships that arrive off Algiers in January 1824. Negotiations with the dey are unsuccessful, though, and the British evacuate their consul. The British then begin a naval blockade and are on the verge of sending a fleet to again bombard Algiers when the dey gives way and agrees to British terms.

March 5, 1824

Southeast Asia: Burma: First Anglo-Burmese War (continued): British declaration of war against Burma. In January 1824 Burmese general Maha Bandula mounts a two-pronged invasion of Bengal from Assam and Manipur. Burmese forces soon threaten Chittagong, and the British declare war on Burma on March 5, 1824. On May 17 the Burmese invade Chittagong and drive British forces from Ramu but fail to exploit this success. Ensuing military operations occur in Arakan, Assam, Manipur, and Cachar, but the truly decisive operations are in Burma proper.

May 10, 1824

Southeast Asia: Burma: First Anglo-Burmese War (continued): British occupation of Rangoon. The British plan to carry the war into Burma, and they assemble in the Andaman Islands a 5,000-man expeditionary force under Commodore Charles Grant and Major General Sir Archibald Campbell. Proceeding up the Rangoon River, it anchors off Rangoon (present-day Yangon) on May 10, 1824. After little opposition, the British land troops and seize the now-deserted city.

May–December 1824

Southeast Asia: Burma: First Anglo-Burmese War (continued): Fighting for Rangoon. Although the British occupy Rangoon (present-day Yangon) proper,

the Burmese have either destroyed or carried off provisions. They now set up defensive positions beyond the city. On May 28 British commander Major General Sir Archibald Campbell orders an attack on some of the outlying Burmese posts. Eventually the British take them all, including Kemmendine on June 10, by land assault supported by gunfire from ships in the river.

It is soon apparent to the British, however, that they have not made adequate provision for resupply, and the Burmese endeavor to deny the British access to food. British troops also fall prey to disease; at one point there are only 3,000 able to fight. Savage combat continues, and Burmese general Maha Bandula arrives with reinforcements from Arakan in August. The British also reinforce.

In this period Campbell takes control of the Burmese provinces of Tavoy and Mergui and the coast of Tenasserim. British forces also capture the old Portuguese fort and factory of Syriam, at the mouth of the Pegu River. In October they occupy Martaban Province.

Thanks to Bandula's troops from Arakan, by the end of November there are 60,000 Burmese surrounding only 5,000 British troops at Rangoon and Kemmendine. The Burmese repeatedly attack Kemmendine without success, and on December 7, 1824, they assault Rangoon in force, only to be defeated by Campbell's counterattack. The Burmese then entrench on the river, where they are attacked by the British on December 15 and are again forced to withdraw.

August 6, 1824

South America: Peru: Bolívar's Campaigns (continued): Peruvian War of Independence: Battle of Junín. The Viceroyalty of Peru is the last Spanish holding in South America. On July 28, 1821, José de San Martín proclaims the independence of Peru in Lima. In February 1824, however, the Royalists regain control of Lima. Simón Bolívar, now leading the liberation movement, assembles a force of some 9,000 men at Trujillo. In June he advances to confront a Spanish force of equal size under General José de Canterac.

The battle occurs on the Junín plains northwest of the Jauja Valley, about 100 miles northeast of Lima. It is a purely cavalry engagement of about an hour's duration. There are some 2,000 men on a side. Battle is initiated by Bolívar's effort to cut off the Royalist withdrawal in the direction of Cuzco. The Spanish cavalry charges Bolívar's cavalry, trying to cover the withdrawing infantry.

The fighting lasts only about an hour and involves close combat with lance and saber but no firearms. About 250 on the Spanish side and 150 on the liberationist side are killed. The battle greatly enhances the morale of the revolutionaries. The Spanish troops continue their withdrawal into the highlands southwest of Lima and experience increasing defections. Patriot general Antonio José de Sucre pursues the Royalists while Bolívar enters Lima and reorganizes the government.

December 9, 1824

South America: Peru: Bolívar's Campaigns (continued): Peruvian War of Independence (continued): Battle of Ayacucho. In late 1824, Royalist forces under Spanish viceroy General José de la Serna still control much of Peru. Patriot general Antonio José de Sucre continues the military offensive, however.

After prolonged maneuvering, the two sides came together in December on the plain of Ayacucho, 186 miles southeast of Lima, at Pampa de La Quinua, close to Ayacucho and near the town of Quinua. In the Quechua language Ayacucho means "dead corner," referring to a slaughter of natives there by the Spanish early in their conquest of Peru. Spanish viceroy José de La Serna y Hirojosa commands the Royalist force of some 9,300 men and seven guns. Sucre has only 5,780 men and two guns. Both sides possess some cavalry.

In the maneuvering before the Battle of Ayacucho (also known as the Battle of La Quinua and the Battle of the Generals), La Serna manages to position his own forces to the north of Sucre, hoping to cut the Patriots off from the sea and also cut off the additional forces that Patriot leader Simón Bolívar is raising in Lima. La Serna then tries to employ his superior numbers to advantage by encircling his opponent. Sucre manages to avoid this and takes up an excellent defensive position on the plain. La Serna then plans to pin Sucre's flanks while finishing off the Patriots with a drive into the center of their line. Sucre cedes the initiative to La Serna, hoping that he can contain that attack and then exploit it with a reserve of three battalions of infantry and five cavalry squadrons.

The battle opens early in the morning of December 9 with the Royalist left wing advancing against the Patriot right, commanded by General José Maria Córdoba. This attack fails, as does another Royalist assault on the Patriot center. A Patriot counterattack drives back the Royalist left and opens a break in their lines that allows Sucre to introduce his infantry and cavalry reserves to seal the victory.

Despite being outnumbered, Sucre has won a complete victory. The entire battle has lasted less than an hour and a half. The Royalists lose 1,400 dead and 700 wounded, while the Patriots sustain 309 dead and 607 wounded. Particularly grievous for the

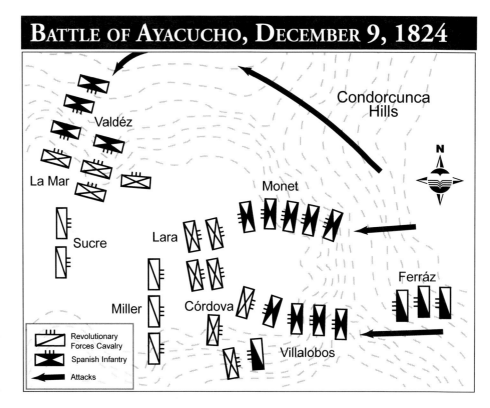

BATTLE OF AYACUCHO, DECEMBER 9, 1824

Royalist cause is the large number of senior officers among the 2,500 Royalists taken prisoner: 15 generals, 16 colonels, and 68 lieutenant colonels. The battle is thus sometimes called the Battle of the Generals. La Serna, who was wounded a half dozen times, is among those captured.

Under the terms of capitulation, La Serna agrees to withdraw all Spanish forces from Peru. Sucre then moves into upper Peru. In August 1825 he declares the province of Chuquisaca independent and renames it Bolivia in Bolívar's honor. Although fighting by small isolated Spanish units continues thereafter, the Battle of Ayacucho marks the effective end of the South American Wars of Independence.

1824

Southern Europe: Greece: Greek War of Independence (continued): Civil war in Greece. Although the Ottomans are repulsed before Messolonghi (Missolonghi), the Greeks fail to take advantage of the respite and dissipate their energies in leadership struggles as Theodoros Kolokotronis opposes Lazaros Kondouriottis. This flares into civil war in 1824 during which Kolokotronis is defeated.

1824–1831

West Africa: First Anglo-Ashanti War. The states of the Gold Coast have placed themselves under British protection. Sir Charles MacCarthy is the governor of the Gold Coast. Leading troops against the Ashanti, he is defeated and killed. Disease prevents the Ashanti from exploiting the situation, and the British send reinforcements to operate with indigenous troops. They are finally victorious in 1827. Four years later, in 1831, the Ashanti formally agree to a treaty whereby they surrender their claims to sovereignty over the coast and accept the Pra River as the border. For the next three decades there is peace.

February 13, 1825

Southeast Asia: Burma: First Anglo-Burmese War (continued): British advance up the Irrawaddy River. British commander in Burma Major General Sir Archibald Campbell decides to advance about 60 miles up the Irrawaddy River to Prome. He sets out by land and water with about 4,000 men on February 13, 1825. The waterborne force, under Brigadier General Willoughby Cotton, proceeds to Danubyu, while Campbell commands the land force toward Prome.

Campbell's force moves faster, but on March 11 he learns that Cotton's assault on Danubyu has failed. Campbell immediately withdraws, linking up with Cotton on March 27.

February 24, 1825

Southern Europe: Greece: Greek War of Independence (continued): Egyptian intervention in Greece. With the Ottoman military intervention in Greece going badly, Sultan Mahmud II appeals for assistance to his powerful vassal, Muhammad Ali of Egypt. He sends a powerful fleet and army to Greece under his son Ibrahim Ali. The Egyptian expeditionary force lands in Greece on February 24, 1825, and soon subdues the entire peninsula. As a result of this intervention, Egypt secures control of all Crete.

April 2, 1825

Southeast Asia: Burma: First Anglo-Burmese War (continued): Battle of Danubyu. On April 2, 1825, the reunited British forces of Major General Sir Archibald Campbell and Brigadier General Willoughby Cotton come under attack by the Burmese. They employ rockets to defeat it. The great Burmese general Maha Bandula is killed, and the British enter Danubyu without resistance.

Campbell then proceeds to Prome, which he occupies on April 25. The British remain there during the rainy season. Burmese forces, now commanded by Maha Nenyo, again surround the British positions.

April 7, 1825–April 23, 1826

Southern Europe: Greece: Greek War of Independence (continued): Second Siege of Messolonghi. A new Ottoman army under Reshid Pasha drives from the north and begins a second siege of the strategically important Greek stronghold of Messolonghi (also Missolonghi), which guards access to the Gulf of Corinth. The siege opens on April 7, 1825. The defenders hold out for an entire year, rejecting Ottoman offers of honorable terms.

Prolonged resistance is possible only because the Greeks are able to resupply the fortress from the sea. When the besiegers close this off, starvation and disease take their toll. A final Ottoman assault occurs on the night of April 22. Few of the defenders of Messolonghi manage to reach the forests of Mount Zygos; most who do perish there.

May–June 5, 1825

Southern Europe: Greece: Greek War of Independence (continued): Siege of Athens. After his victory at Messolonghi (Missolonghi), Ottoman general Reshid Pasha leads his army to Athens and lays siege to the Acropolis. The Greeks ignore the advice of British admiral Lord Thomas Cochrane, who now commands the Greek Navy, and British general Sir George Church. The British commanders therefore escape to their warships off Athens. The Greek garrison surrenders on June 5, accorded the honors of war.

The Turks now control virtually all Greece, and the Greek nationalists appeal to Britain. The British government, worried that Russia might intervene unilaterally and end up dominating Greece, seeks to work out a policy acceptable to all the Great Powers.

August 6, 1825

South America: Bolivia: Bolívar's Campaigns (continued): Republic of Bolivia proclaimed. Following his victory over the Royalists in Peru, General Antonio José de Sucre, Simón Bolívar's lieutenant, moves south into the Presidency of Charcas, west of Brazil. On August 6, 1825, he establishes the Republic of Bolivia.

November–December 2, 1825

Southeast Asia: Burma: First Anglo-Burmese War (continued): Battle of Prome. On November 10 British forces at Prome defeat a Burmese attack led by Maha Nemyo. By November 1825 the Burmese have some 60,000 men in position around Prome, which is defended by a combined British and Indian force of 5,000 men under Major General Sir Archibald Campbell. On November 10 the Burmese attack; they are repulsed, thanks to superior British discipline and firepower.

On December 1 Campbell counterattacks with his own land forces. Supported by naval gunfire, British forces drive the Burmese from their entrenchments. Burmese commander Maha Nemyo is among those killed.

December 10, 1825–January 18, 1826

South Asia: India: British siege of Bhurtpore. This city in northern India, unsuccessfully besieged in 1805 by the British during the Second Maratha War (1803–1805), experiences a disputed succession over who is the rightful rajah. New British commander in chief in India General Stapleton Stapleton-Cotton (later Viscount Combermere), who arrived in Calcutta only in October 1815, seizes the opportunity to win military recognition.

In early December, Stapleton-Cotton moves against the city with three divisions of troops and the largest siege train thus far employed by the British in India. The British arrive at Bhurtpore on December 10. Following more than a month of artillery bombardment, the British explode two huge mines under the walls on January 18, 1826. Their infantry then storms the breaches, taking the city. British losses are 1,000 dead and wounded. The defenders suffer some 8,000 casualties.

1825–1828

South America: Argentina-Brazil War. Argentina lends aid to a revolt against Brazil in the Banda Oriental (Eastern Bank, constituting present-day Uruguay and known to Brazil as the Provincia Cisplatina), which Brazil incorporated into its territory when it achieved independence from Portugal in 1822. Argentina now wants to reacquire the area, with Argentina and the Banda Oriental constituting the United Provinces of the Río de la Plata.

Argentinean and Uruguayan exiles win the Battle of Sarandí (October 12, 1825). Emperor Pedro I of Brazil orders a blockade of the Río de la Plata and its ports of Buenos Aires and Montevideo. The Argentines first move their main naval base to Ensenada and then to Carmen de Patagones. A Brazilian attempt to take Carmen de Patagones fails in 1827.

Argentine forces under General Carlos María de Alvear cross the Río de la Plata into Brazilian territory. In the major battle of the Argentina-Brazil War (also known as the Cisplatine War), they engage and defeat Brazilian forces under the Viscount of Barbacena in the Battle of Ituzaingó on February 20, 1827. The major naval battle is Monte Santiago (April 7–8, 1827), a Brazilian victory.

The war exacts a heavy financial toll on both sides, disrupting important foreign trade. Brazil cannot afford mercenary troops acquired in Ireland and Germany or the 60 warships necessary to maintain the naval blockade of the Río de la Plata.

With Britain and France acting as intermediaries, the two sides then enter into peace talks. In the Treaty of Montevideo of August 27, 1828, the disputed province of the Banda Oriental is constituted as the independent state of Uruguay and thus is permanently lost to both Argentina and Brazil. The eastern portion of territory, known as the Misiones Orientales, is awarded to Brazil. Brazil's loss of the Provincia Cisplatina is a factor in the abdication of Dom Pedro I in 1831.

1825–1830

Southeast Asia: Netherlands East Indies: Great Java War. The last native prince on Java, Dipo Negara, leads a revolt against Dutch rule in the Netherlands East Indies (Indonesia). Guerrilla warfare rages for five years. Finally put down by the Dutch in 1830, the rebellion costs the lives of 15,000 Dutch soldiers. Native Javanese losses are unknown.

January 19, 1826

Southeast Asia: Burma: First Anglo-Burmese War (continued): Battle of Malun. Following their defeat in the Battle of Prome, the surviving Burmese withdraw to Malun on the Irrawaddy River, where they again entrench. In late December the Burmese again open peace negotiations, agreeing to British conditions. When the Burmese king refuses to ratify the treaty, however, the war continues.

British forces under Major General Sir Archibald Campbell attack and defeat the Burmese at Malun on January 19, 1826. The Burmese mount a final stand in defense of their capital of Ava, at the city of Pagan. The British defeat them there on February 9.

February 24, 1826

Southeast Asia: Burma: First Anglo-Burmese War (continued): Treaty of Yandabo. With the British now only four days' march from Ava, the Burmese king finally agrees to peace on British terms. The Treaty of Yandabo (February 24, 1826) ends the war. The Burmese not only agree to pay the British East India Company a large indemnity but also to surrender Assam, Arakan, and the entire Tenasserim coast. British forces remain in the Rangoon (Yangon) area for several years until the treaty's financial conditions are met. The war ends Burmese military predominance in Southeast Asia.

March 10, 1826

Southern Europe: Portugal: Death of King John VI. John VI is succeeded by his legitimate heir and eldest son, Don Pedro I, emperor of Brazil, who is briefly King Pedro IV of Portugal. With neither the Portuguese nor the Brazilians desiring a unified monarchy, Pedro abdicates the Portuguese Crown in favor of his seven-year-old daughter, Maria da Glória of Portugal, on condition that when of age she marry his younger brother, Miguel. In April 1826, in an attempt to reconcile the absolutists and liberals, Pedro revises the constitution of 1822 to give each a role in government. He then returns to Brazil, leaving the throne to Maria, with Miguel as regent.

April 5, 1826

Southern Europe: Greece: Greek War of Independence (continued): Russian ultimatum to the Sublime Porte. Nicholas I, czar of Russia since the death of Alexander I in 1825, is extremely devout; he believes that it is his duty to answer the call of his Orthodox coreligionists in Greece against the Ottomans. Nicholas therefore takes up the Greek cause. He is joined by the British and French governments, which become involved in large part to forestall Russian expansion into the Mediterranean. On April 5 the Russian government demands that the Sublime Porte return to the status quo in the Danubian Principalities and also dispatch a special envoy to St. Petersburg to discuss relations. Under pressure from France and Austria, the Ottomans agree.

June 15–16, 1826

Southwest Asia: Ottoman Empire. The opposition of the Janissaries to military reform leads Sultan Mahmud II to plot their destruction. Their proven inefficiency in battle provides justification for the step. In May, Mahmud decrees the establishment of a new military corps, which will be open to the Janissaries. Seeing this as a threat to their position, the Janissaries rebel.

Mahmud is prepared and, with the support of the small loyal corps, shells the Janissary barracks. The people of Constantinople do the rest. Some 6,000–10,000 Janissaries are massacred.

July 16, 1826–February 21, 1828

Southwest Asia: War between Persia and Russia. The war has its genesis in a boundary dispute between the two empires. There is no formal declaration of war, but on July 16, 1826, a Persian army of 35,000 men led by governor of Azerbaijan Prince Abbas Mirza crosses the border into the Khanate of Talysh and Karabakh. The Khans quickly switch sides and surrender to the Persians their principal cities of

Lenkoran, Quba, and Baku. Believing that he has insufficient military resources available to meet the Persians, Russian governor of the Caucasus Aleksey Yermolov orders the abandonment of Ganja (Kirovabad), the most populous city in the region.

General Ivan Fedorovich Paskievich replaces Yermolov and, with additional resources, launches a counteroffensive. On September 26, 1826, Paskievich and 15,000 Russians meet and defeat Abbas Mirza with 30,000 Persians near Ganja. The Russians force the Persians back across the Araks River and into Persia.

Fighting is suspended during the winter of 1826–1827 but resumes in May 1827. Paskievich advances toward Yerevan (Erivan) in eastern Armenia, taking other cities en route. The Russians capture Yerevan on October 1 following a week-long siege. They capture Tabriz two weeks later, forcing the shah to sue for peace. The war is brought to an end by the Treaty of Turkmanchai on February 21, 1828.

December 1826
Southern Europe: Portugal: British military intervention. With Portugal in upheaval due to a successionist crisis, the British government dispatches an expeditionary force of 5,000 men under General Sir William Clinton to support the constitutional government backed by General João Carlos de Saldanha. Miguel, serving as regent for his seven-year-old bride Maria da Glória, daughter of Emperor Pedro I of Brazil, bows to force; the British withdraw on April 28, 1828.

1826
Central Asia: Afghanistan. Dost Mohammad of the Bārakzay clan captures Kabul and then gradually expands his control over the rest of Afghanistan, ruling that nation during 1835–1839.

1826–1829
Southeast Asia: Laos: War between Laos and Siam. King Chao Anou of Vientiane is determined to free Laos from Siamese rule. Building up his army, he takes advantage of Siamese problems with the British to invade Siam in 1826. He drives almost to Bangkok before the surprised Siamese can react and are able under their capable general P'ya Bodin to halt the Lao army.

Later in 1826 P'ya Bodin leads Siamese forces in an invasion of Laos. In the week-long bitterly contested Battle of Nong-Bona-Lamp'on in 1827, the Siamese force their way across the Mekong River into Laos and destroy the Lao army. King Chao Anou flees to Vietnam.

The Siamese destroy the capital of Vientiane and deport large segments of the Lao population to an area of Siam that had been depopulated during Siam's wars with Burma. The Siamese annex Laos outright in 1828. Although Chao Anou makes an effort to reclaim his throne in 1829, it is unsuccessful, and he is captured.

1826–1835
East Asia: China: Khokand invasions of Xinjiang. Khokand Khanate leader Jahangir invades Xinjiang in 1826. His forces are expelled by a Qing army of 36,000 men in 1828. The Khokand invasion of 1826 and another in 1830 lead the Qing to make agreements in 1832 that, in practice, allow Khokandi merchants in Xinjiang exemption from taxes and from Qing law. The concessions to the Khokandis cost the Qing little, since tax revenue from trade in Xinjiang is negligible. They are, however, a model on which the Qing draw when making concessions to the British in the Treaty of Nanjing of 1842.

February 20, 1827
South America: Argentina-Brazil War (continued): Battle of Ituzaingó. A combined Argentinean-Uruguayan army of 6,000–9,500 men confronts a slightly larger Brazilian army along the Santa Maria River in southern Brazil in the Battle of Ituzaingó (known to Brazil as the Passo do Rosário). General Carlos María de Alvear commands the combined Argentinean-Uruguayan army, while General Felisberto Caldeira Brant, Marquis of Barbacena, leads the Brazilian side. In late January 1827 after Alvear had invaded southern Brazil in order to bring on a confrontation with the Brazilian army, Barbacena moves to meet him.

Alvear has carefully chosen a defensive position in order to maximize his advantage in cavalry. The Brazilian army arrives on February 19, and despite advice that he delay and rest his men, Barbacena attacks the next day, believing that he is engaging only the rear guard of the Argentinean-Uruguayan forces.

Barbacena sends his cavalry and infantry across the river against I Corps under the command of Uruguayan leader Juan Antonio Lavalleja and attempts to encircle it. Although the Uruguayans are initially driven back, Alvear soon counterattacks across open fields with his principal cavalry force, forcing the Brazilians to withdraw.

Brazilian losses are 800–1,300 men (200 killed), while the Argentinean-Uruguayan side loses 400–560 (141 killed). Although this is the largest land battle of the war, neither side gains any strategic advantage, and the war continues.

April 7–8, 1827

South America: Argentina-Brazil War (continued): Battle of Monte Santiago. Although there are numerous small naval engagements in the war, the principal naval battle occurs on April 7–8, 1827, off the coast of Santiago. Brazilian admiral Rodrigo Pinto Guedes commands 12 ships on the first day and 14–16 on the next; Argentinean admiral Francis Drummond has only 4 ships. Brazil's ships are both larger and more powerful, but Drummond hopes to take advantage of the superior speed and maneuverability of his ships to launch a surprise attack and escape before the Brazilians can react.

The Brazilians are able to block the Argentineans from escaping, however; in the ensuing battle the Argentineans lose two ships sunk and another badly damaged. They also suffer 150 casualties including Drummond, who is mortally wounded. Brazil loses only 40 men killed or wounded. The losses sustained by the Argentine Navy in this battle, along with their previous loss of another major combatant, the *25 de Mayo,* in the Battle of Lara-Quilmes (February 24, 1827), gives the Brazilians complete naval superiority.

July 6, 1827

Southern Europe: Greece: Greek War of Independence (continued): Treaty of London. With Ottoman and Egyptian forces now fully in control of Greece, representatives of the French, British, and Russian governments conclude the Treaty of London. It calls on the Ottomans to agree to an armistice and on the Egyptians to withdraw. Should the Porte refuse, the three powers pledge to come to the aid of the Greeks with their naval forces. In the meantime, the British make a strong but ultimately unsuccessful diplomatic effort to get Egyptian ruler Muhammad Ali to remove his forces from Greece.

On August 16 the same three powers send a note to the Porte demanding an armistice, which the Ottomans reject on August 29. With that, the British, French, and Russian governments issue orders to their naval commanders in the Mediterranean to cut off all waterborne Ottoman and Egyptian resupply to Greece.

October 20, 1827

Southern Europe: Greece: Greek War of Independence (continued): Battle of Navarino Bay. In late August 1827, despite warnings from Britain, France, and Russia not to do so, Egypt sends a large squadron with reinforcements to Navarino Bay, Greece. It arrives on September 8, joining several Ottoman ships already there. On September 12 a British squadron under Vice Admiral Sir Edward Codrington arrives at Navarino Bay. The French and Russian governments have also dispatched squadrons to Greece.

Codrington is under orders from the British government to interdict reinforcements and supplies to the Ottoman forces in Greece. His instructions call on him to try to secure an armistice and use force only as a last resort. Codrington, however, is a staunch supporter of Greek independence, and his hands have been freed regarding force because the Ottoman government had rejected conditions presented by the allied governments to the Porte in the Treaty of London.

On September 25 Codrington and French admiral Henry Gauthier de Rigny meet with Ibrahim Pasha, the Egyptian commander in Greece, to discuss a mediation arrangement already accepted by the Greeks. Ibrahim Pasha agrees to an armistice while awaiting instructions from the sultan. Leaving a frigate at Navarino Bay to watch the Egyptian and Ottoman ships there, Codrington then withdraws to the British-controlled Ionian island of Zante (Zakynthos).

Ibrahim learns that while he is expected to observe a cease-fire, Greek naval units under British mercenary commanders (Admiral Lord Cochrane has charge of the entire Greek Navy) are continuing operations in the Gulf of Corinth, at Epirus, and at the port of Patras. On September 29–30 a Greek steamer warship, the *Karteria,* sinks nine Ottoman ships off Salona (Split) in Dalmatia. Codrington sends messages to warn these British officers, who are not under his command, to desist from such operations. These have little effect.

Outraged, Ibrahim first protests to Codrington and then decides to act. On October 1 he orders ships from Navarino Bay to assist the Ottoman garrison at

The Battle of Navarino Bay on October 20, 1827, in which the combined British, French, and Russian squadrons destroyed a combined Egyptian and Ottoman squadron. The last great battle of the Age of Sail, it helped secure Greek independence. (Stapleton Collection/Corbis)

Patras. They are intercepted by Codrington's squadron at the entrance to the Gulf and forced to return to Navarino. On the night of October 3–4, though, Ibrahim personally leads another relief effort. Although his forces manage to avoid detection by the British picket ship at Navarino Bay in the darkness, a strong lee wind prevents him from entering the Gulf. He is forced to anchor off Papas and wait for the storm to end. Codrington then comes up with his squadron and, firing warning shots, forces Ibrahim to return to Navarino Bay.

In the meantime, Ibrahim continues land operations. These include the wholesale burning of Greek villages and fields, the fires from which are clearly visible from the allied ships. A British landing party reports to Codrington that the Greek population of Messina is close to starvation.

On October 13 both a French squadron under de Rigny and a Russian squadron under Admiral Count L. Heidin (Heyden) join Codrington off Navarino Bay. Both of these commanders are inferior in rank to Codrington, who also has the most ships, and they agree to serve under his command.

On October 20, 1827, following futile attempts to contact Ibrahim Pasha, Codrington consults with the other allied commanders and makes the fateful decision to enter Navarino Bay with the combined British, French, and Russian squadrons. The allies have 11 ships of the line and 15 other warships. Codrington flies his flag in the ship of the line *Asia* (84 guns). He also has 2 74-gun ships of the line, 4 frigates, and 4 brigs. Admiral de Rigny has 4 74-gun ships of the line, 1 frigate, and 2 schooners. Admiral Heidin's Russian squadron consists of 4 74-gun ships of the

BATTLE OF NAVARINO BAY, OCTOBER 20, 1827

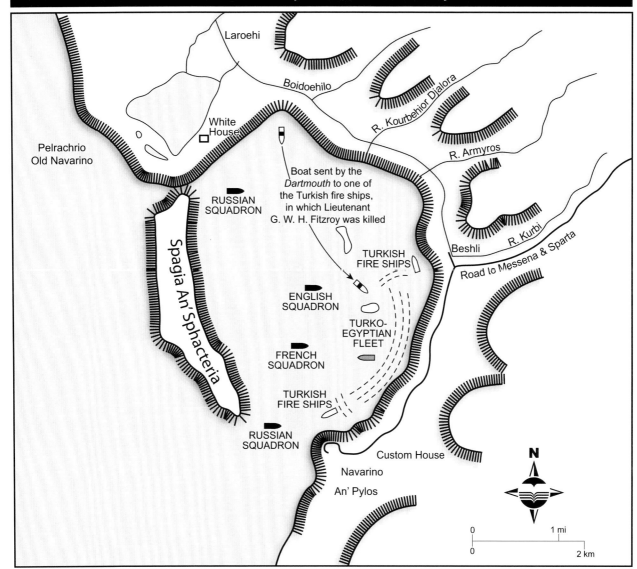

Laroehi

Boidoehilo

R. Kourbehior Dialora

R. Armyros

White House

Pelrachrio
Old Navarino

Boat sent by the *Dartmouth* to one of the Turkish fire ships, in which Lieutenant G. W. H. Fitzroy was killed

RUSSIAN SQUADRON

Spagia An' Sphacteria

TURKISH FIRE SHIPS

Beshli   R. Kurbi

Road to Messena & Sparta

ENGLISH SQUADRON

TURKO-EGYPTIAN FLEET

FRENCH SQUADRON

TURKISH FIRE SHIPS

RUSSIAN SQUADRON

Custom House

N

Navarino
An' Pylos

0   1 mi
0   2 km

line and 4 frigates. The allies thus have 11 ships of the line and 15 other warships.

In Navarino Harbor the Egyptians and Ottomans have 65 or 66 warships: 3 Ottoman ships of the line (2 of 84 guns each and 1 of 76), 4 Egyptian frigates of 64 guns each, 15 Ottoman frigates of 48 guns each, 18 Ottoman and 8 Egyptian corvettes of 14 to 18 guns each, 4 Ottoman and 8 Egyptian brigs of 19 guns each, and 5 or 6 Egyptian fire brigs. There are also some Ottoman transports and smaller craft.

About noon on October 20 the allied ships sail in two lines into Navarino Bay. The British and French form one line, the Russians the other. The Ottomans demand that Codrington withdraw, but the British admiral replies that he is there to give orders, not receive them. He threatens that if any shots are fired at the allied ships, he will destroy the Ottoman-Egyptian fleet.

The Egyptian and Ottoman ships lie at anchor in a long horseshoe-shaped formation with their flanks protected by shore batteries. The allied ships drop anchor in the midst of this formation. Codrington dispatches the frigate *Dartmouth* to an Ottoman ship in position to command the entrance of the bay with an order that it move. The captain of the *Dartmouth* sends a dispatch boat to the Ottoman ship, which then opens musket fire on it, killing an officer and several seamen. Firing then immediately becomes general, with shore batteries also opening up on the allied ships.

The ensuing four-hour engagement, essentially a series of individual gun duels by floating batteries at close range without overall plan, is really more of a slaughter than a battle. Three-quarters of the ships in the Ottoman-Egyptian fleet are either destroyed by allied fire or set alight by their own crews to prevent their capture. Only one, the *Sultane,* surrenders. Allied personnel losses are 177 killed and 469 wounded; the allies estimate Ottoman and Egyptian killed or wounded in excess of 4,000 men.

News of the allied victory is received with great popular enthusiasm across Europe. The Sublime Porte, furious at what has transpired, demands reparations. Recalled to Britain, Codrington is acquitted on a charge of disobeying orders.

The Battle of Navarino Bay removes any impediment to the Russian Black Sea Fleet, and in April 1828 Russia declares war on the Ottoman Empire. That August, Egypt withdraws from hostilities, virtually ending the war, and in the May 1832 Treaty of London, Greece secures its independence. The Battle of Navarino Bay, which makes all this possible, is also noteworthy as the last major engagement by ships of the line in the age of fighting sail.

1827–1829

North Africa: Algiers: French naval blockade of Algiers. Tensions between France and Algiers peak when Dey Husain of Algiers, while airing his grievances against France, strikes French consul Pierre Duval three times with a fly swatter on April 30, 1827. This brings a French naval blockade of the port city. Then, on August 3, 1829, Algerine shore batteries fire on a French ship flying a white flag and carrying negotiators.

1827–1829

South America: Bolivia and Ecuador: Peruvian invasion. In 1827 Peruvian president José de La Mar launches a program of aggressive expansionism, sending Peruvian forces into Bolivia and forcing President Antonio José de Sucre from power. On January 28, 1829, La Mar sends his army into Ecuador, then part of the Republic of Gran Colombia. A Peruvian naval squadron captures Guayaquil. However, on February 27 Sucre, who had taken refuge in Ecuador, combines with Ecuadorian colonel Juan José Flores to defeat the Peruvians in the Battle of Tarqui. The Ecuadorian forces retake Guayaquil the next day, ending La Mar's plans to expand Peruvian territory northward. Ecuador becomes independent in 1830.

February 21, 1828

Southwest Asia: War between Russia and Persia (continued): Treaty of Turkomanchai. Russia secures major gains, including part of Armenia with the city of Yerevan (Erivan). Persia also recognizes Russia's exclusive rights to maintain ships on the Caspian Sea, grants Russia important commercial concessions, and pays a sizable indemnity in gold.

April 26, 1828

Eastern Europe: War between Russia and the Ottoman Empire. On April 26, 1828, Czar Nicholas I of Russia declares war on the Ottoman Empire in the hope of expanding his territory at Ottoman expense but also to aid the Orthodox Christian Greeks in their war of independence against the Turks.

May–December 1828

Central Europe: War between Russia and the Ottoman Empire (continued). The Russians mount a general invasion of Ottoman territory in the Balkans. Because Russia's war with Persia is just over, only about 100,000 men are immediately available. This three-pronged offensive, directed by Czar Nicholas I in person (much to the chagrin of his generals), clears Moldavia and Wallachia but barely crosses the Danube into present-day Bulgaria, where it runs afoul of the Ottoman south-bank fortresses of Shumla, Silistra, and Varna.

The Russians lay siege to Silistra and capture Varna, following a three-month siege, on October 12. General exhaustion, poor logistics, and an outbreak of the plague then bring the Russian offensive to a halt for the winter.

In the Caucasus region, the Russians enjoy greater success. General Ivan Fedorovich Paskievich leads a Russian army from Tiflis to captures Kars before defeating the Turks at Akhalzic (Akhsltzikke) on August 27. Meanwhile, the Russian Black Sea fleet captures the port of Poti. Strong Kurdish opposition, however, beings the Russian advance to a halt along the upper Euphrates River.

June 1828–1834

Southern Europe: Portugal: Miguelite War. On the death of his father, King John VI in March 1826, Emperor Pedro I of Brazil, chooses to inherit his title as King Pedro IV of Portugal, ignoring restrictions of his own constitution. He issues a liberal constitution on April 26, but with neither Portugal nor Brazil desiring a unified monarchy, on May 28 he abdicates the Portuguese Crown in favor of his daughter, Maria II. As she is only seven years old, Pedro names his brother Dom Miguel as regent, on the pledge that he will marry her. Pedro then returns to Brazil, although his indecision over the Crowns of Brazil and Portugal bring him waning popularity.

In May 1828 Miguel seizes power in Portugal and has himself proclaimed king on July 4. Maria II flees to Britain. This begins the Miguelite War (also known as the Portuguese Civil War and the War of the Two Brothers). It is a struggle for the succession between progressive constitutionalists, who wish to introduce the reforms that the French Revolution brought to most of Western Europe, and the authoritarian absolutists, supported by conservative landowners and the Catholic Church, who oppose significant change. The Miguelite War lasts until 1834.

On seizing the throne, Miguel annuls his brother's constitution. This does not go unchallenged. The army garrison at Porto (Oporto) revolts, and under troops loyal to General João Carlos de Saldanha, the constitutionalists establish a rival government at Porto.

Although the rebellion against absolutist rule spreads to other cities, Miguel puts it down. Five years of repression follow during which thousands of Portuguese liberals are either arrested or flee the country.

August 7, 1828

North America: Mexico: Spanish invasion of Mexico. On August 7, 1828, a 3,000-man Spanish expeditionary force under the command of General Isidro Barradas lands at Tampico. The seizure of this Mexican port city on August 21 marks the beginning of a campaign to retake Mexico for Spain.

General Antonio López de Santa Anna Pérez de Lebrón leads Mexican forces against the invaders. Unable to mount an effective assault, Santa Anna lays siege to Tampico. Cut off from resupply and his numbers diminished by disease, Barradas surrenders on September 11, 1828. Santa Anna is widely hailed in Mexico as the savior of the republic.

August 9, 1828

Southern Europe: Greece: Greek War of Independence (continued): Egyptian evacuation of Greece. The British and French governments conclude a convention with Egyptian ruler Muhammad Ali whereby he agrees to withdraw his forces from Greece. The French dispatch an expeditionary force, and under its supervision the Egyptians evacuate Greece during the winter of 1828–1829. This virtually ends the war.

February 27, 1829

South America: Bolivia and Ecuador: Peruvian invasion (continued): Battle of Tarqui. Peruvian forces commanded by General José de La Mar and numbering some 5,000 infantry and cavalry invade Ecuador (then part of the Republic of Gran Colombia) on January 28, 1829. A month later, however, Ecuadorian forces totaling 3,800 infantry and 600 cavalry under Bolivian president-in-exile Colonel Antonio José de Sucre meet the Peruvians in the Battle of Tarqui. The Peruvians occupy a strong position on high ground, with Sucre hoping to mount a surprise dawn attack. The Ecuadorian cavalry encounters the Peruvians prematurely, though, and the battle is on.

With the coming of daylight, the Ecuadorians manage to attack through woods that the Peruvians had thought impassable and therefore did not defend. The Peruvians are routed. The Ecuadorians sustain casualties of 54 killed and 200 wounded; the Peruvians lose 2,500, including a large number of prisoners. The battle is the decisive event in the war. The next day the Ecuadorian army retakes Guayaquil. Ecuador becomes formally independent in 1830.

May 22, 1829

Southern Europe: Greece: Greek War of Independence (continued): London Protocol. The ambassadors of the Great Powers, meeting in London, decide that Greece south of a line from the Gulf of Volo to the Gulf of Arta, with Euboea and the Cyclades (without Crete), is to be an autonomous tributary kingdom of the Ottoman Empire, with a ruling prince who is not to be chosen from the ruling families of Britain, France, or Russia.

June–August 1829
Central Europe: Balkans: War between Russia and the Ottoman Empire (continued): Russian military advance on Adrianople. New Russian commander in the Balkans General Hans Karl Friedrich Anton von Diebitsch-Zabalkansky begins a general offensive against Ottoman forces commanded by Grand Vizier Mustafa Reshid Pasha. The campaign begins slowly in the spring. Diebitsch leaves behind sufficient troops to continue the siege of Silistra. The fortress will surrender on June 11.

Meanwhile, west of Varna in the Battle of Kulevcha (May 31–June 11), Diebitsch defeats Rashid and the Turks. The battle is one of the most important of the war; it opens the way for the Russians to cross the Balkan (Hacmus) Mountains on June 15, the farthest advance for a Russian army thus far. Marching rapidly south, Diebitsch's army outmaneuvers the Turks and takes the city of Adrianople on August 20.

At the same time, General Ivan Fedorovich Paskievich, operating on the Asiatic front, takes both Kars and Erzerum from the Turks. On the verge of collapse and with Constantinople itself now seemingly threatened with capture, the Turks sue for peace.

September 14, 1829
Central Europe: Balkans: War between Russia and the Ottoman Empire (continued): Treaty of Adrianople. Both sides are eager for peace. With their army wracked by disease, the Russians are in no position to press an attack on Constantinople. They also fear British and French intervention should they try. The terms of the peace are therefore surprisingly lenient on the Turks.

In the Treaty of Adrianople (also known as the Treaty of Edirne) of September 14, 1829, Russia abandons its conquests in Europe but gains control of the entire mouth of the Danube. It also secures the fortresses of Akhaltsikhe and Akhalkalaki in Georgia. The Turks recognize Russian possession of Georgia and the khanates of Yerevan (Erivan) and Nakhichevan that had been ceded by Persia to Russia the year before. Russia is to occupy the Danubian provinces pending payment of an indemnity of 14 million ducats over a 10-year period. The hospodars of Moldavia and Wallachia are to receive life appointments, and the Ottomans are to raze all fortresses and remove all Muslims from the two provinces.

The Sublime Porte also agrees to abide by the London Protocol of March 1829 regarding Greece. The pact signals the demise of the Ottoman Empire and gives a false impression of Russian military prowess, when in reality their military effort has been inept.

1829–1833
East Africa: Present-day Kenya. Mombasa defies efforts by Sayyid Said, ruler of Muscat, to take it over. During 1824–1826, the leaders of Mombasa invite in the British and agree to become a British protectorate to avoid Muscati rule. The British, to avoid alienating their ally Said, depart the city in 1826. In 1829 and again in 1833, Said attacks Mombassa. Each time, however, Mombassa defeats the Muscat forces.

June 14, 1830
North Africa: French conquest of Algiers: French expeditionary force sent to Algiers. Using the pretext of an insult to French consul Pierre Duval, who had been struck with a fly swatter by Dey Husain in 1827, French king Charles X authorizes the sending of an expeditionary force to Algiers to remove that threat to French Mediterranean shipping. This is an expedition of conquest rather than a punitive operation, however. The real reason behind the king's decision is to secure a major foreign success that will shore up the unpopular French government headed by the Prince de Polignac and enable it to win the upcoming elections.

On May 25 a large French fleet of some 100 warships, including 11 ships of the line, under the command of Admiral Baron Victor Guy Duperré departs Toulon. The warships escort no fewer than 572 hired merchantmen lifting some 34,000 troops, 83 guns, and horses, equipment, and supplies. Marshal Louis Auguste Victor, Count de Ghaisnes de Bourmont, has command of the land force. The troops begin coming ashore at Sidi Farruj, about 18 miles west of Algiers, on June 14 and establish a beachhead.

July 5, 1830
North Africa: French conquest of Algiers (continued): Capture of Algiers. Thanks to superior artillery and organization, on June 19 in the Battle of Staoueli, a French land force of 34,000 men easily defeats an Algerian force of 43,000 men and pushes

toward Algiers. The French enter the city on July 5. Dey Husain is allowed to keep his personal fortune and agrees to go into exile.

The operation, although it does not result in the triumph that the ministry had sought in the July French election (the opposition actually increases its numbers in the Chambers), is one of the few such enterprises to turn a profit. The dey's ample gold and silver reserves (estimated at 55 million francs) more than pay for the entire cost of the enterprise (48 million francs).

July 28–30, 1830
Western Europe: France: Revolution in Paris. The July Revolution against increasingly autocratic Bourbon king Charles X (r. 1824–1830) sweeps into power his cousin, Louis Philippe, Duc d'Orléans, as "King of the French."

August 25, 1830
Western Europe: Belgian Revolution. Inspired by the French Revolution of 1830 and a stirring performance of Daniel Francis Auber's opera *La Muette de Portici* with its calls for liberty at the Brussels opera house, crowds spill into the streets, and revolution begins in Belgium. The primary causes are sharp differences in language and religion between the Flemish-speaking Protestant Dutch population and the Francophile Catholic Walloons as well as unequal distribution of civil offices in favor of the Dutch. The citizens soon drive out the Dutch troops. The Belgians proclaim their independence from Dutch rule on October 4.

October 27, 1830
Western Europe: Belgium: Dutch bombardment of Antwerp. Dutch forces under General David Hendryk Chassé occupy the citadel of Antwerp, although the Belgians continue to hold the city itself. Chassé's bombardment of the city strengthens anti-Dutch sentiment among the Belgian population.

November 29, 1830
Central Europe: Poland: November Uprising. In 1815 Napoleon's former Grand Duchy of Warsaw passed under Russian control. Czar Alexander I granted the new Kingdom of Poland considerable freedoms, including a constitution (Russia had none at the time), linguistic freedom, and its own institutions, to include an army. Russia and Poland are united only in

the person of the czar, who is also the king of Poland. Over time, however, the Polish freedoms are whittled away, and the Poles grow unhappy with Russian rule.

On November 29, 1830, cadets at the military academy in Warsaw begin a revolt known as the November Uprising or the Cadet Revolution. Many Poles are upset over purported Russian plans to use the Polish Army to crush the 1830 revolutions in France and Belgium. Other Poles soon join the cadets, and a moderate Provisional Government is established. It sends representatives to meet with the Russians, who, however, refuse any concessions. Czar Nicholas I demands complete submission to Russian authority.

With moderation discredited, the radicals seize power in Poland, and on January 25, 1831, the Sejm passes the Act of Dethronization of Nicholas I, ending the Polish-Russian personal union and amounting to a declaration of war against Russia.

Although the insurgents assemble some 70,000 troops led by a number of officers who had learned the military art serving under Napoleon, their efforts are seriously compromised by internal divisions over who should lead Poland.

December 20, 1830
Western Europe: Belgium: Independence of Belgium. On November 4, 1830, representatives of the Great Powers meeting in London order an armistice in the fighting between the Dutch and the Belgians. Then, on December 20, 1830, the same Great Power representatives dissolve the United Kingdom of the Netherlands, and Belgium becomes independent. On June 4, 1831, Leopold of Saxe-Coburg becomes King Leopold I of the Belgians.

February 25–26, 1831
Central Europe: Poland: Russo-Polish War: Battle of Olszynka Grochowska. On February 4 Russian general Hans Karl Friedrich Anton von Diebitsch-Zabalkansky leads 115,000 troops in an advance on Warsaw. The first major battle takes place close to the village of Stoczek near Łuków on February 14, 1831. Polish cavalry defeat a Russian division, but this small victory does not deter the Russians. Subsequent clashes at Dobre, Wawer, and Białołęka are also inconclusive.

The Poles then marshal their forces under the command of Józef Chłopicki on the right bank of the Vistula to defend Warsaw. In the resulting Battle of Olszynka Grochowska of February 25, 1831, some 40,000 Poles defeat a Russian army of 60,000 men under Diebitsch. The Poles suffer some 7,000 casualties, the Russians at least 9,500. Warsaw is saved, and Diebitsch is forced to retreat eastward to Siedlce.

February–March 1831

Southern Europe: Italy: Widespread revolutions. Inspired by Giuseppe Mazzini and his nationalist organization Young Italy, revolutionaries seize power in Parma, Modena, and the Papal States. The revolts are easily crushed by Italian government forces, assisted by Austrian troops.

May 26, 1831

Central Europe: Poland: Russo-Polish War (continued): Battle of Ostroleka. The Poles hope for foreign intervention, and there is considerable popular sympathy for their cause among the people of France and Britain. The governments of these countries have no wish to intervene, however, and Austria and Prussia adopt a position of benevolent neutrality toward Russia. They close their borders with Poland to prevent war matériel from reaching the Poles.

The Poles fight on, but the struggle increasingly degenerates into guerrilla warfare, which exacts a heavy toll from the civilian population from Russian reprisals. Although the Poles inflict a number of defeats on new Russian forces under Grand Duke Michael, the Russians commit substantially more forces and outnumber the Poles about 180,000 to 70,000. This numerical superiority soon tells.

In the Battle of Ostroleka on May 26, 1831, the Poles under General Jan Zigmunt Skrzneki engage in a hard-fought, day-long battle with a Russian army commanded by General Hans Karl Friedrich Anton von Diebitsch-Zabalkansky. Although the battle is indecisive, it also claims 8,000 Polish lives, considerably depleting their forces. The Poles are forced to withdraw.

Heavy personnel losses, some through resignations, coupled with constant changes in leadership cause many Poles to lose hope. The more radical Polish elements call for genuine change, including land reform, to reignite popular support. The Sejm (parliament) holds back, fearful that this will lead to charges of social revolution in Poland and further alienate the European governments.

August 2, 1831

Western Europe: Belgium. Refusing to recognize the wishes of the Belgian people and the dictate of the Great Powers, on August 2, 1831, King William I of the Netherlands leads 50,000 Dutch troops into Belgium to restore Dutch rule. The Dutch are at first victorious over the improvised Belgian forces, but the French government sends Marshal Étienne Maurice Gérard and 60,000 French troops. They force the Dutch army to retire.

The French also lay siege to the citadel of Antwerp, still held by Dutch general David Hendryk Chassé. In December 1832 the French, assisted by a British naval squadron, force Chassé to surrender. An armistice is proclaimed on May 21, 1833.

September 6–8, 1831

Central Europe: Poland: Russo-Polish War (continued): Battle of Warsaw. Russian forces, now commanded by General Ivan Fedorovich Paskievich following the death of General Hans Karl Friedrich Anton von Diebitsch-Zabalkansky, converge on Warsaw. General Jan Zigmunt Skrzynecki fails to prevent the Russian forces from joining, and the Sejm appoints General Henryk Dembinski to temporary command. The revolutionary government nears collapse among widespread rioting.

Despite a desperate defense by Polish troops led by General Józef Sowiński, the Warsaw suburb of Wola falls to the Russians on September 6. The next day the Russians attack the second line of Warsaw's defensive works. Head of the Polish government General Jan Stefan Krukowiecki surrenders that night, although the city still holds out. The defenders and government officials then withdraw to the Modlin Fortress on the Vistula River and from there to Plock. Warsaw surrenders on September 8.

With the news that a crack Polish corps, unable to join the main army, has crossed the frontier into Galicia and surrendered to the Austrians, it is obvious that the end is near. On October 5 the remainder of the Polish army—more than 20,000 men—crosses the frontier into Prussia and surrenders at Brodnica. Only 1 officer surrenders to the Russians.

Those leaders of the revolt whom the Russians are able to catch are sent into exile in Siberia. The remainder flee abroad, where they continue to agitate for Polish independence. Some 10,000 Poles settle in France; many others go to the United States, where their growing numbers become a powerful lobby that helps bring about Poland's independence during World War I.

Czar Nicholas I decrees that henceforth Poland is an integral part of Russia. Poland loses all the special rights that it had supposedly enjoyed; its administration is entrusted entirely to Russian officials. Warsaw becomes little more than a military garrison, its university closed.

1831–1834

Southeast Asia: Siam: Siamese invasion of Cambodia and Siamese-Vietnamese War. Siamese forces commanded by General P'ya Bodin enjoy initial success in their invasion of Cambodia, defeating the Khmers in the Battle of Kompong Chhang in 1832. Khmer king Ang Chan seeks sanctuary in Vietnam.

The Vietnamese then intervene. Their 15,000-man army coupled with an uprising against the Siamese by the Khmers cause the Siamese to withdraw. Vietnam now controls Cambodia.

January 1832

Southern Europe: Italy: Renewed revolutionary agitation. Following unrest in Romagna, in January 1832 Austrian troops occupy the province. In March, French troops take Ancona. Abortive revolutions continue in Italy over the next several years.

March 1832

Southern Europe: Greece. The Great Powers select Prince Otto of Bavaria as ruler of Greece. They also extend the frontiers of Greece to a line between Volo and Arta.

April–August 1832

North America: United States: Black Hawk War. This last Native American War in the Old Northwest is led by Black Hawk (Makataimesh-Ekiakiak). A strong opponent of white settlement, Black Hawk is forced across the Mississippi River by Illinois militia in 1831. In April 1832 Black Hawk returns with some 500 mounted warriors and 500 women and children in hopes of regaining their traditional lands. Some 1,600 militiamen march against him.

On May 14, 300 militia under Major Isaiah Stillman seize and kill several of Black Hawk's truce em-

issaries. In response Black Hawk attacks their camp with only 40 warriors and scatters the militia. Stillman's Run, as it is called, ends any possibility of peace.

Additional Illinois militia are called up and, in late June the army sends troops under Major General Winfield Scott. Although Native Americans kill more than 200 white settlers following Stillman's Run, Black Hawk knows that he cannot win. He attempts to withdraw with his people to the Mississippi. Near present-day Madison, Wisconsin, on July 21 they run into army regulars under Brigadier General James D. Henry. In the Battle of Wisconsin Heights, 30–90 warriors are killed. Black Hawk then withdraws to the juncture of the Bad Axe and Mississippi rivers.

In the Battle of Bad Axe on August 2, Black Hawk is forced to fight Colonel Zachary Taylor and 400 regulars and 900 militia. Some 150 warriors and 150 women and children perish attempting to cross the Mississippi. Black Hawk escapes with only some 150 of his original band. Black Hawk is captured on August 25 and held hostage to ensure compliance with the terms of the Treaty of Fort Armstrong of September 21, 1832. Under its terms, the Fox and Sauk Indians cede approximately one-fifth of present-day Iowa.

May–July 1832

Southwest Asia: Beginning of the First Turko-Egyptian War. As a reward for his assistance to Sultan Mahmud II in Greece, Egyptian ruler Muhammad Ali demands that he be given all Syria. Mahmud rejects his demand. Muhammad Ali then picks a quarrel with the pasha of Acre and sends his son Ibrahim Ali and an Egyptian army to occupy the country, thus beginning the First Turko-Egyptian War (1832–1833). Ibrahim enjoys immediate success, taking Acre (May 27), Damascus (June 15), and Aleppo (July 16).

July 1832

Southwest Asia: First Turko-Egyptian War (continued): Egyptian invasion of Anatolia. On July 29 the Egyptian army under Ibrahim Ali defeats an Ottoman army near Alexandretta. This launches an invasion of Anatolia. The sultan appeals to the British government for assistance, but the British are more immediately concerned about the situation in Belgium and are not yet fully aware of Egyptian strategic goals.

July 9, 1832

Southern Europe: Portugal: Miguelite War (continued): Siege of Porto. In Brazil, deteriorating relations between Emperor Pedro I and wealthy planters lead to Pedro's abdication in April 1831 in favor of his son, Pedro II. Pedro I then sails for Britain, where he organizes a military expedition and sails for the Azores, then controlled by the Constitutionalists, to set up a government-in-exile.

In July 1832 with the backing of liberals in Spain and Britain, Pedro, now styling himself King Pedro IV of Portugal, leads an expeditionary force of some 7,000 men at Porto (Oporto). Beginning on July 9, King Miguel I, at the head of a much larger force, lays siege to Porto. The siege lasts for more than two years, until August 1834. General João Carlos de Saldanha finally breaks the siege following the capture of Lisbon.

December 21, 1832

Southwest Asia: First Turko-Egyptian War (continued): Battle of Konia. Invading Anatolia at Konia in a seven-hour battle on December 21, 1832, the Egyptian army under Ibrahim Ali routs the main Turkish army under Grand Vizier Mehmed Rashid Pasha, who is taken prisoner. With virtually no remaining Ottoman forces opposing him, Ibrahim advances to Brusa. He is on the point of overthrowing Sultan Mahmud II when the Russians intervene. They offer assistance to Mahmud and warn Egyptian ruler Muhammad Ali to cease and desist.

1832

Southeast Asia: Xieng-Khouang. Vietnam conquers and annexes the eastern Lao kingdom of Xieng-Khouang

1832–1837

North Africa: French conquest of Algeria (continued): Fighting against Abd el Kader. Not all of the local officials of Algiers rally to the French. Particularly effective in opposing the French is Abd el Kader (Abd al-Qadir, Abdelkader), emir of Mascara in western Algeria. Capable and chivalrous, he rallies the faithful and wages a highly successful guerrilla war against the French, calling on the faithful to do war against Christianity. On June 1, 1837, however, he concludes with French general Thomas Robert Bugeaud the Treaty of Tafna. Some French military operations continue, however.

February 20, 1833

Southwest Asia: First Turko-Egyptian War (continued). To demonstrate Russian resolve and pressure Egypt into peace, a Russian naval squadron arrives in the Bosporus. The British and French governments, alarmed by the Russian move, press for mediation.

April 8, 1833

Southwest Asia: First Turko-Egyptian War (continued): Convention of Kutahia. In this agreement, the French government secures the cession by the Ottoman Empire to Egypt of both Syria and Adana (ancient Antioch). Sultan Mahmud II balks, hoping to retain Adana. When the Russians land troops on the Asiatic side of the Bosporus and the British and French assemble naval units in the eastern Mediterranean off the coast of Smyrna, it appears that the war will widen. On May 4, however, the sultan agrees to surrender Adana, and the crisis dissipates.

July 5, 1833

Eastern Atlantic Ocean: Miguelite War (continued): Fourth Battle of Cape St. Vincent. In July 1831 following persecution by King Miguel I's government of French citizens in Portugal, France seizes the Miguelite fleet in the Tagus. Supporters of young Queen Maria II, who had fled Portugal when Miguel seized power, also purchase some ships in Britain. On June 8, 1833, Royal Navy captain Charles Napier (who, to avoid provisions of the Foreign Enlistment Act, assumes the alias of Carlos de Ponza) takes command of the anti-Miguelite naval forces as vice admiral of the Portuguese navy.

In June 1833 in a critical decision of the Portuguese civil war, Pedro IV, although still besieged at Porto, now dispatches to Faro, in the Algarve region of southern Portugal, forces under General António Severin de Noronha, Duke of Terceira, escorted by Napier's warships. On July 2 Napier sails in search of the Miguelite fleet. Napier commands six warships—three frigates and three smaller ships—mounting a total of 176 guns. On July 5 off Cape St. Vincent, he encounters the Miguelite navy of three ships of the line and seven smaller ships mounting a total of 372 guns. The ensuing engagement is known as the Fourth Battle of Cape St. Vincent.

Outgunned two to one and thus unlikely to win a gunnery duel with his superior opponent, Napier orders his ships to close and their crews to board the

Miguelite ships. The brief but intense action is thus decided by hand-to-hand combat. Napier's crews capture all three Miguelite ships of the line along with a frigate and a corvette. The captured crews agree to fight for Queen Maria II. The crew of another ship also switches sides the next day. What is left of the Miguelite force flees to Lisbon or Madeira.

Napier's losses are 30 killed (3 of them captains) and some 60 wounded, while Miguelite losses are 200–300. Dom Pedro rewards Napier with the title of Viscount Cape St. Vincent. Napier is stricken from the Royal Navy list but will be restored to it in March 1836.

July 8, 1833
Southwest Asia: Treaty of Unkiar Skelessi. This mutual assistance pact between Russia and the Ottoman Empire, concluded on July 8, 1833, is to last for eight years. Each party is to aid the other in case of attack. A secret article relieves the Turks of this obligation in return for keeping the Dardanelles closed to all foreign warships.

On July 10 Russia withdraws its forces from the Bosporus. France and Britain both protest the treaty, which they interpret to mean that the Dardanelles will remain open to Russian warships. The Ottoman Empire now endeavors to rebuilds its army with the assistance of Prussian military advisers.

July 24, 1833
Southern Europe: Portugal: Miguelite War (continued): Seizure of Lisbon. After landing at Faro, the forces of General António Severin de Noronha, Duke of Terceira, march north through the Alentejo toward Lisbon, defeating the Miguelite forces in the Battle of Almada. Pedro IV's naval forces under Admiral Charles Napier, although hard hit by cholera, assist in Pedro's capture of Lisbon on July 24, 1833. The liberals now control Portugal's two major cities, Lisbon and Porto (Oporto). The absolutists, however, retain control of the countryside, dominated by the rural aristocracy and the Catholic Church. Maria da Glória is again recognized as queen as Maria II, this time with Dom Pedro as regent.

On August 25, 1833, the Miguelites bring Lisbon under siege. They attack the city in September, but the liberal defenses hold. General João Carlos de Saldanha raises the siege on October 10, 1833, forcing the Miguelites to withdraw to the east.

January 31–February 1, 1834
Southern Europe: Italy. A brief abortive revolution occurs in Piedmont and Savoy, led by Italian nationalist Giuseppe Mazzini and involving sailor Giuseppe Garibaldi.

See Leaders: Garibaldi, Giuseppe

April 22, 1834
Southern Europe: Portugal: Miguelite War (continued): Quadruple Alliance. The anti-Miguelite forces are solidified by the Quadruple Alliance signed on April 22, 1834, by Portugal, Spain, Great Britain, and France. The four governments agree to banish Dom Miguel from Portugal and Don Carlos from Spain. Spain agrees to keep troops in Portugal until the end

Italian patriot Giuseppe Garibaldi (1807–1882) dedicated his life to the unification of Italy. An inspirational leader of irregular troops, he conquered southern Italy and Sicily. (Perry-Castaneda Library)

of the Miguelite War, while Portugal promises to provide a force for operations against Don Carlos in Spain. Britain agrees to provide naval support.

May 16, 1834

Southern Europe: Portugal: Miguelite War (continued): Battle of Aceiceira. In the final battle of the Miguelite War, forces loyal to King Pedro IV and Queen Maria II commanded by General António Severin de Noronha, Duke of Terceira, defeat forces loyal to King Miguel under General Miguel Luís Vaz Pereira Pinto Guedes. Although they still command 18,000 men, Miguel's generals are unwilling to continue the war. They force him to seek terms of capitulation at Évora-Monte on May 24.

Miguel renounces all claims to the throne of Portugal in return for an annual pension. He also agrees to go into exile, never to return to Portugal. The Miguelite War is over, although Miguel's supporters continue to cause difficulties into the 1850s. Pedro restores the Constitutional Charter but dies on September 24, 1834. Maria da Glória, however, continues her interrupted reign as Queen Maria II of Portugal.

1834

Southern Africa: Boer conflict with the Bantu. Tensions increase between the British government and the Boers, the original white Dutch settlers in South Africa. Boer resentment of British rule is heightened by the abolition of slavery in 1833 and what many Boers come to believe is inadequate compensation as well as restrictive settlement policies of the British government. As a result, the Boers increasing seek to escape British control.

In 1834 the Bantu tribes (chiefly the Xosa) fiercely contest illicit Boer incursions on their land. Only with great difficulty do the Boers drive off the Bantu.

1834–1839

Southern Europe: Spain: First Carlist War. On June 30, 1833, King Ferdinand VII of Spain, on the urging of his wife Queen Maria Cristina, sets aside Salic Law to secure the succession of his infant daughter, Isabella. He thus deprives his brother Don Carlos of the throne.

After the death of Ferdinand on September 19, 1833, Carlos leads a revolt. His followers are known

as Carlists, while the government supporters are called the Constitutionalists or Isabelines.

In April 1834 France, Britain, and Portugal enter into an agreement with the Spanish government (the Quadruple Alliance) to defeat the Carlists. Britain supplies the so-called Spanish Legion, some 9,600 mercenaries led by Sir George de Lacy Evans, while France hires out its Foreign Legion to the Spanish government.

With Spain's own army largely inept, the French Foreign Legion plays the key role in the government victory and especially distinguishes itself in the Battle of Terapegui, near Pampeluna (April 26, 1836), and the Battle of Huesca (March 24, 1837). The legion pays a high price, however. When it departs Spain at the end of the revolt, it has lost half its strength. The First Carlist War officially comes to an end in the Convention of Vergara on August 31, 1839. Don Carlos flees to France.

October 1, 1835

North America: Mexico: Texas War of Independence: Battle of Gonzales. Many factors pull Texas away from Mexico. The Mexican government outlaws slavery in 1831, although exceptions are granted for Texas in practice. The Mexican government is in constant turmoil, and there are disagreements about tariffs, representation, immigration, and army garrisons. Matters come to a head in 1835 when Mexican president General Antonio López de Santa Anna Pérez de Lebrón abolishes the federal Constitution of 1824 and proclaims a new unitary constitution in its place that will sweep away states' rights. This causes widespread unrest. Revolts break out in Yucatan, Zacatecas, and Coahuila and in Texas.

Throughout 1835 there are altercations in Texas, and Santa Anna decides to send additional troops and punish Texas as he had Zacatecas. Ordered to retrieve a cannon given by the Mexican government to the Texas Militia earlier, Lieutenant Francisco Castañeda and 100 dragoons encounter Colonel John Henry Moore and 140 Texas militiamen with the gun at Gonzales, near the confluence of the San Marcos and Guadalupe rivers. Although shots are fired, there are no casualties in this first battle of the Texas War of Independence (1835–1836). Castañeda falls back to San Antonio.

December 28, 1835

North America: United States: Second Seminole War: Dade Massacre. The Second Seminole War (1835–1843) is the longest and most expensive of all Native American wars in the United States. Since the acquisition of Florida from Spain in 1819, there have been growing demands for removal of the Seminole Indians from Florida to the West to make their lands available for white settlement. The Seminoles are pressured into signing several treaties calling for their relocation on western lands. Many Seminoles, however, resist this.

On June 19, 1835, violence occurs at Hickory Sink when white settlers beat Seminoles accused of stealing a cow, which the Seminoles claim is theirs. Other Seminoles arrive, and in the ensuing clash, three whites are wounded; one Native American is killed and another wounded. In August, Seminoles kill one of the whites they hold responsible for the beatings earlier. By September many Seminoles have rallied to Osceola, leader of those opposing removal. By December 1835 hundreds of Seminoles have sought protection at several U.S. Army forts and are soon removed to the West.

The Second Seminole War begins with the so-called Dade Massacre of December 28, 1835. Major Frances L. Dade is leading two companies of soldiers from Fort Brooke to reinforce Fort King when hostile Seminoles ambush and wipe out the column. Only 2 soldiers of 108 make it back to Fort Brooke, and 1 of these dies of wounds several days later. Hostile Seminole bands soon control much of Florida. They attack isolated farms and settlements and even army posts. By September 1836 they control much of Florida.

1835–1836

North Africa: Tripolitania. Ottoman naval forces and troops reestablish their control over Tripolitania (present-day Lybia).

1835–1837

Southern Africa: The Great Trek. Restive under British control and what they consider to be restrictive policies, some 12,000 Boers undertake a great migration north to carve out their own independent states. One group proceeds north to the Vaal River and the other to the northeast to Natal and Zululand. Follow-ing fierce struggles, the Boers at the Vaal defeat the resident Bantu people.

February 23–March 6, 1836

North America: Mexico: Texas War of Independence (continued): Siege of the Alamo. Mexican president General Antonio López de Santa Anna Pérez de Lebrón and some 3,000 Mexican Army troops lay siege to the Alamo in San Antonio. Although the 183–189 defenders under the command of William Barret Travis and Jim Bowie repulse several attacks, superior Mexican numbers and artillery prevail; the Alamo is taken on March 6. The defenders are all slain. In the attack, the Mexicans suffer some 600–1,000 casualties.

March 2, 1836

North America: Mexico: Texas War of Independence (continued). Texas declares its independence from Mexico. General Sam Houston leads the Texan military forces.

March 27, 1836

North America: Mexico: Texas War of Independence (continued). Goliad Massacre. Mexican general José Urrea moves into Texas from Matamoros. Never defeated in Texas, he makes his way north along the coast to allow the Mexican Navy to land supplies. Urrea wins the Battle of Agua Dulce on March 2, 1836.

Urrea's flying column then catches Texas Colonel James Fannin, who had been slow to move from Goliad, and about 300 of his men on the open prairie at a slight depression near Coleto Creek on March 19. Although the Texans repulse several Mexican charges, they are desperately short of food and water. When Urrea brings up reinforcements and artillery, Fannin surrenders the next day.

About 342 of the Texan troops captured during the entirety of the Goliad Campaign are executed a week later on March 27, 1836, over Urrea's protest and under the direct orders of Mexican president General Antonio López de Santa Anna Pérez de Lebrón. This event is known as the Goliad Massacre.

April 21, 1836

North America: Mexico: Texas War of Independence (continued): Battle of San Jacinto. Texas general Sam Houston, with a force of some 900 men, surprises and routs a Mexican army of 1,400 men commanded by President of Mexico General Antonio López de Santa Anna Pérez de Lebrón. The Texans lose only 9 killed or mortally wounded; 30 receive lesser wounds including Houston, who has an ankle shattered. The Mexicans suffer 630 killed and 730 taken prisoner; Santa Anna is among those captured. While in captivity, he recognizes the independence of Texas. Although this action is repudiated by the Mexican government, Texas independence is a recognized fact. On July 4, 1836, the U.S. government recognizes Texas, with Houston now its president. This step greatly angers Mexicans.

July 6, 1836
North Africa: Algeria. French forces under General Thomas Robert Bugeaud defeat Algerian forces under Emir Abd el Kader (Abd al-Qadir, Abdelkader).

November 11, 1836
South America: Beginning of the War of the Peruvian-Bolivian Confederation. In 1835 Bolivian dictator Andreas Santa Cruz and Peruvian president Luis Orbegosa establish a confederation of their two countries. Chile and Argentina oppose this, and Chile declares war on November 11, 1836. Chilean forces are defeated in their first invasion of Bolivia but then decisively defeat the Bolivian army in the Battle of Yungay, January 20, 1839, breaking up the confederation.

1836–1837
North America: United States: Second Seminole War (continued). In the early fighting the U.S. army suffers from lack of supplies; a high rate of illness forces the abandonment of some forts. However, Seminole leader Osceola becomes ill with malaria, and the Seminoles fragment into disparate bands.

In January 1836 Major General Winfield Scott takes command of U.S. troops in Florida. He has little success, however, and his efforts that spring to draw the Seminoles into conventional battle end in failure, which leads to a court of inquiry. He is cleared, however.

In May, Florida governor Richard Call, also a militia brigadier general, takes charge in the field. He accomplishes little and in December turns over command to U.S. Army brigadier general Thomas S. Jesup. Fighting continues in the form of numerous small engagements, sieges, and ambushes.

On March 6, 1837, in the Treaty of Fort Dade, a number of Seminoles and their allies agree to assemble at Fort Brooke for relocation west of the Mississippi. Jesup proves the most successful U.S. commander of the war. On October 27, 1837, he captures Osceola but under a flag of truce.

1836–1838
Central Asia: War between Persia and Afghanistan. On the prompting of Russia, which is alarmed by British gains in South Asia, Persian ruler Mohammed Shah invades Afghanistan. The Persians march through Khorasan (Khurasan) into Herat Province. The Persian advance is delayed, however, by the need to come to terms with the Turkoman tribes to the north.

When the Persians finally do invest the city of Herat, Captain Eldred Potter of the East India Company's Bombay Army effectively organizes its defense. The initial Persian assault is defeated, and the attackers then settle in for a siege. Under heavy British pressure, they raise it 10 months later, on September 28, 1838, and begin their withdrawal from Afghanistan.

June 1, 1837
North Africa: French conquest of Algeria (continued): Treaty of Tafna. On June 1, 1837, Algerian nationalist leader Abd el Kader (Abd al-Qadir, Abdelkader) concludes with French general Thomas Robert Bugeaud the Treaty of Tafna. Abd el Kader recognizes French sovereignty in Oran and Algiers while he officially controls perhaps two-thirds of the country (chiefly the interior). Although justified by the military situation on the ground, the treaty is poorly received in France, where there is a firestorm of opposition to it. Bugeaud is accused of having compromised the dignity of France. The new wellspring of support for a strong military showing in Algeria leads the French government to send the troop reinforcements it had previously denied its commanders and to make a major military effort in the eastern part of the country, at Constantine.

See Leaders: Bugeaud de la Piconnerie, Thomas-Robert

October 13, 1837
North Africa: French conquest of Algeria (continued): French storming of Constantine. The French

decide on a major effort against the city of Constantine in eastern Algeria, about 50 miles inland from the Mediterranean. The city had previously rebuffed a French assault.

On October 1 General C. M. D. Damremont leads 20,000 troops and 60 guns toward the city, which is held by about 7,500 defenders. Damremont arrives on October 6; he immediately begins siege operations and subjects the city to heavy bombardment. On October 12, however, Damremont is struck in the chest and killed by a cannonball. The next day Damremont's successor, General Sylvain-Charles, Comte Valée, orders a simultaneous assault by three separate divisions. After hard fighting, the city falls to the French. Valée is rewarded with a marshal's baton and is appointed governor-general, serving until 1840.

November 1837

North America: Canada: Papineau's Rebellion. French Canadian leader Louis Joseph Papineau, believing that British officials are ignoring the interests of French Canadian citizens, leads a brief rebellion against the Crown in Lower Canada (present-day Québec Province). British forces easily suppress the rebels in a clash at St. Denis on November 22. Papineau flees abroad.

December 2, 1837

North America: Canada: Mackenzie's Rebellion. Seeking to establish a republican form of government in Canada, on December 2 William Lyon Mackenzie and a number of followers mount an abortive rebellion in Toronto, Upper Canada (now Ontario). British troops easily crush the revolt, and Mackenzie flees.

December 25, 1837

North America: United States: Second Seminole War (continued): Battle of Okeechobee. On December 25, 1837, U.S. Army colonel Zachary Taylor and 1,000 men (mostly regulars but some volunteers and Native American allies) engage some 400 Seminoles led by Wildcat, Sam Jones, and Alligator in a pitched battle on the shores of Lake Okeechobee. In this largest battle of the Second Seminole War, Taylor sends his men forward in two lines, the volunteers leading. The volunteers break and run, but the regulars hold firm, scattering the Seminoles in a bayonet charge.

The battle, while celebrated as a U.S. victory, is inconclusive. The Seminoles and their African American allies merely withdraw into the swamps. Taylor

In November 1837 French Canadian leader Louis Joseph Papineau led a rebellion against Britain in an effort to secure independence for Canada. (T.C. Doane/Library and Archives Canada)

loses as many as 26 killed and 112 wounded against Seminole losses of only 11 dead and 15 wounded. Costly guerrilla warfare continues.

December 29, 1837

North America: United States: *Caroline* Incident. William Lyon Mackenzie, fleeing after a failed attempt at rebellion to establish a republic in Canada, takes refuge on Navy Island, on the Canadian side of the Niagara River. American supporters furnish money, arms, and supplies via the steamboat *Caroline*. On December 29 Canadian loyalist Colonel Sir Allan MacNab and Royal Navy captain Andrew Drew lead a party of militia across the boundary into the United States and seize the *Caroline*. Setting the ship on fire, they cast it adrift to go over Niagara Falls. One American is killed. This leads to the dispatch of troops to the border, but Major General Winfield Scott's astute diplomacy defuses the crisis.

1837

East Africa: Present-day Kenya: Muscat secures Mombasa. A succession crisis in Mombasa allows the ruler of Muscat, Sayyid Said, to take the city and install a Muscati garrison there.

1837–1860

Southeast Asia: Operations against pirates. During these years, the Dutch, British, and Spanish all mount operations against pirates operating principally in Indonesian waters. Occasionally the three colonial powers cooperate.

February 12, 1838

North America: Aroostook War. The Aroostook War (also spelled Aroostock and known as the Pork and Beans War, the Coon-Canuck War, the Lumberjacks' War, and the Northeastern Boundary Dispute) between the United States and Canada is an armed confrontation between Americans and Canadians over lumbering along the disputed international border between New Brunswick and Maine. Some three dozen people die in the dispute, but once again, astute diplomacy by U.S. major general Winfield Scott averts wider trouble. The conflict results in an international agreement over the border in the 1842 Webster-Ashburton Treaty.

February 1838

Southern Africa: Fighting between the Boers and the Zulu in Natal. Prompted by the British abolition of slavery in their colonies, some 10,000 Boers move north to escape British rule. During this so-called Great Trek of 1835–1837, a number of Boers, led by Piet Retief, move into Natal. In February 1838 a number of Boer negotiators, again led by Retief, are massacred at Durban by Zulu forces led by Dingane.

At the same time, the Zulu attack several thousand Trekkers who have just crossed the Drakensburg Mountains, inflicting several hundred casualties.

April 16, 1838

North America: Mexico: Pastry War. To secure payment of 600,000 francs that French citizens residing in Mexico claim they are owed, the French send a naval expedition to Mexico. The French warships blockade Mexico City's principal port of Veracruz on April 16, 1838, shutting off sizable customs revenues to the Mexican government. This action leads to the so-called Pastry War.

July 19, 1838

Central Asia: Afghanistan: Tripartite Treaty. Anxious to prevent further Russian and Persian inroads into Afghanistan, the British East India Company reaches an agreement with ruler of the Punjab Ranjit Singh and with Shah Shuja, former ruler of Afghanistan, to restore the latter to the throne. This brings the First Afghan War (1839–1842).

December 1, 1838

North America: Mexico: Pastry War. With negotiations to end the French naval blockade of Veracruz at an impasse, on November 27, 1838, the French open a bombardment of the port city. This soon forces the surrender of the fortress of San Juan de Ulúa as well as the city of Veracruz. Mexico declares war on France on December 1, 1838, and orders the expulsion of all French citizens from Mexican territory.

Because among the claims mentioned as justification for the French action is one by a French pastry chef in Mexico City, the Mexicans derisively refer to this conflict as the Pastry War. The French continue the blockade for 11 months. After the claims are settled, they withdraw on March 9, 1839.

December 16, 1838

Southern Africa: Battle of the Blood River. On December 16, 1838, a major battle occurs near the Ncome (Buffalo) River between a Boer force led by Andries Pretorius and Zulu warriors, led by Dingane's generals Dambuza (Nzobo) and Ndlela kaSompisi. The Boers score a lopsided victory, reportedly sustaining only 3 wounded, while the Zulus suffer more than 3,000 casualties. Supposedly the Ncome River ran red with the blood of the slain, hence the name Battle of the Blood River.

1838

Southeast Asia: Burma. A Mon rebellion is crushed by King Tharawaddy.

1838–1843

North America: United States: Second Seminole War (continued). In March 1838 U.S. Army brigadier general Thomas S. Jesup reverses policy and promises fugitive blacks allied with the Seminoles that they will be given freedom if they join the army and fight against their former allies. Some 400 do so. During the 18 months that Jesup is in command, more than 2,000 Seminoles are captured and another 300 are killed.

In May 1838 Brigadier General Zachary Taylor takes command. Taylor wants to use classic pacification methods, dividing the disaffected area into districts 20 miles square, each with its own stockade and garrison that would comb the district on alternate days. With the War Department unwilling to provide the resources to make it work and the Seminole raids resuming, Taylor asks to be relieved of his command.

In April 1839 Major General Alexander Macomb replaces Taylor. Although Macomb burns a number of Seminole villages, the Native American attacks continue. Brigadier General Walker Keith Armistead is the next commander; he is also largely unsuccessful in efforts to bring the war to an end.

In August 1841 Colonel William J. Worth assumes command. He introduces aggressive tactics that include the destruction of Seminole crops. In July 1842 negotiations finally lead to an agreement that allows the approximately 600 remaining Seminoles to stay in far southern Florida.

January 19, 1839
East Africa: Present-day Yemen: British acquisition of Aden. On January 19, 1839, the British East India Company lands Royal Marines to take control of the port of Aden. This is part of the wider British policy of securing ports along the route to India. Aden, ruled as a part of British India and known as the Aden Settlement until 1937, remains under British control to 1967.

January 20, 1839
South America: War of the Peruvian-Bolivian Confederation (continued): Battle of Yungay. The war, which began in November 1835, drags on for several years without conclusive result. Finally, on January 20, 1839, in the Battle of Yungay, an invading Chilean army of some 5,400 men under Manuel Bulnes attacks and defeats a 6,000-man Peruvian-Bolivian Confederation army led by Andrés de Santa Cruz. The Chilean forces go on to occupy Lima in April, and the Confederation comes to an end.

April 19, 1839
Western Europe: Belgium: Treaty of London. The Great Powers and the United Kingdom of the Netherlands sign the Treaty of London, also known as the Convention of 1839. The major powers recognize and guarantee the independence and neutrality of Belgium and confirm the independence of Luxembourg. Article VII requires Belgium to remain neu-

tral in perpetuity and by implication commits the signatory powers to protect that neutrality in the event of invasion.

April 1839
Southwest Asia: Second Ottoman-Egyptian War. Having rebuilt its army with Prussian military advisers, in April 1839 Ottoman forces under Hafiz Pasha invade Syria, beginning the Second Ottoman-Egyptian War (1839–1841).

June 24, 1839
Southwest Asia: Second Ottoman-Egyptian War (continued): Battle of Nezib. Largely as a consequence of ignoring the advice of his Prussian advisers, led by Helmuth von Moltke, invading Ottoman forces under Hafiz Pasha are completely defeated by Egyptian forces under Ibrahim Ali in the Battle of Nezib of June 24, 1839.

July 1, 1839
North Africa: Second Ottoman-Egyptian War (continued): Surrender of the Ottoman fleet. After sailing to Alexandria, the Ottoman fleet surrenders to the Egyptians, probably through the treachery of its commander.

July 1, 1839
Southwest Asia: Ottoman Empire. Sultan Mahmud II dies and is succeeded by Abdul Mejid, who is amenable to concessions to Egypt.

August 23, 1839
East Asia: China: First Opium War: Beginning of the war and the British seizure of Hong Kong. The First Opium War (1839–1842), also known as the First Anglo-Chinese War, is caused by trade disagreements between Qing officials and British merchants trading in Canton, the only port allowed to foreign merchants by the Qing dynasty. The British import from China vast quantities of tea, as well as silk goods and fine porcelain. The British have little that the Chinese want in return except silver, which the British are forced to acquire elsewhere at considerable expense.

In an effort to offset the adverse trade balance with China and the outflow of silver, the British embark on the widespread smuggling of opium into China. Opium is produced in India under special government monopoly on the condition that it be sold in China. The trade is illegal under Chinese law and

British warships bombard Canton in May 1841 during the First Opium War (1839–1842), caused by British determination to sell opium in China despite the Chinese government's ban on it. (Hulton Archive/Getty Images)

carried out in defiance of efforts by Qing dynasty officials to end it. This and defiance of Chinese law brings war.

Lin Zexu heads the Qing government's attempt to end the opium trade. He eventually forces British chief superintendent of trade in China Charles Elliot to hand over to Chinese authorities some 20,000 chests of opium, each containing about 120 pounds of the drug.

In July 1839 rioting British sailors destroy a temple near Kowloon and murder a man who tries to stop them. British authorities reject a Qing demand to hand the men over for trial. The British subsequently try six of the men themselves in Canton but immediately release them on their return to Britain.

Meanwhile, in an effort to end the opium trade, Qing authorities insist that all merchants sign a bond agreeing to obey Chinese law and place themselves under its jurisdiction. They must also promise, on pain of death, not to smuggle opium. Elliot then orders the British community to withdraw from Canton and prohibits trade with the Chinese. But some merchants who do not deal in opium are willing to sign the bond and remain.

With war between Britain and the Chinese central government looming, on August 23, 1839, the British seize the trading outpost of Hong Kong as a base for military operations. Fighting begins on November 3, 1839. On January 14, 1840, the Qing emperor asks all foreigners in China to end assistance to the British in China.

October 15, 1839–1840

North Africa: French conquest of Algeria (continued): Renewal of fighting and return of Bugeaud. Claiming that the French have broken the 1837

Treaty of Tfana, Emir Abd el Kader (Abd al-Qadir, Abdelkader) again takes the field. He declares jihad on October 15, 1839.

In December 1840 French general Thomas Robert Bugeaud returns to Algeria as its first governor-general. The government of King Louis Philippe, enjoying widespread popular support in France for its imperialist venture in Algeria, supplies Bugeaud with troop reinforcements, which will ultimately bring French strength in Algeria to some 160,000 men.

Bugeaud, the first major French African colonial administrator, proves an able organizer as well as an effective military commander. He establishes native military units and new tactical formations, including highly mobile flying columns operating from fixed bases spread across Algeria. His new formations of zouaves, spahis, chasseurs d'Afrique, and the French Foreign Legion excite widespread interest and enthusiasm worldwide. In 1843 Bugeaud is rewarded for his accomplishments in Algeria with advancement to marshal of France.

1839

Central Asia: First Anglo-Afghan War: Opening campaign. Prior to the First Anglo-Afghan War (1839–1842), the British intervene in Afghanistan to restore Shah Shuja to the throne in accordance with the Tripartite Treaty. They hope thereby to prevent further Persian and Russian encroachments. Governor-general in India George Eden, 1st Earl of Auckland, spells out the British position in the October 1838 Simla Manifesto, which states that Britain must have a trustworthy ally on India's western frontier to ensure the safety of British India. He pledges to support Shah Shuja in recovering his throne and states that when this is accomplished, British troops will be withdrawn. The British maintain, for public relations purposes, that General Sir John Keane's 21,000-man Army of the Indus is merely supporting Shah Shuja's small army in retaking his throne. It is clear from the onset, however, that Shah Shuja is entirely dependent on the presence of British troops.

British and Indian forces invade Afghanistan from the Punjab in December 1838. With them is William Hay Macnaghten, new chief British representative to Afghanistan. The British reach Quetta in late March 1839, occupy Kandahar in April without a fight, storm the fortress of Ghazni on July 21, and capture Kabul on August 7. Dost Mohammad flees, and Shuja replaces him as ruler after an absence of almost 30 years.

Although some British troops quit Afghanistan, it is soon clear that Shuja will continue in power only as long as the British remain. The Afghans resent the fact that the British allow the families of the occupying troops to join them in Afghanistan, indicating that the British have no intention of withdrawing any time soon.

After unsuccessfully attacking the British forces, Dost Mohammad surrenders to them. He is exiled to India in late 1840.

1839–1847

Central Asia: Russia invades and conquers Khiva. In 1839 Russian general Basil A. Perovsky invades the Khanate of Khiva (parts of present-day Kazakhstan, Uzbekistan, and Turkmenistan). He is defeated and withdraws. The Russians then adopt a gradualist approach, first establishing a fort on the northeastern edge of the Aral Sea at the mouth of the Jaxartes (Syr-darya) River in 1847. The Russians gradually push toward Tashkent.

January 30, 1840

Southern Africa: Battle of Magango. Mpande, the brother of Zulu leader Dingane, rebels and allies himself with the Boers. In the Battle of Magango on January 30, 1840, Mpande's general Nongalaza defeats the royal Zulu army. Dingane flees to Swaziland. Mpande succeeds Dingane and grants the Boers possession of all of southern Natal. The Boers then establish there the short-lived Voortrekker Republic (1838–1843).

July 15, 1840

Southwest Asia: Second Ottoman-Egyptian War (continued): Treaty of London. Fearing that after the Battle of Nezib the Ottoman Empire will collapse, Britain, Austria, Prussia, and Russia agree to force a settlement on Egyptian ruler Muhammad Ali, pledging to support Sultan Abdul Mejid should it prove necessary. The powers offer Muhammad Ali Egypt as a hereditary possession and southern Syria for his lifetime, but he is to give up Crete, northern Syria, Mecca, and Medina and return the Ottoman fleet.

Muhammad Ali, trusting in the support of France, rejects these terms, whereupon the British induce

Sultan Abdul Mejid to depose Muhammad Ali. There is a strong reaction in Paris and even talk of war with Britain. The resignation of bellicose French premier Adolphe Thiers on October 20, however, signals King Louis Philippe's opposition to war with Britain, and the crisis passes.

July–September 1840

Southwest Asia: Second Ottoman-Egyptian War (continued): Uprising in Lebanon. In early summer, Maronite Christians in Lebanon revolt against Egyptian rule. Muhammad Ali dispatches Ibrahim Pasha with 15,000 troops to burn their coastal towns and villages. By July 1, 1840, British commodore Charles John Napier is patrolling with a naval squadron off the coast. In August he appears off Beirut and calls upon Egyptian governor Suleiman Pasha to quit Syria. There is, however, little that Napier can do until September, when he is reinforced.

September–November 1840

Southwest Asia: Second Ottoman-Egyptian War (continued): British military intervention. The rejection by Egyptian ruler Muhammad Ali of the terms of the Treaty of London and his military operations in Lebanon induce the British and Austrians to commence operations against Egypt. British commodore Charles John Napier is joined by an allied fleet under British admiral Sir Robert Stopford. While most of the ships are British, there are also some Ottoman and Austrian warships. Open warfare begins on September 11.

October 10, 1840

Southwest Asia: Second Ottoman-Egyptian War (continued): Battle of Nahr-el-Kelb. Due to the illness of British Army brigadier general Sir Charles Smith, British admiral Sir Robert Stopford orders Commodore Charles John Napier to lead the land force. The allies send 1,500 British marines and Ottoman troops ashore at Junieh. Stopford bombards Beirut, killing many civilians. Napier meanwhile leads a land assault on the Egyptian base of Sidon in southern Lebanon, taking it on September 28.

The Egyptians quit Beirut on October 3, and the allies occupy it a week later. Napier then plans to attack the Egyptians at Nahr-el-Kelb. With Smith recovered, Stopford orders Napier to withdraw and turn command of the land force over to him. Aware that this will cause the allies to lose the tactical initiative, Napier disobeys the order and continues the attack.

In the ensuing Battle of Nahr-el-Kelb (also known as the Battle of Kelbson) of October 10, the British and Ottomans win a hard-fought victory over Ibrahim Ali. It is one of history's few land battles commanded by a naval officer. The allies promptly cut the sea communications of Ibrahim Ali with Egypt.

November 3, 1840

Southwest Asia: Second Ottoman-Egyptian War (continued): Allied shelling and occupation of Acre. By the end of October, Acre (Akko) is the only coastal position remaining in Egyptian hands. On November 3 British Mediterranean Fleet commander Admiral Sir Robert Stopford moves his own and allied Ottoman and Austrian ships into position to bombard the city. The ships fire a total of 48,000 shot and shell into Acre; 1 shell explodes the main magazine in the southern part of Acre, killing 1,100 people. That same night the allies occupy Acre. British losses in the entire operation amount to 18 killed and 41 wounded.

November 27, 1840

North Africa: Egypt: Second Ottoman-Egyptian War (continued): Alexandria Convention. With the defeat of Egyptian forces under Ibrahim Ali in Lebanon, British Mediterranean Fleet commander Admiral Sir Robert Stopford is worried about the possibility of a complete collapse of Muhammad Ali in Egypt and ensuing chaos. Stopford dispatches Commodore Charles John Napier to command the British squadron at Alexandria and monitor the situation.

Again exceeding his instructions, Napier arrives at Alexandria on November 25 and enforces a naval blockade. On November 27 and again on his own authority, Napier negotiates peace with Muhammad Ali.

In the Alexandria Convention, Napier guarantees Muhammad Ali hereditary sovereignty of Egypt. Muhammad Ali is forced to renounce all claims to Crete and Syria, acknowledge the suzerainty of the Ottoman sultan, and return the Ottoman fleet. In return, Napier pledges to evacuate Ibrahim's forces back to Alexandria. Although Stopford repudiates the arrangement when he learns of it, the convention closely resembles the Treaty of London of July, and the British government promptly approves it. Ibrahim's forces evacuate Syria and return to Egypt in February 1841.

1840–1843
Southern Europe: Iberian Peninsula: Spain: Civil war. General Baldomero Espartero seizes power in Spain, driving out both Maria Cristina and Queen Isabella. Although he suppresses revolts in both October 1841 and November–December 1842, a third revolt in July–August 1843, led by General Ramón Narváez, is successful. Espartero flees Spain, and Isabella resumes her reign under the influence of Narváez.

February 26, 1841
East Asia: China: First Opium War (continued): British capture of the Bogue Forts. Seeking to force the Qing dynasty government to terms, the British government and the British East India Company agree on an expedition against Canton. In June 1840 an expeditionary force departs Singapore under Captain Sir James John Gordon Bremer. It consists of 1 ship of the line, 5 smaller warships, 2 Indian steam warships, and 26 transports and storeships lifting about 3,600 troops. Other British warships subsequently join.

Bremer first attacks and seizes Chusan Island. The British then blockade the Ningbo (Ningpo) and Pearl (Canton) rivers. British emissary Captain Charles Elliot demands compensation for losses suffered by the British from interrupted trade. The Qing government refuses, and on February 26, 1841, the British attack and seize the Bogue Forts defending the entrance to the Pearl River, the waterway between Hong Kong and Canton.

May 24, 1841
East Asia: China: First Opium War (continued). A successful British amphibious assault leads to their capture of Canton.

July 13, 1841
Southwest Asia: Straits Convention. The Great Powers, including France (marking its return to the concert of major European powers), reach agreement that both the Bosporus and Dardanelles will be closed to all non-Ottoman warships in time of peace.

August–December 1841
East Asia: China: First Opium War (continued): British operations along the Chinese coast. Following the British capture of Canton, there is a lull in the fighting. During August–December 1841, however, the British carry out a number of amphibious operations along the China coast. They take Xiamen (Amoy) on August 26 and Ningbo (Ningpo) on October 13.

November 18, 1841
South America: Peruvian invasion of Bolivia: Battle of Ingavi. In an effort to annex part of Bolivia, Peruvian president Augustín Gamarra invades that country on September 24, 1841. Though commanding 5,400 men, he is utterly defeated by a Bolivian army of 4,100 under President José Ballivián in the Battle of Ingavi on November 18, 1841. Some 3,400 Peruvians are taken prisoner. Combined killed or wounded on the two sides amount to some 1,500 men. Gamarra is among the Peruvian dead, the first Latin American 19th-century head of state to die on the battlefield.

To pressure the Peruvians to make peace, Bolivian forces then invade that country. Peru agrees to peace on June 7, 1842.

November 1841
Central Asia: Afghanistan: First Anglo-Afghan War (continued): Uprising against the British in Kabul. By late 1841 disaffected Afghans join former shah Dost Mohammad's son, Mohammad Akbar Khan, in Bamian. In November 1841 rioting occurs in Kabul, and a senior British officer is killed. Substantial remaining British forces stationed just outside the city remain inert as British envoy Sir William Macnaghten attempts to negotiate with Mohammad Akbar.

In a secret meeting, Macnaghten offers to install Akbar as Afghanistan's vizier in exchange for allowing the British to remain in the country. Akbar, however, orders Macnaghten arrested; on his way to prison, an angry mob kills him. The crowd parades his dismembered corpse through Kabul.

1841–1845
Southeast Asia: Siamese-Vietnamese War. The Vietnamese, having driven the Siamese from Cambodia in 1834, remain there themselves. In 1841 the Cambodians revolt against the Vietnamese and this time invite Siamese assistance.

In the ensuing 1841–1845 war, the Siamese maintain a slight advantage. In 1845 the two powers agree to establish joint rule over Cambodia, with Siam predominant.

January 1, 1842

Central Asia: Afghanistan: First Anglo-Afghan War (continued): British capitulation in Kabul. Elderly and unwell, British commander in Afghanistan Major General William Elphinstone proves ineffective as a leader. On January 1, 1842, he reaches agreement with the Afghans that provides for the safe exodus of the British garrison and its dependents from the country.

January 13, 1842

Central Asia: Afghanistan: First Anglo-Afghan War (continued): Gandamak Massacre. In accordance with the agreement reached with the Afghans, on January 6, 1842, British commander Major General William Elphinstone leads the British garrison and its dependents from Kabul to return to India. There are about 4,500 military personnel (one British battalion and the remainder Indian units) and more than 10,000 civilian dependents.

Five days later Elphinstone's demoralized force is surprised and attacked by Ghilzai warriors in the snow along a 30-mile stretch of the Khyber Pass road near Gandamak. Almost all of the British combatants are massacred. Very few are taken prisoner, and of these only a handful survive captivity. Supposedly only one Briton escapes to Jalalabad.

The Gandamak Massacre helps establish Afghanistan's reputation as a graveyard for foreign armies. With the British gone, Shah Shuja survives only a few months. He is assassinated in April 1842.

April–September 1842

Central Asia: Afghanistan: First Anglo-Afghan War (continued): British invasion of Afghanistan. The Gandamak Massacre enrages the British and prompts a swift and brutal reaction. In February 1842 Major General Sir George Pollock assumes command of British forces in Peshawar, restoring their morale. At the head of a punitive force, Pollock forces his way through the Khyber Pass to Jalalabad, defeating an Afghan force of 10,000 men for the loss of only 135 men and relieving Jalalabad on April 16.

Both Pollock and Major General Sir William Nott, who has advanced from India to Kandahar through Quetta, then take advantage of poorly written orders to advance on Kabul. Pollock reaches Kabul on September 15 after fighting the Battles of Jugdulluck Pass and Tezeen. Nott arrives on September 17 after fighting the Battle of Ghuzmee. At Kabul, British forces release 95 British prisoners. Afghan leader Dost Mohammad flees toward Turkestan with other prisoners.

A small British force catches up with Dost Mohammad and secures the release of the remaining captives. The East India Company decides that it is unsafe to keep British forces in Afghanistan, however, and orders Pollock and Nott to withdraw to India. They comply in October after destroying both the citadel and the grand bazaar of Kabul. Although the British have to fight their way through the Khyber Pass again, the withdrawal is trumpeted as another great British victory.

Dost Mohammad nevertheless resumes the Afghan throne, ruling from 1842 to 1863. The loss of life and property increases the bitter Afghan resentment of foreign influence. The Russians, moreover, advance steadily southward toward Afghanistan, setting up the British invasion of 1878 and the Second Anglo-Afghan War.

June 19, 1842

East Asia: China: First Opium War (continued). Recommencing military operations in the spring of 1842, British forces capture Shanghai on June 19, then move up the Changjiang (Yangtze, Yangxi) River to take Zhenjiang (Chenkiang) on July 21. This success threatens Nanjing (Nanking), and the Qing government sues for peace.

August 29, 1842

East Asia: China: First Opium War (continued): Treaty of Nanjing. Under the unequal Treaty of Nanjing (Treaty of Nanking) that ends the war, the Qing government cedes Hong Kong Island to the British; agrees to fixed tariffs on British goods; opens the ports of Canton, Xiamen, Fuzhou, Shanghai, and Ningbo (Ningpo) to British merchants; and agrees to pay a heavy indemnity of $20 million for seized British opium and war costs.

In the separate Treaty of the Bogue (October 1843), the Qing Empire extends to Britain most-favored nation status and agrees that British subjects are to enjoy extraterritorial privileges in the treaty ports. In 1844 the Qing conclude similar treaties with the United States and France.

The First Opium War is a terrible blow to the Qing dynasty. The ease with which the British and their modern weapons defeat the far more numerous Chinese forces sharply undermines the government's authority and contributes substantially to the great Taiping Rebellion (1850–1864).

October 20, 1842

North America: California: U.S. seizure of Monterey. Commander of the U.S. Pacific Squadron Commodore Thomas ap Catesby Jones, reading in the newspapers of a strong note by the Mexican government to President John Tyler and assuming that war between the United States and Mexico is inevitable, arrives off Monterey, California, on October 19, 1842. He forces the Mexican governor to surrender the city the next day. On October 21 Jones learns from other papers that war has not been declared. He returns Monterey to Mexican control and departs. The affair leads to considerable acrimony in U.S.-Mexican relations.

1842–1843

West Africa: Ivory Coast. French forces occupy the ports of the Ivory Coast.

1842–1843

Southern Africa: British-Boer war over Natal. Conflict erupts between the Boers and the British, with the British repulsing a Boer attack on Durban. In 1843 British forces invade and occupy Natal, bringing to an end the short-lived Voortrekker Republic (1838–1843).

February 15, 1843

South Asia: India: Conquest of Sindh: Baluchi attack on Hyderabad. Angered by humiliating terms imposed by the British after the First Afghan War (1839–1843) and their threats, some 8,000 Baluchis attack the British residence of Hyderabad. The residency is held by a small number of British troops commanded by the young and able Major James Outram. Major General Sir Charles James Napier, commander of the British forces within the Bombay Presidency, immediately sets out to relieve Hyderabad.

February 16, 1843

South America: Argentine-Uruguay War. The Argentine-Uruguay War (1843–1852), known in

Uruguay as the Great War, is a confusing struggle that involves strife within both Uruguay and Argentina and intervention by France, Britain, and Brazil. The war begins when Argentine dictator Juan Manuel de Rosas attempts to annex Uruguay, supporting Manuel Oribe against elected president José Fructuoso Rivera.

The war centers on a prolonged and largely ineffective siege by Oribe of Fructuoso Rivera in Montevideo. The siege begins on February 16, 1843, and continues for nine years, until February 1852. During the war there are two Uruguayan governments: the Colorados at Montevideo and the Blancos at Cerrito, near Montevideo. The Colorados, supported by the British and French, are liberal federalists and are centered on Montevideo; the conservative, predominantly Catholic, and nationalist Blancos control much of the rest of Uruguay, with the assistance of Rosas.

In an effort to maintain free trade, both Britain and France intervene with naval forces. They blockade Buenos Aires in December 1845 and also protect access to Montevideo from the sea. Their efforts are largely ineffective, however, and in 1850 both Britain and France withdraw. It appears that Montevideo's fate is sealed, but an uprising in Argentina led by Justo José de Urquiza against Rosas changes the situation completely. Brazil meanwhile, fearing that Argentina will annex Uruguay, intervenes in May 1851, providing Urquiza and the Colorados with both money and naval forces. In the Battle of Monte Caseros (February 3, 1852), Urquiza defeats Rosas and drives him from power. This brings the siege of Montevideo and the war to an end.

Uruguayan leaders, grateful for Brazil's support, sign a series of treaties in 1851 that include a perpetual alliance between the two countries, the right of Brazil to intervene in Uruguayan internal affairs, and the cession of some Uruguayan territory.

February 17, 1843

South Asia: India: Conquest of Sindh (continued): Battle of Miani. Major General Sir Charles James Napier, commander of the British forces within the Bombay Presidency, marches to relieve the Baluchi siege of the British residency of Hyderabad. Initially securing military control of the region by forcing an agreement with the Sindh emirs, his forces attack the fortress at Imamgarh. Shortly thereafter a popular revolt breaks out. Musket in hand but leading only 2,800 men, Napier attacks and defeats some 30,000 Baluchis in the decisive Battle of Miani (also known to the British as the Battle of Meeanee) on February 17, 1843. The British suffer 256 casualties; the Baluchis lose 5,000–6,000. Miani is the decisive victory that leads to the British annexation of Sindh. Napier goes on to take Hyderabad.

March–August 1843

South Asia: India: Conquest of Sindh (continued): Napier's campaign. While he never commands more than 5,000 men, during March–May, 1843, British major general Sir Charles James Napier marches some 600 miles in Sindh and in a series of actions defeats opposing forces totaling more than 60,000 men. During June to August his men march a further 250 miles and disperse at least 12,000 enemy troops. In all his forces inflict some 12,000 casualties. Napier is said to have sent back to headquarters the short famous pun message of "Peccavi" (Latin for "I have sinned").

Napier's conquest of Sindh (excluding the state of Khairpur) secures both the western frontier of India and the Indus River. Napier also begins construction on the new port of Karachi. That city then replaces Hyderabad as the capital of Sindh.

May 16, 1843

North Africa: French conquest of Algeria (continued): Battle of Smala. Henri d'Orléans, Duc d'Aumal (and son of King Louis Philippe), is leading a 500-man flying column on a routine reconnaissance when they discover an Algerian rebel encampment of up to 30,000 men, women, and children under Abd el Kader (Abd al-Qadir, Abdelkader). The French immediately attack and disperse the camp, taking 3,000 prisoners and considerable stores. Abd el Kader takes refuge in Morocco.

During the next year, the French reduce Moroccan support for the Algerian rebels by raiding across the border and shelling Tangier and Mogadir.

September 14, 1843

Southern Europe: Greece: Revolt. A revolt forces King Otto I to grant constitutional government.

February 27, 1844

Caribbean Basin: Santo Domingo: Revolt against Haitian rule and proclamation of the Dominican Republic. On February 27, 1844, thereafter recognized as Dominican Independence Day, rebels seize the Ozama fortress in the capital of Santo Domingo. The Haitian garrison is taken by surprise and flees. Within two days, all Haitian officials have left Santo Domingo. A junta takes control of and declares the Dominican Republic independent.

February 28, 1844

North America: United States: Peacemaker explosion. The revolutionary U.S. steam sloop *Princeton* is the first screw propeller warship in any navy. Commanded by Captain Robert F. Stockton, it mounts two 12-inch wrought-iron guns: the Oregon (designed by John Ericsson and manufactured in England) and the Peacemaker (ordered by Stockton and built in the United States). During a demonstration cruise down the Potomac, Stockton orders the Peacemaker fired. The gun blows up, killing Secretary of the Navy Thomas W. Gilmer, Secretary of State Abel P. Upshur, and six others. President John Tyler, who is below at the time of the incident, is uninjured.

The explosion creates renewed interest in manufacturing techniques for heavy ordnance. It also brings a restriction on powder charges, which remains in effect into the American Civil War and probably affects the outcome of the battle between USS *Monitor* and CSS *Virginia* (*Merrimac*).

August 14, 1844

North Africa: Morocco: French conquest of Algeria (continued): Battle of Isly. Sultan of Morocco Abd al-Rahunan is providing substantial assistance to Algerian insurgents under Emir Abd el Kader (Abd al-Qadir, Abdelkader) who continue to resist the French conquest of Algeria. In retaliation, French warships shell Tangier on August 6, 1844. Meanwhile, the French governor-general in Algeria, Marshal Thomas Robert Bugeaud, assembles a force of 11,000 men. During the night of August 12–13, 1844, he moves against a large Moroccan force of up to 45,000 men (20,000–25,000 cavalry) under Abd al-Rahunan assembled along the Isly River on the Moroccan-Algerian border. The Battle of Isly occurs the next day, August 14, not far from Oujda.

Bugeaud forms his infantry into a large lozenge-shaped formation composed of hollow squares with the cavalry in the center and artillery protecting its flanks. Abd al-Rahunan launches his cavalry against the French, but he in unable to penetrate the infantry formations. With the Moroccan cavalry now separated into smaller units, Bugeaud launches his own cavalry and disperses the Moroccan horsemen. He then moves against and defeats the Moroccan infantry and takes the Moroccan camp.

The Moroccans suffer some 800 dead and the loss of 18 guns as well as considerable equipment and property. Isly proves to be the decisive battle of the war, although some fighting continues thereafter.

September 10, 1844
North Africa: French conquest of Algeria (continued): Morocco: Treaty of Tangier. Following the crushing French victory in the Battle of Isly of August 14, 1844, Moroccan sultan Abd al-Rahunan agrees to recognize Algeria as a French possession. In return, the French withdraw their military forces from Morocco.

March 1, 1845
North America: United States: Annexation of Texas. Following protracted negotiations, the Republic of Texas is, at its request, formally annexed to the United States. There is considerable opposition to this among much of the population in the northern United States because Texas permits slavery. The treaty formalizing the annexation fails to win the required two-thirds majority in the U.S. Senate, however; the vote is 35–16 for approval. The annexation bill is then resubmitted as a joint resolution with the support of President-elect James Polk. Although it passes the Senate by only a narrow margin (27–25), President John Tyler signs the resolution on March 1, 1845, bringing Texas into the union.

March 11, 1845–January 11, 1846
Australasia: New Zealand: Flagstaff War. On February 6, 1840, the British and Māori tribes conclude the Treaty of Waitangi, establishing the legal basis for the British presence in New Zealand. The Māori believe that the treaty guarantees them continued possession of their land and preservation of their customs; many British hold that it opens New Zealand to white settlement. On May 21, 1840, the British government formally annexes New Zealand and establishes the capital at Auckland.

Officials of the New Zealand Company announce that the Treaty of Taitangi does not apply to them

and continue to bring in settlers. In June 1843 a dispute over landownership known as the Wairau Affray brings the deaths of 23 Englishmen and 4 Māori. In June 1844, told by American and French traders that the British flag on Flagstaff Hill at Kororareka signifies slavery for his people, Māori leader Hone Heke chops it down. In August, Governor Robert FitzRoy arrives with troops and restores calm in a conference of Māori chiefs.

The calm does not last, shattered by the steady stream of European settlers and the belief among the Māori that they will lose their lands. Hone Heke cuts down the flagpole a second time and a third time. Each time it is replaced. On March 11, 1845, the Māori attack the guard post at the new flagpole, killing the defenders and cutting down the flagpole for a fourth time. They also attack the town of Kororareka, forcing its evacuation and burning most of it.

During the ensuing Flagstaff War (also known as Hone Heke's Rebellion and the Northern War), some Māori fight on the government side. The last battle occurs on September 11, 1856, after which the Māori sue for peace. No one is arrested, and no Māori land is confiscated. British casualties are 82 killed and 164 wounded. The Māori put their own losses at 60 killed and 80 wounded.

June 15, 1845
North America: United States: Mexican-American War: U.S. troops ordered into Texas. James K. Polk campaigned for the U.S. presidency on a platform of Manifest Destiny, that it was the destiny of the United States to expand west to the Pacific and south at least as far as the Rio Grande. Mexico threatened war if the United States annexed Texas, but it had not done so. Still, relations are badly strained when Polk takes office on March 4, 1845. He further angers Mexicans by trying to buy California. When the offer is rejected, Polk baits Mexico into war over the southern border of Texas, with the real prize being California.

On June 15, 1845, after Texas has formally accepted annexation and prior to the Mexican-American War (1846–1848), Polk orders Major General Zachary Taylor and his Army of Observation from Fort Jesup, Louisiana, into Texas to occupy a point "on or near the Rio Grande" and protect the new U.S. state from possible Mexican attack. Taylor advances into

Texas on July 26 and establishes a base on the south bank of the Nueces River, near Corpus Christi. By mid-October, Taylor has under his command some 3,500 men, about half of the regular U.S. Army.

September 22–25, 1845

North Africa: French conquest of Algeria (continued): Battle of Sidi-Brahim. The battle is between a French infantry battalion and a cavalry squadron on one side and Algerian insurgents under Emir Abd el Kader (Abd al-Qadir, Abdelkader) on the other. Cornered, the French seek refuge in a mausoleum, where they are besieged during September 22–25, 1845. The French eventually run out of ammunition, and only seven French infantrymen survive.

December 11, 1845

South Asia: India: First Anglo-Sikh War. Following the death of Ranjit Singh in 1839, tensions increase both within the Punjab and between the Punjab and British India. To consolidate public support, the leaders of the Punjab embark on a war with the British. On December 11, 1845, in the First Anglo-Sikh War (1845–1846), a Sikh army of some 20,000 men crosses the Sutlej River into British India. British commander in chief in India General Sir Hugh Gough marches against the Sikhs with 11,000 men.

December 18, 1845

South Asia: India: First Anglo-Sikh War (continued): Battle of Mudki. On the evening of December 18 some 10,000 Sikhs with 22 guns led by Lal Singh attack 11,000 British under British commander in chief in India General Sir Hugh Gough, who has 42 guns. Because much of the Battle of Mudki takes place at night, it becomes known as Midnight Mudki.

Gough and the British are victorious. Sikh casualties are unknown, but the British sustain heavy casualties: 215 dead and 657 wounded. Two brigade commanders are among the dead.

December 21–22, 1845

South Asia: India: First Anglo-Sikh War (continued): Battle of Ferozeshah. British forces now advance into the Punjab. British governor-general of India Sir Henry Hardinge joins the British forces to serve as second-in-command under General Sir Hugh Gough. It is by no means clear, however, who is in charge. The British side counts 16,700 men and 69 guns. The

Sikhs, led by Lal Singh, have 15,000 men and 90 guns.

The British attack is delayed until late afternoon because of a disagreement between Hardinge and Gough. The Sikhs are well entrenched, and the ensuing battle is one of the hardest fought in the history of British India. It could have gone either way, although the British finally take the Sikh position.

Early the next morning, Tej Singh arrives with 10,000 additional Sikh troops and 40 guns. He attacks the British in a halfhearted effort. The British hold, and the Sikhs withdraw across the Sutlej River. The British suffer 694 dead and 1,721 wounded in the two encounters. Sikh losses are unknown but are presumed heavy. Highly critical of Gough's frontal attack tactics, Hardinge is preparing to remove him from command when circumstances render that step unnecessary.

January 28, 1846

South Asia: India: First Anglo-Sikh War (continued): Battle of Aliwal. A Sikh detachment under Runjodh Singh Majithia (Runjoor Singh) with 7,000 men and 20 guns crosses the Sutlej River and, on January 21, 1846, moves against the British cantonments at Ludhiana. The Sikhs burn part of the cantonments and threaten the British supply lines. British commanders Governor-General Sir Henry Hardinge and commander in chief of British forces in India General Sir Hugh Gough dispatch a division under Sir Harry Smith to remove this threat.

The two sides clash as Smith moves on Ludhiana on January 21; the Sikhs capture much of Smith's baggage train. Smith reaches Ludhiana, however, and, rested and reinforced, marches against the Sikhs with 12,000 men and 32 guns.

The Sikhs are awaiting reinforcements at Aliwal on the Sutlej River. Runjodh Singh Majithia now commands 20,000 men and 69 guns. The Sikh position close to the Sutlej, however, makes it difficult for them to maneuver and risks disaster in a defeat. Smith attacks the Sikh center at Aliwal and threatens the fords across the Sutlej. The British turn the Sikh position.

Unlike other battles, the Sikh retreat turns into a rout; the Sikhs abandon 67 of their guns and all their baggage, tents, and supplies. They also suffer 2,000 casualties. British losses are about 850 men.

February 10, 1846

South Asia: India: First Anglo-Sikh War (continued): Battle of Sobraon. British commander in chief in India General Sir Hugh Gough and governor-general in India Sir Henry Hardinge cross the Sutlej River with 20,000 men and 70 guns (half of them heavy siege guns) to advance on a Sikh army of some 30,000 men and 65 guns entrenched at a bend of the Sutlej. Unfortunately for the Sikhs, the largely incompetent Tej Singh and Lal Singh retain overall direction of the Sikh armies. The Sikh position at Sobraon is linked to the western (Punjabi) bank of the river by a single pontoon bridge; several days of heavy rains have swollen the river, making the bridge vulnerable to being swept away.

The battle opens on February 10 with a two-hour ineffective artillery duel, after which Gough sends in his infantry. The fighting is intense, but finally the British forces break through at several points on the Sikh right, with cavalry and horse artillery pushing through a breach in the line to engage the Sikh center. Tej Singh quits the battlefield early, and in the general Sikh retreat that follows the single pontoon bridge collapses. The cause—whether by deliberate sabotage orders from Tej Singh, because he orders his own artillery on the west bank to fire on it (the Sikh versions), or because it gives way under the weight of the people trying to cross it (the British version)—remains unknown.

The bridge collapse traps 20,000 men of the Sikh army on the east bank of the Sutlej. Most of the Sikhs fight to the death. The British, enraged by the massacre of some of their wounded earlier in the battle, are happy to cooperate. British horse artillery along the riverbank exacts a heavy toll on Sikhs trying to flee. The Sikhs lose about 10,000 men and 67 guns.

The British cross the river that evening, and by February 13 Gough's army is only 30 miles from the Sikh capital of Lahore. Remaining Sikh forces cannot concentrate quickly enough to defend the capital, and the Sikhs decide to end the war, which is concluded in the Treaty of Lahore of March 11.

February 1846

Central Europe: Austrian Empire: Kraków Insurrection. An insurrection in the Polish city of Kraków (Cracow), then part of Austria, fails to spread beyond the city and is speedily crushed by Austrian troops. On November 16 Austria assumes direct rule, establishing what is known as the Grand Duchy of Kraków.

March 11, 1846

South Asia: India: First Anglo-Sikh War (continued): Treaty of Lahore. In the Treaty of Lahore, the British secure effective control of the Punjab. The Sikhs cede outright to the East India Company the valuable agricultural lands of the Jullundur Doab (between the Sutlej and Chenab rivers). They also permit a Resident British officer at Lahore with subordinates in other major cities who will indirectly govern the Punjab. The Sikhs must also pay a heavy indemnity of £1.2 million and agree to reduce their army to 20,000 infantry and 12,000 cavalry.

Because they cannot immediately raise such a sum, Gulab Singh, ruler of Jammu, is allowed to purchase Kashmir from the Punjab by paying £750,000 to the British East India Company. The British also secure the Koh-i-noor diamond.

March 24, 1846

North America: Mexican-American War (continued): U.S. troops arrive at the Rio Grande. A day after he receives word that the Mexican government refuses to see U.S. minister John Slidell (who is bearing a U.S. financial offer for the recognition of the Rio Grande as the southern boundary of Texas and for the purchase of New Mexico and California), on January 13, 1846, U.S. president James K. Polk orders Major General Zachary Taylor to move his Army of Observation from the Nueces River to "positions on or near the left bank" of the Rio Grande. This is in effect an act of war since the Nueces River has been the southern boundary of Texas for a century, and the Republic of Texas never exercised authority beyond the Nueces. Taylor receives the orders on February 3 but does not begin his advance until March 8.

On March 24 Taylor's forces arrive on the left (north) bank of the Rio Grande opposite the Mexican city of Matamoros, where the Mexicans have a garrison of about 5,700 men. During the next month, both sides fortify. Taylor establishes Camp Texas, while Mexican commander General Pedro de Ampudia builds Fort Paredes. Ampudia demands that Taylor return with his troops to the Nueces, declaring that otherwise "arms and arms alone must decide the question." Taylor refuses and requests that U.S. warships blockade the mouth of the Rio Grande.

April 25, 1846

North America: Mexican-American War (continued): Clash between Mexican and U.S. cavalry. On April 24, 1846, General Mariano Arista replaces General Pedro de Ampudia as commander of Mexican forces at Matamoros. Both sides are spoiling for a fight. U.S. major general Zachary Taylor refuses to withdraw his army back to the Nueces River, and the Mexican minister of war has ordered Arista to attack and immediately sends some 1,600 cavalry north of the Rio Grande. The next day they overwhelm a force of 63 U.S. Army dragoons. Eleven Americans are killed and 5 wounded; the remainder are captured. On April 26 Taylor sends a report to Washington that "hostilities may now be considered as commenced."

May 3–9, 1846

North America: Mexican-American War (continued). During April 30–May 1 General Mariano Arista leads 6,000 Mexican troops across the Rio Grande and advances on Fort Texas, which he lays siege to on May 3. Major Jacob Brown commands the U.S. fort. The siege is raised on May 9, although Brown is among those killed in the fighting. The fort is renamed in his honor and becomes the present-day city of Brownsville, Texas.

May 8, 1846

North America: Mexican-American War (continued): Battle of Palo Alto. After first rushing to Point Isabel to strengthen its defenses, on May 7 U.S. major general Zachary Taylor starts back to Fort Texas with about 2,300 men and 400 wagons to relieve the siege by Mexican forces there. Midway, at Palo Alto, he encounters some 3,200 Mexican troops under General Mariano Arista. Against greater Mexican numbers and superiority in cavalry, U.S. forces enjoy the advantage in artillery, especially heavy 18-pounder guns intended for Fort Texas. The four-hour battle, largely an artillery cannonade, ends in a U.S. victory. U.S. losses are 9 killed, 44 wounded, and 2 missing, while the Mexicans lose 102 killed, 129 wounded, and 26 missing. After spending much of the night burying their dead, Mexican forces withdraw early the next morning for Resaca de la Palma.

May 9, 1846

North America: Mexican-American War (continued): Battle of Resaca de la Palma. Despite being outnumbered by Mexican forces under General Mariano Arista, U.S. commander Major General Zachary Taylor pursues the withdrawing Mexicans. In midafternoon on May 9 he encounters Arista's 4,000 men occupying an excellent natural defensive position at Resaca de la Palma, a ravine with dense chaparral.

Taylor attacks with his 1,700 men. The Americans finally drive the Mexicans from their position. The Mexicans counterattack twice and are beaten back each time. They then flee, abandoning 474 muskets and carbines, 8 guns, and substantial baggage. U.S. losses are 23 killed and 89 wounded. Official Mexican figures are 154 killed, 205 wounded, and 156 missing. Many of the latter probably drowned trying the cross the Rio Grande. Taylor claims to have buried 200 Mexican dead. That same evening, Taylor raises the Mexican siege of Fort Texas.

May 13, 1846

North America: Mexican-American War (continued): U.S. declaration of war. On May 11 President James K. Polk sends a message to Congress detailing the "wrongs" committed by Mexico against the United States and announcing that "Mexico has passed the boundary of the United States, has invaded our territory and shed American blood upon American soil." He asks for a declaration of war, which is passed overwhelmingly by the two houses of Congress on May 11 and 12. The next day the United States declares war.

The Mexicans are optimistic, and many European observers believe that the 32,000-man European-trained Mexican Army is more than a match for the 7,365-man U.S. Army. To fight the war, the United States relies primarily on volunteers, with most serving only 6- and 12-month enlistments. Ultimately the U.S. fields 31,000 regulars and marines and some 104,000 volunteers. The Mexican Army is never more than 36,000 men. Mexico has no navy to speak of, while the United States has 70 warships. The U.S. industrial base is far stronger than that of Mexico, and its population is more than twice that of Mexico (17 million to 7 million).

There are three principal theaters of war: California, northern Mexico, and central Mexico. The U.S.

Navy also plays a vital role, blockading the Mexican coasts and preventing military supplies from reaching Mexico while maintaining lines of communication and supply for the U.S. army.

May 18, 1846

North America: Mexican-American War (continued): Northern theater: U.S. troops occupy Matamoros. General Mariano Arista evacuates the town of Matamoros on May 17–18, 1846, and U.S. troops under Major General Zachary Taylor cross the Rio Grande and occupy Matamoros the next day. Taylor delays in Matamoros for three months, awaiting supplies and training volunteer reinforcements.

June 14, 1846

North America: Mexican-American War (continued): California theater: American capture of Sonoma. In June 1846 a number of Californios, unhappy with the rule of the central government of Mexico, join U.S. settlers to organize a rebellion to overthrow the Mexican government in Sonoma, California. This effort receives assistance from U.S. Army captain John C. Frémont, then in California on an exploring expedition with a small number of men. In the Bear Flag Revolt of June 14, 1846, the rebels take possession of Sonoma and hoist a white flag with a bear painted on it.

June 15, 1846

North America: Oregon Treaty. This treaty between the United States and Britain settles the long-standing boundary dispute between Canada and the United States over the northern border of the Oregon Territory, which had led to the slogan in the United States of "Fifty-four forty, or fight!" Although in a December 1845 speech President James K. Polk had claimed the whole of Oregon for the United States, he is anxious to restore harmonious relations with Britain during the war with Mexico. Britain's repeal of the Corn Laws is another incentive. The border is set at an extension of the existing 49th parallel line to the middle of the channel between Vancouver Island and the mainland and then southward through the Strait of Juan de Fuca to the Pacific.

July 7, 1846

North America: Mexican-American War (continued): California theater (continued): U.S. forces take possession of Monterey. Learning of hostilities, Com-modore John D. Sloat, commanding the U.S. Pacific Squadron, sends forces ashore and seizes Monterey on July 7 and declares California annexed to the United States. Californios, however, rise against this and soon retake Monterey and much of the rest of California.

August 18, 1846

North America: Mexican-American War (continued): California theater (continued): U.S. capture of Santa Fe. On the outbreak of war, U.S. president James K. Polk orders Colonel Stephen W. Kearny from Fort Leavenworth, Kansas, to Santa Fe, New Mexico. Kearny departs on June 26 at the head of the 1,700-man so-called Army of the West (including 300 regulars of the 1st Dragoons and 860 men of the 1st Missouri Mounted Volunteers). Kearny occupies Santa Fe on August 18.

September 20–24, 1846

North America: Mexican-American War (continued): Northern theater (continued): Battle of Monterrey. With his army increased to 14,500 men—most of them volunteers—Major General Zachary Taylor begins an ascent of the Rio Grande with approximately half of his force on July 6. On July 14 he reaches Camargo on the San Juan River, a tributary of the Rio Grande, and establishes it as his supply base.

On August 19 Taylor begins his advance on Monterrey, the principal city of northern Mexico. He does not take heavy siege guns with him. He plans to circle around Monterrey and cut off the Mexican supply lines. Taylor's 6,400 men reach the city on September 19. Taylor sends Brigadier General William J. Worth's division around the city to cut the road south to Saltillo. After seizing several fortified heights, they are to attack from that direction. Monterrey is held by 10,000 defenders (7,000 regulars and 3,000 militia) under General Pedro de Ampudia.

U.S. president James K. Polk provides Mexico a new leader in the meantime when he allows the return of former president and Mexican army commander General Antonio López de Santa Anna from exile. Santa Anna claims that he will treat with the United States, but on his return to Mexico City in September he vows to continue the war. He is promptly elected president.

Santa Anna orders Ampudia to establish a defensive line at Saltillo, but Ampudia believes that his men are close to mutiny from constant withdrawals. He is determined to win at Monterrey.

Taylor's two-pronged attack into the city on September 20 goes badly. Following three days of fighting, however, Ampudia agrees to surrender if his men are allowed to leave the city with the full honors of war. Taylor agrees on September 24; the formal surrender takes place the next day. Taylor also agrees to an eight-week armistice.

Losses in the fighting are 120 killed and 333 wounded on the U.S. side and 439 killed, wounded, and missing on the Mexican side. The Battle of Monterrey solidifies the U.S. hold on northern Mexico and sets the stage for the subsequent Battle of Buena Vista. News of the armistice infuriates President James Polk, however, and causes him to lose confidence in Taylor.

September 1846–1849

Southern Europe: Iberian Peninsula: Spain: Second Carlist War. The Carlists (who began as supporters of Don Carlos, brother of the deceased King Ferdinand VII, who abolished the Salic Law in order that his daughter might succeed to the throne), again rise up against the central government, this time seeking to bring about the marriage of Queen Isabella II with the Carlist pretender, Carlos, Count of Montemolín. The fighting is centered in Catalonia. General Ramón María Narváez crushes an uprising in Galicia, while Fernando Fernández de Córdova, captain general of Catalonia, puts down the revolt there early in 1849. The war results in between 3,000 and 10,000 casualties. In June the government announces an amnesty for the Carlists.

December 6, 1846

North America: Mexican-American War (continued): California theater (continued): Battle of San Pascual. U.S. president James K. Polk advances Stephen W. Kearny to Brigadier General and orders him to California to augment U.S. forces there. Leaving most of his force to pacify New Mexico, Kearny sets out on September 25. Believing a false report that California has already been secured, Kearny detaches most of his remaining force and presses ahead with only 121 men. They arrive in California in early December, having marched more than 2,000 miles from Fort Leavenworth, Kansas, since May. Kearny's men join U.S. Marines under Lieutenant Archibald Gillespie.

In the Battle of San Pascual on December 6, 1846, U.S. forces clash with some 75 Californios led by Major Andrés Pico. The Californios win the battle, killing 21 Americans and wounding 17 (including both Kearny and Gillespie) while losing probably 6 dead and 12 wounded. Kearny immediately appeals to new Pacific Squadron commodore Robert F. Stockton at San Diego for reinforcements. Stockton dispatches more than 200 sailors and marines. They disperse the Californios and allow Kearny's force to proceed to San Diego.

December 14, 1846

North America: Mexican-American War (continued): Northern theater (continued): Doniphan's March. Colonel Alexander W. Doniphan's 1st Regiment of Missouri Mounted Volunteers accompanies Colonel Stephen W. Kearny from Fort Leavenworth, Kansas, to Santa Fe, New Mexico. The next month when Kearny continues on to California, Doniphan, a lawyer in civilian life, sets up a governmental structure for the new U.S. territory, and his men garrison much of New Mexico.

On arrival of reinforcements and a new commander, on December 14 Doniphan departs Santa Fe with 800 men of his regiment for El Paso del Norte (present-day Ciudad Juárez, Mexico), 250 miles distant, in order to reinforce Brigadier General John E. Wool in the state of Chihuahua.

December 16, 1846

North America: Mexican-American War (continued): Northern theater (continued): U.S. occupation of Saltillo. Following their capture of Monterrey, U.S. forces under Major General Zachary Taylor move south to Saltillo. There, on December 31, Taylor is joined by 3,000 troops under Brigadier General John E. Wool, marching from San Antonio.

December 25, 1846

North America: Mexican-American War (continued): Northern theater (continued): Doniphan's March (continued): Battle of Brazito. On December 25, some nine miles south of present-day Las Cruces, New Mexico, Colonel Alexander W. Doniphan's 1st Regiment of Missouri Mounted Volunteers is caught by surprise by some 1,200 Mexican Army troops led by Colonel Antonio Ponce de León.

Although heavily outnumbered, Doniphan halts a series of Mexican charges. The Battle of Brazito costs the Mexicans about 50 killed and 150 wounded, while the Americans suffer only 7 wounded. Two days later Doniphan captures El Paso del Norte (present-day Ciudad Juárez, Mexico), with no resistance.

1846–1847
Southern Africa: War of the Axe. Tensions between the British and the Xhosa in the region between the Keiskama and Great Kei rivers erupt in March 1846 when a Khoikhoi escort is killed while transporting a Xhosa thief to Grahamstown to be tried for stealing an axe. The war begins when the Xhosa refuse to surrender the murderer. The Ngqika is the principal tribe in the war, assisted by the Tambukies. On June 7, 1846, British forces defeat the Xhosa in battle on the Gwangu River, but the war continues for a total duration of 21 months, until the beginning of 1848.

January 9, 1847
North America: Mexican-American War (continued): California theater (continued): Battle of La Mesa. On January 9, 1847, near present-day Pasadena, California, American forces under Brigadier General Stephen W. Kearny defeat a group of outnumbered and outgunned Californios in the Battle of La Mesa. One American and 25 Californios are killed. The next day, Kearny retakes Los Angeles from the Californios.

January 13, 1847
North America: Mexican-American War (continued): California theater (continued): Capitulation of Cahuenga. The Capitulation (Treaty) of Cahuenga is signed by (now) Lieutenant Colonel John C. Frémont and Mexican governor-general Andres Pico in what is now North Hollywood, Los Angeles. The treaty ends organized resistance to U.S. rule in California.

January–March 1847
North America: Mexican-American War (continued): Northern theater (continued): Preparations to invade Veracruz. Following the Battle of Monterrey, there is a strategic debate in Washington. Commanding general of the army Major General Winfield Scott prefers an amphibious landing at Veracruz, Mexico City's port, and then a march overland 260 miles to the capital. President James K. Polk favors an advance on Mexico City from the north by troops under Major General Zachary Taylor. Polk is already unhappy with Taylor for his handling of the Battle of Monterrey when Taylor rejects the notion that he

can move 300 miles across desert to San Luis Potosi and then another 200 miles to Mexico City. Taylor's counterproposal is an advance from Veracruz, much as Scott has recommended.

Polk, a Democrat, does not wish for political reasons to name Scott, a Whig, as commander but reluctantly does so. Polk authorizes Scott to take units for the expeditionary force from Taylor, who will then be restricted to defensive operations. Scott departs Washington at the end of November 1846. He stops at Point Isabel to take some of Taylor's best troops, making a lifelong enemy of Taylor, and then sails for Tampico, where he establishes his headquarters on February 18, 1847. He assembles some 10,000 men for the Veracruz landing.

February 22–23, 1847
North America: Mexican-American War (continued): Northern theater (continued): Battle of Buena Vista. Major General Winfield Scott's preparations to invade Veracruz leave Major General Zachary Taylor 5,000 men—a minority of them regulars—to defend northern Mexico. Learning through a captured dispatch of the American plans, Mexican president General Antonio López de Santa Anna sees an opportunity to defeat Taylor and Scott in detail.

Santa Anna sets out northward to attack Taylor on the same route from San Luis Potosi (but in reverse) that Taylor had earlier rejected. Santa Anna moves the 300 miles across the desert with some 20,000 largely untrained troops; only 16,000 complete the grueling march. Forewarned, Taylor selects an excellent defensive position on high ground to help offset Santa Anna's 6,000 cavalry. Santa Anna arrives near Saltillo on February 19. The Mexicans outnumber the Americans 3 to 1.

During the first day of fighting, February 22, Santa Anna's cavalry drive in Taylor's outlying forces. Although the Mexicans fight well, they are exhausted from their long march. The main fighting occurs the next day, February 23; the Americans are victorious.

Colonel Jefferson Davis's 1st Mississippi Volunteer Regiment plays a pivotal role, defeating a Mexican cavalry charge. Army regulars under Brigadier General John E. Wool who rushed to reinforce Taylor are also vital to the American success. The American rear guard at Saltillo, moreover, defeats an effort by Mexican cavalry to envelop the American forces. The far-better-served American artillery is the key to the battle's outcome, though. The Mexicans are driven off, and Santa Anna begins another forced march, this time to Veracruz.

The Battle of Buena Vista marks the end of major fighting in northern Mexico. The fighting now shifts to the central part of the country. American casualties in the battle total 267 killed, 456 wounded, and 23 missing. The Mexicans lose perhaps 500 dead and 1,000 wounded and 2 guns captured.

February 28, 1847

North America: Mexican-American War (continued): Northern theater (continued): Doniphan's March (continued): Battle of Sacramento. Colonel Alexander W. Doniphan's 1st Regiment of Missouri Mounted Volunteers, reinforced by two batteries of artillery, continues its march south, deep into Chihuahua Province. On February 28 at Sacramento, 15 miles north of Chihuahua, Doniphan, outnumbered more than 4 to 1, executes a daring flanking maneuver and defeats 4,200 Mexican infantry and cavalry under Major General José Antonio de Heredia. The Mexicans suffer 169 killed, 300 wounded, and 79 taken prisoner. U.S. losses are 4 killed and 8 wounded. Doniphan continues south and captures the provincial capital of Chihuahua City on March 2.

March 9, 1847

North America: Mexican-American War (continued): Central theater: U.S. forces arrive at Veracruz. Major General Winfield Scott arrives with his expeditionary force off the Gulf Coast port of Veracruz. The large number of transports are escorted by American warships under Commodore David Conner. Using 65 surfboats shipped in the holds of transports, within 24 hours and against only slight opposition the navy puts ashore Scott's entire force of more than 10,000 men, along with their artillery, horses, vehicles, and supplies on a beach three miles from Veracruz. It is the largest amphibious landing in U.S. military history until World War II.

Sailors land heavy guns, which are then sited to bombard the port city. Following a five-day bombardment, the Mexican garrison of 5,000 men surrenders on March 27. Scott puts American losses of killed or wounded at 64, although some sources claim 82. Mexican losses are more difficult to determine. A neutral British observer claims that those killed number 100 civilians and 80 soldiers. (A recent Mexican study claims that 350 soldiers and 400 civilians died and 250 people were injured.) At the same time, Mexico City is undergoing political upheaval. Mexican internal discord greatly assists the Americans throughout the war.

April 15, 1847

Southeast Asia: Vietnam: Incident at Tourane. The persecution of Christian missionaries by Emperor Minh Mang (r. 1820–1841) leads the French government to send two warships to the Vietnamese port of Tourane (Danang). They demand not only the release of the priests but also freedom of worship for Catholics in Vietnam. This leads to an incident on April 15, 1847, in which the French warships fire on and sink three of four Vietnamese ships as they approach. Persecution of Catholics is one justification for the subsequent French intervention in Indochina.

April 18, 1847

North America: Mexican-American War (continued): Central theater (continued): Scott's Mexico City Campaign and Battle of Cerro Gordo. Mexican general Antonio López de Santa Anna endeavors to pin U.S. forces under Major General Winfield Scott on the coast in the yellow fever belt. Immediately after securing Veracruz as his principal base, Scott moves inland, however. His subsequent march to Mexico City ranks among the most brilliant in U.S. military history.

With less than 10,000 men (fewer than half the number of men he requested), hampered by numerous problems not of his own making, and often forced to live off the land, Scott marches his men 260 miles without a reverse in six months. His occupation policies include payment for horses and supplies taken from the Mexicans. While these are not always followed, they help secure his line of communication back to Veracruz.

On April 17, 1847, the Americans reach the fortified pass of Cerro Gordo, held by Santa Anna and 12,000 men. U.S. engineers, including Captain Robert E. Lee, discover a flanking trail. Scott moves his main body along this route, enveloping most of the Mexican defenders and routing them. The Mexicans lose some 1,000 killed or wounded and 3,000 taken prisoner. The Americans also capture 43 guns, 4,000 firearms, and considerable baggage. American losses are 63 killed and 353 wounded. The victory enables

Scott to move out of the yellow fever zone and pursue the retreating Mexicans toward Jalapa.

May 15, 1847
North America: Mexican-American War (continued): Central theater (continued): Scott's Mexico City Campaign (continued): Occupation of Puebla. On May 15, 1847, Major General Winfield Scott's army occupies the city of Puebla, some 75 miles from Mexico City. There it remains for three months. This halt is necessary because Scott's army loses 40 percent of its strength. With their enlistments up, 4,000 volunteers return home.

May 21, 1847
North America: Mexican-American War (continued): Northern theater (continued): Doniphan's March (continued). Receiving orders on April 23 from Major General Zachary Taylor to join his command, Colonel Alexander W. Doniphan's 1st Regiment of Missouri Mounted Volunteers leaves Chihuahua City and marches another 750 miles in difficult conditions to Saltillo. The regiment arrives at Saltillo on May 21. With their enlistments now up, the men continue on to Matamoros and board ships to travel to New Orleans. They return to St. Louis in early June 1847, having traveled some 5,500 miles by land and water in slightly more than one year.

July 17, 1847
Southern Europe: Italy: Austrian occupation of Ferrara. This military occupation of Ferrara greatly inflames Italian nationalists, who increasing resent the Austrian domination of Italy.

August 7, 1847
North America: Mexican-American War (continued): Central theater (continued): Scott's Mexico City Campaign (continued): Resumption of the advance on Mexico City. Having received replacements for the 4,000 volunteers whose terms of enlistment had expired and with his supply lines back to Veracruz now under constant Mexican Army harassment, on August 7, 1847, U.S. major general Winfield Scott resumes his march on Mexico City. In a daring step, Scott leaves behind a small garrison and his sick at Puebla and cuts himself off from his base to advance on Mexico City by living off the land.

General Antonio López de Santa Anna has gathered some 36,000 men and 100 guns to defend the city. Scott has 10,000 men. On August 15 at Ayutla, some 15 miles west of the Mexican capital, Scott discovers that Santa Anna has taken advantage of terrain, especially lakes and marshland, and heavily fortified the area. Scott therefore circles to approach Mexico City from the south, only to encounter strong Mexican troop concentrations near Contreras and Churubusco.

August 19–20, 1847
North America: Mexican-American War (continued): Central theater (continued): Scott's Mexico City Campaign (continued): Battles of Contreras and Churubusco. In circling to the south in their final approach to Mexico City, U.S. forces under Major General Winfied Scott wage two significant battles against Mexican troops under General Antonio López de Santa Anna on August 19–20, 1847. The first occurs near the villages of Contreras and Padierna some 10 miles southwest of the capital. The second is 7 miles to the northeast around the town of Churubusco. They should properly be considered two parts of the same battle. The Americans have to contend with artillerists of the San Patricio Battalion, made up in part of U.S. deserters; some 80 are taken prisoner, and 51 are subsequently court-martialed and hanged.

The Americans win both battles, and Mexican forces flee north to Mexico City. Santa Anna suffers an estimated 4,197 killed or wounded, 2,637 taken prisoner, and 3,000 missing, nearly a third of his force. Scott's losses are 133 killed and 865 wounded, or about 12 percent of 8,500 men engaged.

August 25–September 6, 1847
North America: Mexican-American War (continued): Central theater (continued): Scott's Mexico City Campaign (continued): Armistice. An armistice is declared on August 25, 1847 to consider peace proposals. The chief clerk of the U.S. State Department and peace commissioner, Nicholas Trist, is instructed by President James K. Polk to obtain the Rio Grande boundary for Texas, together with New Mexico and California. The Mexican leaders reject these terms; with the failure of talks on September 6, fighting resumes.

September 8, 1847
North America: Mexican-American War (continued): Central theater (continued): Battle of Molino

del Rey. On September 8 Major General Winfield Scott flings his forces against the Mexican defenders of a gun foundry and fort near the Chapultepec palace and military academy. Brigadier General William J. Worth's 3,400-man division is the U.S. attack force. It suffers heavy casualties from some 8,000 well-entrenched Mexican defenders. The Americans prevail but with the highest casualties in percentage of force engaged of any battle of the war.

U.S. losses on September 8, 1847, are 117 killed, 653 wounded, and 18 missing. The Mexicans sustain around 2,000 killed or wounded and 700 captured. The battle brings recriminations on the U.S. side. Worth is criticized for inadequate reconnaissance to detect the location of Mexican artillery positions.

September 13–14, 1847

North America: Mexican-American War (continued): Central theater (continued): Battle of Chapultepec and capture of Mexico City. The last barrier to Mexico City is the fortified hill of Chapultepec, with its summer palace and the Mexican military academy. U.S. major general Winfield Scott commands some 7,180 effectives. Mexican general Antonio López de Santa Anna commands some 15,000 men in defense of the capital. About 1,000 of these, including 51 military academy cadets, defend Chapultepec under the command of General Nicolás Bravo.

Scott opens an artillery bombardment on September 12 and then launches an assault early the next morning, complete with scaling ladders. General Bravo surrenders after about two hours at about 9:30. Fighting also occurs at the fortified gates of Belén and San Cosme.

U.S. casualties are 116 killed and 669 wounded. The Mexicans lose about 3,000 killed or wounded and 800 taken prisoner. Among the dead are 6 cadets, remembered in Mexican history as los Niños Héros (the Boy Heroes). The fall of Chapultepec opens the way for the American capture of Mexico City.

Major General Winfield Scott leads U.S. forces into Mexico City on September 14, 1847, the culmination of his brilliant campaign from the coast at Veracruz without a reverse. (Library of Congress)

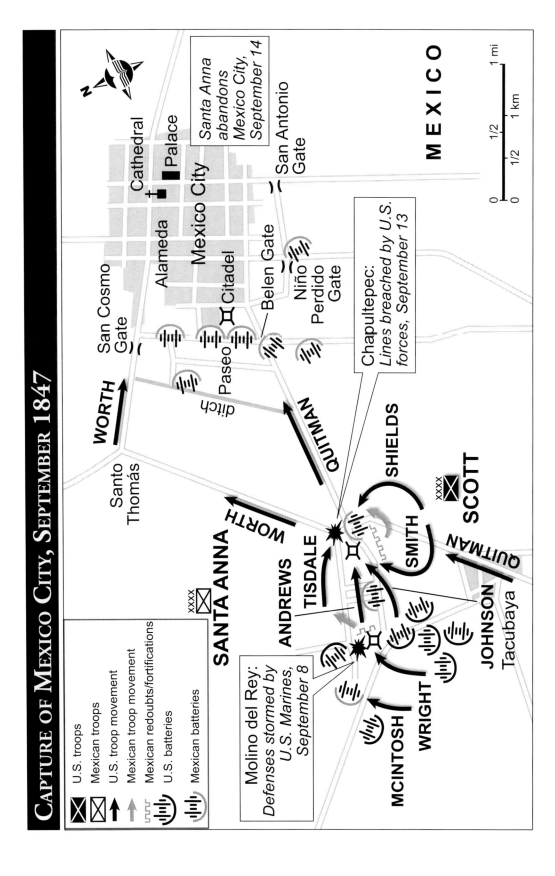

CAPTURE OF MEXICO CITY, SEPTEMBER 1847

Legend:
- ☒ U.S. troops
- ☒ Mexican troops
- ↑ U.S. troop movement
- ↑ Mexican troop movement
- Mexican redoubts/fortifications
- U.S. batteries
- Mexican batteries

Santa Anna abandons Mexico City, September 14

Chapultepec: Lines breached by U.S. forces, September 13

Molino del Rey: Defenses stormed by U.S. Marines, September 8

Cathedral
Palace
Alameda
Mexico City
Citadel
San Cosmo Gate
San Antonio Gate
Belen Gate
Niño Perdido Gate
Paseo
ditch
Santo Thomás

WORTH
QUITMAN
WORTH
SHIELDS
SMITH
QUITMAN
SCOTT
SANTA ANNA
TISDALE
ANDREWS
JOHNSON
Tacubaya
MCINTOSH
WRIGHT

MEXICO

0   1/2   1 mi
0   1/2   1 km

Mexico City officials persuade General Santa Anna to evacuate the city to spare it destruction and civilian casualties. On September 14 General Scott accepts the unconditional surrender of the city, which is then occupied by U.S. troops. With the fall of the Mexican capital, peace talks begin again.

September 1847–February 1848
North America: Mexican-American War (continued): Central theater (continued): Prolonged peace negotiations. Following the U.S. capture of Mexico City, peace negotiations open at Guadalupe Hidalgo, north of the capital. Given the U.S. terms, months pass before any Mexican government is willing to negotiate seriously. U.S. president James K. Polk blames his negotiator, Nicholas Trist, and expeditionary force commander, Major General Winfield Scott, for the lack of progress. Polk actually orders Trist home and orders Scott to resume the war. Trist and Scott, now in serious negotiations with the Mexican side, ignore the presidential orders.

December 23, 1847
North Africa: Algeria: French conquest of Algeria (continued). Algerian insurgent leader Emir Abd el Kader (Abd al-Qadir, Abdelkader) surrenders on the pledge that he will be allowed to proceed to Alexandria or Acre (Akko). The promise is not kept; he is sent to France, where he and his family are kept at various locations, including the Château of Amboise. Finally released under Emperor Napoleon III in 1852 on the pledge that he will never again take up arms against France, Abd el Kader settles in Syria. On several occasions he is instrumental in saving the lives of thousands of Christians and also writes an important philosophical treatise. He dies in Damascus in 1883.

February 2, 1848
North America: Mexican-American War (continued): Central theater (continued): Treaty of Guadalupe Hidalgo. U.S. State Department chief clerk Nicholas Trist proves an able negotiator. Aided by bribes, he finalizes the Treaty of Guadalupe Hidalgo on February 2, 1848. Mexico cedes to the United States all Texas to the Rio Grande boundary, New Mexico (including the future states of New Mexico, Arizona, Colorado, Utah, and Nevada), and upper California

(including San Diego). The United States agrees to assume unpaid claims by U.S. citizens against Mexico and pays $15 million in addition. The U.S. Senate ratifies the treaty on July 4.

U.S. president James K. Polk then does his best to try to humiliate Major General Winfield Scott, who has won the war, and Trist, who has won the peace. Scott is replaced as commanding general, and Trist is fired. Congress, however, votes Scott a gold medal, which Polk is then forced to present.

U.S. forces evacuate Mexico City on June 12 and Veracruz on August 2, 1848. The major issue with the new territorial acquisitions becomes whether they will be slave or free. In this sense, the Mexican-American War helps bring on the American Civil War in 1861.

February 22–24, 1848
Western Europe: France: Revolution in Paris. In reaction to the corruption and *immobilisme* of the regime of King Louis Philippe, a revolution occurs in Paris. It brings the establishment of the Second French Republic but also begins a period of great political and social unrest in France and throughout Europe, for revolutions in France and Italy prove the catalyst for widespread revolts elsewhere in Europe.

March 3, 1848
Central Europe: Austrian Empire: Hungary: Hungarian Revolution. Sparked by events in Paris in February 1848, on March 3 Hungarian nationalist leader Lajos (Louis) Kossuth delivers a speech in the Hungarian parliament in Bratislava attacking heavy-handed Austrian rule and demanding liberal reforms: a constitution for the Habsburg Empire and the establishment of a responsible ministry in Hungary. This brings on the Hungarian Revolution (1848).

March 13, 1848
Central Europe: Austria: Revolt in Vienna. Under the weak rule of Emperor Ferdinand I, unrest simmers within the Austrian Empire and in Hungary, Italy, and even Austria itself. In Vienna, inspired by events in Paris and in Bratislava, students led by Professor Anton Füster demand reform in Austria itself, including an end to censorship. Workers soon join them, and Prince Klemens von Metternich, who has dominated imperial affairs for nearly 40 years, resigns. He soon flees Austria for exile in England. Ferdinand I prom-

ises reforms, but much of the Habsburg Empire and Germany erupt in revolution.

March 15, 1848
Central Europe: Prussia: Beginning of the Prussian Revolution: Beginning of the March Days in Berlin. Rioting on this day in Berlin leads King Frederick William IV to promise (again) that he will grant a constitution. Governments in several of the lesser German states also collapse, and there are widespread calls for an all-German assembly to meet. Many leading liberals believe that the time has come to create a unified German state.

March 15, 1848
Central Europe: Hungary: Revolutionary agitation in Budapest. Events within the Austrian Empire simply move too fast for Vienna to avoid concessions. Students and peasants, gathered in Budapest for a mid-March trade fair, now take the lead. On March 15 the radical young poet Sándor (Alexander) Petöfi addresses a large crowd, which then seizes control of city hall and the university. They also march on the Viceroyal Council building, demanding freedom of the press and other reforms, which the council grants.

A Hungarian Diet hurriedly meets in Pzsony and, under the leadership of Lajos Kossuth, enacts a host of reforms, known as the April Laws, before dissolving on April 11. In effect a new constitution, these 31 laws provide for a host of reforms and establish Hungary as a constitutional monarchy, with the monarchy constrained by an annually convened parliament. They also provide for complete constitutional separation of Hungary from Austria, although the Austrian emperor is still king in Hungary.

March 18–22, 1848
Southern Europe: Italy: Milan rebels against Austrian rule. The revolutionary activity of 1848 actually begins in Italy in late 1847 when Grand Duke Leopold of Tuscany and King Charles Albert of Sardinia (Piedmont-Sardinia) are forced to grant constitutions. In January 1848 the people of Palermo riot against their reactionary ruler, King Ferdinand II, and he too is forced to grant a constitution. On March 18, 1848, revolt flares in Milan, capital of Lombardy, which is then part of the Austrian Empire.

The so-called Five Days of Milan end with 82-year-old Habsburg field marshal Count Johann Josef Wenzel Radetzky von Radetz withdrawing Austrian troops from the city. They retreat to the stronghold at the foot of the Alps, known as the Quadrilateral and comprising the cities of Mantua, Verona, Peschiera, and Legnago.

See Leaders: Radetzky, Josef

March 22, 1848
Southern Europe: Italy: Kingdom of Sardinia declares war on Austria. With unrest and the seeming success of revolutionaries in Milan, Venice, and other parts of Italy, King Charles Albert of the Kingdom of Sardinia (Piedmont-Sardinia) seeks to lead an Italian war of liberation. He declares war against Austria on March 22, 1848, boasting, "*Italia fera da se*" (Italy will do it by itself). Thousands of volunteers from other parts of Italy, including troops from the Papal States, rush to join the 60,000-man Sardinian army.

March 26, 1848
Southern Europe: Italy: Republic of Venice proclaimed. Fortified by what is happening in Milan, Venetian revolutionaries seize control of the arsenal and organize both a civic guard and a provisional government. The Austrians evacuate Venice on March 26, and Venice is declared a republic under the leadership of revolutionary Daniele Manin.

March–August 1848
Northern Europe: Denmark: Revolt of Schleswig and Holstein. In March 1848 King Frederick VII of Denmark announces a new liberal constitution for Denmark that, to meet the demands of Danish nationalists, will also apply to Schleswig. The duchies of Holstein and Schleswig are both ruled by Denmark. Leaders in Holstein, however, demand not only that the constitution be scrapped but that Schleswig be allowed to join it as a member of the German Confederation. Denmark rejects this demand, and in March 1848, encouraged by Prussia, the Germans of Holstein and southern Schleswig rebel.

Prussian troops under General Friedrich Heinrich von Wrangel then occupy the two duchies in what is called the First Schleswig-Holstein War. Most of the major powers support Denmark. Sweden sends troops to assist Denmark, and Britain threatens naval action. Austria and Russia also support Denmark. On August 28, 1848, peace is restored in the Convention of Malmo, but Denmark does not secure full rights in the two provinces until 1850.

April 10, 1848

Central Europe: Hungary: Declaration of Hungarian independence. Hungarian nationalist leader Lajos (Louis) Kossuth proclaims the independence of Hungary.

April 18, 1848

South Asia: India: Second Anglo-Sikh War. Following the First Anglo-Sikh War (1845–1846), the British dominate the Punjab. They rule indirectly through officials controlling the native rulers and generals. Humiliated and angered by the punitive provisions of the Treaty of Lahore of March 1846 and realizing that they have come the closest of the Indian peoples to defeating the British, the Sikhs seek the opportunity for revenge.

Simmering unrest breaks into the open in April 1848, leading to the Second Anglo-Sikh War (1848–1849). On April 18 two British lieutenants, one of them the new political agent for the city, arrive at Multan. They are attacked and wounded by irregular troops and a mob. Their escort flees, and the two men are murdered the next day. News of the killings spreads and excites open opposition to the British elsewhere. A number of Sikh troops desert their regiments and join those prepared to resist the British under the leadership of the Viceroy of Multan, Dewan Mulraj.

June 17, 1848

Central Europe: Bohemia: Bombardment of Prague. The first reversal for the revolutionaries of 1848 within the Austrian Empire occurs in Bohemia, where Habsburg general Alfred zu Windischgrätz uses animosity between the Czech majority and the German minority (which controls much of the country) as the excuse to bombard and subdue the Bohemian capital of Prague. A Pan-Slav congress meeting there is dispersed, and Austrian forces soon reestablish Habsburg control over all Bohemia.

Mid-June 1848

Southern Europe: Italy: Austrian forces go on the offensive. In northern Italy, Austrian forces under Field Marshal Count Johann Josef Wenzel Radetzky von Radetz go on the offensive. They quickly reestablish Habsburg control in Lombardy and in most of Venetia except the city of Venice.

June 23–26, 1848

Western Europe: France: The June Days. An uprising of workers in Paris, following closure of the National Workshops, is suppressed with considerable bloodshed by General Louis Eugène Cavaignac, who receives and then relinquishes temporary dictatorial powers.

July 24–25, 1848

Southern Europe: Italy: Battle of Custozza. Troops of the Kingdom of Sardinia (Piedmont-Sardinia) battling the Austrians are badly trained and poorly equipped and led. Sharp divisions also develop among the allied Italian contingents. Under heavy Austrian pressure, Pope Pius IX withdraws the papal forces, announcing neutrality in a war with another Catholic power.

Field Marshal Count Johann Josef Wenzel Radetzky von Radetz now turns his attention to the Sardinian and allied forces, defeating them in the Battle of Custozza on July 25, 1848. Sardinian king Charles Albert appeals to France, but following the violence of the unrest in Paris known as the June Days, it is in no position to intervene.

August 9, 1848

Southern Europe: Italy: Armistice of Salasco. Following the defeat of Piedmontese and allied Italian forces by the Austrians in the Battle of Custozza and with no support forthcoming from France, on August 9, 1848, General Carlo Canera di Salasco, King Charles Albert of Sardinia's (Piedmont-Sardinia) chief of staff, concludes an armistice with the Habsburg forces. The Piedmontese surrender Lombardy (with the expectation of regaining it later).

August 18, 1848–January 22, 1849

South Asia: India: Second Anglo-Sikh War (continued): Siege of Multan. Lieutenant Herbert Edwardes, British political agent in Bannu, raises loyal troops and defeats viceroy of Multan Dewan Mulraj's army near the Chenab River on June 18. This forces the Sikhs back into Multan. Reinforced, Edwardes brings the city under siege on August 18.

British major general William S. Whish takes command of siege operations. British governor-general Sir Frederick Currie and commander in chief of British forces General Sir Hugh Gough, however, refuse to order up major troop formations until the end of the monsoon season in early November. They send only small detachments to suppress Mulraj's rebellion. The largest of these, under Sikh commander Sher Singh, rebels against the British at Multan on September 14.

August 19, 1848

Southern Africa: Battle of Boomplaats. Increasing tension between the Boers of the Orange River colony and the British leads to the Battle of Boomplaats, near Jagersfontein, on August 19, 1848. Some 1,200 British soldiers under Sir Harry Smith defeat a force of 300 Boers led by Andries Pretorius. The British suffer 22 casualties, the Boers but 7. After the battle, the Boers withdraw across the Vaal River.

September 11, 1848

Central Europe: Hungary: Austrian invasion of Hungary and war between Austria and Hungary. Even as Vienna makes concessions to the Hungarians, it is preparing to crush the revolution. Vienna gives charge of the Slovakian-Croatian border with Hungary to General Josip Jelačić (Joseph Jellachich). A Croat who is completely loyal to the Austrian court but hopes to advance the cause of the Croats, Jelačić despises the Hungarian radical leaders. The situation in Hungary is further complicated by demands of its subordinate Kingdom of Croatia-Slovenia. The nationalist Croats demand the same rights that the Hungarians have achieved, and they appeal directly to Vienna. Understandably, the Habsburgs endeavor to play the Magyars and other minorities against one another.

The intractable problem is that Hungary's many minorities actually form (counting Transylvania) a majority of the kingdom's population. The new constitution, however, makes Magyar rather than Latin the official language of the state. It contains no provision for the minorities, as the Magyars plan a unitary state. The Hungarian capital is also moved from Bratislava to Budapest.

Negotiations between Budapest and Vienna reach a near stalemate, with Vienna taking the part of the non-Magyar half of the Hungarian population.

On September 11, 1848, therefore, General Jelačić crosses the Hungarian border with 30,000–35,000 poorly equipped Croatian troops to put down the rebellion in Hungary.

September 29, 1848

Central Europe: Hungary: War between Austria and Hungary (continued): Battle of Pákozd. The disparate forces that constitute the Hungarian army steadily withdraw before General Josip Jelačić's Croatian forces loyal to the Austrian Crown. Finally, in little more than a skirmish fought some 30 miles southwest of Budapest, Hungarian forces under the command of General János Móga stand and fight. They defeat Jelačić's army.

This small engagement is a landmark in Hungarian history. It is described as Hungary's Valmy (a reference to the victory of French revolutionary forces over the Prussians in September 1792) and proves that the new Hungarian national army is willing and able to fight. An armistice is then arranged between the Royal Hungarian and Imperial Royal Croatian armies. Jelačić withdraws from Hungary toward Vienna and a juncture with the other imperial forces under General Alfred zu Windischgrätz.

October 3, 1848

Central Europe: Hungary: War between Austria and Hungary (continued). Habsburg emperor Ferdinand I issues a manifesto dismissing the Hungarian parliament, subjecting Hungary to military rule, and appointing General Josip Jelačić its military governor.

October 6, 1848

Central Europe: Austria: War between Austria and Hungary (continued): Revolution in Vienna. Students and other radicals in Vienna, sympathetic with the revolutionaries in Hungary and upset with the imperial court's decision to send Austrian troops to support General Josip Jelačić, convince troops in Vienna not to obey their orders. On October 6 a grenadier battalion defies the order of Minister of War General Count Theodor Baillet von Latour to move toward the Hungarian border. A bloody clash occurs when troops loyal to Latour and the grenadiers fire on one another.

Within hours, crowds of Viennese drive some 14,000 imperial troops from Vienna. Latour is hanged from a lamppost, and Emperor Ferdinand I, the court, and other government officials flee to Olmütz (Olomouc) in Moravia. The Austrian Reichstag (parliament) remains behind, but power in the city now passes into the hands of revolutionary committees.

October 30, 1848

Central Europe: Austria: War between Austria and Hungary (continued): Battle of Schwechat. Hungarian Army troops from the east and Austrian imperial forces from the north under General Alfred zu Windischgrätz advance on Vienna. Windischgrätz assembles 70,000 men and moves swiftly; the far smaller and less-organized Hungarian force is slow to move and, in fact, stops at the Hungarian-Austrian border because its commander, General János Móga, and many of his officers hope to avoid further inter-Habsburg fighting and war against Hungary's king. The Viennese revolutionaries are also reluctant to call in the Hungarians, so several weeks are lost.

When the Hungarians do decide to cross the border with some 25,000 men and 40 guns, they encounter the considerably superior united forces of Windischgrätz and General Josip Jelačić, who attack them at Schwechat, just east of Vienna, on October 30. The Hungarians are unaccustomed to the heavy Austrian artillery barrage and are soon in precipitous flight. Many do not halt until they reach the Hungarian border.

Móga, who falls from his horse and is injured during the battle, resigns his command. On November 1 Lajos Kossuth, acting as president of the Hungarian National Defense Committee, appoints Artúr Görgey, barely 30 years old, to command Hungarian forces in the west. Kossuth and Görgey work feverishly to create, almost from scratch, an effective Hungarian military force. By the beginning of 1849 they have created an army of 170,000 men, which surpasses the local Austrian forces in both numbers and equipment.

See Leaders: Görgey, Artúr

October 31, 1848

Central Europe: War between Austrian and Hungary (continued): Imperial forces take Vienna. Following the Battle of Schwechat, Austrian general Alfred zu Windischgrätz turns to the west and attacks the revolutionaries in Vienna with his army of Czech, Moravian, Galician, and Croatian forces. The city is looted; a few revolutionaries are executed, and others are imprisoned.

November 9, 1848

South Asia: India: Second Anglo-Sikh War (continued): British invasion of the Punjab. With the end of the monsoon season, British commander in chief General Sir Hugh Gough orders up major British units. Beginning on November 9, 1848, he undertakes a major invasion of the Punjab.

November 10, 1848

Central Europe: Germany: End of the Prussian Revolution. On November 9, 1848, with the return of Prussian troops following the armistice of Malmö with Denmark, Prussian king Frederick William IV declares Berlin to be in a state of siege. He banishes the Constituent Assembly then meeting at Brandenburg-on-the-Havel. The assembly declares these measures illegal. The next day, November 10, however, Prussian troops under General Count Friedrich von Wrangel occupy the city and expel the deputies. When the assembly meets again on December 4, the king orders it dissolved and announces that he will impose his own constitutional arrangement (the Prussian Constitution of 1850).

November 16, 1848

Southern Europe: Italy: Insurrection in Rome. In September 1848 Pope Pius IX appoints a liberal, Count Pellegrino Rossi, as prime minister. Rossi's reforms are insufficient for many, and he is assassinated on November 15 by a fanatical democrat. On November 16 there is a popular uprising in the city. On November 25, Pope Pius IX flees Rome.

November 17, 1848

Central Europe: War between Austria and Hungary (continued): Austrian forces capture Kolozsvár. In the east, Austrian forces under General Baron Anton Puchner invade Transylvania. On November 17, 1848, they capture its capital, Kolozsvár. Hungarian leader Lajos Kossuth appoints Polish revolutionary hero József Bem as Hungarian military commander in Transylvania. Next to Artúr Görgey, Bem proves to be Hungary's most effective military leader of the war. Operating virtually independently, he soon controls most of that province. This allows Görgey to concentrate on the major Austrian threat from the west. Without Bem's able leadership, the war would have been lost in late 1848.

November 22, 1848
South Asia: India: Second Anglo-Sikh War (continued): Battle of Ramnagar. British commander in chief General Sir Hugh Gough leads the principal British army of some 12,000 men and 60 guns in an invasion of the Punjab. He moves first against rebellious Sikh forces commanded by Sher Singh, positioned on the Chenab River with perhaps 20,000 men and 50 guns. The two forces spar for several weeks.

Battle is finally joined on November 22 when the Sikhs repel a British cavalry attack on their bridgehead at Ramnagar. Although Gough drives his enemy back across the Chenab River, the Sikhs are heartened by their successful defense of the bridgehead, which they regard as a major victory.

December 2, 1848
Central Europe: Austria: Accession of Emperor Franz Joseph I. At Olmütz (Olomouc) in Moravia on December 2, new Austrian chief minister General Prince Felix of Schwarzenberg persuades the weak-willed Emperor Ferdinand I to abdicate. His brother, the mild-mannered Archduke Franz Karl, renounces the throne, and his son, 18-year-old Franz Joseph, becomes emperor of Austria. He will rule until 1916. Schwarzenberg pursues policies combining both centralized government and absolutism, with his ultimate goal being the creation of a great German reich under Habsburg control.

December 13, 1848
Central Europe: War between Austria and Hungary (continued). Imperial forces under General Alfred zu Windischgrätz invade Hungary from the west. Other Austrian forces invade from the north and south. Only Hungarian forces under General Józef Bem to the east in Transylvania defend successfully; the other Hungarian armies are driven slowly back, and on December 30 one of them suffers defeat at Mór, west of Budapest. Kossuth and most of the government officials abandon Budapest for Debrecen, in eastern Hungary. Hungarian army commander General Artúr Görgey, his forces now outnumbered two to one and having broken with Lajos Kossuth and the

revolutionary government, withdraws into the mountains to the north, leaving central and eastern Hungary defenseless.

December 20, 1848
Western Europe: France. Louis Napoleon Bonaparte, nephew of Emperor Napoleon I, is elected president of France.

January 5, 1849
Central Europe: Hungary: War between Austria and Hungary (continued): Austrian troops occupy Budapest. Imperial forces under General Alfred zu Windischgrätz march into Budapest. Hungarian leader Lajos Kossuth names Polish general Henryk Dembiński as commander of the army, replacing General Artúr Görgey. Dembiński's appointment fuels Austrian claims that the Hungarian revolution is part of an international conspiracy. Windischgrätz reports that the war is over and that the Hungarian revolution has been crushed. Indeed, he devotes his energies to the administrative reorganization of Hungary.

At Debrecen meanwhile, Hungarian leader Lajos Kossuth tries to rally his people to continue the struggle. Although the Hungarian Parliament remains in session, most of its members either rally to the Austrians or sit at home. Kossuth and the National Defense Committee issue laws by decree. At the end of January, though, General Görgey's army suddenly reappears from the north, breaks through the Austrian forces, and joins the remainder of the Hungarian army in the northeast.

January 13, 1849
South Asia: India: Second Anglo-Sikh War (continued): Battle of Chilianwala. Following the Battle of Ramnagar in November 1848, British commander in chief General Sir Hugh Gough forces his way across the Chenab River in December. British governor-general in India James Andrew Broun-Ramsay, Earl of Dalhousie, initially orders Gough to halt to allow forces under Major General William S. Walsh, then besieging Multan, to join him. With that siege dragging on, however, Dalhousie orders Gough to seek out and destroy Sher Singh's army before it can effect a juncture with another Sikh army under Chattar Singh.

Gough runs into Sher Singh's army at Chilianwala, near the Jhelum River, on January 13, 1849. The British have 16,000 men and 66 guns, the Sikhs perhaps 23,000 men and 60 guns. Gough, known for his frontal assaults, attacks the Sikh army late in the day. The battle is hard-fought action, and many of Gough's troops attack without benefit of artillery support; they sustain heavy casualties and lose both colors and guns.

The British have somewhat the better of it overall, suffering 2,578 killed, 1,651 wounded, and 104 missing. Sikh casualties are estimated at 3,600 killed or wounded. The Sikhs also lose 12 of their guns. The two armies face off for an additional three days, and then both withdraw.

Because Sher Singh is able to continue north and link up with Chattar Singh near Rawalpindi, the battle must be considered a strategic British defeat. Alarm at the heavy losses that Gough has incurred leads to his relief and replacement by General Charles James Napier.

February 8, 1849
Southern Europe: Italy: Proclamation of a Roman Republic. Following the meeting of a constituent assembly on February 8, Rome is declared a republic. The effects of this are great, especially in northern Italy, where King Charles Albert goes to war against Austria again.

February 21, 1849
South Asia: India: Second Anglo-Sikh War (continued): Battle of Gujarat. British forces under Major General William S. Whish are at last successful in the siege of Multan. On January 22, 1849, British siege guns breach the walls, and infantry storm the city. Whish is now able to reinforce the principal British army in the Punjab under British commander in chief General Sir Hugh Gough, who is anxious to move before he can be replaced.

Gough now commands 24,000 men and more than 100 guns. Sikh commander Sher Singh tries to get his cavalry in behind Gough's force but fails, defeated by British cavalry. On February 13 in the Battle of Gujarat, Gough attacks Sher Singh's 20,000 Sikhs, supported by some 1,500 Afghans and 60 guns. Gough opens the battle with a three-hour artillery bombardment that drives the Sikhs from their entrenchments. Gough then sends in cavalry and

horse artillery to exploit the situation. The pursuit continues for four hours. The British lose 96 killed and 682 wounded. Sikh casualties are estimated at 2,000 killed or wounded.

The British victory at Gujarat is the decisive battle of the war. On March 12 Chattar Singh and Sher Singh surrender near Rawalpindi; some 20,000 men lay down their arms. Dost Mohammad Khan of Afghanistan, who had sent some forces into the Punjab to fight the British, now withdraws them. On March 30 Duleep Singh signs away all claims to rule the Punjab. The territory is then annexed by the British East India Company and becomes the North-West Frontier Province.

February 26–27, 1849
Central Europe: Hungary: War between Austria and Hungary (continued): Battle of Kápolna. Northeast of Budapest on February 26 and 27, 1849, Austrian forces under General Alfred zu Windischgrätz defeat the main Hungarian army under General Henryk Dembiński. This leads to the appointment of General Artúr Görgey to command the army despite the wishes of Hungarian leader Lajos Kossuth.

March 23, 1849
Southern Europe: Italy: War between Austria and the Kingdom of Sardinia: Battle of Novara. In northern Italy, King Charles Albert of Sardinia (Piedmont-Sardinia), faced with events in Rome and under considerable pressure from radicals in Piedmont, renounces the Armistice of Salasco and goes to war with Austria again. Austrian field marshal Count Johann Josef Wenzel Radetzky von Radetz puts together 70,000 men and defeats Charles Albert's army in the Battle of Novara. Charles Albert is forced to sign a second armistice and abdicate the throne in favor of his son, Victor Emmanuel II. (Peace is not secured formally until August 9, with Piedmont-Sardinia agreeing to pay to Austria an indemnity of 65 million francs.) This leaves in northern Italy only the city of Venice holding out against the Austrians and permits Radetzky to send part of his force north, there to combine with other Habsburg forces against the Hungarians.

March 27, 1848
Central Europe: Germany: Frankfurt Assembly approves a constitution for Germany. Since May 18,

1848, delegates from the German states have been meeting at Frankfurt in an effort to create a unified German state. Sharp differences emerge over both what constitutes Germany and the constitutional arrangement to be drawn. These issues become moot as the old conservative German governments recover their authority.

Nonetheless, the deputies reach a decision in March. The so-called Little Germans (Kleindeutch) win out, with German states able to enter the new Germany with their German provinces alone. Austria rejects this. On March 27 the deputies approve a constitution that creates a federal government with representative institutions under a hereditary "Emperor of the Germans." The latter has considerable executive powers, including command of the military, but only a suspensive three-year veto. Ministers are responsible to the upper house of Parliament.

The deputies vote to offer the Crown to Frederick William IV of Prussia. Although he very much wants to be the head of a united Germany, he rejects what he calls a "crown from the gutter." The Frankfurt Assembly collapses.

March 29, 1849

Southern Europe: Italy: Reorganization of the government of the Roman Republic. News of the defeat of the army of Piedmont-Sardinia in the Battle of Custozza leads revolutionaries in Rome to reorganize the government along moderate, conciliatory lines. Giuseppe Mazzini is the best-known figure. Nonetheless, both the French and Austrian governments consider intervention.

April–Early May 1849

Central Europe: Hungary: War between Austria and Hungary (continued). Hungarian army commander General Artúr Görgey outmaneuvers the Austrians, and in April and early May wins a series of small military victories, liberating much of Hungary. The army fights its way into Budapest, although the Austrians continue to hold Castle Hill. On April 22 Hungarian forces relieve the Austrian siege of the fortress of Kamárom on the Danube. Soon the Viennese are fortifying the Austrian capital in anticipation of a Hungarian attack. In truth, the Hungarians lack the population, industrial resources, and military might to win the war.

April 14, 1849

Central Europe: Hungary: War between Austria and Hungary (continued): Hungary declares independence. On April 14, 1849, the Hungarian Parliament at Debrecen declares the complete independence of Hungary and elects Lajos Kossuth as governor-president. The declaration makes little difference in the war and leads to an even more pronounced split with Hungarian army commander Artúr Görgey, who favors a negotiated settlement.

April 24, 1849

Southern Europe: Italy: French military operations against Rome. The governments of Austria and France are both considering military intervention to put down the Republic in Rome and restore Pope Pius IX to full authority, but France moves first. On April 14, 1849, the French assembly votes funds for a military expedition. The move is supposedly to forestall Austrian intervention but in reality is prompted by President Louis Napoleon Bonaparte's hopes of winning the support of French Catholics. On August 24 some 8,000 French troops under Marshal Nicolas Oudinot land at Cività Vecchia, Italy, and begin the march on Rome.

April 29–30, 1849

Southern Europe: Italy: French military operations against Rome (continued): First French assault. Believing that the republicans in Rome enjoy only limited support, Marshal Nicolas Oudinot orders an assault on the city on April 29–30. The French are repulsed by the defenders led by Giuseppe Garibaldi. The republicans also deflect attacks by the Neapolitan army at Palestrina (May 9) and at Velletri (May 19).

May 21, 1849

Central Europe: Hungary: War between Austria and Hungary (continued): Hungarian forces take Castle Hill in Buda. Although the Hungarians control the rest of the city, a few thousand Austrian troops under General Heinrich Hentzi hold out on Castle Hill in Buda. Hungarian army commander General Artúr Görgey moves against Castle Hill, but the siege takes three weeks. The Austrians surrender only on May 21, thanks to their tenacious defense but also because the Hungarians lack siege artillery. Lajos Kossuth enters Budapest that same day. Görgey's decision to take Castle Hill instead of immediately moving against Vienna is his one and only major strategic error of the war. It probably costs the Hungarians their last chance to force the Austrians into negotiations.

May 29, 1849

Southern Europe: Italy: French military operations against Rome (continued): Treaty arranged by Ferdinand de Lesseps. Frenchman Ferdinand de Lesseps (later builder of the Suez Canal), sent by the French government to negotiate with the republican government of Rome, signs a treaty that provides for the French military to be allowed into the city in return for French acceptance of the new republican institutions and a guarantee to protect it against other foreign intervention. De Lesseps is, however, abruptly recalled on June 1, and the treaty is disavowed. French president Louis Napoleon Bonaparte reinforces Marshal Nicolas Oudinot and orders him to take Rome by force.

May–August 24, 1849

Southern Europe: Italy: Austrian siege of Venice. Although republican Venice had come under blockade by Austrian forces months earlier, on May 26, 1849, the Venetian defenders are forced to abandon Fort Marghera. Food is soon scarce. On June 19 the powder magazine blows up. The next month, cholera breaks out and ravages the city. The Austrians then begin to shell the city, and when the Sardinian fleet withdraws from the Adriatic, the Austrians are also able to attack by sea.

On August 24, 1849, with food and ammunition exhausted, leader of the Republic of Venice Daniele Manin negotiates the city's capitulation. He secures amnesty for all except himself and a few others (including Neapolitan general Guglielmo Pepe, who had assisted in the city's defense), who are allowed to go into exile. Manin departs Venice three days later on a French ship; he will die in exile in France.

June 3, 1849

Southern Europe: Italy: French military operations against Rome (continued): Second French assault on Rome. On June 3, 1849, French troops under Marshal Nicolas Oudinot mount a second assault on the city, attacking without warning. In desperate fighting the defenders, led by Giuseppe Garibaldi, again repulse the French. This forces Oudinot to commence siege operations.

June 17, 1849

Central Europe: Hungary: Russian military intervention. Czar Nicholas II of Russia needs little urging, for he believes that monarchs should aid one another to put down revolutions and is angered that Polish generals serve with the Hungarian forces. Prepared to intervene earlier, he waits for an Austrian request. The Austrians, humiliated at having to ask, delay but finally do so.

On May 9, 1849, therefore, Czar Nicholas II promises aid to Austria, and on June 17 Field Marshal Prince Ivan Paskievich leads a Russian army of some 200,000 men in an invasion of Hungary from Poland and the Danubian Principalities. At the same time, General Julius Jacob von Haynau, who replaces General Alfred zu Windischgrätz, invades Hungary from the west with a well-equipped Austrian army of about 175,000 men. Against these two forces, the Hungarians can muster only about 170,000 men with only about one-third the field artillery of their opponents.

June 30, 1849

Southern Europe: Italy: French military operations against Rome (continued): Garibaldi-Oudinot agreement. Spain has also sent some 9,000 troops at the request of the pope to aid in the siege of Rome. Realizing that the situation is hopeless, the commander of the republican defenders of Rome, Giuseppe Garibaldi, comes to terms with French commander Marshal Nicolas Oudinot. Garibaldi and some 4,000 volunteers march out of the city on July 2. Moving north, they hope to join the defenders of the Republic of Venice. They are pursued by French, Austrian, Spanish, and Italian loyalist forces, however, and most are captured, killed, or dispersed. Garibaldi is among those able to escape. He travels to America, where he is in exile until 1854.

June–July 1849

Central Europe: Hungary: Austrian and Russian invasions of Hungary and series of Hungarian military defeats. In late June and early July, Austrian forces under General Julius Jacob von Haynau defeat the main Hungarian army under General Artúr Görgey in a series of battles near the fortress of Komárom. On July 8 the Hungarian government again abandons Budapest. Other military defeats follows for the Hungarians; most come at the hands of the Austrians, the

Russian generals proving prove far less adroit than their Austrian counterparts.

The Hungarian cause is not helped by squabbling between General Görgey and Hungarian governor-president Lajos Kossuth. Görgey maneuvers brilliantly but manages only to preserve his forces largely intact for the Hungarian defeat. The other Hungarian armies, including that of General Józef Bem in Transylvania, are defeated one by one. On July 28 Kossuth and the Hungarian government extend full ethnic rights to all the minorities in Hungary. It is too late.

August 9, 1849

Central Europe: Hungary: Battle of Temesvár. By early August 1849 the remaining Hungarian forces are congregated in the southeastern part of the country. Surprisingly, Hungarian governor-president Lajos Kossuth gives overall command of the army back to General Henryk Dembiński, whose subsequent poor maneuvering renders inevitable the final Hungarian defeat. General Julius Jacob von Haynau commands the Austrian side during the final battle at Temesvár on August 9, 1849. General Józef Bem commands the Hungarians, who have only their southern forces available here and who lose several hundred killed and some 6,000 taken prisoner. The rest of the army simply dissolves. The Austrians lose fewer than 50 killed.

August 13, 1849

Central Europe: Hungary: Surrender of Hungarian forces at Világos. Only the Hungarian army of General Artúr Görgey remains. It and the government are at Arad. On August 11 Kossuth resigns his position and appoints Görgey military dictator of Hungary, and on August 17 Kossuth flees in disguise across the southern border into Ottoman territory along with a few thousand Hungarian soldiers, the entire Polish legion, and some civilians. On August 13 meanwhile, Görgey shows his contempt for the Austrians by surrendering to the Russians at Világos (now Şiria, Ro-

mania) with some 34,000 officers and men and 144 guns. He evidently hopes that they will be allowed to enter Russian service. Except for Görgey himself, the Russians hand all of them over to the Austrians, who execute a number of the leading officers. The Austrians also show little mercy to the remainder or, for that matter, to the civilian population. When the fortress of Komárom surrenders on October 5, the Hungarian War of Independence is over. The next day the Austrians commence the execution of Hungarian revolutionary leaders in their hands.

1849

Southeast Asia: Netherlands East Indies. The Dutch put down a revolt in Java in the Netherlands East Indies (Indonesia) against their rule.

1849–1851

Caribbean Basin: Cuba. Spanish colonel Narciso I. López, in exile in the United States, attempts three filibustering expeditions against Cuba to free the island from Spanish rule. In the first, in August 1849, U.S. authorities intervene to halt the expedition. In the second, López and a number of southern volunteers land at Cárdenas, Cuba, on May 19, 1850, but are driven off. In the third attempt López, with another group of American volunteers, lands near Havana during August 11–21, 1851. The Cuban people fail to rise up. López and his followers are captured. López and 51 American followers are then executed at Havana. This causes widespread outrage in the United States.

1849–1854

Central Asia: Russian conquest of the Syr Darya River Valley. The Syr Darya River is the longest in Central Asia. (The river, which passes through present-day Uzbekistan, Tajikistan, and Kazakhstan, also marked the northernmost limit of Alexander the Great's empire.) The Russia conquest ends Persian suzerainty over this part of Central Asia and brings Russian influence to the border of Persian Khorasan.

The Rise of Military Professionalism

Overview of 1850–1900

The half century from 1850 to 1900 is marked by three major trends that had profound impact on warfare. These are total war, the rise of military professionalism, and heightened technological change. The period also encompasses a number of important wars, including the Taiping Rebellion in China, the American Civil War, the wars for German and Italian unification, the Boer War, and the Spanish-American War. The period ends with heightened tensions among the Great Powers, as seen in the race for overseas markets and colonial empires in Africa and Asia and a not-unrelated naval building contest between Britain and Germany.

The American Civil War inaugurates a new era of total war, one in which the entire society is organized for war and where the nation's entire assets—including population, agriculture, and above all industrial base—all factor into the outcome. In this new era, the aim is not simply the destruction of an enemy's armed forces but the devastation of its economic and even political and social order.

The period is also marked by a dramatic rise in military professionalism. The exemplar is the Prussian General Staff. Following the success of Prussia against Austria (1866) and France (1870–1871), the military establishments of many nations, which had heretofore regarded France as their model, now seek to emulate the Prussian staff system. The hallmarks of the Prussian staff system are careful research, thorough planning, effective preparation (to include the mobilization of resources), and the application of professional logistical concepts in warfare.

Count Alfred von Schlieffen, who became chief of the German General Staff in 1891 and held that position until 1906, figures prominently among military theorists of this period. Perhaps the most widely read and highly regarded military theorist of his day, Schlieffen had a profound impact on the development of modern maneuver warfare. Much of his professional reading and writing was in ancient history. (His classic work was *Cannae,* a study of the 216 BCE battle during the Second Punic War.)

Faced with the collapse of Bismarck's alliance system, which had heretofore kept France isolated, Schlieffen developed a flexible strategy for dealing with a two-front war against France and Russia. His plan centered on a holding action against a slow-to-mobilize Russia, while Germany delivered a knockout blow against the more formidable opponent of France. The Schlieffen Plan failed in World War I and has since been much discussed and debated. In fairness to Schlieffen, however, his successor Helmuth von Moltke (the Younger) dramatically altered the ratio of forces in the West and, when Russia moved faster and in greater strength than anticipated, also modified the plan as the offensive against France was in progress.

See Leaders: Schlieffen, Alfred von

In France, Colonel Charles J. J. J. Ardant du Picq analyzed warfare in the 1850s and 1860s. Du Picq's real influence came after his death, however; he was killed at age 49 in August 1870 by a German shell during the Franco-Prussian War. His writings were subsequently published as *Les Études sur le combat antique et modern* (The Study of Ancient and Modern Combat). They stress greater training by a smaller professional military establishment (as opposed to mass conscript forces) and tactical and strategic aggressiveness. His writing had a profound influence on the officers who led French military forces during World War I, including Ferdinand Foch.

See Leaders: Ardant du Picq, Charles

Among naval strategists, the most important by far was U.S. Navy captain (later rear admiral) Alfred Thayer Mahan. The son of West Point professor Dennis Hart Mahan, the younger Mahan elected to make a career of the navy rather than the army. His major contribution came as a naval historian, theorist, and strategist. Following service in the American Civil War, Mahan wrote extensively, first on that conflict and then on naval history in general. His seminal work, *The Influence of Sea Power upon History, 1660–1783* (1890), was at once both immensely flattering to and influential with the British, for it dealt with the period of their rise as the world's major naval power. It was also widely influential in Germany, where it became the justification for Kaiser Wilhelm II's mistaken plan to build a powerful battle fleet to challenge Britain for world naval mastery. Mahan was less influential in his own country but nonetheless enjoyed influential followers there, including Theodore Roosevelt. Mahan stressed that naval power was the key to world power and that the only way to achieve mastery at sea was through powerful battle fleets centered on battleships. He thus eschewed the *guerre de course* strategy that had been pursued by the United States.

See Leaders: Mahan, Alfred Thayer

Generalleutnant Count Alfred von Schlieffen (1833–1913) was chief of the German General Staff during 1891–1906 and originated the plan associated with his name to deal with the threat of a two-front war with France and Russia. (Hulton Archive/Getty Images)

Technological Changes and Advancements

The changes in technology during 1850–1900 were immense. The Crimean War (1853–1856) began with the old-style warfare of muskets, brightly colored uniforms, cavalry charges, and wooden ships; it ended with trench warfare, the rifle, explosive shell, the telegraph, long-range rifled artillery, the ironclad warship, and mine warfare at sea.

Weapons. Building on greatly improved, more precise machine tools and manufacturing techniques, this period experienced a quantum jump in the effectiveness of small arms. Although in the American Civil War the Union Army alone employed more than 80 different types of shoulder arms, the standard weapon was the muzzle-loading .58-caliber rifle. This was 4.75 feet long, weighed nine pounds, and utilized a cylindro-conoidal lead minié ball bullet fired by a percussion cap. Trained infantrymen could fire three rounds a minute and stop an infantry attack at 200–250 yards. The rifle was effective at more than half a mile.

In the 1870s reliable breech-loading repeating rifles came into general use, and in the 1880s smokeless powder was introduced. The new powder had great advantages over the earlier black powder. It reduced bore fouling and did not impair visibility, which made aiming easier. It also allowed defending riflemen to conceal themselves from enemy observation, as the British discovered in the South African War (Boer War) of 1899–1902 and the Americans learned during the 1898 Spanish-American War. In Cuba, the Spanish defenders had little trouble locating and firing against the positions of the American infantry, firing black-powder Trapdoor Springfields, and the artillery, also using black-powder cartridges. The Americans, however, had difficulty locating the Spanish infantry firing Mauser rifles and their newer model artillery pieces utilizing smokeless powder. Indeed, smokeless powder led to interest in camouflage among the world's armies.

> *See* Weapons: Rifle, Breech Loader
> *See* Weapons: Smokeless Gunpowder
> *See* Weapons: Camouflage

In the 1880s bolt-action magazine rifles were introduced. With these, an individual soldier could fire rounds at the speed he could work the bolt mechanism. Other innovations included the solid-brass cartridge case and the hard-jacketed bullet. The precisely dimensioned cartridge case eased mechanical loading and extraction, which was essential in the new machine guns that fired at rates of 240 and more rounds per minute. The solid-jacketed bullet also facilitated the loading process and left less of itself behind in the bore than the old lead bullet. The shape of bullets also changed. The spitzer, or boat-tail bullet, was both smaller and aerodynamically more stable and hence had greater velocity and range than its predecessor.

> *See* Weapons: Cartridge

The new firearms that appeared at the end of the century would see service, with but slight modification, for a half century or more. Magazine rifles included the British Lee-Enfield (1881), the French Lebel (1886), the Austrian Mannlicher (1886), the German Mauser (1889), and the American Springfield (1903). Almost every weapon brought increases in both range and velocity. Such weapons had a combat-effective range of 400 yards or more, and shooting matches at a range of 1,000 yards were a common occurrence. The British Army especially stressed aimed long-range rifle fire, the importance of which would be revealed in the early battles in France in World War I.

Alfred Thayer Mahan (1840–1914) was a naval officer, historian, and strategist who argued tirelessly for construction of a powerful U.S. battle fleet and acquisition of overseas bases. (Library of Congress)

> *See* Weapons: Lebel Rifle

These new rifles and their improved ammunition continued to widen the advantage of the defense over the offense. Although the bayonet remained in service, it was largely just a tool for camp use. It saw little service as an offensive weapon simply because the attackers rarely got close enough to utilize it.

The appearance of a new infantry weapon also revolutionized warfare and significantly added to the advantages of the defensive over the offensive. New machine tools, improved metallurgical techniques, and closer tolerances made possible the machine gun. The Gatling gun paved the way. Designed by American Richard Jordan Gatling in 1862 during the American Civil War, it saw limited use in that conflict. It was used more extensively in the Indian Wars in the American West. Aware of problems resulting from the buildup of heat on firing, Gatling developed a gun with six rotating barrels around a central axis. Each barrel fired in turn, and each had its own bolt and firing pin.

> *See* Weapons: Gatling Gun

The Gatling gun was soon rendered obsolete by the Maxim gun, patented in 1884 by American Hiram Maxim who was working for the British firm of Vickers. The Maxim gun was the first modern machine gun and a truly efficient killer. Using recoil energy, the Maxim was extraordinarily reliable and easily transportable. It weighed only 100 pounds, was water-cooled, and had a five-man crew.

Fighting in Africa provided ample examples of the Maxim gun's firepower. The British employed the Maxim gun with great success against both the Zulus in South Africa and the Dervishes in the Sudan. In the Battle of Omdurman in the Sudan on September 2, 1898, the British slew some 10,000 Sudanese and wounded as many more, a large number of these from 20 Maxim guns, while losing only 48 dead themselves. Hilaire Belloc wrote, "Whatever happens, we have got the Maxim gun, and they have not." Maxim was later knighted by Queen Victoria for his services to humanity—it was thought that the machine gun would make wars shorter, hence more humane.

See Weapons: Maxim Gun

New powerful explosives appeared in TNT (1863) and dynamite (1866). Artillery also underwent important changes during this period because of the improved manufacturing techniques and tremendous advances in metallurgy, especially steel alloys. The period began with virtually all muzzle-loading smoothbore weapons. Although there were numerous problems, muzzle-loading rifled guns found increased favor during the American Civil War, and by the end of the conflict they accounted for perhaps 20 percent of battlefield guns. The century ended, however, with virtually all artillery pieces being rifled breech-loading guns. Smoothbore mortars were the major exception.

See Weapons: TNT
See Weapons: Dynamite
See Weapons: Napoleon Gun
See Weapons: Breech-Loading Field Artillery

In 1860 the German firm of Krupp began casting rifled steel guns, which the French would have done well to acquire but did not purchase before the Franco-Prussian War. In 1891 both France and Germany developed recoil systems whereby the gun barrel recoiled in slides against springs that returned the barrel to its original position. This meant not only a faster rate of fire but also less manpower needed to work the guns. More reliable mechanical fuses, steel-coated projectiles, and high-explosive fillers for the shells also appeared. Such guns were both more quick-fired and far more accurate than their predecessors. New slower-burning powder also produced more thrust against the shell and less pressure on the gun itself, making possible significant savings in weight.

See Weapons: Bormann Fuse

Up to this point, artillery was essentially a direct-fire antipersonnel weapon. Artillerymen could fire at what they could see on the battlefield. This was its primary employment in the American Civil War. When troops were out of sight of enemy guns, they were essentially safe. An important change occurred in artillery tactics with the introduction of aimed indirect fire.

The first real attempt at this occurred in the American Civil War, but it was not until 1882, when the Russian Carl Guk developed a system for firing on an unseen target using a compass, an aiming point, and a forward observer, that this was truly practical. The Japanese refined this method, and in their 1904–1905 war with Russia they employed indirect fire with great success.

By the 1890s most European armies had standardized the techniques of artillery fire, allowing for the massing of fire on remote targets. During the South African War (Boer War), the Boers concealed their artillery pieces instead of exposing them as in British practice. Smokeless powder meant that the gun's position would be more difficult to locate when it was fired regardless.

Communications: The Telegraph and Telephone. The telegraph, followed by the telephone, brought a communications revolution, making possible the rapid transmission of messages over vast distances and the co-ordination of disparate military elements from a central command point. Cable laid on the ocean floor provided rapid strategic communication between home governments and far-flung military and naval forces. The telegraph proved its worth in the American Civil War and in the Austro-Prussian War of 1866, when General Helmuth von Moltke employed it to coordinate the simultaneous movement of three Prussian field armies into Bohemia. The importance of the telegraph is demonstrated by the efforts of soldiers both North and South to intercept enemy telegraph messages and/or destroy wire during the American Civil War and by U.S. Navy efforts to cut telegraph cables connecting the Philippines and Cuba with Spain during the Spanish-American War of 1898.

Such rapid communication with units in the field had profound impact on grand strategy. It allowed governments, for ill or good, to more closely supervise and order field operations. The telegraph also enabled the rapid transmission by war correspondents of dispatches that might influence government leaders and the general public on the formation of policy. Such news dispatches by the first real war correspondents, during the Crimean War, did have a salutary effect for future generations of soldiers.

Modern photography also came into play in this as well. Both media served to reveal the actual conditions endured by the common soldier and the true nature of war. This led to improvements in medical care and the everyday life of men in the field.

See Weapons: Telegraph

The telephone, invented by Alexander Graham Bell in 1876, enabled instant voice communication. The telephone first went to war in the Spanish-American War of 1898, when President William McKinley had a war room at the White House. Often overlooked in communication, the typewriter also wrought tremendous change, as did the seemingly innocuous development of carbon paper. Both were of great assistance in the management of mass armies of the next century.

See Weapons: Telephone

Care of the Wounded. The horrible suffering of British troops, especially the wounded, during the Crimean War in the winter of 1854–1855 brought a great hue and cry for improvements when it was made known to the British public by the first real war correspondents. This not only led to improved logistical support but also brought the arrival of Florence Nightingale and several dozen of her nurses along with modern military nursing and hospital care. The terrible bloodletting and suffering of the wounded in the Battle of Solferino during the war of France and Piedmont-Sardinia with Austria in 1859 sparked the formation of the International Red Cross.

Great advances were made in sanitation as well. Proper location of latrines was one factor in the change. In the American Civil War, sickness killed 10 times more men than battle; the greatest killer was diarrhea. The Spanish-American War brought confirmation of the cause of yellow fever, and this centuries-long scourge of the tropics was soon eradicated.

Logistics. Logistics, often overlooked in the study of war and development of strategy, also underwent great change in the period. The key was the harnessing of steam power both on land and at sea. On land, this meant the railroad. Railroads were vital in moving and supplying the new mass, conscript armies. Large quantities of military supplies and equipment as well as troops could be moved swiftly in this fashion, as was demonstrated early in the American Civil War when Confederate general Joseph E. Johnston was able to bring up 10,000 men from the Shenandoah Valley to Manassas Junction in the first troop movement by rail in U.S. history. This was undoubtedly a key factor in the Confederate victory in the First Battle of Bull Run (Manassas) of July 21, 1861. The North, with much more track, enjoyed far greater advantage from the railroad than did the South. Because of the importance of railroads, disruption of an enemy's rail system was a principal goal of military planners on both sides in the war. The railroad was also important to Prussia in enabling its rapid victory over Austria in 1866.

See Weapons: Railroad

Land Warfare

Tactics. The introduction, in the 1850s, of long-range rifled muskets of far greater reliability of fire gave tremendous superiority to the defense over the offense. These muskets created a dilemma for any attacker that persisted well into the next century, but was either not appreciated or well understood by the generals. Standard tactics in the American Civil War saw attackers formed in ranks two men deep and advancing shoulder-to-shoulder. Officers were expected to lead from the front, encouraging their men by example. Other officers and noncommissioned officers were positioned in the rear to guard against straggling. Attackers normally moved forward in cadenced step measured by the beat of a drum, with the men halting at intervals to fire and reload. The second rank, positioned a half step to the side of the front rank, fired over the shoulders of the first. Occasionally the attackers advanced on the double. Because of the black powder utilized in the firearms of the day, the battlefield soon became thickly shrouded in dense smoke, with commanders having little idea of what was transpiring. Although contemporary tactical manuals called for attacks to be concluded with the bayonet, this rarely occurred because the two lines usually did not close to such a distance to make it possible. Union surgical records of the war show that only half of 1 percent of war wounds were inflicted with the bayonet.

To compensate attackers for the increased firepower of the percussion rifle by defenders, step rates were increased in the 1850s. Thus, there was a double quick time of 165 steps per minute. But the more rapid step rates did not compensate attackers for the losses that the rifled musket could inflict on them while advancing in close order over distance. During the American Civil War, double quick time and the run, especially over extended distances, wore out the attackers, a problem that is mentioned frequently in after-action reports as an excuse for failure.

Defending infantry was also usually drawn up in double line. The men fired either standing erect or from a kneeling position, or they fired from field entrenchments if there was time to prepare them. The percussion cap and the conoidal minié bullet made infantry fire of the American Civil War about twice as deadly as it had been in the Mexican-American War, less than two decades earlier.

This led to the extensive use, especially after the great slaughter of the Battle of Antietam (September 17, 1862), of field entrenchments by the defenders. Massed fire from such earthworks could be absolutely deadly, especially if it included artillery firing grape and canister. It could destroy an attacking force before it had closed to any appreciable distance. Frontal assaults against well-trained troops rarely succeeded. Indeed, the complex earthen defenses of the American Civil War foreshadowed the trench systems that typified the Western Front in World War I. Generally speaking, in order to ensure success in an offensive operation, the attackers had to possess, at the point of attack, a manpower advantage of up to three to one.

Naval Warfare

Ironclad Warships. Although iron canal boats had been introduced in the late 18th century, the Crimean War saw the first ironclad warships. These were a handful of French floating batteries, wooden ships mounting heavy guns and protected by facing iron plates bolted in place.

See Weapons: Ironclad Warships

The logical extension of the ironclad floating battery was an ironclad oceangoing warship. Britain, which had the most to lose by going to a new weapons system that would render obsolete its navy, then by far the world's largest, resisted. The French took the lead with their *Gloire* of 1860.

See Weapons: *Gloire*

If the English were slow to enter this new arms race, the construction of the *Gloire* created sufficient impetus for them to proceed. Once the British embarked on the construction of armored warships, their technological edge in metallurgy quickly told. The British *Warrior* (1862) was both a true oceangoing ship and a dramatic improvement over the French *Gloire.*

See Weapons: *Warrior,* HMS

The first appearance of a modern ironclad warship in a sea fight came on March 6, 1862, in Hampton Roads, Virginia, during the American Civil War. The Confederate ironclad ram *Virginia* (the raised and rebuilt U.S. Navy screw frigate *Merrimac*) engaged and sank the U.S. Navy sailing frigate *Congress* and the sloop *Cumberland.* The first clash between ironclads and the first use of the turret in naval warfare occurred the next day with the appearance of the Union ironclad *Monitor* and the drawn battle between it and the *Virginia.*

See Weapons: Naval Gun Turret

The revolutionary *Warrior* in drydock at Portsmouth, England, toward the end of its 1872–1875 refit. The *Warrior* was the world's first iron-hulled, armor-plated warship. (U.S. Naval Historical Center)

Those who favored the revolving turret and supporters of broadside armament remained divided for some time. Interest in the ram was renewed as a consequence of the naval Battle of Lissa (July 20, 1866), and bigger, more powerful guns helped decide the matter in favor of the turret. If ramming was a tactical aim, then warships had to fire ahead as they prepared to attack; heavier guns also meant that ships needed fewer of them, and that these should have the widest arc of fire possible. For many years ramming and bows-on fighting (in which ramming was an important part) heavily influenced naval design.

As ship design changed, so too did propulsion systems. Warships continued to carry sail rigs into the 1890s. Down to 1870, most of the world's merchant fleets were sailing ships. As late as 1880, there was as much tonnage driven by wind as by steam. More powerful marine engines soon made the use of screw propellers truly practical, though. Improved metallurgical techniques led to a series of innovations after 1870 including the compound engine, which greatly improved on the simple single-expansion engine. The appearance of the triple-expansion steam engine in the 1880s was a great advance in propulsion. It developed steam in three stages and greatly improved engine economy. Instead of a normal pressure of 25–30 pounds per square inch (psi), it could produce steam at 60 psi. This meant that vessels could go much greater distances without recoaling. This was the last step before the introduction of the steam turbine. Engines became smaller, and an improved condenser appeared.

These inventions reduced the consumption of coal and the cost of operating steamships. Equally important, by reducing the space required for coal and water, more space was available for cargo, crews, and ordnance.

During Queen Victoria's diamond jubilee in 1897, the greatest of all Victorian naval reviews, a novel new craft made its appearance. This was the yacht *Turbina,* powered by the steam turbine engine developed by the firm of Parsons. In this system, steam heated by means of a water-pipe boiler was passed through a series of nozzles. Gaining velocity, it was then directed onto a series of blades on the periphery of a rotor. The velocity of the steam passed along these blades, turning the rotor and powering the propellers.

See Weapons: *Turbina,* HMS

The revolutionary steam turbine engine was both faster and more reliable than the reciprocating engine it replaced, which tended to shake itself to pieces. It also avoided design and protection problems resulting from the growing height of the reciprocal engine's large pistons. As the *Turbina* was faster than either the torpedo boats or torpedo boat destroyers in the review, the Admiralty ordered a turbine-powered destroyer, the *Viper,* launched in 1899.

At sea, the race between guns and armor continued. The British battleship *Inflexible* of 11,880 tons, completed in 1881, mounted four 16-inch muzzle-loading Armstrong guns set two each in two turrets, off the center line so as to allow ahead fire. The *Inflexible* has the distinction of carrying the thickest armor of any battleship ever built. Its citadel had two layers of 12-inch iron plate backed by 36 inches of teak, which altogether weighed 1,100 pounds per square foot. By the end of the century, though, battleships had dramatically increased in size and destructive firepower, and they carried thinner, more resilient armor. The modern steel battleship, now employing breech-loading guns of up to 12-inches set in turrets, held sway.

See Weapons: Breech-Loading Modern Heavy Guns at Sea

Naval ordnance experts simultaneously developed armor-piercing projectiles as the answer to armored warships. In 1881 Hadfield of Sheffield began manufacturing cast-steel projectiles; four years later Hadfield patented a compound armor-piercing shell. Other types of hardened shells followed, including one of chrome steel.

See Weapons: Armor-Piercing Shell

Naval Mine Warfare. In war it is traditionally the weaker power that experiments with new methods, and the Crimean War and American Civil War were no exceptions. The Russians experimented with mines during the Crimean War in order to keep allied ships from its Baltic ports. Although several British ships struck the mines, the latter were so small as to be ineffective. Seeking to overcome superior Union numbers and superior manufacturing resources, the Confederacy also experimented widely with the naval mine. Mines in the American Civil War, then known as torpedoes and exploded either by contact or electronically from shore, actually sank a significant number of Union ships.

American Civil War mine powder charges ranged from some 50 pounds to up to a ton. On the James River in Virginia on May 6, 1864, one of the largest of these torpedoes, detonated electrically from shore, blew up the 542-ton Union gunboat *Commodore Jones.* The explosion claimed some 40 lives. The *Commodore Jones* was the first ship sunk by an electrically detonated mine in the history of warfare.

See Weapons: Mines, Sea

Torpedoes were also placed at the end of a long spar mounted in the bow of a fast launch and were used by both sides as offensive weapons. Thus, during the American Civil War a small Union launch was able to sink the Confederate ironclad *Albemarle* by means of a spar torpedo. The success of such devices led to efforts to develop a propelled mine for use at sea.

The first modern automotive mine, or torpedo, was developed by a Captain Luppis of the Austro-Hungarian Navy in 1865. It was perfected two years later by the Scottish engineer Robert Whitehead, who managed an engine works in Fiume. Automotive torpedoes powered by compressed air were delivered by small, fast, and narrow seagoing warships known as torpedo boats. By the end of the century, automotive torpedoes could sink the largest battleships.

See Weapons: Torpedo
See Weapons: Torpedo Boat

To counter the threat, navies developed the somewhat larger but equally fast torpedo boat destroyer (later simply called the destroyer). These warships were charged with patrolling on the periphery of the battle fleet to search out and destroy enemy torpedo boats.

See Weapons: Destroyer

The ideal delivery system for the torpedo, however, was a new type of warship: the submarine. The first true submarine had appeared in the American Revolutionary War, but the first sinking of a warship by a submersible occurred during the American Civil War off Charleston, South Carolina, on February 17, 1864. The Confederate *H. L. Hunley* employed a spar torpedo against the Union screw sloop *Housatonic*; both the *H. L. Hunley* and the *Housatonic* went down in the engagement.

The first real modern submarine was the *Holland VI*, built by an Irish immigrant to the United States, John P. Holland. His sixth submarine, which made its first surface run in 1898 and is usually known simply as the *Holland*, was the forerunner of all modern submarines. It combined an internal combustion 45-horsepower gasoline engine for running on the surface with hatches open and an electric motor for submerged cruising. The gasoline engine powered a generator that recharged the batteries.

See Weapons: *Holland,* USS

By the end of the century, some naval observers believed that the new powerful automotive torpedoes carried by surface ships and submarines had rendered the battleship obsolete.

Naval Ordnance. The second half of the 19th century saw the introduction aboard ship of increasingly large breech-loading recoiling guns. Heavier guns meant larger projectiles, and this necessitated greater thicknesses of armor. It was not feasible, however, to place heavy armor over the entire ship. One of the chief advantages of the monitor design, for instance, was that the turret could be heavily armored while the rest of the ship could have less armor protection.

A shift to guns of steel accompanied the enormous increases in gun size. At the same time that the Royal Navy went to the breech loader, it adopted the all-steel gun. A steel jacket was shrunk over a steel tube, and layers of steel hoops were then shrunk over this. The system of jackets and hoops over the steel tube was followed by one in which steel wire was spun on under tension, which varied with the distance from the bore. This helped eliminate barrel droop. Such wire guns continued in British service until the 1930s.

Bore lengths of the guns increased from 35 to even 45 calibers. The first great French Navy steel gun was the 48-ton, 13.4-inch Model 1875. The next step up for France came with 371-millimeter (14.6-inch) guns for its battleships *Amiral Baudin* and *Formidable.* Such larger guns required both mechanized ammunition hoists and complex breech-loading gear.

Cordite, which came into widespread use in the 1890s, removed one of the obstacles to accurate long-range gunfire at sea: the massive clouds of smoke that accompanied firing. This was particularly important to accurate fire by the new quick-firing guns against fast-moving torpedo boats. The new powders also had a considerable advantage in weight: a 12-inch gun required only 88.5 pounds of cordite to produce the same muzzle velocity as 295 pounds of prism brown powder.

Capital ships all had mixed armaments to enable them to fight at short, intermediate, and long ranges. Naval theorists held that battles would occur at relatively short ranges, well within the range of secondary armaments that could be used to smother an opponent with rapid fire. This conclusion seemed to be borne out by the sea fights at the end of the century. In the battles of Manila and Santiago during the Spanish-American War, U.S. warships closed to within 2,000 yards of the Spanish vessels in ideal calm conditions yet scored only 3 percent hits.

The development of small-caliber (4- to 6-inch) quick-firing guns was of great importance to warships of the period. Smaller rapid-fire guns had been an integral part of ship armament for some time. All navies utilized machine guns, but the new rapid-fire larger-caliber guns were intended to destroy torpedo boats before they could close to effective range.

See Weapons: Quick-Firing Naval Gun

Tactics. In naval engagements, the line-ahead formation was preferred, as it is allowed maximum fire from the largest turreted guns.

Crossing the T remained the preferred method of engaging an enemy battle line. Here a commander at sea sought to maneuver his own ships in line-ahead formation in order to bring maximum broadsides' firepower on the lead ships in an enemy formation, whereas the latter could only bring their forward guns into play. To achieve that, superior speed was essential.

Chronology (continued)

January–March 1850
Southern Europe: Greece: British naval blockade. When the Greek government fails to pay interest on an international loan and compensation to some British citizens, the British government orders a naval blockade of Greece in January 1850. The blockade is lifted in March following conclusion of a compromise agreement.

November 29, 1850
Central Europe: Moravia: Punctuation of Olmütz. King Frederick William IV wants to be the ruler of a united Germany but on his own terms. He proposes a federation of German princes, without Austria but within a Middle European bloc that would include Austria. This scheme is unacceptable to both Austrian first minister Prince Felix of Schwarzenberg and Russian czar Nicholas I. At a conference at Olmütz (Olomouc) in Moravia, Frederick William, Nicholas, and Emperor Franz Josef of Austria agree on the Punctuation of Olmütz, known to Prussians as the Humiliation of Olmütz. This restores the loose-knit German Confederation of 1815. Thousands of disgruntled Germans (the Forty-Eighters) emigrate, many of them to the United States. The failure of Germans to unify by democratic, peaceful means opens the way to Otto von Bismarck's subsequent iron-and-blood approach.

1850–1853
South Africa: Eighth Xhosa War. The Xhosa Wars are a series of nine separate conflicts between the European settlers and the native Xhosa people of what is now the Eastern Cape in South Africa. Beginning in 1779, the wars extend to 1879; the end result is that the Xhosa people lose most of their land and their independence. Fighting on the European side is conducted mostly by volunteer units.

The most serious of these wars is the Eighth Xhosa War of 1850–1853. The cause is the decision by Cape governor Sir Harry Smith to reduce the power of the Xhosa chiefs. The Xhosa prophet Mlanjeni apparently initiates the war, however.

During the war, the British troopship *Birkenhead,* carrying 490 troops to fight in the war (638 people in all), strikes a submerged rock and is wrecked at Danger Point, Gansbaai, on February 26, 1852. The ship secures a place in history because of the gallantry of the men, who stand fast when ordered to do so, allowing the women and children to escape in the boats before trying to save themselves, thus creating the Birkenhead Drill of "Women and children first!" A total of 445 men lose their lives.

1850–1854

Central Asia: Persia. Russian conquests in the Syr Darya Valley expand Russian territory to the Persian frontier.

1850–1855

Central Asia: Afghanistan. Dost Mohammad Khan reestablishes Afghan control of the outlying areas of Afghanistan, including Balkh (in 1850) and Kandahar (in 1855).

1850–1864

West Africa: Jihad by Muslim leader Al-Hajj Omar ibn Said Talst. In 1850 Omar, the leader of well-armed Muslim followers, begins a series of small wars against neighboring non-Muslim states. His headquarters is located near the town of Dinguiray, near the headwaters of the Niger River. By 1852 Omar has expanded the fighting into a jihad (holy war) against all non-Muslims and even those Muslims who refuse to accept his teachings. Over the next decade, Omar's fanatical troops conquer the territory between the headwaters of the Niger and Timbuktu and there create a unified empire.

During 1856–1859 his troops encounter the French. Omar's forces are repulsed by French troops under Colonel Louis Léon César Faidherbe, governor of French Senegal. They then turn east, taking Timbuktu in 1863. Omar is killed in 1864 while putting down a rebellion. The state that he created dominates the western Sudan until it is conquered by the French at the end of the 19th century.

1850–1865

North America: United States: Indian Wars. The U.S. Army fights dozens of small wars, battles, and skirmishes with Native American tribes in the American West. The acquisition of California in 1848 and the discovery of gold there lures many American citizens to cross the Great Plains and Rocky Mountains by land from the east. The building of the transcontinental railroad in the 1860s and the establishment of settler farms on traditional Native American lands

brings even more conflict. Native Americans roam the plains freely to hunt buffalo, the staple of their subsistence, and do not believe in private landownership, let alone fenced lands. Conflict is inevitable.

During the 1850s the vast majority of the U.S. Army's 16,000–17,000 men is located in the vast American West. There are numerous small posts of company strength or so patrolling and seeking to keep the peace. This involves the army in numerous small wars against the Apache, Arapaho, Cheyenne, Comanche, Kiowa, Mojave, Navaho, Seminole, Sioux, and other Native American tribes. Both sides are guilty of atrocities, although most of those committed by whites are perpetrated by militiamen rather than regular soldiers.

January 1851

East Asia: China: Proclamation of the Taiping Rebellion. The Taiping Rebellion (1851–1864) is sparked by agrarian unrest during the reigns of Qing dynasty emperors Daoguang (Tao-kuang) (1821–1850) and Xianfeng (Hsien-feng) (1851–1861) and is caused by the decline in arable land per capita of population, natural disasters, and absentee landlordism. The leader of the revolt is Hong Xiuquan (Hung Hsiu-ch'üan), a failed civil service examination candidate from Guangdong (Kwangtung) Province. Hong claims that the ruling Manchus have lost their mandate from heaven following the defeat of Chinese forces by Britain in the Opium War of 1840–1842. Hong vows to end Manchu rule and establish in its place a new government, the Taiping Tianguo (Heavenly Kingdom of Great Peace). A self-proclaimed Christian, Hong borrows certain Protestant teachings, including the Ten Commandments. He holds that he has divine authority to regulate all earthly affairs. The Taipings ban gambling and the consumption of alcohol and opium. Because the latter is so important in their trade with China, the Western governments support the imperial government's efforts to overthrow the Taipings.

In January 1851 Hong proclaims a revolt against the Manchu Qing dynasty. It begins in Guangxi (Kwangsi) Province and expands into Hubei (Hupei) Province and Hunan Province. Soon Hong has at his disposal a well-trained and highly motivated army of 50,000 men and women (an important part of Taiping teaching is equality for women). Later, the army grows to upwards of a half million. Its strength rests in its high morale, strict discipline (the troops had to obey a set of 62 rules), and religious conformity. The Taipings also possess effective military commanders, especially Yang Xiuqing (Yang Hsiu-ch'ing), who leads rebel military forces against the Imperial Army in the Changjiang (Yangtze, Yangxi) River Valley.

December 2, 1851
Western Europe: France: Coup d'état. Popularly elected president Louis Napoleon Bonaparte seizes power in a nearly bloodless coup d'état, well planned and executed under the orders of his half brother, Comte Auguste de Morny. Parisians awake on the morning of December 2 to find the army in control of key locations in the city. There are some republican uprisings, most notably in Paris on December 4, but these are easily suppressed and the participants arrested. The coup is approved by plebiscite on December 21, the announced results being 7.5 million in favor of giving the president the right to draw up a new constitution and 640,000 against.

December 2, 1852
Western Europe: France. The Second Empire is formally established, with Louis Napoleon Bonaparte becoming Emperor Napoleon III.

1852–1853
Central Europe: Balkans: Ottoman forces invade Montenegro. In 1852 Ottoman forces under Omar Pasha invade Montenegro but are defeated by Montenegrin forces under Prince Danilo Ostrag. Faced with an Austrian threat of intervention, the Turks withdraw.

1852–1853
Southeast Asia: Burma: Second Anglo-Burmese War. Following a series of incidents in which British merchant ship captains have been arrested and forced to purchase their freedom, Commodore George Robert Lambert proceeds from Calcutta to Rangoon (present-day Yangon) in November 1851 with two warships to resolve matters. Lambert, informed of other breaches by the Burmese of the 1826 Treaty of Yandabo, sends to India for instructions. He also provokes a confrontation by demanding the removal of the governor.

The governor resists, and in January 1852 Lambert institutes a blockade of the port of Rangoon, thus be-

ginning the Second Anglo-Burmese War. The British dispatch an 8,100-man expeditionary force under Lieutenant General Sir Henry T. Godwin. It captures Martaban (April 5) and then Rangoon (April 12). Following heavy fighting, the Burmese army retires northward. The British then capture Bassein (May 19) and Pegu (June 3). After heavy fighting around the Shwemawdaw Pagoda, Godwin's troops occupy Prome (October 9).

Early in December, British East India Company officials inform Burmese king Pagan Min that the province of Pegu will henceforth form part of the British dominions. The proclamation of annexation is issued on January 20, 1853, bringing the war to a close without any formal peace treaty. The British rename Pegu as Lower Burma.

1852–1854
South Africa: Establishment of the Boer Republics. When the United Kingdom abolished slavery in all its colonies, during 1835–1837 some 10,000 Boers moved northeast and north from the Cape Colony in their Great Trek in search of new land where they might be free of British control. The Boers then establish Natal along the African coast to the northeast. Britain annexes Natal in 1843, but in the 1850s the Boers organize as independent republics the Orange Free State and the South African Republic (Zuid-Afrikaansche Republiek [ZAR], informally known as the Transvaal) north of the Vaal River. The British recognize the ZAR in 1852 and the Orange Free State in 1854.

January 12, 1853
East Asia: China: Taiping Rebellion (continued): Capture of Wuchang. In late December 1852, Taiping forces lay siege to Wuchang in Hubei (Hupei) Province. Following a 20-day siege, they take the city on January 12, 1853. The Taiping now control the upper Changjiang (Yangtze, Yangxi) River and its trade, enabling them to cut off the interior from the coast.

March 20, 1853
East Asia: China: Taiping Rebellion (continued): Capture of Nanjing. After taking the city of Wuchang in Hubei Province in January 1853, the Taiping commit a major strategic error. Instead of moving

CAPTURE OF NANJING, MARCH 20, 1853

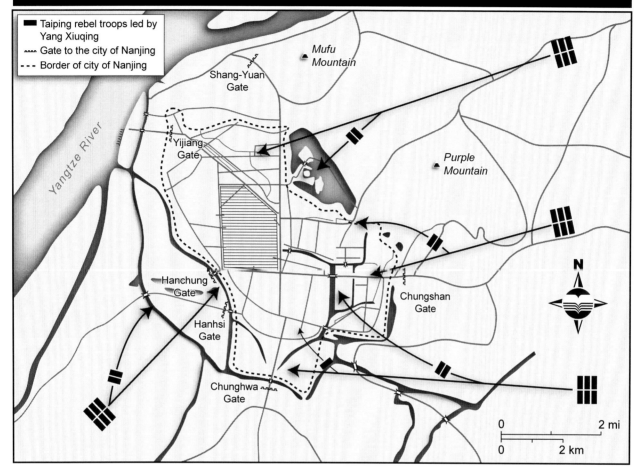

■ Taiping rebel troops led by Yang Xiuqing
⌒ Gate to the city of Nanjing
--- Border of city of Nanjing

Shang-Yuan Gate
Mufu Mountain
Yijiang Gate
Yangtze River
Purple Mountain
Hanchung Gate
Hanhsi Gate
Chungshan Gate
Chunghwa Gate

0   2 mi
0   2 km

against Beijing in Hebei (Hopeh) Province, they proceed down the Changjiang (Yangtze, Yangxi) River against the city of Nanjing. This decision costs them their best chance of taking the imperial capital and overthrowing the Manchus. The Taiping apparently take this course because of reports of a large imperial force protecting Beijing.

In early February 1853 some 500,000 Taiping depart Wuchang, cross the Yangtze River, and burn their floating bridges behind them in order to delay an advancing imperial force. While part of the army moves by land on the north side of the river, the majority moves downriver toward Nanjing in some 20,000 requisitioned craft.

The Taiping easily capture Jiujiang (Kiukiang) in western Jiangxi Province and Anqing (Anking), the capital of Anhui (Anhwei) Province. After securing

provisions from storehouses there, they continue on to Nanjing, the capital of Jiangsu Province.

The Taiping arrive before Nanjing on March 6, 1853. The city population has swelled to three-quarters of a million people. Although ill-prepared for a siege, the defenders manage to hold the Taiping at bay for 13 days. On March 19, however, the Taiping deploy hundreds of horses carrying effigies of soldiers bearing torches before the west wall. Expecting an attack from that quarter, defending soldiers crowd onto the wall. They realize too late that it is a ruse; two great explosions from Taiping mines breach the wall. Although a third mine explodes late, killing many of the attacking troops, the Taiping troops nonetheless secure access to the city. The Taiping may also have been aided by spies. Reportedly, they had sent some 3,000 of their number into the city disguised as Buddhist monks. News of the death of the imperial commander in Nanjing, Lu Jianying (lu Chien-ying), demoralizes the defenders, many of whom abandon their posts.

On March 20 the Taiping assault the inner Imperial City, defended by 40,000 Manchu troops, and take it in costly human wave assaults. The Taipings massacre some 30,000 of the defenders, who refuse to surrender.

The rebels make Nanjing their capital and there proclaim a new dynasty, the Taiping Tianguo (T'ien-kuo) (Heavenly Kingdom of Great Peace). Hong is the ruler. The Taiping never rigorously implement the egalitarian social programs that had drawn so many poor Chinese to their ranks. Furthermore, the revolutionary nature of the Taiping policies and religion proved repugnant to the Chinese landholding elite, who now willingly come to the aid of the Qing government. These factors and the endemic bloody infighting within the ranks of the Taiping leadership doom their regime to eventual failure.

July 8, 1853

East Asia: Japan: Perry opens Japan. The mistreatment of American shipwrecked sailors by Japan and the desire for trade and a coaling station prompt the U.S. government to order U.S. Navy commodore Matthew Calbraith Perry to Japan. Sailing from Norfolk, Virginia, he arrives with his squadron of four modern steam warships at Uraga Harbor, near Edo (present-day Tokyo), on July 8, 1853. He is there met by representatives of the Tokugawa Shogunate. They order him to proceed to Nagasaki, the only Japanese port open to foreigners. Perry refuses and demands permission to present a letter from U.S. president Millard Fillmore.

With Perry threatening a naval bombardment, the Japanese, fearing the modern weaponry of his so-called Black Ships, agree to let him land. He comes ashore and presents his letter to Japanese officials. It requests the establishment of diplomatic relations between Japan and the United States, better treatment for American shipwrecked sailors, and the opening of one or two treaty ports. Perry then departs, promising to return the next spring with a more powerful squadron for a reply.

See Leaders: Perry, Matthew Calbraith

U.S. Navy captain Matthew Calbraith Perry (1794–1858) was a naval reformer and advocate of steam power. He is best remembered, however, for his expeditions to Japan in 1853 and 1854 that opened that country to the West. (Library of Congress)

October 4, 1853

Eastern Europe: Russia: Crimean War: Background to the conflict and Turkish declaration of war against Russia. The Crimean War (1853–1856) is chiefly remembered today for a mistaken cavalry charge and the courage of one woman, Florence Nightingale. It is, however, an important event in European history that witnesses considerable military change. The chief cause of the war is the desire of Russian czar Nicholas I to secure the Ottoman possessions in Europe and, specifically, to gain control over the Straits connecting the Black Sea to the Mediterranean, a long-term Russian goal.

Toward this end, the Russian government approaches Britain and other powers about dividing up the Ottoman Empire, the "sick man of Europe." Britain, however, sees Russian control of the Straits as a threat to its naval dominance in the Mediterranean. France, ruled by Emperor Napoleon III who has been snubbed by Nicholas, also takes an aggressive stance. Napoleon III even orders a French naval squadron to Istanbul.

The catalyst for war, though, is a dispute over of control of the shrines in the Holy Land, which thanks to that nation's aggressive stance, are placed by Sultan Abdülmecid I (r. 1839–1861) under France and the Roman Catholic Church. Nicholas demands that the Greek Orthodox Church control the religious sites. St. Petersburg then dispatches an ultimatum demanding the right to act as protector of the Ottoman Empire's 12 million Christian subjects, the vast majority of whom are Orthodox. This would allow Russia to intervene almost at will in Ottoman affairs.

When the Ottomans reject this demand, Russia sends troops into Ottoman-controlled Moldavia and Wallachia (the Danubian Principalities, today joined as Romania). Russian leaders believe that Austria will not object to Russian acquisition of several Ottoman border provinces, given Russia's support in crushing the Hungarian Revolution of 1848–1849. Frantic diplomatic activity by representatives of Britain, France, Austria, and Prussia in Vienna fail to avert war.

Britain sends a naval squadron to Istanbul. Confident of the support of Britain and France, Sultan Abdülmecid I rejects a possible compromise. The Ottoman Empire declares war on Russia on October 4, 1853, and sends an army under able commander Omar Pasha (Croatian-born Michael Lattas) across the Danube against the Russians.

October 15, 1853

North America: Mexico: First Walker filibustering expedition. U.S. soldier of fortune William Walker dreams of leading a private campaign to conquer parts of Mexico and Central America. He launches his first filibustering expedition on October 15, 1853, leaving California with 45 men to conquer the Mexican territories of Baja California and Sonora. He and his men capture La Paz, the capital of sparsely populated Baja California, and declare it the capital of the Republic of Lower California. He is unable to secure Sonora, however.

Lack of supplies and opposition by the Mexican government eventually force Walker to return to California, where he is arrested and placed on trial for conducting an illegal war. Given the attitude of the times and the prevalence of Manifest Destiny, a jury promptly acquits him.

November 4, 1853

Eastern Europe: Crimean War (continued): Balkan Front: Battle of Oltenița. Ottoman forces under Omar Pasha cross the Danube and defeat the Russians at Oltenița.

November 30, 1853

Black Sea: Crimean War (continued): Battle of Sinope. In late November 1853 Ottoman vice admiral Osman Pasha is en route north along the western Black Sea coast with a force of seven sailing frigates, two corvettes, and several transports to resupply Ottoman land forces. Osman flies his flag in the 60-gun frigate *Avni Illah.* Caught by a storm in the Black Sea, he takes his ships into the Ottoman port of Sinope (Sinop). Although Osman's largest guns are only 24-pounders, the anchorage is protected by 84 guns, some of them possibly landed from the ships.

Russian admiral Paul S. Nakhimov now arrives at Sinope with three ships of the line of 84 guns each: the *Imperatritsa Maria* (flagship), *Chesma,* and *Rostislav.* He also has two frigates. He secures from Sevastopol three additional ships of the line: the 120-gun *Veliky Knyaz Konstantin, Tri Sviatitelia,* and *Parizh.* Their main armament comprises new 68-pounder shell guns.

A thick mist on the morning of November 30 masks the approach of the Russian ships into the harbor. The Ottomans barely have time to clear for action before battle is joined at 10:00 a.m. Within half an hour, the *Veliky Knyaz Konstantin* has sunk an Ottoman frigate and silenced the Ottoman shore batteries. The battle nevertheless rages until 4:00 p.m. Only one Ottoman vessel, the paddle steamer *Taif* of 12 guns, manages to escape; the remaining ships are all sunk. The Russians admit to 37 dead; Ottoman losses are upwards of 3,000 men.

Although the Turks are badly outgunned at Sinope, the inequity of the losses conclusively demonstrates the superiority of shell over shot against wooden ships. The Russian *Imperatritsa Maria* had been struck by 84 cannonballs without major damage, for example, while the Ottoman fleet was destroyed. The battle heightens world interest in the construction of ironclad warships for protection against shell.

The battle also produces a wellspring of support in Britain and France for the Ottoman Empire. The British press labels this legitimate act of war "a foul outrage" and a "massacre."

1853

East Africa: Abyssinia: Battle of Gorgora. Lij Kassa, chief of Kwara in western Amhara, sharply increases his power. Two other princes, Ras Ali and Ras Ubié, combine against him. Lij Kassa defeats them both in 1853 at Gorgora, on the south shore of Lake Tana, in Abysinnia (Ethiopia). Ras Ubié retreats into Tigré; Ras Ali retires to Begemeder, where he dies.

1853–1881

East Asia: China: Regional unrest throughout China. The collapse of imperial authority during the great Taiping Rebellion (1851–1864) encourages widespread unrest throughout China. During 1853–1868 Nian (Nien) rebels organize bandit bands to ravage the provinces of Anhui, northern Jiangsu (Kiangsu), and Shandong (Shantung).

Chinese Muslims in Yunnan Province revolt and form a government in Dali (1855–1873). A separate Muslim rebellion occurs in the northeastern areas of Ningxia, Gansu, and Qinghai (1862–1877). This cuts the Qing off from Xinjiang, where an adventurer named Yakub Beg forms an independent government with its capital in Kashgar (1865–1877).

In the southwestern province of Guizhou, the oppressive policies of Qing officials spark a rebellion of the Miao, joined by Han Chinese and local Chinese Muslims (1855–1881). The central government is also seriously handicapped by having to fight simultaneously against inroads in China by the Western powers led by Britain.

January 3, 1854

Black Sea: Crimean War (continued): British and French warships enter the Black Sea. The annihilation of the Turkish Squadron at Sinope (Sinop) in November 1853 brings a wave of popular support in Britain and France for the Ottoman Empire and leads London and Paris to dispatch naval assets there. On January 3, 1854, French and British warships enter the Black Sea; on March 12 both nations agree to protect the Ottoman Empire's coasts and shipping against Russian attack.

January–February 1854

Southern Europe: Greece: Crimean War (continued): Greek invasion of Thessaly and Epirus. Taking advantage of the fighting between Russia and the Ottoman Empire, the Greek government sends troops to occupy Thessaly and Epirus.

February 13, 1854

East Asia: Japan. Commodore Matthew Calbraith Perry duly returns to Edo (present-day Tokyo) Bay, Japan, as promised, this time with seven warships (nearly twice as many as on his first visit). Pressed by Perry, the Tokugawa Shogunate reluctantly signs the Convention of Kanagawa on March 31, 1854. It establishes an American consulate and includes a Japanese pledge to protect shipwrecked American sailors. It also opens two Japanese ports for restricted trade with the United States. Other nations, including Britain and Russia, then negotiate similar treaties with Japan.

March 20, 1854

Central Europe: Balkans: Bulgaria: Crimean War (continued). Following the orders of Czar Nicholas I, Russian marshal Ivan Paskievich crosses the Danube with a strong army and invades Bulgaria. His aim is to capture Silistra, on the south bank of the Danube. The Russians begin a siege of that fortified city on March 20.

March 28, 1854

Eastern Europe: Russia: Crimean War (continued): Britain and France declare war on Russia. Czar Nicholas I had hoped that the war would be restricted to Russia and the Ottoman Empire, but Britain and France join the Turks. These two powers conclude a mutual alliance with the Ottoman Empire on April 10.

April 1854–February 1857

Southern Europe: Greece. British and French forces occupy the Greek port of Piraeus, next to Athens, effectively preventing Greece from sending assistance to Russia in the Crimean War.

June 9, 1854

Eastern Europe: Bulgaria: Crimean War (continued): Russia raises the siege of Silistra. A British-French expeditionary force lands at the Bulgarian port Varna on the Black Sea. The city becomes the headquarters for their forces in the war. Although Austria does not declare war, it refuses to guarantee its neutrality and, with Ottoman permission, sends an army of 50,000 men into the Danube provinces (Moldavia and Wallachia). These two factors convince the Russians to withdraw. They raise the siege of Silistra on June 9 and retire across the Danube. The Habsburg army will remain in the Danube provinces until 1857.

Although it appears that the war will end at this point, London is concerned that the Russian fleet remains a threat to British maritime interests in the Mediterranean. British public opinion, moreover, demands a decisive victory. Paris is also anxious for glory and prestige for French arms. The allies therefore put forward a four-part peace proposal: Russia is to give up its protectorate over the Danubian Principalities, abandon any claim to interfere in Ottoman affairs on behalf of Orthodox Christians, agree to a revision of the Straits Convention of 1841, and agree to free access for all nations on the Danube. When the Russians reject the allied demands, the war continues.

June–August 1854
Northern Europe: Baltic Sea: Crimean War (continued): Allied naval operations in the Baltic. With most of their naval strength deployed in the Black Sea, the British and French governments are concerned about the threat posed by 27 Russian ships of the line in the Baltic. To prevent the Russian ships from departing the Baltic, London assembles a fleet of 25 ships under Vice Admiral Sir Charles Napier and dispatches it from Portsmouth on March 10, 1854, even before war is declared.

Kronstadt is too powerful for Napier to take, so his orders call on him to seal the Baltic and destroy such Russian ships as possible. Napier therefore divides his force into three squadrons so as to watch the Gulf of Gdańsk (Danzig), the Gulf of Riga, and the mouth of the Gulf of Finland. Operations are limited to small raids and the destruction of several Russian dockyards and forts.

July 1854
Southern Europe: Iberia: Spain. Spanish generals Leopoldo O'Donnell and Baldomero Espartero topple the government of Queen Mother Christina and

force her to flee abroad. Fourteen years of unrest follow.

August 10–14, 1854
Northern Europe: Baltic Sea: Crimean War (continued): Allied operation against Bombarsund in the Åland Islands. In June the French send a fleet to the Baltic under Vice Admiral Parseval Deschenes. The French also agree to provide 11,000 troops for raiding operations if the British provide the transports.

On June 21, 26, and 27 the allies shell Bombarsund, one of the fortified towns in the Åland Islands guarding the Gulf of Finland. They have little success. On August 10 British vice admiral Sir Charles Napier returns and lands some 6,000 French troops under General Achille Baraguay d'Hilliers in two locations. Working their way overland, they bombard the town from the land side while the British ships shell the Russian lines. After four days the 2,400-man Russian garrison surrenders and is taken off as prisoners of war. Allied troops destroy the fortifications, but with winter approaching, the allied fleets return home.

August 1854–March 1857
Central Europe: Balkans: Crimean War (continued): Austrian forces occupy Moldavia and Wallachia (Romania).

September 13, 1854
Eastern Europe: Crimean War (continued): Crimean Front: British and French forces land in the Crimea. The British and French now decide to move against the center of Russian power on the Black Sea: the naval base of Sevastopol, on the Crimean Peninsula. The ensuing expedition is poorly planned, with little thought given to conditions that the troops are likely to encounter in the Crimea or to matters of resupply.

On September 7, 1854, a vast allied force of some 150 ships and transports sets out for the Crimea with the intent of taking Sevastopol by coup de main. Major General Fitzroy James Henry Somerset, Lord Raglan, commands the British forces of some 26,000 men. French marshal Armand Jacques Leroy de Saint-Arnaud has charge of the French contingent of 28,000 men. There are also some 7,000 Ottoman troops. The two commanders begin landing their troops on September 13.

The Russian commander in the Crimea, Prince Alexander Sergeievich Menshikov, makes no effort to oppose the allied landing at Calamita Bay, about 35 miles north of Sevastopol. Nonetheless, the allies dither so long that the Russians are able to throw up defenses on the land side. Although the allies win a number of land victories, they are thus unable to take Sevastopol that autumn as they planned.

September 20, 1854

Eastern Europe: Crimean War (continued): Crimean Front: Battle of the Alma River. A week after their first troops come ashore, the allies at last get under way. On September 19 they head south toward Sevastopol with 60,000 infantry, 1,000 British cavalry, and 128 guns. Allied warships keep pace with the troops offshore. The march involves the crossing of three rivers, and it is on the second of these, the Alma, that Russian commander in the Crimea Prince Alexander Sergeievich Menshikov decides to make his stand.

Menshikov positions his 36,400 men on the south side of the river, about 15 miles north of Sevastopol. The allied troops get across the river without much problem. Supported by the guns of the fleet, the French on the allied right are able to take the high ground without too much difficulty. The British units on the allied left, however, get bunched up and have difficulty advancing uphill against the Russians' Greater Redoubt. With the Russians finally driven from the high ground, Menshikov withdraws unmolested. The British wanted to pursue, but the French had left their packs on the other side of the river and could not have joined them. The allies suffer perhaps 3,342 casualties, most of them British troops; the Russians sustain 5,709 casualties. Incompetent leaders and missed opportunities mark the military operations of both sides in the war.

September 26, 1854

Eastern Europe: Russia: Crimean War (continued): Crimean Front: Siege of Sevastopol. Following the Battle of the Alma River, allied troops move south against Sevastopol. The Russians, however, scuttle six ships of the line, three frigates, and six steamers in the harbor channel north of the city, preventing an allied naval attack from that direction. The allies opt for a flanking march east of the city and then move southwest to secure the port of Balaklava (Balaclava) and isolate Sevastopol from the eastern (land) side.

The allies bypass the inadequate Russian defenses on the city's southern edge, settling instead for siege operations. On September 29 French commander Marshal Armand Jacques Leroy de Saint-Arnaud dies of cholera and is succeeded by General François Certain Canrobert.

Russian commander in the Crimea Prince Alexander Sergeievich Menshikov leaves a small force in Sevastopol and marches north. He crosses the allied march route to join Russian reinforcements arriving at Bakhchisarai.

With Menshikov gone, the defense of Sevastopol is led by Russian vice admirals Vladimir Kornilov and Pavel Nakhimov, assisted by able chief engineer Lieutenant Colonel Eduard Todleben. The Russians have slightly more than 35,000 men, most of them seamen but also marines, militia, and workers. By mid-October the allies have some 120 guns ready to fire on Sevastopol; thanks to the cannon removed from their warships before they were scuttled, the Russians have three times that number.

Allied shelling commences on October 17, 1854. Russian counterfire destroys a French magazine, silencing their guns, but British fire then sets off the magazine in the Russians' Malakoff Redoubt, killing Vice Admiral Kornilov and silencing most of its guns. The allies might then have mounted an infantry assault but choose not to do so, and the opportunity soon passes.

October 25, 1854

Eastern Europe: Crimean War (continued): Crimean Front: Battle of Balaklava. The Russians initiate battle near the small seaport of Balaklava (Balaclava), a key allied supply base some eight miles southwest of Sevastopol, when their commander in the Crimea Prince Alexander Sergeievich Menchikov attempts to drive a force between Sevastopol and Balaklava. The battle pits some 23,000 Russians under General Pavel Liprandi, Menshikov's second-in-command, against some 20,000 allied troops under British commander in chief Major General Fitzroy James Henry Somerset, Lord Raglan. The Russians are able to penetrate the allied lines and capture some Ottoman guns, but their cavalry exploitation is halted by the British Heavy Cavalry Brigade.

The battle is best known, however, for the charge of the British Light Brigade under Brigadier General James Thomas Brudenell, Lord Cardigan. Thanks to

Commencement of the Siege of Sevastopol by Thomas Packer. (Photos.com)

a poorly worded order from Raglan and the stupidity of Cardigan and British cavalry commander Major General G. C. Bingham, Lord Lucan, in interpreting it, the 673-man Light Brigade charges the Russian artillery at the end of the valley. In the process it runs a gauntlet of fire from guns on each side as well as from the guns in front of them. The brigade reaches and rides through the Russian artillery position at the end of the valley and then regroups; the survivors ride back again. They are saved only by the intervention of the equally brave French 4th Chasseurs d'Afrique, who attack the flanking Russian guns. The charge of the Light Brigade is best summed up by French eyewitness General Pierre F. J. Bosquet: "It is magnificent, but it is not war."

The action costs the British 247 men and 497 horses. Often used as an example of British senior officer incompetence, the event is immortalized in Alfred Lord Tennyson's poem "The Charge of the Light Brigade."

The Battle of Balaklava is, however, indecisive; it ends with the Russians controlling the Vorontosov Ridge that commands the Balaklava-Sevastopol road, while the allies control Balaklava itself. The

entire battle claims some 350 British and 250 French casualties. Russian casualties are unknown but probably numbered several hundred.

November 5, 1854
Eastern Europe: Crimea: Crimean War (continued): Crimean Front: Battle of Inkerman. The third major battle of the war, apart from the siege of Sevastopol, occurs at Inkerman only a few miles east of Sevastopol on November 5, 1854. Russian commander in the Crimea Prince Alexander Sergeievich Menchikov, having received substantial reinforcements, again attempts to break through the allied cordon around Sevastopol. His second-in-command, General Pavel Liprandi, has actual charge of the Russian troops in the battle: some 31,000 infantry and 4,000 cavalry.

The Russians feint an attack on the French to hold them in place while concentrating most of their resources against some 8,200 British troops. French general Pierre F. J. Bosquet is not fooled, however, and the timely arrival of his 7,500-man division saves the British.

The battle is the most costly of the war, claiming perhaps 5,000 Russians killed and another 7,000

BATTLE OF INKERMAN, NOVEMBER 5, 1854

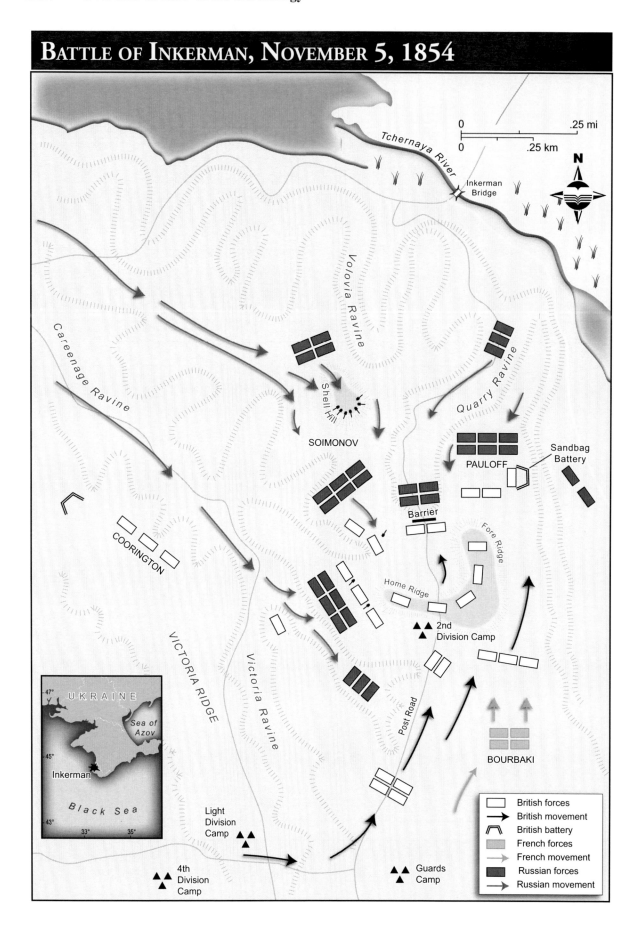

Tchernaya River

Inkerman Bridge

0   .25 mi

0   .25 km

N

Volovia Ravine

Quarry Ravine

Shell Hill

SOIMONOV

PAULOFF

Sandbag Battery

Carenage Ravine

Barrier

Fore Ridge

COORINGTON

Home Ridge

2nd Division Camp

VICTORIA RIDGE

Victoria Ravine

Post Road

BOURBAKI

UKRAINE

Sea of Azov

Inkerman

Black Sea

Light Division Camp

4th Division Camp

Guards Camp

	British forces
	British movement
	British battery
	French forces
	French movement
	Russian forces
	Russian movement

The Battle of Inkerman on November 5, 1854, the third major engagement of the Crimean War and its most costly in terms of casualties, was an inconlusive allied victory that did, however, purchase more time for the Russians to fortify Sevastopol. (Photos.com)

wounded for only 3,300 allied killed or wounded. The British lose 635 killed and 1,938 wounded; French losses are 175 killed and 1,625 wounded. British commander General Fitzroy James Henry Somerset, Lord Raglan, is promoted to field marshal after the battle. Inkerman does, however, purchase the Russians additional time to build up the defenses of Sevastopol and prevents an allied assault on the city before winter.

November 1854–March 1855
Eastern Europe: Crimean War (continued): Crimean Front: Siege of Sevastopol (continued): Winter conditions. Suffering on both sides in the winter of 1854–1855 is severe. Given their command of the sea, the allies should have had no problem adequately supplying their forces, while the Russians had a long, difficult overland supply route to the area. Incom-

petence, poor planning, and a major winter storm on November 14 that wrecks some 21 transports at Balaklava (Balaclava) laden with food, clothing, and medical supplies take their toll, however, especially on the British forces. Food is scarce, much of the clothing is summer issue, and tents prove hopelessly inadequate. Scurvy, dysentery, and cholera carry off many. Adding insult to injury, there are no hospitals to care for the sick. Perhaps four-fifths of the allied dead in the war are from disease.

The horrors of the situation are revealed to the British people by the first real war correspondents and photographers (William Howard Russell and Robert Fenton, respectively). Various commissions are sent out to investigate, with the most important being the Sanitary Commission. The investigations bring changes. The end of winter, the reorganization of supply services, and the work of Florence Nightingale (the "lady with the lamp") and her 38 volunteer nurses at Scutari, across the Black Sea in the Ottoman Empire, all bring relief. Indeed, one of the major results of the Crimean War is the general upgrading of military medical services.

The French supply services are much better handled. By February, when the British are down to 12,000 men able to fight, the French have 78,000.

1854–1877
South Africa. Sporadic warfare occurs between the Zulus and Boer settlers as the latter seek to expand their holdings eastward.

January 26, 1855
Eastern Europe: Crimean War (continued): Sardinia enters the war on the allied side. Prime Minister Count Camillo Benso di Cavour of the Kingdom of Sardinia (Piedmont-Sardinia) sees Sardinian participation in the war as a means of securing British and French support for his country's aspirations in Italy. Sardinia declares war on Russia on January 26, 1855, dispatching 10,000 men to the Crimea under General Alfonso Ferrero La Marmora.

February 11, 1855
East Africa: Abyssinia: Lij Kassa proclaimed Emperor Tewodros (Theodore) II. Following his victory in the Battle of Gorgora of 1853, Lij Kassa is ruler of Amhara. He goes on to conquer both Gojam and Tigré and proclaims himself ruler of all of Abyssinia (present-day Ethiopia). Crowned emperor on February 11, 1855, he takes the name of

SIEGE OF SEVASTOPOL, NOVEMBER 1854–MARCH 1855

Legend:
- City fortifications
- Allied command:
  - → Allied advance
  - Allied artillery
  - ■ British infantry
  - ⊠ French forces
  - ▭ Turkish forces
  - Russian artillery
  - ⊠ Russian forces

0 2 4 mi
0 2 4 km

Black Sea

RUSSIAN CAMP

Great Harbor

Sevastopol

4TH DIV

5TH DIV

LIGHT DIV

2ND DIV

3RD DIV

4TH DIV

3RD DIV

FRENCH CAMP

BRITISH CAMP

RUSSIAN CAMP

BRITISH CAVALRY

1ST DIV

TURKISH CAMP

Balaklava

Black Sea

N

Tewodros (Theodore) II to fulfill the prophecy that a man named Tewodros will restore the Ethiopian Empire to greatness. He rules until 1868.

Theodore II makes major efforts to modernize Abyssinia and reform its government. Among other changes, he moves the capital from Gondar to Magdala. Described as highly intelligent, generous to a fault, and magnanimous to his enemies, he is also increasingly mentally unstable (especially follow-ing the death of his beloved wife) and subject to outbursts of anger and great religious zeal.

February 17, 1855
Eastern Europe: Crimean War (continued): Crimean Front: Siege of Sevastopol (continued): Battle of Eupatoria. Russian forces, now commanded by Prince Michael Gorchakov, make a dilatory effort to disrupt the improved allied road and rail lines supply-

ing forces besieging Sevastopol. The Russians are defeated in the Battle of Eupatoria (Yevpatoriya) on February 17, and the allies push their siege lines closer.

March 18, 1855
Central Asia: Afghanistan: Treaty of Peshawar. The Treaty of Peshawar of March 18, 1855, officially brings to a close the Second Anglo-Sikh War (1848–1849). In it, the East India Company recognizes Dost Mohammad Khan as emir of all Afghanistan. The treaty is designed in part to impede Persian designs on Herat. Despite his earlier anti-British policies, Dost Mohammad now enjoys full British support and declares his intention to take Herat.

April 8–18, 1855
Eastern Europe: Crimean War (continued): Crimean Front: Siege of Sevastopol (continued): Easter bombardment. During April 8–18, 1855, the allied besiegers subject Sevastopol to heavy shelling. They destroy a large part of the defenses and kill an estimated 6,000 defenders drawn up to meet an expected allied assault.

Meanwhile, the allied governments and their field commanders squabble over the proper course of action to follow. French commander General François Certain Canrobert, disgusted and frustrated, resigns his command. General Jean Jacques Pélissier succeeds him.

May 24, 1855
Eastern Europe: Crimean War (continued): Crimean Front: Siege of Sevastopol (continued): Allied capture of Kerch. On May 24 in a well-executed allied operation, a naval force of 9 ships of the line and 50 smaller ships lands more than 15,500 troops (7,000 French, 5,000 Ottomans, 3,500 British, and some Sardinians) on the Kerch Peninsula of eastern Ukraine, a few miles below the port of Kerch. Taken by surprise, the Russians blow up their fortifications, scuttle some ships, and retire. The allies take Kerch without opposition. Their ships then proceed into the Sea of Azov, clearing it of Russian ships, destroying supplies, and cutting Russian communications with the interior.

June 7–18, 1855
Eastern Europe: Crimean War (continued): Crimean Front: Siege of Sevastopol (continued): A major allied assault on the fortress results in the capture of a portion of the outer Russian defensive works on June 7. Allied casualties amount to some 6,900; the Russians sustain 8,500 casualties.

Another allied assault takes place on June 17–18 against the two Russian strong points. The British assault the Redan Redoubt, and the French attack the Malakoff Redoubt. The Russians repulse both attacks. The allies lose 4,000 men, the Russians 5,500. British commander in chief Major General Fitzroy James Henry Somerset, Lord Raglan, broken by the failure, dies 10 days later. General Sir James Simpson succeeds him.

June 1855
Northern Europe: Baltic Sea: Crimean War (continued): First mine-sweeping operation. In June 1855 the allies are surveying approaches to the principal Russian naval base of Kronstadt when they discover a large Russian minefield. In probably the first mine-sweeping operation in history, the allies recover several Russian mines. One small British ship strikes a mine but is little damaged.

June–November, 1855
Eurasia: Caucasus: Crimean War (continued): Operations on the Caucasus Front and Siege of Kars. In the last major military operation of the war, Czar Alexander II orders General Michael Muraviev to conduct military operations against the Ottomans in Asia Minor in an effort to reduce allied pressure on Sevastopol. Muraviev puts together a force of 40,000 men; the centerpiece of his operations is the June–November 1855 siege of the fortress city of Kars, in the northeastern Ottoman Empire.

The 30,000-man Ottoman garrison at Kars, commanded by British general Sir William Fenwick Williams (Williams Pasha), repulses an assault in June. The Russians then settle in for siege. Upon learning of the siege, Ottoman general Omar Pasha indeed requests the redeployment of Ottoman troops from Sevastopol in order to relieve Kars.

On September 6 Omar Pasha departs the Crimea for Batumi with 45,000 men. His arrival leads Muraviev to try another assault, on September 19, 1855. About half of the 13,000-man Russian assault force is killed in the attack. Williams and the Turks, now in dire straits, hold on, however.

Instead of marching on Kars, though, Omar Pasha engages the Russians in Mingrelia and captures Sukhumi. A second Ottoman army of some 15,000 men commanded by Selim Pasha, Omar's son, lands at Trabzon and moves south to Erzerum to prevent further Russian advances into Asia Minor. The Russians detach some men from Kars to attack the Turks, but Selim Pasha defeats them in the Battle of the Ingur River on November 6.

Selim Pasha is unable to reach Kars in time, however. The garrison there succumbs to starvation and cholera. Williams surrenders on November 26, 1855.

July 9, 1855

Northern Europe: Baltic Sea: Crimean War (continued): First mining of a warship while under way. To protect their coastal forts on the Baltic Sea, the Russians employ a number of sea mines. On July 9, 1855, several miles off Kronstadt, the paddle packet/survey vessel *Merlin* becomes the first ship to be mined in naval warfare. Although the *Merlin* strikes and sets off two Russian mines, they are small, and the ship is little damaged.

August 9–11, 1855

Northern Europe: Baltic Sea: Crimean War (continued): Allied naval bombardment of Sveaborg. The allies have a strong naval force in the Baltic. Vice Admiral Richard Saunders Dundas, former British commander in the Black Sea, now commands British ships in the Baltic, while Rear Admiral Pénaud commands French ships there. Although the allies pay lip service to an attempt against Kronstadt, Dundas is determined not to squander men or ships there. He is well aware of the limited effect that bombardment would have against the masonry and stone forts of Sevastopol, while his own ships would be exposed to return fire from the Russian heavy guns.

Although Dundas rejects an Admiralty plan for an attack on Kronstadt, he agrees to a joint attack against the five-island complex known as Sveaborg fortress in Helsinki Harbor. Here the Russians have more than 800 guns and 12,000 men. Beginning on August 9 the allied fleet shells the Sveaborg complex for three days and two nights, lobbing thousands of shot, shell, and rockets. Heavy explosions ashore indicate several magazines blown up. The allies claim to have killed 2,000 Russians, but the actual tally is 55 killed and 199 wounded. This ends naval operations in the Baltic.

The British also maintain a squadron in the White Sea to blockade Archangel. An Anglo-French squadron also sees some action in the Pacific.

August 16, 1855

Eastern Europe: Russia: Crimea: Crimean War (continued): Crimean Front: Siege of Sevastopol (continued): Battle of Traktir Ridge. Under constant allied shelling, the Russian forces in Sevastopol sustain losses of perhaps 250 people a day during the month of July. With Sevastopol not able to hold out much longer, Russian forces operating outside Sevastopol under Prince Michael Gorchakov make one last effort to secure access to the beleaguered fortress.

In the Battle of Traktir Ridge, Gorchakov hurls two Russian corps against some 37,000 French and Sardinian defenders holding the high ground above the Chernaya River. After a five-hour fight the Russians withdraw, leaving behind some 3,300 casualties. Allied losses are only 1,400. It is the last Russian effort to relieve Sevastopol.

September 8, 1855

Eastern Europe: Russia: Crimea: Crimean War (continued): Crimean Front: Siege of Sevastopol (continued): Storming of the Malakoff. Following their defeat of the Russians in the Battle of Traktir Ridge, the allies are confident of taking Sevastopol. Heavy allied shelling reduces the Malakoff strong point, and French commander General Aimable Jean Jacques Pélissier plans a final assault.

After an intense three-day bombardment, an entire French corps attacks the Melakoff without signal, through the coordination of watches, exactly at noon on September 8, 1855. The Russians contest every foot of ground, but the French prevail. Although the British again fail in their simultaneous effort to take the Redan Redoubt, the Russians crowded in that work now become targets for French guns at the Malakoff and are forced to evacuate.

That night the Russians evacuate Sevastopol. After setting fire to and blowing up what remains, the Russians cross over bridges to the north side. On September 9 the allies take possession of their empty prize.

In the final assault, the allies suffer some 10,000 casualties, the Russians about 13,000. With their objective at last realized, the allied governments lose interest in further prosecution of the war. No operations are taken against the remaining Russian forces in the peninsula under Prince Michael Gorchakov.

October 17, 1855

Black Sea: Ukraine: Crimean War (continued): Crimean Front: Battle of the Kinburn Forts. The

Battle of Sinope (Sinop) in November 1853 led to renewed interest in iron as armor for wooden vessels. In early 1855 French emperor Napoleon III proposes a system of iron protection for ships, and British chief naval engineer Thomas Lloyd demonstrates that four inches of iron can protect against large solid shot. The French then undertake construction of five *batteries flottantes cuirassées* (armored floating batteries).

On October 17, 1855, three of these new armed watercraft—the *Dévastation, Lave,* and *Tonnante*—mount an attack on Russia's Kinburn forts in an estuary at the mouth of the Dnieper and Bug rivers. Protected by 4-inch iron plate backed by 17 inches of wood, each of the floating batteries mounts 16 50-pounder and 2 12-pounder guns.

The Kinburn forts, three of which are of stone and two of sand, house 81 guns and mortars in all. From a range of between 900 and 1,200 yards, in an engagement lasting from 9:30 a.m. until noon the French armored floating batteries fire 3,177 shot and shell and reduce the Russian forts to rubble. Although repeatedly hulled themselves, the floating batteries are largely impervious to the Russian fire. The *Dévastation* absorbs 67 hits, and the *Tonnante* absorbs 66 hits. Two men are killed and 24 wounded, but the casualties resulted from two hot shot entering gun ports and another entering through an imperfect main hatch. The floating batteries' armor is only dented.

At noon, allied ships of the line shell what remains of the forts from 1,600 yards; in less than 90 minutes the Russians surrender. Undoubtedly, the success of the batteries is magnified because they are Emperor Napoleon III's special project, but many observers conclude that the Kinburn battle proves the effectiveness of wrought iron and marks the end of the old ships of the line.

1855–1858

North America: United States: Third Seminole War. The third and final war waged by U.S. forces to remove the Seminole Indians from Florida to Indian Territory in the West begins in 1855. As with the previous two Seminole wars, the Third Seminole War (1855–1858) is sparked by white encroachment on Seminole lands in southern Florida. It starts on December 20, 1855, when an 11-man reconnaissance patrol from Fort Myers under Lieutenant George Hartsuff is attacked in Big Cyprus Swamp by the

Seminole band headed by Chief Holata Micco (Billy Bowlegs). Four soldiers are killed. The Seminoles then carry out numerous raids on isolated farms and plantations.

Clashes continue through 1856, but the 700 soldiers in southern Florida and local militiamen are unable to defeat the elusive Seminoles, who take full advantage of their knowledge of the swamps. In late 1856 Colonel William S. Harney, a veteran of the Second Seminole War, assumes command in Florida. He employs an attrition strategy, ordering constant army patrols and the use of shallow-draft whale boats to penetrate deep into the Everglades.

In March 1858 most of the several hundred surviving Seminoles led by Billy Bowlegs accept a cash payment and removal. The Sam Jones band of fewer than 150 Seminoles is, however, allowed to remain in the Everglades.

1855–1860

Central America: Filibustering by William Walker in Nicaragua and Honduras. Having failed in Mexico in 1853, American soldier of fortune William Walker leads a new private campaign to conquer parts of Central America. Civil war rages in Nicaragua, and Walker is hired as a mercenary by one of the factions. Evading U.S. authorities, he sails from San Francisco on May 4, 1855, with 57 men. Landing in Nicaragua, he is reinforced by 170 locals and some 100 Americans.

On September 1 Walker defeats the Nicaraguan national army at La Virgen. After taking control of a steamer on Lake Nicaragua, in October Walker captures the capital of Granada. In May 1856 U.S. president Franklin Pierce's administration recognizes Walker's regime. Walker actively recruits more than 1,000 U.S. and European mercenaries with the goal of conquering all Central America.

Walker is opposed by wealthy American Cornelius Vanderbilt, who wants to monopolize trade and travel between the eastern United States and California across Nicaragua with his Accessory Transit Company, whose charter Walker revokes. Vanderbilt pressures the U.S. government to withdraw its recognition of Walker's regime and helps arm Nicaragua's neighbors.

In April 1856 troops from Costa Rica invade Nicaraguan territory and defeat Walker in the Battle of Rivas. Juan Santamaría plays a prominent role.

In July 1856 following a sham election, Walker officially becomes president of Nicaragua. To increase his support from the southern U.S. states, he opens Nicaragua to slavery, which had been abolished in 1824. Walker's forces, reduced by defection and disease, are no match for their opponents, however. Walker surrenders to the U.S. Navy on May 1, 1857, and is returned to New York City.

On November 25, 1857, Walker returns to Nicaragua. He is quickly deported and taken by the U.S. Navy. After writing an account of his adventures he is off again, this time to Honduras in August 1860. There he is arrested by British naval authorities and turned over to the Honduran government, which executes him by firing squad on September 12, 1860. The Walker adventures are seen by many in Latin America as proof of undue meddling in their affairs by the United States.

February 1, 1856

Central Europe: Crimean War (continued): Preliminary Peace of Vienna. With both sides exhausted, Austria threatens to join the conflict. Czar Alexander II is more amenable to a peace settlement than Nicholas I had been, and on February 1, 1856, the Russians agree to peace during talks in Vienna.

The Crimean War claims about a quarter million dead, perhaps three quarters of these to sickness and disease. The French lose some 100,000 dead, the British 20,000, the Sardinians 2,000, the Turks 30,000, and the Russians perhaps 110,000.

The final peace treaty is hammered out in the Congress in Paris during February–March 1856.

February 25–March 30, 1856

Western Europe: Crimean War (continued): Congress of Paris. Preliminary terms having already been agreed to at Vienna on February 1, 1856, the formal peace conference opens in Paris on February 25. Emperor Napoleon III, his nation having provided most of the allied land contingent in the war (and the majority of the allied dead), insists on the conference location. It is certainly one of the high-water marks of the emperor's reign.

The Great Powers agree to admit the Ottoman Empire to the concert of Europe and to respect its independence and territorial integrity; Russia is thus forced to give up its aspirations regarding the Ottoman Empire. Russia also loses control of the mouth of the Danube and is forced to cede the southern part of Bessarabia to the Ottoman Empire, return Kars to the Ottoman Empire, and demilitarize the Black Sea. The Danubian Principalities are placed under a joint guaranty of the powers with their exact status to be determined later. An international commission is appointed to ensure safe navigation on the Danube River.

Many in Russia interpret the war's outcome as another sign of that nation's backwardness in the political, economic, and military spheres. Czar Alexander II, in fact, initiates a series of reforms (known as the Great Reforms) as a direct consequence of the war.

Another consequence of the Crimean War is the Declaration of Paris, which outlaws paper blockades and privateering and places restrictions on commerce raiding in general. Of the world's major naval powers, only the United States and Spain refuse to sign this declaration.

May 21–September 15, 1856

North America: United States: Bleeding Kansas. In a prelude to the American Civil War, violence erupts within Kansas over the issue of whether this territory will enter the Union as a free or slave state. A proslavery mob sacks the Free-State stronghold city of Lawrence on May 21, destroying much property. Abolitionist fanatic John Brown then leads a raid on a proslavery settlement on Pottwatomie Creek during May 24–25, hacking 4 men to death with swords. Free-Staters seize the town of Franklin on August 13, while proslavery men drive Brown and his followers from Osawatomie on August 30. In the disorders, 20 people die and much property is destroyed. In mid-September, federal troops restore order.

October 8, 1856

East Asia: China: Seizure of the ship *Arrow* and beginning of the Second Opium War. On October 8, 1856, Chinese officials seize the lorcha *Arrow* and arrest its crew on smuggling charges. The Chinese-owned *Arrow* is registered in Hong Kong and flies the British flag. This action therefore brings an immediate British demand for the return of the ship and its crew, leading to the Second Opium War (1856–1860), also known as the *Arrow* War.

On October 14 Ye Mingchen (Yeh Ming-ch'en), Chinese imperial governor of the provinces of Guangdong (Kwangtung) and Guangxi (Kwangsi) at Canton and also imperial commissioner in charge of barbarian (non-Chinese) affairs, releases a few members of the crew but also claims that the British lack jurisdiction. Indeed, the *Arrow*'s right to fly the British flag is questionable because its Hong Kong registry has expired.

British officials consult with Rear Admiral Sir Michael Seymour, who wants to use force. They decide on an ultimatum with a 24-hour deadline. Despite last-minute concessions by Ye, on October 23 Seymour's men storm ashore and capture the barrier forts, Canton's main defenses located on both sides of the Pearl River some 12 miles from the city proper. The British spike the guns and burn the interior buildings. Seymour then proceeds to Canton.

On October 27 British ships open fire on the city, battering its walls and opening a breach through which British seamen enter the city to sack Commissioner Ye's residence. Lacking sufficient resources to remain, the British withdraw. Ye now orders all foreigners to leave Canton.

November 1, 1856

Southwest Asia: Anglo-Persian War. As part of the Great Game (the struggle for influence in Central Asia between Russia and Britain), the British seek to maintain Afghanistan as an independent state and a buffer between Russia and India. Despite warnings from Britain, Persia, now under a degree of Russian influence, sends troops to take Herat, Afghanistan, on October 25, 1856. The Persians had threatened this in the past but had backed down under British pressure. Apparently, the Persians believe that this time the British will not fight.

In response to the Persian move, however, the British governor-general in India, acting on orders from London, declares war on Persia on November 1, 1856. The Anglo-Persian War (1856–1857) on the British side is waged largely by East India Company forces. Because of their experience in the First Afghan War (1839–1843), the British are reluctant to send troops through Afghanistan to relieve Herat. They opt instead for operations directly against Persia along the Persian Gulf coast. An East India Company squadron captures the Reshire Fort on December 7. The British occupy Karak Island and Bushire on December 10 and then await reinforcements.

1856

South Africa: Zululand civil war. Zulu leader Mpande, having ruled since 1840 (the longest-reigning Zulu king), dies in 1872, and a succession struggle occurs

between his sons Cetewayo and Mbulazi. Cetewayo, with 20,000 men, defeats Mbulazi's 7,000 men in the decisive Battle of the Tugela River in December 1856. Mbulazi is killed.

1856–1857

South Africa: Xhosa Wars (continued): Cattle Killings. The desperate Xhosa people listen to 16-year-old prophetess Nongqawuse, who tells them that if they kill all of their cattle and destroy their food stocks, the ancestors of the Xhosa will return to help drive out the European settlers. The result is the near self-destruction of the Xhosa, about two-thirds of whom die of starvation.

February 7, 1857

Southwest Asia: Anglo-Persian War (continued): Battle of Khushab. With the arrival of troop reinforcements, British major general Sir James Outram leads an advance inland from Bushire to Brazjun, which the Persians simply abandon. The British destroy substantial Persian supplies at Brazjun, but Outram decides not to adopt the risky course of pursuing the Persians into the mountains. He begins a return march to the coast instead.

On February 7, 1857, en route to Bushire, a Persian force of some 8,000 men under Khanlar Mirza attempts to block Outram's force of 4,600 men at Khushab. Although the British have only some 400 cavalry to 2,000 for the Persians, the British cavalry charges the Persian infantry, and the British go on to win a major victory in what turns out to be the largest battle of the war. Pursuit of the Persians is impractical, and the British continue on to Bushire.

February–April 1857

Southwest Asia: Anglo-Persian War (continued): Additional British campaigning and end of the war. The British now shift their forces to the north of the Persian Gulf and the well-defended city of Mohammerah on the Euphrates River. Mohammerah is on the border with the Ottoman Empire, whose territory British forces are ordered not to violate. Following a British naval bombardment, however, the Persians abandon Mohammerah and withdraw 100 miles up the Karun River to Ahvaz. The British pursue, attacking Ahvaz by land and water and taking it on April 1, 1857. The British return to Mohammerah on April 4. There they learn that a peace agreement has been reached in Paris on March 4.

In the treaty ending the war, the Persians agree to withdraw from Herat, sign a commercial treaty, and cooperate in ending the slave trade in the Persian Gulf. Herat returns to more direct Afghan administration when Dost Mohammad Khan retakes it in 1863.

May 10, 1857

South Asia: India: Great Sepoy Mutiny. British military power in India consists of two elements: a large native Indian force (Sepoys) of some 311,000 men controlled by the East India Company and a relatively small number of British Army personnel totaling only some 45,500 officers and men. There is growing unrest among the Sepoy units, the consequence of low pay, ineffective administration, and efforts by some British officers to convert the Sepoys to Christianity.

The rebellion, however, is sparked by introduction of the new Minié rifle cartridge, which is bitten off prior to loading and is greased. The grease, it turns out, includes tallow, or fat from cows, which are sacred to Hindus, and lard from pigs, which Muslims consider unclean. The result is the Great Sepoy Mutiny (1857–1858), also known as the First War of Indian Independence, the Indian Mutiny, or the Sepoy Rebellion. Most of the violence is confined to north central India. Although there have been previous mutinies, that of 1857 is unprecedented in both scale and ferocity.

The first outbreak occurs among members of the 3rd Bengal Light Cavalry Regiment at Meerut, some 25 miles from Delhi. On May 9, 1857, the British publicly disgrace and imprison 95 members of the regiment who refuse to use the new cartridges. The next day, most members of the regiment attack their British officers and free the imprisoned men. All then set about killing British military personnel. They also kill 20 civilians, including women and children. Although there are actually more British than Indian troops at Meerut, the British commanders are slow to react, and the mutineers are able to flee without pursuit to Delhi.

May 11, 1857

South Asia: India: Great Sepoy Mutiny (continued): Massacre at Delhi. On May 11, 1857, the Sepoy mutineers from Meerut reach Delhi. They are joined there by other Indian troops and a good many of the poor in the city. They set about killing all Europe-

ans they can find. Those Europeans who are able to escape find refuge with British army cantonments outside the city. A few British officers and men hold the arsenal in Delhi. When it is about to be captured, they blow it up, killing themselves and a large number of the attackers.

The rebels declare their allegiance to Bahadur Shah Zafar, who proclaims himself emperor of all India. Soon the great majority of the Bengal Army of some 86,000 men, the largest of the Indian armies, is in revolt against the British.

May 30, 1857

South Asia: India: Great Sepoy Mutiny (continued): Beginning of the Siege of Lucknow. Rebellion also erupts in the city of Lucknow, the capital of the former state of Oudh (now known as Awadh, a region in the state of Uttar Pradesh), annexed little more than a year before. The prolonged Siege of Lucknow (May 30–November 18) is one of the most important events in the mutiny. The energetic British commissioner resident at Lucknow, Sir Henry Lawrence, has sufficient time to fortify the residency compound and lay in supplies for the many British who seek refuge there.

June 27, 1857

South Asia: India: Great Sepoy Mutiny (continued): Cawnpore Massacre. At the beginning of June, Dandu Panth (Nana Sahib), rajh of Bitpur, leads the Sepoys in Cawnpore (now Kanpur) in a three-week siege of the British garrison there during June 6–26. The British commander, Major General Sir Hugh Wheeler, had relied on his good relations with Nana Sahib and had done little to prepare fortifications or lay in supplies and ammunition. With little food or water, he is forced to surrender on June 26. He accepts Nana Sahib's generous terms that include safe passage to Allahabad.

On June 27, however, when the troops and some 200 women and children are embarking on the riverboats, firing breaks out. Most of the men are killed, and the surviving women and children are imprisoned. Only 4 of the British soldiers escape. On July 15, with British forces approaching Cawnpore, authorities in the town order the women and children killed. They are hacked to death by local butchers.

The British exact a terrible revenge on the Sepoys (who were not responsible for the murders but did not try to intervene) and on others in the city. Cawnpore becomes a rallying cry for the British and their allies during the remainder of the mutiny.

June 1857–April 1858

North America: United States: Utah War. U.S. president James Buchanan, concerned about the practice of polygamy and an apparent theocracy in the Utah Territory under the Church of Jesus Christ of Latter-day Saints (the Mormons), led by Brigham Young, in June 1857 declares Utah to be in a state of rebellion and calls up troops. The next month Buchanan appoints Alfred Cumming as new territorial governor of Utah, but fails to notify Young. Command of the 2,500 troops sent to Utah falls to U.S. Army colonel Albert Sidney Johnston.

Each side misunderstands the other's intentions, leading to the Utah War (also known as the Utah Expedition and Mormon Expedition). Informed of the troop movement, Young mobilizes the Utah militia and prepares for war. Mormon militia units attack and burn several army supply trains. With the arrival of winter, Johnston decides to delay his advance into Utah Territory and establishes camps in Wyoming. In the spring of 1858, 3,000 reinforcements arrive.

Meanwhile, with the permission of Buchanan, Thomas L. Kane arrives in Utah in February 1858 as a mediator. He persuades Young to accept Cumming as governor if there is a peaceful transition. He then gets Cumming to proceed to Salt Lake City without military escort. Cumming is received peacefully, and in April Young surrenders the title of governor to him. The troops arrive shortly thereafter and establish themselves in Camp Floyd, more than 30 miles from Salt Lake City. There is no violence, and the troops depart in 1860.

July 1–September 14, 1857

South Asia: India: Great Sepoy Mutiny (continued): Siege of Delhi. The British reaction to the mutiny is delayed because their garrisons have been scattered to hill stations for the summer months. It also takes time for London to organize the movement of reinforcements to India. In late May two British columns begin a slow movement toward Delhi, meeting at Karnal. This force contains not only British troops but also loyal Sepoys and Gurkha forces serving under contract with the British.

On July 1 the British begin the siege of Delhi. For much of the siege the British are in fact outnumbered. Not until August do the British have sufficient man-

power to undertake offensive action. A siege train also arrives, and on September 7 the British are able to begin artillery fire on the city, opening breaches in the walls and silencing the mutineer artillery.

Finally, on September 14 after three days of artillery preparation, 4,000 men in four columns storm the city. In heavy fighting over a six-day period, the British take possession of Delhi on September 21. They lose 1,574 men, including their commander, Brigadier General John Nicholson.

Considerable looting and reprisals follow, and innumerable Muslim cultural works are destroyed. Bahadur Shah is taken prisoner; a British officer shoots his two sons and one grandson out-of-hand in reprisal for the British women and children murdered at Cawnpore. The capture of Delhi ends the dream of a reconstituted Mogul (Mughal) Empire.

Shortly after the fall of Delhi, the British organize a column from Delhi to relieve a force besieged in Agra. It then presses on to Cawnpore, also recently recaptured.

September 25, 1857

South Asia: India: Great Sepoy Mutiny (continued): First Relief of Lucknow. The British commissioner resident in Lucknow, Sir Henry Lawrence, fortifies the residency compound and lays in supplies. The British force numbers some 1,700 men, including loyal Sepoys. Initial assaults on the compound fail, and the rebels settle in for a siege. Lawrence is killed by artillery fire on July 4 and is succeeded in command by Brigadier General John Inglis. The rebels attempt to breach the walls with explosives; they tunnel underneath the walls, leading to some underground combat. After three months of siege, the defenders are reduced to 350 British soldiers, 300 loyal Sepoys, and 550 noncombatants.

On September 25 a British relief column of 2,500 men from Allahabad under Sir Henry Havelock, joined by Sir James Outram (technically the superior officer), arrives at Lucknow, having fought its way from Cawnpore and defeated the rebels in a series of increasingly larger battles. Although the relief force is able to break through the 30,000–60,000 besiegers to the British compound in what is known as the First Relief of Lucknow, which takes place in the state of Awadh (also known as Oudh, in present-day Uttar Pradesh), it is not strong enough to extricate itself. The relief effort costs the column 535 casualties. The survivors are thus forced to join the besieged garrison. Outram now assumes command of the defense of the compound as the siege continues.

November 16, 1857
South Asia: India: Great Sepoy Mutiny (continued): Second Relief of Lucknow. In October a larger relief force of 4,500 men under the new commander in chief in India, Sir Colin Campbell, advances from Cawnpore. It begins moving into Lucknow on November 14. The troops are finally able to break through on November 16. The British claim 2,000 Sepoy dead in the operation. November 16 sees the largest number of Victoria Crosses (24) awarded for a single day's action.

December 6, 1857
South Asia: India: Great Sepoy Mutiny (continued): Second Battle of Cawnpore. Campbell considers Lucknow to be indefensible and on November 19, 1857, commences an evacuation of all the British there to Cawnpore. Sir Henry Havelock dies of dysentery on November 23. In the Second Battle of Cawnpore on December 6, Campbell defeats a large rebel force under Tantya Tope (Tantia Topi), probably the most capable of rebel military leaders, attempting to recapture the city.

March 21, 1858
South Asia: India: Great Sepoy Mutiny (continued): British recapture of Lucknow. Early in 1858 British commander in chief in India Sir Colin Campbell, now heavily reinforced, again advances on Lucknow with a large force, determined to suppress the rebellion in the state of Awadh (also known as Oudh, in present-day Uttar Pradesh). Campbell is aided by 10,000 Gurkhas under Nepalese prime minister Jang Bahadur, who has remained loyal to Britain throughout the rebellion in India. Following a methodical advance to Lucknow and a week of fighting, Campbell's forces drive the rebels from the city on March 21, 1858, with but few casualties to his own troops.

Large numbers of rebels are now dispersed throughout Awadh, however. Campbell continues operations into the autumn to crush scattered pockets of resistance.

March–June 1858
South Asia: India: Great Sepoy Mutiny (continued): British operations in Central India. Jhansi, a Maratha-ruled princely state in Bundelkhand, is an early center of the rebellion. British officials and their families take refuge in the fort there and surrender on the promise of evacuation, only to be massacred on leaving it. By the end of June 1857, the British have lost control of much of Bundelkhand and eastern Rajastan. Not until March 1858 is Sir Hugh Rose, with two brigades of loyal Bengal Army troops, about 3,000 men known as the Central India Field Force, able to advance on and lay siege to Jhansi on March 21.

During the siege a large rebel force under Tantya Tope (Tantia Topi) arrives at Jhansi. On April 1 Rose commits half of his besieging force to battle against Tantya Tope. The British defeat Tantya Tope, although he escapes. Two days later, on April 3, Rose's forces carry Jhansi by assault. The titular head of the rebellion there, Rani Lakshmi Bai, the widow of the former raja, escapes the city in disguise. Rose goes on to take both Kunch (on May 1) and Kalpi (on May 22). Over a five-month span, Rose wins 13 battles against the rebels.

On June 1, 1858, Rani Lakshmi Bai, Tantya Tope, and Maratha rebels capture the fortress city of Gwalior from the rulers of Scindia, who have remained loyal to the British. Rose quickly advances on Gwalior with his Central India Field Force. The Battle of Gwalior takes place during June 16–19. Rani Lakshmi Bai, who is sometimes compared to Joan of Arc (Jeanne d'Arc), is shot and killed during the fighting on June 17. Tantya Tope escapes but is later captured. He is executed on April 18, 1859.

The British victory at Gwalior, for all intents and purposes, brings the rebellion to a close. British mopping-up operations continue for some time thereafter, accompanied by harsh reprisals.

April 1858
Central Europe: Balkans: Ottoman invasion of Montenegro. Following a number of border clashes, Ottoman forces numbering between 7,000 and 13,000 men invade Montenegro. They are again defeated, this time by a Montenegrin army of some 7,500 men led by Mirko Petrović, brother of Prince Danilo Ostrag. The battle occurs at Grahovac between April 28 and May 1, 1858.

May 20, 1858
East Asia: China: Second Opium War (continued): British-French attack on the Dagu (Taku or Peiho)

INDIA, 1858

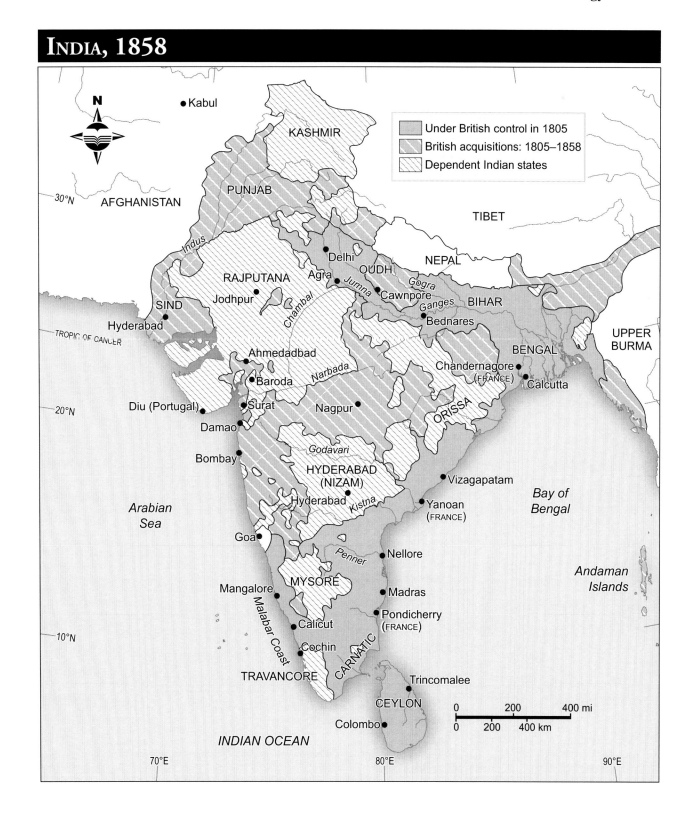

Under British control in 1805
British acquisitions: 1805–1858
Dependent Indian states

Kabul

KASHMIR

AFGHANISTAN

30°N

PUNJAB

TIBET

Indus

RAJPUTANA

Delhi

OUDH

NEPAL

Agra

Jumna

Gogra

Jodhpur

Cawnpore

Ganges

BIHAR

SIND

Chambal

Hyderabad

Bednares

TROPIC OF CANCER

BENGAL

Ahmedadbad

Narbada

Chandernagore
(FRANCE)

Calcutta

UPPER
BURMA

20°N

Diu (Portugal)

Baroda

Surat

Nagpur

ORISSA

Damao

Godavari

Bombay

HYDERABAD
(NIZAM)

Vizagapatam

Arabian
Sea

Hyderabad

Kistna

Yanoan
(FRANCE)

Bay of
Bengal

Goa

Penner

Nellore

Andaman
Islands

Mangalore

MYSORE

Madras

Malabar Coast

Calicut

Pondicherry
(FRANCE)

10°N

Cochin

CARNATIC

Trincomalee

TRAVANCORE

CEYLON

Colombo

0   200   400 mi
0   200   400 km

INDIAN OCEAN

70°E

80°E

90°E

Forts, which guard the approach to Tianjin and Beijing. French forces join the British against the Qing, using the excuse of the murder of French missionary Auguste Chapdelaine. On May 20, 1858, British and French forces operating under the command of British rear admiral Sir Michael Seymour attack the Dagu Forts on the Hai (Baihe) River about 36 miles from Tianjin (Tientsin). Some 1,200 men in landing parties go ashore to spike the guns and destroy Chinese shore installations.

June 25, 1858

East Asia: China: Second Opium War (continued): Treaty of Tianjin. Beginning on May 29, 1858, the Chinese government negotiates with the British, French, U.S., and Russian governments. On June 25 the two sides reach agreement in the Treaty of Tianjin (Tientsin). This involves the opening of treaty ports, establishment of Western embassies in Beijing (then closed to foreigners), and other concessions. The Qing government refuses to ratify the treaty, and the war continues.

The Qing are forced, however, in the Treaty of Aigun of May 1858 to cede the left bank of the Amur River to Russia.

July 20, 1858

Southern Europe: Italy: War of Austria with France and the Kingdom of Sardinia: Background and Pact of Plombières. Despite the failure of the Revolutions of 1848–1849 to expel the Austrians, sentiment for Italian unification remains strong throughout the peninsula. The revolutions bring home a number of important lessons: the republicans have lost support as a consequence of their failure; the pope is an unsuitable leader for the unification movement; throwing off Austrian domination will require the intervention of an outside power, most likely France; and the best hope of leadership within Italy in this struggle is the Kingdom of Sardinia (the island of Sardinia and Piedmont in northwestern Italy), which has demonstrated its steadfastness and leadership by going to war against Austria.

In November 1852 Count Camillo Benso di Cavour becomes the prime minister of Piedmont-Sardinia. He embarks on a series of political, social, and economic reforms to make the kingdom a model of parliamentary monarchy and an exemplar for the rest of Italy. He also takes his country into the Crimean War

to gain the support of Britain and France, and he uses the Congress of Paris at the end of that conflict to expound on the problems of Italy.

In 1856 leading Italian nationalists form the National Society to support the unification of Italy under the Kingdom of Sardinia. On January 14, 1858, Italian nationalist Felice Orsini, angered by the failure of Napoleon III (in his youth a participant in the Italian revolutionary movement) to support the unification movement, attempts to assassinate the emperor. This event seems to have goaded Napoleon into action; on July 20, 1858, he meets with Cavour at Plombières in southeastern France and concludes a secret pact with Piedmont-Sardinia.

The Pact of Plombières between France and Piedmont-Sardinia provides that the two will goad Austria into war against Piedmont-Sardinia, at which point France will come to its assistance with 200,000 men. France and Piedmont-Sardinia will then fight together until Italy is "free from sea to sea" and they establish a kingdom of northern Italy consisting of Piedmont-Sardinia, Lombardy, Venetia, Parma, Modena, and the papal legations of Ravenna, Ferrara, and Bologna. Napoleon seeks a federation of Italian states under French influence to include the new kingdom of northern Italy as well as a kingdom of central Italy (Tuscany with Umbria and the Marches), Rome and its surrounding territory, and the Kingdom of Naples. All these are to be under the presidency of the pope. In return for French aid against Austria, Piedmont-Sardinia will give Nice and Savoy to France.

To cement the pact, Princess Clotilde, daughter of King Victor Emmanuel II, is betrothed to Prince Joseph Charles Bonaparte, cousin of Napoleon III; they are married on January 30, 1859. The formal treaty is signed on December 10, 1858, after Napoleon assures himself of the goodwill of Russian czar Alexander II.

August 2, 1858

South Asia: India: Passage of the Government of India Act by the British Parliament. The Great Sepoy Mutiny brings to an end the century-long rule of India by the East India Company. Its authority is now taken over by the British Crown and vested in the India Office, a new British government department headed by the cabinet-level post of secretary of state for India, who is charged with the formation of policy. (In 1877 Queen Victoria takes the title of Empress of India.)

The new British regime ends attempts at Westernization and makes religious toleration stated policy. It attempts to reform administration in India and integrate the higher Indian castes and rulers into the government. Educated Indians are also admitted into the lower levels of the civil service.

Bahadur Shah meanwhile is tried for treason by a British military commission assembled at Delhi and is exiled to Rangoon, bringing the Mogul (Mughal) dynasty to an end.

September 1, 1858

Southeast Asia: Vietnam: French land troops at Tourane. French emperor Napoleon III adopts an aggressive policy in Asia. Defense of the Catholic Church is one of the pillars of his regime, especially because of the exhortations of his pious wife, Eugénie. An entente with the United Kingdom makes this possible, and Vietnamese persecution of Catholics provides the excuse.

In 1856 a French warship bombards the port of Tourane (Danang). In mid-July 1857 Napoleon III decides to intervene in Indochina. Following their successful participation with the British in operations against the Qing in 1857–1858, French naval forces under Admiral Rigault de Genouilly proceed to Vietnam.

The French decide to move against southern Vietnam first; it is the newest part of the country, and its inhabitants are not as wedded to Vietnamese institutions. Napoleon III hopes to secure a treaty port similar to Hong Kong. Rigault de Genouilly's squadron of 14 warships carrying 3,000 troops anchors off Tourane on August 31, 1858. Believing that military action will bring fruitful negotiations, on September 1 he lands his men, including 300 Filipino troops sent by Spain. The invaders take Tourane's forts after only perfunctory Vietnamese resistance, seizing them and the port and beginning the first phase of the French conquest of Indochina. Within a few months, however, heat, disease, and a lack of supplies force the French from Tourane.

1858–1860

North America: Mexico: Civil war. The struggle in Mexico is between the Conservative party led by Félix Zuloaga, which holds the capital of Mexico City, and the reformist Liberal party led by Benito Juárez, which sets up a rival government at Veracruz. Much of this centers on attitudes toward the Catholic Church.

The Liberals pass legislation to limit the influence of the Catholic Church by introducing civil marriage and nationalizing Church property in what becomes known as La Reforma (The Reform). The United States recognizes the Juárez government in April 1859. Liberal forces then win the decisive Battle of Calpulalpam on December 22, 1860, establishing themselves as the sole government of Mexico. With Mexico's finances now in an absolute shambles, Jáurez suspends payments on foreign debts, which involve British, French, and Spanish citizens and invites foreign intervention.

1858–1868

South Africa: Orange Free State Wars. Led by King Mosheshu, in 1858 the Basuto begin a decade-long struggle with the Orange Free State to drive the Boers from their ancestral lands. Initially the Basuto enjoy success, but on the renewal of fighting the Boers are successful and annex large parts of Basutoland during 1864–1866. After additional fighting during 1867–1868 and further Boer territorial gains, the British annex Basutoland to prevent additional Boer acquisitions.

February 17, 1859

Southeast Asia: Vietnam: French seize Saigon. After being forced from Tourane (present-day Danang) in late 1858, French admiral Rigault de Genouilly shifts his attention southward to the fishing village of Saigon (present-day Ho Chi Minh City). It is selected because of its proximity, its promise as a deep-water port, and the fact that it could be important in controlling the southern rice trade. Following a brief struggle, Saigon falls to the French on February 17, 1859.

March 9, 1859

Southern Europe: Italy: Franco-Austrian War: Creating the war and Sardinian mobilization. In January 1859, French emperor Napoleon III complains about the plight of Italy and unsatisfactory relations with Austria, while articles in the official French press attack Austrian rule in Italy. Many ardent French Catholics express alarm over the direction of events and possible threat to the papacy, while British diplomats try without success to reverse the drift toward war. Yet Napoleon finds his Italian policy opposed by his wife Eugénie and a majority of his cabinet ministers. Again he wavers.

On March 9 Piedmont-Sardinian premier Count Camillo Benso di Cavour mobilizes the Sardinian Army, calling up reserves but also recruiting volunteers, many of whom are from Lombardy, in a direct provocation to Austria. This begins the Franco-Austrian War (also known as the Second War of Italian Independence and the Austro-Sardinian War).

April 20, 1859
Southern Europe: Italy: Franco-Austrian War (continued): Austrian ultimatum to Piedmont-Sardinia. Following the Piedmont-Sardinia mobilization of March 9, Emperor Franz Joseph II authorizes the mobilization of the Austrian Army on April 9. Then, with Napoleon III of France backtracking, on April 20 Austria makes a fatal mistake by sending an ultimatum to Piedmont-Sardinia, giving that nation three days to demobilize. Cavour, believing the opportunity for war lost, had on April 19 already ordered demobilization. Without a direct telegraph link between Turin (Turnio) and Vienna, though, Austrian leaders are unaware of this. The Austrian ultimatum appears as an act of diplomatic bullying and gives Cavour the excuse he needs for war. Piedmont-Sardinia rejects the ultimatum, and on April 29 Habsburg forces invade Piedmont.

May 3, 1859
Southern Europe: Italy: Franco-Austrian War (continued). France declares war on Austria on May 3, 1859. For three weeks, however, inept Austrian commander Field Marshal Count Franz Gyulai marches and countermarches, failing to take advantage of his superior numbers and giving time for French troops to come up. French emperor Napoleon III arrives by sea at Genoa on May 12 to take personal command of his troops in Italy.

May 20, 1859
Southern Europe: Italy: Franco-Austrian War (continued): Battle of Montebello. In the first real engagement of the war, Austrian commander Field Marshal Count Franz Gyulai, who has failed to undertake any major offensive action during the previous three

weeks and perhaps under prodding from Vienna, orders General Count Stadion's corps to mount a reconnaissance in force toward Voghera in Lombardy on May 20. About noon, this Habsburg force of some 27,000 men encounters near Montebello a French infantry division and some Piedmontese cavalry, totaling perhaps 8,000 men. French division commander General Elias Forey audaciously attacks. Only a portion of the Habsburg force comes into battle, and after two hours of fighting the French drive the Austrians from Montebello. Stadion withdraws his corps all the way to Stradella.

The Austrians sustain some 1,300 casualties, the allies only 730. Assuming the far larger Habsburg army will resume the attack the next day, Forey also withdraws, toward Voghera. While not a major battle, Montebello brings great prestige to the French. It serves as a major morale boost for the allies and a corresponding depressant for the Austrians.

May 30–31, 1859
Southern Europe: Italy: Franco-Austrian War (continued): Battle of Palestro. Following their victory at Montebello and with all the French troops and their equipment having arrived, the allies take the offensive. They plan to advance on Novara and then to Milan. Covering the allied right, part of the Piedmontese army advances to Robbio.

On the morning of May 30 this Piedmontese force crosses the Sesia River and, following hard fighting, takes Palestro, Confienza, and Vinzaglio. The next day Habsburg general Fredrick Zobel counterattacks at the village of Palestro with his two infantry divisions of some 14,000 men and 42 guns against the Piedmontese under King Victor Emmanuel II. The previous night, the king had called up reinforcements in the form of a French Zouave regiment so that the allies now number 21,000 men and 36 guns.

In the Battle of Palestro the allies repulse the Austrians, suffering some 600 casualties against Austrian losses of 1,600, of which nearly half are missing. The allies, however, have failed to utilize their superior resources (they have 50,000 men within several hours' march) and do not pursue the retreating Austrians.

June 4, 1859
Southern Europe: Italy: Franco-Austrian War (continued): Battle of Magenta. In one of the two major

battles of the war, the commanders on both sides manage to concentrate only a portion of their forces. The battle pits some 54,000 French troops against 58,000 Austrians. French emperor Napoleon III plans a pincer movement against the Austrians at Magenta by maneuvering the II Corps of General Marie Edmé Patrice Maurice de MacMahon on the left bank of the Ticino while the Imperial Guard and III and IV Corps cross the Ticino farther south. The French do not expect the Austrians to react prior to the closing of the pincers.

The Austrians have already decided to retreat to the northeast. They are even slower in their withdrawal than MacMahon is in his advance, though, and the two sides clash on the morning of June 4. MacMahon's corps manages to break through and win the battle, mainly because of the elan of the French infantry, the highly effective fire of French rifled artillery, and the inept performance of Habsburg commander Field Marshal Count Franz Gyulai. The Austrians withdraw in good order, unmolested, to Robecco.

French casualties total 657 killed, 3,203 wounded, and 655 taken prisoner or missing. The Austrians lose 1,368 killed, 4,538 wounded, and 4,500 taken prisoner. Although horrified by the slaughter of the battle, a relieved Napoleon III creates MacMahon a marshal of France and confers on him the title of Duke of Magenta. General Achille Baraguey d'Hilliers, commander of the Imperial Guard, also is rewarded with a marshal's baton in recognition of the role played by the Guard in the victory. On June 8 Napoleon III and Sardinian king Victor Emmanuel II make a triumphal entry into Milan.

See Leaders: MacMahon, Marie Edmé Patrice Maurice de

June 8, 1859
Southern Europe: Italy: Franco-Austrian War (continued): Battle of Melegnano. French emperor Napoleon III orders Marshal Achille Baraguey d'Hilliers, supported on his right by General Adolphe Niel's IV Corps and on his left by Marshal Marie Edmé Patrice Maurice de MacMahon's II Corps, to attack Austrian forces 18 miles to the southeast of Milan at Melegnano. It takes the French all day to reach the town, and the battle opens in early evening on June 8, 1859.

Poor tactics ensure that the French are unable to trap the isolated Austrians. Baraguay d'Hilliers fails to wait for MacMahon's II Corps to close on Melegnano, immediately launching an infantry attack without adequate artillery support. Habsburg general Ritter Ludwig August von Benedek's VIII Corps is heavily entrenched and barricaded in the little medieval town. Their Lorenz rifles exact a heavy toll on the attackers. The French II Corps does not arrive in time to take part in the battle, and that night the Austrian defenders withdraw in good order. The French sustain 948 casualties, the Austrians about 1,480. The battle is a waste. The Austrians had planned to withdraw the next day in any case, and the French fail to exploit the situation by pursuing Benedek. Instead, they return to Milan.

June 24, 1859
Southern Europe: Italy: Franco-Austrian War (continued): Battle of Solferino. Habsburg emperor Franz Joseph II dismisses his commander in Italy, the inept Field Marshal Count Franz Gyulai. Assuming personal command of the Austrian forces, Franz Joseph moves to meet the French and Piedmontese forces. The ensuing Battle of Solferino is the culminating engagement of the Italian Campaign of 1859.

Thanks to poor reconnaissance, the battle comes as a surprise to both sides. As with other battles of the war, Solferino is marked by little recognition on the part of the generals of the tremendous defensive firepower of the rifled musket behind field entrenchments and by poor coordination of forces. Forces are committed to battle en masse as they arrive in large frontal assaults with the bayonet.

The forces involved are quite large; indeed, Solferino is the largest battle in Europe since Leipzig in 1813. The French and Piedmontese have six army corps of some 138,000 men and 366 guns, while the Austrians commit seven army corps with 129,000 men and 429 guns. The allies thus enjoy superiority in numbers and in cavalry. The Austrians have the advantage of defensive positions and greater numbers of artillery.

The battle is concentrated along the Mincio River, from the Lago de Garda to Mantua, and centered on the town of Solferino. General Marie Edmé Patrice Maurice de MacMahon commands the French forces. French emperor Napoleon III, king of Sardinia Victor

BATTLE OF SOLFERINO, JUNE 24, 1859

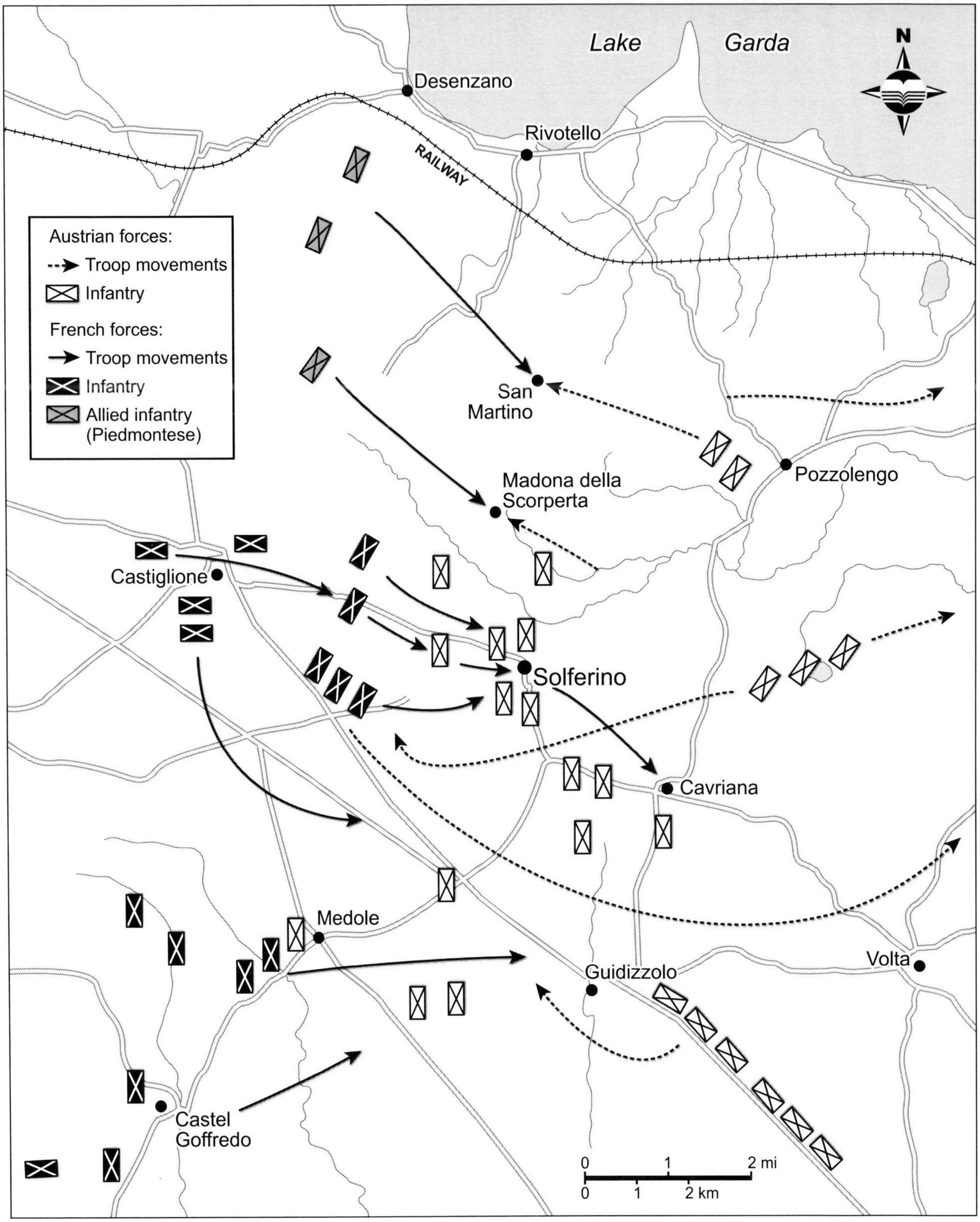

Lake Garda

Desenzano

Rivotello

RAILWAY

N

Austrian forces:
- - -▶ Troop movements
⊠ Infantry

French forces:
──▶ Troop movements
⊠ Infantry
⊠ Allied infantry
(Piedmontese)

San Martino

Pozzolengo

Madona della Scorperta

Castiglione

Solferino

Cavriana

Medole

Guidizzolo

Volta

Castel Goffredo

0   1   2 mi
0   1   2 km

Napoleon III at the Battle of Solferino by Jean-Louis-Ernest Meissonier, 1863. Soldiers from France and Piedmont-Sardinia defeated the Austrians here in a sanguinary fight on June 24, 1859. The suffering of the wounded in the battle spurred the creation of the International Red Cross. (Library of Congress)

Emmanuel II, and Habsburg emperor Franz Joseph are all present.

Fighting begins at 4:00 a.m., when the advance guards of each side stumble upon one another. Much of the ensuing combat is hand-to-hand. The battle is decided by the bravery of the attacking French and Piedmontese infantry. Fighting ends at about 8:00 p.m. with the collapse of the Austrian center. With their center broken and their left unable to overcome the French, the Austrians begin a general withdrawal. They are saved from a rout only by the effective leadership of General Ritter Ludwig August von Benedek.

Although the allies trumpet a great victory, it is a hollow one. Both sides are exhausted. The allies suffer 17,292 casualties (French losses are 1,622 killed, 8,530 wounded, and 1,518 captured or missing; the Piedmontese lose 691 dead, 3,572 wounded, and 1,359 captured or missing). At 22,007 casualties, Austrian losses are even higher: 2,202 dead, 11,167 wounded, and 8,638 captured or missing.

The Battle of Solferino has another major effect. The suffering of the wounded there is the more horrible from totally inadequate ambulance services. Many of the wounded lie under a hot sun for three days, a number of them robbed of their possessions by local peasants, until they are attended to.

Swiss businessman Henri Dunant, who had traveled to Solferino to talk with Napoleon III, witnessed the battle and its aftermath. In 1862 he publishes a small book about his experiences. Titled *Un Souvenir de Solférino,* it deals principally with the efforts to tend to the wounded in the small town of Castilogne. In his book, Dunant suggests that each country form societies to care for those wounded from battle. This leads in 1864 to the formation in Geneva of the International Committee of the Red Cross.

See Leaders: Benedek, Ludwig August von

June 25, 1859
East Asia: China: Second Opium War (continued): Attack on the Dagu Forts. Fighting resumes in 1859 after the Qing government refuses to permit the establishment of a British embassy in Beijing as promised in the Treaty of Tianjin (June 1858). On June 25, 1859, British and French naval forces, now under the

Austrian general Ludwig von Benedek (1804–1881) was a veteran of fighting in Italy but proved inept in the July 3, 1866, Battle of Königgrätz, the decisive encounter of the Austro-Prussian War. (Anne S. K. Military History Collection, Brown University Library)

command of Rear Admiral Sir James Hope, again attack the Chinese Dagu (Taku or Peiho) Forts located on the Hai (Beihe) River about 36 miles from Tianjin (Tientsin). These works, destroyed in 1858, have been rebuilt by the Chinese.

The Chinese put up an effective defense and force the landing parties to retire. Commodore Josiah Tattnall, commanding the U.S. Asiatic Squadron, declares that "blood is thicker than water" and provides covering fire to the withdrawing allied force. The British lose three gunboats as well as 89 men killed and 345 wounded. French losses are 4 killed and 10 wounded. Chinese casualties are unknown.

July 11, 1859
Southern Europe: Italy: Franco-Austrian War (continued): Meeting at Villafranca. Following the Bat-

tle of Solferino, Emperor Napoleon III of France is appalled by the great bloodshed resulting from his policies. He is also concerned about a Prussian mobilization and possible military intervention by that country on the Rhine while his best troops are committed in Italy. Habsburg troops now occupy strong defensive positions in the so-called Quadrilateral: the fortresses of Mantua, Peschiera, Verona, and Legnano. It is also apparent that he has misread the strength of the Italian unification movement, and the likely result of a total Austrian defeat is a unitary Italian state rather than the loose confederation he has envisioned. In addition, French public opinion has now turned against the war.

In light of all of this, Napoleon III abandons his ally King Victor Emmanuel II of Piedmont-Sardinia and his pledge to free Italy "from sea to sea" to conclude an armistice with the Austrians on July 8, 1859. Napoleon III then meets with Austrian emperor Franz Josef at Villafranca on July 11. Franz Joseph agrees to turn over to France all Lombardy except the fortress cities of Mantua and Peschiera, with the understanding that France will then cede the territory to Piedmont-Sardinia. Austria retains control of Venetia. The rulers of Modena, Parma, and Tuscany—all unseated by nationalist uprisings during the war—are to be returned to their thrones. The terms are formally ratified by the Treaty of Zürich (November 10, 1859).

Italian nationalists are outraged by Villafranca, and Piedmont-Sardinian prime minister Count Camillo Benso di Cavour foolishly urges Victor Emmanuel to continue the war alone. When the king refuses, Cavour resigns in disgust.

October 16–18, 1859
North America: United States: John Brown's Raid. Abolitionist John Brown and 18 followers seize the Federal Arsenal at Harpers Ferry, Virginia, hoping to spark a slave insurrection and then arm them with the seized weapons. The assault is badly planned, and the insurrection fails to occur. A number of Brown's men are killed in the raid, and marines under U.S. Army colonel Robert E. Lee capture Brown and his followers. They are charged with murder, conspiracy, and treason against Virginia.

Brown rejects his counsel's suggestion of an insanity plea. He is convicted and hanged in December. The raid alarms whites in the South and leads to the establishment of militia companies.

October 1859–April 1860
North Africa: War between Spain and Morocco. Incidents along the border between the Spanish North African enclave of Ceuta and Morocco lead Spain to declare war on Morocco in October 1859. In February 1860 Spanish forces enjoy success in the fighting and occupy Tetuán. The war ends with British mediation in April 1860. Morocco pays Spain an indemnity, and Spain receives Ifni and the Spanish Sahara.

1859
Indian Ocean: Madagascar. French forces establish control over coastal areas of Madagascar.

March 24, 1860
Southern Europe: Italy: Treaty of Turin. In the late summer of 1859 popularly elected assemblies in Parma, Modena, Tuscany, and the Ramagna call for the union of their states with Piedmont-Sardinia. The Sardinian government, however, does not dare to accept without the approval of French emperor Napoleon III. In January 1860 Count Camillo Benso di Cavour returns as Piedmontese prime minister. He negotiates the annexation of these areas. Napoleon III insists on and receives from Piedmont both Nice and Savoy in return for his approval. In early March, plebiscites in Parma, Modena, Tuscany, and the Ramagna duly approve annexation to Piedmont. Another plebiscite, on March 24, 1860, confirms the transfer of Nice and Savoy to France through the Treaty of Turin.

May 1860–January 1861
Southeast Asia: Vietnam: Siege of Saigon. France continues to add to its holdings in southern Vietnam, but the French naval squadron there is recalled to China. The French leave behind in Saigon a garrison of some 1,000 men. Almost immediately a Vietnamese force of 12,000 men besieges the French there. The siege lasts from March 1860 to February 1861, during which time the garrison is completely cut off from outside contact.

When fighting in China concludes at the end of 1860, France is again free to concentrate its Far Eastern resources in Indochina. Admiral Léonard Victor Joseph Charner and 3,000 troops arrive and relieve Saigon after winning the Battle of Chi-hoa on February 25, 1861.

Emperor Tu Duc, deprived of rice from the French-controlled South and facing a rebellion in the North, is obliged to sign a treaty with France. It provides for an indemnity of 20 million francs, three treaty ports in Annam and Tonkin (Tongking), and French possession of the eastern provinces of Cochin China, including Saigon. The French continue to expand their control in the South; by 1867 they have conquered all of Cochin China. They have also learned that the Mekong is not navigable to the interior of China. Tu Duc also stirs up resistance to the French, with continuing guerrilla activity.

May 11, 1860
Southern Europe: Sicily: Garibaldi's Sicilian Expedition. Following an abortive uprising led by Rosolino Pilo in Sicily against King Francis II on March 4, 1860, Italian nationalist Giuseppe Garibaldi handpicks a force of some 1,150 men (and at least 1 woman) to carry on the work of Italian unification. This force is known as the One Thousand (in Italian, Mille) or the Red Shirts (for their makeshift uniform). Most had served under Garibaldi in the war against Austria and respect his leadership.

Garibaldi receives secret financial support and arms from Piedmontese premier Count Camillo Benso di Cavour and then embarks with his men on a filibustering expedition to Sicily. Sailing from Genoa in two steamers on May 5, the men come ashore at Marsala in western Sicily on May 11.

May 15, 1860
Southern Europe: Sicily: Garibaldi's Sicilian Expedition (continued): Battle of Calatafimi. Almost immediately upon the arrival of Giuseppe Garibaldi's One Thousand at Marsala, several Neapolitan Navy gunboats come up. Although they are delayed by the presence of several British warships, the Neapolitan ships destroy one steamer and capture the other. Garibaldi, however, is able to get all his men ashore and begin the march inland.

Garibaldi announces that he is assuming the dictatorship of Sicily in the name of Victor Emmanuel II, "King of Italy." Although Francis II has an army of some 100,000 men, he is hated by his subjects; Garibaldi gathers recruits as he proceeds toward Palermo. At Calatafimi on May 15 he does battle with

THE UNIFICATION OF ITALY, 1859–1870

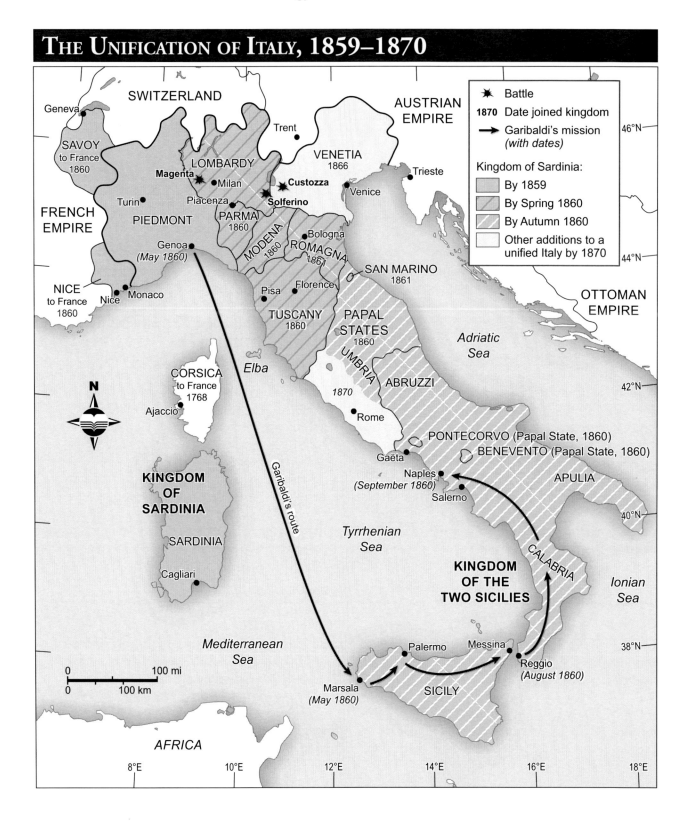

some 2,000 men of the Neapolitan Army under General Francisco Landi.

In a sharp action, Garibaldi recklessly exposes himself to enemy fire to rally his men. The One Thousand are victorious. They suffer some 30 dead and 150 wounded, 100 of them so badly that they cannot proceed. The Neapolitan forces flee to Palermo, arriving there on May 17.

May 27–29, 1860
Southern Europe: Sicily: Garibaldi's Sicilian Expedition (continued): Battle for Palermo. Morale among Giuseppe Garibaldi's men is greatly boosted by their victory at Calatafimi. Increasing numbers of Sicilians also rally to him. Garibaldi moves on the capital city of Palermo. It is held by some 22,000 Neapolitan troops under the command of 75-year-old General Ferdinando Lanza. On May 27, although he has only about 750 men able to fight, Garibaldi attacks.

A significant portion of Palermo's 180,000 residents rally to Garibaldi, including some 2,000 prisoners liberated from the local jails. The Neapolitans are driven back from a number of key positions on the first day of fighting. Lanza then shells that part of the city that had been lost, leading to some 600 civilian deaths during a three-day span. By May 28, though, Garibaldi controls much of Palermo. On May 29 the One Thousand defeat a Neapolitan counterattack, and Lanza requests a truce.

When two battalions of well-trained and well-equipped Bavarian mercenaries in the employ of the Bourbons arrive, however, the situation looks bleak for Garibaldi. His men are almost out of ammunition. He is saved by Lanza's decision to surrender on May 30.

An armistice is hastily arranged by British admiral George Rodney Mundy. On June 6 Garibaldi arranges a convention for the withdrawal by sea from Palermo of some 22,000 royal troops, to be effected by June 19.

July 20, 1860
Southern Europe: Sicily: Garibaldi's Sicilian Expedition (continued): Battle of Milazzo. In late June in a bid to win moderate support for his regime, Bourbon king Francis II forms a liberal ministry and introduces the liberal constitution of 1848. It is too late. With the fall of Palermo, only Syracuse, Augusta, Milazzo, and Messina remain under Bourbon

control. Prime Minister of Piedmont Count Camillo Benso di Cavour, worried by the pace of Garibaldi's victories and unsure of his intentions, sends an envoy calling for the immediate annexation of Sicily to Piedmont. Garibaldi rejects the overture, pending completion of his mission.

Garibaldi now creates the Southern Army, reinforced by volunteers from throughout Italy and some regular Piedmontese troops sent by Cavour. Against these, Francis II musters some 24,000 men at Messina and the other fortress cities. Garibaldi also has to contend with peasant revolts against the landowners.

On July 20 Garibaldi and 4,000 of his men attack Milazzo, held by perhaps 3,000 Bourbon troops under General Bosco. Garibaldi's side suffers 750 killed or wounded. The Neapolitan troops, fighting from cover, sustain only 150 casualties, but they are eventually forced to surrender. Under terms of the capitulation, the defenders are allowed to depart on July 24 with the full honors of war, leaving Garibaldi the fortress guns, munitions, and stores. Shortly thereafter the city of Messina surrenders, leaving only 4,000 in the citadel and other forts. All remaining Sicilian strongholds capitulate by the end of September.

August 21, 1860
East Asia: China: Second Opium War (continued): Renewed British and French offensive and capture of the Dagu Forts. The British and French governments commit additional resources to the fighting. In May 1860 they assemble at Hong Kong 11,000 British troops under Lieutenant General Sir James Hope Grant and 7,000 French troops under Lieutenant General Charles Guillaume Marie Apollinaire Antoine Cousin Montauban. These forces then move north to carry out a landing at Beitang (Pei Tang) on August 1. On August 21 they mount a successful attack on the Dagu (Taku or Peiho) Forts located on the Hai (Beihe) River, about 36 miles from Tianjin (Tientsin).

August 22, 1860
Southern Europe: Italy: Garibaldi crosses the Strait of Messina and lands in Calabria. Italian nationalist Giuseppe Garibaldi, having taken virtually all Sicily, is adamant about crossing into southern Italy and defeating the remaining Neapolitan forces. Premier of

Piedmont-Sardinia Count Camillo Benso di Cavour, at first strongly opposed to the move, now encourages Garibaldi.

Garibaldi crosses the narrow Strait of Messina on August 22, 1860, with an initial force of 4,000 men. He faces in southern Calabria perhaps 20,000 well-equipped Neapolitian Army troops. Apart from some relatively minor battles, Garibaldi's progression to Naples is an easy one, however.

King Francis II still has some 40,000 men. Plans to block Garibaldi on the plain between Eboli and Salerno evaporate, however. On September 5 the entire Neopolitan cabinet resigns. Two days later Garibaldi enters Naples in triumph. Francis II flees to the fortress of Gaeta.

Garibaldi plans to defeat the remaining Neapolitan troops, march on Rome, and proceed to conquer Venetia.

September 8, 1860

Southern Europe: Italy: Uprising in the Papal States in favor of Italian unification and intervention by Piedmont-Sardinia. Although Italian nationalist Giuseppe Garibaldi has always professed loyalty to King Victor Emmanuel II, Piedmont-Sardinian premier Count Camillo Benso di Cavour is worried about the international impact of Garibaldi's future plans. He fears that a march on Rome will bring the intervention of France while a march on Venetia will assuredly mean another war with Austria. An uprising in the Papal States on September 8, 1860, gives Cavour the opportunity to take leadership of the campaign for Italian unification out of Giuseppe Garibaldi's hands.

When the papacy rejects Cavour's demands that it disband its foreign military force, on September 10 Cavour sends Piedmontese forces south into papal territory. The British government supports Cavour, as it fears a Muratist (French) restoration in Naples.

September 18, 1860

Southern Europe: Italy: Battle of Castelfidaro. Piedmontese forces march into the Papal States on September 10, 1860. There is fighting at other places, but the principal battle occurs on September 18 at Castelfidaro, a dozen miles south of Ancona. Although the overall Piedmontese forces are considerably larger than those of the papacy, at Castelfidaro each side deploys only about 3,000 men. The Pedmontese are commanded by General Enrico Cialdini, the papal side by expatriate French general and commander of the papal army Louis Christophe Léon Juchault de Lamorcière.

The Piedmontese lose several dozen dead and about 140 wounded. Papal losses are not much greater, but the battle is decisive and the papal forces dissolve virtually overnight. The Piedmontese forces then advance into Neapolitan territory and link up with Garibaldi's troops.

October 1, 1860

Southern Europe: Italy: Battle of the Volturno. King Francis II hopes that with his sizable remaining Neapolitan forces he can defeat Italian nationalist Giuseppe Garibaldi and his army before the Piedmontese army moving through the Papal States can arrive. The battle occurs on a front of some 14 miles along the Volturno (Volturnus) River, north of Naples in northern Campania between Capua and Maddaloni. General Giosuè Ritucci commands some 31,200 Neapolitan troops; Garibaldi has only about 20,000.

Ritucci attacks at dawn on October 1, and the battle rages most of the day. It ends in a Neapolitan defeat. Garibaldi's casualties are 300 killed, 1,328 wounded, and 389 missing. Bourbon losses are not known with any certainty but are presumed to be no fewer than 1,000 killed or wounded; 2,000 prisoners are taken the next day. Garibaldi's men also capture seven Neapolitan guns.

October 6, 1860

East Asia: China: Second Opium War (continued): British and French forces capture Beijing. Following their capture of the Dagu (Taku or Peiho) Forts before Tianjin (Tientsin) on August 21, British troops under Lieutenant General Sir James Hope Grant and French troops under Lieutenant General Charles Guillaume Marie Apollinaire Antoine Cousin Montauban proceed to Beijing. En route they push aside a Qing army of some 30,000 men. They arrive at the imperial capital on September 26. The allied troops assault and capture the city by October 6. They then set fire to the Summer Palace and the Old Summer Palace following considerable looting. British commander Lieutenant General Sir James Hope Grant orders the burning of the Old Summer Palace in reprisal for the earlier ill-treatment of British diplomat Sir Harry Smith Parkes and his party when they had attempted to negotiate an end to the fighting and had been seized and tortured that September.

October 18, 1860
East Asia: China: Second Opium War (continued): Treaty of Beijing. Following the capture of Beijing, the Chinese imperial government is forced to sue for peace. In the Treaty of Beijing, China ratifies the earlier Treaty of Tianjin (1858). The treaty legalizes the import of opium. Britain, France, Russia, and the United States receive the right to legations in Beijing, then a closed city. The Chinese also agree to open 10 additional ports for foreign trade, including Niuzhuang, Danshui, Hankou, and Nanjing. Foreign ships receive the right to free navigation on the Changjiang (Yangtze, Yangxi) River, and foreigners are allowed to move freely inside China for travel, trade, or missionary activities. Western citizens residing in China, including those of the United States, secure extraterritorial protections from Qing civil and criminal law.

The Qing government is forced to pay an indemnity of 8 million taels of silver. It also has to surrender to the British the territory of Kowloon on the Chinese mainland opposite Hong Kong as well as grant special rights to the French. The Russians take advantage of the Qing's weakness to seize the left bank of the Amur River and the Maritime Provinces, establishing the port of Vladivostok in 1860–1861.

October 21–22, 1860
Southern Europe: Italy. Naples and Sicily vote by plebiscite to join Piedmont-Sardinia. Favorable votes also occur in the Marches (November 4) and Umbria (November 5). On October 26 at Teano in northern Campania, Garibaldi and King Victor Emmanuel II meet. Garibaldi requests that he be allowed to remain for one year as dictator in the former Kingdom of the Two Sicilies (Naples and Sicily) and that his officers be absorbed into the new Italian Army. Victor Emmanuel refuses both requests, whereupon Garibaldi returns to his home at Caprera.

November 3, 1860–February 14, 1861
Southern Europe: Italy: Siege of Gaeta. Beginning on November 3, 1860, Piedmontese forces lay siege to Gaeta, where the former Neapolitan king, Francis II, has taken refuge with his remaining forces. The siege is protracted by the actions of the French. Emperor Napoleon III orders French Mediterranean Squadron commander Vice Admiral Marie Charles Adelbert Le Barbier de Tinan to position his ships between the Italian ships and the shore forts. The French ships are withdrawn on January 10 under growing British diplomatic pressure. Gaeta surrenders on February 14. Francis II goes into exile in Austria.

December 20, 1860
North America: United States: American Civil War. Causes of the war and the secession of South Carolina from the Union. By 1860 North and South in the United States are completely estranged. The essentially agricultural South is the world's largest producer of raw cotton. The vast majority of this crop is exported, chiefly to the United Kingdom.

Some 85 percent of industry is located in the North. Northerners therefore want a high tariff to protect their goods against cheap British manufactures. Banking, insurance companies, and railroads are all concentrated in the North as well, and the West is increasingly tied to the North by the expanding railroad net.

There is a large growing population imbalance between the two regions as well. New immigrants, unable to compete with slave labor in the South, settle primarily in the North.

Increasingly, Southerners believe that their way of life is threatened as abolitionist movements gain strength worldwide. Most Southerners support the right of a state to secede from the Union, whereas Northerners reject this. Institutions, including churches and political parties, split along regional lines.

The election of Republican Party candidate Abraham Lincoln as president of the United States in November 1860 prompts the secession of the so-called Deep South. The Republican platform calls for no more slavery in the territories but no interference with slavery in the states. Carolina nonetheless votes to secede on December 20, 1860. Alabama, Georgia, Florida, Mississippi, Louisiana, and Texas all follow suit, leading to the American Civil War (1861–1865).

See Leaders: Lincoln, Abraham

1860
West Africa: Cameroon. The Germans establish trading posts along the coast of Cameroon (Kamerun).

Unversally acknowledged as one of the greatest of U.S. presidents, Abraham Lincoln (1809–1865) was an adroit politician and masterful communicator. Determined to preserve the Union at all costs, he had scant military experience but proved to be a highly effective war leader during the American Civil War. (Chaiba Media)

1860–1861
South America: Colombia: Civil war. Tomás Cipriano de Mosquera, rebel leader in Colombia (New Granada), emerges victorious in a civil war and becomes president of the New Granadine Confederation (July 18, 1861–February 4, 1863).

1860–1862
East Asia: China: Taiping Rebellion (continued): Imperial Chinese victories under Frederick Townsend Ward. With the end of the Second Opium War (*Arrow War*) in 1860, Viceroy Zeng Guofan (Tseng Kuo-fan) and Li Hongzhang (Li Hung-chang) work to reform and revitalize the imperial government. They also attempt to subdue the Taiping regime to the south. Despite its promises of reform, the Taiping regime has become increasingly repressive, the key factor in its subsequent demise.

With the Taipings threatening Shanghai, in 1860 wealthy Shanghai merchants finance a mercenary army. It is initially composed of foreigners and commanded by Frederick Townsend Ward, who arrives in the city with his brother that same year. Ward is an American merchant marine officer and soldier of fortune from Salem, Massachusetts, who had been a filibuster in Mexico and had fought in the Crimean War as an officer in the French Army. His Foreign Arms Corps, which begins with about 100 men and a military reverse, steadily grows in size and comes to be known as the Ever Victorious Army for a series of successful military campaigns.

In 1861 Ward is made a brigadier general in the Imperial Army. During a four-month span he and his army, assisted by British and French forces returning from their operations at Beijing, win 11 victories and clear a swath of territory about 30 miles wide around Shanghai. On August 20, 1862, however, Ward is mortally wounded while leading an assault on the walled city of Cixi (Tzeki) in Zhejiang (Chekiang).

See Leaders: Zeng Guofan

1860–1872
Australasia: New Zealand: Second Maori War (Taranaki Wars). Angered by the continued encroachments by British settlers on their lands, the Maori tribesmen of New Zealand wage a guerrilla war that lasts for a dozen years. Both militia and regular British troops take part in the fighting against the Maori.

British major general Duncan Alexander, commanding a force of almost 4,000 men, defeats the Maori on the Katikara River on January 4, 1863, and at Rangaria on November 29. However, he is defeated, with considerable casualties, at Gate Pa on April 29, 1864. In January 1865 Alexander refuses to attack Weroroa *pas*, considering it too strongly held. British governor-general of New Zealand Sir George Grey then takes personal command; he attacks and reduces Weroroa *pas* after three days of hard fighting. Alexander returns to Britain.

After 1865 British troops are gradually withdrawn, and the fighting is conducted by locally raised forces. A brief truce allows the Maori to keep the land still in their possession, but fighting soon resumes in the form of guerrilla warfare. By 1872 the settlers have taken most of their land they desire. Perhaps 54,000 Maori, or half of their population, have died.

With the outcome clear, the war is settled by diplomacy. The Maori receive recognition of the right to their remaining land.

Leaders

Ardant du Picq, Charles

Birth Date: October 19, 1821
Death Date: August 19, 1870

French Army officer and military theorist. Charles Jean Jacques Joseph Ardant du Picq was born at Périgueux on October 19, 1821. He graduated from the French Military Academy at Saint-Cyr in 1844 as a sublieutenant, having been assigned to the 67th Infantry Regiment. Promoted to captain in August 1852, he served in the 9th Light Cavalry Battalion during the Crimean War (1853–1856) and was taken prisoner in the storm of the central bastion of Sevastopol in September 1855. Following his release at the end of the war, he saw service in both Syria during 1860–1861 and Algeria during 1864–1866. Promoted to colonel in 1869, he took command of the 10th Infantry Regiment and, while leading it in battle during the Franco-Prussian War, was mortally wounded by a shell explosion near Gravelotte on August 15, 1870. Ardant du Picq died at Metz on August 19.

Ardant du Picq was the author of the one of the most original books of military theory of the 19th century, the posthumous *Les Études sur le combat antique et moderne* (Studies of Ancient and Modern Combat), usually known simply by its English title as *Battle Studies* and published in 1880. Before his death he had published only his study of ancient warfare in 1867. The larger work, a military classic, is largely unknown today. His work stresses the importance of moral and psychological principles in battle, which Napoleon had stated as being as to all others three to one. Ardant du Picq claimed that such factors did not change through history. Regardless of the time in which they live, men in combat are capable of just so much exertion, sacrifice, and effort. In his writing, he stresses the need for inspiration and capable leadership. He also places great importance on fire power, insisting that attackers should fire to "the last possible moment" without which they would not reach their objective. Ardant du Picq's writing was highly influential in the offensive doctrine (*offensive à outrance*) championed by Colonel François Loyzeau de Grandmaison and future marshal of France Ferdinand Foch during World War I.

SPENCER C. TUCKER

References
Ardant du Picq, Charles Jean Jacques Joseph. *Battle Studies: Ancient and Modern Battle.* Translated by John N. Greely and Robert C. Cotton. Harrisburg, PA: Stackpole, 1958.
Van Creveld, Martin. *The Art of War: War and Military Thought.* London: Cassell, 2000.

Arnold, Benedict

Birth Date: January 14, 1741
Death Date: June 14, 1801

American Revolutionary War general, first for the Americans and then for the British. Born in Norwich, Connecticut, on January 14, 1741, Benedict Arnold was both difficult and rebellious as a youth. At age 15 he enlisted in the Connecticut militia and served in the French and Indian War (1754–1763), although he did not

Continental Army major general Benedict Arnold initially served the revolutionary cause with great skill. His subsequent plot to betray West Point and hand over lieutenant General George Washington to the British failed, whereupon he fought as a British Army brigadier general. (Library of Congress)

see battle. Later he became a pharmacist and a bookseller in New Haven. In 1774 he was elected captain of a Connecticut militia company.

With the beginning of the American Revolutionary War, Arnold joined the Patriot cause. Proud, vain, and extremely sensitive to criticism, he was nonetheless an effective planner and a brilliant field leader. He conceived a plan to attack British-held Fort Ticonderoga and secure its cannon to use against the British in the siege of Boston. Commissioned a militia colonel by Massachusetts, he teamed with Ethan Allen, who had the same idea, to take Ticonderoga on May 10, 1775.

In the summer of 1775 various plans were developed for a Patriot invasion of Canada. Arnold submitted his own plan to Continental Army commander General George Washington and secured command of the smaller of two columns sent into Canada. Commissioned a colonel in the Continental Army, Arnold led 1,000 men on an epic march through the Maine wilderness against Quebec (Québec), which he narrowly missed seizing and with it all Canada. He was wounded in the leg in the December 31, 1775, Battle of Quebec. In January 1776 Congress appointed him a brigadier general.

Arnold remained in Canada until the spring of 1776 and the arrival of British reinforcements. He then oversaw the building of and then commanded the little fleet of some 15 gondolas and galleys that met the British in one of the most important battles of the war, on Lake Champlain on October 11–13, 1776. Although Arnold's fleet was destroyed, he had delayed the British advance south down Lake Champlain, preventing an invasion of New York that autumn and perhaps saving the Patriot cause.

Brave, even reckless, in battle, Arnold nonetheless made enemies through his lack of tact and imperious manner. He also failed to understand the workings of state and national politics as they affected the military. When he fell victim to a quota system and was unfairly passed over for appointment as major general, he saw only the work of enemies and a nation's ingratitude. Congress finally advanced him to major general in May 1777 but did not restore his seniority. A bitter Arnold temporarily resigned his commission in July. Named by Washington to go north and assist in stopping British lieutenant general John Burgoyne's invasion of New York, Arnold returned to service.

Arnold raised the siege of Fort Stanwix (Fort Schuyler) at the end of the Mohawk Valley in New York in August 1777, then played a key role in stopping the main British force under Burgoyne. In the First Battle of Saratoga (Freeman's Farm) on September 19 Arnold commanded the American left wing and brought Burgoyne's advance to a halt. Arnold also openly quarreled with American commander Major General Horatio Gates, leading Gates to remove him from command. Arnold disobeyed Gates's order to remain in camp and rallied American forces to help win the Second Battle of Saratoga (Bemis Heights) on October 7, 1777, where he was again injured in the same leg that had been wounded at Quebec.

Restored to seniority on the major generals' list by Congress in November 1777, Arnold became military governor of Philadelphia in 1778, where he was soon accused of questionable financial dealings. There he also fell in love with Peggy Shippen, a beautiful, ambitious, and disgruntled young lady of Loyalist persuasion. Living beyond their means, together they conceived a plan to betray their nation to the British. This called for Arnold to secure command of West Point and deliver the fortress, its garrison, and probably Washington himself to the British. Arnold secured the West Point command on August 3, 1780, but a series of accidents led to the plot's discovery late the next month.

Arnold escaped and accepted a commission as a brigadier general in the British Army. He fought principally in Virginia, where he took Richmond in January 1781 and destroyed much property. He also led a bloody raid on New London, Connecticut, in September 1781. Quite possibly the finest field commander on either side in the war, Arnold never found the fame he sought. Departing for England in December 1781, he soon found himself retired as a colonel on half-pay. He made several attempts to secure an active British Army commission but was unsuccessful. Arnold died in London on June 14, 1801, his name synonymous with "traitor."

SPENCER C. TUCKER

References

Flexner, James Thomas. *The Traitor and the Spy: Benedict Arnold and John Andre.* Boston: Little, Brown, 1975.

Martin, James Kirby. *Benedict Arnold, Revolutionary Hero: An American Warrior Reconsidered.* New York: New York University Press, 1997.

Bagration, Peter Ivanovich

Birth Date: 1765
Death Date: September 24, 1812

Russian general, best known for his service during the French Revolution and Napoleonic Wars. Born in 1765 into a noble family in Georgia, Peter Ivanovich Bagration joined the Russian Army in 1782. He subsequently fought in some 20 campaigns and 150 battles. Certainly one of the very best Russian generals of the period, he inspired his men by his personal bravery in battle and generosity to them, but his fiery temperament made him impetuous and a difficult subordinate.

Bagration first saw action in fighting in the Caucasus against the Turks in the Russo-Turkish War of 1787–1792. He then campaigned in Poland under Marshal Aleksandr Suvorov, where Bagration's role in the siege of Warsaw in 1794 led to his elevation to general. He first gained international renown for his role in the Wars of the French Revolution in campaigning in Italy and Switzerland again under Suvorov, specifically for his capture of Brescia on April 21, 1799, and role in the Battle of Trebbia on June 17–19, 1799. During Marshal Mikhail Kutuzov's retreat before Napoleon Bonaparte in 1805, Bagration distinguished himself at Hollabrunn on November 16, and his 6,000-man rear guard held off 30,000 French cavalry under Marshal Joachim Murat. In the December 2, 1805, Battle of Austerlitz, Bagration's men held on the allied right against French troops under Marshal Jean Lannes. Bagration again commanded the Russian rear guard in the Russian retreat after the battle. He participated in the hard-fought battles at Eylau on February 8, 1807, and Heilsberg on June 10. At Friedland on June 14, 1807, he again distinguished himself.

Following the Treaty of Tilsit that restored peace between Russia and France, in 1808 Bagratian marched a Russian army across the frozen Gulf of Finland to capture the Åland Islands from Sweden. In 1809 he again fought against the Turks with success, this time in Moldavia.

During Napoleon's invasion of Russia in 1812, Bagration commanded the Russian Second Army of the West. Following Prince Mikhail Barclay de Tolly's withdrawal from Smolensk, Bagration accused his superior of treason (on his deathbed, Bagration acknowledged that Barclay had done the right thing after all). In the September 7, 1812, Battle of Borodino, Bagration commanded the Russian center and left. He was mortally wounded in the battle by a French musket ball that shattered his left shin. Bagratian died at Simy, east of Moscow, on September 24, 1812. As a highly effective leader of rearguard actions, he has often been compared to French marshal Michel Ney. The great Soviet World War II Belarusian offensive of 1944 that resulted in the destruction of German Army Group Center was named for Bagration.

SPENCER C. TUCKER

References

Chandler, David. *The Campaigns of Napoleon.* New York: Macmillan, 1966.

Riehn, Richard K. *1812: Napoleon's Russian Campaign.* New York: McGraw-Hill, 1990.

Barclay de Tolly, Mikhail Bogdanovich

Birth Date: December 27, 1761
Death Date: May 26, 1818

Russian field marshal. Born at Luhde-Grosshof in Livonia of Scots descent on December 27, 1761, Mikhail Bogdanovich Barclay de Tolly joined the Russian Army as a private in 1776. His enterprise, bravery, and demonstrated ability won him steady promotion. Barclay de Tolley first saw combat in fighting against the Turks during 1788–1789. He then fought against the Swedes in 1792 and the Poles during 1792–1794. He won promotion to general in 1799 and distinguished himself in the Battle of Pułtusk on December 26, 1806. He commanded a division in the Battle of Eylau on February 7–8, 1807, and was badly wounded. His role in the battle gained the attention of Czar Alexander I and brought his advancement to lieutenant general. During 1808–1809 Barclay de Tolly campaigned in Finland against the Swedes. In 1810 he was appointed minister of war. In this position he carried out numerous reforms that greatly improved the capability of the Russian Army. He well understood the limits of these, and in the event of a French invasion of Russia he advocated drawing the French deep into Russian territory and awaiting a favorable opportunity to engage the invaders.

Appointed to command the First Army of the West on Napoleon Bonaparte's invasion of June 1812, Barclay de Tolly several times avoided Napoleon's efforts to envelop his forces, drawing the French deeper into Russia. Such a strategy was highly unpopular at court, however, and led directly to Barclay de Tolly's replacement as Russian commander by Field Marshal Prince Mikhail Kutuzov.

Barclay de Tolly commanded the right wing of the Russian Army in the Battle of Borodino on September 7, 1812, but he resigned from the army soon thereafter. Recalled to active service in 1813 for the German War of Liberation, he commanded a corps in the Battle of Dresden on August 26–27 and the Battle of Leipzig on October 16–19. His role in the latter victory led to his being made a count. He led Russian forces in the invasion of France in 1814 and on the Russian occupation of Paris was promoted to field marshal.

On Napoleon's return to France in 1815, Alexander I appointed Barclay de Tolly commander of the Russian Army. Russian forces did not see action in the Hundred Days, but on the second abdication and final exile of Napoleon, the czar created Barclay de Tolly a prince. Barclay de Tolly died on May 26, 1818, at Insterburg (Chernyakhovsk) in East Prussia. A gifted administrator and military reformer, he was also a brave soldier and capable field commander, and he deserves much credit for the final defeat of the French in 1814.

SPENCER C. TUCKER

References

Cate, Curtis. *The War of the Two Emperors: The Duel between Napoleon and Alexander, Russia 1812.* New York: Random House, 1985.

Josselson, Michael, and Diana Josselson. *The Commander: A Life of Barclay de Tolly.* New York: Oxford University Press, 1980.

Riehn, Richard K. *1812: Napoleon's Russian Campaign.* New York: McGraw-Hill, 1990.

Barry, John

Birth Date: ca. 1745
Death Date: September 13, 1803

U.S. naval officer, considered the Father of the U.S. Navy. Born in County Wexford, Ireland, around 1745, John Barry immigrated to Philadelphia in 1761 and joined the merchant marine at an early age. When the American Revolutionary War broke out in 1775, he sold his ship *Black Prince* to the Continental Navy and was commissioned a captain. On April 6, 1775, he captured the British tender *Edward,* the first Royal Navy vessel taken by a Continental Navy ship. Over the next few years he held a succession of naval commands and established himself as one of the most aggressive American naval leaders. While awaiting a new ship he raised an artillery company from his crew in the autumn of 1776, which served with distinction on land in the Battle of Trenton (December 26, 1776) and the Battle of Princeton (January 3, 1777) and won commendation from General George Washington.

In the spring of 1781 Barry received his most important command, that of the frigate *Alliance.* He departed Boston carrying diplomatic envoys and en route defeated and captured three British brigs. On the return trip he conveyed the Marquis de Lafayette back to America before commencing a successful Caribbean cruise and securing more prizes. The *Alliance* fired the final shots of the war at sea and crippled HMS *Sybil* off Cape Canaveral on March 10, 1783.

After the war Barry successfully lobbied Congress to provide pensions for veteran sailors. He also engaged in the lucrative China trade before being appointed senior captain of the newly created U.S. Navy in March 1794. In this capacity he supervised construction of the large 44-gun frigate *United States,* which he commanded throughout the undeclared Quasi-War with France (1798–1800). He successfully captured several French privateers and also dueled with the batteries at Bass Terre before taking charge of all American naval forces in the Caribbean. His final official duty was ferrying diplomatic envoys to France for peace negotiations.

Poor health forced Barry to resign from the navy in 1801. He died in Philadelphia on September 13, 1803, having imparted traditions of aggressive leadership and victory to the nascent U.S. Navy.

JOHN C. FREDRIKSEN

References

Clark, William B. *Gallant John Barry: The Story of a National Hero of Two Wars.* New York: Macmillan, 1938.

Miller, Nathan. *Sea of Glory: The Continenal Navy Fights for Independence, 1775–1783.* New York: David McKay, 1974.

Morgan, William James. "John Barry: A Most Fervent Patriot." In *Command under Sail: Makers of the American Naval Tradition, 1775–1840,* edited by James C. Bradford, 46–67. Annapolis, MD: Naval Institute Press, 1985.

Beauharnais, Eugène de

Birth Date: September 3, 1781
Death Date: February 21, 1824

French general. Born in Paris on September 3, 1781, Eugène de Beauharnais was the son of Alexandre Vicomte de Beauharnais, guillotined in 1794 during the Reign of Terror, and his wife Joséphine de Tascher de la Pagerie, who became the mistress and then the first wife of Napoleon Bonaparte. Eugène entered the army at age 13 and fought in the Vendée. Taking an immediate liking to Napoleon, Eugène served as his aide-de-camp in the Italian Campaign of 1796–1797 and the Egyptian Campaign of 1798–1799. He assisted Napoleon in his coup d'état of November 1799 and was made a captain of dragoons, leading his squadron under his stepfather in the Battle of Marengo on June 14, 1800. By 1804 Eugène he was made a member of the French royal family as Prince Eugène de Beauharnais and a general.

In June 1805 Napoleon appointed Eugène viceroy of Italy and in January 1806 officially adopted him. In 1809 Eugène was made commander of the Army of Italy. Defeated by Austrian forces under Archduke John in the battles of Sacile on April 16 and Caldiero on April 29–30, Eugène was nonetheless victorious at San Daniele on May 11. He won the important victory of the Raab on June 14. Following the Battle of Aspern-Essling, Napoleon recalled the Army of Italy, and Eugène fought with the emperor at Wagram on July 5–6.

During the 1812 Russian Campaign, Eugène led the largely Italian IV Corps and fought with distinction in the Battle of Borodino on September 7 and the Battle of Maloyaroslavets on October 24–25. During the retreat from Russia on January 13, 1813, he assumed command of what remained of the Grande Armée from Napoleon's brother-in-law Marshal Joachim Murat, who fled to Italy. During the 1813 War of German Liberation, Eugène played a major role in the French victory at Lützen on May 2 and was then sent to organize the defense of Italy. Victorious in the Battle of Mincio on February 8, 1814, he was nonetheless forced to conclude an armistice with Austria and Naples on April 16.

Eugène then retired to the court of his father-in-law, King Maximilian I of Bavaria. Created the prince of Eichstädt and duke of Leuchtenberg, he lived in Munich until his death on February 21, 1824. A bold, daring, and resourceful military commander, he was also a capable administrator and was well liked by his men. Unlike many members of Napoleon's family, Eugène remained loyal to Napoleon, who both loved him and thought most highly of him.

SPENCER C. TUCKER

References

Beauharnais, Eugène. *Mémoires et correspondences politiques et militaires.* Paris: Michel Lévy frères, 1858–1860.

Connelly, Owen. *Napoleon's Satellite Kingdoms.* New York: Free Press, 1965.

Steward, Desmond. *Napoleon's Family.* New York: Viking, 1986.

Benedek, Ludwig August von

Birth Date: July 14, 1804
Death Date: April 27, 1881

Austrian field marshal. Born at Ödenburg (Sopron), Hungary, the son of a doctor, on July 14, 1804, Ritter Ludwig August von Benedek graduated from the Maria Theresa Military Academy in 1822 and was commissioned in the Austrian Army. In 1833 he was appointed to the General Staff.

Benedek took part in the operation to put down a revolt by Poles against Austrian rule in western Galicia in 1846. Serving under Field Marshal Josef Radetzky, Benedek distinguished himself in fighting during the Revolutions of 1848–1849, first against the Sardinian Army at Curtalone (May 29, 1848), at Vicenza (June 10), at Custozza (July 25), at Mortara (March 21, 1849), and at Novara (March 23) and then against the Hungarians during April–August 1849.

Benedek then served as a chief of staff to Radetzky during 1850–1857. During the Italian War of 1859 between Austria on the one hand and Sardinia and France on the other, Benedek commanded a corps and distinguished himself in covering the Austrian retreat over the Mincio River bridges following the Battle of Solferino on June 14, 1859. Emperor Franz Joseph then promoted Bendedek to *Feldzeugmeister* (field marshal), advancing him over a half dozen other officers and appointing him quartermaster general of the army during 1860–1864 and commander of Austria's largest field army, the Army of Italy, in Venetia during 1861–1866. As the son of a provincial doctor and thus not of the nobility, Benedek proved popular with his men and the public, especially with his jabs at "blue bloods" and "bookworms" among the officer corps.

On the outbreak of the Austro-Prussian War of 1866, Franz Joseph named Benedek to be commander of the North Army, the main Austrian forces in Bohemia in June. The emperor did this despite Benedek's unfamiliarity with the area and over his own objections. On July 3, 1866, in the decisive battle of the war, Benedek's army was defeated by the Prussians under General Helmuth von Moltke at Königgratz, although Benedek's forces were able to withdraw in good order. Benedek was then relieved of his command and court-martialed, but Franz Joseph halted the proceedings. Benedek was allowed to retire from the army to Graz, where he died on April 27, 1881. A bold and resourceful junior commander, Benedek proved indecisive in supreme command, although in his defense his service had prepared him for action in Italy, not in Bohemia.

SPENCER C. TUCKER

References

Craig, Gordon A. *The Battle of Königgratz: Prussia's Victory over Austria, 1866.* Westport, CT: Greenwood, 1975.

Rothenberg, Gunther E. *The Army of Francis Joseph.* West Lafayette, IN: Purdue University Press, 1976.

Wawro, Geoffrey. *The Austro-Prussian War: Austria's War with Prussia and Italy in 1866.* New York: Cambridge University Press, 1996.

Bernadotte, Jean Baptiste Jules

Birth Date: January 26, 1763
Death Date: March 8, 1844

Marshal of France and king of Sweden as Charles XIV. Born at Pau on January 26, 1763, the son of a lawyer, Jean Baptiste Bernadotte enlisted in the French Army in September 1780. His rapid advance through the ranks was made possible by the great expansion of the army and the departure of Royalist officers during the Wars of the French Revolution. Bernadotte was promoted to regimental sergeant major in February 1790, *sous-lieutenant* (second lieutenant) in November 1791, and major in February 1794. In April 1794 he commanded a demibrigade in the Army of the North.

Bernadotte played an important role in the victory by General Jean-Baptiste Jourdan over the Austrians in the Battle of Fleurus on June 26, 1794, for which Bernadotte was promoted to general of brigade. That October he was promoted to general of division. In January 1797 he joined the French Army of Italy commanded by Napoleon Bonaparte. Briefly ambassador to Vienna during February–April 1798, in August Bernadotte married Desirée Clary. From July to September 1799 he was minister of war. During April 1800–September 1802 he was commander of the French Army of the West. Named marshal of France in May 1804, he served as governor of Hanover during May 1804–August 1805.

Bernadotte commanded I Corps in Napoleon's victory over the Austrians and Russians in the Battle of Austerlitz on December 2, 1805. Created Prince de Porte-Corvo in June 1806, Bernadotte commanded I Corps in the 1806 war against Prussia but was not present at the battles of Jena-Auerstädt on October 14, 1806, despite Napoleon's orders and for which he was censored by the emperor. Bernadotte partially redeemed himself by a victory over the Russians at Mohrungen on January 25, 1807. In June 1807 he was wounded in the neck by a musket ball during fighting with the Russians in the Battle of Spanden. From July 1807 to March 1809 he was governor of the Hanseatic towns. In 1809 he commanded I Corps in the war against Austria and fought in the Battle of Wagram on July 3, 1809. Quarreling with Napoleon regarding his conduct in the battle, Bernadotte resigned his commission on July 8 and returned to Paris. He was then briefly commander of the Army of Antwerp during August–September 1809.

On August 21, 1810, the Swedish Parliament elected Bernadotte crown prince of Sweden, based on his record as an effective administrator and good relations with the Swedes while he was in northern Germany. He soon became quite popular in Sweden. After Napoleon occupied Swedish Pomerania in January 1812, in April Bernadotte first allied Sweden with Russia and then in March–April 1813 with Britain and Prussia against Napoleon. During June 1813–July 1814 Bernadotte commanded the allied Army of the North against France. In the German War of Liberation of 1813 he was victorious over French forces at Gross Beeren on August 23, 1813, and Dennewitz on September 6. He participated in the Battle of the Nations at Leipzig on October 16–18. Arriving on the field late in the battle, he helped turn the French retreat into a rout. During December 1813–January 1814 he invaded Denmark and forced it to cede Norway to Sweden. He then commanded Swedish forces that occupied Norway during May–June 1814. In February 1818 Bernadotte formally succeeded to the Swedish throne as King Charles XIV. He died at Stockholm on March 8, 1844. Bernadotte's record as a general was uneven, although he performed very well in the German War of Liberation. An effective king of Sweden, he proved to be a moderate who did much to modernize his adopted country.

SPENCER C. TUCKER

References

Barton, D. Pluckett. *The Amazing Career of Bernadotte, 1763–1844.* London: Murray, 1930.

Heathcote, T. A. "Serjent Bell-Jame—Bernadotte." In *Napoleon's Marshals,* edited by David Chandler, 18–41. New York: Macmillan, 1987.

Palmer, Alan. *Bernadotte: Napoleon's Marshal, Sweden's King.* London: John Murray, 1990.

One of Napoleon's marshals, Jean Baptiste Bernadotte (1763–1844) was elected crown prince of Sweden in 1810. He led that nation into the war against Napoleon in 1813 and became king of Sweden as Charles XIV in 1818. (Photos.com)

Blücher, Gebhard Leberecht von

Birth Date: December 16, 1742
Death Date: September 12, 1819

Prussian field marshal. Born in Rostock, Mecklenburg, on December 16, 1742, Gebhard Leberecht von Blücher enlisted in a Swedish cavalry regiment in 1757 during the Seven Years' War (1756–1763) and fought against the Prussians until he was captured in 1760. He then changed sides and was commissioned a cornet in the Prussian Army. Soon earning a reputation for boldness and personal bravery as a resourceful cavalry officer, he fought against Sweden until the end of the war. He was also noted for his heavy drinking, gambling, and womanizing, qualities that were not acceptable in the army during the reign of Frederick II (Frederick the Great; r. 1740–1786).

Disliking garrison life and passed over for promotion, Blücher retired from the army in 1773 to farm. Recalled to service as a major in 1786 at his own request after the death of Frederick II, Blücher served with distinction against the French in the early battles of the French Revolution and the Napoleonic Wars. As commander of the 8th Hussars, he was victorious over the French in the Battle of Landau on May 28, 1794, and was promoted to major general.

Following peace between Prussia and France in 1795, Blücher became military governor of Münster, openly criticizing Prussia's failure to enter the war on the side of Austria and Russia. In 1805 he wrote a tract titled *Thoughts on the Organization of a National Army* in which he urged Prussia to adopt a program of universal military service.

In 1806 when Prussia again declared war on France, Blücher performed effectively during the Prussian withdrawal before Napoleon. Fighting under Friedrich Wilhelm, the Duke of Brunswick at the Battle of Auerstadt, Blücher carried out repeated cavalry charges against the French, attempting to cover Brunswick's retreat on October 14, 1806. Blücher was one of the few Prussian generals to emerge from the war with his reputation intact. During 1807–1811 he was military governor of Pomerania, after which he retired.

At age 71 Blücher again came out of retirement in 1813 to fight in the War of German Liberation only to lose both at Lützen on May 1–2 and Bautzen on May 20. He triumphed at Katzbach on August 26, however, and was the Prussian commander in the Battle of the Nations (Leipzig) on October 16–18, 1813.

Promoted to field marshal, Blücher led Prussian forces across the Rhine and into France on January 1, 1814. Although checked by Napoleon on numerous occasions during the drive on Paris, Blücher always resumed the advance. On March 30 he joined forces with other allied troops to win the Battle of Montmartre in the capital, bringing Napoleon's abdication on April 6.

Blücher then again retired to his Silesian estates. With Napoleon's return from Elba, Blücher again came out of retirement on March 8, 1815, at age 72 to command the Prussian Army in the field. Defeated in the Battle of Ligny on June 16, 1815, Blücher marched his men to support the English under Arthur Wellesley, the Duke of Wellington, at Waterloo rather than retreat back on his base at Namur. Wellington later called it "the decision of the century," for the arrival of the Prussians decided the Battle of Waterloo, Napoleon's final defeat, on June 18, 1815.

Created Prince of Wahlstadt, Blücher then retired from the army for a final time. He died at Kribolwitz in Silesia on September 12, 1819. Although rough, uneducated, and a man of substantial vices and appetites, Blücher was well respected by his men, who knew him as "Alte Vorwarts" (Old Forward). Personally courageous, he was also a bold and resourceful commonsensical commander who relied heavily on a highly effective staff. Blücher restored confidence in the Prussian Army, which had been badly shaken by its early defeats at the hands of Napoleon.

SPENCER C. TUCKER

References

Petre, Francis L. *Napoleon's Last Campaign in Germany.* London: Arms and Armour, 1977.

Warner, Richard. *Napoleon's Enemies.* London: Osprey, 1977.

Bolívar, Simón

Birth Date: July 24, 1783
Death Date: December 17, 1830

South American revolutionary leader, general, and liberator. Born into a wealthy family in Caracas, Venezuela, on July 24, 1783, Simón Bolívar was orphaned at age six and was raised by an uncle and educated by tutors. He traveled to Spain in 1799 to complete his education and there married a young Spanish noblewoman in 1802. He returned with his wife in 1803 to Venezuela, where she died of yellow fever. Bolívar returned to Spain in 1804. After visiting France, he returned to Venezuela in 1807.

Napoleon Bonaparte's removal of the Bourbons from the Spanish throne in 1808 brought upheaval to the Spanish colonies in Latin America, whereupon Bolívar joined the Latin American movement seeking independence. Dispatched on a diplomatic mission to Britain by the Venezuelan Junta in 1810, Bolívar was unable to secure assistance and returned to Venezuela in March 1811 with Francesco Miranda, who had led an unsuccessful revolution in Venezuela in 1806. Bolívar joined the army of the new republic (declared on July 5,

1811). He commanded the fortress of Porto Cabello, but when Miranda was forced to surrender to the Spanish in July, Bolívar fled to Cartagena de Indias.

Securing a military command in New Grenada (now Colombia), Bolívar led an invasion of Venezuela in May 1813 and defeated the Spanish in six hard-fought battles known as the Campaña Admirable. He entered Mérida on May 23 and was proclaimed El Liberador. Bolívar took Caracas on August 6 and was confirmed as El Liberador. Civil war soon broke out. Bolívar won a series of battles but was defeated at La Puerta in July and forced to flee to New Grenada. Gaining control of forces there, he liberated Bogotá, only to be defeated by Spanish troops at Santa Maria and forced into exile in Jamaica in 1815. There he requested and received assistance from Haitian leader Alexandre Pétion in return for a promise to free the slaves.

Returning to Venezuela in December 1816, Bolívar fought a series of battles but was again defeated at La Puerta on March 15, 1818, and withdrew into the Orinoco region, where he raised a new force. Joined by several thousand British and Irish volunteers who were veterans of the Napoleonic Wars and linking up with other revolutionary forces, he crossed the Andes by the Pisba Pass and caught Spanish forces completely by surprise, winning the important Battle of Boyacá on June 11, 1819, and taking Bogotá on August 10. On the creation in September 1821 of Gran Colombia, a federation comprising much of present-day Venezuela, Colombia, Panama, and Ecuador, he became its president. Victories over the Spanish in the Battle of Carabobo (June 25, 1821) and the Battle of Pichincha (May 24, 1822) consolidated his authority in Venezuela and Ecuador.

In September 1823 Bolívar arrived in Lima to raise a new army. In the Battle of Junín on August 6, 1824, he defeated royalist forces, then departed to liberate Upper Peru, which was renamed Bolivia by its people. Bolívar wrote the new state's constitution, which provided for a republican form of government with a strong presidency. Bolívar's subsequent efforts to bring about Latin American unity were unsuccessful. Disheartened by the secession of Venezuela from the Gran Colombia in 1829, Bolívar, now in failing health, resigned his presidency on April 27, 1830. Intending to travel to Europe, he died near Santa Marta, Colombia, of tuberculosis on December 17, 1830.

Tenacious, bold, and resourceful, Bolívar was a great motivator of men. He was a staunch republican who favored limited government, property rights, and the rule of law. Not a brilliant tactician as a general, he was more important as an inspirational leader. Credited with having led the fight for the independence of the present nations of Venezuela, Colombia, Ecuador, Panama, and Bolivia, Bolívar was disappointed in his efforts to achieve continental unity. He is today regarded as one of Latin America's greatest heroes.

SPENCER C. TUCKER

References

Bolívar, Simón. *El Libertador: The Writings of Simón Bolívar.* Edited by David Bushnell. Translated by Frederick H. Fornoff. New York: Oxford University Press, 2003.

Lynch, John. *Simón Bolívar: A Life.* New Haven, CT: Yale University Press, 2006.

Masur, Gerhard. *Simon Bolivar.* Albuquerque: University of New Mexico Press, 1948.

Bonaparte, Napoleon

Birth Date: August 15, 1769
Death Date: May 5, 1821

French general and emperor. Napoleon Bonaparte (Napoleone di Buonaparte) was born in Ajaccio, Corsica, on August 15, 1769. His parents, Carlo and Letizia Buonaparte, were members of the lesser nobility. Genoa had ceded Corsica to France the year before, so Napoleon was born a citizen of France. Because of his father's status and his mother's influence with the local French military commander, Napoleon was granted an appointment to the Brienne military school in France. He was a student there for five years during 1779–1784. Considered a foreigner by his classmates, he was alone much of the time. While not a gifted student, he developed his prodigious powers of concentration and memory.

Napoleon studied at the École militaire in Paris during 1784–1785 and was commissioned in the army and assigned to the La Fère Artillery Regiment in Valence in September 1785 at the age of 16. There he was greatly influenced by the noted artillerist Baron J. P. Du Teil. After a year with his regiment, Napoleon secured a leave with pay to return to Corsica in September 1786, which he extended. He then returned to his regiment, now at Auxonne, in June 1788.

The French Revolution of 1789 made possible Napoleon's rapid advancement and brilliant military career. War began in the spring of 1792, and with two brief exceptions (1802–1803 and 1814–1815), 23 years of war followed. Napoleon dominated 17 of these. Essentially middle class in outlook, Napoleon welcomed the coming of the Revolution, but except for two periods (February–September 1791 and May–September 1792), he was in Corsica for most of the next three years (late 1789–June 1793). During one period in Paris he observed the near assault on King Louis XVI on June 20, 1792, and the overthrow of the monarchy and massacre of the Swiss Guards on August 10, 1792. He and his brothers Joseph and Lucien hoped to advance the family position on the island but ran afoul of Corsican nationalist Pascal Paoli, and the family fled to France.

French general Napoleon Bonaparte (1769–1821). An important reformer and one of the greatest military commanders in history, Napoleon knew how to motivate men and manipulate events, but he proved utterly incapable of listening to the wise counsel of others or curbing his personal ambition when it was in the interests of his nation for him to do so. Painting of Napoleon at the Bridge of Arcole in 1796 by Baron Antoine-Jean Gros, ca. 1801. (Chaiba Media)

The collapse of Napoleon's Corsican ambitions and expulsion from the island in June 1793 was undoubtedly the turning point in his career. He now had to provide for his family (including his mother and six brothers and sisters). Finding employment as an artillery officer in the siege by the French Army of the Royal Navy and French Royalists of Toulon during September 4–December 19, Napoleon developed the artillery plan that drove the British from the port on December 19. In the final stage of the attack, he was wounded lightly in the thigh by a bayonet.

Recognized for this success, Napoleon was advanced from captain to brigadier general in December 1793 and given command of the artillery in the French Army of Italy in February 1794. Following the fall of Maximilian Robespierre on July 27, Napoleon was briefly arrested and imprisoned as a suspected Jacobin during August 6–September 14. Following his release, he secured appointment to the Topographical Bureau in Paris. He was then second-in-command of the Army of the Interior and in this capacity utilized artillery to put down the Royalist uprising of 13 Vendémiaire on October 5, 1795. His "whiff of grapeshot" killed several hundred people but saved the convention. Napoleon received command of the Army of the Interior until given command of the Army of Italy in March 1796. Before his departure for Italy, he married the widow Joséphine de Beauharnais. Taking the offensive on his arrival in April, he showed that he knew how to motivate men. He forced an armistice on the Piedmontese and defeated the Austrians at Lodi on May 10 and entered Milan on May 15. He secured all Lombardy and then won a series of other battles over the Austrians, including Arcole on November 15–17 and Rivoli on

January 14–15, 1797. Advancing into Austria, he imposed on the Austrians the preliminary Peace of Leoben on May 12. From Italy, he instigated General Pierre Augereau's coup of 18 Fructidor on September 4, 1797, against Royalists who sought to overthrow the Directory. Napoleon then dictated the terms of the Treaty of Campo Formio with Austria on December 17 that secured the Austrian Netherlands (Belgium and Luxembourg) for France and Austrian recognition of a northern Italian (Cisalpine) republic under French influence.

Napoleon's reward for his brilliant success was command of an expedition against Egypt that stopped at Malta en route, seizing that island and its large treasury on June 10, 1798. Landing at Alexandria on July 1, Napoleon defeated the Mamluks in the Battle of the Pyramids (First Battle of Aboukir) on July 21 but was then cut off in Egypt by the destruction of most of his fleet by Admiral Horatio Nelson in the Battle of the Nile (Battle of Aboukir Bay) on August 1. His forces overran all Egypt and set up headquarters in Cairo. After reorganizing and modernizing the Egyptian government, Napoleon invaded Syria to forestall a Turkish attack in February 1799 but failed to take the city of Acre by siege during March 15–May 17.

Returning to Egypt, Napoleon defeated an Anglo-Turkish force in the Second Battle of Aboukir on July 25, 1799. Learning of unrest in France, he abandoned his army in Egypt and, with a small party, sailed in a fast frigate on August 1, eluding British ships. Returning to France on October 9, he took the leading role in the coup d'état of 18 Brumaire on November 9, 1799.

Elected first consul under the Constitution of the Year VIII in February 1800, Bonaparte solidified his still-precarious position in France and abroad by invading Italy and defeating the Austrians in the narrowly won Battle of Marengo on June 14, 1800. Following General Jean Moreau's brilliant victory over the Austrians in Germany at Hohenlinden on December 3, Austria sued for peace in the Treaty of Lunéville on February 3, 1801.

Napoleon ended hostilities with England at Amiens in March 1802. Europe was now at peace for the first time in a decade, and Napoleon was rewarded by being made consul for life in May. He refused to work to secure a lasting peace; indeed, his actions gave Britain every excuse to resume the war in May 1803. He then prepared for an invasion of Britain. He was crowned emperor of the French in Paris as Napoleon I on December 2, 1804, and king of Italy on May 26, 1805.

On the opening of hostilities with Austria in July, Napoleon quickly broke up the camp at Boulogne and marched his forces across Germany, surprising the Austrians and forcing the surrender of an entire army at Ulm on October 20; he then captured Vienna on November 13. Advancing against a larger Austrian and Russian force in Moravia, he tricked the allies into attacking him and won his most brilliant victory, at Austerlitz on December 2. He then forced peace terms on Austria at Bratislava on December 26.

Napoleon dissolved the Holy Roman Empire and reorganized much of Germany into the Confederation of the Rhine under French control in July 1806. His passage of French troops through Prussian territory (Ansbach) in 1805 on the way to attack the Austrians and his offer to cede back Hanover to England without first consulting Prussia led the latter to declare war on France in September 1806. Napoleon advanced into Germany along two main axes to meet the Prussian forces moving to attack him. Marshal Louis Davout defeated the main Prussian army under the Duke of Brunswick at Auerstädt, while the same day Napoleon defeated another Prussian army at Jena on October 14. These two battles in effect decided the campaign, although other battles followed. Russian support for Prussia drew Napoleon into Poland, where he did battle with the Russians, suffering a check against them at Eylau on February 8, 1807, and then achieving success at Friedland on June 14, which led Czar Alexander I to conclude the Peace of Tilsit on July 7.

As part of the treaty, Russia agreed to join Napoleon's Continental System, designed to prohibit British exports to Europe. Napoleon promulgated the system in his Berlin Decree in November and Milan Decree in December. His efforts to impose this economic system on all Europe led to unrest in Portugal and Napoleon's decision to take over both Portugal and Spain. This in turn created a popular uprising in Madrid against the French (El Dos de Mayo) on May 2, 1808, and brought the Peninsular War, with Britain sending an expeditionary force. Napoleon now began to feel the effects of strategic overreach.

Austria judged this the right time to go to war against France again, believing that all Germany would join it. This did not happen. Napoleon took Vienna on May 12, 1809, but suffered defeat at Aspern-Essling on May 21–22, which he reversed with a decisive victory at Wagram on July 5–6. He dictated peace in the Treaty of Schönbrunn in October. Desperate for an heir, he set aside Joséphine and married Archduchess Marie Louise on April 1, 1810. She gave birth to their son, Napoleon Francis Joseph Charles, the king of Rome, on March 20, 1811.

Russia meanwhile was unhappy with the fruits of its French alliance and Napoleon's demands that it adhere to the Continental System. It then withdrew from the Continental System in December 1810. Napoleon resolved to punish the czar and all through 1811 put together the Grande Armée, invading Russia with a half million men on June 24, 1812. He took Smolensk on August 7 but ignored the warnings of his advisers and decided to push on for Moscow, which he believed would bring the czar to terms. At Borodino on September 7 Napoleon fought the bloodiest battle of the century. The Russians were able to withdraw in good order, however. Although Napoleon captured Moscow on September 14, the czar refused to treat with him. Napoleon waited too long (six weeks) before withdrawing. Russian winter and Russian army attacks destroyed Napoleon's Grande Armée.

Napoleon left the army and returned to Paris to raise a new force on December 16. He could secure men but was not able to recover from the loss of officers, noncommissioned officers, and trained horses in the Russian fiasco. He then advanced into Germany in 1813 to fight what became known as the German War of Liberation. He won costly battles at Lützen on May 2 and Bautzen on May 20–21, but a prolonged truce during June–August, when he did not negotiate seriously, allowed his enemies to become stronger, especially with the addition of Austria, which Napoleon did not believe would join the coalition against him. Although he was victorious in the Battle of Dresden on August 26–27, he was defeated in the largest battle of the Napoleonic Wars, at Leipzig (the Battle of the Nations) on October 16–19. Napoleon then rejected peace terms that would have given France a Rhine frontier.

In the winter of 1813–1814 Napoleon waged a brilliant campaign, winning a number of battles with dwindling resources, but he was unable to stop the allies from occupying Paris on March 30, 1814. He prepared to fight on, but his marshals united against this and demanded his abdication at Fontainebleau on April 4. Exiled to Elba by the Treaty of Fontainebleau, he busied himself with his small kingdom. With France in some unrest over decisions by the new government of Bourbon king Louis XVIII and with the allies in sharp disagreement over the peace settlement at the Congress of Vienna, Napoleon escaped from Elba and arrived back in France on March 1, 1815. Troops sent to arrest him rallied to their former commander, and Napoleon returned to Paris and issued yet another constitution, this one more liberal, in an effort to win popular support. Resolved to strike before his enemies could again coalesce against him, he invaded Belgium on June 1 and won a victory over the Prussians at Ligny on June 16 and over the British at Quatre Bras on June 16, but he detached a large body to pursue the withdrawing Prussians, who marched to aid the British at Waterloo, enabling the allies to win that battle on June 18 and bring the Napoleonic Wars to a close. Napoleon abdicated for a second time and surrendered to the English, who sent him to the island of St. Helena in the South Atlantic on October 15, where he died from gastric cancer on May 5, 1821. In 1840 his remains were returned to France and entombed at Les Invalides in Paris.

A brilliant strategist and meticulous planner and until his later years in power seemingly indifferent to fatigue, Napoleon was not a great military innovator. His major operational innovation was the corps formation. Taking advantage of theories developed by others, he waged wars of rapid movement that would culminate in one decisive battle. On occasion he was lucky or saved by subordinates. He knew how to motivate men, and they responded by calling him affectionately "The Little Corporal." A master propagandist, he took the credit for success and blamed others for his failures. He introduced many reforms in France and was a great lawgiver in the Napoleonic Codes, which he had a sizable role in drafting. Napoleon rarely listened to sound advice from his advisers, as in the case of his invasion of Russia, and he put his own aspirations ahead of the legitimate interests of France. A hundred years later, General Ferdinand Foch wrote of him, "He forgot that a man cannot be god; that above the individual is the nation, and above mankind the moral law; he forgot that war is not the highest aim, for peace is above war." Despite his failings, Napoleon was certainly one of the great captains in all history.

SPENCER C. TUCKER

References

Chandler, David G. *The Campaigns of Napoleon.* New York: Macmillan, 1966.

Connelly, Owen. *Blundering to Glory: Napoleon's Military Campaigns.* Wilmington, DE: Scholarly Resources, 1990.

Lefebvre, Georges. *Napoleon.* 2 vols. Translated by Henry F. Stockhold and J. E. Anderson. New York: Columbia University Press, 1969.

Schom, Alan. *Napoleon Bonaparte.* New York: HarperCollins, 1997.

Thompson, J. M. *Napoleon Bonaparte.* New York: Oxford University Press, 1952.

Bugeaud de la Piconnerie, Thomas-Robert

Birth Date: October 15, 1784
Death Date: June 10, 1849

Marshal of France. Thomas-Robert Bugeaud was born on October 15, 1784, into a noble family in Limoges, France. The youngest of 13 children, he ran away from home and for some years worked as an agricultural laborer. He enlisted as a private in the light infantry of the Imperial Guard during the Napoleonic Wars and fought in the Battle of Austerlitz on December 2, 1805. Commissioned the next year, he took part in the Battle of Jena (October 14, 1806) and the Battle of Eylau (February 8, 1807). Sent to Spain, he was in Madrid during the uprising of December 2, 1808. He won promotion to the rank of captain during the Second Siege of Saragossa (December 20, 1808–February 20, 1809). In the course of subsequent fighting in the Peninsular Campaign, he was promoted to major and took command of a regiment. With the first restoration of Louis XVIII, Bugeaud sided with the Bourbons and became a colonel, but he rallied to Napoleon during the Hundred Days and saw service in the Alps region.

With the overthrow of Napoleon and the second restoration, Bugeaud was dismissed from the army. He settled in the Périgueux region and occupied himself with agricultural pursuits. With the July Revolution in 1830, he returned to military service. An unflagging supporter of new king Louis Philippe, Bugeaud received command of a regiment, and in 1831 he was commissioned *maréchal de camp.* Elected to the Chamber of Deputies the same year, he was an outspoken opponent of democracy and helped crush the riots in Paris in 1834.

Bugeaud had opposed the French expedition to Algiers in 1830. Initially sent to Algeria in a subordinate capacity, he ultimately played the key role in the French pacification of that vast territory. After a highly successful six-week campaign, which included the defeat of Algerian forces under Emir Abd el Kader (Abd al-Qadir, Abdelkader) at Sikkah on July 6, 1836, Bugeaud returned to France a lieutenant general. The next year he signed the generous Armistice of Tafna on June 1, 1837, with Algerian nationalist leader Abd el Kader. Necessary because of the political and military situation, it nonetheless led to much criticism of Bugeaud in France.

On December 19, 1840, Bugeaud returned to Algeria as its first governor-general. The next year he instituted his system of light, highly mobile flying columns, which proved highly effective against Abd el Kader's forces. Bugeaud also employed native troops. Well respected by his men, he was known as "Père Bugeaud" (Father Bugeaud). In 1842 he undertook the construction of a network of roads to help secure the pacification of the country. In 1843 he was made marshal of France. His great victory over Abd el Kader's allied Moroccan forces in the Battle of Isly on August 14, 1844, led to his being made a duke.

In 1845 following the French defeat at Sidi Brahim on September 22–25, Bugeaud again took the field. He was almost constantly campaigning until his final departure from Algeria in July 1846, brought about over differences with the French government's refusal to adopt his program of military colonization. During Bugeaud's years in Algeria the number of French settlers increased from 17,000 to 100,000.

During the Revolution of 1848 Bugeaud took command of the army but was unable to prevent the overthrow of Louis Philippe. Approached about being a candidate for the presidency to oppose Louis Napoleon, Bugeaud refused. Following service as commander of the Army of the Alps, established during 1848–1849 in consequence of events in Italy, he retired and died in Paris of cholera on June 10, 1849. One of France's greatest colonial soldiers and administrators, Bugeaud was a model for Joseph Gallieni and Hubert Lyautey. Although conservative in his political views, Bugeaud had considerable sympathy for the Algerian peasants and sought to protect them from the excesses of French colonial administration.

Spencer C. Tucker

References

Azan, Paul. *L'armée d'Afrique de 1830 à 1852.* Paris: Plon, 1936.
———. *Bugeaud et l'Algérie; Par l'épée et par la charrue.* Paris: N.p., 1930.
Bugeaud d'Ideville, Count H. *Memoirs of Marshal Bugeaud.* 2 vols. Edited by Charlotte M. Yonge. London: Hurst and Blackett, 1881.
Sullivan, Anthony Thrall. *Thomas-Robert Bugeaud. France and Algeria, 1784–1849, Politics, Power, and the Good Society.* Hamden, CT: Archon Books, 1983.

Burgoyne, John

Birth Date: February 4, 1722
Death Date: June 4, 1792

British general. Born in Park Prospect, Westminster, London, on February 4, 1722, John Burgoyne attended the Westminster School and joined the British Army in 1740. In 1743 he eloped with Lady Charlotte Stanley, the 15-year-old daughter of the 11th Earl of Derby. Estranged from her parents and beset with debts, he sold his commission and moved to France in 1746. He and his wife lived there and in Italy.

Returning to England, Burgoyne reconciled with his wife's father in 1755 and, largely through his influence, rejoined the army in 1756. Advanced to lieutenant colonel in 1758, he took part in operations along the French coast during 1758–1759 during the Seven Years' War (1756–1763). He won election to Parliament in 1761. As a brigadier general in 1762 he served in Portugal to fight the Spanish invasion of that country, winning recognition for his unit's capture of the fortified Portuguese town of Villa Velha on October 5. From 1768 he was again in Parliament, where he achieved recognition by attacking Robert Clive and demanding an inquiry into the affairs of the British East India Company. At the same time Burgoyne achieved recognition as a librettist and dramatist. His play, *The Maid of the Oaks,* was produced in 1775. He also continued his reckless gambling.

Promoted to major general, Burgoyne was dispatched to North America on the outbreak of the American Revolutionary War. He arrived in Boston, Massachusetts, in May 1775 and observed the Battle of Bunker Hill (Breed's Hill). He returned to England on the excuse of illness in December 1775 with the goal of securing an independent command in America. Successful in this effort, in 1776 he was named second-in-command to British commander in Canada Lieutenant General Sir Guy Carleton for an invasion of New York from Canada. Following the Battle of Valcour Island on October 11–13 and the capture of Crown Point, however, Carleton halted the invasion and returned with his forces to Canada.

Burgoyne then returned to London, where he undermined his chief, Carleton, and received approval from Secretary of State for the Colonies Lord George Germain to lead another invasion of New York with the aim of securing the Hudson River and cutting off New England. Burgoyne planned a three-pronged invasion. He would lead the main effort south along the Lake Champlain-Hudson corridor. A diversionary attack by Lieutenant Colonel Barry St. Leger was to attack from Oswego in the west and draw off American forces. Burgoyne also counted on forces under British commander in America Lieutenant General William Howe to move north up the Hudson, meeting his own force in the vicinity of Albany, but Howe had his own plans, also approved by Germain, to act against Philadelphia, and informed Burgoyne of them, telling his colleague that he would have available in New York City at most one corps, elements of which might be able to support Burgoyne to some degree.

Burgoyne pressed ahead nonetheless. Setting out from Canada in June 1777 with some 7,000 men, he captured Fort Ticonderoga on July 6, moving south toward Albany. St. Leger's force meanwhile was blocked by the Americans (Howe's corps got only above Hyde Park on the Hudson). Burgoyne pressed ahead, but a large force sent to forage for supplies met disaster in the Battle of Bennington on August 16. Burgoyne was halted near Saratoga, New York, and in the Battle of Freeman's Farm on September 19 and the Battle of Bemis Heights on October 7 was defeated by the Americans under Major General Horatio Gates and forced to surrender on October 17, 1777. This American victory led France to enter the war openly on the American side.

Allowed to depart from Boston in April 1778, Burgoyne returned to London. He demanded but never secured both a court-martial and a court of inquiry into his conduct, but these were denied him. Prime Minister Lord North and Germain feared that any investigation would turn into a broader critique of war policy. Burgoyne published his version of events, *A State of the Expedition from Canada,* in 1780. When his political ally, Lord Rockingham, became prime minister in 1782, Burgoyne was appointed commander in chief in Ireland, but with the defeat of the Rockingham government the next year, Burgoyne was again stripped of his posts and withdrew into private life, devoting himself to literary pursuits. His comedy *The Heiress* (1786) proved quite popular. Known as "Gentleman Johnny," Burgoyne died in London on June 4, 1792. A capable soldier who was well liked by his men because of his concern for their welfare, he developed an overly complicated plan that failed to take into consideration the realities of campaigning in the interior of North America.

SPENCER C. TUCKER

References
Hargrove, Richard J. *General John Burgoyne.* Newark: University of Delaware Press, 1983.
Howson, Gerald. *Burgoyne of Saratoga: A Biography.* New York: Times Books, 1979.
Lunt, James. *John Burgoyne of Saratoga.* New York: Harcourt Brace Jovanovich, 1975.
Mintz, Max M. *The Generals of Saratoga: John Burgoyne and Horatio Gates.* New Haven, CT: Yale University Press, 1990.

Carnot, Lazare

Birth Date: May 13, 1753
Death Date: August 2, 1823

French general and government minister. Born in Nolay, Burgundy, the son of a lawyer on May 13, 1753, Lazare Nicolas Marguerite Carnot graduated from the Mézières engineering school and was commissioned in the French Army engineers in 1773.

Stationed at Arras, Carnot there met future revolutionary leader Maximilien Robespierre. Promoted to captain in 1783, Carnot welcomed the French Revolution of 1789 and won election to the Legislative Assembly in 1791. Identified as both a staunch republican and a radical, he won election to and served in the National Convention during 1792–1794. In January 1793 he voted for the execution of King Louis XVI. Carnot was subsequently elected by the convention as one of the 12 members of the Committee of Public Safety, the body that in effect ruled France during the Reign of Terror (1793–1794). Carnot's responsibility on the committee was military affairs.

Although decisions by the Committee of Public Safety were reached collectively, Carnot clearly played the key role in developing the committee's military policy, to include mass conscription for French males of military age (the *levée en masse*) and the organization of the home front as the nation-in-arms. This included sending proconsuls, known as the deputies-on-mission, into the provinces, the equivalent of later-day commissars. Carnot blended the large numbers of untrained recruits with seasoned veterans to create the 14 field armies of the French Republic that would sweep over much of Europe. He also had a major role in the development of military strategy and new simplified tactics that took advantage of superior French numbers. These emphasized light infantry and mixed order. In addition, he increased the numbers of horse artillery. Although his services were necessarily required in Paris, Carnot occasionally accompanied the army in the field, as in the victory over an Austrian-allied force at Wattigries on October 15–16, 1793.

Unlike so many of his colleagues on the Committee of Public Safety, Carnot survived the Thermidorean Reaction to the Reign of Terror. He served in the French Directory during 1795–1797 and briefly worked in the Ministry of War under Napoleon Bonaparte in 1800. Carnot disapproved of the empire and retired from government to write. He published two books on geometry and also, in 1812, published an important military treatise, *Défense des places fortes* (Defense of Strong Points).

In January 1814 Carnot returned to military service as a major general, and Napoleon gave him charge of the defense of Antwerp during January–May 1814. Carnot rallied to Napoleon during the Hundred Days (April–June 1815), when he served as minister of the interior. This mistaken decision resulted in Carnot's exile from France on the return to power of King Louis XVIII that July.

Carnot died in Magdeburg, in Prussian Saxony (Germany), on August 2, 1823. His role in saving the French Republic from military defeat in the immediate period following the execution of King Louis XVI was indeed substantial, and he well deserved the gratitude of his nation and the title given him of "The Organizer of Victory."

SPENCER C. TUCKER

References

Adler, Ken. *Engineering the Revolution: Arms and Enlightenment in France, 1763–1815.* Princeton, NJ: Princeton University Press, 1997.

Brown, Howard G. *War and the Bureaucratic State: Politics and Army Administration in France, 1791–1799.* Oxford: Oxford University Press, 1995.

Dupre, Huntley. *Lazare Carnot: Republican Patriot.* Philadelphia, PA: Porcupine, 1975.

Lynn, John A. *The Bayonets of the Republic: Motivation and Tactics in the Army of Revolutionary France, 1791–94.* Urbana: University of Illinois Press, 1994.

Palmer, R. R. *Twelve Who Ruled: The Year of the Terror in the French Revolution.* Princeton, NJ: Princeton University Press, 1941.

Charles, Archduke of Austria

Birth Date: September 5, 1771
Death Date: April 30, 1847

Austrian archduke and field marshal. Charles, born Karl Ludwig Johann Josef Lorenz in Florence on September 5, 1771, was the third son of the emperor Leopold II and his wife Infanta Maria Luisa of Spain. Charles grew up in Tuscany, in Vienna, and in the Austrian Netherlands. He received his military training in the Austrian Netherlands under the Duke of Saxe-Teschen and first saw service in the Wars of the French Revolution, beginning in 1792. Charles commanded a brigade in the Battle of Jemappes on November 6, 1792. In the campaign of 1793 he distinguished himself in fighting at Aldenhoven (near Aachen) on March 1 and at the Battle of Neerwinden on March 18 but suffered defeat in the Battle of Wattignies on October 15–16 and was present in the important Battle of Fleurus on June 16, 1794, another Austrian defeat that gave the French control of Belgium.

In 1796 Charles was named field marshal general and given command of the Austrian Army of the Rhine. That year he performed with distinction against French generals Jean Victor Marie Moreau and Jean Baptiste Jourdan, defeating them in the Battle of Amberg (August 24) and the Battle Würzburg (September 3) and forcing the French back across the Rhine.

In 1797 Charles was ordered to Italy to deal with the French general Napoleon Bonaparte. Outnumbered there, Charles skillfully extracted Austrian forces. In fighting in 1799 he was victorious against Jourdan in the Battles of Ostrach on March 21 and Stockach on March 25. Charles then invaded Switzerland, there defeating French general André Masséna in the First Battle of Zürich on June 4–7. Charles next campaigned in western Germany and again forced the French back across the Rhine River.

Poor health forced Charles into temporary military retirement as governor of Bohemia. He was recalled to check a French drive by Moreau on Vienna, but Moreau's brillant victory in the Battle of Hohenlinden on December 3, 1800, foredoomed that effort, and Charles was forced to conclude the armistice of Steyr on December 25.

When Austria again went to war against France in 1805, Charles commanded forces in Italy but was attacked and defeated by French forces under Masséna in the Battle of Caldiero on October 28–31. Following the Austrian defeat in the war, in 1806 Charles was entrusted with command of the Austrian Army as well as the head of the War Council. He threw himself into the task of reorganizing and reforming the army, the proof of which would be seen in 1809. He adopted much of the French system, including the concept of the nation in arms and many of the French tactics.

In the campaign of 1809 Charles achieved early successes before meeting defeat at Eggmühl. But then he defeated Napoleon himself in the Battle of Aspern-Essling on May 22, only to be defeated, but not routed, in the Battle of Wagram on July 5–6. With the Austrian defeat in the war, Charles resigned his military positions. Command of Austrian forces in the final years of the Napoleonic Wars was vested in Prince Karl zu Schwarzenberg, who benefited greatly from Charles's earlier military reforms.

Charles passed the remainder of his life in retirement apart from government service, although he was for a brief time governor of Mainz. In 1822 he became Duke of Saxe-Teaschen. He also wrote extensively on military matters. Charles died in Vienna on April 30, 1847.

A brilliant administrator and capable strategist and field commander, Charles was also an important military theorist. In his writings he stressed defensive operations, believing that the retention of strong points, rather than the defeat of enemy forces in the field, held the key to victory. At the same time he was capable of executing bold offensive operations, as is best shown in his brilliant campaign of 1796.

SPENCER C. TUCKER

References

Arnold, James R. *Crisis on the Danube: Napoleon's Austrian Campaign of 1809.* New York: Paragon House, 1990.

Petre, F. Lorraine. *Napoleon and the Archduke Charles: A History of the Franco-Austrian Campaign in the Valley of the Danube in 1809.* London: Arms and Armour, 1976.

Rothenberg, Gunther E. *Napoleon's Great Adversaries: The Archduke Charles and the Austrian Army, 1792–1814.* London: Batsford, 1992.

Clausewitz, Carl Philipp Gottfried von

Birth Date: June 1, 1780
Death Date: November 16, 1831

Prussian general and important military theorist. Born in Burg near Magdeburg, Prussia, on June 1, 1780, Carl Philipp Gottfried von Clausewitz was the son of a retired army officer who claimed nobility. Clausewitz entered the Prussian Army at age 12 and campaigned with the Prussian and Austrian force that invaded France in 1792 to begin the Wars of the French Revolution. After Prussia left the war in 1795 he spent six years in garrison duties, during which time he bettered his education. In 1801 he entered the War College in Berlin, studying under Gerhard Johann David von Scharnhorst. On graduation Clausewitz was appointed an aide to Prince August of Prussia in 1804 and thus witnessed the destruction of Prussia's armies at the hands of Napoleon Bonaparte and the French in 1806, fighting in the Prussian defeat at Auerstädt on October 14. Clausewitz was taken prisoner at Prenzlau on October 28.

Following his exchange in 1807, Clausewitz assisted both Scharnhorst and August von Gneisenau in the reform of the Prussian Army during 1807–1811. At the same time Clausewitz was an instructor to Crown Prince Friedrich Wilhelm. Angry when King Friedrich Wilhelm III agreed to supply a contingent of troops to Napoleon for the French invasion of Russia, Clausewitz resigned his commission and left Prussia. During the 1812 Campaign he was first an observer and then a staff officer in the Russian forces. He remained with the Russian Army through the 1813 War of German Liberation and then rejoined the Prussian Army in 1814. During Napoleon's return to France in the Hundred Days, Clausewitz participated in the Waterloo Campaign as a staff officer in III Corps.

In 1818 Clausewitz was appointed director of the Kriegsakademie (War College) in Berlin. Reflecting on his experiences in the Wars of the French Revolution and the Napoleonic Wars, he began work on his seminal work that would be published posthumously as *Von Krieg* (*On War*). In it Clausewitz sought to discover the fundamental principles of war. In perhaps his best-known maxim he defined war as "the continuation of politics [or policy] by other means." Clausewitz believed that in order to be successful in war, a commander had to be attuned to political realities and their possible effect on the conduct of operations. He noted that in war where two powers are of more or less equal strength, victory will go to that side with the greater will to win. Success in war rests on a trinity of forces: the government, the military, and the people. If the people should lose faith in a war, then the first task of the government is to extradite itself from the conflict. In order to be victorious in war, it is essential to recognize the center of gravity of the other side, then direct all energy there. Clausewitz also examined such key factors as friction, genius, the fog of war, and the unpredictability of war. In addition to *On War,* Clausewitz also wrote numerous essays and studies of various Napoleonic campaigns, including 1812.

Clausewitz was not happy with *On War* but never had the opportunity to revise it. In 1830 he was assigned to the Russian border as major general and chief of staff of Prussian forces stationed on the Russian frontier to prevent Poles fleeing the revolution there from escaping into Prussia. He contracted cholera and died in Wrocław, Silesia, on November 16, 1831.

Although Clausewitz had instructed his wife not to publish his book until he had revised it, friends persuaded her to do so. The work did not receive significant attention until after the Prussian military victory over France in 1871. Although interest in it has ebbed and flowed depending on the time period, *On War* remains the chief work of Western military theory with a wide applicability today. As such, it has been translated into a great many languages and is widely studied in military academies around the world.

SPENCER C. TUCKER

References

Clausewitz, Carl von. *On War.* Edited and translated by Michael Howard and Peter Paret. Princeton, NJ: Princeton University Press, 1976.

Paret, Peter. *Clausewitz and the State.* Oxford: Oxford University Press, 1976.

Parkinson, Roger. *Clausewitz: A Biography.* New York: Stein and Day, 1971.

Clinton, Sir Henry

Birth Date: April 30, 1730
Death Date: December 23, 1795

British general. Born on April 30, 1730, in Newfoundland where his father, Royal Navy captain George Clinton, was the governor, Henry Clinton moved with his family to New York in 1743 when his father, now a rear admiral, took up appointment as governor there. Henry Clinton attended school on Long Island and in 1745 was commissioned a militia lieutenant. Following a year's service in New York, he was promoted to captain.

In 1749 Clinton traveled to England and two years later became a lieutenant in the Coldstream Guards in 1751. By 1758 he was a lieutenant colonel in the Grenadier Guards. Beginning in 1760 he saw action in Germany during the Seven Years' War (1756–1763), serving as an aide to Charles, Prince (later duke) of Brunswick, commander of the allied corps. Promoted to colonel in June 1762, Clinton was wounded in the Battle of Johannisberg on August 30, 1762. Returning to England, he was promoted to brigadier general in June 1763 and to major general in May 1772. He was also elected to Parliament. In 1774 he spent six months in the Balkans observing Russian preparations for war against the Turks.

With the outbreak of fighting in America, in 1775 Clinton was ordered there along with major generals John Burgoyne and William Howe. The three arrived in Boston in May and urged the British commander in North America, Lieutenant General Thomas Gage, to attack the Americans on Breed's Hill. Although his proposal to attack the rear of the American position was rejected, Clinton led the final assault on the American forces in person on June 17. With Gage's departure, Howe assumed command with Clinton as second-in-command with the local rank of lieutenant general in September.

Clinton commanded British forces in an expedition against Charleston, South Carolina. With the failure of the British naval attack on Fort Moultrie on June 28, 1776, however, Clinton withdrew his troops on July 21 and returned to New York. Disappointed at the failure of the expedition and being at odds with Howe, Clinton sailed to England with the intention of resigning from the service. Persuaded to change his mind, he returned to New York in July 1777 to find Howe about to strike against Philadelphia. With only 7,000 men, Clinton assumed command in New York but conducted operations up the Hudson River as far as Hyde Park in support of Lieutenant General John Burgoyne's drive southward from Canada to Albany that, however, ended in the latter's surrender at Saratoga on October 17.

Succeeding Howe as commander of British forces in May 1778, Clinton evacuated Philadelphia. He then held off Continental Army commander General George Washington's assault on his withdrawing troops at Monmouth, New Jersey, on June 28. Clinton concentrated his forces in New York and kept to the defensive the remainder of the year. He undertook limited offensive action in Georgia in 1778, Virginia in May 1779, and Connecticut in June 1779.

Shifting the focus of military operations to the American South, in 1780 Clinton mounted the largest British offensive since 1777, to take Charleston. Following a protracted siege during February 11–May 12, Charleston surrendered in what was the greatest Continental Army defeat of the war. Clinton then returned to New York, leaving Lieutenant General Charles, Lord Cornwallis, in command in the South. After inconclusive campaigning, Cornwallis withdrew to the port of Yorktown, Virginia, where the French fleet and American and French land forces began siege operations. Clinton mounted a relief operation but arrived on October 24 five days after Cornwallis had surrendered. Clinton then returned to New York.

Openly critical of the British government's handling of the war, Clinton was replaced as commander in chief in America by Lieutenant General Sir Guy Carleton on May 5, 1782. Returning to Britain, Clinton failed to secure the inquiry that he hoped would clear his name. Gradually returned to favor, he won election to Parliament in 1790, was promoted to full general in October 1793, and was appointed governor of Gibraltar in July 1794. He died at Gibraltar on December 23, 1795. Intelligent and for the most part effective, Clinton often found it difficult to get along with others. He lacked capable subordinates, but as commander in chief he demonstrated a lack of initiative and boldness.

SPENCER C. TUCKER

References

Clinton, Henry. *The American Rebellion: Sir Henry Clinton's Narrative of His Campaigns, 1775–1782, with an Appendix of Original Documents.* Edited by William B. Willcox. New Haven, CT: Yale University Press, 1954.

Willcox, William Bradford. *Portrait of a General: Sir Henry Clinton in the War of Independence.* New York: Knopf, 1964.

Cochrane, Thomas

Birth Date: December 14, 1775
Death Date: October 31, 1860

Admiral in the service of Britain, Chile, Brazil, and Greece. Born on December 14, 1775, at Ainsfield, Lanarkshire, eldest son of the ninth Earl of Dundonald, Thomas Cochrane entered the Royal Navy at age 17 in a ship commanded by his uncle, Alexander Cochrane.

Varied duties led in 1800 to Thomas Cochrane's command of the brig *Speedy* in which he captured the much larger Spanish frigate *El Gamo* and other prizes before surrendering to a superior French force near Gibraltar in 1802. While commanding the frigate *Pallas* (32 guns), he preyed on French merchantmen until his ship succumbed to damage in 1806. That same year he was elected to Parliament from Honiton and in 1807 won a seat from Westminster. In the House of Commons he attacked abuses in the navy and became an outspoken critic of the Admiralty.

Back at sea in command of the frigate *Imperieuse,* Cochrane added to an already impressive list of prizes. In 1809 he led a daring fire ship attack against the Aix Roads off Brest. On his return to England he was knighted, but his criticism of his commander, Admiral Lord James Gambier, for his timidity in the attack led to a court-martial that exonerated Gambier. This incident, combined with his actions in Parliament, effectively destroyed Cochrane's reputation with the Admiralty, ending his active service in the Royal Navy for almost 40 years.

Over the next few months Cochrane used his seat in Parliament to expose naval incompetence and corruption. But just as it appeared in 1813 that he would join his uncle on the North American station, he was implicated in a stock scandal, convicted of fraud, and sentenced to a year in prison. Although innocent, he was dropped from the navy, expelled from the House of Commons, and removed from the knighthood.

After his imprisonment Cochrane was returned to the House of Commons by his Westminster constituents and there continued his attack on the Admiralty, which he believed had orchestrated his downfall. Mired in residual legal troubles, he accepted an offer from Chile to command its navy in the struggle for independence from Spain.

Arriving at Valparaiso in 1818, Cochrane took charge of the seven-ship fleet, including a captured 40-gun Spanish frigate. Renamed *O'Higgins,* it became his flagship. For several months Cochrane harassed the Spanish. In June 1820 he led a spectacular amphibious attack on the fortified port of Valdivia, netting many prisoners and much matériel. His capture that November of the Spanish frigate *Esmeralda,* during which he was wounded, led to the capitulation of Lima and greatly facilitated the liberation of Chile and Peru. After a falling out with General José de San Martín, with whom he had collaborated at Valdivia, Cochrane accepted command of the Brazilian Navy. Again with a small fleet he worked wonders against the Portuguese Navy and contributed to the independence of another South American state. However, plagued by the intrigues of Latin American politics, he resigned and returned to England.

Contacted by the Greeks to command yet another nascent navy, Cochrane insisted on lavish guarantees of new equipment, specifically English-built steam vessels. An early proponent of steam warships, he was frustrated when these failed to arrive. His ineffectual tenure in Greece was tainted by scandal that seemed to follow him wherever he went. Disheartened, he returned to England to pursue reinstatement in the Royal Navy.

In 1832 he was reinstated in the Royal Navy with the rank of rear admiral. Upon the death of his father the previous year Cochrane became 10th Earl of Dundonald. He devoted attention to innovation, particularly refinement of steam technology and development of the screw propeller. Promoted to vice admiral in 1841, he saw his last active service as commander of the West Indies and North American stations during 1848–1851, when he was elevated to full admiral; in 1847 he was reinstated as a knight in the order of Bath.

Too old for service during the 1853–1856 Crimean War, Cochrane offered a plan to use sulfur gas against Sebastopol or Kronstadt, but this was rejected on humanitarian grounds. Without doubt a gifted innovator and a truly talented naval commander, Cochrane's inability to escape controversy precluded a much loftier place in history. He did, however, gain enduring romantic stature as a dashing and unconventional sailor, a rebel, and a liberator. Cochrane died at London on October 31, 1860.

DAVID COFFEY

References

Cochrane, Thomas, and H. Fox Bourne. *The Life of Thomas, Lord Cochrane, Tenth Earl of Dundonald.* 2 vols. London: R. Bentley, 1869.

Lloyd, Christopher. *Lord Cochrane, Seaman, Radical, Liberator: A Life of Thomas, Lord Cochrane, Tenth Earl of Dundonald.* Reprint ed. New York: Henry Holt, 1998.

Thomas, Donald S. *Cochrane: Britannia's Sea Wolf.* London: Cassell, 1999.

Worcester, Donald E. *Sea Power and Chilean Independence.* Gainesville: University of Florida Press, 1962.

Cornwallis, Charles

Birth Date: October 31, 1738
Death Date: October 5, 1805

British general. Born in London on October 31, 1738, the eldest son of the 1st Earl Cornwallis, Charles Cornwallis was educated at Eton and joined the British Army as an ensign in 1756. He served with British forces in Hanover during the Seven Years' War (1756–1763), fighting in the Battle of Minden on August 1, 1759. Promoted to captain, he returned with his regiment to England and was elected to the House of Commons in 1760. He returned to the war the next year and fought in several battles in Germany. In 1762 on the death of his father, he assumed his seat in the House of Lords.

Cornwallis was advanced to colonel in 1766 and major general in 1775. Although sympathetic to the Patriot cause, he volunteered for service in America and arrived there in February 1776 with seven regiments of reinforcements to participate in the unsuccessful British assault on Charleston on June 16–July 25. He then fought under Major General William Howe in the New York campaign, distinguishing himself in the battles of Kip's Bay on September 15, Fort Washington on November 14–15, and Fort Lee, New Jersey, on November 18. Cornwallis had overall command of the British outpost forces in New Jersey that were defeated by General George Washington's Continental Army at Trenton on December 26, 1776, and Princeton on January 3, 1777.

In Howe's Philadelphia campaign, Cornwallis commanded the main British forces in the Battle of Brandywine on September 11, 1777. Cornwallis then sailed to Britain on leave but returned to America in April 1778 as a lieutenant general and second-in-command there to Lieutenant General Henry Clinton. Cornwallis took part in the Battle of Monmouth on June 28 but returned to Britain to be with his dying wife. Returning to America, he enthusiastically supported Clinton's southern strategy and played a key role in it. Following the siege and capture of Charleston during February 11–May 12, 1780, Clinton returned to New York, leaving Cornwallis in command in the south.

Cornwallis busied himself with administrative matters in Charleston until August, when he hurried to Camden to meet an American force moving south under Major General Horatio Gates, defeating it soundly in the Battle of Camden, South Carolina, on August 16, 1780. British defeats sustained by subordinates at Kings Mountain on October 7 and Cowpens on January 17, 1781, greatly reduced his strength, however. Although he defeated Major General Nathanael Greene's Continentals in the Battle of Guilford Courthouse on March 15, 1781, this came at the cost of casualties amounting to a quarter of his force.

Moving north into Virginia, Cornwallis assumed command of British forces there and then decided to withdraw his forces to the coast, ending up at the tobacco port of Yorktown. There his army was cut off from resupply by water by the arrival of a powerful French fleet under Admiral Comte de Grasse, which defeated a British fleet in the pivotal naval Battle of the Chesapeake (Battle of the Capes) on September 5, 1781. Meanwhile, French and Continental Army forces under General George Washington and the Comte de Rochambeau laid siege to Yorktown from the land side, forcing Cornwallis to surrender on October 19 with his army. This American victory brought down the British government and for all intents and purposes ended the war.

Cornwallis went on to be a highly effective and fair-minded reformist governor-general of India during 1786–1793. He commanded British forces in person in the Third Mysore War (1790–1792), taking Bangalore and forcing Tipu Sahib (Tipu Sultan) to surrender following the siege of Seringapatan on March 16, 1792. Cornwallis was created the 1st Marquess Cornwallis in 1793. He was then commander in chief in Ireland during 1798–1801, where he put down the Irish Rebellion of 1798 in connection with a French invasion attempt. He treated the Irish leniently and resigned in 1801 when King George III refused to grant Catholic emancipation.

Cornwallis returned to India as governor-general in 1805 and died in Ghazipur on October 5. A brave and capable general, he was far more effective as a field commander than he was a strategist. His greatest talents lay in administration, where he was highly effective.

SPENCER C. TUCKER

References

Buchanan, John. *The Road to Guilford Courthouse.* New York: Wiley, 1997.

Wickwire, Francis, and Mary Wickwire. *Cornwallis: The American Adventure.* Boston: Houghton Mifflin, 1970.

———. *Cornwallis: The Imperial Years.* Chapel Hill: University of North Carolina Press, 1980.

Davout, Louis Nicolas

Birth Date: May 10, 1770
Death Date: June 1, 1823

Napoleonic marshal, known as the "Iron Marshal." Born at Annoux (Yonne) into a noble Burgundian family on May 10, 1770, Louis Nicolas Davout studied at the military school at Auxerre and then at the Royal Military School in Paris. In February 1788 he was commissioned into the Royal Champagne Cavalry. Promoted to general of brigade in July 1793, he was taken prisoner at Mannheim in September 1795 and then exchanged. During 1798–1799 he campaigned with Napoleon Bonaparte in Egypt. Captured by the Royal Navy en route to France in March 1800, Davout was subsequently freed. Promoted to general of division in July 1800, he was named a marshal of the empire in May 1804.

Davout commanded III Corps and held the French right in Napoleon's victory over the Austrians and Russians in the great Battle of Austerlitz on December 2, 1805, and the same unit in the campaign of 1806 against Prussia, when he played a key role in the victory of Auerstädt on October 14, 1806, his corps driving from the field a Prussian force twice as large. He fought against the Russians and was slightly wounded in the Battle of Eylau on February 7, 1807. Appointed by Napoleon as governor of the Grand Duchy of Warsaw in July, Davout was created duke of Auerstädt in March 1808. He held semi-independent command during the Ratisbon phase of the 1809 campaign, distinguishing himself and making possible the French victories at Eckmühl on April 22 and Ratisbon on April 23, and he again distinguished himself at Wagram on July 5–6. In August, Napoleon created him prince of Eckmühl.

Appointed to command the Army of Germany in January 1810, Davout entered Russia in June 1812 in command of I Corps, a virtual army of 72,000 men. He was wounded in the Battle of Borodino on September 7 and then commanded the rear guard in the French withdrawal from Russia in October. During the 1813 German War of Liberation he defended Dresden on March 9–19 and then assumed command at Hamburg, holding it against a much larger German force for six months. On the abdication of Napoleon, Davout evacuated Hamburg on the orders of French king Louis XVIII and was exiled to his estates.

Davout rallied to Napoleon in the Hundred Days in 1815 and became minister of war during March–June. Appointed military governor of Paris on June 24, Davout evacuated the capital and took command of the Army of the Loire on July 5. Resubmitting to King Louis XVIII, Davout was again exiled to his estates. Restored to the dignity of marshal of France in August 1817 and readmitted to the French peerage in March 1819, Davout died in Paris of consumption on June 1, 1823. A highly effective field commander, he was perhaps second in talent only to Napoleon. Perhaps the least liked of Napoleon's marshals, Davout was also the most feared and respected as an adversary. Unfortunately for the emperor, he did not adequately utilize Davout's talents at the end of the empire.

SPENCER C. TUCKER

References

Chandelr, David G. "Davout." In *Napoleon's Marshals,* edited by David G. Chandler, 92–117. New York: Macmillan, 1987.

Gallagher, John. *The Iron Marshal: A Biography of Louis Davout.* Mechanicsburg, PA: Stackpole, 2000.

Gillespie, John C. *The Iron Marshal: A Biography of Louis N. Davout.* Carbondale, IL: Southern Illinois University Press, 1976.

Decatur, Stephen, Jr.

Birth Date: January 5, 1779
Death Date: March 23, 1820

U.S. Navy captain. Born January 5, 1779, at Sinepuxent, Maryland, the son of a highly successful privateer captain of the American Revolutionary War, Stephen Decatur was raised in Philadelphia and briefly attended the University of Pennsylvania before securing a warrant as midshipman in the navy in April 1798. Assigned to the frigate *United States,* he served on that ship under Captain John Barry during the 1798–1800 Quasi-War with France and was promoted to lieutenant in May 1799.

In May 1801 Decatur joined the Mediterranean Squadron on the frigate *Essex* and in August 1802 transferred to the frigate *New York.* In May 1803 he was ordered to Boston to supervise the fitting out of the brig *Argus,* which he sailed to the Mediterranean, there taking command of the schooner *Enterprise* in November 1803. The United States was then at war with Tripoli, and in December the *Enterprise* captured the Tripolitan ketch *Matisco,* which was taken into the U.S. Navy as the *Intrepid.*

On February 16, 1804, in a daring mission Lieutenant Decatur sailed the *Intrepid* into Tripoli Harbor and there destroyed the captured U.S. frigate *Philadelphia.* The operation was carried out without losing a single man. This celebrated act made Decatur an American hero, and on the recommendation of Commodore Edward Preble, brought his promotion to captain. At age 25 Decatur became the youngest U.S. Navy captain ever.

During the August 3, 1804, bombardment of Tripoli in which Decatur commanded a gunboat division, he learned that a Tripolitan captain had shot and killed his younger brother James after having surrendered his gunboat to the American lieutenant. With only 10 men in an American gunboat, Decatur sought out and boarded the Tripolitan boat. While Decatur fought with the gunboat's captain, a Tripolitan sailor tried to strike him from behind. Reuben James, one of Decatur's sailors, stepped forward and took the blow, saving him. Decatur then shot the Tripolitan dead. In the fighting, 24 Tripolitans were killed while the Americans suffered only 4 wounded.

Decatur later commanded in succession the frigates *Constitution* and *Congress.* At the conclusion of the Tripolitan War he returned to the United States a hero in 1805. He then oversaw gunboat construction and commanded the Gosport (Norfolk) Navy Yard. He took command of the crippled frigate *Chesapeake* after it had been fired into and disabled by the British ship *Leopard* on June 22, 1807, and he sat on the subsequent court-martial of Commodore James Barron, which found that Barron had neglected to prepare *Chesapeake* for action and suspended him from the service.

During the War of 1812 Decatur commanded the frigate *United States,* capturing the British frigate *Macedonian* off the Azores on October 8, 1812, in only 90 minutes and returning with it to the United States. The *Macedonian* was the first British frigate captured by the Americans in the war. The British blockade prevented Decatur's return to sea for two years. Having taken command of the *President* at New York, he finally escaped on the night of January 14, 1815. The frigate sustained damage on passing over the bar, however, and was pursued and captured the next day by the British blockading squadron. The surrender of the *President* remains the one blemish on Decatur's otherwise distinguished career, only because he did not fight his ship to the last.

After the war Decatur led a nine-ship American squadron with his flag in the frigate *Guerriere* to the Mediterranean to punish Algiers and, after taking several Algerine warships, dictated peace terms to that North African state. He returned to the United States to become a member of the new three-man Board of Naval Commissioners. A feud with Captain James Barron led to a duel between the two men on March 22, 1820, at Bladensburg, Maryland. Both men were wounded, Decatur mortally. He died the next day at Washington, D.C.

One of the greatest of American naval heroes, Decatur was energetic, brave, and intensely patriotic. An extraordinarily effective leader, he treated his men fairly and led by example. As a commander, he demonstrated great strategic sense, a flair for timing, diplomatic skill, and firmness of purpose.

SPENCER C. TUCKER

References

Anthony, Irwin. *Decatur.* New York: Scribner, 1931.

Lewis, Charles Lee. *The Romantic Decatur.* Philadelphia: University of Pennsylvania Press, 1937.

Schroeder, John H. "Stephen Decatur: Heroic Ideal of the Young Navy." In *Command under Sail: Makers of the American Naval Tradition, 1775–1850,* edited by James C. Bradford, 199–219. Annapolis, MD: Naval Institute Press, 1985.

Tucker, Spencer C. *Stephen Decatur: "A Life Most Bold and Daring."* Annapolis, MD: Naval Institute Press, 2004.

Dumouriez, Charles-François du Perier

Birth Date: January 25, 1739
Death Date: March 14, 1823

French general. Born into an aristocratic military family in Cambrai on January 25, 1739, Charles Dumouriez first saw military action in Germany in 1757 during the Seven Years' War (1756–1763), when he was also wounded and received a commission in the cavalry. At heart an adventurer, he left the army in 1762 to carry out secret diplomatic assignments for King Louis XV in Corsica, Portugal, and Spain. In 1770 as a colonel Dumouriez was dispatched on a secret effort to assist the Poles against the Russians. In 1772 he went on a mission to Hamburg. He then spent some time imprisoned in the Bastille in Paris for plotting against the Duc d'Augillion.

Dumouriez soon returned to military service. Among his duties was the study of new Prussian tactics. He also advanced his specialist knowledge through his friendship with French military theorist Jacques-Antoine Guibert. Dumouriez was commandant of the Cherbourg garrison during 1778–1790, during which time the French Revolution began.

Immediately drawn into revolutionary politics, Dumouriez was soon a major general. A careerist, he saw the revolution as an opportunity to advance his own career. In 1790 the Marquis de Lafayette sent him to the Austrian Netherlands to advise rebels there. Thereafter this region became foremost in Dumouriez's strategic thinking. After seven months as commander of the 12th Military District in 1791, he returned to Paris a strong advocate of the war policy advanced by the Girondin ministry and was made minister of foreign affairs on March 15, 1792. He pushed his plan to annex the Austrian Netherlands on the beginning of war with Austria and Prussia in April 1792. When the undisciplined French troops were sent reeling back into France, Dumouriez lost his post in June.

Now a lieutenant general, Dumouriez was assigned to the Army of the North. When Lafayette, its commander, failed in his attempted coup and surrendered to the Austrians, Dumouriez assumed command of the Army of the North on August 16. Ordered to send part of his force south to deal with the advance of Prussian forces under the Duke of Brunswick, Dumouriez skillfully delayed the Prussian advance. His front turned, he joined his army to the Army of the Center under General François-Christophe Kellermann and acted in reserve during the defeat of the Prussians in the Battle of Valmy on September 20 that halted the Prussian drive on Paris and saved the revolution.

Dumouriez then went to Paris, where he urged a great offensive against the Austrian Netherlands. Securing approval, he defeated the Austrians in the great Battle of Jemappes near Mons on November 6. The French treated the area as conquered territory, offending the inhabitants by their actions. The invasion also brought English and Dutch hostility. The government ordered Dumouriez to invade the Dutch Netherlands, but an Austrian counterattack forced him to abandon the effort and meet the Austrians, who defeated him at Neerwinden on March 18, 1793. Dumouriez then opened negotiations with the Austrians and concluded an agreement whereby the Austrians allowed the French to withdraw and Dumouriez was to march on Paris, overthrow the National Convention, and restore the monarchy. Dumouriez saw himself as the regent to the young Louis XVII. When the Paris government sent deputies to investigate, Dumouriez arrested them. Unable to convince his men to follow him, he defected to the Austrians on April 5. His treason led to a wide purge of French generals and the deaths of a number of them.

Dumouriez finally settled in England, where he became a salaried adviser to the British government on the overthrow of Napoleon. Dumouriez hoped for but did not receive reward from the restored French king Louis XVIII after 1815, who refused him reentry to France. Dumouriez lived out the rest of his life in England, dying at Turville Park, Buckinghamshire, on March 14, 1823. A competent general, he also put his personal interests ahead of those of his nation, but French political leader Louis Adolphe Thiers wrote of him, "If he abandoned us, he had also saved us."

SPENCER C. TUCKER

References

Chuquet, Arthur. *Dumouriez.* Paris: Hachette, 1914.
Rose, John H. *Dumouriez and the Defence of England against Napoleon.* London: John Lane, 1909.

Gage, Thomas

Birth Date: 1719 or 1720
Death Date: April 19, 1787

British general. Born in late 1719 or early 1720, Thomas Gage was the second son of Irish viscount Thomas Gage. His elder brother William inherited the family estate and subsequently assisted the younger Gage in his military career. Gage was educated at the Westminster School, and sometime after leaving school in 1736 he was commissioned an ensign. He fought in the War of the Austrian Succession (1740–1748) and saw action at the Battle of Fontenoy in Belgium on May 10, 1745.

During the Jacobite Rebellion, Gage served under the Duke of Cumberland in the Battle of Culloden on April 16, 1746. Gage then returned to the continent for the remainder of the War of the Austrian Succession, serving in Flanders and Holland. In 1748 he purchased a major's commission and later advanced to lieutenant colonel in March 1751.

At the beginning of the French and Indian War (1754–1763) Gage went to Virginia with his regiment, the 44th Foot. He took part in Major General Edward Braddock's ill-fated Fort Duquesne expedition, commanding the advanced guard in the British defeat by the French and Indians in the Battle of the Monongahela on July 9, 1755. Gage was slightly wounded in the battle and became close friends with George Washington during the retreat. Gage was temporarily commander of the 44th Regiment (its commander was killed in the battle), but efforts by his friends to secure him its colonelcy failed.

Gage was second-in-command to Governor William Shirley in the unsuccessful Mohawk Valley Campaign in August–September 1756. Gage also took part in Lord Loudoun's successful assault on Fort Louisbourg in June–September 1757. Gage then raised a local light regiment (the 8th Foot), earning his colonelcy in 1757. He was wounded leading the advance guard in the unsuccessful British attack on Fort Ticonderoga in July 1758. Ordered by British commander in chief in North America Major General Jeffery Amherst to attack French Fort La Galette in New York, Gage decided when he reached Niagara that he had insufficient forces for the task and turned back, thereby incurring Amherst's displeasure. During the winter of 1759–1760 Gage commanded at Albany and then had charge of the rear guard during Amherst's advance on Montreal (Montréal) in March–September 1760.

Gage was the governor of Lower Canada at Quebec (Québec) during 1761–1763 and proved to be both a fair and able administrator. In 1761 he won promotion to major general. In November 1763 he succeeded Amherst as commander in North America, with his headquarters at New York. Promoted to lieutenant general in December 1770, Gage returned briefly to Britain during June 1773–May 1774 but was ordered back to the restive American colonies as both British commander in chief and governor of Massachusetts in May 1774 at Boston. Unlike the ministry in London, Gage was well informed about conditions in America and pessimistic about the prospects for an easy British victory over the Patriots if it came to war. He soon requested additional troops. London regarded him as an alarmist or worse. Gage several times sent troops out from Boston to destroy Patriot stocks of arms and munitions, but a similar effort at Concord sparked the American Revolutionary War on April 19, 1775. Following the Pyrrhic victory by the British in the Battle of Bunker Hill (Breed's Hill) on June 17, Gage was recalled to Britain. He turned over his command to Major General William Howe on October 10 and sailed for Britain, where he was formally relieved of his post in North America on April 18, 1776.

Gage returned to active duty in 1781 and organized militia in Kent against a possible French invasion. Promoted to general in November 1782, he died at his home in Portland on April 19, 1787. A capable but prudent commander and an exceptionally able administrator, Gage knew America well, and the ministry in London would have been well served to have followed his advice.

SPENCER C. TUCKER

References

Alden, John Richard. *General Gage in America: Being Principally a History of His Role in the American Revolution.* New York: Greenwood, 1969.

Gage, Thomas. *Correspondence of General Thomas Gage with the Secretary of State, 1763–1775.* 2 vols. Edited by Clarence Edwin Carter. Hamden, CT: Archon Books, 1969.

Garibaldi, Giuseppe

Birth Date: July 4, 1807
Death Date: June 2, 1882

Italian patriot and general. Born in Nice on July 4, 1807, Giuseppe Garibaldi became a merchant seaman, then enlisted in the navy of the Kingdom of Sardinia (Piedmont-Sardinia) in 1833. He became dedicated to the cause of Italian unification and was a close associate of Giuseppe Mazzini, joining his Young Italy movement that sought to bring about unification and a democratic government. Involved with Mazzini in a plot to overthrow the Sardinian monarchy, Garibaldi was forced to flee abroad and was sentenced to death in absentia in 1834.

Arriving in South America, Garibaldi became a privateer captain for the Brazilian state of Rio Grande do Sul. Transferring his allegiance to Uruguay in 1843, he raised a unit of expatriate Italians to fight against Argentina during 1843–1847. He won an early battle at Sant-Antonio in 1846 but sailed for Europe upon learning of the revolutionary upheavals of 1847–1848 and arrived at Nice in June 1848. He wrote to King Charles Albert offering to fight in the Sardinian Army against Austria. Not receiving a reply, Garibaldi joined the fight against the Austrians at Milan and led a small number of patriots out of that city following its surrender on August 9. He then waged a guerrilla campaign against the occupying Austrians that lasted for several weeks but was forced into Switzerland.

Invited to Rome to lead Republican forces there, Garibaldi arrived in that city on December 12, 1848, and took command of its defenses, repulsing the initial French Army attack on Rome on April 29–30, 1849, and then Neapolitan troops at Palestrina on May 9 and Velletri on May 19 and a second French assault on Rome on June 3. The French reinforced and settled down to a siege of Rome. Realizing that the situation was hopeless, Garibaldi concluded an agreement with French commander Marshal Nicolas Oudinot on June 30 that allowed him and some 4,000 volunteers of his men to march out of the city on July 2. Hoping to join his men to the defenders of the Republic of Venice, Garibaldi marched north, but most of his men were killed, captured, or dispersed by far more numerous French, Austrian, Spanish, and loyalist Italian pursuing forces.

During 1849–1854 Garibaldi was in exile in America. Reaching agreement with the Sardinian government, he returned there and, on the outbreak of war with Austria in March 1859, assumed command of a brigade in the Sardinian Army as a major general. He won a victory at Varese on May 26 and liberated considerable territory before the armistice of Villafranca ended hostilities in July. Under the terms of the armistice, Sardina secured Lombardy but not Venetia. Disgusted with the outcome, Garibaldi went to Tuscany to assist the revolutionary government there and plan a march on Rome. Forbidden to embark on the latter course by Sardinian king Victor Emmanuel I, Garibaldi resigned his commission in the Sardinian Army.

In May 1860 Garibaldi sailed in a handful of steamers from Genoa with 1,000 handpicked followers, known as the Red Shirts, to assist a revolt in Sicily. He won a victory at Calatafimi on May 15 and then on May 27–30 captured Parma, which was held by 20,000 men. Crossing over the Strait of Messina to Naples on August 18–19, he entered Naples on September 7, then waited for the Sardinian Army to march south, agreeing to surrender his conquests to Sardinia and enabling the new Kingdom of Italy to annex the former kingdom of Naples. Declining all honors, he retired to his home on Caprera Island.

In 1861 on the outbreak of the American Civil War, Garibaldi offered his services to the Union side, providing he be placed in command of all the forces. President Abraham Lincoln declined the offer. In 1862 Garibaldi again tried to seize Rome, now garrisoned by the French Army, but was prevented from doing so by troops of the Kingdom of Italy and was wounded and captured in May. In 1866 when Italy allied with Prussia against Austria, Garibaldi again led a small force against the Austrians but was defeated at Bececca on July 21, 1866. He again attempted to seize Rome but was defeated at Mentana by a French and papal force on November 3, 1867. In early September 1870 on the outbreak of war between France and Prussia, the French troops were re-called from Rome, and Italian troops marched in on September 20. Pope Pius IX shut himself up as the "prisoner in the Vatican." Garibaldi had realized his dream, for Rome now became the capital of a united Italy.

Recruiting 20,000 Italian volunteers, Garibaldi entered the Franco-Prussian War on the side of the French Republic, fighting in the Battle of Belfort on January 15–17, 1871. Elected to the new National Assembly of the French Republic that same year, he soon resigned and returned to Italy, where he was elected to the Italian parliament in 1874. Garibaldi died on the island of Caprera off Sardinia on June 2, 1882.

A staunch patriot and a brave and capable commander of irregular troops, Garibaldi was probably the best-known revolutionary of the 18th century. A lifelong advocate of democratic government, he was however out of his element in regular warfare and the higher levels of government and diplomacy.

SPENCER C. TUCKER

References

Hibbert, Christopher. *Garibaldi and His Enemies: The Clash of Arms and Personalities in the Making of Italy.* Boston: Little, Brown, 1966.

Mack Smith, Denis. *Garibaldi.* Englewood Cliffs, NJ: Prentice-Hall, 1957.

Martin, George. *The Red Shirt and the Cross of Savoy: The Story of Italy's Risorgimento (1748–1871).* New York: Dodd, Mead, 1969.

Trevelyan, George M. *Garibaldi and the Thousand.* London: Longman, Green, 1909.

Gneisenau, August von

Birth Date: October 27, 1760
Death Date: August 23, 1831

Prussian field marshal and military reformer. Born at Schildau, Saxony, on October 27, 1760, August Wilhelm Anton von Gneisenau was the son of an artillery officer. He studied at Erfurt University and then joined the Austrian Army and served in its cavalry during 1778–1780. He then joined the army of Bayreuth-Anspach and, as a lieutenant, served in Canada during 1782–1783 in mercenary forces employed by Britain during the American Revolutionary War.

In 1786 Gneisenau joined the Prussian Army as a captain and was assigned to the King's Suite, a nascent general staff. By 1790 Gneisenau was a staff captain, and in 1795 he led the 15th Fusiliers in the Third Partition of Poland. He fought in the 1806–1807 Prussian war against France and was wounded in the Battle of Jena on October 14, 1806. He won wide recognition for leading the Prussian defense of Colberg, Pomerania, during May 20–July 2, 1807, which won him promotion to lieutenant colonel.

Following the disastrous Treaties of Tilsit on July 7–9, 1807, King Frederick William III appointed a Military Reorganization Commission under Gerhard von Scharnhorst. As a member of the commission, Gneisenau helped produce such proposals as an effective reserve system, officer promotion on the basis of performance rather than seniority, an end to corporal punishment, and the establishment of a true general staff.

Following extensive travel abroad in Britain, Russia, and Sweden, Gneisenau returned to Prussia to become chief of staff to Prussian Army commander General Gerhard von Blücher in June 1813, serving with him in the War of German Liberation. Gneisenau played a major role in victories at Katzbach on August 26, 1813, and at Leipzig on October 16–19, 1813, for which he was created a count. He continued with Blücher in the invasion of France in the spring of 1814 and the subsequent capture of Paris. The two men were a perfect complement to one another. Gneisenau was with Blücher the next year in the Waterloo Campaign and fought in the Battle of Ligny on June 16, 1815. When Blücher was wounded, Gneisenau took the important decision following this Prussian defeat not to retire back on the Prussian base, making it possible to march to and support the British at Waterloo on June 18.

Upset by what he considered the lenient treatment of France and the postponement by the conservative Prussian establishment of many of the liberal reforms that he advocated, Gneisenau resigned from military service in 1816. He spent the last 15 years of his life in a series of largely honorific posts, including mayor of Berlin in 1818. Advanced to field marshal in 1825 on the 10th anniversary of the Battle of Waterloo, Gneisenau commanded the Prussian Army of Observation sent to the eastern frontier during the abortive Polish Revolution of 1831. He died in Posen (Poznan), Pomerania, Prussia, of cholera on August 23, 1831. Gneisenau was brave, intelligent, and a capable commander. He was also a staunch supporter of German unification. A brilliant staff officer, he saw most of his reforms set aside by the conservative establishment, not to be implemented until the middle of the 19th century and the rebuilding of the Prussian Army under Helmuth von Moltke.

SPENCER C. TUCKER

References

Craig, Gordon Alexander. *The Politics of the Prussian Army.* Oxford, UK: Clarendon, 1955.

Paret, Peter. *Yorck and the Era of Prussian Reform, 1807–1815.* Princeton, NJ: Princeton University Press, 1966.

Simon, Walter Michael. *The Failure of the Prussian Reform Movement.* Ithaca, NY: Cornell University Press, 1955.

White, Jonathan Randall. *The Prussian Army, 1640–1871.* Landham, MD: University Press of America, 1996.

Görgey, Artúr

Birth Date: January 30, 1818
Death Date: May 21, 1916

Staunch Hungarian patriot and leading general during the War for Hungarian Independence (1848–1849). Artúr Görgey was born on January 30, 1818, in Toporcz, Hungary (present-day Toporec, Slovakia), into a Saxon noble family that had converted to Lutheranism. Görgey entered the Austrian military in 1837 as a member of the Bodyguard of Hungarian Nobles at Vienna, where he also pursued university studies. On his father's death in 1845 Görgey could no longer financially afford to remain in the military and left the army to study chemistry at the University of Prague. He soon abandoned his plan of becoming a professor and returned home to try his hand at managing the family estates.

Görgey found his true calling with the Hungarian Revolution of 1848. He joined the Hungarian cause as a captain. Initially involved in weapons acquisition, he was soon promoted to major and given command of national guard units north of the Tisza River. While involved in fighting to prevent Croat forces from crossing the Danube below Pest, Görgey took prisoner the prominent Hungarian noble Count Jenö Zichy. Görgey caused him to be brought before a court-martial. Found guilty, Zichy was hanged as a traitor.

Görgey soon proved himself a capable commander. His most notable early military success was a victory over the Croats in the Battle of Ozora on October 6, 1848. On November 1 president of the Hungarian National Defense Committee Lajos Kossuth named Görgey, barely 30 years old, commander of the Hungarian Army of the Upper Danube facing Austrian general Prince Alfred zu Windischgrätz. Kossuth and Görgey were similar in background but very unlike in temperament. Kossuth, the lawyer, was warm, passionate, and eloquent. Görgey, the soldier, was cold, aloof, and puritanical. He distrusted Kossuth's radicalism and civilian leaders in general. Kossuth sought a total military victory, while Görgey hoped for a negotiated peace. The two men soon clashed on virtually all aspects of strategy, with unfortunate results for the Hungarian cause.

When Windischgrätz advanced across the Latja River, Görgey withdrew toward Vác despite protests from Kossuth. On January 5, 1849, perturbed by what he believed to be undue political interference, Görgey issued a proclamation blaming recent military reverses on the government and virtually separating himself from its authority. He then retired with his forces into the mountains to the north and operated independently.

Following the defeat of the principal Hungarian forces under General Henryk Dembriński in the Battle of Kápolna (Görgey's corps arrived too late to influence the outcome), Görgey took full command of Hungarian forces. Throughout the spring of 1849 he waged a brilliant campaign against Windischgrätz. That April, Görgey was victorious at Gödöllö, Isazeg, and Nagysalló (present-day Tekovské Lužany in Slovakia). He also relieved the fortress of Komárom and was again victorious at Vác. Unfortunately, he failed to follow up this military success with an advance on Vienna, preferring instead to lay siege to the Hungarian capital of Buda.

Görgey was not in sympathy with Kossuth's separation of ties with Austria on April 14 and rejected the proffered position of field marshal, although he did assume the portfolio of minister of war while at the same time commanding Hungarian troops in the field. The Russian Army invaded Hungary in June. That month and in July, Görgey suffered a series of defeats inflicted by Austrian forces under General Julius Jacob von Haynau. On August 11 Kossuth resigned and named Görgey military dictator. Convinced that he could not break through the Russian lines, two days later Görgey surrendered his army of some 34,000 men to the Russians at Világos. The Russians then handed the Hungarians over to the Austrians. Most of the officers were court-martialed and executed. Czar Nicholas I secured an amnesty only for Görgey. Kept confined at Klagenfurt, Görgey worked as a chemist until he was pardoned and allowed to return to Hungary in 1867.

Görgey often found himself the object of ridicule, most Hungarians apparently agreeing with Kossuth's charge that Görgey had undermined the state by surrendering at Világos and delivering his officers and men to Austrian retribution while he secured amnesty. Görgey attempted to justify his actions in *Mein Leben and Würken in Ungarn, 1848–1849* (My Life and Acts in Hungary in the Years 1848–1849), published in 1852. The matter continues to be a source of debate in Hungarian historiography. Görgey worked as a railroad engineer before retiring to Visegrád, where he lived quietly until his death on May 21, 1916. It was only then that his military reputation began to undergo a degree of rehabilitation.

A capable commander and brilliant strategist, Görgey was also headstrong and an unfortunate choice to command a revolutionary army. His enmity with Hungarian political leader Kossuth undoubtedly served to advance the Hungarian military defeat.

SPENCER C. TUCKER

References

Görgey, Artúr. *My Life and Acts in Hungary in the Years 1848 and 1849.* New York: Harper, 1852.

Sugarm, Peter F., Péter Hanák, and Tibor Frank. *A History of Hungary.* Bloomington: Indiana University Press, 1990.

Greene, Nathanael

Birth Date: July 27, 1742
Death Date: June 19, 1786

Continental Army general. Born at Potowomut (Warwick), Rhode Island, on July 27, 1742, into a Quaker family, Nathanael Greene had little formal education but from his own love of reading became well educated by the standards of the day. In 1770 he assumed leadership of the family-owned ironworks and other businesses. He served in the Rhode Island General Assembly during 1771–1774. His interest in military affairs led him to help establish a militia unit, the Kentish Guards, in 1774. Because he walked with a slight limp as a result of a birth defect, the men refused to elect him an officer, and he enlisted as a private.

Known as a staunch Patriot, Greene believed early that America must become independent of Britain. Several days after the beginning of the American Revolutionary War on April 19, 1775, the Rhode Island General

Assembly selected him as one of two commissioners to meet with representatives of Connecticut concerning a common defense. The General Assembly also ordered the raising of a brigade of 1,500 men. After others had turned down the post and although he had no military experience, Greene was named its commander.

Greene led his brigade in the siege of Boston. Congress confirmed him as a brigadier general in the Continental Army in June 1775, and he quickly distinguished himself. He was soon one of Continental Army commander General George Washington's closest advisers.

Ordered with his brigade to New York in April 1776, Greene helped prepare defenses on Long Island but was ill and absent during the Battle of Long Island on August 27. Advanced to major general that same month, he saw his first action in the Battle of Harlem Heights on September 16. Following withdrawal of most of the Continental Army forces from New York to New Jersey, he urged retention of Fort Washington on the New York side of the Hudson, an unfortunate decision in which Washington concurred that led to one of the worst Continental Army defeats of the war on November 16.

Greene commanded Fort Lee, on the New Jersey side of the Hudson, but escaped with his garrison just ahead of a British attacking force on November 20, 1776. He played an important role in the Battle of Trenton (December 26, 1776) and the Battle of Princeton (January 3, 1777) and he led the principal Continental Army attacking column at Germantown on October 4, 1777.

On Washington's urging, Greene reluctantly accepted appointment as quartermaster general of the army. In this position he rendered highly effective and absolutely essential service during March 1778–July 1780, but he chafed to return to line duties. He commanded the right wing in the Battle of Monmouth on June 28, 1778, and he took part in the Battle of Newport, Rhode Island, on August 29. Following the treason of Major General Benedict Arnold in 1780, Greene took command of West Point.

Following Major General Horatio Gates's disastrous defeat in the south in the Battle of Camden on August 16, 1780, Washington named Greene as Gates's successor. Greene found the army in the south both vastly outnumbered and wretchedly equipped. He then adopted the risky tactic of dividing his army while he retrained and rebuilt his forces. He also made highly effective use of militia forces. Following Brigadier General Daniel Morgan's victory in the Battle of Cowpens on January 17, 1781, Greene led a brilliant long withdrawal north over the Dan River into Virginia, escaping pursuing British forces under Lieutenant General Charles, Earl Cornwallis. Following subsequent extensive maneuvering, Greene engaged Cornwallis in battle at Guilford Courthouse, North Carolina, on March 15, 1781. Although Greene was defeated, heavy British losses in the battle led Cornwallis to shift his operations to Virginia, culminating in his surrender at Yorktown on October 19.

Greene meanwhile went on the offensive but suffered a rebuff against forces under British lieutenant colonel Lord Rawdon in the Battle of Hobkirk's Hill, South Carolina, on April 25, 1781. This battle prompted Greene to remark, "We fight, get beat, rise, and fight again." Greene was next forced to break off a siege of the British outpost at Ninety Six and retreat on June 20. Although he did not win a battle during the period April–July 1781, he forced the British from all of Georgia and South Carolina, with the exception of Savannah and the area around Charleston. In late August, Greene, now reinforced, attacked Rawdon's successor, Lieutenant Colonel Alexander Stewart, in the Battle of Eutaw Springs on September 8. Stewart was so weakened by this hardest-fought of all southern battles of the war that he was obliged to withdraw to near Charleston, which Greene occupied following the British evacuation in December 1782.

Considered the finest general on the American side in the war second only to Washington, Greene was a superb organizer, trainer of men, and administrator. A stern taskmaster, he was fair and highly regarded by his soldiers. He was also a brilliant strategist, and his Southern Campaign remains an American military masterpiece.

Following the war, Greene retired from the military to an estate, Mulberry Grove, north of Savannah, Georgia. He died of sunstroke on June 19, 1786, at only 43 years old. Had he not died so young, Greene might have played a prominent role in the new republic.

SPENCER C. TUCKER

References

Alderman, Clifford Lindsey. *Retreat to Victory: The Life of Nathanael Greene.* Philadelphia: Chilton Books, 1967.

Golway, Terry. *Washington's General: Nathanel Greene and the Triumph of the American Revolution.* New York: Henry Holt, 2005.

Thane, Elswyth. *The Fighting Quaker: Nathanael Greene.* New York: Hawthorn Books, 1972.

Hood, Alexander

Birth Date: December 2, 1727
Death Date: May 2, 1814

British admiral. Born at Butleigh, Somerset, on December 2, 1727, Alexander Hood joined the navy in 1740 during the War of the Austrian Succession (1740–1748). Promoted to lieutenant in December 1746, he went on half-pay after the war until 1755. He returned to active service during the Seven Years' War (1756–1763) and was promoted to commander in March 1756 and to post captain in June 1756. His ship sailed as part of the Channel Fleet in 1759, and he fought in the Battle of Quiberon Bay on November 20.

In 1766 Hood became treasurer of Greenwich Hospital. During the American Revolutionary War (1775–1783) he commanded a ship at the Battle of Ushant on July 27, 1778. In the subsequent court-martial of Admiral Augustus Keppel, Hood admitted that he tampered with his ship's log. This discredited Hood's testimony, and public opinion turned against him, nearly ruining his career. Promoted to rear admiral in September 1780, he served in the relief of Gibraltar in 1782.

Appointed vice admiral in September 1787 and knighted the following year, Hood became second-in-command of Lord Richard Howe's Channel Fleet at the outbreak of hostilities with France in 1793 in the Wars of the French Revolution. Promoted to full admiral in April 1794, Hood fought in the Battle of the Glorious First of June that year. In recognition of the victory, he was created a peer of Ireland with the title of Baron Bridport of Cricket St. Thomas in Somerset.

With Howe in poor health, Bridport assumed temporary command of the Channel Fleet in 1795 and commanded it in the Battle of Belle Isle on June 23. Although the victory was not decisive, Bridport's Irish peerage was converted into an English peerage in recognition. The Channel Fleet, still under his temporary command, then broke into detachments, with the nucleus remaining at Spithead.

The next year a French invasion force sailed from Brest to invade Ireland in December 1796. Only poor weather saved the British, for Bridport did not put to sea until January 3, 1797, and by then the invasion had failed. Mutinies then gripped the Channel Fleet, paralyzing it in Spithead during April–May 1797. Following this mutiny, Bridport became the official commander of the fleet that remained more continuously off Brest than ever before, but even then a French fleet escaped in April 1799. Bridport expected an invasion of Ireland, but instead the French sailed to the Mediterranean.

Bridport relinquished his command in April 1800. Advanced to viscount in 1801, he never held another naval appointment. He died on May 2, 1814.

KEVIN D. McCRANIE

References

Hood, Dorothy. *The Admirals Hood.* London: Hutchinson, 1942.

Saxby, Richard. "The Blockade of Brest in the French Revolutionary War." *Mariner's Mirror* 78(1) (February 1992): 25–35.

———. "Lord Bridport and the Spithead Mutiny." *Mariner's Mirror* 79(2) (May 1993): 170–178.

Hood, Samuel

Birth Date: December 12, 1724
Death Date: January 27, 1816

British admiral. Born on December 12, 1724, the son of Samuel Hood, vicar of Butleigh in Somerset and prebendary of Wells, the younger Samuel Hood entered the navy in 1741 during the War of the Austrian Succession (1740–1748) as a captain's servant. After service in several ships he became a midshipman in November 1743 and was promoted to lieutenant in 1746. He was on half-pay from November 1748 until 1753. In 1754 he took command of the sloop *Jamaica* on the North American station.

In 1756 Hood was promoted to captain and returned to England. During 1757–1758 he then served in other ships in the blockade of France. His ship, the frigate *Vestal* (32 guns), captured the French frigate *Bellona* (32 guns) off Cape Finisterrre in 1759. He served in the Mediterranean during 1760–1763 and afterward was appointed to command the ship of the line *Thunderer* (74 guns) at Portsmouth in 1763. Transferred to the North American station in this ship in 1765, he was named commodore commanding that station in the *Romney* (50 guns) in 1767. Returning to England, he commanded guardships at Portsmouth during 1771–1776, then was appointed to command the third-rate ship of the line *Courageux* (74 guns). Named commissioner at Portsmouth and governor of the Naval Academy, he was created a baronet in 1778.

Hood was promoted to rear admiral in 1780 and was sent to reinforce Admiral Sir George Brydges Rodney in the West Indies. Hood participated in the expedition against St. Eustatius in 1781 and then blockaded Martinique, where he fought a brief engagement with the superior fleet of French admiral François Joseph Paul, Comte de Grasse-Tilly, in April 1781. Sent to reinforce Rear Admiral Thomas Graves at New York, Hood commanded the rear ships in the Second Battle of the Chesapeake on September 5, 1781, which was inconclusive but nonetheless sealed the fate of British troops at Yorktown.

Returning to the West Indies, Hood briefly occupied Basseterre at Nevis and joined Rodney for the Battle of the Saintes against de Grasse on April 12, 1782, where Hood captured the French flagship *Ville de Paris* (110 guns).

Made a baron in 1782, Hood returned to Parliament in 1784, was promoted to vice admiral in 1787, and commanded at Portsmouth during 1787–1788. Named to the Board of Admiralty in 1788, he served until his appointment to command the Mediterranean Fleet in 1793. There he oversaw the occupation of Toulon and the capture of Corsica. Hood was promoted to admiral in 1794 and returned to England. Created Viscount Hood of Catherington in 1796, he was named governor of Greenwich Hospital, where he served until his death on January 27, 1816. A capable commander and a fine tactician, Hood had only limited opportunities for higher command.

STEVEN W. GUERRIER

References

Clowes, William Laird. *The Royal Navy: A History from the Earliest Times to the Present.* 7 vols. Boston: Little, Brown; London: S. Low, Marsten, 1897–1903.

Laughton, J. K. "Hood, Samuel, Viscount Hood." In *Dictionary of National Biography,* Vol. 27, edited by Sidney Lee, 263–270. London: Smith, Elder, 1891.

Le Fevre, Peter. *Precursors of Nelson: British Admirals of the Eighteenth Century.* Mechanicsburg, PA: Stackpole, 2000.

Lyon, David. *Sea Battles in Close-Up: The Age of Nelson.* Annapolis, MD: Naval Institute Press, 1996.

Howe, Sir William

Birth Date: August 10, 1729
Death Date: July 12, 1814

British general. Born in London, England, on August 10, 1729, William Howe was the younger brother of future admiral Lord Richard Howe. Educated at Eton, William Howe was commissioned in the British Army as a cornet in September 1746, was promoted to lieutenant in 1747, and rose rapidly in rank and responsibility. He served in North America during the French and Indian War (1754–1763) and as a lieutenant colonel commanded a regiment in the Siege of Louisbourg on June 2–July 27, 1758. While still in North America he was elected to Parliament to succeed his brother George Augustus, who was killed at Fort Ticonderoga in July 1758. Howe served in Parliament for 22 years, much of it in absentia during 1758–1780. He led the ascent to the Plains of Abraham outside of Quebec (Québec) on the night of September 12–13, 1759, and distinguished himself in the subsequent battle on September 13. He then commanded a brigade in the advance on Montreal (Montréal) in September 1760 and another brigade in the siege of Belle Isle in 1761.

Howe participated in the siege of Havana, Cuba, during June–August 1762 and, as a colonel, commanded a regiment in Ireland in 1764. He was then appointed lieutenant governor of the Isle of Wight in 1766 and was promoted to major general in 1772. He also developed a new system of infantry training, subsequently adopted by the British Army in 1774.

Howe returned to North America in May 1775 as second-in-command of British forces with the outbreak of fighting in the American Revolutionary War (1775–1783) and led in person the bloody British assault on Breed's Hill (Bunker Hill) on June 17. Although the British won this battle, the high casualties sustained may have given Howe pause, for he never again vigorously pressed home his attacks. He succeeded Lieutenant General Thomas Gage as commander of British troops in North America on the latter's return to Britain on October 10.

Howe withdrew British forces from Boston to Halifax, Nova Scotia, on March 17, 1776, closing out the first phase of the war. He and his brother, Vice Admiral Richard Howe, who commanded British naval forces in North American waters, had great sympathy for the colonial cause and, acting with the authority of King George III, endeavored without success to reach a peace agreement with the Continental Congress in 1776.

Negotiations having failed, William Howe, supported by Richard Howe's ships, then led an expeditionary force against New York, landing on Staten Island on July 3 and then defeating the Americans in battles on Long Island on August 27 and capturing New York on September 12. William Howe again was victorious at Harlem Heights on September 16 and White Plains on October 28. His forces scored a major triumph in capturing Fort Washington, New York, and Fort Lee, New Jersey, on November 12–16. He was subsequently knighted for his capture of New York. He then leisurely pursued the remains of General George Washington's Continental Army across New Jersey before going into winter quarters. Washington's successful counterstrokes during December 1776–January 1777 subsequently forced Howe to abandon most of New Jersey.

Sailing from New York City, Howe opened the 1777 campaign with a naval descent into Chesapeake Bay, landing at the Head of Elk (Elkton, Maryland) on August 25 prior to driving against the Patriot capital at Philadelphia. Defeating Washington's forces in the Battle of Brandywine Creek on September 11, Howe took Philadelphia on September 26 and then defeated a Continental Army attack on his encampment outside of Philadelphia at Germantown on October 4. After clearing the lower Delaware in conjunction with his brother's ships, Howe then remained largely inert at Philadelphia.

Howe came under considerable criticism for the British defeats at Trenton on December 26, 1776, and Princeton on January 2–3, 1777, and the failure to coordinate with Lieutenant General John Burgoyne's assault on Albany that met defeat at Saratoga in September–October 1777. Howe was unfairly blamed for Burgoyne's failure, as Minister for the Colonies Lord George Germain had approved both diametrically opposed plans, and Howe had kept Burgoyne fully informed of his intentions. Dispirited over his failure to win the war,

Howe resigned his commission on April 14, 1778; turned over command to Lieutenant General Henry Clinton; and returned to England in May, there to criticize the British government for what he charged was insufficient support for the war effort.

Promoted to lieutenant general in 1782 and full general in October 1793, Howe held several important commands. He succeeded to the earldom on his brother Richard's death in 1799. Plagued by poor health, he resigned all his posts in 1803. Howe died at Plymouth, England, on July 12, 1814. Personally brave and a commander of great tactical ability, he was popular with his officers and men. He was also slow and deliberate in his movements. In his defense, Howe argued with some validity that London had not allowed him either the resources necessary to win the war or to set its strategy.

SPENCER C. TUCKER

References

Anderson, Thoyer Steele. *The Command of the Howe Brothers during the American Revolution.* New York: Octagon, 1972.

Gruber, Ira D. *The Howe Brothers and the American Revolution.* New York: Atheneum, 1972.

Partridge, Bellamy. *Sir Billy Howe.* London: Longman, Green, 1932.

Jackson, Andrew

Birth Date: March 15, 1767
Death Date: June 8, 1845

U.S. general and president (1829–1837). Born on March 15, 1767, the son of poor Scotch Irish immigrant parents in the Waxhaws Settlement on the South Carolina frontier, Andrew Jackson received little formal education. During the American Revolutionary War (1775–1783) he fought in guerrilla operations against the British in South Carolina during 1780–1781 and was captured in 1781. A drunken British officer slashed his face with a saber, and he contracted smallpox while a prisoner. Also, his mother and both older brothers died during the war. These events no doubt influenced Jackson's subsequent strong Anglophobia.

Following the war Jackson first read and then practiced law in North Carolina and later in Tennessee in 1788, where he became highly successful. He became state prosecuting attorney in 1788 and, although poor investments almost led to bankruptcy, was a delegate to the state constitutional convention in 1796 and Tennessee's first representative in the U.S. House of Representatives during 1796–1797. Appointed U.S. senator in 1797, Jackson soon resigned because of financial problems in 1798. He then served as a superior court judge during 1798–1804, again resigning because of financial difficulties.

Jackson found his calling when he was elected major general of the Tennessee Militia in 1802. Jackson and his men entered federal service at the beginning of war with Britain in June 1812. Jackson led his troops to Natchez, Mississippi, in preparation for an invasion of Florida, which was canceled by decision of Congress. He then marched his men back to Tennessee, earning the nickname of "Old Hickory" for his toughness.

When a dispute between Creek Indian factions of Alabama and Mississippi expanded to attacks on white settlements in the autumn of 1813, Jackson led his men against the Creeks. A strict disciplinarian, he drilled his men, believing that militia, if well trained and adequately supplied, could be an effective fighting force. After carefully stockpiling supplies, he began a campaign against the Creeks in November when their own food supplies were low. Part of his force, under Brigadier General John Coffee, defeated the Creeks at Tallasahatchee, Alabama, on November 3, while Jackson himself won a lesser victory at Talladega on November 9. After reorganizing his forces, Jackson invaded the Creek heartland in March 1814, taking the main Creek encampment in the Battle of Horseshoe Bend (Tohopeka) on March 27, 1814.

Appointed major general in the regular army in May 1814, Jackson assumed command of the Seventh Military District. He improved the defenses of Mobile, Alabama, and then defended it against a British naval attack on September 15. He then marched into Florida without official authorization. Taking Pensacola on November 7, he destroyed its fortifications and then hastened to New Orleans in December to defend the city against a British attack. Jackson assembled a force of regulars and hastily assembled an army of militia and volunteers that repulsed British lieutenant general Sir Edward Pakenham's assault on January 7, 1815, making Jackson a national hero.

With the end of the war on December 24, 1814, Jackson assumed command of the Southern Division of the army at New Orleans. Using the outbreak of the First Seminole War (1817–1818) as a pretext, he invaded Spanish Florida. Exceeding his authority, he not only seized Pensacola on May 24, 1818, but also created an international incident in April by hanging two British nationals for allegedly supplying the Seminoles with arms. The James Monroe administration used Jackson's actions to induce Spain to sell Florida to the United States in 1819.

Resigning his commission in June 1821, Jackson served briefly as governor of Florida during March–October 1821 before returning to his plantation home, the Hermitage, near Nashville. Elected to the U.S. Senate from Tennessee in 1823, he resigned after one session to run for president. In the November 1824 election he won a plurality of the popular vote and electoral votes but lost the election in the House of Representatives to John Quincy Adams. Jackson's supporters worked to bring about electoral changes that then led to his election to the presidency by wide margins in 1828 and 1832.

As president, Jackson maintained U.S. neutrality but encouraged his friend Sam Houston in the Texas War of Independence (1835–1836). Jackson secured congressional approval for the Indian Removal Bill that forced many Native Americans, especially the Cherokees, to move west of the Mississippi River. This act led to both the Black Hawk War (1832) in Illinois and the Second Seminole War (1835–1843) in Florida. Among other events during his presidency were the South Carolina Nullification Crisis and the demise of the second Bank of the United States. On the completion of his second term in 1837, Jackson returned to Nashville. He died at the Hermitage on June 8, 1845. While he began his military career as a rank amateur, Jackson proved to be a military genius. A strict disciplinarian and careful planner, he understood the need for thorough training before committing his men to battle.

SPENCER C. TUCKER

References

Remini, Robert V. *Andrew Jackson and the Course of American Empire, 1767–1821.* New York: Harper and Row, 1977.

———. *Andrew Jackson and the Course of American Freedom, 1822–1832.* New York: Harper and Row, 1981.

———. *Andrew Jackson and His Indian Wars.* New York: Viking Penguin, 2001.

Jervis, John

Birth Date: January 9, 1735
Death Date: March 14, 1823

British admiral of the fleet, known as "Old Jarvey." Born in Stone, Staffordshire, on January 9, 1735, John Jervis entered the navy as a midshipman in 1749 and was promoted to lieutenant in 1755, commander in 1759, and post captain in 1760. He served on active duty until the end of the Seven Years' War (1756–1763), when he was placed on half-pay.

Recalled to active service at the beginning of the American Revolutionary War in 1775, Jervis took command of the ship of the line *Foudroyant* (80 guns) and fought in the Battle of Ushant on July 27, 1778. In 1782 he captured the French ship of the line *Pégase* for which he was knighted. First elected to Parliament in 1783 as a Whig, he was promoted to rear admiral in 1787 and vice admiral in 1793. On the renewal of war with France in 1793 he commanded the naval force that captured Guadeloupe and Martinique in 1794. In poor health, he returned to Britain in February 1795. Promoted to admiral that July, he took command of English forces in the Mediterranean in November.

Jervis soon found himself in difficulty, thanks to Napoleon Bonaparte's victories in northern Italy and the loss of its ports coupled with the threat posed by an alliance between France and Spain. Jervis withdrew to the Atlantic in December 1796, keeping watch on the Spanish at Cádiz. With 15 ships of the line he intercepted and defeated a Spanish fleet of 27 ships of the line off Cape St. Vincent on February 14, 1797, capturing 4 of them.

Created Earl St. Vincent and granted a pension for this victory, he continued to command in the Mediterranean. Later in 1797 he put down with severity a mutiny in his fleet, prompted by mutinies at the Nore and Spithead. Declining health forced St. Vincent to resign his command in mid-1799. His health restored, the next year he took command of the Channel Fleet but aroused much opposition because of his overly strict discipline. The fleet was almost continuously off Brest, in the process revolutionizing blockade operations.

During 1801–1803 St. Vincent was first lord of the Admiralty. He improved the royal dockyards and attacked corruption and inefficiency but came under criticism for neglecting preparedness. Refusing command of the Channel Fleet in 1803, he took up that post again during 1806–1807, maintaining the blockade of Brest until 1807, when he retired at his own request. He never held another command, although on the coronation of King George IV in 1821 St. Vincent was promoted to admiral of the fleet. He died at home in Sussex on March 14, 1823.

Spencer C. Tucker

References

Arthur, Charles B. *The Remaking of the English Navy by Admiral St. Vincent: The Great Unclaimed Naval Revolution (1795–1805).* Lanham, MD: University Press of America, 1986.

Berckman, Evelyn. *Nelson's Dear Lord: A Portrait of St. Vincent.* London: MacMillan, 1962.

James, William. *Old Oak: The Life of John Jervis, Earl of St. Vincent.* New York: Longman, Green, 1950.

Tucker, Jedediah Stephens. *Memoirs of the Right Hon. The Earl of St. Vincent.* 2 vols. London: R. Bentley, 1844.

Jomini, Antoine Henri

Birth Date: March 6, 1779
Death Date: March 22, 1869

Military writer who sought to determine the principles guiding the conduct of war. Born into a middle-class family on March 6, 1779, in Payerne in the French-speaking Canton of Vaud, Switzerland, Antoine Henri Jomini gave up a career in banking in Paris to secure an unpaid staff position in the French Army. During the Peace of Amiens (1802–1803) he returned to banking. He became acquainted with Marshal Michel Ney, who was impressed with Jomini's quickness of mind and helped him publish his first military writings, treating the campaigns of Frederick II of Prussia, in which Jomini made certain comparisons to the campaigns of Napoleon Bonaparte.

Jomini joined Ney's staff in 1805 and saw action and won praise for his roles at Ulm in October 1805 and at Austerlitz on December 2. Napoleon then invited Jomini, now a colonel, to join his personal staff. Taking part in the 1806 campaigns against Prussia and then Russia, Jomini served in the Battle of Jena (October 14, 1806) and the Battle of Eylau (February 7–8, 1807).

Jomini then returned to Ney's staff and accompanied him to Spain as chief of staff during 1808–1809, but Jomini's disagreements with the marshal led him to return to France in November 1809. Jomini had a clear understanding of Napoleon's strategic viewpoint, and Napoleon, who appreciated the value of his writings, brought Jomini into his staff. Jomini served as an assistant to Napoleon's chief of staff Marshal Louis Alexandre Berthier, although he disliked Jomini. Jomini was promoted to *général de brigade* in November 1810.

Jomini was an open admirer of Russian czar Alexander I, and during Napoleon's invasion of Russia in 1812 he kept Jomini in the rear areas as governor of Vilna and later of Smolensk. In the spring of 1813 Jomini rejoined Ney's staff and saw service in the Battle of Lützen (May 1–2) and the Battle of Bautzen (May 21). Berthier had Jomini arrested on a minor technicality for being late with his corps reports, causing Jomini to defect to the Russians on August 14. During the remainder of the Napoleonic Wars, Jomini served as a military adviser to Czar Alexander I. On Alexander's death Jomini advised his successor, Czar Nicholas I, who promoted him to general in chief.

Following the Napoleonic Wars, Jomini devoted himself largely to writing, although he did see some action during the Russo-Turkish War of 1828–1829. He was undoubtedly the most prolific and recognized military writer of the 19th century, and his best-known work was *Préis sur l'art de la guerre* (Summary of the Art of War), published in 1838. Jomini retired to Passy (near Chaumont), France, and died there on March 22, 1869. A student of the Enlightenment, he believed that there were principles underlying the conduct of war and that by studying them one could learn effective generalship. He also believed that once a war was begun, the government should yield full control of its conduct to its generals. Jomini enjoyed such widespread and continuing interest because he wrote in French, the international scientific language of the day, and because his formulaic approach to the study of war had then, and still has today, a tremendous appeal. Certainly his writings about the Napoleonic era influenced an entire generation of military officers including those who fought the American Civil War, with whom he had more influence than his better-known contemporaries such as Carl von Clausewitz. Jomini's great contribution lay in his clarification of the principles of military science and stress on the importance of strategy. His emphasis on careful planning made clear the vital role of military intelligence.

SPENCER C. TUCKER

References

Brinton, Crane, Gordon A. Craig, and Felix Gilbert. "Jomini." In *Makers of Modern Strategy: Military Thought from Machiavelli to Hitler,* edited by Edward Mead Earle, 77–92. Princeton, NJ: Princeton University Press, 1971.

Howard, Michael. *The Theory and Practice of War.* Bloomington: Indiana University Press, 1975.

Jomini, Antoine. *Summary of the Art of War.* Harrisburg, PA: Stackpole, 1965.

Jones, John Paul

Birth Date: July 6, 1747
Death Date: July 18, 1792

U.S. naval officer. Born John Paul in Kirkcudbrightshire, Scotland, on July 6, 1747, Paul joined the merchant marine at an early age. An accomplished sailor, he rose to command his own ship at the age of 21 but was a draconian disciplinarian. On two occasions his harsh measures resulted in the death of sailors, and he fled to Virginia under the assumed name of John Paul Jones in December 1773. When the American Revolutionary War began two years later he made his way to Philadelphia, where the Continental Congress appointed him a lieutenant in the newly formed Continental Navy.

Jones accompanied Commodore Esek Hopkins in an expedition to Nassau in March 1776 and subsequently commanded the sloop *Providence.* After several successful cruises Jones was entrusted with a larger vessel, the *Alfred,* and took additional prizes off Nova Scotia. However, by December 1776 American naval fortunes were at a nadir, and Jones was unable to secure either promotion or a bigger warship. He left for France in November 1777 in the sloop *Ranger.* There he took advantage of the recent Franco-American alliance to secure command of a warship under construction. Jones's strategy was to raid Britain's territorial waters. He arrived at Nantes, France, in late 1777 only to learn that the ship in question had been sold. While cruising Quiberon Bay, his ship received the first official salute to the American flag from French warships on February 14, 1778.

Jones led the *Ranger* into the Irish Sea and brazenly captured the town of Whitehaven for several hours, an event that roundly embarrassed the British government. Two months later the *Ranger* met and defeated the Royal Navy sloop *Drake* on April 20, 1778, the first British warship taken during the war in home waters.

Jones then spent several weeks refitting in France. Meanwhile, Benjamin Franklin, the American representative in Paris, arranged for him to captain the former French East Indiaman *Duc de Duras* (42 guns), and Jones subsequently renamed it the *Bonhomme Richard* in honor of his patron. Jones departed France in concert with the *Alliance* (36 guns) and two smaller French vessels and circumnavigated the British Isles, taking 17 prizes. Pursuing a British convoy, he undertook a desperate night engagement with the escorting 50-gun Royal Navy frigate *Serapis* off Flamborough Head on September 23, 1779. Both ships, lashed together, pounded each other at point-blank range until the British captain called upon Jones to surrender. Jones responded, "No, I'll sink, but I'll be damned if I will strike." This was later recalled as "I have not yet begun to fight." Within the hour, the *Serapis* struck.

Jones spent the remainder of the war constructing warships and negotiating prize money in France. He also received a gold medal from Congress, the only naval officer so honored.

Jones hoped to become the first American admiral and was assigned command of what was to be the first American 74-gun ship, the *America,* but Congress awarded that ship to France as a gift in September 1782. Finding no employment in America at the end of the war, Jones accepted appointment from Russian empress Catherine II (the Great) as an admiral of the Black Sea Fleet in 1788. He commanded a squadron that year against the Turks, but internecine court politics led to his being placed on two-year suspension from duty and induced him to leave Russia in the late summer of 1789. Jones wound up in Paris and died there on July 18, 1792. His remains were located in an unmarked grave in 1905 and were returned to the United States and reinterred on the U.S. Naval Academy grounds in 1913. An excellent seaman who was both brave and resolute, Jones was America's first great naval hero.

JOHN C. FREDRIKSEN

References

Callo, Joseph. *John Paul Jones: America's First Sea Warrior.* Annapolis, MD: Naval Institute Press, 2006.

Morison, Samuel E. *John Paul Jones: A Sailor's Biography.* Boston: Little, Brown, 1959.

Thomas, Evan. *John Paul Jones: Sailor, Hero, Father of the American Navy.* New York: Simon and Schuster, 2003.

Knox, Henry

Birth Date: July 25, 1750
Death Date: October 25, 1806

American general and U.S. secretary of war. Born in Boston, Massachusetts, on July 25, 1750, Henry Knox was forced by the death of his father to go to work at age 12 in a bookstore. He went on to establish his own bookstore in 1771. Largely self-educated, he read widely, especially in the practice of artillery. He joined the Massachusetts militia in 1765 and continued in it, although a hunting accident in 1772 cost him two fingers on his left hand. With the beginning of the American Revolutionary War (1775–1783), he fought in the Battle of Breed's Hill (Bunker Hill) on June 17, 1775. In the prolonged siege of Boston during April 19, 1775–May 17, 1776, Knox became close to Continental Army commander General George Washington. Commissioned a colonel of artillery, Knox supervised the removal and transport by sledge of 55 cannon from Fort Ticonderoga to the Boston area during December 5, 1775–January 25, 1776. The subsequent emplacement of these guns on the heights around the city led to the British evacuation of Boston, ending the first phase of the American Revolutionary War. Knox remained thereafter one of Washington's closest military associates.

Knox fought in the Battle of Long Island on August 27, 1776, and helped supervise removal of much of the Continental Army artillery in the retreat across New Jersey. He then participated in organizing and also fought in the Battle of Trenton (December 26, 1776) and the Battle of Princeton (January 3, 1777), gaining promotion to brigadier general on December 17, 1776.

Knox helped establish both the Springfield Arsenal and the Academy Artillery School (precursor to the U.S. Military Academy). He fought in the Battle of Brandywine on September 11, 1777, and at Germantown on October 4. He was with the army at Valley Forge during the winter of 1777–1778, when he greatly improved the training and efficiency of the Continental Army artillery. He fought in the Battle of Monmouth on June 28, 1778, and then played a major role in the Yorktown Campaign of September–October 19, 1781. On Washington's strong recommendation, Knox was promoted to major general, the youngest in the army in March 1782, with promotion backdated to November 1781. After commanding at West Point, Knox took over from Washington as commander in chief of the army in December 1783 until he retired in June 1784.

Knox cofounded the Society of the Cincinnati, an organization of former Continental Army officers in May 1783. Congress appointed Knox secretary of war in 1785 in which post he helped quell Shays' Rebellion in 1786. When the nation adopted the Constitution and Washington became president of the United States in 1789, he asked Knox to remain as secretary of war.

Knox pressed for a stronger federal military and proposed a system of universal military training. Congress ultimately passed the Militia Act of 1792, a greatly diluted version of Knox's original plan. Two disastrous campaigns against the northwestern Native Americans followed in 1790 and 1791, but Knox oversaw the creation of the Legion of the United States under Major General Anthony Wayne with its victory over the Native Americans in the Battle of Fallen Timbers on August 20, 1794. Knox also presided over the creation of the U.S. Navy when Congress authorized construction of six frigates in 1794. Knox resigned his office in December 1794 and retired to his estate at Thomaston, Massachusetts (now Maine). Briefly reappointed a major general during the Quasi-War with France during 1798–1800, he died suddenly at his estate on October 25, 1806. Intelligent and an able administrator, Knox rendered highly effective service.

SPENCER C. TUCKER

References

Callahan, North. *Henry Knox: George Washington's General.* South Brunswick, NY: A. S. Barnes, 1958.

Kohn, Richard. *Eagle and Sword: The Federalists and the Creation of the Military Establishment in America, 1783–1802.* New York: Free Press, 1975.

Palmer, Dave R. *1794: America, Its Army, and the Birth of the Nation.* Novato, CA: Presidio, 1994.

Kutuzov, Mikhail Illarionovich Golenischev

Birth Date: September 16, 1745
Death Date: April 28, 1813

Russian general. Born in St. Petersburg, Russia, on September 16, 1745, Mikhail Illarionovich Golenischev Kutuzov was the son of a Russian general. He received his education at the St. Petersburg Engineering and Artillery School. Commissioned an officer in 1761, he first saw action in Poland as an artillery officer during the Russian intervention there (1764–1769). He was transferred to the Crimea to fight in the First Russo-Turkish War during 1768–1774. Badly wounded in the Battle of Alushta in 1774, he lost the sight of his right eye. Promoted to major general, he fought in the Second Russo-Turkish War during 1787–1792 and was again wounded in the Battle of Ochakov on December 17, 1789, but recovered to participate in the capture of Izmail on December 22, 1790.

Kutuzov then held a succession of important administrative posts including ambassador to Constantinople (Istanbul), governor of Finland, ambassador to Prussia, governor of Lithuania, and military governor of St. Petersburg during 1793–1802. Retiring from the military in 1802, he was recalled in 1805 to command the Russian contingent of the allied Russo-Austrian forces in the Third Coalition. He won a delaying battle against the French at Dürrenstein on November 11 but was overruled by Czar Alexander I and forced to order an attack on the French in the Battle of Austerlitz against Napoleon on December 2, 1805, in which the allies were badly defeated. Alexander subsequently relieved Kutuzov from command, making him military governor of Kiev in 1806 and then of Vilnius in 1809. Kutuzov was appointed commander of the Russian army in Moldavia against the Turks in 1811 and destroyed a Turkish army at Rushchuk, bringing the Russian annexation of Bessarabia.

When Napoleon's Grande Armée invaded Russia in June 1812, Kutuzov urged the czar to pull back his armies, drawing Napoleon deep into Russia until such point as the emperor's supply lines were overextended and the Russians could stage an effective counterattack. Reluctantly Alexander followed his advice, appointing Kutuzov to replace General Barclay de Tolly as Russian commander in August. Finally forced to fight to defend Moscow, Kutuzov engaged the French at Borodino on September 7, where he was defeated in one of history's bloodiest battles. Napoleon's reluctance to commit his reserves, however, enabled Kutuzov to withdraw the remainder of his army, and although the French then occupied Moscow, it was a hollow victory.

Kutuzov rebuilt the army, which, in the subsequent French withdrawal in October, decimated the Grande Armée. Kutuzov directed the pursuit of French forces into Poland, where he died of exhaustion at Bunzlau, Silesia (later Boleslawiec, Poland), on April 28, 1813. Cunning and skillful as a strategist, in the closing years of his military career Kutuzov was both indolent and an alcoholic, but he was deeply respected by his men and helped bring about the defeat of Napoleon Bonaparte and the collapse of his empire.

SPENCER C. TUCKER

References

Duffy, Christopher. *Napoleon against Russia, 1812.* London: Sphere, 1972.

Palmer, Alan. *Napoleon in Russia: The 1812 Campaign.* New York: Simon and Schuster, 1967.

Parkinson, Roger. *The Fox of the North: The Life of Kutuzov, the General of War and Peace.* New York: David McKay, 1976.

Lafayette, Marie-Joseph

Birth Date: September 6, 1757
Death Date: May 20, 1834

French nobleman, Continental Army general, French Army general, and French political leader. Born at Chavaniac, Auvergne, France, on September 6, 1757, Marie-Joseph-Paul-Yves-Roch-Gilbert du Motier, Marquis de Lafayette (La Fayette), was a member of one of the greatest noble families of France. His father was killed in the Battle of Minden on August 1, 1759, during the Seven Years' War (1756–1763), and on the death of both his mother and grandfather in 1770, young Lafayette inherited an immense fortune. Lafayette joined a French infantry regiment in April 1771 but transferred to the dragoons in 1773. He married wealthy heiress Anastasie Adrienne de Noailles on April 11, 1774, and shortly thereafter was promoted to captain and transferred to Metz, where he learned of the American Declaration of Independence in the summer of 1776. Inspired by the ideas it expressed and seeking military experience, he secured from American representatives in Paris a commission in the Continental Army.

Lafayette crossed into Spain in April 1777 and there outfitted a ship at his own expense, sailing to America despite the protests of his family and the French court. Arriving in Philadelphia in July, he offered his services without pay and received a commission as a major general. Joining the staff of Continental Army commander General George Washington, the two men became very close, Washington in effect becoming Lafayette's adopted father.

Lafayette distinguished himself and was slightly wounded in the Battle of Brandywine Creek on September 11, 1777. He spent the winter at Valley Forge. He also fought well in the Battle of Barren Hill (May 18, 1778) and the Battle of Monmouth (June 28, 1778), then served as liaison between American and French forces attempting to take Newport, Rhode Island, in July–August. Congress granted Lafayette leave in October 1778 to return to France, where he received a hero's welcome and helped arrange for the French expeditionary force under Lieutenant General Jean Baptiste Donatien de Vimeur, Comte de Rochambeau.

Returning to the United States in April 1780, Lafayette served as a liaison between Washington and Rochambeau. In February 1781 Lafayette took command of the Virginia Light Corps and with it disrupted British brigadier general Benedict Arnold's raids in Virginia and harried the numerically superior British forces there. Lafayette played an important role in the Yorktown Campaign as commander of one of the American divisions.

Returning to France in December 1781, Lafayette received an appointment as major general in the French Army. After a brief trip to the United States during July–December 1784, where he was lionized, he played a leading role in the early period of the French Revolution. A member of the Assembly of Notables in 1787, he also represented Auvergne in the States General in 1789. Appointed commander of the National Guard in July 1789, he helped save the royal family from the mob in October. Promoted to lieutenant general in 1791, he took command of the French Army of the Center in the spring of 1792. Under suspicion from the radical Jacobins who in August overthrew the constitutional monarchy he had helped to create, Lafayette fled France, only to be imprisoned by the Austrians. Released in 1797, he returned to France, living on his wife's estate at La Grange-Bléneau. He supported Napoleon Bonaparte's liberal constitution in 1815 and then helped secure his second abdication. Following the return to France of King Louis XVIII, Lafayette entered the Chamber of Deputies in 1818. He made a farewell tour of the United States in 1824 and played an important role in the July Revolution of 1830 in France against King Charles X, when he again commanded the National Guard and also rallied support for Louis Philippe, Duc d'Orléans, to be king. Later Lafayette denounced Louis Philippe for failing to fulfill his promises. Lafayette died in Paris on May 20, 1834. Intelligent and an effective military commander who was genuinely concerned for his men, Lafayette remained a lifelong advocate of the principles of liberty and self-government espoused by the American Revolution, which he sought in vain to bring to his own country.

SPENCER C. TUCKER

References

Gottschalk, Louis. *Lafayette in America.* Chicago: University of Chicago Press, 1975.

Kramer, Lloyd S. *Lafayette in Two Worlds: Public Cultures and Personal Identities in an Age of Revolutions.* Chapel Hill: University of North Carolina Press, 1999.

Taillemite, Étienne. *La Fayette.* Paris: Fayard, 1989.

Lannes, Jean

Birth Date: April 10, 1769
Death Date: May 31, 1809

Napoleonic marshal. Born in Lectoure, Gascony, on April 10, 1769, Jean Lannes was apprenticed to a dyer before volunteering to serve in the Revolutionary Army at Giers in June 1792. The chaotic circumstances of the French Revolution opened great opportunities for men of talent, making it possible for individuals of talent such as Lannes to rise rapidly from obscurity to prominence. Lannes fought in the Army of the Pyrenees against Spain before transferring to General Napoleon Bonaparte's Army of Italy in 1795. Rising rapidly through the ranks, Lannes was promoted to *général de brigade* in 1796. He distinguished himself in fighting at Dego on April 15, Lodi on May 10, and Bossano on September 8. He was wounded three times in the fighting at Arcole on November 15–17.

Lannes accompanied Napoleon on the Egyptian expedition during 1798–1799, first on his staff and then in command of a division. Lannes was shot in the head and left for dead in the siege of Acre on May 8, 1799, and it took him five months to recover from the wound and the subsequent onset of illness. His leadership at Acre earned him provisional promotion to *général de division.* Lannes was again wounded, in the thigh, in the Second Battle of Aboukir on July 25.

Lannes supported Napoleon's seizure of power in the coup of 18 Brumaire (November 9, 1799) and was rewarded with the post of inspector general of the Consular Guard and then confirmed as *général de division* in May 1800. He performed with great distinction in independent command in the Battle of Montebello on June 9 and at Marengo on June 14.

Dispatched on a diplomatic mission to Portugal in 1802, Lannes proved unsuited for that post and returned to France to assist in preparations for a possible French invasion of England during 1803–1804. Advanced to marshal of the empire in May 1804, he took part in the Ulm campaign in 1805 and fought in Napoleon's great victory over the Austrians and Russians at Austerlitz on December 2, 1805.

Lannes again commanded the French vanguard in the war against Prussia in 1806. His unit was the first to arrive on the field in the Battle of Jena on October 14. He was again wounded in fighting at Pułtusk in December; it took him five months to recover. He took part in the siege of Gdańsk (Danzig) during March 10–May 25, 1807, and then fought in the Battle of Friedland, where he again commanded the center of the French line on June 14, 1807, and distinguished himself against numerically superior Russian forces.

Created Duke of Montebello in 1808, Lannes then served in Spain, where he was victorious in the Battle of Tudelo on November 30. He then took command of the French siege of Saragossa, securing that city's surrender on February 20, 1809. Two months later he was fighting with Napoleon in the Danube campaign against Austria. Seizing a scaling ladder, Lannes personally led hesitating troops in assaulting the walls of Ratisbon, ending in the capture of the city on April 23. He was seriously wounded in the Battle of Aspern-Essling on May 22, 1809, when a spent cannonball smashed both his legs, and his right leg had to be amputated. Pneumonia set in, and Lannes succumbed nine days later on May 31, the first of Napoleon's marshals to die of wounds in battle. An aggressive, capable officer known for his complete loyalty to Napoleon, Lannes was particularly effective on detached service and often commanded the advance guard. Certainly one of the most capable of Napoleon's marshals and a brilliant independent commander, Lannes was known both as the "Roland of the Army" and the "Bravest of the Brave."

SPENCER C. TUCKER

References

Chriswan, Margaret. *The Emperor's Friend: Marshal Jean Lannes.* Westport, CT: Greenwood, 2001.
Horward, Donald D. "'The Roland of the Army': Lannes." In *Napoleon's Marshals,* edited by David G. Chandler, 190–215. New York: Macmillan, 1987.

Lincoln, Abraham

Birth Date: February 12, 1809
Death Date: April 15, 1865

U.S. war president. Born in modest circumstances near Hodgenville, Kentucky, on February 12, 1809, Abraham Lincoln moved with his family to Illinois in 1830. Lincoln was largely self-taught, and his sole military experience came as a volunteer in the Black Hawk War in 1832. Elected a captain, he saw no fighting. Lincoln read for the law and passed the Illinois state bar in 1836, then moved to Springfield in 1847 to practice. He served in the Illinois state legislature during 1834–1840 and was elected to one term in the U.S. House of Representatives during 1847–1849, where he was a critic of the Mexican-American War (1846–1848).

Becoming a highly successful lawyer, Lincoln reentered politics and joined the new Republican Party in 1856. He was his party's candidate for the U.S. Senate from Illinois in 1858. Lincoln engaged in a series of debates with his Democratic opponent Stephen A. Douglas in the summer and autumn. Douglas won the election, but Lincoln's strong stand against slavery made him a national figure. Lincoln won the Republican Party nomination for president in May 1860. His humble birth, reputation for honesty, superb wit, and debating skill were all powerful assets. The Democratic Party split on the issue of slavery gave Lincoln the presidency in November 1860 with a plurality of the popular vote but a majority of the electoral vote.

Lincoln's election led to the secession of the Deep South from the Union and the formation of the Confederate States of America. Southern leaders dreamed of an empire based on Negro slavery to extend down into Mexico, and the Republican Party platform, while not championing abolition where slavery already existed, opposed any extension of slavery in the territories.

Lincoln took office on March 4, 1861, determined to preserve the Union. He delayed taking action for a month until finally forced to undertake the reprovisioning of Fort Sumter in Charleston Harbor, South Carolina. Confederate batteries opened fire to prevent this on April 12, thus beginning the American Civil War (1861–1865).

Lincoln immediately responded with a call for 75,000 volunteers and a naval blockade of the South. Throughout the long war Lincoln played the pivotal role. He had a good grasp of the necessary overall strategy. From the very beginning he established the objective as preserving the Union. Abolition of slavery came a distant second. Lincoln made few military decisions himself and few strategic mistakes. He saw that the main objective must be the destruction of the Confederate armies rather than seizing territory. He also astutely avoided war with Britain over the *Trent* Affair in November–December 1861.

Lincoln did have a problem finding the right military commander. Five different men would command his principal field force, the Army of the Potomac. Lincoln was also to be disappointed in major generals George B. McClellan and Henry Halleck as generals-in-chief. Not until Lieutenant General Ulysses S. Grant took that post in April 1864 did Lincoln have the correct man. With military events finally going the Union's way, Lincoln formulated liberal peace terms for the South to reenter the Union. He also issued the Emancipation Proclamation that abolished slavery in areas still in rebellion on January 1, 1863, and he pushed for passage of the 13th Amendment to abolish slavery altogether (ratified in December 1865 after his death).

Lincoln won reelection in a hard-fought campaign against McClellan, the Democratic Party candidate, in November 1864. General Robert E. Lee surrendered the principal Confederate field army, the Army of Northern Virginia, at Appomattox Court House, Virginia, on April 9, 1865, virtually ending the war. Before Lincoln could carry out his lenient Reconstruction plans, he was shot by the Southern sympathizer and actor John Wilkes Booth at Ford's Theater in Washington, D.C., on April 14, dying the next morning. Lincoln's accomplishments were significant. The Great Communicator, he mobilized the North behind the war and used its far superior resources to achieve military victory. Lincoln was certainly one of the great war leaders in history.

SPENCER C. TUCKER

References

Borrit, Gabor S., ed. *Lincoln the War President: The Gettysburg Lectures.* New York: Oxford University Press, 1992.

Donald, David Herbert. *Lincoln.* New York: Simon and Schuster, 1995.

Oates, Stephen B. *With Malice toward None: The Life of Abraham Lincoln.* New York: Harper and Row, 1977.

MacMahon, Marie Edmé Patrice Maurice de

Birth Date: June 13, 1808
Death Date: October 17, 1893

French general and president of the Third Republic of France. Born on June 13, 1808, in Sully, Department of the Saône-et-Loire, the descendant of Irish Jacobite immigrants to France and the 16th of 17 children, Marie Edmé Patrice Maurice de MacMahon was educated at the College of Louis le Grand and the French Military Academy of St. Cyr. Commissioned on his graduation from the latter in 1827, he was sent to Algiers when the French invaded that North African state in 1830. MacMahon distinguished himself in the capture of the city of Constantine in October 1837, when he was also wounded. He took command of the French Foreign Legion in 1843 and was promoted to general of division in 1852.

MacMahon won distinction during the Crimean War (1853–1856), especially in the storming of the Malakoff Redoubt on September 8, 1855, during the siege of Sevastopol. He then returned to Algeria. During the Italian War of 1859 in which France and the Kingdom of Sardinia (Piedmont-Sardinia) fought Austria, MacMahon commanded II Corps (the Army of Italy). He played a key role in the important French victory in the Battle of Magenta on June 4, 1859, leading Emperor Napoleon III to advance him to marshal and make him duke of Magenta.

Following the war MacMahon again returned to Algeria, where he served as governor-general until the beginning of the Franco-Prussian War, when he received command of the three-corps Army of Alsace on July 31, 1870. Defeated in the Battle of Fröschwiller on August 6, he withdrew his army to Châlons-sur-Marne. MacMahon then led the 120,000-man French Army of the Rhine with Napoleon III in company in an effort to try to relieve Marshal Achille Bazaine's army trapped at Metz, but the Prussians reacted promptly, and their Third Army intercepted MacMahon along the Meuse River on August 29, forcing him to fall back on Sedan. The Prussians brought up additional forces in the new Fourth Army. MacMahon's indecisiveness allowed the Prussians to completely surround his army and lay siege to Sedan on September 1. MacMahon was wounded early in the battle and thus escaped responsibility for its outcome. General Emmanuel de Wimpffen succeeded to the command, and with the French cause soon hopeless, Napoleon III insisted on the opening of talks and surrender on September 2.

Taken prisoner by the Prussians, MacMahon was released in the spring of 1871. He then commanded the government troops that crushed the Commune of Paris on May 21–28. Respected for his soldierly skills and integrity, MacMahon was selected by the royalist Nationalist Assembly of the Third Republic as a caretaker president on the resignation of provisional president Adolphe Thiers on May 24, 1873. The Assembly planned to restore the monarchy but was unable to decide on a successor to the throne. To provide sufficient time to resolve this impasse, the deputies elected MacMahon to a seven-year term. MacMahon became accustomed to the presidency and sought to exercise real power. In the Seize Mai Crisis (May 16) of 1877 he dismissed Premier Jules Simon and appointed his own man, the Orleanist Duc de Broglie, to succeed him. A struggle with the Assembly followed, but after Assembly elections in October went against him, MacMahon, who had actively interjected himself into the campaign, resigned on January 28, 1879. He died in Paris on October 17, 1893. A brave soldier and capable commander of smaller bodies of troops, MacMahon was indecisive and a failure as an army commander. His actions as president brought a weakening of that office, which had detrimental effect on both the Third and Fourth Republics.

Spencer C. Tucker

References

Chapman, Guy. *The Third Republic of France: The First Phase, 1871–1894.* New York: St. Martin's, 1962.

Howard, Michael. *The Franco-Prussian War.* New York: Routledge, 2001.

Wawro, Geoffrey. *The Franco-Prussian War: The German Conquest of France in 1870–1871.* New York: Cambridge University Press, 2003.

Mahan, Alfred Thayer

Birth Date: September 27, 1840
Death Date: December 1, 1914

Prominent naval historian and strategist and staunch proponent of U.S. imperialism. Born at West Point, New York, on September 27, 1840, Alfred Thayer Mahan was the son of West Point professor Dennis Hart Mahan, who initiated the study of military theory in the United States and exerted a profound impact on officers in the Civil War.

The younger Mahan attended Columbia College for two years and then entered the U.S. Naval Academy, Annapolis, graduating second in his class in 1859. He served in the U.S. Brazil Squadron and during the American Civil War (1861–1865) was posted to the South Atlantic Blockading Squadron. He was promoted to lieutenant commander in 1865 and commander in 1872. In 1883 he published *The Gulf and Inland Waters,* a book treating U.S. Navy operations during the war. This impressed Captain Stephen Luce, and in 1885 Luce, president of the newly established Naval War College, invited Mahan to lecture there on naval tactics and history. Mahan was promoted to captain that same year.

In 1890 Mahan published his lectures under the title *The Influence of Sea Power upon History, 1660–1783.* This important book is a history of British naval development in its most crucial period, a treatise on war at sea, and a ringing defense of a large navy. It had particular influence in Britain, Germany, and Japan, but Mahan's lectures and magazine articles on current strategic problems also won an ever-widening audience in the United States with such individuals as Theodore Roosevelt.

Mahan argued that the United States needed a strong navy to compete for the world's trade. He claimed that there was no instance of a great commercial power retaining its leadership without a large navy. He also criticized traditional U.S. single-ship commerce raiding (*guerre de course*), which could not win control of the seas. Mahan argued for a seagoing fleet, an overbearing force that could beat down an enemy's battle line with its strength in battleships operating in squadrons. Mahan believed in the concentration of forces, urging that the fleet be kept in one ocean only. He also called for U.S. naval bases in the Caribbean and in the Pacific. Mahan overlooked new technology, such as the torpedo and the submarine, and he was not concerned about speed in battleships.

Mahan was president of the Naval War College during 1886–1889 and 1889–1893. He commanded the cruiser *Chicago,* flagship of the European Station during 1893–1896, and was publicly feted in Europe and recognized with honorary degrees from Oxford and Cambridge. An important apostle of the new navalism, Mahan retired from the navy in 1896 to devote himself full-time to writing.

Mahan was called back to active duty with the navy in an advisory role during the 1898 Spanish-American War. He was a delegate to the 1899 Hague Peace Conference, and he was promoted to rear admiral on the retired list in 1906. Mahan wrote a dozen books on naval warfare and more than 50 articles in leading journals, and he was elected president of the American Historical Association in 1902. He died in Washington, D.C., on December 1, 1914.

SPENCER C. TUCKER

References

Hughes, Wayne P. *Mahan: Tactics and Principles of Strategy.* Newport, RI: Naval War College, 1990.

Livezey, William E. *Mahan and Sea Power.* Norman: University of Oklahoma Press, 1947.

Mahan, Alfred Thayer. *The Influence of Sea Power upon History, 1660–1783.* Boston: Little, Brown, 1890.

Puleston, William D. *Mahan: The Life and Work of Captain Alfred Thayer Mahan.* New Haven, CT: Yale University Press, 1939.

Quester, George R. *Mahan and American Naval Thought since 1914.* Newport, RI: Naval War College, 1990.

Mahan, Dennis Hart

Birth Date: April 2, 1802
Death Date: September 16, 1871

West Point professor who initiated the study of military theory in the United States and taught many of the generals who commanded on both sides in the American Civil War. Born on April 2, 1802, in New York City of Irish immigrants, Dennis Hart Mahan was a frail boy who wanted to be an artist. He grew up in Norfolk, Virginia.

Mahan sought admission to the United States Military Academy, West Point, because drawing was part of the curriculum. Entering West Point in 1820, he soon attracted Superintendent Sylvanus Thayer's attention as a brilliant student, and from Mahan's second year Thayer made him acting assistant professor of mathematics. Mahan graduated first in his class of 32 in 1824 and was commissioned in the engineers. He remained at the academy to teach, but in 1826 Thayer selected him to go to Europe to study military and civil engineering. Mahan spent much of his time in France, then the world's center for military engineering. There he inspected military fortifications and completed a course in the School of Application for Engineers and Artillery at Metz. When he returned to West Point in 1830, he became acting professor of engineering. Two years later he was professor of civil and military engineering, and in 1838 he became dean of the faculty.

Mahan taught the capstone course in Thayer's curriculum, the fourth-year course in civil and military engineering, known by 1843 as Engineering and the Science of War. This included civil and military architecture, field fortification, and artillery science. Significantly, Mahan insisted that there be added to his professorial title the phrase "and the Art of War." Indeed, he initiated the American branch of the study of military theory.

An exacting professor and most unmilitary figure who refused to wear a uniform, Mahan stressed the necessity of officers acquiring a broad historical and theoretical knowledge of war. Because no textbooks in English were available, Mahan produced his own. His many published books helped establish military engineering in the United States. They included *Complete Treatise on Field Fortification* (1836), *Elementary Course of Civil Engineering* (1837), *Summary of the Course of Permanent Fortification and of the Attack and Defense of Permanent Works* (1850), and *An Elementary Course of Military Engineering* (1867). His most important book was *An Elementary Treatise on Advanced-Guard, Out-Post, and Detachment Service of Troops,* which first appeared in 1847. In addition to its use at West Point, the book was also widely used for militia and volunteer training before the American Civil War. Mahan stressed that war was a science and could therefore be learned. Knowledge of military history was the key. As Mahan recognized, there were exceptions, and "it is in discovering these cases that the talent of the general is shown." Mahan was heavily influenced by French writer Antoine Henri Jomini, an admirer of Napoleon. Both men stressed the Napoleonic principle of fire and maneuver, culminating in one big battle.

A staunch Unionist, Mahan continued as professor of engineering at the United States Military Academy until 1871, when the academic board decided that his advanced age necessitated his retirement. Mahan died shortly thereafter on September 16, 1871.

SPENCER C. TUCKER

References

Ambrose, Stephen E. *Duty, Honor, Country: A History of West Point.* Baltimore: Johns Hopkins University Press, 1966.

Dupuy, R. Ernest. *Men of West Point: The First 150 Years of the United States Military Academy.* New York: Sloane, 1951.

Grant, John, James Lynch, and Ronald Bailey. *West Point: The First 200 Years.* Guilford, CT: Globe Pequot, 2002.

Masséna, André

Birth Date: May 6, 1758
Death Date: April 4, 1817

French marshal. André Masséna was born in Nice on May 6, 1758. Of Italian extraction and the son of a shop-keeper of Italian extraction, his father died when Masséna was six years old, and when his mother remarried, he went to live with relatives. He went to sea as a cabin boy in 1771, and in 1775 he enlisted in the Royal Italian Regiment in the French Army. He rose to sergeant before leaving the army after marrying the daughter of a surgeon in 1789. He then made his living by smuggling. Rejoining the army in 1791, he rose rapidly in rank because of his ability and the pressing need for officers in the Wars of the French Revolution beginning in 1792. Promoted to captain of guides in the French Army of Italy, he subsequently saw service in the Siege of Toulon during September 7–December 19, 1793, and was advanced to general of division that December.

Masséna enjoyed success in the fighting in northern Italy in 1794 and took command of one of the three divisions of the Army of Italy in November 1795. Following his victory at Loano on November 22–24, commander of the Army of Italy General Napoleon Bonaparte gave him command of the center division of the army during the 1796 campaign. Masséna was victorious at Montenotte on April 12 and Dego on April 14. He led the subsequent advance on Turin, played a key role in the French victory at Lodi Bridge on May 10, and subsequently fought with distinction in the Battle of Castiglione (August 5, 1797), the Battle of Bassano (September 8, 1797), and the Battle of Rivoli (January 14–15, 1797). He also played a key role in the subsequent French advance on Vienna during March–April 1797.

In February 1798 Masséna was again in Italy, serving under the overall command of Marshal Louis Alexandre Berthier, but Masséna's troops at Rome mutinied from lack of pay. In November 1798 he commanded a corps under Barthelmy Catherin Joubert in Switzerland, succeeding him in command after the latter's defeat in the Battle of Stockach on March 25, 1799. Defeating an allied assault on Zürich on June 4, Masséna then withdrew to regroup. Taking the offensive, he defeated the Russians in the Second Battle of Zürich on September 26, pursing the Russians northward across the Rhine River.

Following his seizure of power in November 1799, Napoleon ordered Masséna to assume command of what remained of the Army of Italy, and Masséna conducted a brilliant defensive operation there during early April 1800, only to be besieged at Genoa during April 24–June 4, where he was forced to surrender.

Following Masséna's repatriation, he went into retirement. Napoleon named him a marshal of the empire (fifth in seniority) on October 18, 1804, and the next year assigned him command of all French forces in Italy. There Masséna boldly attacked larger Austrian forces commanded by Archduke Charles of Lorraine. Although Masséna was rebuffed at Caldiero near Verona on October 30, he drove the Austrians back into the Julian Alps and then pacified Calabria during July–December 1806.

Created Duke of Rivoli by Napoleon in March 1808, Masséna took command of IV Corps and fought in the campaign against Austria the next year at Abensburg-Eggmühl. He then fought with distinction in the Battle of Aspern-Essling on May 21–22. In the subsequent Battle of Wagram on July 5–6, although he was injured by a fall from a horse and had to direct operations from a carriage, he directed the holding action that allowed Napoleon to carry out a flanking attack that gave Napoleon victory over Archduke Charles.

In January 1810 Napoleon conferred on Masséna the title of Prince of Essling and that April assigned him command of the Army of Portugal. Leading an advance into Portugal from Spain that June, Masséna captured the Ciudad Rodrigo fortress on July 10 and then suffered defeat by Arthur Wellesley, Viscount Wellington, at Buçaco (Bussaco) on September 27. Masséna fought Wellington again at Fuentes de Oñoro on May 3–5, 1811, but was forced to withdraw because of a lack of supplies. Replaced later in May by Marshal Auguste Marmont, Masséna never again held a field command but served as governor of the military district at Toulon. He gave his allegiance to Louis XVIII in March 1815. Masséna reluctantly rallied to Napoleon during the latter's effort to return to power in the Hundred Days during April–June 1815, but poor health forced Masséna to resign. He was retired without pension in January 1816. Masséna died in Paris on April 4, 1817.

A gifted strategist and an energetic field commander, Masséna was among the best of Napoleon's generals. Wellington in particular had a high opinion of Masséna.

SPENCER C. TUCKER

References

Buffery, David. *Wellington against Masséna: The Third Invasion of Portugal, 1810–1811.* London: Pen and Sword, 2007.

Marshall-Cornwall, James. *Marshal Masséna.* London: Oxford University Press, 1965.

Moreau, Jean Victor Marie

Birth Date: February 14, 1763
Death Date: September 2, 1813

French general. Born at Morlaix in Brittany on February 14, 1763, Jean Victor Marie Moreau was the son of a lawyer. He himself studied law at Rennes but left school to join the National Guard on the beginning of the French Revolution in 1789. Raising an artillery company, he became its captain in 1789. Transferring to the infantry, he was elected lieutenant colonel of an infantry regiment in 1791 and saw action with his unit in the Army of the North. Distinguishing himself in the Battle of Neerwinden on March 18, 1793, he was promoted to *général de brigade* in December and to *général de division* on April 14, 1794.

Moreau received command of the Army of the North in March 1795 and then the Army of the Rhine and the Moselle in March 1796. He again distinguished himself in fighting in Germany in 1796. Temporarily suspended from command for suspected Royalist sympathies after the failure of the attempted Royalist coup of 18 Fructidor on September 4, 1797, he was restored to command on September 9. Temporarily in command of the French Army of Italy, he was defeated at Magnano on April 5, 1799, and was succeeded by the new army commander General Barthelemi-Catherine Joubert. Following Joubert's death in the Battle of Novi on August 15, Moreau again commanded the Army of Italy. Returning to Paris on September 21, he was approached by plotters to take Joubert's place as the "sword" for a coup against the Directory. Moreau declined and suggested Napoleon Bonaparte as a more likely candidate for the successful coup of 18 Brumaire on November 9, 1799. Bonaparte became first consul for his role in this event.

Rewarded with command of the Armies of the Rhine and Helvetia (Switzerland), Moreau won a brilliant victory over the Austrians in the Battle of Hohenlinden on December 3, 1800, accomplishing it at less cost than Napoleon's victory at Marengo on June 14, 1800. The victory of Hohenlinden forced the Austrians to sue for peace, which they had rejected after the Battle of Marengo.

Napoleon was undoubtedly jealous of Moreau's military successes and regarded him as a threat to his own reputation. Moreau was implicated, no doubt unjustly, in a Royalist plot to unseat Napoleon in 1804. Moreau was arrested on April 14. Protesting his innocence, he was sentenced to exile for life. He lived in the United States in Morrisville, Pennsylvania, during 1804–1813, returning to Europe to accept a commission from Czar Alexander of Russia in 1813 and serve as military adviser to the czar during the German War of Liberation in 1813. Moreau was mortally wounded in the Battle of Dresden on August 27, reportedly by artillery fire from the Imperial Guard. He died at Lahn on September 2 and was buried in St. Petersburg. Personally brave and well respected by his men, Moreau was a splendid field commander and general who was essentially apolitical. His reputation as a general rivaled that of Napoleon.

SPENCER C. TUCKER

References

Lambin, Émile. *Moreau.* Paris: Le François, 1869.

Phillippart, John. *Memoirs of General Moreau.* Philadelphia: M. Carey, 1816.

Picard, Ernest. *Bonaparte et Moreau.* Paris: Plon-Nourrit, 1905.

Murat, Joachim

Birth Date: March 25, 1767
Death Date: October 13, 1815

Napoleonic marshal and king of Naples. Born in La Bastide-Fortunière (later La Bastide-Murat), Department of Lot, in Gascony, France, on March 25, 1767, Joachim Murat was the son of an innkeeper. Murat gave up studies for the priesthood to join the French Army in February 1787. The Wars of the French Revolution brought him rapid promotion. A noncommissioned officer in April 1792, he gained a commission in October and then advanced to major in the Army of the North in 1793.

Murat first met Napoleon Bonaparte during the unrest of 13 Vendémiaire when he secured the necessary artillery for Napoleon's "whiff of grapeshot" that put down the Royalist insurrection against the Directory on October 5, 1795. Murat then joined Napoleon's staff and campaigned with him in Italy during 1796–1797, being promoted to *général de brigade* in May 1796 and receiving command of a cavalry brigade under General Michel Ney, which Murat led most effectively.

Accompanying Napoleon on the Egyptian campaign, Murat fought in the Battle of the Pyramids (First Battle of Aboukir) on July 25, 1798, where he was wounded in the jaw while leading an attack. For his important role in the battle, he was advanced to *général de division* in August. Returning to France with Napoleon, Murat played an important role in the latter's coup d'état on November 9–10, 1799. Appointed commander of the Consular Guard in January 1800, Murat married Caroline Bonaparte, sister of Napoleon, on January 18, 1800.

Murat participated in virtually all of Napoleon's subsequent campaigns as cavalry commander and served with distinction in the Battle of Marengo on June 14, 1800. Dispatched by Napoleon to Italy as commander of the French Army of Italy, Murat wrested the Papal States from Naples and imposed terms on the Neapolitans in February 1801. Made governor of Paris in January 1804, he was part of the tribunal that tried and ordered the execution of the Duc d'Enghien.

Murat was appointed *maréchal de l'empire* (second in seniority) in May 1804. He became governor-general of Paris in July 1804 and was also named grand admiral with the title of prince in February 1805. He screened the French advance, leading to the Austrian capitulation at Ulm on October 17, 1805, but angered Napoleon by breaking off the pursuit of Austro-Russian forces to occupy Vienna, where Murat and Marshal Jean Lannes bluffed the Austrians into believing that an armistice had been signed, preventing the destruction of the Danube bridge. Murat accepted the armistice of Hollabrunn on November 15, 1805, and in the Battle of Austerlitz on December 2, 1805, led a celebrated charge. Napoleon rewarded him by creating him Grand Duke of Cleve and Berg.

Murat fought with distinction against the Prussians in the Battle of Jena on October 14, 1806, and then captured Erfurt and Prenzlau and forced the Prussian surrender at Lübeck on November 7. After occupying Warsaw, he fought in the Battle of Eylau against the Russians on February 7–8, 1807, where his perhaps epic cavalry charge of some 5,000 men, one of the largest of the era, plugged a gaping hole in the center of the French line and preserved Napoleon's army from destruction. Murat then directed the successful siege of Königsberg (Kaliningrad) on June 11–16.

Appointed to command in Spain as imperial lieutenant in February 1808, Murat brutally crushed the insurrection in Madrid against the French (El Dos de Mayo) on May 2, 1808. Napoleon then sent him to Italy and made him king of Naples on August 1. Murat's effort to conquer Sicily in 1809 failed against British opposition.

Murat took part in Napoleon's 1812 campaign in Russia, commanding the advance guard. Among other battles, Murat fought at Smolensk on August 17–19 and Borodino on September 7, where he tried and failed to convince the emperor to commit the Imperial Guard and win decisive victory. Promoted to lieutenant general of the Grande Armée, Murat took charge of the French withdrawal from Russia on Napoleon's departure on December 5 but then relinquished the command to Eugène de Beauharnais to depart for Italy in an effort to retain his kingdom there.

Murat entered into negotiations with the Austrians and the British in Sicily, but unable to secure what he thought was sufficient reward, he returned to fight with Napoleon in Germany in the Battle of Dresden (August 26–27, 1813) and the Battle of Leipzig (October 16–19). Murat then departed for Italy and reopened negotiations with the Austrians and the British, reaching agreement on January 26, 1814, to provide 30,000 men against France. Following Napoleon's abdication in April, Murat found that the allies did not trust him, and he rallied to Napoleon on the latter's return from Elba in 1815, seeking to drive Austria from Italy. After early success, Murat was defeated at Tolentino on May 2, 1815, and fled to France on May 21. When Napoleon refused to receive him and the British also refused a request for asylum, Murat arrived in Corsica on August 24. There he organized a small force in an effort to regain his kingdom. Defeated at Pizzo in Calabria on October 7, he was arrested, tried, and executed by a firing squad at Pizzo in Calabria on October 13, 1815. Brave to the end, he himself gave the firing order: "Aim for the heart; spare the face!" Although a failure in independent command and seemingly incapable of correct judgment, Murat was an exceptional subordinate and one of history's most brilliant cavalry commanders. He played a key role in Napoleon's battlefield successes.

SPENCER C. TUCKER

References

Atteridge, A. H. *Marshal Murat, King of Naples.* Uckfield, UK: Naval and Military Press, 2006.

Cole, Hubert. *The Betrayers: Joachim & Caroline Murat; A Dual Biography of Napoleon's Sister and Her Husband.* New York: Saturday Review Press, 1972.

Pickles, Tirn. "Prince Joachim Murat." In *Napoleon's Marshals,* edited by David Chandler, 332–356. New York: Macmillan, 1987.

Nelson, Horatio

Birth Date: September 19, 1758
Death Date: October 21, 1805

British admiral. Born the son of a clergyman at Burnham Thorpe in Norfolk on September 19, 1758, Horatio Nelson went to sea at age 12 with his maternal uncle Captain Maurice Suckling, who ensured that his nephew had varied training including service as an ordinary sailor in a merchant ship and on an expedition to the Arctic during 1771–1774. Partly because of his uncle's influence and partly from his own transparent merit, Nelson rose swiftly in his profession and became a post captain at the early age of 20. During the American Revolutionary War (1775–1783) he saw much active service, mainly in the West Indies.

After five unhappy years ashore following a peacetime commission in the West Indies, on the outbreak of the war with Revolutionary France in 1793 Nelson was appointed to command the ship of the line *Agamemnon.* He participated in the capture of Corsica in 1794, landing with men and guns to assist with the siege and capture of two key ports; he lost the sight of his right eye in the process.

Nelson commanded a detached squadron off the coast of Italy as a commodore in 1796, hampering the advance of the victorious French armies under the brilliant young general Napoleon Bonaparte. Fame came at last to Nelson when he played a decisive role in the British victory over the Spanish fleet in the Battle of Cape St. Vincent on February 14, 1797, blocking the escape of part of the Spanish fleet and capturing two ships. Promoted to rear admiral and knighted, five months later he suffered a serious setback on July 24 when, ordered to attack the Spanish town of Santa Cruz in Tenerife, one of the Canary Islands, he was repulsed with heavy losses and lost his right arm.

Nelson returned to active service after only a few months' convalescence and received command of a detached squadron in the Mediterranean. He led it to a stunning victory over the French fleet in the Battle of the Nile on August 1, 1798, in which his prebattle planning was crucial. Showered with praise and rewards including a peerage from Britain, he let the adulation go to his head and became embroiled in an ugly civil war in Naples, one of Britain's few remaining allies in the Mediterranean. He also fell very publicly in love with Emma, Lady Hamilton, wife of the British ambassador.

Recalled home in near disgrace in 1800, Nelson was promoted to vice admiral in January 1801 and was sent back to sea again as second-in-command of a special fleet assembled to challenge the Armed Neutrality of the North, which was threatening Britain's trade interests in the Baltic. In the ensuing Battle of Copenhagen on April 2, 1801, he again showed his leadership qualities, winning a very hard-fought victory against a determined and gallant foe.

Nelson's passionate love affair with Emma Hamilton continued, and when she bore him a daughter he left his wife and set up home with Emma and her husband during the brief period of peace following the Treaty of Amiens in March 1802. When war began again in May 1803 Nelson received command in the Mediterranean over the heads of more senior admirals.

In this challenging post Nelson showed that he was far more than just a fighting admiral. He maintained his fleet at sea off the French port of Toulon for nearly two years during June 1803–April 1805 without once going into port, and he patiently trained his men, keeping them healthy and amused. When Admiral Pierre Jean Pierre Baptiste Silvestre, Comte de Villeneuve, and the French fleet escaped from Toulon in April 1805 and sailed to the West Indies, Nelson pursued relentlessly and drove them back into European waters. After a brief spell of leave with Emma and their daughter Horatia, he returned to take command of the British fleet off Cádiz and led it to a decisive victory over the combined French and Spanish fleets in the Battle of Trafalgar on October 21, 1805. At the height of the action he was struck down by a musket ball while pacing the quarterdeck of his flagship, *Victory.* Carried below, he died about three hours later. His death was extravagantly mourned both in his own fleet and at home in England, where his body was given a lavish state funeral and buried in St. Paul's Cathedral, London. An affectionate man with an endearing, almost boyish, enthusiasm, Nelson was loved by most of those who served with him. Although physically nondescript, he exuded energy and charisma and inspired his followers with his own extraordinary physical courage. But his administrative ability and his capacity for making meticulous plans were also important components of his success, as was his lifelong experience as a practical seaman. Nelson was traditionally portrayed as an isolated genius, and it is now recognized that he was in fact a member of one of the most gifted generations of officers that the Royal Navy has ever produced. Nonetheless, he still stood out then, and two centuries after his death he continues to fascinate and inspire.

COLIN WHITE

References
Bennett, Geoffrey. *Nelson, the Commander.* London: Batsford, 1972.
Oman, Carola. *Nelson.* London: Hodder and Stoughton, 1947.
Pocock, Tom. *Horatio Nelson.* London: Bodley Head, 1987.
White, Colin, ed. *The Nelson Companion.* Gloucester, UK: Suttons, 1995.

Ney, Michel

Birth Date: January 10, 1769
Death Date: December 7, 1815

Napoleonic marshal. Born on January 10, 1769, at Saarlouis in Alsace, France, Michel Ney was the son of a cooper. He enlisted in the 5th Hussars in February 1787, became a fine horsemen and fencer, and was extraordinarily brave in battle. The Wars of the French Revolution gave him the opportunity to advance in rank commensurate with his abilities. He was promoted to regimental sergeant major in April 1792 and then was commissioned as a sublieutenant in October. Ney fought at Jemappes on November 6, 1792. He became a captain in April 1794 and was wounded in the shoulder in the Siege of Maastricht on December 22.

Reports of Ney's great bravery led the Directory to promote him to *général de brigade* in August 1796. He won the Battle of Kirchberg on April 19, 1797, but was taken prisoner by the Austrians at Giessen on April 21, 1797. Soon released in a prisoner exchange, he was promoted to *général de division* in March 1799. In the campaign against the Russians in Switzerland while leading cavalry, Ney was wounded three times in the Battle of Winterthur on May 27. Transferred to the Rhine front against the Austrians, he distinguished himself in General Jean Moreau's brilliant victory at Hohenlinden on December 3, 1800. Napoleon Bonaparte then entrusted Ney with the post of inspector general of all French cavalry in January 1801. Napoleon then sent Ney as military commander and political representative to repair French relations with Switzerland in 1802.

In 1803 Napoleon gave Ney command of VI Corps, which he trained effectively in preparation for Napoleon's threatened invasion of England. Appointed a *maréchal de l'empire* in May 1804, in the subsequent war against Austria Ney commanded VI Corps and personally led a cavalry charge on October 14, 1805, to win at Elchingen, which led to the Austrian surrender at Ulm. He then captured Innsbruck in November.

During the war against Prussia, Ney again commanded VI Corps in the French victory in the Battle of Jena on October 14, 1806. He then captured the Prussian fortress of Magdeburg on November 8. In fighting against Russia he continued in command of VI Corps in the Battle of Eylau (February 8, 1807) and the Battle of Friedland (June 14, 1807).

Napoleon created Ney the Duc d'Elchingen in June 1808 and then ordered him to join the French Army of Spain in August. Ney and his VI Corps were then sent to join the French Army of Portugal in April 1810. Ney captured Ciudad Rodrigo on July 10, but his corps suffered heavy casualties at Busaco on September 27. Later in the campaign, Marshal André Masséna dismissed Ney for insubordination on March 23, 1811.

Ney returned to France to command the camp of Boulogne. He commanded III Corps in the invasion of Russia, fighting at Smolensk on August 17, where he was wounded. He fought with distinction in the great Battle of Borodino outside Moscow on September 7, 1812, urging Napoleon, in vain, to commit the Imperial Guard and score a decisive victory. Given command of the rear guard in the retreat from Moscow on November 3, Ney performed brilliantly, undoubtedly saving the lives of thousands of French soldiers, for which Napoleon called him "Bravest of the Brave" and created Ney the Prince of Moscow on March 28, 1813.

In 1813 during the War of German Liberation, Ney commanded III Corps in the Battle of Lützen on May 2 and the French left at Bautzen on May 20–21, but his delay and lack of cavalry prevented him from trapping the Prussians there. Severely wounded on October 18 during the Battle of Leipzig (October 16–19), Ney returned to France.

Ney led the group of marshals at Fontainebleau who demanded that Napoleon abdicate on April 4, 1814. Given command of the French cavalry by King Louis XVIII on May 20, 1814, on Napoleon's escape from Elba the king entrusted Ney with troops sent to arrest Napoleon. Ney vowed that he would bring the former emperor back to Paris in "an iron cage," but when his troops deserted en masse to Napoleon at Auxerre, Ney did likewise on March 12, 1815. During the Hundred Days, Ney fought at Quatre Bras on June 16 and at Waterloo on June 18, where he led the final charge of the Old Guard. Unable to get himself killed at Waterloo, he was subsequently caught in the provinces on August 3 and brought to Paris. Tried by the Court of Peers, he was found guilty and shot by a firing squad near the Luxembourg Gardens in Paris on December 7, 1815, being given the right to issue the order to fire. Known for his great courage and fiery temper, Ney was an effective trainer and led by example. He was not well suited to high independent command, however.

SPENCER C. TUCKER

References

Atteridge, A. H. *Marshal Ney: The Bravest of the Brave.* Uckfield, UK: Military and Naval Press, 2001.

Horricks, Raymond. *Marshal Ney: The Romance and the Real.* London: Archway, 1988.

Young, Peter. "The Bravest of the Brave—Ney." In *Napoleon's Marshals,* edited by David Chandler, 358–380. New York: Macmillan, 1987.

Perry, Matthew Calbraith

Birth Date: April 10, 1794
Death Date: March 4, 1858

U.S. Navy officer and diplomat. Born in South Kingston, Rhode Island, on April 10, 1794, Matthew Calbraith Perry was the son of American Revolutionary War and Quasi-War captain Christopher R. Perry. Matthew followed his older brother, Oliver Hazard Perry, to sea, securing a midshipman's warrant in January 1809. Matthew sailed with his older brother in the schooner *Revenge* during 1809–1811 and then served in the frigate *President* under Commodore John Rodgers in 1811–1812 during the engagement with HMS *Little Belt* on May 17, 1811, and early in the War of 1812 and then was transferred to the frigate *United States* under Commodore Stephen Decatur during 1813–1815. Perry was promoted to lieutenant in July 1813 but spent the balance of the conflict blockaded at New London, Connecticut. After the war he commanded the brig *Chippewa* in Commodore William Bainbridge's squadron during the brief naval war with Algiers in 1815.

During the next 30 years Perry fulfilled numerous and far-ranging naval and diplomatic activities. He was promoted to commander in March 1826 and captain in February 1837. Perry hunted slave ships off the African coast in the corvette *Cyane* during 1819–1820, then chased down pirates in the West Indies. He later commanded the schooner *Shark* during 1821–1824 and assisted in the founding of Liberia. He was the first lieutenant in the ship of the line *North Carolina* in the Mediterranean Squadron during 1824–1828 and then commanded the Boston Navy Yard. He commanded the sloop *Concord* during 1830–1833 and then the Brooklyn Navy Yard during 1833–1842, where he established his reputation as a naval reformer. Perry was active in the education movement for seamen. He also established the first U.S. naval testing laboratory. Perry also outfitted the U.S. Exploring Expedition led by Charles Wilkes. However, Perry's biggest contribution to the service was his forceful advocacy of steam power. He helped design the steamer *Fulton II* in 1837 and then commanded it during 1838–1840. He subsequently supervised construction of the steam frigates *Mississippi* in 1841 and *Missouri* in 1842. Perry then took command of the African Squadron, where he had a conspicuous role in suppressing the slave trade during 1843–1845.

Perry's only command experience in war came during the Mexican-American War of 1846–1848. Originally posted to Commodore David Conner's Gulf Squadron as second-in-command, Perry captained the frigate *Mississippi.* He then captured the port of Frontera, demonstrated against Tabasco, and participated in the Tampico expedition. Perry then returned in the *Mississippi* to the Norfolk Navy Yard for repairs and thus missed the actual Veracruz landing on March 9, 1847, but returned with orders relieving Conner of command of the squadron on March 20. Perry then supported the siege of Veracruz on March 22–29 and operated up the Tuxpan River on April 18–22 and the Tabasco River on June 14–22, where he was the first ashore and led a land operation against Tabasco on June 16. After the war he was general superintendent of mail steamers during 1848–1852.

Having wrested the Pacific coast from Mexico, the United States looked for markets in Asia. A major stumbling block was Japan, which had sealed itself off from the outside world for nearly two and a half centuries. President Millard Fillmore authorized Perry to open diplomatic relations with that country, and Perry's squadron of four so-called Black Ships arrived at Japan on July 8, 1853. Perry parleyed with reluctant local officials and promised to return the following year. When he did so with an even larger force in February 1854, the Tokugawa shogunate reluctantly signed the Treaty of Kanagawa on March 31, 1854, which established an American consulate and opened two ports. However, that government's inability to control the influx of foreigners into Japan contributed to its overthrow by the Meiji emperor in 1868.

Perry returned to the United States in January 1855 and concluded his seafaring career. After several years with the Naval Efficiency Board and having prepared his three-volume *Narrative of the Expedition of an American Squadron to the China Seas and Japan,* he died in New York City on March 4, 1858. Known as "Old Bruin," Perry was one of the most important officers in the history of the U.S. Navy.

JOHN C. FREDRIKSEN AND SPENCER C. TUCKER

References

Barrows, Edward M. *The Great Commodore: The Exploits of Matthew Calbraith Perry.* Indianapolis: Bobbs-Merrill, 1935.

Morison, Samuel E. *"Old Bruin": Commodore Matthew C. Perry, 1794–1858.* Boston: Little, Brown, 1967.

Pineau, Roger, ed. *The Japan Expedition, 1852–1854: The Personal Journal of Commodore Matthew C. Perry.* Washington, DC: Smithsonian Institution Press, 1968.

Schroeder, John. *Matthew Calbraith Perry: Antebellum Sailor and Diplomat.* Annapolis, MD: Naval Institute Press, 2001.

Perry, Oliver Hazard

Birth Date: August 2, 1785
Death Date: August 23, 1819

U.S. naval officer. Born in South Kingston, Rhode Island, on August 2, 1785, Oliver Hazard Perry joined the navy as a midshipman in 1799 and sailed under his father, Captain Christopher R. Perry, in the frigate *General Greene* during the Quasi-War with France in 1798–1800. A capable sailor who learned his profession well, the younger Perry served during 1802–1803 with Commodore John Rodgers in the Mediterranean during the 1801–1805 war with Tripoli. Perry then commanded the schooner *Nautilus* (12 guns) during 1804–1806 at only age 20. He spent four years supervising gunboat construction at Newport, Rhode Island. He was promoted to lieutenant in 1807, and his next sea command was the schooner *Revenge,* which was lost when it struck a reef in fog while surveying Newport Harbor on February 2, 1811. Perry was suspended from duty but then cleared by a court of inquiry.

When the War of 1812 began in June 1812, Perry was in command of the gunboat flotilla at Newport but petitioned the Navy Department for a more important command. Advanced to commander in August, he was transferred to Lake Ontario under Commodore Isaac Chauncey in the spring of 1813. Shortly thereafter, Chauncey ordered Perry to Presque Isle (Erie), Pennsylvania, with orders to construct a fleet on Lake Erie. Throughout the spring and summer, Perry accomplished exactly that task despite the remoteness of his station. He alienated his second-in-command, Jesse Duncan Elliott, who had been in charge prior to Perry's arrival and apparently resented the intrusion. As Perry's fleet neared completion, he consulted closely with Major General William Henry Harrison, commander of U.S. western forces. Control of Lake Erie would be essential to American reconquest of the frontier.

The long-anticipated Battle of Lake Erie occurred when Perry's fleet fell in with a British squadron under Captain Robert H. Barclay on September 10, 1813. During the initial phases of the battle, Perry impetuously allowed his flagship, the brig *Lawrence,* to outdistance the fleet and engage the entire British force alone. Elliott, with the second brig, *Niagara,* remained in the distance and offered no support. At length the *Lawrence* was forced to strike, but not before Perry transferred his flag to the *Niagara* and led it into the fray. This new infusion of firepower forced the entire British squadron to capitulate. His report to the secretary of the navy became famous: "We have met the enemy and they are ours. Two ships, two brigs, one schooner, one sloop." The battle secured control of Lake Erie for the United States and made Perry a national hero. He then transported Harrison's army into Canada where it won the Battle of the Thames, with Perry serving ashore and leading a charge on October 5. Voted the thanks of Congress and promoted to captain in January 1814, Perry took part in efforts to harass the British as they withdrew down the Potomac River following their attack on Washington.

After the war Perry supervised the fitting out of the frigate *Java* and then commanded it in the Mediterranean during 1816–1817. During the cruise he struck Captain John Heath, commander of marines on the frigate. Perry reported the action immediately. A court of inquiry censured Heath and reprimanded Perry. Heath demanded satisfaction, and the two fought a duel on October 19, 1818. However, Perry refused to fire, and Heath missed. Continuing friction with Elliott resulted in a challenge from that officer as well, but Perry refused a duel and instead pressed charges against him in August 1818. For political reasons, no trial was ever held, but the affair poisoned the officer corps for years thereafter.

In 1819 Perry commanded the corvette *John Adams* on a successful diplomatic mission to Venezuela. Perry died of yellow fever at the mouth of the Orinoco River during the return trip on August 23, 1819. He was a capable, resourceful, and brave officer who won one of the most decisive battles in U.S. naval history, and his death at only age 34 cut short a promising career.

JOHN C. FREDRIKSEN AND SPENCER C. TUCKER

References

Dillon, Richard. *We Have Met the Enemy: Oliver Hazard Perry, Wilderness Commodore.* New York: McGraw-Hill, 1978.

Mahon, John K. "Oliver Hazard Perry: Savior of the Northwest." In *Command under Sail: Makers of the American Naval Tradition, 1775–1840,* edited by James C. Bradford, 126–146. Annapolis, MD: Naval Institute Press, 1985.

Skaggs, David C., and Gerald T. Altoff. *A Signal Victory: The Lake Erie Campaign, 1812–1813.* Annapolis, MD: Naval Institute Press, 1997.

Porter, David

Birth Date: February 1, 1780
Death Date: March 3, 1843

U.S. Navy officer. Born in Boston, Massachusetts, on February 1, 1780, into a maritime family (his father commanded sloops during the American Revolutionary War), David Porter went to sea with his father to the West Indies in 1796. On a later voyage he was impressed by the Royal Navy but managed to escape. Porter entered the U.S. Navy as a midshipman in January 1798 aboard the frigate *Constellation* commanded by Captain Thomas Truxtun, who befriended Porter and was a role model. Porter first earned recognition during the Quasi-War with France (1798–1800) during the battle between the *Constellation* and the French frigate *l'Insurgent,* which ended in the capture of the latter on February 9, 1799. Porter took command of the prize ship. He was then promoted to lieutenant in October.

Ordered to sail the schooner *Enterprise* to the Mediterranean, Porter won praise for his handling of the ship. During the Tripolitan War of 1801–1805 he was first assigned to the frigate *New York* and then served on the frigate *Philadelphia.* He was aboard the latter ship when it ran aground off Tripoli and was captured on October 31, 1803. Porter remained a prisoner until the end of the war. After his release he was promoted to master commandant (commander) in April 1806. He was then captain of the frigate *Constitution* and later the *Enterprise* before returning to the United States to oversee the New Orleans Naval Station during 1808–1810.

Porter then took command of the frigate *Essex* (32 guns) in July 1811 and was promoted to captain in July 1812. During the War of 1812 (1812–1815) he raided British commerce in the South Atlantic, taking nine prizes including the sloop of war *Alert* (16 guns) on August 13, 1812, the first British warship taken in the conflict. After a brief return to Philadelphia with his prizes, Porter sailed again in October, making the first voyage by a U.S. Navy ship around Cape Horn and largely destroying the British whaling fleet in the Galapagos Islands. While in the Pacific he also claimed the Marquesas Islands on November 19, 1813, although the U.S. government refused to recognize this action.

The *Essex* was off Valparaiso, Chile, on March 28, 1814, when it engaged and was defeated by the British frigate *Phoebe* (36 guns) and sloop *Cherub* (20 guns). Porter was handicapped by the fact that while his ship had 46 guns, 40 of these were short-range carronades, while the British ships were armed primarily with long guns. The *Phoebe* alone mounted 30 long guns able to fire beyond the ability of the *Essex* to respond. In the battle the *Essex* suffered 60 percent casualties before Porter struck.

Following the war Porter served as a member of the new Board of Naval Commissioners until 1822, when he assumed command of the West India Squadron charged with suppressing Caribbean piracy. While he was generally successful, Commodore Porter's inflated sense of honor led to a court of inquiry in 1824 for his invasion of Fajardo, Puerto Rico, after the Spanish governor there had insulted one of his officers. The court found him guilty, but the sentence was light: six-months' suspension from duty. Porter nonetheless believed that he had been betrayed and resigned his commission.

Porter accepted command of the Mexican Navy during 1826–1829. President Andrew Jackson then appointed him consul to Algiers in 1830, then chargé d'affaires and minister to the Ottoman Empire in 1831. Porter died in Istanbul (Constantinople) on March 3, 1843. His body was returned to the United States to be buried in Philadelphia. Porter's son, David Dixon Porter, and his foster son, David G. Farragut, both became admirals during the American Civil War.

SPENCER C. TUCKER

References

Long, David F. *Nothing Too Daring: A Biography of Commodore David Porter.* Annapolis, MD: Naval Institute Press, 1970.

Turnbull, Archibald Douglas. *Commodore David Porter, 1780–1843.* New York: Century, 1929.

Radetzky, Josef

Birth Date: November 2, 1766
Death Date: January 5, 1858

Austrian general and chief of the general staff. Born into a noble family in Trebnice, south of Prague in Bohemia, on November 2, 1766, Josef Wenceslas Radetzky enlisted in the Austrian Army as a cadet in 1784 and was commissioned a lieutenant in 1787. He first saw action and distinguished himself by his courage under fire in war with Turkey during 1788–1792. Radetzky then fought in the French Revolution and the Napoleonic Wars beginning in 1792. He led a cavalry charge in the Battle of Fleurus in the Austrian Netherlands on June 26, 1794. Promoted to captain, he was then a staff officer during Austrian fighting against General Napoleon Bonaparte's French Army of Italy in 1796.

During the War of the Second Coalition, Radetzky was a colonel. He saw action in the battles at Trebbia on June 19, 1799; Novi on August 15; Marengo, where he was wounded, on June 14, 1800; and Hohenlinden on December 3. Promoted to major general in 1805, he served under Archduke Charles in Italy. With the renewal of war between Austria and France in 1809, Radetzky saw action at Aspern-Essling on May 21–22, and he commanded the Austrian rear guard in the Battle of Wagram on July 5–6. For his services he was promoted to field marshal lieutenant and was made chief of the General Staff in 1809.

Although Radetzky accomplished a great deal as chief of the General Staff during 1809–1812—including the establishment of training schools, more thorough training, and the organization of militia—many other reforms failed because of conservative opposition and lack of funding. Still, his reforms meant that Austria was able to field against Napoleon a force of 200,000 men to be commanded by Field Marshal Karl zu Schwarzenberg, for whom Radetzky served as chief of staff in 1813. Radetzky fully supported the Trachtenberg Plan whereby the allied commanders would seek to avoid direct battle with Napoleon himself while concentrating on attacks against his lines of communication and isolated smaller detached French units. Radetzky helped plan the campaign that saw Napoleon defeated at Leipzig on October 16–19 and the French expelled from Germany.

Following the defeat of Napoleon, Radetzky was one of the Austrian representatives to the Congress of Vienna during 1814–1815. He then held a number of minor posts and wrote. Semiretired, he was advanced to general of cavalry in 1829. Recalled to troop command, he put down the revolutions against Austrian control in Lombardy and Venetia. Promoted to full field marshal in 1836, he was again called upon during the Revolutions of 1848. Following five days of fighting in Milan on March 18–23, Radetzky withdrew his troops from the city back into the easily defended Quadrilateral (fortresses at Legnano, Mantua, Presciera, and Verona). Both Lombardy and Venetia temporarily freed themselves from Austrian control, but Radetzky, once reinforced, led Austrian forces in the defeat of the Kingdom of Piedmont-Sardinia at Custozza on July 24–25, 1848. He recaptured Milan, invaded Piedmont, and defeated, this time decisively, the army of King Charles Albert of Piedmont-Sardinia in the Battle of Novara on March 23, 1849, forcing the latter's abdication.

As Austrian governor of Lombardy-Venetia during 1850–1857, Radetzky did all he could to repress Italian nationalism. He died on January 5, 1858. Intelligent, brave, and imaginative, Radetzky was a highly effective commander of troops and was well respected by his men, who called him "Father Radetzky." Although he carried out a number of military reforms, he was prevented from realizing others. His successes late in his career delayed the disintegration of the Austrian Empire.

SPENCER C. TUCKER

References

Regele, Oskar. *Feldmarschall Radetzky: Leben, Leistung, Erbe.* Wien, Germany: Herald, 1957.
Rothenberg, Gunther E. *The Army of Francis Joseph.* Lafayette, IN: Purdue University Press, 1976.
Sked, Alan. *The Decline and Fall of the Hapsburg Empire, 1815–1918.* New York: Longman, 2001.

San Martín, José Francisco de

Birth Date: February 25, 1778
Death Date: August 17, 1850

South American independence leader. Born at Yopayú in the viceroyalty of Río de la Plata (northeastern Argentina) on February 25, 1778, José Francisco de San Martín was the son of a Spanish Army officer. He returned to Spain with his family in 1785 and there joined the Spanish Army in 1790. He served in the army for more than 20 years, distinguishing himself in fighting against the French during the Peninsular War and attaining the rank of lieutenant colonel.

Despite his long service in the Spanish Army, San Martín believed that Spain's Latin American colonies should be independent. Learning of the independence movements there, he resigned his commission in 1812 and joined those supporting a war for Latin American independence. He arrived in Buenos Aires in March 1812 and associated himself with the revolutionary government. His previous military experience secured him command of a mounted unit. In December 1813 he became a commander in the revolutionary army in northern Argentina.

Latin American revolutionary leaders believed that their success depended on securing Peru, a center of loyalist support. The Royalists there had already defeated three Argentinean invasions of upper Peru (later Bolivia). San Martín now planned a cross-Andean invasion to liberate Chile, which could then be used as a base for a seaborne invasion of Peru.

San Martín resigned from the revolutionary army in January 1817 and was appointed governor of Cuyo Province in western Argentina at the base of the Andes. Establishing a base at Mendoza, he conferred with Chilean exiles and built a military force of Argentineans, Chileans, and slaves who had been promised freedom on exchange for their military service.

San Martín's Army of the Andres, numbering 2,500 infantry, 700 cavalry, and 21 guns, then departed Mendoza and made its way north through the Andes passes into Chile during January 24–February 8, 1817, catching Spanish forces there completely by surprise. Defeating a small Spanish force in the Battle of Chacabuco on February 12–13, 1817, San Martín's army occupied Santiago on February 15. San Martín then named his friend and ally Bernardo O'Higgins to direct political affairs in Chile. On the arrival of a large Spanish force from Peru under General Mariano Osorio in early 1818, San Martín engaged Osorio and was narrowly defeated by him in the Battle of Cancha-Rayada on March 16. San Martín then struck back and this time routed Osorio in the Battle of Maipo on April 5, securing Chilean independence. Chilean leaders then offered San Martín the position of supreme ruler of Chile, but he declined in order to continue the war against the Spanish in Peru.

For 18 months San Martín carefully prepared an invasion force for Peru. Now actively supported by the Chilean and Argentinean governments and with a flotilla of ships commanded by Englishman Thomas Cochrane, Earl of Dundonald, to transport his men, San Martín set out for Peru with 4,500 men by sea in August 1820. He landed about 100 miles south of Lima, but because the Spanish forces in Peru were larger than his own, he refused to accept battle unless it was on favorable terms, hoping that his presence would spark popular uprisings. In the meantime, he planned to whittle down the Spanish through guerrilla warfare. Indeed, the Spanish soon evacuated Lima in June 1821. Entering Lima, San Martín declared Peruvian independence on July 21, 1821.

Peruvians were sharply divided politically, and San Martín was forced to take power as protector of Peru. He instituted policies that angered the rich, including the imposition of taxes, an end to Indian tribute, and freedom for children of slaves. Threatened by unrest and the continued presence in Peru of the larger Spanish force, San Martín met with fellow Latin American revolutionary leader Simón Bolívar at Guayaquil on July 26–27, 1822. Although there is some disagreement on this (and no record of the meeting was kept), it appears that San Martín agreed to hand over the liberation of Peru to Bolívar. Returning to Lima, San Martín resigned in September 1822 and departed for Argentina. He then began a self-imposed European exile, dying in Boulogne-sur-Mer, France, on August 17, 1850. Idealistic, selfless, and a sincere patriot and capable military leader, San Martín supported constitutional monarchies for Latin America (Bolívar favored independent republics).

SPENCER C. TUCKER

References

Lynch, John. *The Spanish American Revolutions, 1808–1826.* New York: Norton, 1986.
Rojas, Richard. *San Martín: Knight of the Andes.* New York: Doubleday, 1945.

Scharnhorst, Gerhard Johann David

Birth Date: November 12, 1755
Death Date: June 8, 1813

Prussian general and military reformer. Born at Bordenau, Lippe, near Hannover on November 12, 1755, Gerhard Johann David Scharnhorst was the son of a small landowner. He joined the Hannoverian Army in 1778, then served as an artillery instructor and helped to write an officers' handbook and a field manual. In the War of the First Coalition (1793–1795) during the Wars of the French Revolution, he saw action in several battles in Flanders. He was then quartermaster general during 1796–1801 and also published several studies, including one on the factors behind French military success.

Scharnhorst, now widely respected, joined the Prussian Army as a lieutenant colonel and was ennobled in 1801. He was then an instructor at the Prussian War College in Berlin during 1801–1804 and also tutor to the crown prince during 1802–1804. Scharnhorst next was deputy quartermaster general and commander of the 3rd Brigade during 1804–1805, then chief of staff to Charles William Ferdinand, the duke of Brunswick, during 1805–1806.

When Prussia went to war against France in 1806, Scharnhorst accompanied Brunswick in the field. He fought at and was wounded in the Prussian defeat in the Battle of Auerstädt on October 14, 1806. He then fought under Prussian general Gebhard Leberecht von Blücher. Captured with Blücher in November, Scharnhorst was exchanged and took part in the Battle of Eylau on February 7–8, 1807. He then carried out attacks in Pomerania before the end of the war with the Treaties of Tilsit in July 1807.

Promoted to major general in 1807, Scharnhorst was appointed both minister of war and chief of the Prussian General Staff in March 1808. He headed the Military Reorganization Commission in Prussia designed to reform the army. Scharnhorst wanted a truly national army. Among the reforms enacted were the ending of corporal punishment and hereditary serfdom. He also made it possible for commoners to become officers. Officer training was also improved, with promotion to be on the basis of merit. Scharnhorst also sought programs in weapons testing, the development of national military industry, and mass conscription as well as a national militia.

Although forced to leave the Prussian Army in 1810 following a Napoleonic edict banning foreigners from serving in it, Scharnhorst returned in 1812 to become Blücher's chief of staff and played an important role in preparing the German War of Liberation against Napoleon in 1813. Scharnhorst saw the Prussian Army perform credibly against the French in the Battle of Lützen (May 1–2, 1813), in which he was wounded, and in the Battle of Bautzen (May 20, 1813). He died on June 8, 1813, at Prague in Bohemia from the effects of his wound while trying to win over the Austrians to the coalition. A superb staff officer and brilliant administrator, Scharnhorst was arguably the prime mover in the reform of the Prussian Army following its defeat by Napoleon.

SPENCER C. TUCKER

References

Clausewitz, Carl von. *Historical and Political Writings.* Edited by Peter Paret. Princeton, NJ: Princeton University Press, 1992.

Craig, Gordon Alexander. *The Politics of the Prussian Army.* Oxford, UK: Clarendon, 1955.

Paret, Peter. *Yorck and the Era of Prussian Reform, 1807–1815.* Princeton, NJ: Princeton University Press, 1966.

White, Jonathan Randall. *The Prussian Army, 1640–1871.* Landham, MD: University Press of America, 1996.

Schlieffen, Alfred von

Birth Date: February 28, 1833
Death Date: January 4, 1913

German Army general and chief of the General Staff. Born in Berlin the son of a Prussian Army officer on February 28, 1833, Alfred von Schlieffen studied law but then decided to pursue a military career and volunteered for the 2nd Guard Uhlans Regiment in 1853. He then became a regular army officer in 1854 and entered the Kriegsakademie in 1858.

Following graduation from the Kriegsakademie in 1861, Schlieffen served on the General Staff and participated in the Austro-Prussian War (1866), including the Battle of Königgratz on July 3, 1866. He also saw action as a staff major during the Franco-Prussian War (1870–1871). During 1876–1884 Schlieffen later commanded the 1st Guards Uhlans Regiment, demonstrating an exacting attention to detail. In 1884 he became head of the Military History Section of the General Staff. Promoted to *Generalmajor* in 1886, he served simultaneously as quartermaster general and deputy chief of staff as a *generalleutnant.* In February 1891 Schlieffen then succeeded General Alfred von Waldersee as chief of the General Staff.

As chief of staff, Schlieffen faced the complex dilemma of defending Germany simultaneously on two fronts against France and Russia. He devoted himself to solving this problem as he continually refined his analysis utilizing historical research, map exercises, staff, rides, and war games. He also emphasized study of the 216 BCE Battle of Cannae as the model of a battle of annihilation by enveloping an enemy army.

Schlieffen combined this model with advanced technology, rapid mobilization, and detailed planning into a concept that theoretically would achieve an operational victory.

In essence, Schlieffen called for a strategic defense against Russia until France could be knocked from the war in a Cannae-like battle near Paris. Toward that end some seven-eighths of the German Army would be committed against France, with the bulk of them on the right wing. To ensure speed in the offensive, Germany would violate neutral Belgium. On the defeat of France, Germany would deploy forces to the east to defeat Russia.

An emotionally cold and solitary man, Schlieffen's intense focus on the technical aspects of warfare reflected an unflattering image of the Industrial Age staff officer with little interest but work. He even read military history to his children before putting them to bed and assigned subordinates military problems to solve during the Christmas holidays. Although Schlieffen retired as chief of the German General Staff in 1906, he never stopped working on the German strategic dilemma of a two-front war until his death in Berlin on January 4, 1913. His dying words—probably apocryphal—were said to have been "keep the right wing strong." Schlieffen's plan, which was fatally modified by his successor, Helmuth von Moltke (the Younger), has nonetheless been criticized in retrospect for its inflexibility and failure to take into account political realities and the logistical limitations of the time.

STEVEN J. RAUCH

References

Bucholz, Arden. *Moltke, Schlieffen, and Prussian War Planning.* New York: Berg, 1991.

Ritter, Gerhard. *The Schlieffen Plan: Critique of a Myth.* New York: Praeger, 1958.

Zuber, Terence. *Inventing the Schlieffen Plan: German War Planning, 1871–1914.* New York: Oxford University Press, 2002.

———. "The Schlieffen Plan Reconsidered." *War in History* 6(3) (July 1999): 262–305.

Schwarzenberg, Karl Philip zu

Birth Date: April 18, 1771
Death Date: October 15, 1820

Austrian general. Born in Vienna on April 18, 1771, into one of the most important noble families of Austria, Prince Charles Karl Philip zu Schwarzenberg developed an interest in the military at an early age. He joined the Austrian cavalry in 1788 and served with distinction in the Austro-Turkish War of 1787–1791.

Promoted to major in 1792, Schwarzenberg fought in the Netherlands in the War of the First Coalition (1792–1795), including the Battle of Neerwinden on March 18, 1793. He distinguished himself by leading his regiment in a highly effective cavalry charge against the French in the Anglo-Austrian victory at Cateau-Cambrésis on April 26, 1794. In subsequent fighting in Germany in 1796, he led his regiment in victories by Archduke Charles at Amberg on August 24 and at Würzburg on September 3. Promoted to *Generalmajor* in 1796, Schwarzenberg led cavalry and light infantry in raids against the French. Advanced to the rank of field marshal lieutenant in 1799, he received command of a division.

Schwarzenberg led his division in the Austrian defeat in the Battle of Hohenlinden on December 3, 1800, but managed to break out and was rewarded by being given command of the rear guard in Archduke Charles's army. In the War of the Third Coalition (1805–1807) Schwarzenberg commanded a corps in Germany and was responsible for the victory in the Haslach on October 11, 1805. He managed to escape the Austrian encirclement at Ulm on October 17–20, leading a difficult march through French-held territory. He urged Emperor Francis II against an early battle with the French, a warning that was fully vindicated by Napoleon's victory at Austerlitz on December 2, 1805.

Schwarzenberg then served as Austrian ambassador to Russia during 1806–1809 but returned to Austria in time to participate in the Battle of Wagram on July 5–6, 1809. Following the Treaty of Schönbrunn in October that ended the war, Schwarzenberg went to France to negotiate the marriage of Archduchess Marie Louise to Napoleon. Schwarzenberg commanded the Austrian corps in Napoleon's Grande Armée during the invasion of Russia in 1812 and was able to save most of it from being destroyed.

Promoted to field marshal, Schwarzenberg was appointed commander in chief of allied forces in Germany in the War of German Liberation in 1813. Defeated in the Battle of Dresden on August 26–27, he led the allies to victory in the great Battle of Leipzig (Battle of the Nations) during October 16–19, 1813, the largest battle in terms of number of men engaged of the Napoleonic Wars and probably the most important battle of the wars, as it forced the French from Germany.

Schwarzenberg commanded the Army of Bohemia in the invasion of France in 1814 and won victories over the French, including at Bray-sur-Seine on February 27 and at Arcis-sur-Aube on March 20–21, the latter battle leading to the allied capture of Paris on March 31. He also commanded Austrian forces in 1815 during the Hundred Days, which, however, ended in the Battle of Waterloo on June 18 before Austrian forces could arrive. Schwarzenberg served as president of the Higher War Council during 1814–1820 but, stricken with paralysis, died at Leipzig on October 15, 1820. A talented, intelligent, skilled, and brave officer in his early military career, Schwarzenberg was also a skilled diplomat as much as a military figure late in his career. He was in fact the ideal commander for the allied forces against Napoleon in 1813 and showed himself adept in overcoming such obstacles as the presence of monarchs at his headquarters.

SPENCER C. TUCKER

References

Arnold, James R. *Crisis on the Danube: Napoleon's Austrian Campaign of 1809.* New York: Paragon House, 1990.

Bancalari, Gustav. *Feldmarschall Carl Philip Fürst Schwartzenberg.* Salzburg: Dieter, 1970.

Hollins, David. *Austrian Commanders of the Napoleonic Wars.* London: Osprey, 2004.

Scott, Winfield

Birth Date: June 13, 1786
Death Date: May 28, 1866

U.S. Army general. Born at Laurel Branch near Petersburg, Virginia, on June 13, 1786, Winfield Scott briefly attended the College of William and Mary in 1805 and then read for the law. In the aftermath of the *Chesapeake-Leopard* Affair (June 22, 1807) he enlisted in a Virginia cavalry troop. He then secured a direct commission as a captain of artillery in 1808 and was assigned to New Orleans. Following a direct letter to President Thomas Jefferson in which Scott sharply criticized the demonstrated incompetence of his commanding officer, Brigadier General James Wilkinson, Scott was suspended without pay for a year during 1809–1810. He then returned to New Orleans during 1811–1812 and was promoted to lieutenant colonel in July 1812.

Assigned to the Niagara frontier at the beginning of the War of 1812, Scott saw combat at the Battle of Queenston Heights on October 13, where he was taken prisoner. Exchanged, he was promoted to colonel in March 1813. Known as a demanding trainer who nonetheless was much concerned for the welfare of his men, Scott led the successful attack on and capture of Fort George, Ontario, on May 27, where he was wounded. Promoted to brigadier general in March 1814, he led a brigade in Major General Jacob Brown's invasion of Canada, distinguishing himself in the Battle of Chippewa on July 5 and the Battle of Lundy's Lane on July 25, where he was wounded twice. His performance in these hard-fought contests, in which U.S. forces bested British regulars, made him a national hero and won him the thanks of Congress, a gold medal, and a brevet promotion to major general.

Following the war Scott wrote the drill manual *Infantry Tactics* that became the standard on the subject in the U.S. Army for a generation. Appointed to command the Northern Department in 1815, he twice traveled to Europe to study its military establishments. He then assumed command of the Eastern Division in 1829. He helped smooth relations with South Carolina in the Nullification Crisis of 1832 and with Britain over the U.S.-Canadian border during 1838–1839. He was also heavily involved in Native American affairs, negotiating the Treaty of Fort Armstrong with the Sauk and Fox tribes in September 1832, commanding U.S. forces against the Seminoles in 1836, and overseeing the Cherokee removal in 1838.

Appointed commanding general of the U.S. Army with the permanent rank of major general in July 1841, Scott supported Major General Zachary Taylor's operations in northern Mexico during the Mexican-American War (1846–1848) and then planned and carried out the march to Mexico City that began with an amphibious landing at Veracruz on March 9, 1847. Outnumbered, moving through hostile territory, often short of supplies, and plagued by political generals, Scott conducted a brilliant campaign. He was victorious at Cerro Gordo on April 18, at Puebla on May 15, at Contreras and Churubusco on August 20, at Molino del Rey on September 8, and at Chapultepec on September 13. He captured Mexico City on September 14 and ignored President James K. Polk's orders to recommence fighting, allowing U.S. envoy Nicholas Trist to secure peace at Guadalupe Hidalgo on February 2, 1848.

Scott's performance in the war brought the thanks of Congress and the enmity of President Polk. Scott returned to the United States in April 1848 to find that Polk had set out to ruin him. Viewing Scott as a political rival, Polk ordered an inquiry into Scott's relationship with his subordinate commanders in the war, especially Major General Gideon Pillow, a political appointee. Although Scott was exonerated, the inquiry ruined his chance at the presidency. Running as the Whig candidate in 1852, he carried only four states.

Brevetted lieutenant general in 1855 (the first to hold that rank since George Washington), Scott was sent west by President Franklin Pierce to end tensions with the British over the Puget Sound area that had escalated into the so-called Pig War and specifically a dispute over San Juan Island. Scott established a good rapport with the British and brought about a peaceful resolution.

As commanding general of the army when the Southern states began secession, Scott urged preparations for war in 1860. Too old himself to exercise command, he tried without success to persuade Colonel Robert E. Lee to accept the field command of the army. One of the few in Washington to understand that the war would be long and difficult, Scott developed a strategic plan to impose a naval blockade of the Confederate coasts while training a large army and then operate with the navy to bisect the South along its great rivers. This so-called Anaconda Plan ultimately brought victory.

After 54 years in military service and the longest tenure as a general officer in U.S. history, Scott retired from the army in November 1861. He moved to West Point, where he wrote his memoirs and died on May 28, 1866. Known as "Old Fuss and Feathers," Scott loved display. A brilliant trainer, careful planner, consummate strategist, successful diplomat, and highly effective field commander, Scott ranks as one of the most important military leaders in U.S. military history.

SPENCER C. TUCKER

References

Eisenhower, John S. D. *Agent of Destiny: The Life and Times of General Winfield Scott.* Norman: University of Oklahoma Press, 1997.

Johnson, Timothy D. *Winfield Scott: The Quest for Military Glory.* Manhattan: University Press of Kansas, 1999.

Scott, Winfield. *Memoirs.* 2 vols. New York: Sheldon, 1864.

Suffren Saint-Tropez, Pierre André de

Birth Date: July 17, 1729
Death Date: December 8, 1788

French admiral. Born in the Château of Saint-Cannat (Bouches-du-Rhône) on July 17, 1729, Pierre André de Suffren Saint-Tropez was the younger son of the Marquis de Saint-Tropez. André Suffren entered the French Navy as a midshipman in October 1743 and took part in the naval campaigns of the War of the Austrian Succession (1740–1748), seeing action in the Battle of Toulon on February 11, 1744. He then saw service in the North American station and took part in the failed Cape Breton expedition in 1746. He was taken prisoner by the British during the Second Battle of Cape Finistere on October 15, 1747.

At the end of the war Suffren entered the service of the Knights of Malta in 1748 but rejoined the French Navy for the Seven Years' War (1756–1763) and served as a lieutenant. He took part in the Battle of Minorca on May 20, 1756, but was again taken prisoner in the Battle of Lagos on August 18, 1759. He was promoted to commander in August 1767 and to captain in February 1772. During the American Revolutionary War (1775–1783) he served in North America as a captain of a ship under Admiral Charles Hector d'Estaing and distinguished himself in the attack on Newport, Rhode Island, on August 5–11, 1778, and in the French capture of Grenada on July 6, 1779.

Following command of the ship of the line *Zélé* (74 guns) in the Atlantic in 1780, Suffren led a squadron of five warships that departed France for India in March 1781. His orders were to sail to the Cape of Good Hope and there aid the Dutch, then continue on to India, where he was to disrupt British shipping and support operations against the British on land. En route he attacked a larger English force at anchor at Puerto Praya in the Cape Verde Islands on April 16, inflicting damage to the English ships sufficient to dissuade the commander from continuing on to strike the Dutch colony at the Cape of Good Hope. Suffren remained off the Cape of Good Hope for two months and then sailed to Mauritius (Île de France), where he joined with a squadron under Admiral Comte d'Orves in October, the combined fleet arriving in Indian waters in January 1782. Following the death of d'Orves on February 9, 1782, Suffren had command of 12 ships of the line.

Suffren then engaged the English fleet under the command of Admiral Sir Edward Hughes in a series of battles off the Indian coast through the spring and summer of 1782: Sadras on February 17, Provedien on April 12, Negapatam on July 6, and Trincomalé on September 3. Although none were decisive victories for Suffren, his aggressive melee tactics kept his opponent on the defensive. Anticipating British admiral Horatio Nelson's tactics, Suffren tried and sometimes succeeded in doubling the British battle lines, catching the enemy ships between two fires. His successes were all the more remarkable in that unlike his British counterpart, Suffren lacked convenient bases and had to contend with flagrant insubordination from some of his captains.

Suffren refitted at Sumatra during November–December 1782 and then returned to India in January 1783, where he attacked Hughes for a fourth time off Cuddalore, forcing the British to raise the siege of that place on June 20. With the end of the war, Suffren had little do and returned to France in March 1784. Promoted to vice admiral, he received command of the Brest squadron during the war scare of 1787. Suffren died in Paris on December 8, 1788. He was not murdered nor did he die from wounds sustained in a duel, as some stories have it, but rather died from a lingering illness. Without doubt the greatest French admiral of the 18th century, Suffren was a bold and innovative commander who had a good sense of tactics and strategy.

SPENCER C. TUCKER

References

Cavaliero, Roderick. *Admiral Satan: The Life and Campaigns of Suffren.* New York: Tauris, 1994.

Masson, Philippe. "Pierre André de Suffren de Saint-Tropez: Admiral Satan." Translated by Jack Sweetman. In *The Great Admirals: Command at Sea, 1587–1945,* edited by Jack Sweetman, 172–191. Annapolis, MD: Naval Institute Press, 1997.

Taillemite, Étienne. *Dictionnaire des marins français.* Paris: Éditions Maritimes, 1982.

Wayne, Anthony

Birth Date: January 1, 1745
Death Date: December 16, 1796

Continental Army officer and later commander of the Legion of the United States. Born in Waynesborough, Chester County, Pennsylvania, of Irish descent on January 1, 1745, Anthony Wayne was educated at the Academy in Philadelphia but left school to become a surveyor. He was later a tanner in his father's business.

Elected to the Pennsylvania colonial assembly in 1774, Wayne resigned upon the outbreak of the American Revolutionary War to raise a volunteer regiment. Although he had no formal military training, in January 1776 he was commissioned colonel of the 4th Pennsylvania Regiment. Wounded in the Battle of Trois Rivières on June 8, 1776, his action in covering the retreat of U.S. forces from Canada won him promotion to brigadier general in February 1777.

Wayne again distinguished himself in the Battle of Brandywine Creek on September 11, 1777, but he was caught by surprise in a British night attack on his camp at Paoli on September 21, 1777. He requested a court-martial, which cleared him of any negligence. Wayne earned praise for his conduct in the Battle of Germantown on October 4, 1777, and performed well in the Battle of Monmouth on June 28, 1778, leading the initial attack and then defending against the British counterattack. He led a bayonet attack that carried the British position at Stony Point, New York, on July 16, 1779, an action that won him the nickname of "Mad Anthony." In January 1781 he ably defused a mutiny of the Pennsylvania line. During the latter stages of the American Revolutionary War he participated in the Yorktown Campaign of May–October 19, 1781, and then campaigned under Major General Nathanael Greene in Georgia until the British evacuated Savannah in July 1782. At the end of the war Wayne was brevetted a major general in September 1783.

After the war Wayne retired to farm in Pennsylvania. He was a member of the Pennsylvania State Assembly in 1785 and was elected to the state convention that ratified the U.S. Constitution. He then relocated to Georgia to manage landholdings that the state had awarded him for his services there during the Revolutionary War in 1782. Unsuccessful in securing election to the U.S. Senate from Georgia, he won election to the U.S. Congress from that state in 1791, but the election was subsequently declared invalid because of voting irregularities.

In April 1792 following two disastrous expeditions against northwestern Native Americans by Brigadier General Josiah Harmar and Governor Arthur St. Clair of the Northwest Territory, President George Washington recalled Wayne as a major general to command the newly authorized 5,000-man Legion of the United States. Wayne took advantage of extended negotiations with the Native Americans to establish a camp at Legionville in western Pennsylvania and properly train the army. He stressed drill, proper sanitation, field fortifications, and marksmanship. Finally, in the summer of 1794 Wayne led the army, supported by Kentucky militia, west into the Ohio Territory. In the Battle of Fallen Timbers on August 20, 1794, he defeated Native American forces led by Shawnee chief Blue Jacket. This victory broke the power of the Native Americans in the eastern part of the Old Northwest and did much to restore the prestige of the U.S. Army, so badly tarnished in the earlier Harmar and St. Clair expeditions. As a result, Wayne is often called the father of the new U.S. regular army. A year later he concluded the Treaty of Greenville with the Native Americans.

In 1796 Wayne secured the relinquishment of British forts in the Great Lakes area to the United States. While on a military excursion from Fort Detroit to Pennsylvania, Wayne died suddenly at Presque Isle (Erie), Pennsylvania, on December 16, 1796.

PAUL G. PIERPAOLI JR. AND SPENCER C. TUCKER

References

Fox, Joseph L. *Anthony Wayne: Washington's Reliable General.* Chicago: Adams Presses, 1988.

Gaff, Alan D. *Bayonets in the Wilderness: Anthony Wayne's Legion in the Old Northwest.* Norman: University of Oklahoma Press, 2004.

Nelson, Paul V. *Anthony Wayne: Soldier of the Early Republic.* Bloomington: Indiana University Press, 1985.

Tucker, Glenn. *Mad Anthony Wayne and the New Nation: The Story of Washington's Front-Line General.* Harrisburg, PA: Stackpole, 1973.

Wellesley, Sir Arthur

Birth Date: May 1, 1769
Death Date: September 14, 1852

British general and prime minister. Born in Dublin, Ireland, on May 1, 1769, Arthur Wellesley was the fifth son of Garrett Wellesley, 1st Earl Mornington. The younger Wellesley was educated at Eton and the French military school at Angers. He then entered the British Army. Family influence secured him a commission as an ensign in the 73rd Highland Regiment in 1787. Promoted to lieutenant by the end of that year, he was soon a captain in command of a company in June 1791. Borrowing money from his brother, Wellesley purchased a major's commission in the 33rd Regiment of Foot and was soon its lieutenant colonel in September 1793.

War had begun between Britain and France in 1793, and Wellesley led his regiment into combat under the Duke of York against the Dutch at Hondschoote on September 8. Wellesley then commanded a brigade in Flanders and in Hanover. Disappointed by the lackluster performance of the British Army, he considered resigning. He served in India during 1797–1805; this was fortuitous, as his elder brother, Richard Wellesley, 2nd Earl Mornington, was governor-general there. Rapid promotion followed. Wellesley took part in the campaign against Sultan Fateh Ali Tipu (Tipu Sultan, Tiger of Mysore) and following the capture of Seringapatam and the death of Tipu became its governor. Wellesley won major victories in the Second Maratha War (1803–1805) and at Poona on March 20, 1803, Ahmadnager on August 11, Assaye on September 23, Aragon on November 28, and Gawilgarh on December 15.

Returning to England as a major general in September 1805, Wellesley commanded a brigade in the abortive Hanover campaign of 1805. He entered the British Parliament from Rye and then married in 1806. He was appointed chief secretary for Ireland in April 1807. Wellesley took part in the campaign against Denmark during July–September 1807 and was victorious at Kjoge on August 29.

Promoted to lieutenant general in 1808, Wellesley received command of a British expeditionary force for an invasion of Spanish Venezuela, but with the revolt against French rule in the Iberian Peninsula, the force was diverted there instead. Temporarily commanding British forces in Portugal at the beginning of the Peninsular War (1808–1814), Wellesley was victorious over French forces under General Jean Junot at Vimiero on August 21, 1808, leading to the liberation of Portugal from the French. Superseded by the cautious British general Sir Hugh Dalrymple, Wellesley was forced to stand on the defensive. Following the conclusion of the Convention of Cintra that provided that the French soldiers would be returned to France in British ships, Wellesley and other British generals were called home and underwent an investigation by Parliament. Cleared of any wrongdoing, Wellesley returned to Portugal as commander of all British forces there on April 22, 1809. He captured Porto (Oporto) on May 12 and also defeated the French at Talavera on July 27–28, but superior French numbers forced him on the defensive. For his success, however, he was ennobled as Viscount Wellington of Talavera. He then oversaw construction of a strong defensive system and kept the French from taking Lisbon during the winter of 1809–1810.

Although constantly suffering from insufficient support from his own government, Wellesley consistently performed well against the more numerous French. A commanding figure who seemed to be everywhere on the battlefield, he most often dressed in civilian clothes without insignia. He was purported to despise his men and was a stern, on occasion brutal, disciplinarian who nonetheless enjoyed the full support and loyalty of his men.

Wellesley defeated French marshals André Masséna and Michel Ney at Bussaco on September 27, 1810, and Masséna's slightly larger force again at Fuentes de Oñoro on May 5, 1811. Taking the offensive in 1812 on the weakening of French forces in Spain occasioned by Napoleon's invasion of Russia, Wellesley was victorious at Ciudad Rodrigo on January 7–20 and Badajoz on March 17–April 9. He was named Earl of Wellington in February 1812.

In one of his greatest victories, Welesley routed Marshal Auguste Marmont's army at Salamanca on July 22 and took Madrid on August 12, for which he was made marquess in October. Outnumbered by reconstituted French forces, he withdrew in late October. Appointed general in chief of the Spanish Army, he reorganized his forces and took the offensive in the spring of 1813. Wellesley then drove the French from Spain, routing a smaller force under King Joseph (Napoleon's brother) in the Battle of Vitoria on June 21, 1813, and then winning the Battle of the Pyrenees on July 25–August 2. Besieging and taking San Sebastián on July 9–September 7, Wellesley invaded southern France. For his accomplishments, he was advanced to field marshal in 1813.

Wellesley defeated Marshal Nicolas Soult at Orthez on February 27, 1814, and then captured the key southwestern port city of Bordeaux on March 17 before taking Toulouse on April 10. As such, his forces played an important role in the defeat of Napoleon, who abdicated on April 4. Created duke in May 1814, Wellesley was appointed British ambassador to the court of restored King Louis XVIII of France during August 1814–January 1815 and then was sent to Austria for the peace conference of the Congress of Vienna.

Following Napoleon's escape from exile in Elba in March 1815, Wellesley was recalled to the command of British and Dutch forces. He was in Brussels when Napoleon invaded Belgium and advanced to meet the French. Wellesley held off attacks by Marshal Ney at Quatre Bras on June 16 but sustained heavy losses in the process. Wellesley then fought Ney and Napoleon in the Battle of Waterloo on June 18 and was joined just in time by Prussian forces under Field Marshal Gebhard Blücher, winning a narrow but decisive victory over the French and bringing finis to the Napoleonic Wars.

After commanding British occupation forces in northern France during 1815–1818, Wellesley returned to Britain and entered politics. Appointed master-general of the ordnance in 1818, he was ambassador to Austria during 1822–1826 and then ambassador to Russia in 1826. He then commanded the British Army in 1827. As prime minister during January 1828–November 1830, Wellesley set himself firmly against parliamentary reform and social change, stances that made him unpopular with many. Indeed, the iron shutters installed on his London residence, Ashby House, to protect it from constant window smashers led to him being called the "Iron Duke." His great accomplishment as prime minister was to secure passage of the Catholic Emancipation Act in 1829. Wellesley served as foreign secretary during 1834–1835 and then again commanded the British Army during 1842–1852. His popularity returned in his later years. He died at Walmar Castle in Kent on September 14, 1852.

Certainly the finest British field commander of the 19th century and one of the greatest British generals of all time, Wellesley was personally brave and unflappable under fire. A brilliant tactician and strategist, he won the respect of his men by his concern for their welfare and by being sparing of them in battle.

SPENCER C. TUCKER

References

Hibbert, Christopher. *Wellington: A Personal History.* Reading, MA: Perseus, 1997.

Longford, Elizabeth. *Wellington: The Year of the Sword.* New York: Harper and Row, 1969.

Rothenberg, Gunther E. *The Art of Warfare in the Age of Napoleon.* Bloomington: Indiana University Press, 1980.

Zeng Guofan

Birth Date: November 26, 1811
Death Date: March 12, 1872

Chinese general. Zeng Guofan (Tseng Kuo-fan) was born to a scholar farming family in Xiang (Hsiang) District, Hunan, China, on November 26, 1811. He studied for the traditional scholarly examinations that were the route to civil service position. Passing the highest academic examination for the *jinshi* (*chin-sin;* doctoral degree) on his second attempt in 1838, Zeng was appointed to the Hanlin Academy in Beijing for 13 years. He concentrated on interpreting the Confucian classics. By the 1850s, however, he had spoken out against government policies.

Following the death of his mother in 1852, Zeng took the then-customary three-year leave at home for mourning but broke off the mourning to raise a military force in Hunan against Taiping (T'ai-p'ing) forces that had entered the province during what became known as the great Taiping Rebellion (1850–1864) against the Qing (Ch'ing) dynasty. One of the major events in Chinese history, it ultimately claimed the lives of some 20 million Chinese.

Zeng attracted a wide following to his army because of his insistence on observance of Confucian principles, including obligation to the soldiers and loyalty to one's superior. Soon this well-disciplined force of volunteers had grown into the Xiang (Hsiang) Army, the chief military force against the Taipings. Zeng also created a naval force of some 240 junks to operate on the region's rivers.

Zeng's forces were victorious in the naval Battle of Xiangtan (Hsiang-t'an) on May 1, 1854, and also recaptured Hubei (Hupeh) in October. The rebels retook Hubei the next year, and Zeng could do little during the next two years, although he secured the position of viceroy of Liangjiang (Liang-chiang) comprising the provinces of Jiangxi (Kiangsi), Anhui, and Jiangsu (Kiangsu) during 1860–1864 and the right to finance his army through the collection of customs duties. His army grew to a force of 120,000 men with a number of capable generals, such as Li Hongzhang (Li Hung-chang) and Zuo Zongtang (Tso Tsung-t'ang). Again defeated at the Battle of Qimen (Ch'i-men) in Anhui Province in mid-1861, Zeng nonetheless continued to campaign and won the loyalty of the peasants and was finally victorious, capturing the Taiping capital of Nanjing (Nanking) and ending the rebellion in 1864. For this he was awarded the title of marquis. Thereafter an administrator, Zeng served as viceroy of Zhili (Chih-li, the old name for Hebei [Hopeh]) during 1865–1870 and again as viceroy of Liangjiang during 1870–1872. He resumed military command during May 1865–October 1866 against the Nian (Nien) Rebellion in northern China but then resigned in favor of his protégé, Li Hongzhang.

Zeng was responsible for a number of reforms, and he supported a program of modernization in China. This included creation of the Jiangnan (Kiangnan) naval arsenal at Shanghai that built several modern warships. He strongly supported study of Chinese classical literature, but it was at his recommendation that the Chinese government first sent students to be educated abroad. Zeng died in Nanjing on March 12, 1872. After his death, the government accorded him the name of Wenzheng (Wen-cheng), the highest title possible under the Qing dynasty. Although not a great field commander, Zeng was certainly the leading Chinese general and civil leader of 19th-century China. Both praised and condemned for this, his efforts ensured the continuation of the Qing dynasty into the 20th century.

SPENCER C. TUCKER

References

Jen, Yu-wen. *The Taiping Revolutionary Movement.* New Haven, CT: Yale University Press, 1973.

Porter, Jonathan. *Tseng Kuo-fan's Private Bureaucracy.* China Research Monographs. Berkeley: Center for Chinese Studies, University of California Press, 1972.

Spence, Jonathan. *God's Chinese Son: The Taiping Heavenly Kingdom of Hong Xiuquan.* New York: Norton, 1997.

Weapons

Air Gun

The air gun is descended from the blowgun, the difference being that the air gun fires its projectiles by means of compressed air rather than by an individual blowing into a tube, as in the blowgun. In the air gun the pressure may be generated by a spring piston, which is released on pulling the trigger. The degree of power provided is directly related to the difficulty of the cocking stroke. Guns of this type are of small caliber and fire either a BB, a small round shot usually formed of copper-coated steel, or a wasp-waisted lead diabolo pellet. Such guns are used for target practice or for hunting small game. More lethal larger-caliber air guns operate from a compressed air reservoir. Multistroke pneumatic air guns require 2 to 10 pump ups from an attached pump lever that then stores the compressed air in a reservoir. When the trigger is pulled, a valve briefly opens, releasing a set amount of air that then propels the projectile down the barrel. Some newer cylinder air guns employ a purchased cylinder gas cylinder, usually with liquefied carbon dioxide.

Guns operating on compressed air are hardly new. In 18th- and 19th-century air guns the reservoir was often the butt of the gun. The operator removed the reservoir from the remainder of the gun and used a pump, similar to today's bicycle pumps, to fill it. A few Austrian Army sharpshooters employed the Girandonoi air rifle during 1793–1802 in the French Revolution and the Napoleonic Wars. A 20-shot repeating rifle, it fired a round .51-caliber ball and had an effective range of about 130 yards. Nineteenth-century English sporting guns featured a ball-type reservoir under the stock.

The largest air guns were the three 15-inch guns on the U.S. dynamite cruiser *Vesuvius*. They saw service during the Spanish-American War of 1898 when they were used to shell Morro Castle, Cuba.

While air guns have very high accuracy, their limited range usually restricts their use to hunting and target practice. The Crossman Corporation is the major U.S. firm manufacturing pump-up rifles and pistols. Most target-practice air guns today are of .177 caliber (4.5 millimeter).

SPENCER C. TUCKER

Reference
Diagram Group. *Weapons: An International Encyclopedia from 5000 BC to 2000 AD.* New York: St. Martin's, 1980.

Armor-Piercing Shell

In the ongoing race between guns and armor at sea, naval ordnance designers developed armor-piercing projectiles to overcome armor in warships. In 1881 Hadfield of Sheffield began manufacturing cast-steel projectiles. In 1885 that same firm patented the Compound Armour Piercing Shell. As with compound armor, it combined a hardened steel point and a resilient body (a completely hardened shell would shatter on impact). Other types of hardened projectiles followed, including one of chrome steel. But most broke up when they struck the new armor.

In 1878 a Captain English of the Royal Engineers came upon capping the tip of the projectile. During tests of shells and armor at Woolwich Arsenal, a number of shells had broken up when fired against steel plate. Quite by accident, a 2.5-inch iron plate was left in front of a steel armor plate. In consequence, a 9-inch Palliser shell passed through the iron plate and penetrated 13 inches into the steel-faced plate. English then proposed manufacturing a shot with a wrought-iron cap of approximately the thickness of the plate that the other shell had passed through. When this was done and the shell was fired, it went entirely through the compound armor. Strangely, nothing was done to exploit this discovery, and it was left to Russian admiral Stepan Makarov to reinvent the capped projectile in 1890.

When the capped shell struck its target, the cap received the full shock of the initial impact and distributed it over the length of the shell. The cap also served to lengthen the time during which the shock was distributed to the shell and acted as a support for the point at the beginning of penetration, softening the plate slightly so as to give the point a better opportunity for penetration.

The U.S. Navy came up with the Johnson capped shell. The French improved on this in their 1896 Holtzer cap. In spite of evidence of the success of the capped shell, the Royal Navy resisted adopting it until 1905. Nonetheless, by World War I all the major navies of the world employed capped armor-piercing projectiles for use against enemy ships. The same process was applied to armor piercing projectiles for land artillery.

SPENCER C. TUCKER

References

Gardiner, Robert, ed., and Andrew D. Lambert, consultant ed. *Steam, Steel & Shellfire: The Steam Warship, 1815–1905.* Annapolis, MD: Naval Institute Press, 1992.

Hogg, Ian V., and John Batchelor. *Naval Gun.* Poole, Dorset, UK: Blandford, 1978.

Bormann Fuse

Artillery shell fuse. A major challenge for artillerists to the mid-19th century was the timely ignition of explosive shells above a target. From the 17th century to the mid-19th century, artillerymen simply packed a fuse channel with fine gunpowder. The action of firing the gun ignited this powder train, which then burned to and set off the explosive charge in the shell. Precise timing was impossible because the powder in the fuse was more tightly packed toward the bottom and thus burned more slowly than at the top. This problem was compounded by the compression of the powder train in the action of the shell being fired.

Imprecision in the timing of the shell explosion had not been a major problem until the development in 1784 of spherical case shot (case or shrapnel). Such projectiles, specifically designed for use against troop concentrations, required precise timing of the explosion to be effective, for with a shell moving at 1,200 feet per second, an error of a quarter of a second would mean 300 feet off the target.

Belgian Army captain (later major-general) Charles G. Bormann provided the solution. After extensive tests in 1851, the Belgian Army adopted the fuse of his design, which then found its way into worldwide general use. In the United States it was widely employed during the American Civil War by both the Union and Confederacy, especially in the 12-pounder Napoleon and the Dahlgren boat howitzers.

The Bormann fuse consisted of a threaded zinc disc about .5 inch thick and 1.5 inches in diameter. Because the fuse train of mealed powder was placed in a channel laterally around the periphery of the fuse, it enabled uniformity in packing the powder and eliminated any effect of the discharge of the gun on the distribution of fuse powder and hence timing. Guided by raised indicators on the fuse's face, the gunner set the fuse by perforating its face with a special punch to expose the powder trail at the appropriate mark. The Bormann fuse allowed a maximum timing of 5.25 seconds for a range of 1,200 yards for the 12-pounder gun.

As with much Southern ordnance, Confederate-manufactured Bormann fuses often proved defective on the battlefield. The main trouble lay in the sealing of the underside of the horseshoe channel containing the powder train. The shock of the discharge of the gun tended to dislodge the plug closing the channel and allowed the flame from the composition to reach the main charge without burning around through the fuse. Attempts to correct the problem were unsuccessful. Following numerous casualties from prematurely exploding shells during the Battle of Fredericksburg, the Confederate Army withdrew the Bormann fuse from service on December 24, 1862.

Union forces did not report comparable problems, and the Bormann fuse saw extensive use until it was eventually phased out of service following the war.

SPENCER C. TUCKER

Reference

Dickey, Thomas S., and Peter C. George. *Field Artillery Projectiles of the American Civil War.* Atlanta: Arsenal Press, 1980.

Breech-Loading Field Artillery

Dramatic improvements in artillery occurred in the second half of the 19th century. The most important of these occurred in the change from muzzle-loading to breech-loading guns. This was made possible by greatly improved manufacturing techniques and tremendous advances in metallurgy, especially steel alloys. Steel guns appeared, machined to close tolerances.

Two efficient means of sealing the breech developed. The first of these employed a brass cartridge case, in effect itself the seal. This became the established process for smaller field pieces employing what was known as fixed ammunition, with projectile, charge, and primer all contained in one case. The second method of sealing the breech was the De Bange system. In it, the projectile, the bag or bags of powder, and the primer (vent tube) were all loaded separately. This system was used in the larger guns and had the advantage of being able to vary the range depending on powder charge utilized. In the De Bange system a mushroom-shaped piece was driven back by the force of the exploding gunpowder against a soft obturator ring in front of the breech block. The obturator ring expanded, sealing the breech.

Sliding breech blocks were developed for quick-firing guns. These moved to one side or downward and allowed the breech to be quickly opened and then closed again. Another system employed an interrupted screw breech. In it, the breech block had a screw thread but with a section cut away. Turning it through a few degrees would either lock or unlock the breech, permitting rapid reloading. Usually the interrupted screw breech was used with the De Bange system.

One of the first modern breech-loading guns was the British 12-pounder (that is, firing a shell weighing 12 pounds) Armstrong field gun of 1859. In this 3-inch–caliber gun, shell and propellent were loaded separately. Some 12-pounder Armstrongs saw service on the Confederate side in the American Civil War (1861–1865). In 1891 both France and Germany developed recoil systems in which the gun recoiled in a slide against springs or hydropneumatic buffers that returned it to its original position. This meant that the artillery piece did not have to be reaimed after each round, which produced far more rapid rates of fire as well as improved accuracy. There were also new mechanical fuses, steel-jacketed projectiles, and new high-explosive fillers. Such guns were quick firing and highly accurate. The howitzer also increased in importance. This midtrajectory weapon could fire at longer ranges than mortars. It came to be the preferred artillery piece in World War I because its high arc of fire allowed highly accurate plunging fire against enemy entrenchments.

Notable light field artillery pieces going into World War I included the French 75 millimeter (mm), the Russian 76.2-mm, the British 13-pounder (3-inch) and 18-pounder (3.3-inch), and the German 77 mm. One trend during the war, however, was the increasing use of heavier guns, which were found necessary to smash through concrete bunkers. Such pieces included the British 4.5-inch and 9.2-inch howitzers and 60-pounder (5-inch) gun; the French howitzer and gun, both of 155-mm caliber; the Russian 122-mm gun; and the German 105-mm howitzer, 150-mm long gun, and 210-mm howitzer. In World War II the standard German and American field howitzers were of 105 mm. Heavier guns included the 155-mm M2 Long Tom used by the Americans and a number of their allies.

In modern artillery, caliber means two different things. It is first the diameter of the bore and second the length of the barrel. Thus, a 16-inch 50-caliber naval gun would have a bore 16 inches in diameter and a gun tube length of 16 inches by 50 or 66.67 feet.

Through the 1860s artillery was essentially a direct-fire antipersonnel weapon. This was its primary employment in the American Civil War. During that conflict, artillerymen usually fired only at what they could actually see. If infantry were out of sight, they were generally safe from enemy artillery fire.

An important change occurred with the advent of aimed indirect fire. In 1882 the Russian Carl Guk published a system for firing on an unseen target using a compass, an aiming point, and a forward observer. Ironically, the Japanese refined Guk's method and employed indirect fire with great success against the Russians in the Russo-Japanese War of 1904–1905.

By the 1890s most European armies had standardized the techniques of artillery fire, allowing for the massing of fire on remote targets. During the 1899–1902 Boer War the Boers concealed their artillery pieces rather than deploy them in the open, as in British practice. The advent of new smokeless powders meant that a gun's position was more difficult to locate when it was fired. At the same time, new slower-burning powder also produced more thrust against the shell and less pressure on the gun itself, allowing greater ranges.

All of these changes greatly increased the lethality of artillery. It, not the rifle or machine gun, was the great killer of World War I; estimates claim that artillery fire caused up to 70 percent of battlefield deaths in the war.

SPENCER C. TUCKER

References

Hogg, Ian V. *The Guns, 1914–1918.* New York: Ballantine Books, 1971.

———. *The Illustrated Encyclopedia of Artillery: An A–Z Guide to Artillery Techniques and Equipment throughout the World.* London: Stanley Paul, 1987.

Jobé, Joseph, ed. *Guns: An Illustrated History of Artillery.* Greenwich, CT: New York Graphic Society, 1971.

Breech-Loading Modern Heavy Guns at Sea

Ordnance experiments in the 1870s involving testing pressures in gun bores revealed that performance could be significantly enhanced by utilizing slower-burning gunpowder and longer barrels. Slow-burning large-grain powder, known as prismatic powder, prolonged the length of time that the charge acted on the projectile and thus increased both muzzle velocity and range. The problem with this was that the projectile left the barrel before all the powder was consumed. This could be solved by longer barrels, but that made muzzle loading next to impossible. The slower-burning powders also required a powder chamber of a diameter larger than that of the bore. All these factors and the need to protect gun crews during the loading process prompted a renewed search for an effective breech-loading gun.

Although breech loaders had been tried at sea in the modern era beginning in 1858 on the *Gloire* and later on the *Warrior,* problems led to them being discarded. In 1864 the Royal Navy reverted definitively to muzzle-loading ordnance, but other nations, especially the French, moved ahead with breech loaders.

The old problem of ineffective sealing at the breech was only slowly overcome. In 1872 a French Army captain named de Bange came up with a plastic gas check that helped prevent escape of gasses at the breech, and in 1875 France adopted the breech loader. At the same time, brass cartridge cases, already used for small arms, came into use for the smaller breech-loading guns.

An accident aboard HMS *Thunderer* in the Sea of Marmora in January 1879 helped prompt the Royal Navy's return to breech loaders. Simultaneous firing was under way, with the main guns fired in salvo; during this, one of the battleship's 12-inch muzzle-loading guns misfired. This was not detected from the force of the discharge of the one gun, and both guns were run back in hydraulically to be reloaded. When they were again fired the double-charged gun blew up, killing 11 men and injuring 35 others. This could not have happened with a breech-loading gun, and in May the Admiralty set up a committee to investigate the merits of breech-loading versus muzzle-loading guns. In August 1879 after a committee of officers examined new breech loaders built by Armstrong in Britain and Krupp in Germany, the Royal Navy decided to utilize the breech loader in three battleships entering service in 1881–1882.

Another change in the period was to guns of steel, which accompanied enormous increases in gun size. Krupp in Germany began producing cast steel rifled guns in 1860. The change to steel guns was made possible by the production of higher-quality steel. At the same time that the Royal Navy went to the breech loader it adopted the all-steel gun in which a steel jacket was shrunk over a steel tube and layers of steel hoops were then shrunk over this. The system of jackets and hoops over an inner steel tube was followed by one in which steel wire was spun on under tension, varying with the distance from the bore. This helped eliminate barrel droop. Such wire guns continued in British service until the 1930s. Bore lengths of the guns increased from 35 to 45 calibers and even to 40 to 45 calibers.

The larger guns of the period required mechanized ammunition hoists and complex breech-loading gear. Their metal carriages recoiled on inclined metal slides that pivoted under the gun port. The slides were trained laterally by means of transverse truck wheels moving on racers, or iron paths set into the ship's deck.

SPENCER C. TUCKER

References

Gardiner, Robert, ed., and Andrew D. Lambert, consultant ed. *Steam, Steel & Shellfire: The Steam Warship, 1815–1905.* Annapolis, MD: Naval Institute Press, 1992.

Hogg, Ian V., and John Batchelor. *Naval Gun.* Poole, Dorset, UK: Blandford, 1978.

Padfield, Peter. *Guns at Sea.* New York: St. Martin's, 1974.

Tucker, Spencer C. *Handbook of 19th Century Naval Warfare.* Annapolis, MD: Naval Institute Press, 2000.

Camouflage

Camouflage is a method of deception whereby men and their equipment are concealed from an enemy both on and off the battlefield. This process had existed since ancient times, with individuals wearing animal skins and employing foliage to conceal their location. With the development of mass armies maneuvering on the battlefield in compact formations, however, camouflage seemed of little worth.

The arrival of the long-range rifle in the second half of the 19th century changed all that. Its bullets were able to reach much farther into the battlefield than ever before, and personal concealment now became a major concern. Also, the development of smokeless powder meant that firing a rifle did not mean the immediate appearance of a telltale cloud of black smoke. It was thus much more difficult for opposing forces at greater range to detect an enemy position. Both developments heightened interest in cover and concealment. Uniforms, heretofore brightly colored in part to instill confidence in one's own side and intimidate an opponent, soon gave way to drab khaki and gray that blended in with the landscape. Cheap and fast chemical dye processes aided the process. Aerial observation, which came into its own in World War I, heightened the need to conceal one's own dispositions, even well behind the front lines.

Camouflage, first widely practiced by the Boers against the British in the Boer War (1899–1902), really came into its own in World War I. Camouflage seeks to reduce the effect of color and blend an object into the background. Properly applied, it also transforms shapes, changing them from rectangular man-made forms to the indiscriminate. Camouflage also involves removing the shine from metal equipment. Faces too might be colored, either by burned cork or by mud. White suits were introduced for alpine troops so that they would blend in against the snow.

Screens of green canvas with different-colored shapes applied to them and the netting were also widely employed beginning in World War I. Dummy tree trunks and other common objects also appeared overnight, replacing real tree trunks on the battlefield. These concealed snipers or observation outposts. At the same time, dummy heads or body shapes were used to attract enemy fire where it could do no harm to real troops.

Ships and aircraft were not immune from this process. Experiments revealed that aircraft were less prone to observation from above if they were painted in a disruptive pattern in matt colors, mainly olive green and very dark green, while the same was true from below if the undersides of fuselages and wings were painted a sky blue or light gray. Aircraft while on the ground were parked in revetments with their own camouflage netting.

At sea, attempts were made to disrupt the silhouette of a vessel by painting it in alternating dark and light gray blocks of color, known as dazzle camouflage. This type of camouflage was intended not to conceal the presence of a vessel, which was impossible, but rather to obscure its size, type, and orientation.

Camouflage reached new levels of sophistication in World War I, reached new levels of sophistication in World War II. Painted screens and face blackening, especially among elite raiding troops, came into wide use, as did helmet nets to hold foliage. Uniforms varied in color depending on the battlefield, from jungle to desert. Factories received paint that appeared to alter their shape from the air, while painted forms could give the impression of a bomb crater on an otherwise undamaged runway. Lights at night in open uninhabited positions were used to attract enemy aircraft, while night-fighter aircraft were painted black to render them more invisible. Aircraft also dropped aluminum strips (chaff) to give false readings on radar. Today there are stealth aircraft and even stealth ships designed so as to be invisible to conventional radar.

As infrared sights and observation equipment came into wider use, new materials were introduced for uniforms and camouflage netting that absorbed, rather than reflected, the infrared rays. Special paint for vehicles and equipment also absorbs infrared. Camouflage continues to be an important element of modern war.

SPENCER C. TUCKER

References

Hartcup, Guy. *Camouflage: A History of Concealment and Deception in War.* New York: Encore Editions, 1980.

Hodges, P. *Royal Navy Warship Camouflage.* London: Almark, 1973.

Stanley, R. M. *To Fool a Glass Eye: Camouflage versus Photoreconnaissance in World War II.* Shrewsbury, UK: Airlife, 1998.

Cartridge

A cartridge is the case containing the charge for a gun, which later for small arms and most artillery consisted of a single entity containing the powder charge, primer, and projectile. At first artillerists simply measured a loose amount of cannon powder to ladle into the bore of the gun. Cartridges came into general use in the second half of the 16th century. They offered the advantage of containing a precise amount of powder, which could vary and be so marked for the range desired. Once the desired sack of powder had been selected, it was rammed to the bottom of the bore and pierced by means of a sharp pick thrust through the touchhole of the gun. Fine gunpowder was then poured into the touchhole, and the gun was fired when this was ignited.

Cartridge cases were most usually of wool, paper, or parchment, but all left some residue in the bore, necessitating cleaning out the bore every few shots with a device known as a worm, which looked like a double corkscrew. The bore also had to be sponged out after every round because burning residue might ignite the next powder charge as it was being loaded. Cartridges were usually made up by gunners in garrison on land or a ship's gunner and his assistants at sea, to be stored until use.

Small-arms cartridges consisted of the entire round of cartridge case, powder, and ball. The individual musketeer ripped open the end of the cartridge case with his teeth and poured a small amount of powder into the flintlock's flash pan. He then poured the remaining powder down the barrel, to be followed by the ball and cartridge casing, which were seated at the base of the bore by means of a rammer. The cartridge case served as wadding to ensure that the ball did not move away from the powder charge when the weapon's muzzle was lowered in firing position.

In 1807 Scottish Presbyterian minister Alexander Forsyth patented a gun lock utilizing newly mercuric fulminates as a priming for firearms. A percussion cap, the inside of which was coated with the mercuric fulminates, was placed over the touchhole of small arms. When struck a blow by a hammer, it would ignite and send a flame down the touchhole to ignite the main charge in the bore. This system revolutionized the firing of small arms by sharply reducing misfires. It worked effectively with smaller individual firearms but not in large cannon with long touchholes. These guns continued to be fired by means of a loose fine powder poured into the touchhole or a quill arrangement of such powder.

A number of individuals in different countries experimented with ways to combine the percussion cap with the cartridge and projectile into one unit. In 1812 Swiss national Samuel J. Pauly patented a cartridge incorporating a metal base with a cavity for detonating powder and a striker to ignite it. It was certainly one of the most important inventions in the history of small arms.

In 1828 Johann Nikolaus von Dreyse of Prussia invented the needle gun. The first practical bolt-action breech-loading rifle, it employed a paper cartridge with the primer situated at the base of the bullet. The charge was detonated by a long, sharp needlelike firing pin that pierced the cartridge and drove through the entire length to crush the primer against the base of the bullet. Adopted by the Prussian Army in 1841, the Dreyse needle gun played an important role in the defeat of the Austrian Army in the Battle of Königgratz in 1866.

In 1829 meanwhile, Frenchman Clement Pottet designed a cartridge incorporating a depression at its base to receive a primer of fulminates. A metal cartridge case with priming on the inside of the rim of the base was patented in 1846. Such rimfire cartridges continue in those for the small-bore .22-caliber rifle of today. Pin-fire cartridges had a pin in the center of the base of the cartridge case that exploded the primer. Mass-production metal cartridge cases appeared in the 1850s, while the French Schneider cartridge of 1858 with a paper upper section and a brass base was utilized in the shotgun shell.

The center-fire brass cartridge case, so-called for the primer situated in the center of its base, won out. This helped facilitate the development of the modern bolt-action and semiautomatic rifles as well as the automatic-fire machine guns that appeared in a large number of types by the 1880s. Metal cartridge cases could also be resized, fitted with a new primer, and reloaded.

Powder bag cartridge charges continued for the largest naval and land guns, but brass fixed one-piece cartridge cases containing the primer, charge, and projectile became the norm for light artillery. These facilitated loading and made possible the so-called quick-firing guns that appeared at the end of the 19th century. Although there have been experiments with other types of cartridge cases, mostly plastics, the vast majority of subsequent changes in ammunition have been in the projectiles and in their propellent charges rather than in the cartridge case itself.

SPENCER C. TUCKER

References

Blair, Claude, ed. *Pollard's History of Firearms.* New York: Macmillan, 1983.
Brown, G. I. *The Big Bang.* Stroud, Gloucestershire, UK: Sutton, 2005.
Hoyden, G. A. *The History and Development of Small Arms Ammunition.* Tacoma, WA: Armory, 1981.

Constitution, USS

The sailing frigate *Constitution* is the oldest U.S. Navy warship still in commission and its most famous warship. It is also the world's oldest warship still afloat. One of six frigates authorized by the U.S. Congress in 1794 to mark the birth of the U.S. Navy, it was designed by Joshua Humphreys and launched at Boston on October 21, 1797. As the United States did not have a ship of the line in service until after the War of 1812, Congress intended that these ships be the largest of their classes in the world, and they were longer, heavier, and more powerfully armed than frigates of other nations. The *Constitution* is 175 feet between perpendiculars (157 feet 10 inches on keel) by 43 feet 6 inches in beam. Its original weight was 1,576 tons. Rated at 44 guns, in 1812 it carried 52 guns (30 24-pounders, 14 12-pounders, and 8 32-pounder carronades). Its contemporary British frigates initially mounted only 18-pounders (the British believed that 24-pounders would take more men to service and that 18-pounders could be fired more rapidly, but the larger crews carried on the American frigates offset this).

The *Constitution* saw service in the Caribbean during 1798–1799 in the Quasi-War with France and in the Mediterranean during 1803–1807 when it was Commodore Edward Preble's flagship in the Tripolitan War and participated in attacks on the Tripoli forts. It was the flagship of the North American Squadron during 1809–1812.

Under Captain Isaac Hull, the ship gained lasting fame in the War of 1812. During July 17–20, 1812, Hull escaped a superior British squadron while becalmed by both rowing and kedging. On August 19, 1812, the *Constitution* was off the Grand Banks when it encountered the British frigate *Guerrière* (38 guns). British shot appeared to bounce harmlessly off the *Constitution*'s live oak hull, leading to its lasting nickname of "Old Ironsides." The *Guerrière* struck; too badly damaged to save, Hull ordered it burned.

On December 29 the *Constitution,* now under Captain William Bainbridge, encountered and defeated in the South Atlantic in less than an hour the British frigate *Java* (38 guns), which was also burned. The *Constitution*'s next captain, Charles Stewart, sailed the ship from Boston in December 1814 and, off Madeira on February 20, 1815, defeated and beat into surrender two smaller Royal Navy ships, the frigate *Cyane* (32 guns) and sloop *Levant* (20 guns).

After the War of 1812 the *Constitution* returned to the Mediterranean and served often as the flagship of the U.S. squadron there. By 1830 the ship was declared unseaworthy and destined to be scrapped, but public outcry, aided by Oliver Wendell Holmes's poem "Old Ironside," forced the government to order it rebuilt. The *Constitution* returned to service in 1835. During 1844–1846 it circumnavigated the globe and in the next decade was on anti–slave trade patrol. At the beginning of the American Civil War it was serving as a training vessel for the U.S. Naval Academy at Annapolis and then at Rhode Island when the academy was moved there. Rebuilt again in 1871, it was laid up in 1882 and deteriorated. Facing scrapping in 1905, the ship was again saved by public pressure. After a complete renovation, in 1931 the *Constitution* was permanently stationed at Boston as a naval monument. In 1997 it set sail for the first time in 116 years. The frigate *Constitution* remains a U.S. Navy icon and an enduring reminder of the age of fighting sail.

SPENCER C. TUCKER

References

Gillmer, Thomas C. *Old Ironsides: The Rise, Decline, and Resurrection of the USS Constitution.* Camden, ME: International Marine, 1997.

Martin, Tyrone. *A Most Fortunate Ship: A Narrative of the USS Constitution.* Rev. ed. Annapolis, MD: Naval Institute Press, 1997.

Dahlgren Gun

Name given to a system of guns developed by U.S. Navy commander John A. Dahlgren and used extensively throughout the American Civil War by both sides. In many ways the Dahlgren gun marked the apogee of the heavy muzzle-loading gun at sea. Dahlgren first arrived at the Washington Navy Yard in 1844 as a lieutenant, assigned there to conduct ordnance-ranging experiments. Soon he was designing new firing locks for guns and had developed a new system of naval ordnance.

In 1849 Dahlgren produced a new boat howitzer for the navy. Cast of bronze, the howitzer appeared as a 12-pounder (light, 660 pounds, and heavy, 750 pounds) and 24-pounder smoothbore (1,300 pounds). There were also 3.4-inch (12-pounder, 870 pounds) and 4-inch (20-pounder, 1,350 pounds) rifles. Dahlgren boat howitzers were the finest guns of their time in the world and remained in service with the U.S. Navy until the 1880s. They were also copied by other navies.

Dahlgren is chiefly remembered, however, for the system of heavy smoothbore muzzle-loading ordnance that bears his name. In January 1850 Dahlgren submitted a draft for a 9-inch gun to the chief of ordnance. The first prototype Dahlgren gun was cast at Fort Pitt Foundry and delivered to the Washington Navy Yard in May 1850. The original 9-incher had a more angular form and only one vent. Later the design was modified in favor of a curved shape and double vent, and in 1856 the side vents were restored. The purpose of the second vent was to extend the life of the gun. Repeated firings enlarged the vent opening, and when this occurred the second vent, which had been filled with zinc, was opened, and the original vent itself sealed with zinc.

Dahlgren guns, with their smooth exterior, curved lines, and preponderant weight of metal at the breech, resembled in appearance soda water bottles and were sometimes so-called. Dahlgren designed them so as to place the greatest weight of metal at the point of greatest strain at the breech. The 9-inch Dahlgren smoothbore remained the most common broadside carriage-mounted gun in the U.S. Navy in the American Civil War; the 11-inch gun, the prototype of which was cast in 1851, was the most widely used pivot-mounted gun. Its 11-inch shell could pierce 4.5 inches of plate iron backed by 20 inches of solid oak.

Dahlgren guns appeared in a variety of sizes: 32-pounder (3,300 and 4,500 pounds), 8-inch (6,500 pounds), 9-inch (12,280 pounds), 10-inch (12,500 pounds for shell and 16,500 pounds for shot), 11-inch (16,000 pounds), 13-inch (34,000 pounds), and 15-inch (42,000 pounds). There was even a 20-inch bore (97,300 pounds) Dahlgren that, however, did not see service aboard ship during the war. The 15-inch Dahlgren was employed aboard Union monitors.

Dahlgrens also appeared as rifled guns, somewhat similar in shape to the smoothbores. Some of these had separate bronze trunnion and breech straps. Dahlgren rifles appeared in the following sizes: 4.4-inch/30-pounder (3,200 pounds), 5.1-inch/50-pounder (5,100 pounds), 6-inch/80-pounder (8,000 pounds), 7.5-inch/150-pounder (16,700 pounds), and 12-inch (45,520 pounds, only three of which were cast). Dahlgren's rifled guns were not as successful as his smoothbores, and in February 1862 most were withdrawn from service.

Apart from the rifles, Dahlgren guns were extraordinarily reliable. They remained the standard muzzle-loading guns in the navy until the introduction of breech-loading heavy guns in 1885.

SPENCER C. TUCKER

References
Dahlgren, John A. *Shells and Shell Guns.* Philadelphia: King and Baird, 1856.
Olmstead, Edwin, Wayne Stark, and Spencer C. Tucker. *The Big Guns: Civil War Siege, Seacoast, and Naval Cannon.* Alexandria Bay, NY: Museum Restoration Service, 1997.
Tucker, Spencer C. *Arming the Fleet: U.S. Naval Ordnance in the Muzzle-Loading Era.* Annapolis, MD: Naval Institute Press, 1989.

Demologos, USS

The U.S. Navy ship *Demologos* (*Fulton I*) was the first steam warship in any nation. In 1813 during the War of 1812, inventor Robert Fulton submitted plans to U.S. president James Madison for a steam warship. Secretary of the Navy William Jones and influential captains supported the idea, and Congress authorized such a vessel in March 1814. Fulton had charge of the construction. Named the *Demologos* ("Voice of the People"), the new vessel was launched at the end of October 1814. After Fulton's death in February 1815, it was renamed the *Fulton* and subsequently the *Fulton I.*

At the time of its commissioning in June 1815, the *Fulton* was the first steam frigate in any navy in the world. Intended as a harbor defense vessel for New York City, it was a catamaran, not a true frigate. Its twin hulls protected a center paddle wheel. Fulton conceived the vessel as a floating battery utilizing steam power as the sole source of motive power, but Captain David Porter, who took command of the *Fulton* while it was under construction, insisted on adding a two-mast lateen sail rig. This alteration required bulwarks on the spar deck capable of protecting men working the sails and added greatly to the ship's displacement without enhancing its fighting qualities.

Weighing 2,475 tons and having a length of 153 feet 2 inches and a width of 56 feet, the *Fulton* was the largest war steamer in the world. Its engine developed 120 horsepower, and it could make 5.5 miles per hour under steam alone. Its 50-inch–thick outer bulwarks were considered shot-proof. The *Fulton* was rated at 30 guns, and the plan was to arm it with large columbiads, but it carried long 32-pounders on its trial run. Discussion of the armament is academic, because with the end of the war the ship was never fully completed for service.

The *Fulton* became a receiving ship at the Brooklyn Navy Yard. It blew up there in June 1829, the result of careless handling of gunpowder in its magazine.

SPENCER C. TUCKER

Reference

Canney, Donald L. *The Old Steam Navy,* Vol. 1, *Frigates, Sloops, and Gunboats, 1815–1885.* Annapolis, MD: Naval Institute Press, 1990.

Destroyer

Destroyers are relatively small, lightly armed and armored (even unprotected) warships capable of high speed. They were specifically developed to deal with the threat posed to the battle fleet by torpedo boats. First known as the torpedo boat destroyer, later the new ship was called simply a destroyer. The precursor was probably the Royal Navy *Polyphemus* of 1881. Known as a torpedo ram, it displaced 2,640 tons, was 240 by 40 feet in size, and was capable of a speed of 18 knots. It carried a 2-pounder gun and 18 torpedoes for its five torpedo tubes.

To counter the large number of torpedo boats built by the rival French and Russian navies, in 1898 the Royal Navy contracted for what became known as a torpedo boat destroyer. Early types, however, lacked the speed to hunt down and destroy torpedo boats. That changed with the *Havock* of 1893, generally regarded as the first modern torpedo boat destroyer. Weighing 275 tons, it was 180 by 19 feet and capable of nearly 27 knots. It was armed with a 12-pounder and three 6-pounder guns as well as three 18-inch torpedo tubes.

Each subsequent design registered improvements. Typical of British destroyers were the 34 River-class (later E-class) destroyers. They averaged 550 tons and 225 by 24 feet and were armed with four 12-pounders and two 18-inch torpedo tubes. Such ships were capable of sustained operations with the battle fleet.

With their excessive vibration, wet conditions, and excessive rolling, destroyers were difficult ships for their crews. Some of these negatives were mitigated in later designs that altered both superstructure and weight displacement. HMS *Viper,* launched in 1899, was the world's first naval vessel powered by the new turbine engine. This 440-ton destroyer was 210 by 21 feet. Armed with one 12-pounder and five 6-pounder guns and two torpedo tubes, it was, at 37 knots, the fastest ship in the fleet.

The U.S. Navy destroyer *Bainbridge* (DD-1), completed in 1902, began the U.S. Navy numbering system for destroyers; the last in this numbering system was DD-997, the Spruance-class *Hayler* in 1983. In 1914 destroyers were the most numerous warships of the world's navies, with Britain operating 221, Germany 90, France 81, Russia 42, and the United States and Japan about 50 each. Destroyers assumed the role of torpedo boats in attacking the capital ships of an enemy fleet, but they also were charged with providing perimeter protection for one's own capital ships against enemy destroyers. During World War I, Allied destroyers provided protection for the vital convoys. With the advent of the submarine, destroyers became the primary antisubmarine vessel. Equipped with depth charges and hydrophones in 1917 and ASDIC (sonar) in 1918, they proved to be highly effective submarine hunters. They also provided gunfire support for amphibious operations.

Destroyers continued in these same roles in World War II in addition to a new role as antiaircraft platforms. Probably the best known of World War II destroyers were the 150 U.S. Navy Fletcher-class ships. Launched during 1942–1945 and displacing 2,325 tons, they were 376 by 40 feet in size and capable of a speed of 38 knots. They carried an armament of five single-mount 5-inch guns along with four 40-millimeter (mm) and four 20-mm guns and 10 21-inch torpedo tubes. They had a crew complement of 273 men. Considered some of the best destroyers ever built, the Fletchers played an important role in the Pacific theater.

Destroyers remained in service after the war and fought in the Korean War. In 1957 the United States launched the *Coontz,* the first purpose-built guided missile destroyers (DDG). The Soviet Union followed the American lead in 1958. In August 1964 two U.S. destroyers were the focus of the Gulf of Tonkin Incidents. During the 1982 Falklands War, British destroyers protected troop ships from Argentine submarine and air attack.

In the first decade of the 21st century, destroyers are the heaviest surface combatants in general use, with only four navies—those of the United States, the Russian Federation, France, and Peru—still operating cruisers and none having battleships in active service. Modern destroyers, also known as guided missile destroyers, are equivalent in tonnage but substantially superior in firepower to World War II-era cruisers.

SPENCER C. TUCKER

References

Gardiner, Robert, ed., and Andrew D. Lambert, consultant ed. *Steam, Steel & Shellfire: The Steam Warship, 1815–1905.* Annapolis, MD: Naval Institute Press, 1992.

George, James L. *History of Warships: From Ancient Times to the Twenty-First Century.* Annapolis, MD: Naval Institute Press, 1998.

Preston, Anthony. *Destroyers.* Englewood Cliffs, NJ: Prentice-Hall, 1977.

Smith, Peter. *Hard Lying: The Birth of the Destroyer, 1893–1913.* Annapolis, MD: Naval Institute Press, 1971.

Tucker, Spencer C. *Handbook of 19th Century Naval Warfare.* Annapolis, MD: Naval Institute Press, 2000.

Dynamite

Dynamite is a powerful explosive invented by Swiss chemist and engineer Alfred Nobel in 1866 and patented a year later. Nobel's involvement in heavy construction work in Stockholm led him to try to develop safer methods of blasting rock. In 1846 Italian chemist Ascanio Sobrero had invented nitroglycerin, which consists of a mix of sulfuric acid, nitric acid, and glycerin. A powerful explosive, nitroglycerin soon found application in commercial mining and blasting operations, but it suffered from the drawback of being highly volatile in its liquid state. Even a slight shock can cause nitroglycerin to explode, and it was thus very dangerous to transport and utilize.

Nobel discovered that nitroglycerin could be stabilized when absorbed in diatomaceous earth (kieselguhr). He named his invention dynamite, after the Greek *dynamos* ("powerful"). It was the first safe and predictable explosive with a greater force than gunpowder and was certainly one of the great inventions of the 19th century.

Dynamite consists of three parts nitroglycerin and one part diatomaceous earth as well as a small amount of sodium carbonate. Dynamite most usually is formed into sticks about an inch in diameter and eight inches long and wrapped in paper. These sticks were in this manner so that they could be easily inserted in holes drilled into rock.

Dynamite is classified as a high explosive, meaning that it detonates instead of deflagrating. Nobel sold his explosive as Nobel's Safety Blasting Powder. In order to detonate the dynamite, Nobel also developed a blasting cap, which he also patented. It was ignited by lighting a fuse.

Dynamite found wide application in such areas as construction, mining all sorts of materials, and digging canals and tunnels. Its military implications were also immense. Dynamite found its way into high-explosive fillers for artillery shells, bombs, and land mines. It was also used in satchel charges.

Nobel made a great fortune from his invention. The Republic of South Africa soon became the largest producer of dynamite, which was widely used in mining for gold. Nobel later used some of his money gained from the invention to establish prizes in the sciences, although the most recognized of these prizes is the Nobel Prize for Peace. Nobel's invention ended centuries of experiment with gunpowder and inaugurated a new era of vastly more powerful high explosives.

SPENCER C. TUCKER

References
Brown, Stephen R. *A Most Damnable Invention: Dynamite, Nitrates, and the Making of the Modern World.* New York: St. Martin's, 2005.
Fordham, Stanley. *High Explosives and Propellents.* Oxford, UK: Pergamon, 1980.

Explosive Shell and the Shell Gun

The introduction of a bursting projectile and a gun specifically designed to project it had tremendous impact on warship design and naval warfare. Solid shot had been the mainstay at sea for centuries. Shot was used to hole a vessel, damage and destroy spars and masts, and create crew casualties. But wooden warships with their thick oak sides could absorb a tremendous number of hits. Even if it penetrated, shot tended to leave regular rounded holes easily plugged by a ship's carpenter, especially as the wooden fibers tended to close after shot had passed through. In any case, it took a great many such holes to sink a large wooden warship. Occasionally ships were lost by a magazine explosion, but most captured vessels were disabled through damage to masts, spars, and rigging or from heavy personnel casualties that enabled them to be taken by boarding.

The antipersonnel effects of shot occurred when it exited the wood and produced showers of splinters. The effects of this were greatest when the force of the shot was only slightly more than that required to pass through the wood. But far too often, shot failed to penetrate the wooden side of a ship at all. Shell was designed not to penetrate. It moved at a slow velocity in order to lodge in the side of a ship and there explode, causing an irregular hole that would be difficult to patch and, in many cases, large enough that it might even sink the vessel. Shot had greater range, but shell was much more destructive.

With improvements in both shells and fusing (crews firing early shells dreaded them because on occasion the shells exploded prematurely, bursting the gun), special guns were developed to fire explosive shell. The French took the lead because they had less to lose and more to gain than the British from the introduction of an entirely new system (the British had by far the world's largest navy). In trials conducted in the 1820s, French Colonel (later general) Henri Paixhans proved the effectiveness of explosive shell against wooden ships.

Shell guns had the great advantage of being lighter than shotguns, as shell was fired with smaller charges. This meant that the weight of metal that a warship fired in broadside might actually be increased at the same time that the weight of its ordnance was reduced. In 1837 the French introduced the Paixhans 80-pounder shell gun as a part of every ship's regular battery. It weighed as much as a 36-pounder shotgun. A frigate armed with a few of the new guns could easily defeat a much larger ship of the line.

In the 1840s shells and shell guns came into general use in the world's navies. In the United States, Lieutenant John Dahlgren developed his own ordnance system for the U.S. Navy. In effect, explosive shell projected by special shell guns rendered wooden ships obsolete and led to the introduction of the ironclad warship. The irony is that with the appearance of the ironclad ship during the American Civil War, Dahlgren's shell guns fired solid shot rather than explosive shell against Confederate ironclads.

SPENCER C. TUCKER

References
Gardiner, Robert, ed., and Andrew D. Lambert, consultant ed. *Steam, Steel & Shellfire: The Steam Warship, 1815–1905.* Annapolis, MD: Naval Institute Press, 1992.

Hogg, Ian V., and John Batchelor. *Naval Gun.* Poole, Dorset, UK: Blandford, 1978.

Tucker, Spencer C. *Arming the Fleet: U.S. Naval Ordnance in the Muzzle-Loading Era.* Annapolis, MD: Naval Institute Press, 1989.

Gatling Gun

The American Civil War (1861–1865) gave rise to a number of new weapons. Among these were several precursors to the modern machine gun, including Wilson Ager's Coffee Mill. It took its name from the means of feeding the ammunition from the top of the weapon by a funnel and crank mechanism, all of which resembled a coffee mill.

Ager's gun had a single barrel. The ammunition was formed of a steel tube that contained powder and a .58-caliber bullet and a nipple at the end for a percussion cap. Steady turning of the crank dropped a round into the chamber, locked the breech block in place, dropped a hammer that fired the round, and ejected the spent case. Ager claimed a firing rate of 100 rounds a minute, although the gun barrel could not have long withstood the heat thus generated.

Ager demonstrated his weapon before President Abraham Lincoln, and the U.S. Army eventually purchased 50 of them. The Coffee Mills proved unreliable, however, in combat use and were never employed en masse. Ultimately they were used in the defensives of Washington.

Confederate Army captain D. R. Williams also invented a mechanical gun. Mounted on a mountain-howitzer carriage, it was a 4-foot-long 1-pounder of 1.57-inch bore. Operated by a hand crank, it utilized paper cartridges and could fire 65 shots a minute. It tended to overheat, and it was also not a true machine weapon in that ammunition was fed into it by hand.

Other such weapons also appeared, but the most famous of mechanical guns was that invented by Richard Jordan Gatling in 1862. Well aware of problems from the buildup of heat, Gatling designed his gun with six rotating barrels around a central axis, each barrel fired in turn and each with its own bolt and firing pin. Thus, in a firing rate of 300 rounds per minute, each barrel would have been utilized only 50 times.

The Gatling gun employed a hopper for the ammunition similar to that of the Coffee Mill. The first Gatling gun also employed steel cylinders with a percussion cap at the end, a round, and paper cartridges with the charge. The production model did away with the percussion cap in favor of a rimfire cartridge. Turning the crank rotated the barrels, dropped in the rounds, and fired each barrel in turn. The chief difference from the Coffee Mill was in the rotating multiple-barrel design.

The U.S. Army's chief of ordnance Colonel John W. Ripley, who was well known for his opposition to innovative weaponry, blocked adoption of the Gatling gun. Gatling's North Carolina birth also seems to have worked against him. Despite Gatling's appeals to Lincoln, the army never adopted the gun. Its only use in the American Civil War came when Major General Benjamin Butler purchased six of them at his own expense and employed them effectively in the Siege of Petersburg at the end of the war.

In 1864 Gatling redesigned the gun so that each barrel had its own chamber, which helped prevent the leakage of gas. Gatling also adopted center-fire cartridges. These and other refinements produced a rate of fire of about 300 rounds per minute. Finally in 1866 the U.S. Army purchased 100 Gatling guns, equally divided between 6-barrel models of 1-inch caliber and 10-barrel models of .50-inch caliber. Gatling worked out a licensing agreement with Colt Arms to produce the gun.

The Gatling gun provided effective service in the Indian Wars in the American West and in the Spanish-American War. The V Corps' Gatling Gun Detachment played an important role in the Santiago Campaign in Cuba, especially in the U.S. victory in the Battle of San Juan Hill of July 1, 1898. They also were utilized in the Puerto Rico Campaign.

Gatling guns also served with the U.S. Navy. Tested by the British government in 1870, the Gatling gun out-shot its competition by a wide margin and was adopted by both the British Army and the Royal Navy in

.42 caliber and .65 caliber, respectively. It remained the standard mechanical rapid-fire weapon until the introduction of the Maxim gun, the first true machine gun.

During the Vietnam War era Gatling-type weapons returned, this time electrically driven. The 20-mm M-61 Vulcan automatic cannon was first designed as an aircraft weapon but was also used as a ground-based antiaircraft weapon. The smaller 7.62-mm M-134 minigun was primarily a helicopter-mounted weapon.

SPENCER C. TUCKER

References

Berk, Joseph. *The Gatling Gun: 19th Century Machine Gun to 21st Century Vulcan.* Boulder, CO: Paladin, 1991.

Wahl, Paul, and Don Toppel. *The Gatling Gun.* New York: Arco, 1965.

Willbanks, James H. *Machine Guns: An Illustrated History of Their Impact.* Santa Barbara, CA: ABC-CLIO, 2004.

Gloire

French leaders most fully understood the implications of the ironclad floating batteries introduced during the Crimean War. Convinced that wooden ships were obsolete, they ordered a halt in construction of wooden ships of the line (the last was laid down in 1855) and began converting their most powerful warships into fast single-gun deck ironclads. The French also carried out a series of armor experiments, seeing a chance to outflank their rival Britain and offset the Royal Navy's numerical superiority with new technology.

Chief French naval constructor Stanislaus Dupuy de Lôme's steam screw frigate *Gloire* began the ironclad revolution. Laid down at Toulon in 1858, the *Gloire* entered service in 1860. Described both as an armored frigate and a cut-down two-deck ship of the line, it was in fact altogether a new class of ship.

The *Gloire* was a three-masted ship of nearly 5,618 tons, measuring 254 feet 5 inches by 55 feet 6 inches. Slightly longer than the wooden steam battleship *Napoleon,* it had finer lines that enabled its French-built 900-horsepower engine to drive it at a high speed of 13.5 knots. Dupuy de Lôme sharply reduced the sail area; these were only to have a secondary role.

Because the French lacked the British iron shipbuilding experience and resources, the *Gloire* was constructed of wood. Indeed, it was built basically along the same lines as its wooden predecessors; the difference was that it was protected by a 4.5-inch iron belt that ran the entire length of the ship and extended from 6 feet below the waterline to the upper deck. The belt was supported by 17 inches of wood. The *Gloire* mounted 14 22-centimeter (cm) (8.8-inch) and 16-cm (6.4-inch) rifled breech-loading guns. It was, however, not a good sea boat. Rolling badly, it also was not the best gun platform. Dupuy de Lôme had in fact not designed the *Gloire* for high-seas operations.

Even before the *Gloire* had entered service, Paris decided in March 1858 to order additional ironclads. The *Gloire*'s sister ships, *Normandie* and *Invincible,* were launched in March 1860 and April 1861. They were followed by the *Magenta* and *Solferino* in June 1861. The *Gloire* certainly began the naval revolution, but the British response, the *Warrior,* which entered service in 1861, was a true iron seagoing vessel and was superior to the *Gloire* in virtually every respect.

SPENCER C. TUCKER

References

Baxter, James Phinney. *The Introduction of the Ironclad Warship.* New York: Archon Books, 1968.

Darrieus, Henri, and Jean Quéguiner. *Historique de la Marine française (1815–1918).* Saint-Malo, France: Éditions l'Ancre de la Marine, 1997.

George, James L. *History of Warships: From Earliest Times to the Twenty-first Century.* Annapolis, MD: Naval Institute Press, 1998.

Tucker, Spencer C. *Handbook of 19th Century Naval Warfare.* Annapolis, MD: Naval Institute Press, 2000.

Holland, USS

Irish immigrant to the United States John P. Holland invented the first really practical submarine. Holland arrived in America in 1873 with a hatred of the English. He hoped that his submarine might end British dominance at sea and perhaps its hold on Ireland. Holland planned to use water ballasts to submerge the submarine and horizontal rudders to make it dive. Navy Department officials were unimpressed, and so Holland approached the Fenian Brotherhood, an organization dedicated to independence for Ireland. In 1876 Holland demonstrated a 30-inch model of his submarine to Fenian supporters at Coney Island, New York, and they agreed to advance money for the project.

The one-man *Holland I* was lozenge-shaped with a length of 24 feet 6 inches and a breadth of 12 feet 6 inches. It had a square conning tower. The submarine sank when launched, unoccupied, on May 22, 1878. It was easily recovered, and a week later Holland took it out on a successful trial.

Holland's next submarine, the *Holland II,* was also funded by the Fenians. Weighing 19 tons, it was powered by a 15-horsepower combustion engine. Utilizing horizontal rudders while under way, it actually dove beneath the surface, unlike its predecessor, which simply sank in place. The *Holland II* was also equipped with a pneumatic cannon to fire a torpedo. Twice Holland entered and won U.S. Navy submarine design competitions, but his steam-powered *Plunger* of 1897 proved unsuccessful. Believing the navy specifications to be unrealistic, Holland decided to build a submarine to his own specifications.

Holland built his sixth submarine, at Elizabeth, New Jersey, during 1896–1897. The *Holland VI,* which made its first surface run in February 1898, is usually known simply as the *Holland.* The forerunner of all modern submarines, it was powered by an internal-combustion 45-horsepower gasoline engine for running on the surface with hatches open and an electric motor for submerged operation. While it was running, the gasoline engine powered a generator that recharged the batteries. The *Holland* was the first submarine to be so equipped, with this system becoming common on submarines for the next half century.

The *Holland* had a length of 53 feet 10 inches and a breadth of 10 feet 3 inches. It displaced only 63.3 tons on the surface and 74 tons submerged. It was armed with a single 18-inch torpedo tube and could carry two reload torpedoes. It was also equipped with an 8-inch pneumatic dynamite gun mounted forward. The *Holland* could travel at 8 knots on the surface and 5–6 knots submerged. It was designed for a crew of five.

Its stability while submerged and greater range put the *Holland* in a class by itself. Recognizing the importance of the design, in April 1900 the navy purchased the submarine, commissioning it that October. Later it was assigned hull number SS-1 as the U.S. Navy's first submarine. In September 1900 during North Atlantic Squadron war games off Newport, Rhode Island, the *Holland* carried out mock torpedo attacks against the battleship *Kearsarge,* during which the latter was ruled to have been sunk. A month earlier, Washington had signed a contract with the Holland Torpedo Boat Company for six additional submarines, the first of which was launched in July 1901. Given names, they were known as the Adder class. The *Holland* itself became a training vessel and was finally scrapped in 1913.

SPENCER C. TUCKER

References

Morris, Richard Knowles. *John P. Holland, 1841–1914, Inventor of the Modern Submarine.* Annapolis, MD: Naval Institute Press, 1965.

U.S. Navy. *Dictionary of American Naval Fighting Ships,* Vol. 3. 8 vols. Washington, DC: Naval History Division, Department of the Navy, 1960–1981.

Ironclad Warships

While steam power was being applied to warships, experiments were also going forward with iron-hulled vessels. The boom in railroad construction in Britain reduced the price of iron and sharply increased the number of men skilled in its manufacture. The first iron vessels were canal boats at the end of the 18th century. In 1838 the British transatlantic liner *Great Britain* proved the durability of iron construction for larger ships, and the next step was to apply this to warships.

The British firm of Laird had already built several iron ships for the East India Company, and in 1839 Laird launched the first iron warship, the *Nemesis,* an iron paddler for the Bengal Marine, the naval arm of the East India Company. The world's first significant iron warship was the steam frigate *Guadeloupe,* built by Laird for Mexico in 1842. It and another Laird iron warship, the *Montezuma,* proved their worth in fighting against Texas. Under fire almost daily over a period of four to five weeks, the *Guadeloupe* was repeatedly hulled, but the shot passed through cleanly with few dangerous splinters (which caused the most personnel casualties on battle involving wooden warships), and the holes were easily patched. Royal Navy officers who served on the two ships thought them excellent fighting vessels.

Iron was brittle, however, and experiments revealed that it tended to fracture under the impact of shot, whereas wood merely absorbed it. This and the loss of the iron-hulled troop ship *Birkenhead* on February 26, 1852, with the death of 455 people, resulted in a temporary move away from iron hulls.

The Crimean War changed this thinking. On November 30, 1853, at Sinop (Sinope), Turkey, a Russian squadron destroyed a Turkish squadron at anchor. The Russians fired both shot and shell, but shell did the most damage, tearing large irregular holes when it exploded in the wooden sides of the Turkish ships. The effect of shell in the battle at Sinop was exaggerated—the Turks were simply overwhelmed in every category—but the battle renewed interest in iron as armor over wooden ships. French emperor Napoleon III took the lead, the first ironclad vessels being literally ironclad in that iron armor was applied as plates over the wooden sides. The emperor, who was knowledgeable about artillery, wanted 10 such vessels for the 1855 campaign, but with French yards able to build only 5, he asked Britain to construct a like number. British chief naval engineer Thomas Lloyd meanwhile demonstrated that four inches of iron could indeed protect against powerful shot.

Virtually rectangular in shape so as to provide a more effective gun platform, the French ironclad floating batteries were some 170 feet by 43 feet in size and were protected by 4-inch iron plate backed by 17 inches of wood. Each mounted 16 50-pounder guns and 2 12-pounders and was capable of a speed of 4 knots under steam. Not seagoing vessels, they were specifically designed to batter Russian land fortifications.

On October 17, 1855, three of the French *batteries flottantes cuirassées* (armored floating batteries), the *Dévastation, Lave,* and *Tonnante,* took part in an attack on Russia's Kinburn forts in an estuary at the mouth of the Dnieper and Bug rivers. The Russian fortifications, three of which were of stone and two of sand, housed 81 guns and mortars. From a range of between 900 and 1,200 yards in an engagement lasting from 9:30 a.m. until noon, the French vessels fired 3,177 shot and shell and reduced the Russian forts to rubble. Although they were repeatedly hulled, the vessels themselves were largely impervious to the Russian fire. The *Dévastation* suffered 67 hits and the *Tonnante* 66. Two men were killed and 24 wounded, but the casualties resulted from two hot shot entering gun ports and another through an imperfect main hatch. The vessels' armor was only dented. At noon an allied fleet of ships of the line shelled what was left of the forts from a range of 1,600 yards, and in less than 90 minutes the Russians surrendered. Undoubtedly, the success of the batteries was magnified because they were the emperor's special project, but many observers concluded that the Kinburn battle proved the effectiveness of wrought iron and marked the end of the old ships of the line.

Britain also built four floating batteries in 1856. Of the same general size as the French vessels, they were each armed with 14 68-pounder guns and were protected by four-inch iron armor, supported by six inches of oak.

Many observers now considered wooden warships to be obsolete, and the next step was to build true ironclad warships as opposed to mere floating batteries. France took the lead because it had far less to lose than the British, who maintained the world's largest wooden navy. The *Gloire* of 1860 began the naval revolution. The British responded with their *Warrior* of 1861, the first iron-hulled armor-plated warship.

The American Civil War (1861–1865) saw the most extensive ironclad construction and helped prompt further ironclad construction. The U.S. Navy *Monitor* of 1861 was the most innovative, although not necessarily the most practical, of the early ironclad designs. During the war the North alone laid down 56 ironclads (52 of them of the turreted or Monitor type). The first clash between ironclad warships occurred in March 1862 during the American Civil War when the *Monitor* and the Confederate ironclad *Virginia* fought to a stalemate in Hampton Roads, Virginia.

SPENCER C. TUCKER

References

Baxter, James P. *The Introduction of the Ironclad Warship.* Cambridge: Harvard University Press, 1933.

George, James L. *History of Warships: From Earliest Times to the Twenty-first Century.* Annapolis, MD: Naval Institute Press, 1998.

Tucker, Spencer C. *Handbook of 19th Century Naval Warfare.* Annapolis, MD: Naval Institute Press, 2000.

Lebel Rifle

In 1886 France was the first nation to add a high-velocity small-bore rifle to its arms inventory. It was also the first standard weapon to incorporate the spitzer bullet. Two years earlier French chemist Paul Vielle developed a successful nitrocellulose powder for small arms; his Poudre B was the first successful smokeless powder adopted by any nation. Weapons utilizing it also had a much higher muzzle velocity than those employing ordinary gunpowder cartridges.

The French government was not slow to capitalize on Vielle's work. Two years later it introduced the 8-millimeter (mm) (.315 caliber) Lebel, based on the earlier 11-mm Gras and officially known as the Fusil d'infanterie Modèle 1886. It was named for Colonel Nicolas Lebel, who chaired the committee that oversaw its development. Because the powder was more powerful, the French were able to reduce the caliber of the weapon and hence the weight of the ammunition, permitting individual soldiers to carry more rounds. With the Lebel, France captured the lead in small-arms development from Germany.

In 1898 the French introduced the spitzer boat-tail bullet in the Lebel. A more aerodynamic bullet, it had a tapered rear that looked a bit like a boat stern. The original bullet was 232 grains and had a flat nose and base. The spitzer was 198 grains. All military bullets are of this streamlined shape today.

The Lebel was an excellent long-range high-velocity (2,380 feet per second) firearm, but it was also heavy, at 9 pounds 3.5 ounces, and in many ways an anachronism mechanically for its eight-round tubular magazine that was difficult to load with a stiff feed sprung. Most new rifles were utilizing box magazines. The Lebel-Berthier 1907/1915 modification replaced the tubular magazine with a box magazine and Mannlicher clip, first for three rounds and then for five. The latter model had a weight of 8 pounds 8 ounces and remained in service until the 1950s.

The technological advances of the longer-range Lebel were obvious, and other nations quickly followed suit. Germany and Austria-Hungary produced an 8-mm smokeless powder rifle in 1888. The standard German infantry rifle of World War I, the 7.92-mm 5-shot Mauser, developed by Peter Paul Mauser, appeared in 1898 and incorporated the clip and magazine into one mechanism. Italy produced its first smokeless powder rifle in 1890. Britain was slower in this regard. Its .303-caliber smokeless powder Lee-Enfield, named for its designer, American James Lee, and its manufacturer, the Royal Small Arms Factor in Enfield, London, appeared only in 1895. The Short Magazine Lee-Enfield (SMLE) Mark III with which the British fought World War I was first produced in 1907. It incorporated a 10-round magazine and was suited to high-volume fire, as the well-trained professional British infantry showed in fighting at Mons in Belgium early in the war. An excellent weapon, it continued in service into World War II. Perhaps half the American troops in France in World War I were supplied with the M1917 American Enfield, which was chambered for .30-06 caliber. The remainder received the excellent M1903 .30-06-caliber Springfield, manufactured at the Springfield Armory in Massachusetts. Comparable in performance to the Lee-Enfield, it utilized a Mauser-type action. The M-1903 Springfield remained in service through the early days of World War II.

SPENCER C. TUCKER

References
Blair, Claude, ed. *Pollard's History of Firearms.* New York: Macmillan, 1983.
Smith, W. H. B. *Small Arms of the World.* 9th ed. Harrisburg, PA: Stackpole, 1969.

Maxim Gun

If any one weapon symbolized World War I, it was the machine gun. Efficient manually operated rapid-firing small arms were in service in the 1860s and 1870s, including the Agar Coffee Mill (ca. 1860) and the Gatling gun (1862) employed at the end of the American Civil War (1861–1865). The French utilized the 25-barrel Mitrailleuse (1869) in the Franco-Prussian War (1870–1871). But the Maxim gun of 1884, named for American Hiram Maxim, was the first truly automatic machine gun. Development of the metallic cartridge made possible rapid loading at the breech.

Maxim's innovation was to use some of the energy of the firing to operate the weapon. Using the recoil energy, which he called blowback, Maxim designed a fully automatic rifle fed by a revolving magazine. He then applied the same principle to a machine gun, which fired as long as the trigger was depressed. In the Maxim gun, the firing of the cartridge drove back the bolt, compressing a spring that in turn drove the bolt forward again, bringing a new round into position for firing. The Maxim gun was both self-loading and self-ejecting.

Maxim demonstrated his prototype machine gun in 1884. It weighed 60 pounds (the Mitrailleuse had weighed 2,000 pounds because it was mounted on a towed field carriage, like an artillery piece). The Maxim was both belt fed and water cooled. It fired a .45-caliber bullet at a rate of up to 600 rounds per minute and could be operated by a crew of only five men. The gun was fired principally by a single gunner. The others assisted in carrying it and in bringing up belts of ammunition for it. Aided by the British firm of Vickers, Maxim had his gun largely perfected before the end of the 1880s.

The British employed the Maxim gun with great success against the Zulus in South Africa and the Dervishes in the Sudan. Rudyard Kipling proclaimed the importance of the new weapon when he wrote, "Whatever else, we have got the Maxim gun, and they have not." Maxim was later knighted by Queen Victoria for "services to humanity" in the false assumption that the machine gun would make wars shorter and thus more humane. Despite the experiences of the Boer War (1899–1902) and the Russo-Japanese War (1904–1905), almost all armies had failed to come to terms with the new lethality of the increased firepower by the start of World War I in 1914. At 450–600 rounds per minute, one machine gun could equal the fire of 40 to 80 riflemen. It also had greater range than the rifle, enabling indirect fire in support of an attack. In the German Army, machine guns initially were deployed in companies as opposed to dispersing them among infantry formations, but as the war progressed the Germans altered their tactics and organization to make the light machine gun the centerpiece of the German infantry squad. Light machine guns, such as the excellent Lewis Gun, appeared later and saw widespread service in World War I.

Spencer C. Tucker

References
Goldsmith, Duff L., and R. Blake Stevens. *The Devil's Paintbrush: Sir Hiram Maxim's Gun.* 2nd ed. Toronto, CA: Collector Grade Publications, 1993.
Willbanks, James H. *Machine Guns: An Illustrated History of Their Impact.* Santa Barbara, CA: ABC-CLIO, 2004.

Mines, Sea

The idea of using explosive devices to sink ships dates to at least the 16th century, but American and Yale University student David Bushnell developed the first practical sea mine. During the American Revolutionary War, he constructed floating contact mines in his workshop near Saybrook, Connecticut. These consisted of kegs of powder triggered by a flintlock. When the keg struck an object, the shock released the hammer and set off the main charge.

On January 5, 1778, Bushnell released his mines in the Delaware River in an effort to destroy British warships downstream. The current was slow, and the mines took more than a week to reach the British anchorage, by which time many of the ships had moved. Also, some boys spotted one of the kegs and tried to retrieve it, and the mine blew up and killed them. Thus warned, the British fired at anything floating in the water, initiating what became known as the Battle of the Kegs.

In 1801 during the Napoleonic Wars, American Robert Fulton tried to interest Napoleon Bonaparte in employing submarine-laid mines of his invention against English shipping in the Thames. After Bonaparte rejected his ideas, Fulton went to London in 1804 to try to sell his scheme there. Prime Minister William Pitt, worried that the concentration of French shipping across the English Channel was for a possible invasion of England, arranged a contract for Fulton to build so-called submarine bombs.

In 1804 and again in 1805, Fulton carried out two attempts against French ships at Boulogne with floating mines set to explode on 10-minute fuses. Deployed from cutters, the mines were secured together in pairs by means of a long line. Fulton hoped that these lines would catch on the cables of the vessels, causing the mines to come to rest against the ship's sides and there explode. Although many mines did indeed explode, the results were insignificant.

On October 15, 1805, Fulton demonstrated his mines in England against a 200-ton captured Danish brig, the *Dorothea*. This trial, of two mines secured to one another by a line and set to explode in 18 minutes, worked. The blast lifted the ship out of the water and broke it completely in two, the first time that a large vessel had been destroyed by a mine.

With Pitt's death in 1806, however, Fulton lost his chief patron. The admiral Earl St. Vincent then dismissed Fulton, calling Pitt "the greatest fool that ever existed, to encourage a mode of war which they who commanded the seas did not want, and which, if successful, would deprive them of it."

Fulton returned to the United States, where he conducted additional experiments with his so-called torpedoes, named for the electric ray fish that shocks its prey. In July 1807 Fulton blew up a 200-ton brig in New York Harbor, although this required several attempts before it was successful. He also advocated defensive mining to close American ports to an attacker in time of war.

Mining was not successful during the War of 1812. In July 1813 Fulton's mines were employed in a half dozen unsuccessful attempts to attack a British 74-gun ship near Norfolk. A similar attempt failed against British ships in Long Island Sound.

In 1839 Russian czar Nicholas I appointed Prussian émigré Moritz-Hermann Jacobi head of a scientific committee to conduct experiments in a galvanic (electronic) mine. As early as 1782 Tiberius Cavallo had demonstrated that gunpowder could be detonated by means of an electric current. He summed up his work in *Treatise on Magnetism in Theory and Practice* (1787). Building on work by Cavallo, Fulton, fellow American Samuel Colt, and Russian baron Pavel L'vovich Schilling von Cannstadt, Jacobi developed working mines by the time of the Crimean War (1854–1856). Jacobi's mines were zinc canisters filled with gunpowder and set off by a detonator, a glass tube filled with acid that when broken ignited the main charge of gunpowder. During the war the Russians used chemical, contact, and electrical command-detonated mines in both the Baltic and Black seas. Crimean War mines were, however, too small to inflict great damage.

Mines came into their own during the American Civil War (1861–1865). Hoping to reduce the sizable Union naval advantage, the Confederacy employed them extensively. Confederate Navy officer and scientist Matthew Fontaine Maury was an early proponent of mines and conducted extensive experiments with them. American Civil War naval mines/torpedoes were of a variety of types but were essentially stationary weapons, a sort of buoy held in place at an appropriate distance from the surface by a cable anchored to the sea bottom by a weight. There were two basic types of detonation: contact and electricity. The first were detonated when the horns surrounding the charge were broken; this set off a chemical reaction that ignited the charge. The second were fired by means of electrical connections from batteries on shore. The first were more certain to explode but were unable to distinguish their victim and hence were also dangerous to friendly vessels. The second type could only be used close to shore. More often than not, early mines failed to explode as a result of faulty detonating equipment or when they became waterlogged or were swept away by the current. Even so, they had a profound psychological effect on Union sailors, producing so-called torpedo fever.

Mines discovered during the February 1862 Union assault on Fort Henry on the Tennessee River were sheet-iron cylinders some 5.5 feet long and pointed at the ends, each containing about 75 pounds of gunpowder. They were fired by contact-type detonators. All those recovered were waterlogged and harmless, however.

On December 12, 1862, the Union ironclad *Cairo* succumbed to a mine in the Yazoo River, but the first ship loss in actual battle was the ironclad *Tecumseh,* which went down during the August 5, 1864, Battle of Mobile Bay. Powder charges in American Civil War mines ranged from approximately 50 pounds to up to a ton. One of the latter type, detonated electronically, sank the Union gunboat *Commodore Jones* in the James River on May 6, 1864.

Mines were also used offensively as spar torpedoes at the end of a spar, or pole. The Confederates built a number of craft designed to operate very low in the water and carry such a spar torpedo in their bows to attack Union warships. On the night of October 5, 1863, one of these craft, the *David,* damaged the Union ironclad *New Ironsides.* The Union also employed such weapons, and on October 18, 1864, the Union *Picket Boat No. 1* sank the Confederate ironclad ram *Albermarle* with a spar torpedo.

The largest ship sunk by a mine during the war was the Union steam sloop *Housatonic.* On February 17, 1864, it sank off Charleston, the victim of a 90-pound spar torpedo from the partially submerged Confederate submarine *H. L. Hunley.* In all, 50 ships were sunk or damaged by mines during the war. Four-fifths of these were Union vessels. On the Confederate side, only the *Albermarle* was lost to a Union mine; the others were victims of their own mines.

In 1868 German scientist Heinrich Hertz developed what became known as the Hertz horn to explode a contact mine. Such mines were typical of those deployed in both world wars. A half dozen horns extended outward from the top part of the mine in various directions. Each horn contained a glass tube with an electrolyte (potassium bichromate solution). This was connected to a carbon plate and a zinc plate. When a ship encountered the horn and broke it, the solution leaked out, connecting the two plates and forming a simple battery that generated sufficient current to ignite the mine's electric detonator.

In the second half of the 19th century, most naval powers pursued mine development. The most notable was the evolution of the spar torpedo into an automotive torpedo, or fish. On the other hand, lesser and continental navies discovered static mines as a low-cost alternative to conventional coastal defenses. Russia and Germany in particular focused on the development of moored contact mines based on Hertz's and Jacobi's actuation mechanisms. By the turn of the century, both countries had sizable stocks of mines.

During the Russo-Japanese War (1904–1905) both sides made extensive use of mines. The Russians employed them to defend the approaches to their Pacific ports and laid the first mines of the war. Russian mines would claim 10 Japanese warships including 2 battleships, more ships than were lost to naval gunfire. The Japanese also laid mines in fields and attempted to lure Russian ships over them. During the war the Russians lost to mines 6 ships, including a battleship. Some of the Russian mine types, such as the M-04, M-08, and M-12, developed prior to World War I saw service for more than 70 years during which their design was licensed to North Korea, Vietnam, and other Soviet Cold War clients.

Encouraged by the results of mine warfare during their war with Japan, the Russians evolved their mine warfare capability with the addition of the purpose-built minelayers *Amur* and *Jenissei* to the fleet in 1906 and the launching of the world's first mine-laying submarine *Krab* in 1904.

World War I witnessed mine warfare at sea on a large scale by both sides. On October 14, 1914, the newly commissioned British battleship *Audacious* sank after having struck a single mine laid by a converted German liner.

The most widely used mine in World War I was the moored contact mine, consisting of a spherical or cylindrical mine case, an anchor to secure the mine in place, and a mooring wire connecting the two to hold the buoyant mine case at a predetermined depth. Most powers relied mostly on the Herz horn type of firing mechanism. The German E-Type moored contact mine was so reliable that the British copied it in 1917. Mines played a key role in the war, and one small minefield may have altered the course of history. In early 1915 the allies assembled a formidable task force to push through the Dardanelles and steam to Constantinople to force Turkey from the war and open up a southern supply route to Russia. On March 18 a small undetected Turkish minefield of 26 1880s vintage German mines claimed several Allied battleships, causing Admiral John de Robeck to break off his effort to force the Dardanelles by naval power alone. The failure to open up a supply corridor to Russia through the Mediterranean undoubtedly prolonged the war and may have led to the Russian Revolutions of 1917.

Both sides also deployed mines extensively as offensive weapons. Charge weights ranged from 60 to 600 pounds. The Germans used both submarines and surface vessels to lay mines off British ports, while the Allies sowed great belts of mines, known as barrages, to inhibit German access to the North Sea. Mines and mine nets claimed 34 of the 178 German submarines lost to enemy action in the war. Of an estimated 310,000 sea mines deployed during the war, 260,000 were laid by the Allies. In return, German mines, mostly laid by submarines, claimed more than 1.5 million of a total of 12 million tons of Allied merchant shipping sunk during the war. Toward the end of the war the British developed the first magnetic influence mine. It was activated by the disruption of the earth's magnetic field generated by the passage of a steel ship.

Development of mines continued after the war. Experiments with acoustic mines, those set off by noise, began in 1937. By World War II, mines were far more sophisticated and capable of rising and falling with the tide or delayed action release from the seabed. The Germans introduced air-laid magnetic mines (UMA/UMB type) with great effect in 1939. They continued to refine these influence mines throughout the war and ultimately incorporated magnetic pressure and acoustic-firing mechanisms. The mines could be adjusted to detect the magnetic fields of even the smallest vessels, which made them a lethal enemy of Allied mine-sweeping forces. For the seaward defense of Europe, the Germans also employed bottom-contact mines, some of them simple antitank mines. These were laid offshore and on stakes to prevent landing craft from reaching shore.

The real operational value of mines lies in their disruptive effects on shipping. British aerial mining of the Kiel Canal and the Danube in 1944 severely disrupted the German material flow to the Western Front and oil supplies from the Romanian oil fields for brief periods of time. The most devastating mine-laying campaign of the war was perhaps the American Operation STARVATION that employed 15,000 air-laid mines in Japanese waters in 1945 and paralyzed what little Japanese maritime traffic remained at that stage.

Limpet mines, though technically time-fused demolition charges, were also employed. Small high-explosive charges usually with small watertight compartments that gave them only the slightest negative buoyancy, limpet mines were usually carried by divers to the hulls of targeted ships and there affixed by magnets, hence the name for the mollusk limpet. Limpet mines were usually exploded by means of a timed fuse.

The Italians employed commandoes to deliver the mines. Human torpedoes, electrically powered underwater vessels, delivered the combat swimmers and their craft's warhead charge to the targets. Just before the end of World War I, Italian commandoes used such techniques to sink the Austro-Hungarian battleship *Viribus Unitis*. Continuing that tradition in World War II, Italian frogmen of the 10th Light Flotilla sank the British battleships *Valiant* and *Queen Elisabeth* in the port of Alexandria on December 18, 1941. A different mode of delivering the charges was selected by the Royal Navy in World War II when several midget submarines (called X-Craft by the British) successfully placed explosive charges on the sea bottom underneath the German battleship *Tirpitz* at its anchorage in a Norwegian fjord on September 22, 1943.

Sea mines of the second half of the 20th century grew ever more sophisticated and remain an important weapon of naval warfare. Today most offensive mines are laid by aircraft, as in the case of the U.S. mining of Haiphong Harbor in North Vietnam during the Vietnam War. Among U.S. mines still in the U.S. inventory are the MK56 ASW (developed in 1966), the MK60 CAPTOR (for encapsulated torpedo), and the MK62 and MK63 Quickstrike and MK67 SLMM (Submarine Launched Mobile Mine).

Mine-sweeping techniques were developed as early as 1900 by several nations. The preferred method usually involved a converted trawler (and later purpose-built mine sweepers) to stream one or two steel wires held at the desired depth and angle by paravanes. Shears were mounted on the sweep wires to cut the mine's mooring wire. This is known as the Oropesa Sweep. Team sweeps were also conducted in the form of a long wire run between two mine-sweeping vessels. Once the swept mines floated to the surface, they were exploded by rifle or shell fire.

During World War II the Allies alone deployed 1,300 mine-sweeping vessels of all types. To counter magnetic mines, mine-sweeping vessels employed large electromagnets to try to explode them at a distance behind the vessels. Degaussing, or the wrapping of ship hulls in cable to reduce their magnetic signature, and the use of wooden-hulled minesweepers assisted in efforts to stymie magnetic mines. Mine hunting, or actively searching for mines with sonar in front of the mine countermeasures vessel, is the standard measure today for hard-to-sweep influence sea mines. Once located, these are dispatched with explosive charges by divers or remote-operated underwater vehicles.

SPENCER C. TUCKER AND DIRK STEFFEN

References

Cowie, J. S. *Mines, Minelayers and Minelaying.* Oxford: Oxford University Press, 1949.

Hartmann, Gregory K., with Scott C. Truver. *Weapons That Wait: Mine Warfare in the U.S. Navy.* Annapolis, MD: Naval Institute Press, 1991.

Hutcheson, Wallace. *Robert Fulton: Pioneer of Undersea Warfare.* Annapolis, MD: Naval Institute Press, 1981.

Ledebur, Gerhard Freiherr von. *Die Seemine.* Munich: J. Lehmanns Verlag, 1977.

Roland, Alex. *Underwater Warfare in the Age of Sail.* Bloomington: Indiana University Press, 1978.

Minié Ball

The minié system revolutionized military small arms in the 1850s. Others had experimented with similar ideas, but in 1849 Captain Claude Étienne Minié designed the bullet named for him. The French were particularly interested in developing a more rapidly fired rifle to deal with the Arabs in Algeria, who sniped at them from long range. The system proved effective, and in 1851 the British Army also adopted it, ordering 23,000 Minié rifled muskets, many of which saw service in the Crimean War of 1854–1856. Ultimately, any rifle with a similar bullet system became known as the minié.

The so-called minié ball, as the bullet was known during the American Civil War, was not a cylindrical ball at all but rather a cylindro-conoidal lead bullet that contained an iron plug set in a hollow in the base of the bullet, which was also cast in a diameter slightly smaller than the gun bore. When inserted into the gun muzzle, the bullet slid easily down the bore, but on the explosion of the gunpowder at the base of the bore, the base plug pushed forward a fraction of a second ahead of the rest of the bullet, expanding its soft lead to grip the rifling and cause the bullet to be fired on an accurate trajectory. A simpler form of the minié bullet had a hollowed-out cone base. This had the same effect of expanding the bullet with the discharge of the powder and sealing the bore.

The minié system combined the ease of loading of the smoothbore musket with the accuracy of the rifle. The new minié ball rifle could be loaded and fired as fast as the old smoothbore musket (perhaps three times a minute), but it had far greater effective range: at least 400 yards as opposed to 100–200 yards for the smoothbore musket. The two developments of the new bullet and reliable percussion primer ignition produced a tremendous increase in long-range defensive infantry firepower.

As is usually the case, tactics lagged behind technology. A great many lives would be lost in the wars of the mid-19th century, especially the American Civil War, because of the failure to appreciate the effects of long-range rifle fire from defensive positions against charging troops.

SPENCER C. TUCKER

References

Blackmore, H. L. "The Percussion System." In *Pollard's History of Firearms,* edited by Claude Blair, 161–187. New York: Macmillan, 1983.

Tunis, Edwin. *Weapons: A Pictorial History.* New York: World Publishing, 1954.

Napoleon Gun

The U.S. 12-pounder smoothbore Napoleon gun was the standard field piece of the Union and Confederate armies in the American Civil War. It was, in effect, the epitome of five centuries of field artillery development. Officially known in the U.S. Army as the light 12-pounder gun, this field piece was most often referred to on both sides in the war as the Napoleon. The gun was named not for French emperor Napoleon I but for his nephew, Emperor Napoleon III (r. 1852–1870). A perceptive student of artillery, Napoleon III conceived a lightweight weapon of uniform caliber that would replace guns and howitzers of differing calibers for field service. Such a weapon would have the great advantage of standardization in ammunition. The new weapon was basically a gun without the powder chamber of the howitzer but able to fire shells at howitzer trajectories if need be. By 1856, gun howitzers had been adopted by France, Prussia, Russia, and other European countries.

The first American Napoleon gun was produced in 1857 by Ames Manufacturing Co. of Chicopee, Massachusetts. During the war five northern foundries cast it. By the time production ceased in 1864, they had produced 1,157 guns, of which almost 500 survive. Seven Confederate arsenals cast some 535 Napoleons during the American Civil War, of which 133 survive.

Dozens of varieties of Napoleons existed. Although some were rifled, the vast majority were smoothbores of bronze (at the end of the war with bronze in short supply, the Tredegar foundry in Richmond cast some Napoleons in iron). Napoleons had a bore diameter of 4.62 inches and a bore length of approximately 64 inches or 14 calibers (the bore being 14 times as long as its bore diameter).

Napoleons were characterized by a smooth exterior appearance without the rings of older guns and with only a slight muzzle swell (the best-known Confederate version had no muzzle swell). They weighed about 1,200 pounds, or 100 times the weight of their round shot. Several dozen of the earliest federal Napoleons had handles over their trunnions for lifting the guns, but these were eliminated in late 1861. Of the surviving federal Napoleons, only five are rifled.

Napoleons fired a variety of ammunition, including solid shot, shell, spherical case, grapeshot, and canister. A powder charge of 2.5 pounds gave its solid shot projectile a range of 1,600 yards, more than sufficient for the line-of-sight firing in mixed country that characterized most American Civil War battles. Grapeshot fired at intermediate ranges was especially effective against cavalry charges, while canister from the Napoleon fired at close ranges proved deadly against attacking infantry.

The Napoleon gun was extraordinarily safe for its crews, with few if any recorded instances of them bursting. By the end of the American Civil War, Napoleons comprised four-fifths of Union artillery. The remaining guns were Parrott rifles.

SPENCER C. TUCKER

References

Hazlett, James C., Edwin Olmstead, and M. Hume Parks. *Field Artillery Weapons of the Civil War.* Newark: Delaware University Press, 1983.

Ripley, Warren. *Artillery and Ammunition of the Civil War.* New York: Van Nostrand Reinhold, 1970.

An African American soldier guards a 12-pounder Napoleon gun on a limber ready for travel. The Napoleon was a favored artillery piece during the American Civil War. (Library of Congress)

Nautilus, French Revolution Submarine

In December 1797 during the Wars of the French Revolution, American inventor Robert Fulton submitted plans to the French Directory in Paris for a so-called plunging boat. Fulton demanded payment of 500,000 francs for the first British ship destroyed and set sums for those sunk thereafter. He reasoned that such payments were justified because the British would consider such a craft to be outside the accepted practices of war and might well treat its crew as pirates if they were to be caught.

In November 1799 General Napoleon Bonaparte came to power in France, and when Fulton supporter P. A. L. Forfait became minister of marine, Fulton began construction of his submarine, which he called the *Nautilus.* Built by the Perrier workshop near the Seine, it was completed in June 1800. The *Nautilus* was a quantum advance over David Busnell's *Turtle* of the American Revolutionary War, although the goal was the same: a means to transport a mine and release it against an enemy vessel.

The cigar-shaped *Nautilus* was some 21 feet long and had a double hull of copper over an iron frame. It also was fitted with a collapsible mast for a sail. Fulton added a deck 6 feet wide by 20 feet long to be used by the three-man crew when the submarine was on the surface. The *Nautilus* was powered by hand cranks that drove a propeller and had a system to control ballast.

Successfully tested on the surface and underwater on the Seine River at Paris on June 13 with Forfait in attendance, the *Nautilus* remained submerged for some 45 minutes. Forfait enthusiastically recommended Fulton's work in a report to Bonaparte. Because the Seine was too shallow, in July Fulton had the *Nautilus* transported to Rouen and then to Le Havre on the English Channel, where that August he submerged it to a depth of 15 feet and remained underwater for an hour. Fulton also successfully tested a contact mine against a barrel target.

Now ready to try the *Nautilus* against the Royal Navy, during September 12–15 Fulton took the submarine out into the English Channel. On two separate occasions he tried to approach English brigs near the Marcou Islands, but each time the ships got under way before he could close the range. The *Nautilus* performed well, although at one point rough water forced Fulton to remain submerged for six hours, the crew receiving air through a metal tube.

Bad weather and approaching winter forced Fulton to end his tests and return to Paris. French mathematicians Gaspard Monge and Pierre Simon de Laplace, who had been in communication with Fulton, recommended his work to Bonaparte, who then met with the three men. Monge and Laplace recommended that Fulton receive additional funding.

In late July 1801 Fulton conducted further tests on the *Nautilus* at Brest, and at one point he took the submarine down to a depth of 25 feet. He also added a window topside at the bow. Fulton spent much of the summer at Brest cruising off the port and looking for English warships. Apparently warned, the British posted extra lookouts and used ships' boats to circle the warships as additional precaution.

Monge and Laplace urged Fulton to bring the submarine to Paris for a demonstration before Bonaparte, but Fulton stunned them by writing on September 20 that the *Nautilus* no longer existed. Dissatisfied with leaks and its means of propulsion, he had taken apart the submarine and sold off its components. This action probably led Bonaparte to remove his support. Fulton then traveled to Britain to sell his services there. The British government was not interested in his submarine, but it did pay him to work on mines for use at sea.

SPENCER C. TUCKER

References

Hutcheson, Wallace. *Robert Fulton: Pioneer of Undersea Warfare.* Annapolis, MD: Naval Institute Press, 1981.

Roland, Alex. *Underwater Warfare in the Age of Sail.* Bloomington: Indiana University Press, 1978.

Tucker, Spencer C. *Handbook of 19th Century Naval Warfare.* Annapolis, MD: Naval Institute Press, 2000.

Naval Gun Turret

Following the decision to arm ships with a few large-bore pivot-mounted guns as their principal armament, the next step was an armored turret to protect the guns and their crews, especially during the lengthy reloading process. During the Crimean War, Royal Navy captain Cowper Coles designed two floating batteries to engage Russian shore batteries at close range. The second of these mounted a 68-pounder protected by a hemispheric iron shield, which during action proved largely impervious to hostile fire.

In March 1859 Coles patented the idea of turrets aboard ship. He advocated guns mounted on the center line of the vessel so as to have wide arcs of fire on either side of the ship and halve the number of guns previously required for broadsides fire. Coles's persistence coupled with the powerful support of Prince Albert led the Admiralty in March 1861 to install an experimental armored turret on the floating battery *Trusty*. The test was a success, for 33 hits from 68-pounder and 100-pounder guns failed to disable it.

The Coles turret turned on a circumferential roller path set in the lower deck, operated by two men with a hand crank. Its upper 4.5 feet of armor came up through the main or upper deck and formed an armored glacis to protect the lower part. The crew and ammunition entered the turret from below through a hollow central cylinder.

The first British seagoing turreted ship was the Coles-inspired *Prince Albert* of 1864. It mounted four 9-inch muzzle-loading rifles, one each in four center-line circular turrets, turned by hand; 18 men could complete a revolution in one minute. The problem of center-line turrets in a ship of high superstructure and sail rig and very low freeboard (the latter the result of a design error) contributed to the disastrous loss at sea of the Coles-designed HMS *Captain* in 1870. Most of its crew drowned, Coles among them.

In the United States, John Ericsson's single revolving turret *Monitor* entered service in March 1862. The *Monitor* and many follow-on types all had very low freeboard. This lessened the amount of armor required to protect the ship and allowed it to be concentrated in the turret. Unlike the *Captain,* however, the *Monitor* had no high superstructure or sail rig.

Ericsson's turret was all above the upper deck, on which it rested. Before the turret could be turned, it had to be lifted by rack and pinion from contact with the deck. A steam engine operating through gearing turned the turret around a central spindle. The *Monitor* was the first revolving turret actually employed in battle, which occurred in its March 9, 1862, engagement with CSS *Virginia.*

Sharp disagreement continued between those who favored the revolving turret and supporters of broadside armament. Renewed interest in the ram—in consequence of the 1866 Battle of Lissa—and larger, more powerful guns helped decide this in favor of the turret. The ram meant that ships had to fire ahead as they prepared to attack an opposing vessel; heavier guns meant that ships needed fewer of them and that these should have the widest possible arc of fire. The elimination of sail rigs and improved shop designs heightened the stability of turreted warships.

Turrets continued to undergo design refinement and received new breech-loading guns as well as heavier armor, indeed the thickest aboard ship. Relatively thin top-of-turret armor on British battle cruisers, however, led to the loss of three of them to German armor-piercing shells in the Battle of Jutland of May 31–June 1, 1916. The battle cruiser turrets also lacked flash protection doors and the means of preventing a shell burst inside the turret from reaching the magazines. The largest battleship ever built, the Japanese *Yamato,* had 25.6-inch steel armor protection on its turrets.

SPENCER C. TUCKER

References
Hawkey, Arthur. *Black Night off Finisterre: The Tragic Tale of an Early British Ironclad.* Annapolis, MD: Naval Institute Press, 1999.

Hogg, Ian V., and John Batchelor. *Naval Gun.* Poole, Dorset, UK: Blandford, 1978.

Hough, Richard. *Fighting Ships.* New York: Putnam, 1969.

Padfield, Peter. *Guns at Sea.* New York: St. Martin's, 1974.

Tucker, Spencer C. *Handbook of 19th Century Naval Warfare.* Annapolis, MD: Naval Institute Press, 2000.

Parrott Gun

The most widely used rifled gun of the American Civil War (1861–1865), designed by Robert P. Parrott, superintendent of the West Point Foundry. Parrott guns were easy to operate and were reliable, accurate, and relatively inexpensive to manufacture. Both sides produced them during the war. The Parrott was essentially a cast-iron rifled gun with a wrought-iron band shrunk over the breech, the point of greatest strain. The band was equal in thickness to half the diameter of the bore.

Parrott's first rifled gun was a 2.9-inch (land diameter) 10-pounder. Prior to the American Civil War, Parrott also produced a 3.67-inch (20-pounder) gun and a 4.2-inch (30-pounder) gun. Neither the army nor the navy adopted the Parrott guns until after the start of the American Civil War. During the war Parrotts were produced in 2.9-inch, 3-inch, 3.3-inch, 3.67-inch, 4.2-inch, 5.3-inch (60-pounder), 6.4-inch (100-pounder army, 80-pounder navy), 8-inch (200-pounder army, 150-pounder navy), and 10-inch (300-pounder army, 250-pounder navy) bore diameters. The guns had spiraled rifling, with from three grooves and lands on the 1.9-inch gun to 15 grooves and lands on the 10-inch gun.

The smallest U.S. Navy Parrott was the 3.67-inch gun. The larger guns were better suited to naval service, where weight was also not as much a factor as in field artillery on land. The 6.4-inch Parrott, for example, weighed some 9,800 pounds. With a powder charge of 10 pounds and at 35 degrees of elevation, it could fire its projectile more than five miles. The U.S. Navy employed the 8-inch Parrott in the turrets of some of its monitors alongside a smoothbore Dahlgren.

The Parrott gun fired an elongated projectile some 3 calibers in length. Cylindro-conical in shape, it had a bronze ring at a contraction in the base. On ignition of the powder charge, the gas expanded the bronze ring into the grooves of the bore, thus imparting a spin to the projectile. Parrott projectiles were fitted with both time and percussion fuses, and there were also variations with hardened noses to pierce armor.

Both the army and navy experienced problems during the war with Parrott guns bursting, most notably in operations against Charleston and Fort Fisher. Parrott blamed these on premature shell explosions rather than defects in the bore, but clearly these early rifled guns experienced greater problems than did the smoothbores, especially from grit and sand in the bores. Fewer navy guns burst, which was probably attributable to an order that all rifled projectiles be thoroughly greased before they were loaded. The navy did subsequently remove its heaviest Parrotts from service, however.

From the beginning of the war through April 1864, nearly 2,000 Parrotts were manufactured for the U.S. Army and the U.S. Navy, representing about one-fifth of Union guns on land and sea. The Confederates produced their own Parrotts at the Tredegar Iron Works in Richmond in 2.9-inch, 3-inch, 3.67-inch, and 4.2-inch sizes.

SPENCER C. TUCKER

References

Hazlett, James C., Edwin Olmstead, and M. Hume Parks. *Field Artillery Weapons of the Civil War.* Newark: Delaware University Press, 1983.

Olmstead, Edwin, Wayne Stark, and Spencer C. Tucker. *The Big Guns: Civil War Siege, Seacoast, and Naval Cannon.* Alexandria Bay, NY: Museum Restoration Service, 1997.

Tucker, Spencer C. *Arming the Fleet: U.S. Naval Ordnance in the Muzzle-Loading Era.* Annapolis, MD: Naval Institute Press, 1989.

Percussion Cap

The chief military invention of the first half of the 19th century was the percussion cap, made possible by the discovery of fulminate of mercury in 1800. In 1807 Scottish Presbyterian minister Alexander Forsyth patented a gun lock utilizing mercuric fulminates as a priming for firearms. The process brought reliability to the discharge of lethal projectiles.

Before this invention, all guns—individual firearms through the largest cannon—were discharged by lighting a priming charge of finely ground gunpowder. This was first accomplished by a burning rope and later by flint and steel, both outside the touchhole at the end of the bore. Mercury fulminate detonated when struck a sharp blow, and Forsyth's system employed what looked like a perfume bottle, known as the scent bottle, that was mounted on the side of the gun at the breech. It contained sufficient fulminates for perhaps 20 shots and was connected by a fire hole that led to the base of the bore. To prime the scent bottle, it was turned upside down, causing some of the fulminates to drop down onto a flash pan. When the trigger was pulled, a hammer dropped down on top of a firing pin at the end of the scent bottle. It came down on the pan, exploding the small amount of fulminates there. The flash from this then passed into the bore of the gun, igniting the main charge.

Joshua Shaw, an English artist living in Philadelphia, simplified the process considerably by 1816. Shaw painted the fulminates on the inside of a small copper cap, which fitted over a nipple containing the fire hole over the base of the bore. When the hammer struck the percussion cap, the exploding fulminates ignited, and the fire raced down the touchhole to explode the main powder charge.

Percussion-cap side arms could be reloaded and fired more rapidly than a flintlock and were reliable in all weather conditions. In 1834 the British Army tested a musket armed with the new percussion cap against the old Brown Bess flintlock. Each weapon fired 6,000 rounds. The percussion cap weapon failed 6 times, while the flintlock failed to fire nearly 1,000 times. As can be readily imagined, the new system produced a tremendous increase in firepower.

Muzzle-loading rifled muskets fired this way were in general service in the world's armies by 1850. The U.S. Army adopted the percussion cap system in 1842, paying Shaw $18,000 for the use of it. The percussion cap muzzle-loading rifled musket was the standard infantry firearm of the American Civil War.

SPENCER C. TUCKER

References

Blackmore, H. L. "The Percussion System." In *Pollard's History of Firearms,* edited by Claude Blair, 161–187. New York: Macmillan, 1986.

Tunis, Edwin. *Weapons: A Pictorial History.* New York: World Publishing, 1954.

Princeton, USS

The U.S. Navy steam sloop *Princeton* was the world's first warship designed and built as a screw steamer. In Britain U.S. Navy captain Robert Stockton witnessed the trials of John Ericsson's screw propeller. Stockton was instrumental in getting Ericsson to come to the United States and in lobbying for a prototype warship to combine the innovations of a new heavy armament and screw propeller.

Congress authorized construction of the 672-ton steam sloop *Princeton,* which was named for Stockton's hometown. Work began in 1841, and the ship was launched in 1843. Ericsson set down the hull lines and general dimensions, while naval constructor John Lenthall drew the detailed working plans. Ericsson also designed the engine and the six-blade screw propeller. Stockton oversaw the construction and designed the ship's sail rig.

The 673-ton second-rate steam sloop *Princeton* had a deck length of 164 feet (156 feet 6 inches between perpendiculars) and a beam of 30 feet 6 inches. It displaced 1,046 tons, and the engine could drive it at seven knots. The ship had a complement of 166 men.

The most technologically advanced warship of its time, the *Princeton* was the first screw propeller warship in any navy, the first warship with machinery entirely below the waterline, and the first to burn anthracite coal and use fan blowers for its furnace fires. The *Princeton*'s armament consisted of two large 12-inch wrought-iron guns and two 42-pounder carronades. On a demonstration cruise down the Potomac River on February 28, 1844, one of these guns, the Peacemaker, designed by Stockton and built in the United States, blew up, killing eight people including two cabinet members.

Stockton continued in command of the *Princeton,* which served in the Home Squadron. The ship performed extensively and well in the Gulf Coast Squadron during the Mexican-American War (1846–1848) and helped establish the value of steamers, especially in blockade duty. After undergoing a refit, it served in the Mediterranean until July 1849. On its return, the *Princeton* was found too rotten for repair and was broken up at the Boston Navy Yard.

SPENCER C. TUCKER

References

Silverstone, Paul H. *The Sailing Navy, 1775–1854.* Annapolis, MD: Naval Institute Press, 2001.

Tucker, Spencer C. "U.S. Navy Steam Sloop *Princeton.*" *American Neptune* 49(2) (Spring 1989): 96–113.

Quick-Firing Naval Gun

The development of relatively small caliber, 4- to 6-inch, quick-firing guns was of great importance to naval warfare at the end of the 19th century. All navies utilized machine guns, but they were of limited range and effectiveness. The quick-firing gun was a larger-caliber weapon specifically developed to deal with the threat of torpedo boat attack and to be able to riddle the unprotected portions of ships.

The quick-firing gun operated on the principle of fixed ammunition, cartridge cases utilized in small arms that contained propellent, primer, and projectile. Fixed ammunition had the advantages of ease and rapidity of loading, protection of the powder charge, reducing erosion on the chamber of the gun, and sealing the breech. Quick-firing guns had sliding breech blocks and a recoil mechanism that rapidly returned the gun into firing position with a minimum of displacement. Besides their rapid rate of fire, such guns required smaller crews, only three men each for the lesser calibers.

The quick-firing gun resulted from an 1881 Royal Navy advertisement for a gun to fire 12 aimed shots a minute. The 47-millimeter (mm) revolving Hotchkiss gun, which fired a 2.37-pound high-explosive shell out to a range of 4,000 yards, was subsequently adopted by several major navies. The 53-mm Hotchkiss fired a 3.5-pound shell out to 5,500 yards but failed to achieve the popularity of the smaller model.

In 1886 57-mm (2.24-inch) 6-pounder single-barrel guns by Hotchkiss and Nordenfelt were introduced in Britain. Later the quick-firing gun was made larger to deal with armored vessels. A 4.7-inch quick-firing gun was tested and proven successful on the cruiser *Piemonte,* constructed in Britain for Italy in 1887. By the end of the decade Hotchkiss had built a 33-pounder and had a design for a 55-pounder; Armstrong had 4.72-inch, 5.5-inch, and even 6-inch rapid-fire guns. Such larger quick-firing guns soon became standard secondary armament on British battleships.

Because of the short battle ranges that prevailed in pre–range finder days, the quick-firing 6-inch gun could easily riddle the unarmored sections of the old battleships. Henceforth, to use wood as material for a ship's superstructure was to invite disaster, as the Chinese learned during their war with Japan in 1894.

Spencer C. Tucker

References

Brodie, Bernard. *Sea Power in the Machine Age.* Princeton, NJ: Princeton University Press, 1941.

Gardiner, Robert, ed., and Andrew D. Lambert, consultant ed. *Steam, Steel & Shellfire: The Steam Warship, 1815–1905.* Annapolis, MD: Naval Institute Press, 1992.

Hogg, Ian V., and John Batchelor. *Naval Gun.* Poole, Dorset, UK: Blandford, 1978.

Tucker, Spencer C. *Handbook of 19th Century Naval Warfare.* Annapolis, MD: Naval Institute Press, 2000.

Railroad

The first practical application of the steam engine to land transportation came in the locomotive designed by Richard Trevithick in England in 1801, but George Stephenson built the first true railway, between Stockton and Darlington, also in England, in 1825. The first U.S. rail line was constructed in 1828.

Prussia was the first nation to grasp the importance of the railroad in war. German writers were quick to point out how rail lines could help their nation in case of war against powerful neighbors. They enabled Prussia, and later Germany, to use railroads in interior lines by which forces could be mobilized and shifted rapidly.

In 1846 the Prussians conducted the first major troop movement by rail, while the American Civil War in 1861 saw the first such movement by rail in war when Confederate forces were transported from the Shenandoah Valley to fight in the First Battle of Bull Run (Manassas). Its much more developed rail net helped the Union side win the American Civil War, while railroads were critical in enabling Prussia to win a rapid victory over Austria in 1866. Armored trains and railroad artillery appeared in the American Civil War and in the Boer War.

At the beginning of World War I France may have survived militarily because of its well-developed rail net that enabled rapid shifting of major units to meet the German foot-bound invasion of northeastern France in August 1914. Russia's ambitious program for a strategic railroad net would have rendered obsolete Germany's Schlieffen Plan for waging a near-simultaneous war against France and Russia, and it was certainly a factor in Germany's decision to declare war in 1914. Germany could not have been able to win a two-front war five years later.

During World War I, railroads moved the bulk of the vast numbers of men and quantities of munitions and supplies to the front. Railroad artillery allowed rapid deployment of the heaviest guns, and railroad cars also served as mobile command posts. The inability of the Russian rail system to meet both civilian and military needs led to food riots in the cities and ultimately to revolution in March 1917.

Rail lines were also of immense importance in World War II, although modern aircraft rendered them much more vulnerable to attack. Disruption of the movement of the enemy's supplies by rail became a primary concern of both sides in war, as in the bombing and resistance activities prior to the Allied landings in Normandy in June 1944, and the rapid restoration of the French rail system thereafter was a top priority for the Western Allies.

During the Cold War, railroads were to be the primary means by which the Soviet Union would deploy its massive armored forces from Russia and Ukraine into Eastern Europe and to the inter-German border. The key challenge for the Soviets was the fact that their railroads used broader-gauge tracks than the railroads of their opponents or the rest of the world. This meant that all rail traffic transiting between east and west had to go through large transloading zones at the Soviet border. North Atlantic Treaty Organization (NATO) intelligence officers made extensive studies of the Soviet and Warsaw Pact rail networks, and targeting officers developed extensive targeting lists against such critical choke points as tunnels, bridges, switching centers, and especially the transloading zones.

Railroads continue to be a major factor in war.

SPENCER C. TUCKER

References

Bishop, Denis, and W. J. K. Davies. *Railways and War before 1918.* London: Blandford, 1972.
———. *Railways and War since 1917.* London: Blandford, 1974.
Westwood, John N. *Railways at War.* San Diego, CA: Howell-North Books, 1981.

Revolver

The development of pistols paralleled that of muskets. Alexander Forsyth's patent of mercury fulminates as priming for firearms in 1807 was a great boon in pistol development as well as that of muskets.

Pistols proliferated in the 19th century. There were many types, but among notable designs were those of American Henry Deringer Jr., who opened a business in Philadelphia in 1806 and routinely made flintlock muskets for the federal government. He was one of the first gun makers to embrace the new percussion cap system, although he did not receive his first government contract for percussion firearms until 1845. Deringer's muzzle-loading rifled percussion cap pistols were of varying bore size and had 1- to 6-inch barrel lengths. The smaller pistols could easily be carried concealed and became de rigueur for many men and women, especially in the more lawless American West and South.

So-called pepperbox pistols also were popular for defensive purposes. They had four to six barrels that were loaded separately from the muzzle end. Most usually, the barrels were bored into a single piece of metal that then rotated on a long steel pin. In some of these pistols the barrels had to be turned by hand, but soon the barrels were turned by double action, that is, the action of pulling the trigger turned the barrel(s) and raised and dropped the hammer to fire the pistol.

In 1836 Samuel Colt of Hartford, Connecticut, formed the Patent Army Manufacturing Company in Patterson, New Jersey. Its first product was a small five-shot .28-caliber revolver, but its most famous early design was the 1838 Colt Holster Model Paterson Revolver No. 5. Better known as the Texas Paterson, it was .36 caliber, had five cylinders, and came in 4- to 12-inch barrel lengths. This was the first revolving cylinder pistol in general use. Each chamber was separately loaded from the muzzle end and had its own nipple for the copper percussion cap. The drum chamber moved each time the hammer was cocked. Colt revolvers were adopted by both the army and navy and saw wide service in both the Mexican War and the American Civil War as well as in fighting with the American Indians in the West.

At the same time, breech-loading revolvers appeared. Screw-off barrels had appeared early in the development of firearms, but in 1812 Swiss national Samuel J. Pauly, working in Paris, developed a pistol in which the barrel swiveled downward to allow it to be loaded. It utilized a self-contained cartridge of Pauly's invention, surely one of the most important developments in the history of small arms. Several types of methods were used to fire it.

The development of metal cartridges led to a change from muzzle-loading to breech-loading firearms. Not only were muzzle-loading rifles turned into breech loaders, but Colt revolvers were similarly transformed. Thus, in the 1870s the Colt Model 1861 navy revolver was converted to a breech loader. In the .57-caliber British aptly named man-stopper revolver of 1870–1880, the cylinder was removed for reloading.

There are three principal means of ejecting spent cartridge cases from the cylinder. In the side-gate type, the cartridge cases are pushed rearward out of the cylinder one at a time by means of a hand-operated rod alongside the barrel. In the break-open type, all cartridge cases are ejected at the same time by means of a star-shaped extractor when the revolver is opened. Finally, there is the swing-out cylinder, in which all cases are ejected simultaneously by hand with a star-shaped extractor after the cylinder is opened.

The first breech-loading revolver designed specifically for metal cartridges was the Smith and Wesson Model No. 1. Manufactured during 1857–1860, it had a rifled barrel and seven chambers and was hinged at the top. It utilized .22-caliber rimfire ammunition. In 1869 Smith and Wesson produced a .44-caliber revolver for the army. Probably the most famous early revolver in U.S. history was the Colt .45 Peacemaker. Still in production, it was widely used in the American West in fighting against the American Indians. The cavalry version had a 7.5-inch barrel and was officially known as the Single Action Army Revolver, Model 1873 Six-shot Caliber .45-inch Colt. Colt also produced another famous side arm during 1898–1944, the Colt New Service Double Action Revolver, in .45 caliber.

For the most part, at the end of the 19th century .38 was the standard army caliber. It remained thus until after the Philippine-American War of 1898–1902 when the army sought a caliber with greater stopping power. Competition led to adoption of the Colt semiautomatic .45-caliber pistol, which became the standard side arm of the U.S. military for the next 70 years.

Among other notable revolvers were designs in the United Kingdom by both Webley and Enfield, produced chiefly in .38 and .44 calibers. During World War II Britain purchased some 1 million Smith and Wesson .38-caliber revolvers. In 1953 Colt introduced its new, more powerful Colt Python in .357 caliber, and a number of other manufacturers followed suit.

SPENCER C. TUCKER

References
Blair, Claude, ed. *Pollard's History of Firearms.* New York: Macmillan, 1983.
Kinard, Jeff. *Pistols: An Illustrated History of Their Impact.* Santa Barbara, CA: ABC-CLIO, 2003.
Myatt, F. *Illustrated Encyclopedia of Pistols and Revolvers.* London: Salamander Books, 1980.
Taylorson, A. *The Revolver.* 3 vols. London: Arms and Armour, 1966–1970.

Rifle, Breech Loader

The first guns were actually breech loaders, but the difficulty of effectively sealing the gases at the breech led to their abandonment and the embrace of the muzzle loader, both for cannon and for small arms. Improvements in metallurgical techniques and closer tolerances were one factor in changing this. The other was the change from a loose propellent charge in connection with the flint-and-steel method of firing to a metal cartridge case that contained both powder and projectile. Hand-made cartridge cases, tailored to the gun so that their fire port matched one drilled through the gun breech, while possible for the very rich were not practical for the equipment of mass armies.

The discovery of fulminate of mercury and the development of Alexander Forsyth's percussion cap did away with the necessity of striking fire outside the gun. The next step was to incorporate the percussion cap into a cartridge holding both gunpowder and the bullet, while a hinged-block or bolt opening made in the breech allowed the cartridge to be inserted there. Pulling the trigger released a steel pin that jabbed into the percussion cap and ignited it and thus the main charge. The first was the pin-fire cartridge in the 1840s, followed by the rimfire cartridge and then the central-fire cartridge by 1860. Prussia took the lead. In the 1840s it adopted the Dreyse breech-loading rifle, better known as the needle gun, a bolt-operated weapon that, however, utilized a paper cartridge.

The Spencer carbine of the American Civil War (1861–1865) was another important step forward. First issued to units of the Union Army, it featured a magazine, loaded through the butt of the rifle stock, that could hold seven metallic rimfire cartridges. These were fed to the breech by means of a compressed spring. When the trigger guard was lowered, the breech block dropped down, ejecting the spent cartridge case. As the trigger guard was returned to its normal position, the breech block moved up, catching a new cartridge and inserting it into the breech. Among the most important weapons utilizing this principle were the .44-caliber rimfire, lever-action, breech-loading rifle designed by American Benjamin Taylor Henry in the late 1850s and the so-called improved Henry, the Model 1866 lever-action Winchester, its most notable improvement over the Henry being the addition of a patented cartridge-loading gate system that allowed for a closed magazine tube and a wooden forearm. The Model 1866 fired the same .44-caliber rimfire round as the Henry rifle; however, cartridge improvements allowed a shorter carbine barrel length. Its follow-on was the Winchester Model 1873, the weapon that is said to have "won the West."

The breech loader could be loaded and fired three times as fast as the old muzzle loader, but its chief advantage was that this could be easily accomplished in the prone position. By the 1870s breech loaders had magazines attached from which rounds could be fed to the breech as fast as the rifleman could aim, fire, and work the reloading mechanism that would eject the spent case, feed a new round into the breech, and cock the firing mechanism by either bolt or lever action.

By the first decade of the 20th century, such fine bolt-action repeating rifles as the German Mauser, Austrian Mannlicher, Russian Mosin-Nagant, British Lee-Enfield, and American Springfield provided riflemen with greatly enhanced firepower at ranges of up to 1,000 yards or more.

SPENCER C. TUCKER

References

Blair, Claude, ed. *Pollard's History of Firearms.* New York: Macmillan, 1983.
Smith, W. H. B. *Small Arms of the World.* 9th ed. Harrisburg, PA: Stackpole, 1969.

Rocket

The war rocket was actually the oldest of all explosively propelled projectiles. The Chinese used rockets, some of them quite sizable, as anticavalry weapons from the early 11th century. War rockets made their way into European arsenals by the 1300s. The French employed them in the Hundred Years' War against the English in the Siege of Orléans in 1429.

The extensive use of rockets by Sultan Fateh Ali Tipu (Tipu Sultan, Tiger of Mysore) of Mysore against the British during the siege of Seringapatam in 1799 gave British artillery officer Sir William Congreve the idea of improving on them. Congreve had already designed a new lightweight gun for ships, introduced in the Royal Navy as the Congreve gun. Congreve developed rockets for both land and naval use. These weighed as little as 2 ounces—"a species of self-moving musket balls"—to more than 300 pounds. In 1806 Congreve rockets were successfully tested at sea in an attack on the French port of Boulogne, and they were used with equal effectiveness in bombarding Copenhagen in 1807. In the latter instance the British fired thousands of Congreve rockets into the city, setting much of it on fire.

Congreve rockets were also employed in the War of 1812 both on land and at sea. His observations of the "rocket's red glare" in the bombardment of Fort McHenry at Baltimore, Maryland, provided Francis Scott Key inspiration in penning the "Star Spangled Banner." Rockets were also employed by the U.S. Army in the Mexican-American War during the Mexico City Campaign and in the American Civil War by Union forces on land in the bombardment of Yorktown and Richmond and at sea to drive off Confederate picket boats at night.

Continued experiments, however, failed to correct the rocket's problems of errant flight and instability. Because rockets often exploded prematurely, crews were reluctant to fire them. Rockets also tended to deteriorate in storage. Their promise as a weapon of war was not fulfilled until World War II, when rockets played a considerable role, especially in ground-to-ground and air-to-ground use.

SPENCER C. TUCKER

Reference

Baker, Davd. *The Rocket: The History and Development of Rocket & Missile Technology.* New York: Crown, 1978.

Shrapnel

Shrapnel, or spherical case shot, was invented in 1784 by Lieutenant (later lieutenant general) Henry Shrapnel (1761–1842) of the British Royal Artillery. Shrapnel came up with the idea in order to extend the range of highly effective case or canister shot against enemy troops.

During the Spanish siege of Gibraltar (1779–1783), the British successfully fired 5.5-inch mortar shells from their 24-pounder long guns, but in 1784 Shrapnel improved on this improvisation by inventing what he called spherical case shot. The new artillery ammunition was later known simply by its designer's name. Spherical case shot, or shrapnel, consisted of a thin-walled hollow round shell filled with a small bursting charge and small iron or lead shot. A time fuse set off the charge in the air, scattering the shot and pieces of the shell casing among opposing troops. The bursting charge was only a small one, allowing the scattered balls and burst casing to continue on the same trajectory as before the explosion (a greater charge would increase the velocity but scattered the balls more widely and reduced their effectiveness). Explosive shell had for some time been utilized in high-trajectory fire mortars but had not before been widely projected in horizontal fire by guns.

Shrapnel shells had thinner walls than other shells and had to be carefully cast. Their weight empty was about half of that for solid shot of the same caliber, but their loaded weight made them comparable to solid shot.

The British first fired shrapnel during the Napoleonic Wars in 1804 in the siege of Surinam and continued to use it thereafter. Early shrapnel had a wooden plug and a paper fuse, but in the 1850s it incorporated the more precise Bormann fuse. Shrapnel was widely used in the American Civil War both on land and in naval actions, most often in the 12-pounder Napoleon and Dahlgren boat howitzers. Shrapnel soon became a staple round in the world's artillery establishments. Britain alone produced 72 million shrapnel shells during World War I.

By the end of the 19th century, shrapnel rounds had evolved to a similar size and shape as the other cylindro-conoidal shells fired by breech-loading artillery. The operating principle was still similar to the original spherical case. The thin-walled projectile was packed with small steel balls and an expelling charge. The expelling charge, however, did not rupture the projectile. Rather, it blew the fuse off the front end and expelled the shrapnel balls forward. Thus, the shrapnel round was something like a huge flying shotgun shell. Because of the imprecise burning times of the black powder time fuses of the era, the adjustment of the proper height of bust was very difficult. Shrapnel was only effective against troops in the open. As trench warfare set in during World War I and field fortifications became more robust, shrapnel became virtually worthless. Meanwhile, advances in both explosives and metallurgy during World War I finally produced high-explosive shells that had both significant blast and fragmentation effects. After World War I, shrapnel completely disappeared, replaced entirely by high-explosive (HE) rounds. Today, the fragmentation produced by an HE round is popularly, but incorrectly, called shrapnel.

SPENCER C. TUCKER AND DAVID T. ZABECKI

References
Bull, Stephen. *Encyclopedia of Military Technology and Innovation.* Westport, CT: Greenwood, 2004.

Ripley, Warren. *Artillery and Ammunition of the Civil War.* New York: Van Nostrand Reinhold, 1970.

Tucker, Spencer C. *Arming the Fleet: U.S. Naval Ordnance in the Muzzle-Loading Era.* Annapolis, MD: Naval Institute Press, 1989.

Smokeless Gunpowder

The standard propellent for firearms, large and small, from its introduction into Europe in the 13th century up to the late 19th century was black powder. Its principal liabilities were the residue it produced on burning (known as fouling), which necessitated considerable windage (the difference between the diameters of the bore and the projectile), and the dense cloud of smoke it gave off on firing. The latter immediately revealed the weapon's location on the battlefield. After a half dozen shots, the smoke also obscured observation of the target. With the development of rapid-firing firearms and artillery, this became a serious liability.

Attempts were made to develop a substitute for black powder, especially after the mid-19th century. In 1846 the French government appointed a commission to report on the feasibility of using nitrated cotton, which was found to burn without smoke and might be suitable for small-arms use. In 1884 French chemist Paul Vielle produced a successful nitrocellulose powder for small arms. His next type, which came to be designated Poudre B, was the first successful smokeless powder adopted by any nation. Weapons utilizing it also had a much higher velocity than those with ordinary gunpowder.

Similar experiments were carried out by Alfred Nobel in Sweden with what came to be known as ballistite, a compound of nitroglycerin and nitrocellulose. Nobel employed camphor to harden the powder grains. The British were aware of Nobel's work and sought to develop a powder using nitroglycerin and acetone as a solvent for guncotton but without using camphor. British scientists used petroleum jelly to help with stabilizing and antifouling. The British powder, formed in pale brown stands, came to be called cordite. The chief problem with cordite was a more rapid erosion of the weapon's bore. These new powders also proved less dangerous in bulk than the old black powder.

Smokeless powder proved its worth in the Boer War (1899–1902). Using it in new German Krupp artillery and long-range Mauser rifles, the Boers were able to open fire at long range on the British positions without revealing their own. This development greatly influenced tactics and led to renewed interest in camouflage.

SPENCER C. TUCKER

References
Blair, Claude, ed. *Pollard's History of Firearms.* New York: Macmillan, 1983.

Cocroft, Wayne. *Dangerous Energy: The Archaeology of Gunpowder.* London: English Heritage Publications, 2000.

Kelly, Jack. *Gunpowder: Alchemy, Bombards, and Pyrotechnics; The History of the Explosive That Changed the World.* New York: Basic Books, 2004.

Partington, James Riddick. *A History of Greek Fire and Gunpowder.* Baltimore: Johns Hopkins University Press, 1998.

Steam Warship

The steam engine revolutionized not only the construction of ships but also the entire practice of naval warfare. It freed ships from the vagaries of the wind and allowed captains to maneuver as the tactical situation required. Although primitive steam engines were known to the ancients, the modern type evolved from the late 17th century to the second half of the 18th century, when it was largely perfected by James Watt, an instrument maker at the University of Glasgow. He patented his steam engine in 1769.

In 1783 a Frenchman, the Marquis de Jouffroy, constructed a practical small stern-wheel steamship, the *Pyroscaphe.* It plied the Sâone River near Lyons. In 1787 American John Fitch tested a steamboat on the Delaware River, and in 1788 Scottish banker Patrick Miller and engineer William Symington tested Britain's first steamboat, the *Charlotte Dundas,* on the Firth of Forth. In 1807 American inventor Robert Fulton built the first commercially successful steamboat, the *Clermont.* It carried passengers on the Hudson River between New York and Albany. Europe's first merchant steamer was Thomas Bell's *Comet* of 1812 on the Clyde River.

The first serious attempt at a steam-powered warship came in the 1790s in Britain when the Earl of Stanhope built the *Kent.* It was powered by paddles (not paddle wheels) or, as he called them, duck feet, that feathered on the return stroke. Tested on the Thames in 1793, its engine proved a failure. In fact, the Royal Navy was slow to embrace a change that would render obsolete its navy, the world's largest. The first steam warship in any nation was Robert Fulton's *Demologos* of 1815, but it was basically a floating battery to defend New York City.

All early steamers were hybrids, employing sail rigs as well as steam power. This practice continued late into the 19th century. Because of the inefficiency of the early steam engines, the first steamers relied on sail the vast majority of the time.

The first Royal Navy steamship was the *Comet* of 1822, employed as a tender and tug. The *Lightning* (1823) and *Meteor* (1824) followed. All three ships were rated at three guns.

In fairness to their critics, early steam vessels had serious shortcomings. Their engines frequently failed, they were slow, and their high rate of fuel consumption reduced cruising range. Side wheels were an inefficient means of propulsion, and their drag inhibited speed when under sail. The large paddle wheels were vulnerable to enemy fire, and they took up much room on the side of the vessel. This prevented standard broadside batteries, forcing location of fewer and larger longer-ranged guns on pivot mounts on the upper deck.

The first steam paddle warships were built for African service: the Royal Navy *Congo* in 1816 and the French *African* and *Voyager* in 1818. The first purpose-built war steamer actually known to have participated in high-intensity combat was the British-built Greek Navy *Karteria* ("Perseverance") during the Greek War of Independence. Armed with four 68-pounders, in 1827 it captured or destroyed some two dozen Turkish vessels and carried out shore bombardment.

Over time the number of steam warships grew. The *Dee* entered Royal Navy service in 1832. At 700 tons, it was twice the size of the previous steamers. Sometimes known as the first practical steam warship, it mounted two 32-pounders. The *Dee* and another steamer, the *Rhadamanthus,* proved their worth in 1832 during a Royal Navy blockade of the Netherlands coast to bring about the withdrawal of Dutch troops from Belgium. By 1837 nearly 30 steamers had been built expressly for the Royal Navy, with others purchased for minor duties.

Steam warships also grew larger and mounted more powerful armaments. The paddler frigate *Gorgon* of 1837 was 1,111 tons and mounted two 10-inch guns and four 32-pounders. It took part in the 1840 Syrian campaign. The paddle-wheel frigate *Cyclops* of 1838 mounted two 98-pounders and four 68-pounders. The Royal Navy built 18 *Gorgon* and 6 *Cyclops* derivatives through 1846.

France was the only other nation to make a serious commitment to steam in this period. The first effective French steam warship was the dispatch boat *Sphinx* of 1829. Of 777 tons, it took part in operations against Algiers in 1830. Over the next 10 years France built 23 similar dispatch boats, and in the 1940s it also built a few larger paddle frigates to match the British Gorgon class.

The *Missouri* and *Mississippi* marked the real beginning of the U.S. steam navy. Launched in 1841, they were 3,200 tons in displacement and mounted two 10-inch pivot guns and eight 8-inch guns in broadside. The *Missouri* was destroyed by fire in 1843, but the *Mississippi* had a distinguished 20-year career.

The change from paddle wheel to screw propulsion was essential for steam-powered warships. Not only was the screw propeller more efficient, but it was concealed from enemy fire. Although there were a number of earlier experiments, in 1836 Francis Petit Smith and John Ericsson, working independently, took out patents for screw propellers. Smith's design was helical in shape. In 1839 Smith fitted his propeller to a ship of his design, the *Archimedes.* It became the first seagoing screw propeller vessel. In a series of cross-Channel races, it proved a match for the Dover paddle-wheel packets. Smith's propeller was also fitted on I. K. Brunel's Atlantic liner, the *Great Britain* of 1843, the first large commercial ship of iron construction.

Ericsson's first design consisted of a pair of contra-rotating drums aft of the rudder. It was tested successfully on the launch *Francis B. Ogden.* Ericsson improved it by removing one of the drums and mounting the propeller before the rudder. One problem with the screw propeller was technical. The single expansion engine, in use until the 1860s, only worked at about 20 pounds per square inch. This slow-running engine was better suited to running the paddle wheel; to run the propeller with sufficient speed required considerable gearing.

The first screw-propeller warship in the world was the U.S. Navy steam sloop *Princeton* of 1843. Ericsson designed the engine and six-blade propeller. The first Royal Navy screw-propelled vessel was the sloop *Rattler* of the same year. Of 888 tons, it mounted one 68-pounder bow gun and four 32-pounders. Doubts over which was the superior form of propulsion—the screw or the paddle wheel—were resolved by tests in 1845. In a series of races the *Rattler* proved faster than its rival, the paddle sloop *Alecto.* Proponents of the paddle-wheel vessel claimed that it had superior towing capabilities; this too was disproved in a tug-of-war between the two ships on April 30, 1845, which the *Rattler* won. The screw-propelled steamship was here to stay.

SPENCER C. TUCKER

References

Brown, D. K. *Before the Ironclad: Development of Ship Design Propulsion and Armament in the Royal Navy, 1815–60.* Annapolis, MD: Naval Institute Press, 1990.

Gardiner, Robert, ed., and Andrew D. Lambert, consultant ed. *Steam, Steel & Shellfire: The Steam Warship, 1815–1905.* Annapolis, MD: Naval Institute Press, 1992.

George, James L. *History of Warships: From Ancient Times to the Twenty-First Century.* Annapolis, MD: Naval Institute Press, 1998.

Perlmutter, Tom. *War Machines, Sea.* London: Octopus Books, 1965.

Telegraph

Telegraph-like systems for the transmission of messages linked parts of the Roman Empire. Signaling stations set up at regular intervals on high ground or on towers could relay messages by flags, mirrors, fires, smoke, or other means. The English operated a system of warning beacons at the time of the Spanish Armada in 1588, while France and then Britain operated semaphore mechanical telegraph systems in the early 19th century. The French system could transmit simple messages across much of Europe in a matter of hours. Such systems were, however, subject to the vagaries of weather or actions by enemy troops and had only limited application at night. They were also costly to operate and maintain.

By about 1830 scientists determined that messages could be transmitted by means of an electrical impulse through wires. While a number of electric telegraphy systems were developed, American Samuel Morse created a system and a code for it that employed short and long breaks in the electrical current (dots and dashes). Morse received a patent for his invention in 1840, and in 1843 the U.S. Congress appropriated funds to build a pilot 40-mile telegraph line from Baltimore to Washington. In 1844 Morse transmitted his first message over this line: "What hath God wrought?"

The telegraph allowed messages to be transmitted over considerable distances within minutes. Applied initially to the control of railroad traffic, the combination of telegraph and railroad brought about great changes in military operations. The telegraph proved of immense military value in the rapid communication of messages and control of troops during the Crimean War in the 1850s, the American Civil War (1861–1865), and the Austro-Prussian War of 1866. Telegraph lines laid under the ocean by 1866 connected Europe with North America and, within decades, the rest of the world.

Telegraphy was widely applied in the Boer War (1899–1902) and was used by both sides in World War I. Indeed, the telegraph remained a means of military communication through World War II. Only after 1950 did telegraph usage decline in the face of competition from the telephone. Today, few except ham radio operators use Morse code. The best-known telegraph signal is S-O-S, a call for assistance consisting of three dots, three dashes, and three dots.

SPENCER C. TUCKER

References

Beauchamp, Ken. *History of Telegraphy.* London: IEE, 2001.
Wilson, Geoffrey. *The Old Telegraphs.* London: Phillimore, 1976.

Telephone

The telephone is a communications device used to send and receive sound, usually speech. The telephone has also been adapted for data communication (telex, fax, and Internet). Telephone equipment consists of a bell, beeper, light, or other device so that the user is alerted to incoming calls and number buttons or (in earlier models) a rotary dial to enter a telephone number for outgoing calls. Work on telephone development was carried out by Innocenzo Manzetti, Antonio Meucci, Johann Philipp Reis, Elisha Gray, Alexander Graham Bell, and Thomas Edison. On March 7, 1876, Bell was granted a U.S. parent for "Improvement in Telegraphy," covering "the method of, and apparatus for, transmitting vocal or other sounds telegraphically . . . by causing electrical undulations, similar in form to the vibrations of the air accompanying the said vocal or other sound."

The telephone was adopted for military use more slowly than the telegraph. There were several reasons for this. The telephone left no physical record of a message, and until World War I, telephone signals were largely local. Yet the telephone could be easily used (no need for trained specialists), allowed fast transmission of messages without code, and encouraged two-way communication. Drawbacks included fragility and susceptibility to interference.

By the early 1880s the British were using telephones over short distances in African colonial campaigns and in India, while the U.S. Army Signal Corps installed experimental telephones in 1878 and soon began to use them at seacoast defenses for fire control. Following telegraph precedents, both man-carried and horse-borne means of laying wire in the field were developed. Hand generator and battery systems were both used, the former in combat conditions and the latter on individual posts.

Britain used telephones during the Boer War (1899–1902). During the Spanish-American war, the U.S. Army Signal Corps established telephone networks within bases, and national military leaders in Washington could call Tampa, Florida, the principal American assembly point for Cuba. In the American West, telegraph lines that connected military posts slowly gave way to telephone networks.

By World War I, the military telephone was widely used. French civilian telephone networks were also utilized, but demand surpassed their capacity. The introduction of telephone repeaters allowed service over longer distances and also allowed the use of thinner, lighter wire. Static trench warfare on the Western Front favored use of telephones, but even when buried deeply, massive heavy artillery fire repeatedly tore up lines. One important problem was security, and listening by induction to enemy telephone signals was widespread by 1915. For subsequent field operations, British and American forces used a combined buzzer and telephone; the British Fullerphone was the best-known example. The British manufactured more than 40,000 trench telephones that were used on all fronts, linked by manual switchboards. The U.S. Army standardized use of a field telephone based on commercial equipment. Dedicated telephone links were soon established between Allied headquarters and both London and Paris. After 1917 a cadre of some 200 so-called Hello Girls operated the switchboards. A huge dedicated network of some 20,000 miles of wire served both telegraph and telephone networks in France.

During World War II, telephones carried two-thirds of communications within the United States and some overseas sites (telegraphy remained the more secure long-distance communication mode). In combat theaters, redundant routing helped ensure communications continuity, although switchboards had changed little since World War I. Britain's Fighter Command connected more than 40 airfields and radar installations during the Battle of Britain with a dedicated telephone network that made use of redundant facilities to maintain connectivity despite battle damage. German and Japanese forces made extensive use of telephones, although the latter's Pacific islands made radio more valuable. In order to improve security, the Germans banned radio use in preparation for their massive Ardennes Offensive of December 1944, using only secure land lines instead. As a result, the Allied decoding ULTRA operation provided no advance warning of the German attack. During the war, British prime minister Winston Churchill and U.S. president Franklin Roosevelt communicated by secure transatlantic links.

By the late 20th century, telephone links were so common as to have become part of the military background—always available and ready—with a steady progression from analog to digital technology.

CHRISTOPHER H. STERLING

References

Fagan, M. D., ed. *A History of Engineering and Science in the Bell System: National Service in War and Peace (1925–1975)*. New York: Bell Telephone Laboratories, 1980.

Lavine, A. Lincoln. *Circuits of Victory*. Garden City, NY: Country Life, 1921.

Scheips, Paul J., ed. *Military Signal Communication*. 2 vols. New York: Arno, 1980.

TNT

Trinitrotoluene, more commonly known as TNT, is a pale yellow crystalline hydrocarbon high-explosive compound. Its chemical formula is $C_7H_5N_3O_6$. TNT is today part of many explosive mixtures. German chemist Joseph Wilbrand invented TNT in 1863, although it was not an immediate success because it was hard to detonate and not as powerful as some other high explosives. TNT is much more stable than nitroglycerin, however, and unlike dynamite, it does not absorb water and thus may be safely stored over long periods. Because of its low melting point (81° C), TNT could be easily melted by hot water and then poured in liquid form into shell casings. TNT is, however, quite toxic. Munitions workers handling it during World War I developed a number of serious health problems until they were equipped with respirators and protective skin grease.

The Germans first adopted TNT as a filler for artillery shells in 1902, and the British followed suit in 1907. TNT is mixed with 40–80 percent ammonium nitrate to form amatol. Mixed with about 20 percent aluminum powder, it forms minol, which the British used in both mines and depth charges. The explosive force of TNT is today the standard measurement for the energy released in nuclear weapons blasts.

SPENCER C. TUCKER

References

Cook, Melvin A. *The Science of High Explosives*. New York: Reinhold, 1958.

Fordham, Stanley. *High Explosives and Propellents*. Oxford, UK: Pergamon, 1980.

Torpedo

The success of stationary mines in the Crimean War (1854–1856) but primarily in the American Civil War (1861–1865), where mines were known as torpedoes for the torpedo fish that gives a shock to its prey, led to efforts to develop a self-propelled mine. The first modern automotive mine or torpedo was developed by Captain Johannes Luppis of the Austro-Hungarian Navy in 1865 and was perfected two years later by the Scottish engineer Robert Whitehead, who managed an engine works in Fiume.

The Luppis-Whitehead torpedo was a long cylinder, streamlined for movement through the water. It had an 18-pound dynamite warhead and was powered by an engine that ran on compressed air. The torpedo moved just below the surface at a speed of six to eight knots and had an effective range of only several hundred yards. Its secret was a balance chamber that enabled the torpedo to keep a constant depth beneath the surface. The Austrian government, strapped financially by the 1866 war against Prussia and Italy, declined to buy the exclusive rights to the invention.

Whitehead then traveled to Britain to demonstrate the weapon, and in 1870 the Admiralty was sufficiently impressed that it purchased rights to his invention for £15,000. Two years later Whitehead opened a torpedo factory in England. The British concentrated on a 16-inch, 1,000-yard-range version driven by contra-rotating screws at a speed of 7 knots or 300 yards at 12 knots.

The torpedo was first used in combat in 1877 when the British frigate *Shah* attacked the Peruvian monitor *Huascar*. The *Shah* launched its torpedo within 600 yards, but the *Huascar* easily changed direction and escaped.

Whitehead made improvements in his torpedo, further streamlining it and fitting it with fins to stabilize its movement toward the target. He also increased the explosive charge threefold by replacing gunpowder with guncotton. A three-cylinder gas-powered engine dramatically improved torpedo speed to 18 knots, making it more difficult for a targeted vessel to escape. The addition of a gyroscope, adapted for torpedo use by the Austrian Ludwig Obry, made the torpedo more accurate. Range also increased so that by 1877 torpedoes could reach 800 yards.

Disappointment over the performance of torpedoes in the Russo-Japanese War (1904–1905) led to a new propellent to replace compressed air. In 1904–1905 both the Whitehead factory at Fiume and the Armstrong Whitworth works at Elswick in Britain came up with heaters to produce hot gas. This had a dramatic effect on both speed and range. A typical 18-inch torpedo driven by compressed air could range out about 800 yards at a speed of 30 knots. The new hot gas torpedo of the same size could travel more than 2,000 yards at 34 knots or 4,400 yards at 28 knots. By 1909 the British Mk VII 18-inch (actually 17.7-inch) torpedo reached 3,500 yards at 45 knots or 5,000 yards at 35 knots. Torpedoes also grew in size. The German 500-millimeter (19.7-inch) Type G of 1906 could reach 6,000 yards at 36 knots, and its charge of 440 pounds was double that of an 18-inch weapon. The British Mk II 21-inch torpedo of 1910 carried a 400-pound charge some 5,000 yards at 35 knots.

The first successful torpedo attack in warfare occurred during the Russo-Turkish War of 1877–1878. On January 26, 1878, off Batum on the Black Sea the Russian torpedo boat *Constantine* fired two torpedoes at a range of some 80 yards to sink the Turkish patrol boat *Intikbah* in Batum Harbor. Torpedoes had a more spectacular result during the Indochina Black Flag/Tonkin Wars (1882–1885). On August 23, 1884, at the Chinese naval base at Fuzhou (Foo Chow), French torpedo boats Nos. *45* and *46* sank the Chinese flagship cruiser and damaged a second vessel. Torpedoes found their natural delivery system in the submarine, and in World War I they wreaked havoc on both warships and merchant ships.

Torpedoes increased in both size and speed. In 1908 a 21-inch diameter torpedo appeared. This soon became the standard size. The British Weymouth Mark II torpedo of 1914 weighed 2,794 pounds, could travel at 29 knots, and had a range of 10,000 yards. To pierce torpedo nets, swung out by ships when they were stationary, some torpedoes were equipped with net-cutting devices. Propellers underwent improvement, and the air blast gyroscope improved stability at long ranges.

The finest torpedo early in World War II was the Japanese Long Lance. Torpedo improvements in World War II included the magnetic pistol, which set off the explosive charge when the torpedo was under a ship; electric drive; acoustic torpedoes that honed in on sound; and a system developed by the Germans whereby the torpedo would circle after its initial straight run in order to improve the chances of hitting a ship in a convoy.

Torpedo developments in the early Cold War period included smaller lighter-weight models for aircraft use, although the standard heavy torpedo was still 21 inches in diameter. The U.S. Mary 44 torpedo was powered by a seawater battery and had active sonar to seek out its target. Most torpedoes employ acoustic homing. Active acoustic torpedoes generate sound and then hone in on the echoes, while passive acoustic types are attracted by sound. Torpedoes have also been developed specifically to operate against other submarines.

Modern torpedoes utilize a variety of drive mechanisms, including electric motors and gas turbines. Some, such as the Russian VA-111 Shkval, utilize supercavitation to produce speeds of more than 200 knots. The U.S. Mark 48 heavy torpedo is 21 inches in diameter and 19 feet in length. It weighs 3,695 pounds and has a warhead of 650 pounds. It has wire guidance and passive and active sonar homing and is detonated by a proximity fuse, and its swash-plate piston engine gives it a speed of some 55 knots and a range of more than 23 miles.

SPENCER C. TUCKER

References

Gray, Edwyn. *The Devil's Device: Robert Whitehead and the History of the Torpedo.* Rev. and updated. Annapolis, MD: Naval Institute Press, 1991.

Jenkins, E. H. *A History of the French Navy: From Its Beginnings to the Present Day.* Annapolis, MD: Naval Institute Press, 1973.

Torpedo Boat

Development of the automotive torpedo meant that for the first time in naval history small vessels could threaten large ships. Torpedo boats launched their so-called fish (torpedo) from the bow, presenting the smallest silhouette to enemy fire. All navies developed such small, fast boats specifically to launch torpedoes, leading to some discussion in the 1880s as to whether the battleship had been rendered obsolete.

The first purpose-built torpedo boat was the Royal Navy *Lightning,* built by the firm of John I. Thornycroft in 1877. Displacing just 27 tons, it was 84.5 feet long and 11 feet in beam. Powered by a 478-horsepower engine, it could make 19 knots and was fitted with a bow-launching tube for a single 14-inch torpedo. The French were almost first. Their *Torpilleur No. 1* was actually ordered in 1875 but not completed until 1878. Heavily influenced by the thinking of the so-called Jeune École that emphasized smaller ships, France built the largest number of torpedo boats. By 1890 France had 220, while Britain had 186, Russia had 152, Germany had 143, and Italy had 129. But torpedoes became standard armament on all classes of warships. All Royal Navy ships launched after 1872 carried them.

Early torpedo boats were too small to be effective. Their poor performance during maneuvers led to the construction of larger vessels. Torpedo boats were made about 50 percent longer while at the same time preserving their slim, narrow lines. These craft were technically capable of ocean work, although their crews often did not think so. In 1889 France ordered larger boats of about 125 tons each to accompany squadrons at sea. In 1895 the 136-ton 144.4-foot *Forban* reached 31 knots, a world record.

The threat posed by torpedo boats was partially countered by the development of quick-firing Nordenfelt and Gatling machine guns, which became part of the standard armament of even the largest warships. At night these were paired with the newly developed searchlight. The torpedo boat destroyer (later simply known as the destroyer) also appeared; its task was to search out and destroy the torpedo boats before they could close within range. During World War I the Italian Navy operated nearly 300 MAS (torpedo-armed motorboats) in the Adriatic Sea against the Austro-Hungarian Navy. The Royal Navy also employed coastal motor boats (CMBs) in home waters and in raids against Ostend and Zeebrugge, Belgium, in April 1918.

The major powers continued to employ torpedo boats during World War II. For the most part these small, fast, highly maneuverable wooden-hulled shallow-draft vessels operated in coastal waters. The Germans had E boats, while the British employed motor torpedo boats (MTBs). Perhaps the best known of all these craft, however, were the U.S. Navy patrol torpedo boats, popularly known as PT boats. They were 77 feet long with an average speed of 27.5 knots in rough waters and mounted two 21-inch torpedo tubes. They also carried two .50-caliber machine guns in twin turrets. During the war the U.S. Navy deployed 350 PT boats in the Pacific theater, 42 in the Mediterranean, and 33 in the English Channel. They were not very effective against Japanese ships because early U.S. torpedoes proved defective and because of the difficulty of firing them accurately while maneuvering at high speed. PT boats were much more effective in coastal work, where they attacked and destroyed large numbers of Japanese landing craft, landed small forces, and—armed with rockets, mortars, or a 40-millimeter gun—provided support to troops ashore. The successors of such craft were effectively employed in riverine operations during the Vietnam War, while North Vietnamese torpedo boats triggered the Gulf of Tonkin Incident of August 1964.

SPENCER C. TUCKER

References

Bulkley, Robert J., Jr. *At Close Quarters: PT Boats in the United States Navy.* Washington, DC: Naval Historical Division, 1962.

Nelson, Curtis L. *Hunters in the Shallows: A History of the PT Boat.* Washington, DC: Brassey's, 1998.

Preston, Anthony. *Destroyers.* Englewood Cliffs, NJ: Prentice-Hall, 1977.

Ropp, Theodore. *The Development of a Modern Navy: French Naval Policy, 1871–1904.* Edited by Stephen S. Roberts. Annapolis, MD: Naval Institute Press, 1987.

Tucker, Spencer C. *Handbook of 19th Century Naval Warfare.* Annapolis, MD: Naval Institute Press, 2000.

Turbina, HMS

In Britain during Queen Victoria's diamond jubilee on June 16, 1897, the greatest of all Victorian naval reviews, a novel new craft made its appearance. This was the yacht *Turbina,* powered by a steam turbine engine developed by Sir Charles Parsons. The yacht in effect took center stage at the review when, with Parsons at the helm, it broke from the stately procession and ran the length of the review line. Torpedo boats and torpedo boat destroyers, sent to catch the *Turbina,* were unable to match its 34-knot speed.

The steam turbine was a rotary engine in which steam that was heated by means of a water-pipe boiler passed through a series of nozzles. Gaining velocity, it was then directed onto a series of blades on the periphery of a rotor. The velocity of the steam passing along these blades turned the rotor and powered the propellers.

The revolutionary steam turbine engine was both faster and more reliable than the reciprocating engine it replaced, which often shook itself apart. It also avoided design and protection problems resulting from the growing height of the reciprocal engine's large pistons. The speed of the *Turbina,* so spectacularly demonstrated at Spithead, led the Admiralty to order a turbine-powered destroyer. HMS *Viper* of 1899 was the world's first steam turbine–powered warship. Other steam-turbine driven destroyers followed, and in 1905 HMS *Dreadnought* became the first steam turbine–driven battleship. The only major differences in propulsion of ships at sea since have been in the introduction of gearing and new working fluids in the gas turbine.

SPENCER C. TUCKER

References

Appleyard, Rollo. *Charles Parsons: His Life and Work.* London: Constable, 1933.

Gardiner, Robert, ed., and Andrew D. Lambert, consultant ed. *Steam, Steel & Shellfire: The Steam Warship, 1815–1905.* Annapolis, MD: Naval Institute Press, 1992.
Preston, Anthony. *Destroyers.* Englewood Cliffs, NJ: Prentice-Hall, 1977.
Tucker, Spencer C. *Handbook of 19th Century Naval Warfare.* Annapolis, MD: Naval Institute Press, 2000.

Turtle Submarine

The first real submarine was invented by American David Bushnell during the American Revolutionary War. Bushnell had already invented a mine, and he now came up with the means to deliver it, building at Saybrook on the Connecticut River in 1775 what he called a "sub-marine." It consisted of two tortoise-like shells made of oak staves similar to those of a barrel clamped together by iron hoops. Resembling an egg in appearance, it rode upright in the water with its smallest end facing down. An entry hatch at the top of the craft had small windows to provide light for the operator below, and a 900-pound keel provided stability. The 7.5- by 6-foot tar-coated craft was reinforced internally against water pressure. Two brass pipes with check valves to prevent flooding provided fresh air and a means of exhaust. A foot-operated valve in the keel admitted water to submerge, and a pump expelled water to ascend. The craft was driven forward and up and down by means of two sets of screwlike paddles manually operated by inside cranks, one on top of the craft and the other in front of the operator. A rudder moved by a tiller steered the vessel. In an emergency the operator could detach 200 pounds of the lead keel, which could also be let down to serve as an anchor. The craft also had a depth gauge and a compass. Because of its appearance, it was known as the *Turtle.*

The new craft's destructive power came in the form of a cask with 150 pounds of gunpowder. A long bolt attached it to the back of the submarine. When withdrawn, the bolt released the mine and activated the timer, which exploded the mine by means of a flint lock after about an hour. The submarine was to dive beneath its target, and the operator would then screw an auger into the target vessel's hull. Once this was accomplished the auger was released, and the mine would float free against the target vessel's hull. The *Turtle*'s chief drawback was that the operator had only 30 minutes of air once it was submerged. This meant that an attack had to be mounted at night or in poor visibility in order to get as close as possible before submerging for the final run to its target.

Bushnell successfully tested the *Turtle* but was too frail to operate it in actual combat conditions and thus recruited his brother. Bushnell's brother fell ill, and a volunteer, Sergeant Ezra Lee, took his place for an attempt on the night of September 6–7, 1776, against Admiral Lord Richard Howe's flagship, the *Eagle,* at New York City. For various reasons the attack failed. Several other attempts to sink British ships in the Hudson were also unsuccessful. The *Turtle* was later destroyed, probably to prevent it from falling into British hands.

SPENCER C. TUCKER

References
Miller, Nathan. *Sea of Glory: The Continenal Navy Fights for Independence, 1775–1783.* New York: David McKay, 1974.
Roland, Alex. *Underwater Warfare in the Age of Sail.* Bloomington: Indiana University Press, 1978.

Victory, HMS

The Royal Navy ship of the line *Victory* of 1778 is the oldest warship in the world still in commission and one of the most famous museum ships. The fifth of five ships in the Royal Navy of that name (the first was the *ex-Great Christopher* purchased in 1560), this first-rate three-deck ship of the line was laid down in 1759.

Launched at Chatham in 1765, it was commissioned in 1778. Displacing approximately 4,000 tons fully loaded, the ship measures 328 feet overall with an extreme beam of 52 feet and a draft of 19 feet 8 inches. Its mainmast is 203 feet tall. The *Victory*'s crew complement at the Battle of Trafalgar in October 1805 was 850 officers and men. Armament consisted of 30 32-pounders, 28 24-pounders, 30 12-pounders, 12 quarterdeck 12-pounders, and 2 68-pounder carronades.

HMS *Victory* served under a succession of Royal Navy commanders, taking part in fighting against France and Spain in the American Revolutionary War, the Wars of the French Revolution, and the Napoleonic Wars. After two years as a hospital ship and two years of refit, it was recommissioned in 1801. *Victory*'s most famous action was undoubtedly as the flagship of Admiral Horatio Nelson in the Battle of Trafalgar in October 1805. Following another refit, from 1824 on it served as the flagship of the Portsmouth Command. In 1922 *Victory* was moved to Portsmouth Naval Shipyard and drydocked and then was restored as a museum ship to its Trafalgar appearance. The *Victory* today is still manned by an active-duty Royal Navy crew and flies the White Ensign of a commissioned Royal Navy ship.

SPENCER C. TUCKER

References

McGowan, Alan. *HMS Victory: Her Construction, Career, and Restoration.* London: Chatham, 1999.
McKay, John. *The 100-gun Ship Victory.* Annapolis, MD: Naval Institute Press, 2000.

Warrior, HMS

The Royal Navy armored frigate *Warrior* was the world's first seagoing iron-hulled warship. The Royal Navy was slow to introduce ironclad ships; after all, it had the world's largest wooden navy. The French decision in 1856 to build six seagoing ironclads brought action, however. News of the construction of the French *Gloire*, which reached Britain in May 1858, created something akin to panic. The British public need not have worried. Britain led the world in metallurgical techniques, and its armor plate was superior to that of France. The British also led in the development of rifled heavy ordnance.

Construction of the *Warrior* demonstrated the British determination to retain the technological lead at sea. As the Royal Dockyards lacked the experience and facilities to build large iron ships, the *Warrior* was ordered in May 1859 from the Thames Ironworks Company of Blackwall, London. The novelty of the construction and modifications to the design brought construction delays. The *Warrior* was launched in December 1860 and entered service in June 1862. At 9,210 tons, 380 feet in length, and 58.5 feet in beam, the *Warrior* was larger than the *Gloire* and any wooden warship.

A quantum leap forward in ship design, the *Warrior* immediately made every other warship in the world obsolete. Whereas the *Gloire* was merely a wooden ship protected by iron plate, the *Warrior* was virtually an iron vessel. The ship was protected by a 4.5-inch band of iron bolted to .625-inch plating and 18 inches of teak running from 6 feet below to 6 feet above the waterline. The ends of the hull were divided into watertight compartments, a major innovation made possible by the iron construction. The heart of the design, however, was the citadel, a 210-foot-long armored box protecting the guns and machinery. Powered by a 1,250-horsepower engine (10 boilers and 40 furnaces), the *Warrior* retained a full sail rig.

The *Warrior* had just one gun deck, but it carried a powerful battery of 10 Armstrong 110-pounder and 4 70-pounder Armstrong breech-loading rifled guns and 26 68-pounder muzzle-loading smoothbores. This was a heavier armament than wooden ships of the line, the guns of which could not penetrate its armor.

With its long, sleek lines, the *Warrior* was the prototype of the new warship. A true seagoing design, the ship was much faster than conventional ships of the line. The *Warrior* could make up to 13.75 knots under sail, 14.33 under steam, and 17.5 knots combined. Properly handled, with its superior speed, armor, and long-range guns, it could have destroyed any ship in the world.

Hulked in 1902, in 1923 the *Warrior* became a jetty at an oil terminal in Wales. Rescued in the 1970s, the ship was then restored and in 1986 was returned to Portsmouth as the largest historic ship in the dockyard complex.

SPENCER C. TUCKER

References

Hamilton, C. I. *Anglo-French Naval Rivalry, 1846–1870.* Oxford: Oxford University Press, 1993.
Lambert, Andrew D. *Warrior: The First and Last Ironclad.* London: Conway, 1987.

Index

Mil Mi-24 Hind helicopter, 2535, 2748–2749

Sikorsky R-4 helicopter, 2311–2312

Helsinki Accords, 2502–2503

Henri II (king of France), 515, 518–519, 520

Henri III (king of France), 532, 533, 539, 542

Henri IV (king of France), 542–543, 543 (image), 831–832

Henry II (king of England), 255, 395–396, 396 (image)

Henry V (king of England), 323–327, 328, 329, 397

Henry VI (king of England), 329–330, 336, 345–347, 348
murder of, 351

Henry VII (king of England), 355–356, 397–398

Henry VIII (king of England), 475, 479, 480 (image), 484, 832–833

Henry the Tudor, 355–356

Heraclius, 195, 195 (image), 197, 199, 201, 398–399

Herzegovina, 1548, 2617

Hess, Rudolf, 1922

Hideyoshi, Toyotomi, 535, 548, 867–869, 868 (image)

Himmler, Heinrich, 1856

Hindenburg, Paul von, 1571, 1571 (image), 1573, 1583, 1603, 1604, 1638, 1675, 1707–1709, 1853

Historic Age (to 600 BCE), 5–22
battlefield tactics during, 9–10
land warfare during, 8–10
naval warfare during, 10
weapons of, 8–10

Historic Age (600–400 BCE), 22–49
battlefield tactics during, 23, 25
land warfare during, 22–23, 25
naval tactics during, 26–27
naval warfare during, 25–26
weapons of, 22–23, 25–26

Historic Age (400–200 BCE), 49–79
battlefield tactics during, 50
land warfare during, 49–50
naval tactics during, 51
naval warfare during, 50–51
weapons of, 49–50

Historic Age (200–1 BCE), 97–122
naval warfare during, 98

overview of, 97–98

Historic Age (200–400 CE), 145–166
overview of, 145

Historiography, 27

Hitler, Adolf, xxx, 1675, 1831, 1853, 1853 (image), 1856, 1867, 1874, 1875–1876, 1882, 1891, 1896–1897, 1903, 1907, 1916, 1917, 1924, 1925, 1928, 1929, 1945, 1949, 1978, 1982, 1985, 1986, 1998, 2000 2001, 2003, 2166–2168
decision to invade the Soviet Union, 1911–1912
failed assassination of, 2039
failures made concerning the Normandy invasion, 2028–2029
orders of for the invasion of Poland, 1884–1885
suicide of, 2080

Ho Chi Minh, 2093, 2095, 2098, 2168–2169, 2169 (image), 2323, 2379

Hobbes, Thomas, xxix

Hodges, Courtney, 2041, 2047, 2062, 2068, 2169–2170, 2170 (image)

Hoffman, Max, 1570, 1574, 1709–1710

Holland, John P., 1203

Holland, 1323

Hollow charges, 2269

Holy League, 482, 529–530, 531

Holy Roman Empire, 226, 228, 262, 263, 615 (map)
end of, 1048
war with France, 489, 490, 492, 493–495, 494 (image), 498, 499, 500, 502, 507, 510–512
See also Peace of Westphalia; Thirty Years' War

Homer, 14

Honduras, 2463, 2510, 2560, 2571, 2581

Hood, Alexander, 973, 1271

Hood, Samuel, 946, 946 (image), 950, 955, 1272

Hooker, Joseph E., 1391, 1393, 1398

Hoover, Herbert, 1604

Hovercraft, 2269–2270

Howard, Charles, 539, 833–834

Howe, Richard, 776, 777 (image), 8334–835, 934

Howe, William, 915, 915 (image), 919–920, 928, 933, 9361273–1274

Hundred Years' War, 299, 303 (image), 311, 312, 314–315, 316, 321, 323–326, 326–327, 328, 329–330, 331–332, 339–340, 340–341
Battle of Agincourt, 324–326, 324 (image), 325 (map)
Battle of Castillon, 343–344
Battle of Formigny, 340
Battle of Patay, 333, 335
Battle of Poitiers, 305–307, 306 (image)
Battle of Sluys, 299–301, 300 (image)
capture of Calais by the English, 304–305
Crécy Campaign, 301–305, 303 (image)
Peace of Arras, 336
Siege of Orléans, 332–333, 332 (image)
Truce of Tours, 337

Hungary, 336–337, 545, 546, 547, 549, 559–560, 560–561, 567, 641, 657, 692, 1185, 1192–1193, 1814, 2353, 2588
civil war in, 498
Hungarian Revolution, 2373–2374, 2374 (image), 2375, 2377–2378
Suleiman the Magnificent's campaign against, 496–498, 497 (image), 500, 509
war with Austria, 1187–1188, 1188–1189, 1191–1192
in World War II, 2021, 2052, 2058

Huns, 169, 171
White Huns, 167, 173, 180
See also Attila the Hun

Hunyadi, János, 336–337, 399–400

Hussein, Saddam, 2528, 2539, 2542, 2579, 2595, 2598, 2599, 2604, 2617, 2635, 2645, 2715–2716, 2716 (image)

Edwards Brothers Malloy
Thorofare, NJ USA
July 10, 2012